The Origins of the
Civil War in Tajikistan

Contemporary Central Asia:
Societies, Politics, and Cultures

Series Editor: Marlene Laruelle, George Washington University

At the crossroads of Russia, China, and the Islamic world, Central Asia remains one of the world's least-understood regions, despite being a significant theater for muscle-flexing by the great powers and regional players. This series, in conjunction with George Washington University's Central Asia Program, offers insight into Central Asia by providing readers unique access to state-of-the-art knowledge on the region. Going beyond the media clichés, the series inscribes the study of Central Asia into the social sciences and hopes to fill the dearth of works on the region for both scholarly knowledge and undergraduate and graduate student education.

Titles in the Series

The Origins of the Civil War in Tajikistan

Nationalism, Islamism and Violent Conflict in Post-Soviet Space

Tim Epkenhans

LEXINGTON BOOKS
Lanham • Boulder • New York • London

Published by Lexington Books
An imprint of The Rowman & Littlefield Publishing Group, Inc.
4501 Forbes Boulevard, Suite 200, Lanham, Maryland 20706
www.rowman.com

Unit A, Whitacre Mews, 26-34 Stannary Street, London SE11 4AB

British Library Cataloguing in Publication Information Available
The hardback edition of this book was previously catalogued by the Library of Congress
as follows:

Library of Congress Control Number: 2016951461
ISBN 9781498532785 (cloth: alk.paper)
ISBN 9781498532808 (pbk. : alk. paper)
ISBN 9781498532792 (electronic)

♾™ The paper used in this publication meets the minimum requirements of American
National Standard for Information Sciences—Permanence of Paper for Printed Library
Materials, ANSI/NISO Z39.48-1992.

Printed in the United States of America

Contents

Acknowledgments

This book is the result of a research project which inadvertently commenced in May 2003 in a small village in the Qarotegin Valley. I had been invited by friends to stay over the weekend with their families and here I first encountered local narratives of the civil war that markedly differed from those of government officials, diplomats and scholars and that should haunt me ever since. Back then, I worked as a diplomat and could not pursue a serious research project. Only few years later, in 2006, my work at the OSCE Academy in Bishkek allowed me to return to Tajikistan and collect with colleagues the Oral History Archive of independent Tajikistan. Although this book does not extensively capitalize on the archive, the interviews I listened to profoundly influenced my understanding of the civil war in Tajikistan.

I had the pleasure to work with marvelous colleagues, who inspired, challenged and encouraged me. Furthermore, I had the privilege to work in academic institutions which supported and facilitated my research interests. At the University of Bamberg, Bert Fragner and Lutz Rzehak inspired me with their enthusiasm, deep knowledge and sincere sympathy for Central Asia and Tajikistan. At the University of Freiburg, a generous grant by the Ministry of Science, Research and Arts of the State of Baden-Württemberg and the Faculty of Philosophy supported my research activities. At the University of Bern, the Faculty for Humanities accepted an earlier version of this manuscript as a habilitation treatise.

Teaching classes on contemporary Central Asia in Basel, Bishkek and Freiburg gave me the opportunity to discuss my thoughts and ideas with committed and critical students who challenged my interpretations and invited me to refine my conceptual thinking.

While working on this manuscript, I had the pleasure to discuss my poorly sorted thoughts on the origins of the Civil War in Tajikistan with colleagues and friends: Dieter von Blarer, Stéphane Dudoignon, Pál Dunay, Olmo Gölz, Michal Hall, Faredun Hodizoda, John Heathershaw, Anke von Kügelgen, Anna Matveeva, Temirlan Moldogaziev, Parviz Mullojonov, Shahnoza Nozimova, Johanna Pink, Mariella Ourghi, Maurus Reinkowski, Sophie Roche, Maxim Ryabkov and Nicola Spakowksi continuously encouraged me with their constructive critique.

Unfortunately, the political situation in Tajikistan has again deteriorated in recent years. In September 2015, the government banned the Islamic Revival Party and imprisoned many of its members. The remaining opposition, independent media and civil society have been silenced since. Hopes and aspirations of a future in an open, pluralistic and democratic society—which many of my Tajik friends and colleagues shared—have been sadly diminished. Considering the political situation, many of my Tajik friends and colleagues with whom I discussed my work, asked me not to mention their names here. With a heavy heart, I comply with their request. Nonetheless, without their support, their readiness to share their knowledge with me, their unwavering friendliness and hospitality, I would have not been able to work on this book.

All of this, however, would be pretty meaningless for me without my family near and far. In particular, my wife Asel and our children Max and Gulbarchyn. Researching violent conflict is a distressing affair and too often it is difficult to disengage from the disturbing narratives, but you were the foothold that kept me grounded. Thank you.

Abbreviations and Glossary

Table A.1

Abbreviation/ Term	Tajik	Explanation/Translation
APC	*Tank* or *BTR/ BMP*	Armoured Personnel Carrier
CC/CPT	*Kumitai markazī*	Central Committee of the Communist Party of the TaSSR, *de jure* the highest body of the CPT.
CSCE		Conference for Security and Cooperation in Europe (the predecessor of the OSCE).
DOSAAF		Russ.: *Dobrovelnoe Obščestvo Sobeystviya Armii, Aviacii i Floty*, "Volunteer Society for Cooperation with the Army, Aviation, and Fleet," a paramilitary organization in the Soviet Union.
Ešon		*ešon* is a Tajik honorific title for important representatives of a Sufi order (*tariqa*) in parts of Central Asia.
GBAO	*Viloyati Muxtori Kūhistoni Badaxšon*	Russ.: *Gorno-Badakhšanskaya avtonomnaya oblast'*; Gorno-Badakhshan Autonomous Province created in 1925.
GKČP		Russ.: *Gosudarstvenniy komitet po* črezvyčaynomu *položeniyu*, "State Committee on the State of Emergency"; the August 1991 Coup against Gorbachev.
GNR		Government of National Reconciliation
GRU		Russ.: *Glavnoe razvedyvatel'noe upravlenie*, "Main Intelligence Directorate," the military intelligence service of the Soviet Armed Forces.
IRPT	*Hizbi nahzati Islomii Toǧikiston*	Islamic Revival Party of Tajikistan

Table A.1

Abbreviation/ Term	Tajik	Explanation/Translation
Ispolkom	*kumitai iğroiya*	Russ.: *Ispolnitelniy komitet,* "Executive Committee" on the various tiers of the administration (province, city, district).
KGB/NSC	KAM (*Kumitai amniyati millī*)	Russ.: *Gosudarstvennye komitety nacional'noy bezopasnosti,* State Committee for National Security, successor of the KGB.
Komsomol		Russ.: *Kommunističeskii Soyuz Molodyoži,* the youth division of the Communist Party established in 1918.
MRD		Motor Rifle Division; Russ.: *Motostrelkovaya diviziya,* in Tajikistan the 201st MRD.
MRR		Motor Rifle Regiment; Russ.: *Motostrelkovyj polk.*
Maxdum		Honorific title for Sufi authorities (Arabic: *maḫdūm*).
Muhoğir		Tajik for "person living in exile," mostly people from the mountainous areas in Tajikistan who were forcibly resettled since the 1920s.
Murid		Tajik for "student, follower," a term predominately used for those who follow Sufi authorities (the *muršid*); usually the status of a *murid* implies the rendition of services for the *muršid.*
Muršid		Tajik for "teacher, master," usually a Sufi authority who instructs a group (or individual) *murid.*
MVD (see also VKD)		Russ.: *Ministerstvo vnutrennikh del,* Ministry of Internal Affairs.
Nohiyya		Tajik term for district, the lowest administrative tier in Soviet and post-Soviet Tajikistan (Russ.: *rayon*).
Oblast		See *viloyat.*
OMON		Russ.: *Otryad Mobilniy Osobovo Naznačeniya,* "Special Purpose Mobile Unit" of the MVD.
Pir		Tajik for "old," honorific title for a representative of a Sufi order (*tariqa*).
Presidium of the Supreme Soviet	*Presidiumi Šūroi Olī* or *riyosati Šūroi Olī*	Permanent body of the Supreme Soviet, elected by the Supreme Soviet and acting on its behalf while not in session.
qoziyot		(Tajik for the office of a judge, from the Arabic *qāḍī,* "judge") Since 1988 the republican quasi-state institution for regulating "Islam" in Tajikistan hived out of the SADUM. Chaired by a *qozikalon* ("Supreme Judge").
Rayon		See *nohiyya.*
RSFSR		Russian Soviet Federative Socialist Republic.

Table A.1

Abbreviation/ Term	Tajik	Explanation/Translation
SADUM		Russ.: *Dukhovnoe upravlenie musul'man Sredney Azii i Kazakhstana*. The Spiritual Administration of the Muslims of Central Asia and Kazakhstan was the central Soviet institution to regulate Islam in Central Asia.
Supreme Soviet	*Šūroi olī*	Between 1938 and 1995 the highest decision-making body in the TaSSR and Republic of Tajikistan.
Tariqa		Tajik for "path" usually used for Sufi brotherhood such as the Naqšbandiyya or Qaderiyya.
TaSSR		Tajik Soviet Socialist Republic.
UTO	INOT	Russ.: *Ob'edinyonnaya tadžikskaya oppoziciya* (OTO), Taj.: *Ittihodiyai nerūhoi oppozitsioni Tоğik*. The "United Tajik Opposition" was established in 1994 by the IRPT, DPT, the Moscow-based Coordination Centre for Opposition Forces and the refugee organization *Umed*. Later La'li Badaxšon (1997) joined the UTO.
Viloyat		Tajik term for province (Russ.: *oblast*). A *viloyat* consists of various districts (Taj.: *nohiyya*, Russ.: *rayon*).
VKD (see MVD)	ī	Ministry of Internal Affairs

Introduction

On 23 May 2003, the population of a small hamlet in the Nurobod district in the Qarotegin Valley gathered at the northern edge of their village in a small grove to remember the day "the War came" to their community ten years ago. In a solemn ceremony the community commemorated their relatives who were killed that day and buried in the grove. No information board pointed out to the importance of the location for the local population and no government official from the district administration conjured stability (*subot*), peace (*tinĝ*) and national unity (*vahdati millī*) in post-conflict Tajikistan. After the ceremony, the men went to the small teahouse while the women met in one of the larger farmhouses. Over tea and *plov* the men recalled for their foreign guests the tragic events of 23 May 1993, when a group of militiamen from the Popular Front advanced upon their hamlet, dislodged the opposition and occupied the village after heavy fighting that killed several civilians and combatants. The narratives of the men in the teahouse had two interconnected layers: First, they remembered what happened in (and to) their community since the late 1980s, during the tumultuous time of independence 1991, the outbreak of the civil war in May 1992 and eventually the fateful day in May 1993 from a local perspective focused on everyday life of their families, friends and neighbors. The second layer tried to rationalize or make sense of the cruel fate that had befallen the village by integrating the local events into the larger master narrative of the civil war. This second layer operated with assumptions why the conflict broke out hinting to issues such as regionalism, ideology and elite conflicts. Over the years, I listened to similar narratives in Dushanbe, Xuĝand, Qūrĝonteppa, Šahrtuz, Kūlob, Xoruĝ and other parts of Tajikistan. These memories of local conflict dynamics often deviate from the master narratives rationalizing the civil war in academic papers and political discourses. The many puzzle pieces I collected draw a complex and

1

intricate picture of the conflict that raised more questions than it answered.[1]
The sequence of events is often contested, biographical data on central
actors is notoriously inaccurate and important details are omitted. In order
to organize the puzzle pieces and reconstruct the historical context of Tajikistan's civil war, I consulted media reports and a hitherto neglected genre:
25 autobiographical accounts by key actors of the turbulent time between
Perestroika, independence and the outbreak of violence in May 1992. These
texts are the central source for the following analysis of the origins of the civil
war in Tajikistan.

OBJECTIVES AND LIMITS

In May 1992 political and social tensions in the former Soviet Republic of
Tajikistan escalated to a devastating civil war, which killed approximately
40,000–100,000 people and displaced more than one million.[2] The enormous
challenge of the Soviet Union's disintegration compounded by inner-elite
conflicts, ideological disputes and state failure triggered a downward spiral
to one of the worst violent conflicts in the post-Soviet space. The origins and
parameters of the Tajik Civil War have been analyzed in various shorter publications since the early 1990s, but arguably the General Peace Accord 1997
and the subsequent peace building in Tajikistan have attracted more scholarly
attention than the origins of the conflict.[3] A detailed monograph on the origins
of the civil war has not been published yet and this manuscript has no other
ambition than to discuss these origins in greater historical detail. My account
focuses on the time period between the Dushanbe riots in February 1990 and
November/December 1992, when the 16th Session of the Supreme Soviet and
the successive "capture" of Dushanbe on 10 December 1992 by the Popular
Front (Taj.: *Fronti xalqī* or Russ.: *Narodniy Front Tadžikistana*) transformed
the nature of the conflict.

As with any historical events, the origins of the Tajik Civil War go back
in history to pre-Soviet Central Asia, to the enforcement of Soviet rule in the
1920s and to seven decades of Soviet transformation. Although I consider the
longue durée perspectives and structural causes as important for the analysis
of Tajikistan's civil war, my focus lies on the events between 1990 and 1992,
the key actors and the many contingencies that shaped the tumultuous time
between Perestroika, Glasnost and independence. While the February riots—
in Tajikistan known as the "Bloody Month of Bahman" (*Bahmanmohi xunin*)[4]
or plainly as the "February Events" (*voqeahoi fevralī*)—mark the outbreak
of politically motivated violence in the unfolding disintegration of the Soviet
system, the 16th Session of the Supreme Soviet in November 1992 eventually
established a new dominant elite and political economy in Tajikistan, thus

deciding the civil war by this time.[5] However, after the militias from Kūlob (a city and region in south-eastern Tajikistan) captured Dushanbe, the conflict was far from over. Instead, the fighting shifted from the densely populated southern lowlands to the "remote" mountainous east, the Qarotegin Valley and its many tributary valleys. The fighting in the east was no less cruel and terrorizing for the local population, but the domestic and international perception gradually changed: The opposition transformed into an "insurgence" sustained by (foreign) Islamist groups in a "traditionally" restive region (referring to earlier Soviet discourses on the Qarotegin Valley). Although peace talks between the government of Rahmonov and the United Tajik Opposition commenced in 1994, it took the two parties until 1997 and significant external pressure by Iran and Russia to agree on the General Peace Accord.

This account does not look for a specific variable all other variables are subordinated to—keeping in mind Stéphane Dudoignon's observation that in the case of the Tajik Civil War one particular variable often conceals other variables.[6] I explain the causes of Tajikistan's civil war with a historical narrative addressing the many contested events, their sequences and how individuals and groups shaped the dynamics of events or responded to them. This historical narrative recognizes long-term structural causes of the conflict originating in the Soviet transformation of Central Asia since the 1920s as well as short-term causes triggered by Perestroika or Glasnost and the rapid dismantling of the Soviet Union. This perspective on the civil war partly grew out of the impression that previous research did not consider the role of individual actors sufficiently. Therefore my analysis is actor oriented and focusses on key individuals who were confronted with sudden changes in the course events, their agency in the unfolding conflict and their adaptation to the changing context of independence, such as Būrī Karim (a reformer and chairman of the State Planning Agency Gosplan), Safaralī Kenğaev (chairman of the Supreme Soviet), Rahmon Nabiev (president of Tajikistan), Abdullo Nurī (founder of the Islamic Revival Party of Tajikistan, IRPT), "Bobo" ("Grandfather"), Sangak Safarov (an ex-convict and field commander from Kūlob), Asliddin Sohibnazar (a reformer and co-founder of the Democratic Party of Tajikistan, DPT), Hoğī Akbar Tūrağonzoda (Tajikistan's *qozikalon*[7]) or Šodmon Yusuf (chairman of the DPT). The attention to individual actors also hints at the many contingencies—personal interests, rivalries and animosities—that have shaped the cause of events. Furthermore, several key actors have composed their memoirs, and these autobiographical texts form the central source corpus of this manuscript. Paired with complementary sources such as the media coverage and interviews, the autobiographical sources provide insights of how Tajik politicians, field commanders and intellectuals perceived and rationalized the outbreak of the civil war within the complex context of post-Soviet decolonization, Islamic revival and nationalist renaissance. By integrating the origins of Tajikistan's conflict into the historical context of the late Soviet era, the interpretation and analysis of the qualitative empirical data reflects on the wider discussion of "new" and "old" wars by Mary Kaldor, Stathis Kalyvas, John Mueller and others.[8]

DESIGNATING THE CIVIL WAR IN TAJIKISTAN

The civil war in Tajikistan is generally designated in Tajik as internal war (*ǧangi doxilī*), civil war (*ǧangi šahravandī* or *graždanī*), fratricidal war (*ǧangi barodarkuš*), a regional war (*ǧangi mintaqavī*) or a suicidal war (*ǧangi xudkušī*). Occasionally, the conflict is labeled the "Second Civil War," while the first one was the enforcement of Soviet rule in Central Asia against the resistance by local groups between 1920 and 1931.[9]

In his first New Year's address on 31 December 1992, Emomalī Rahmonov—then since a few weeks Chairman of the Supreme Soviet—called the civil war a "fratricidal and destructive war."[10] While these labels are largely uncontested, more controversial and judgmental designations circulate as well: Prominently, Rahmonov referred in his *The Tajiks in the Mirror of History* to the civil war as a "senseless war (*ǧangi bema'nī*)."[11] Rahmonov was not the first to label the conflict as senseless, notably Safaralī Kenǧaev characterized the civil war as senseless in his memoirs a few years earlier.[12] The notion of a "senseless war" has been decidedly challenged by Būrī Karim who insisted that the civil war was "destructive and not fought without an objective but was related to the soul, blood, homeland and honor (*ǧon, xun, Vatan, nomus*)"[13] and insisted that the conflict broke out because of "ideological, kinship (*qavmī*) and national conflicts."[14] The notion of senselessness implies a cruel contingency and chance. It is particularly difficult to understand for the surviving members of a family that their father, brother, sister, mother, son or daughter was killed "by chance" and without any consoling reason. Individuals and societies try to make sense out of horrifying events or they tend to suppress the memory and commemoration.[15] A similar strategy of making sense out of horrifying events, however without recognizing one's own collective or individual responsibility, is the description of the civil war as imposed by others. For instance, Abdullo Nurī, the late chairman of the IRPT, stated in an interview with *Radioi Ozodī* (the Tajik service of Radio Free Europe) that the "war was imposed on us (*boloi mo tahmil šuda bud*)."[16] Hoǧī Akbar Tūraǧonzoda likewise asserted that the "war was planned outside of Tajikistan and imposed (*tahmil*) on the nation."[17] As one of the few, Ibrohim Usmonov, a former advisor to Rahmonov and member of the National Reconciliation Commission, explicated that the civil war was *not* imposed from outside but triggered by domestic forces.[18]

The question of how to label the civil war in Tajikistan is far more than a philological exercise but indicates how different groups or individuals remember, commemorate and understand the civil war—a highly contentious issue in post-conflict Tajikistan. The contentiousness derives from the fact that there is no official commemoration of the conflict, instead the re-establishment of "order" and "peace" is remembered. No central memorial or commemoration day remembers the victims or the conflict as such. While there is no official commemoration at the national level, local communities, which have suffered from extreme violence between 1992 and 1997, do commemorate the conflict informally as narrated in the introduction: Former kolkhoz and sovkhoz (collective farms) communities in Qūrġonteppa or the Qarotegin Valley remember the day the "war came" to their community. In most reports, the immediate fighting took place within a relatively short time, from a few hours to a few days but transformed in the aftermath into a protracted conflict with random eruptions of violence and a vicious cycle of revenge and counter revenge.

TAJIKISTAN IN THE 20TH CENTURY: A HISTORY OF VIOLENCE

The experience of violence was no novelty for the Tajik society in 1992. Throughout the 20th century, Tajikistan's population experienced periods of intense physical and permanent structural violence. In the 1920s local armed groups—the *bosmačī*—resisted in the eastern and southern parts of the country the establishment of Soviet rule. Although the Red Army repressed the uprising in central parts of the Tajik Socialist Soviet Republic (TaSSR), the insurgence continued in the remote mountain valleys until 1931.[19] The Stalinist collectivization from 1928 onward compounded the plight of the local population and triggered an exodus of approximately half a million people from southern Tajikistan to Afghanistan. In less than a decade after the revolution, eastern Bukhara lost according to Soviet statistics 42.5% of its population—in some districts such as Kūlob, Qūrġonteppa, Hisor or Qubodiyon more than 60% of the population perished or migrated.[20] With the consolidation of Soviet rule in the TaSSR, the traditional elites, above all religious authorities (*ulamo*[21]) and landowners (*bey* or *beg*), were systematically repressed, expropriated and often arrested. From 1926 on, the Soviet administration initiated the large-scale agricultural transformation of the Vaxš valley (*Vaxšstroy*) for cotton cultivation. A dense irrigation system fundamentally changed the ecosystem of the sparsely populated southern lowlands and since cotton cultivation needs a high input of manual labor, the Soviet authorities resettled large parts of the population from the mountainous parts of the country, that is, the Qarotegin Valley, Zarafšon, Mastčoh and Badaxšon.[22] The resettlement was insufficiently prepared and many people perished due to the harsh climate, diseases and poor accommodation.[23]

In 1937/1938 Stalin's Great Terror reached also the empire's periphery and killed the first generation of Bolshevik activists in the TaSSR: The 1st Secretary of the CPT, Širinšoh Šohtemur (1899–1937), the former chairman of the revolutionary committee (RevKom), Nusratullo Maxsum (1881–1937), Ūrunboy Ašūrov (1903–1938) and Abdullo Rahimboev (1896–1938) were arrested, tortured, exhibited on show trials and executed. The Great Terror was followed by Nazi Germany's invasion of the Soviet Union. In the Great Patriotic War approximately 300,000 Tajiks were mobilized to serve in the Soviet Armed Forces and some 50,000 Tajik military personnel and 70,000 civilians perished in the war, corresponding with 7.8% of the entire population.[24] Until today "Victory Day" is commemorated in Tajikistan with military parades and an address by the president or minister of defense to the veterans at the central memorial in Dushanbe's spacious Victory Park.

In the 1950s and especially after Stalin's demise in 1953, the TaSSR's urban population experienced decades of reduced physical violence. Dushanbe emerged as a Soviet urban space with a high level of ethnic diversity. For rural communities, especially those of the mountainous Qarotegin Valley, the Badaxšon, Mastčoh and Zarafšon valleys, the 1950s however meant again large-scale resettlement campaigns to the cotton-cultivated areas in southern and northern Tajikistan. The resettlement did not break up communities since the collective farms were often organized according to ethnic or regional origins. Larger resettled communities, such as the Ġarmī population, had their own social "gravity" and maintained only limited interaction (for instance intermarriage) with other groups. Internally resettled communities in the TaSSR adopted the term *muhoġir* (Tajik for emigrant, refugee or evacuee—today used for labor migrants in Russia) and exile strengthened the imagined or real bonds with what was considered and imagined home. *Muhoġir* communities cultivated their specific regional identity sometimes with a nostalgic romanticization of the alleged pristine mountainous environment they had been deported from. The resettlement dramatically changed the regional and ethnic distribution of the population. While in the 1920s two-thirds of the population lived in mountainous areas, the ratio rapidly changed and in 1989 less than a quarter of the population lived in the mountainous regions.[25] In 1926, the region around Qūrġonteppa had according to the Soviet census only 33,000 inhabitants; in the early 1950s the population had increased to 250,000, in 1970 to 650,000 and in 1989 to more than one million people.[26] Migration also changed the political and economic weight of certain regions: Kūlob continuously lost political (representation in the republican administration) and economic (resource allocation) influence to Qūrġonteppa.

In the late 1960s the economic development lost its pace, investment in the agricultural sector faltered, while the ambitious industrial projects, such as the USSR's second largest Aluminum smelter in Tursunzoda, were prestige projects with operational costs exceeding profits. Simultaneously economic growth did not keep pace with the population growth in particular among Tajikistan's titular ethnic population, which registered the highest population growth rates and the lowest rural out-migration in the entire Soviet Union.[27] Especially in the agricultural areas in southern Tajikistan competition over the limited resources intensified and resulted in local conflicts and tensions. As in other parts of the USSR, youth violence increased in suburban and urban Tajikistan, deeply worrying the Brezhnevite "middle" class (the "Soviet baby boomers"[28]), overwhelmingly cadres in the public administration. Many sources, however, portray the 1960s and 70s as a time of remarkable stability, peace and progress. For many Tajik men born between the late 1950s and the mid-1960s these relatively peaceful years were disrupted by the experience of extreme violence during the Soviet military campaign in Afghanistan. In the nine years of occupation, many Tajiks served as conscripts in the Soviet military intelligence service (GRU) or the civilian administration in Kabul. Many veterans of the Afghan war, the *Afgancy* or in the official Soviet terminology "Internationalist Soldiers" (*voiny internacionalisty*), returned with disturbing memories from Afghanistan and had difficulties reintegrating into the Soviet society. Tajik *Afgancy* played a significant role in the nationalist movements of the late 1980s and many became involved in the fighting during the civil war.[29]

THE ORIGINS OF THE CIVIL WAR: THE STATE OF RESEARCH RECONSIDERED

A set of interpretations on the origins of Tajikistan's Civil War has emerged framing the conflict within the complex context of the USSR's disintegration, which is considered the main catalyst for the outbreak of violence in Tajikistan. Most accounts identify several determinants for the origins of the civil war, namely (1) regionalism and Soviet administrative practice, (2) ideological disputes and the role of Islam in the Tajik society, (3) the catastrophic economic downturn and the intensifying competition over local resources and finally (4) the fragmentation of elites. Most prominently, the civil war is described as a conflict between regional solidarity groups or networks that possess distinct perceptions of regional identities, usually referred to as "regionalism" (Taj.: *mahalgaroī* or *mahalčigī*; Rus.: *mestničestvo*).[30]

Not only scholarly works refer to regionalism as one of the central causes of the civil war, also the primary sources and Tajik informants highlight the importance of regionalism. There are variations how regionalism is narrated: as primordial "clans" which "survived" the Soviet transformation of the Tajik society; or as regional-based solidarity networks which emerged within the Soviet administrative system and which were manipulated through political and social exclusion or interference by the center (Moscow).[31] In this book I argue that regional solidarity networks *were* important, both for the outbreak of the conflict and the mobilization. However, in reference to John Mueller, I consider *mahalgaroī* in Tajikistan's civil war as an "ordering device than as an impelling force"[32] and not causative for the conflict. To some extent, the regionalism motive in the Tajik conflict resembles in the form (tropes and narratives) and function (rationalization) the motive of ethnicity in other civil wars.[33] Although ethnicity was addressed in the political confrontations (with an post-colonial twist toward the Russian and an hostile "Othering" of the Uzbek minorities), conflicting ethnic identities were not causative for the outbreak of violence and the key actors in Tajikistan were very well aware that the conflict was first of all an inner Tajik one. Furthermore, regionalist sentiment facilitated the mobilization and dynamics of the conflict, but it should not be understood as a Tajik exotic peculiarity. The extended family ties, provenience from a certain neighborhood or village (*mahalla, qišloq*), district (*nohiyya*) or region (*viloyat*), marriage patterns, membership in a professional association or a specific occupation generate symbolic capital and subsequently mutual trust in other societies as well.[34]

In late Soviet Tajikistan, within the context of Glasnost and the nationalist awakening, the urban civil society and emerging independent media discussed next to political reforms the very idea of Tajikistan—its authentic history, religion, language and culture. Both, political reforms and the imagination of Tajikistan were contentious issues and controversially discussed in the media as well as during the political rallies on the streets and squares of Dushanbe.[35] Perhaps, Dov Lynch's statement that the civil war in Tajikistan was not "a conflict over the 'idea' of Tajikistan"[36] should be therefore modified: Although Tajikistan's intelligentsia and political nomenklatura shared similar assumptions on the ethnogenesis of the Tajiks and the emergence of Tajik statehood, they were far from united on the question where to locate national history, culture and language in a larger regional context or on their societal and political vision of a future Tajikistan. The urban intelligentsia was a product of the Soviet social mobilization and local processes which have shaped the political economy of the TaSSR since the 1940s. During Perestroika and Glasnost, intellectuals and political activists started to reconsider their dependencies and engaged in an anti-colonial analysis of the situation which contributed to the increasing polarization of the Tajik society along several contentious subjects, such as language, regional ownership or history. Especially reformers and the intelligentsia had distanced themselves from the Communist Party's old guard and started to establish civil associations and political clubs discussing the status of the Tajik language, the question of Tajikistan's Iranian and Islamic heritage, center-periphery relations and the regional ownership. The demand for economic reforms, however vague and inconsistent, generated additional tensions between the CPT nomenklatura, the nationalist intelligentsia, urban reformers, rural functionaries in the agro-industrial complex and representatives of the socially and economically marginalized regions.

The 1970s and 1980s saw the emergence of radically alternative concepts of political and social order among young Muslim activists, some of them organized in the *harakat* (movement), the proto Islamic Revival Party of Tajikistan (IRPT). These activists demanded the reintegration of Islam into Tajikistan's public sphere and national narrative and challenged the dominant patterns of resource allocation. The idea of an Islamic political system became a highly contentious issue after the Iranian Revolution 1979 and the Soviet nomenklatura responded with an increasingly belligerent defamation campaign against Islam and Islamic activism. The alleged secular-religious divide eventually shaped the master narrative of Tajikistan's conflict in the early 1990s and the secular government started to conceptualize Islam as external to the authentic Tajik identity.

Next to regionalism and ideology, the economic and social development of the TaSSR is widely regarded as an important factor contributing to the increasing tensions in the Tajik society. The TaSSR was the least developed and most externally dependent of the 15 Soviet republics and received significant subsidies from Moscow, according to some calculations up to 46% of the annual budget.[37] Investment in the labor-intensive agricultural sector contracted since the 1970s and did not compensate for the increasing degradation of agricultural areas and the attrition of the irrigation system. Ambitious large-scale industrial projects were economically unsustainable and increased the uneven development between the marginalized eastern parts and central/ southern parts of the TaSSR. The overrepresentation of non-Central Asian nationalities (Russians, Byelorussians, Ukrainians and Germans) in industrial employment fueled animosities among the different ethnic groups in the TaSSR. In the agrarian sector, high population growth and limited rural out-migration among the Tajik and Uzbek communities intensified local competition over limited resources and arable land. The economic crisis of the Soviet Union in the late 1980s was aggravated by the erratic economic policies of the TaSSR's nomenklatura and the collapse of the USSR led to a dramatic economic downturn on the macro-economic level with a catastrophic impact on the household level. The economic crisis had a local micro-economic impact and was understood in terms of a conflict over limited resources between regionally defined groups and therefore contributed to the perception that regionalism triggered the conflict.[38]

In May 1992, Tajikistan spiraled down to complete state failure and many accounts hold Tajikistan's wider nomenklatura responsible for the dynamics of the conflict. In complicity with organized crime, the nomenklatura dismantled state institutions and facilitated the increasing privatization of violence by non-state actors. These violent non-state actors transformed the conflict to an instrumentalist struggle of local elite groups and opportunistic individuals in a weak institutional environment. Markowitz emphasizes the fragmentation and ultimately defection of the security forces on the local and regional tiers.[39] Idil Tunçer-Kılavuz assumes a top-down mobilization in May 1992 in which President Rahmon Nabiev mobilized his networks in the region and therefore intentionally "chose the war option in order to maintain the support of the hardliners."[40] Although the assumption of a top-down mobilization should not be categorically dismissed, the conjecture of an intentional decision by Nabiev to "choose" the war option dramatically overestimates his situative capacity and influence in May 1992 and underestimates the many contingencies and the local deviances as well as the agency of local actors. We have relatively little understanding of local processes and cleavages—the "disjunction between center and periphery"[41]—in the Tajik conflict. The journalistic and academic accounts provide rather unsystematic insights into the local dynamics and underline the complex nature of the conflict. In civil conflicts, local cleavages are often articulated in terms of the master narrative, but a closer analysis and a more systematic evaluation of available sources may reveal important deviations from the established conceptualizations as Kalyvas assumes: "Because the meaning of rebellions is often articulated by elites in the language of national cleavages, many observers erroneously code them as actually mobilizing popular support along those cleavages."[42] Violent non-state actors in complicity with the former nomenklatura were arguably the main drivers of violence in the early stage of the conflict, but as I try to show here, they were not merely 'activated' but had agency and even enunciated their own narratives of legitimacy. The empirical qualitative data presented and analyzed here might provide insights into how local actors (the micro level) refer to "master narratives" or adopt the particular parameters of the conflict.

In most memoirs and official narratives of the Tajik Civil War, the Tajiks are presented as a peaceful, sedentary, cultured and diligent people and the civil war as "imposed" by foreign forces. Notably both, the government of Emomalī Rahmonov and the United Tajik Opposition (UTO) under the leadership of Abdullo Nurī, agreed on the hidden foreign hand, which imposed the civil war on the Tajik people. Undoubtedly, Uzbekistan and

Russia provided military and financial assistance to the Popular Front and individual field commanders. Russian and Uzbek authorities carefully prepared the convention of the 16th Session of the Supreme Soviet in Xuǧand and orchestrated Rahmonov's election to its chairman. In 1993 the Uzbek Air Force supported the Rahmonov government with airstrikes against the opposition positions in the Qarotegin Valley. Vice versa, the opposition received weapons and training from Gulbuddin Hekmatyar's *Ḥezb-e Islāmī* or the Northern Alliance under Ahmad Shah Massoud and financial support from Iran. The influence of external actors in the conflict is undisputable and Russia, Iran and Uzbekistan had an impact on the course of the conflict from 1993 on.[43] However, the immediate *outbreak* of the civil war in May 1992 was neither a "plot" nor a "conspiracy" by foreign powers designed to deprive the Tajiks of their statehood and independence, but triggered by local actors. In 1992, there were no external sources of legitimation or funding for the conflicting groups. Instead, Uzbekistan and Russia got gradually involved in Tajikistan's civil war in the autumn months of 1992, but their early engagement was improvised. Russian special forces and officers of the 201st Motor Rifle Division deployed in Tajikistan took matters into their own hands and did not act on directives by Moscow. Therefore, the involvement of foreign powers will be less addressed here.

Instead, the following account offers a detailed historical narrative with a particular focus on individual actors, their motivation, legitimation strategies and response to the rapid transformation. While reading through the sources and the secondary literature, three subjects recur repeatedly which have not been sufficiently addressed in the relevant literature: A post-colonial perspective on the Glasnost discussions among the Tajik intelligentsia, concepts of masculinity in the legitimation of violent non-state actors in the civil war and eventually the contingencies in the outbreak of the civil war.

Contingency is a contested category in history and Reinhart Koselleck calls contingency "ahistorical," indicating inconsistencies both in its determining factors as well as in the incommensurability of its consequences. Koselleck concedes that the notion of contingency eventually contains a specific historical aspect and postulates that in modern historiography, contingency indicates the absence of moral or rational public policy. I do not understand the concept of contingency as contrary to theoretical models reflecting on mobilization and macro-political results behind the course of events. Instead, I consider contingency as a useful category to bridge the micro and macro levels of contemplation and to emphasize the importance of individual actors and catalysts.[44] The discussion about the controversial designation of the Tajik Civil War as "senseless" highlights the problem of contingency and structural (i.e., rational) causes of the conflict. Various authors are well aware of the contingencies but make circuitous efforts to refute chance in the events.

Būrī Karim, for instance, maintains in an ambivalent narrative that the events
were *not* contingent (*tasadufī*) but a manifestation of the people's hopes and
aspirations: "The Tajik people have entered the political stage, the first time
deliberately and consciously, with the complete awareness of the anomaly, the
deception and indifference of the rulers."[45] The reference to contingency does
neither intend to view violence in the Tajik Civil War as fundamentally "irrational" nor suspend the search for structural causes such as Soviet administrative practice, uneven economic development, elite fragmentation or identity
politics, but should remind us of the complexity of the civil war and the often
cruel contingencies that shape violent conflicts.[46]

Field commanders and warlords in the Tajik Civil War were exclusively
male. Women participated in the emerging civil associations and were
involved in the political confrontation, such as the poet Gulruxsor Safieva,
the lawyer Oynihol Bobonazarova or the Communist Party deputy Adolat
Rahmonova, but not a single source reports about the active involvement of
women as combatants in the civil war (but sadly numerous accounts report
about violence *against* women).[47] Many male politicians and field commanders refer in their legitimation narratives explicitly to "concepts of masculinity,"[48] in particular to the idea of *ğavonmardī* (Tajik for "manliness").
Chapter 7 deals in greater detail with the issue of violence and masculinity in
the Tajik Civil War.

Last but not least, my account on the origins of the civil war in Tajikistan
adopts a post-colonial perspective to the discussion among the Tajik intelligentsia locating a brief post-colonial moment during the final years of
the Soviet Union. A younger generation of Tajik intellectuals and political
activists suddenly scrutinized the intellectual dependencies on the center
(Moscow) and reformulated the Soviet paradigms on history, culture, language and religion. The post-colonial moment never fully blossomed in
Tajikistan and the outbreak of violence in May 1992 suspended this period.[49]

THE SOURCES: AUTOBIOGRAPHIES

In general, archival sources covering the events in Tajikistan between 1990
and 1993 are not accessible yet and considering the destruction of the Tajik
KGB/Communist Party archive in May 1992, the amount of archival sources
for the administrative and political history of Tajikistan might be limited
anyway. Instead, the main source corpus for this study are 25 autobiographical texts published by key actors since 1992. These accounts have been randomly used for mining information on the events, but often without a proper
contextualization addressing validity, narrative strategies or the authors'
agenda.[50] The texts consulted here have been published predominately in

Tajik, sometimes with Russian text fragments, due to the political situation often outside Tajikistan with a low print run. Only a few titles are available in Tajikistan but scattered in libraries throughout Central Asia, Europe and North America. Moreover the Tajik government and its academic institutions have started to sort out "disagreeable" literature in order to manipulate the commemoration of the recent history and the discourse on the civil war.[51]

The accounts under consideration here significantly differ from the established literary genre of autobiography and life writing popular in the wider Persianate context, represented in Tajikistan for instance by Sadriddin Aynī's *Yoddoštho (Memoirs)* or Ǧalol Ikromī's *Onči az sar guzašt (Those things which have happened)*.[52] Although Būrī Karim, Safaralī Kenǧaev and Asliddin Sohibnazar have literary ambitions, their texts provide predominately a digest of the events, highly polemic and hastily composed with little editing competing for the interpretative predominance of the events covered. Although the authors, who were at the same time key actors in the unfolding events, claim that their analyses reflect the "objective truth," they reproduce an individual, biased and partial interpretation of the events legitimizing their personal decisions and actions.

Most of the memoirs expect from the reader extensive background knowledge on the political, social and historical developments in the TaSSR. The information provided—numbers, dates, places and personal names—are notoriously inaccurate and often exaggerated indicating the partisan interpretation. Although the narratives usually follow a chronological sequence, there are sudden fissures and unrelated digressions and flashbacks.

While the historical value of autobiographical texts is undisputed, their interpretation (fiction/nonfiction), verification, contextualization in collective reproducible horizon of experience (the "social imaginaries") or representation of the "Self" (or "Selfhood") is discussed extensively in the relevant literature.[53] In reference to Charles Taylor's concept of social imaginaries, autobiographies reflect the forms of social constraint individuals are exposed to and show in their narratives acquired dispositions (beyond questions of credibility or validity). Self-construction is guided by larger sociological structures determining the individuals' sense of the possibilities of their intended actions.[54] In these terms, autobiographical writing is not primarily the retrospective reconstruction of the author's life or the events covered, but the self-perception, self-reflection and construction of an identity and social role model, which also reflects flexible and shifting attitudes of personal identities, influenced by the rules and dynamics of the social fields.[55] Greyerz points out that personal/autobiographical narratives reproduce and create discourses which are embedded in a collective context and that the reconstruction in self-narratives allows us to analyze the "specific cultural, linguistic, material and, last but not least, social embeddedness. Ultimately a majority of these texts [...] probably tell us more about groups than they do about individuals."[56] Similarly, Fulbrook and Rublack conclude that

> [o]ne does not have to follow down a post-modernist route to realize the significance of the fact that no account of the self can be produced which is not constructed in terms of social discourses: that the very concepts people use to describe themselves, the ways in which they choose to structure and to account for their past lives, the values, norms, and common-sense explanations to which they appeal in providing meaning to their narratives, are intrinsically products of the times through which they have lived.[57]

Thus, the narratives refer to the social and cultural embeddedness of their authors and help us to understand the social and political transformation of Tajikistan since the 1980s. Importantly, the authors' accounts represent a *retrospective* interpretation and rationalization of the events and a legitimation of their actions. This raises the question of accuracy of the memories and the authenticity of the motivations and intentions depicted in the accounts. Complementary sources (media reports or interviews) either support or disprove the representation of the events in the autobiographical accounts, but arguably more important for the analysis of the origins of Tajikistan's civil war is the interpretation of the particular tropes and rhetorical figures in these narratives. Some of the autobiographical texts need to be singled out, either for their particular relevance as source material or their aggressive polemic.

Būrī Karim's Faryodi solho

Būrī Karim[ov], born in 1957 in the Leninsky district close to Dushanbe, was a career functionary in Gosplan (*Gosudarstvenniy Komitet po Planirovaniyu*, the republican State Planning Committee) and between 1988 and 1990 minister for transport as well as deputy chairman of the Council of Ministers (which today corresponds with the office of a vice prime minister). Karim belonged to a relatively small group of CPT officials, which demanded more substantial (or radical) reforms in the TaSSR since the late 1980s. During the February 1990 Events, Karim emerged briefly as one of the popular leaders of the opposition. However, with the subsequent suppression of the protests and the nomenklatura's prevalence, Karim was politically sidelined. His voluminous *Faryodi solho* (*The Cry of Years*), published in Moscow 1997, is a biographical account organized as collage of diary entries, copies of official documents, newspaper articles, photos and comments by Karim covering the period between the mid-1980s and 1997.[58] His intention was to offer advice (*pand*) for the future generation, to remind them of the historical greatness of the Tajik people but also their bitter (*talx*) moments such as the conquest of Alexander the Great, the invasion of the Arabs, the destruction under the Mongols and finally the Russian conquest in the 19th century.[59] One of Karim's central concerns was to refute the nomenklatura's version of the events and to show the truth (*haqiqat*), but notably he conceded that he has difficulties to be objective in his account.[60] Due to the diary character and the frequent incorporation of newspaper/magazine articles, Karim's account is relatively reliable with dates and the sequence of events and less polemic in its tone (compared to the other texts). Already marginalized in 1990, Karim played a minor political role in the political developments after 1991 but remained a mindful observant of Tajikistan's trials and tribulations until today.

Hikmatullo Nasriddinov's Tarkiš

Tarkiš (*Explosion*) depicts the events between the late 1980s and 1992 from the perspective of Hikmatullo Nasriddinov, an ambitious politician and CPT Deputy from Kūlob. Born 1939 in Mūʿminonbod, Nasriddinov had been minister for agricultural water management between 1986 and 1992 and was one of the presidential candidates in the 1991 elections. He published *Tarkiš* in 1995 and many of my Tajik colleagues and informants consider his account as fairly accurate and balanced. Although Nasriddinov maintained that he wrote *Tarkiš* in order to expose the prevalent regionalism in the TaSSR/ Tajikistan, his account ventures far beyond the issue of regionalism and provides thoughtful insights to the political field and center-periphery relations in the TaSSR.[61] Nasriddinov lost his political influence with the outbreak of the civil war but remained a politician with modest fortune in the post-conflict Tajikistan.[62]

Asliddin Sohibnazar's Subhi Sitorakuš

Arguably, Sohibnazar's two-volume *Subhi sitorakuš* (*The Morning the Star Is Killed*) is the most elaborated, ambitious and personal narrative on the origins of Tajikistan's civil war. Sohibnazar, born 1939 in Kūhdara in the Rohatī district east of Dushanbe, had been a senior planning official in the agro-industrial complex and deputy of the Supreme Soviet. As a radical reformer, he left the Communist Party and established with like-minded intellectuals the Democratic Party of Tajikistan (DPT). As one of the few democratic deputies in the Supreme Soviet and member of the Presidium of the Supreme Soviet, Sohibnazar was one of the key political actors in Tajikistan until December 1992. His autobiographical account covers the time period from the late 1980s to the mid-1990s, however, with frequent retrospect excursions discussing his career in the later TaSSR.[63] Sohibnazar employs a range of remarkable narrative strategies to increase the impression of his memoir's credibility and authenticity. For instance, he introduces several authoritative witnesses for the events, such as the omniscient Russian KGB operative "Andrey," who predicts in detail the developments in Tajikistan, or the Tajik racketeer "Mūso," who is involved in the early violence and "knows" the masterminds behind the outbreak of the civil war.[64] Although Sohibnazar's account is not free from polemics, his dense narrative on the political trials and tribulations between 1989 and 1992 is a highly relevant source for the reconstruction of the conflict's origins.

Ibrohim Usmonov's Soli Nabiev

Ibrohim Usmonov, born 1948 in the Ašt *nohiyya* in Leninobod, has been a professor for journalism, former minister of communication (1992–1993), chairman of Tajikistan's Radio and TV Committee (1994), advisor to President Rahmon (until 2004) as well as a central figure in the peace negotiations between 1994 and 1997. He published his first account on the developments between 1991 and 1992 under the title *Soli Nabiev* (*The Year of Nabiev*) already in 1995. Although Usmonov refers in *Soli Nabiev* to his personal perception of the evolving political crisis in Tajikistan, his account is more of a political analysis than memoirs in a strict sense. Albeit he does not conceal his sympathies with the Communist Party, his judgement and evaluation is in general balanced and consistent considering the polarization of the society during these years. Usmonov continued to publish extensively on Tajikistan's recent history and was one of Rahmonov's key advisors in the peace negotiations with the UTO and member of the Peace and Reconciliation Commission after 1997. In 2013, Usmonov established the *Dialogue of Civilizations* format in Dushanbe in which prominent key actors, such as Davlat Usmon, Būrī Karim and others, have talked about their memories of the conflict.

Hoğī Akbar Tūrağonzoda's Miyoni obu ateš. . .

Hoğī Akbar Tūrağonzoda (born 1954 in Vahdatobod) was between 1988 and 1993 the *qozikalon*, formally the highest religious authority in the administration of Islam in Tajikistan. In many respects, Tūrağonzoda epitomized the political and social transformation of Perestroika in the religious field: As a young, versatile and charismatic descendant from a prominent religious family, he represented a new generation of religious specialists in Central Asia. Tūrağonzoda ably blended his appeals for a "return" to a normative understanding of the Hanafi Sunni tradition with nationalist imaginaries and a Perestroika/Glasnost discourse on economic and political change. Initially, he tried to remain independent in the unfolding political struggle, however in the increasing polarization of the Tajik society, he finally joined the opposition in spring 1992. As for today, Tūrağonzoda composed only a short account of the events between 1991 and 1992 under the title *Miyoni obu ateš* (*Between Water and Fire*) during his exile in Tehran.[65] Despite its brevity, the account offers valuable insights into Tūrağonzoda's conceptual thinking and his relationship with other important actors (such as Rahmon Nabiev and Safaralī Kenğaev). Since he has remained a public and controversial figure in Tajikistan, his frequent interventions—interviews and writings—are an important complementary source as well.

Three autobiographical accounts have to be singled out in this brief introduction for their aggressive polemics, exaggerations and limited factual validity: Šodmon Yusuf's *Tajikistan: The Price of Freedom*, Safaralī Kenğaev's three-volume *Coup d'état in Tajikistan* and Narzullo Dūstov's *A Wound in the Body of the Homeland*. While Yusuf is a representative of the reformist opposition, Kenğaev and Dūstov operated within the Popular Front. The three accounts share similar strategies of defamation and fraudulent misrepresentation, which deeply undermine the authenticity and validity of these sources but provide interesting insights into the political conflicts and the polarization.

Šodmon Yusuf's Tāğīkestān: Bahā-ye āzādī

Šodmon Yusuf, a former research fellow in the Philosophy Department of the Tajik Academy of Science and Communist Party organizer, was born in 1949 into a *muhoğir*-family (originally from Darband in the Qarotegin Valley) in a small village close to Šahrituz in southern Tajikistan. After post-graduate studies in Moscow, he returned to the TaSSR in 1987 but soon disassociated himself from the CPT. He sympathized with the Rastoxez movement and eventually became one of the co-founders the DPT in 1990. Yusuf published his autobiographical account *Tāğīkestān. Bahā-ye āzādī* (*Tajikistan: The Price of Freedom*) during his exile in Iran and apparently exile shaped his narrative. His coverage of the events between 1989 and 1992 comes in form of an embittered pamphlet against Russian/Soviet rule in the TaSSR "exposing" numerous conspiracies (mostly set in motion by the Uzbeks), genocides and atrocities against the Tajik people undermining some of the original concerns of his report, namely the plight of the civilian population in the Qūrġonteppa area during the first months of the civil war. Yusuf's *Tāğīkestān* is one of the most partisan accounts with gross exaggerations, countless inaccuracies and many false reports villainizing opponents and even de-humanizing them.

Safaralī Kenğaev's Tabadduloti Toğikiston

Kenğaev published several autobiographical accounts between the late 1980s and the mid-1990s. *Sūzi dil* (*Burning Heart*) covers the Perestroika time and the three-volume *Tabadduloti Toǧikiston* *(Revolution/Coup d'état in Tajikistan)*[66] is the most detailed accounts of the civil war by one of the leading political actors. Kenǧaev (1942–1999) was born into a Yaǧnobī family in Čoryakkoron, a suburb in western Dushanbe and presented himself as a staunch *homo sovieticus* rooted in the Soviet system. He graduated as 1965 with a law degree from the Tajik State University and started to work in the Public Persecutor's Office in Dushanbe. He quickly made a career and was promoted as district prosecutor and eventually to the republican transport sector prosecutor, when he was elected to the Supreme Soviet in 1990. Energetic, self-conscious and unscrupulous, he emerged as a central actor in the tumultuous time and organized the successful election campaign of Rahmon Nabiev for the presidential elections in November 1991 who in turn awarded him with the position of the chairman of the Supreme Soviet. In this position he significantly contributed to the increasing polarization of the political factions and his public assault on the minister of interior in April 1992 is considered a catalyst and provocation that contributed to the outbreak of violence. Kenǧaev, as his memoirs demonstrate, was a complex character, who referred to a mixture of strategies and methods originating in the Soviet political economy, to some extent an outsider to the system, a political adventurer with little ideological baggage. Kenǧaev's memoirs are— similar to Yusuf's account—partisan, biased, manipulative and highly unreliable. Kenǧaev maliciously defamed the entire political nomenklatura of the later TaSSR and independent Tajikistan including some of his political allies and his memoirs reflect the uncompromising polarization and confrontation dominating Tajikistan's politics.

Narzullo Dūstov's Zahm bar ǧismi vatan

Narzullo Dūstov, a confidant of Kenǧaev and Nabiev's vice president between December 1991 and May 1992, was born in 1940 in Qalʿai Xumb (Darvoz). Dūstov made a career in the TaSSR's transport sector and was director of the *avtobaza* No. 2 when he was elected to the Supreme Soviet in 1990. In September 1991, Nabiev selected him as running mate in the election campaign for the presidential office. Dūstov was appointed minister of transportation in 1993, but joined Mahmud Xudoyberdiev in his ill-fated attempted to seize Xuǧand in 1998.[67] His 1995 account *Zahm bar ǧismi vatan* (*A Wound in the Body of the Homeland*) is by far the most biased and erratic account on the Tajik Civil War and Dūstov's agitation against the Islamist opposition as *vahhobī* (Wahhabis) extremists exceeds even Kenǧaev's rancor and defamation. His account provides little reliable information and his narrative is saturated with conspiracy theories and untenable defamations.

The IRPT's Counter Discourse

Memoirs of the late Muhammadšarif Himmatzoda and Abdullo Nurī have not been published yet. Davlat Usmon reportedly finished his memoirs, but it will be difficult to publish them in the current political situation. Despite being politically marginalized and finally banned in 2015, the IRPT nonetheless published a counter-discourse on the Tajik Civil War. The IRPT's weekly *Nağot* had frequently featured articles on the events between 1990 and 1993 and the IRPT's Presidium had composed its standardized history, political legend and counter narrative on the origins of the party and its role in the conflict.[68] With the death of the IRPT's founder, Abdullo Nurī, in 2006, the IRPT had stepped up the publication of its history with a clear focus on Nurī's contribution to the peace process culminating in the General Peace Accord in 1997. In 2013 representatives of the IRPT published several memoirs and shorter biographical works on the occasion of the IRPT's 40th anniversary.[69] The continuous political pressure by the Tajik government—physical attacks on IRPT representatives, defamation campaigns in the state media, law suits and so forth—had certainly contributed to the intensified but often destitute effort by the IRPT to formulate a counter narrative on the events. Most of the memoirs published so far offer a rather docile reading of the *harakat* and IRPT's role in the final years of the USSR. Although controversial issues— such as the *domullo* Hindustonī's opposition toward Islamic activism—are addressed in the memoirs, the *harakat*/IRPT is mostly portrayed as a dissident cultural association and not as an Islamist political party, which maintained its armed militia during the conflict.[70]

Complementary Sources

The most important complementary sources are the media coverage on the events and the many interviews with key actors and eyewitnesses. For more than a decade after the General Peace Accord of 1997, neither the government nor the civil society encouraged the public commemoration of the events leading to the civil war, instead peace, stability and order were celebrated. Since 2009, however, one can observe a significant change in Tajikistan's otherwise timid public: On the eve of the 20th anniversary of the February 1990 events the independent Tajik media began to publish interviews with eyewitnesses and articles on the dramatic events. The Tajik branch of Radio Free Europe/ Radio Liberty, *Radioi Ozodī*, was particularly active in the initial coverage on Tajikistan's recent history, but also the domestic media (except for the government-controlled outlets such as *Minbari xalq* and *Ğumhuriyat*) joined the commemoration: *Ozodagon*, *Millat*, *Farağ*, *Nigoh*, *SSSR*, *Toğikiston*, the Asia Plus Agency (with the radio station and newspaper *Asia Plus*) and the

IRPT newspaper *Naǧot* frequently publish extensive articles and interviews on the civil war in the past years. In case dates and the sequence of events are contested, I usually refer to Davlat Nazriev and Igor Sattarov's voluminous and meticulously collected chronicle of the years 1991–1993.[71]

STRUCTURE

This book follows a chronological order, but overlapping topics, such as "regionalism," "Islam" or biographies of key actors are presented outside the chronological order in separate (sub-)chapters. The first chapter offers a historical introduction to Perestroika and Glasnost in the TaSSR. The chapter does not claim to offer an exhaustive and detailed history of the final decade of Soviet Tajikistan, but highlights developments I consider important for the understanding of the cleavages and tensions in the Tajik society. Shifting debates on national history, language and dependencies to the Soviet system condensed during the late 1980s to a short but pronounced post-colonial moment in the later TaSSR. The political tensions, the inability of the Tajik intelligentsia to negotiate an inclusive idea of Tajik nationalism and finally the outbreak of violence in May 1992 suspended this short post-colonial moment. The second chapter reviews regionalism in the TaSSR and how regionalism is narrated in the relevant sources. I argue that regionalist solidarity groups and networks *were* important in Tajikistan, but they did not generate categorical solidarity or loyalty. Moreover, the frequent reference to "regionalism" as the central catalyst for the civil war is often an attempt to rationalize the outbreak of the conflict and relativize the many contingencies. The third chapter revisits the February 1990 events in detail and covers the time period until spring 1991. Since conspiracy theories are ubiquitous in the autobiographical accounts, I will briefly introduce some of the pervasive conspiracy theories in this chapter as well. The fourth chapter covers the time period between independence in September 1991 and March 1992: President Mahkamov had to resign after the failed August coup in Moscow and continuous protests on the streets of Dushanbe changed the political landscape in Tajikistan. Instead of a reformist Glasnost supporter, a Brezhnevite cadre, Rahmon Nabiev, was elected president in November. The fifth chapter considers how Soviet institutions regulated Islam and how religious specialists (the *ulamo*) responded to the appropriation and manipulation by the state in the TaSSR. While the religious field experienced since the 1950s significant changes and "revivals," the 1970s saw the emergence of a younger generation of political activists who expressed their societal vision in religious terms. The political nomenklatura and established *ulamo* soon stigmatized these Islamic activists as religious extremists. The sixth chapter returns to the chronological order and looks at the increasing polarization of the Tajik society during the protests on Ozodī Square and Šahidon Square between March and May. The seventh chapter analyses concepts of masculinity in Tajikistan and how male violent non-state actors shaped the dynamics of the civil war. The eighth chapter narrates the outbreak and initial stages of the civil war between May and November 1992. The chapter particularly focusses on the many divisions in the two major factions. The ninth chapter presents the 16th Session of the Supreme Soviet in Xuğand, which (at least from the narrative of the Rahmonov government) re-established legitimate order in Tajikistan. The conclusive Epilogue eventually deals with the commemoration of the civil war in post-conflict Tajikistan.

TERMINOLOGY

The official terminology of the political, social and cultural spheres of the TaSSR is a complex and at times intricate affair due to the inflationary use of acronyms and sesquipedalian titles. Tajikistan's official designation as a Soviet Republic was Soviet Socialist Republic of Tajikistan (Tajik: *Respublikai Sovetii Socialistii Toğikiston*) and the most powerful office was the first secretary of the Central Committee of the Communist Party of the Soviet Socialist Republic of Tajikistan. To keep the balance between accuracy and redundancy, I decided to abbreviate most of the recurring terms, for instance TaSSR for the Soviet Socialist Republic of Tajikistan or CC/CPT for Central Committee of the Communist Party of the TaSSR.

I frequently use the term "nomenklatura" for those individuals who occupied leading positions in the various tiers—union, republican, provincial and district level—of the Soviet administration covering different portfolios such as government, security, industry, agriculture, health, education or culture.[72] The term nomenklatura implies that these individuals were members of a distinct social group, usually appointed by the Communist Party and part of larger patron-client networks.[73] Likewise, the terms "intellectuals" and "intelligentsia" appear frequently. Intelligentsia (Taj./Russ.: *intelligenciya*[74]) is related to the nomenklatura since the USSR's constitution of 1977 and the TaSSR's constitution of 1978 stipulate that the socialist society consists of three distinct social groups: the workers, peasants and the intelligentsia.[75] As for the TaSSR, the emergence of the intelligentsia as a cognizable but heterogenous social group is embedded in the societal transformation since the 1960s. Prerequisite for being a member of the intelligentsia was usually the formal nomination to a position in the academic-scientific and cultural institutions.

Soviet Tajikistan was a multi-ethnic society: In 1989, only 62.3% of the population were ethnic Tajik, 23.5% were Uzbeks and some 10% non-Central

Asian nationalities, such as Russians (7.6%), Tatars, Germans, Ukrainians, Koreans and so forth. Since independence, the ethnic diversity has continuously receded due to emigration. In 2000, 80% of the population were considered ethnic Tajik and in 2010 84.3%. The percentage of the ethnic Russian population declined from 1.1% (in 2000) to 0.5% in 2010.[76] The term "Tajik" refers here in general to the citizens of Tajikistan regardless of their ethnicity. In case ethnicity seems to be relevant, I will refer to it explicitly.

Islam, Muslim religious elites and Islamic activists or Islamists recur frequently in this text. Instead of using terms such as "clergy" borrowed from the Greek-Latin Christian tradition, I apply either the original Tajik/Arabic terms for Islamic religious specialists (*mullo, domullo, imom-xatib, ešon* and so forth) or collectively the plural term *ulamo* (from the Arabic *"ulamā"*) for scholars of the Islamic sciences. There has been an on-going debate about the correct terminology to describe political interpretations of Islam, for instance as fundamentalism, political Islam, radical Islam or Islamism. I prefer here the term Islamism as "fundamentalism" too strongly stresses the aspect of a scripturalist interpretation of Islam and "political Islam" gives a too exclusive weight to the question of political agenda. "Islamism" is to be understood as a trend of thought in the Islamic world from the late 19th century onwards that, by implicitly struggling with the challenges of the "West" and "modernity", seeks for a return to the intellectual and religious fundamentals of Islam, intends to form the entire society according to these insights and gives (limited or unlimited) precedence to the necessity of enforcing this new-old order.[77] For those individuals, who have appropriated this Islamist thought, I use for the Tajik context the term Islamic activist or Islamist. Finally, I borrow the term Islamicate from Marshall Hodgson's seminal study *The Venture of Islam* for phenomena, which originated in regions dominated by Muslims but which were not necessarily religious as such.[78]

TRANSLITERATION AND TECHNICAL REMARKS

This thesis is predominately based on Tajik sources written in the Tajik-Cyrillic alphabet. For the reproduction of Tajik, I apply a simplified transliteration with six special characters for terms and proper names according to their Tajik-Cyrillic and not Russian-Cyrillic spelling, for instance Rahmonov and not Rakhmonov.[79] Since the late 1980s many Tajiks have changed their surnames out of nationalist sentiment. Intellectuals and politicians demonstratively omit the Slavic suffix *–ov* or replace it with the Persian/Tajik suffix *–zoda*.[80] The incumbent president of Tajikistan, Emomalī Rahmonov, decreed in 2007 that his surname shall be Rahmon from then on and several members of his retinue followed suit. At times, the Soviet/Russian, Soviet/Tajik or post-Soviet variations of proper names are used simultaneously in the literature creating some confusion. Besides, the TaSSR/Tajikistan has experienced a continuous naming and renaming of toponyms: First the Bolshevists introduced ideologically adequate names, and then Stalinism had its day—even the TaSSR's capital, Dushanbe was "elevated" to Stalinobod between 1923 and 1961. In the 1960s the memory of Stalinism was erased and in the late 1980s nationalist sentiment and independence initiated again a reconsideration of toponyms. Since the 2000s, President Rahmonov is again changing names conjuring his imagination of the Tajik nation. As a rule, I cite all proper names and toponyms in Tajik as given in the sources but usually provide their current (2016) variation in Tajik as well.[81]

NOTES

1. The Oral History Archive of independent Tajikistan is accessible for researchers at the OSCE Academy in Bishkek and at the University of Freiburg.
2. There is no reliable data on the casualties of the conflict. Many accounts operate with 50,000 dead. Jesse Driscoll uses the conservative figure 41,300 in his study *Warlords and coalition politics in post-Soviet states* (New York: Cambridge University Press, 2015), 70. During a round table discussion in Dushanbe in December 2013, discussants gave 27,000 to 150,000 casualties (see www.ozodi.org/content /article/25208268.html. Accessed December 21, 2013).
3. On the Civil War see: Muriel Atkin, "The Politics of Polarization in Tajikistan," In *Central Asia: Its strategic importance and future prospects.* Edited by Hafeez Malik (New York: St. Martin's Press, 1994); Valentin Buškov and D. Mikul'skiy, *Anatimiya graždanskoy voyny v Tadžikistane: etno-social'niye processy i političeskaya bor'ba: 1992–1996* (Moskva, 1996); Driscoll, *Warlords*; Stéphane Dudoignon, *Communal solidarity and social conflicts in late 20th century Central Asia: The case of the Tajik civil war* (Tokyo, 1998); Dov Lynch, "The Tajik Civil War and Peace Process," *Civil Wars* 4, no. 4 (2001); Lawrence Markowitz, *State erosion: Unlootable resources and unruly elites in Central Asia* (Ithaca, N.Y.: Cornell University Press 2013); Olivier Roy, *The new Central Asia: Geopolitics and the birth of nations* (London: Tauris, 2007); Barnett Rubin, "The Fragmentation of Tajikistan," *Survival* 35, no. 4 (1993): 71–91; İdil Tunçer-Kılavuz, *Power, networks and violent conflict in Central Asia: comparison of Tajikistan and Uzbekistan* (London: Routledge, 2014). For the politics of peacebuilding see John Heathershaw, *Post-conflict Tajikistan: The politics of peacebuilding and the emergence of legitimate order* (London: Routledge, 2009).
4. *Bahman* is the 11th month (*moh*) of the Iranian calendar (21 January to 19 February).
5. See Barnett Rubin, "Russian Hegemony and State Breakdown in the Periphery: Causes and consequences of the Civil War in Tajikistan," In *Post-Soviet political order: Conflict and state building.* Edited by Barnett R. Rubin and Jack L. Snyder (London: Routledge, 1998).

6. Cf. Stéphane Dudoignon, "Une Segmentation peut en Cacher une Autre: Regionalismes et Clivages politico-economiques au Tadjikistan," *Cahiers d'étues sur la Méditerranée orientale et le monde turco-iranien*, no. 18 (1994): 73–129.

7. *Qozikalon*, Tajik for "supreme judge," was until 1993 the highest office among the registered *ulamo* (Islamic scholars) in Tajikistan.

8. See Mary Kaldor, *New and old wars. Organized violence in a global era* (Stanford: Standford University Press, 2012); Stathis Kalyvas, "'New' and 'Old' Civil Wars. A Valid Distinction?" *World Politics* 54 (2001): 99–188.

9. For the first civil war, see Mullo I. Irkaev, *Istoriya Graždanskoy Voyny v Tadžikistane* (Dušanbe: Irfon, 1971).

10. Emomalī Rahmonov, *Istiqloliyati Toğikiston va Ehyoi millat*. Vol. 1 (Dušanbe: Irfon, 2002), 18.

11. Emomalī Rahmonov, *Toğikon dar oinai ta'rix: Az Oriyon to Somoniyon*. Vol. 1 (Dušanbe: Irfon, 1999), 8.

12. Safaralī Kenğaev, *Tabadduloti Toğikiston 2* (Toškand: Fondi Kenğaev, 1994), 102 & 337.

13. Būrī Karim, *Faryodi solho* (Moskva: Transdornauka, 1997), 23.

14. Karim, *Faryodi*, 456.

15. See Benedict Anderson, *Imagined communities: Reflections on the origin and spread of nationalism* (London: Verso, 2006), 191–210; Christian Meier, *Das Gebot zu vergessen und die Unabweisbarkeit des Erinnerns: Vom öffentlichen Umgang mit schlimmer Vergangenheit* (München: Siedler, 2010).

16. A. Qayumzod, *40 soli muboriza, muqovimat va talošho* (Dušanbe: Muattar, 2013), 37.

17. Hoğī Akbar Tūrağonzoda, "Ivazšavii hokim naboyad nišonai noamnī bošad," *Nigoh*, July 10, 2013, 16. For a similar perception see Šādmān Yūsuf, *Tāğikistān. Bahā-ye āzādī* (Tehrān: Daftar-e našr-e farhang-e Eslāmī, 1994/1995), 9–10.

18 See www.bbc.co.uk/tajik/news/2013/05/130517_mm_usmanov_civil_war .shtml. Accessed May 17, 2013.

19. Cf. Glenda Frazer, "Basmachi (Part I)" *Central Asian Survey* 6, no. 1 (1987): 1–73 and "Basmachi (Part II)" *Central Asian Survey* 6, no. 2 (1987): 7–42.. *Bosmačī* (Russ.: *basmačestvo*) is originally a Turkish word with the meaning "bandit, marauder," *bosmačigī* is usually used for the heterogeneous resistance movement in parts of Central Asia in the 1920s.

20. Cf. K. Abdullaev, *Ot Sin'czyanya do Xorasana. Iz istorii sredneaziatskoy emigracii XX veka* (Dushanbe: Irfon, 2009); Beatrice Penati. "The Reconquest of East Bukhara: The Struggle Against the Basmachi as a Prelude to Sovietization," *Central Asian Survey* 26, no. 4 (2007): 521–538.

21. The Arabic plural term *"ulama"* (Tajik: *ulamo*) means generally "scholars" but is used almost exclusively for the Islamic sciences.

22. The Qarotegin (or Rašt/Ğarm) Valley is a mountainous area east of Dushanbe dominated by the Surxob/Vaxš River basin. The Zarafšon River (in its upper reach: Mastčoh) rises in the fringes of the Pamir and flows west in the direction of Panğakent through Aynī and the Zarafšon/Turkestan Mountains. Badaxšon is in the eastern Pamir, today the Autonomous Province of Mountain Badaxšon (Russ.: *Gorno-Badakhšanskaya avtonomnaya oblast'*, GBAO).

23. Š. I. Kurbanova, *Pereselenie. Kak eto bylo* (Dušanbe: Irfon, 1993); Botakoz Kassymbekova, "Humans as Territory: Forced Resettlement and the Making of Soviet Tajikistan, 1920–38," *Central Asian Survey* 30, no. 3–4 (2011): 349–70.

24. See Vadim Erlikhman, *Poteri narodonaseleniia v XX veke: Spravochnik* (Moskva: Russkaia panorama, 2004), 22–35.

25. Aziz Niyazi, "Migration, Demography and Socio-Ecological Processes in Tajikistan," In *migration in Central Asia: Its history and current problems*. Edited by H. Komatsu et al., (Tokyo: Japan Center for Area Studies, 2000), 169–171.

26. Cf. Muhammad Osimī, ed., *Enziklopediyai sovetii Tоǧik*. Vol. 8 (Dušanbe: SIEST, 1988); TAJSTAT, ed., *Demografiyai solonai ǧumhurii Toǧikiston* (Dušanbe: RMT MKH, 2013), 26.

27. Ajay Patnaik, "Agriculture and Rural Out-Migration in Central Asia, 1960–91," *Europe-Asia Studies* 47, no. 1 (1995): 147–69.

28. Donald Raleigh, *Soviet baby boomers: An oral history of Russia's Cold War generation* (Oxford: Oxford University Press, 2012), 220–267.

29. See Mullonazar Xolnazar, *Dar čašmoni xotiraho* (Dušanbe: Kayhon, 2011).

30. See Kirill Nourzhanov and Christian Bleuer, *Tajikistan: A political and social history* (Canberra: ANU Press, 2013); Shirin Akiner, *Tajikistan: Disintegration or reconciliation?* (London: Royal Institute of International Affairs, 2001); Kathleen Collins, *Clan politics and regime transition in Central Asia* (Cambridge: Cambridge University Press, 2006).

31. The Tajik sources often use the term *markaz* ("center") for the USSR's political leadership in Moscow.

32. John Mueller, "The Banality of 'Ethnic War,'" *International Security* 25, no. 1 (2000): 62.

33. See Rogers Brubaker and David Laitin, "Ethnic and Nationalist Violence," *Annual Review of Sociology* 24 (1998): 423–452.

34. Cf. Pierre Bourdieu, *Distinction: A social critique of the judgement of taste* (New York: Routledge, 2008).

35. See Nassim Jawad and Shahrbanou Tadjbakhsh, *Tajikistan: A forgotten civil war* (London: Minority Rights Group, 1995).

36. Lynch, "Tajik Civil War," 49.

37. Cf. World Bank Group, ed., *Statističeskiy sbornik, 1993 god* (Washington, DC: World Bank, 1992).

38. Lynch, "Tajik Civil War," 55.

39. Cf. Markowitz, *State*, passim and Driscoll, *Warlords*, passim. For a definition of violent non-state actors see Ulrich Schneckener, "Fragile Statehood, Armed Non-State Actors and Security Governance," In *Private actors and security governance*. Edited by Alan Bryden and Marina Caparini (Wien: Lit, 2006), 25; "[…] armed (or violent) non-state actors are (1) willing and able to use violence for pursuing their objectives; and (2) not integrated into formalised state institutions such as regular armies, presidential guards, police or special forces. They may, however, be supported by state actors whether in an official or informal manner. There may also be state officials who are directly or indirectly involved in the activities of armed non-state actors —sometimes for political purposes, but often for personal interests (i.e., corruption, clientelism)."

40. İdil Tunçer-Kılavuz, "Understanding Civil War: A Comparison of Tajikistan and Uzbekistan," *Europe-Asia Studies* 63, no. 2 (2011): 280.

41. Stathis Kalyvas, "The Ontology of 'Political Violence': Action and Identity in Civil Wars," *Perspectives on Politics* 1, no. 3 (2003): 476.

42. Kalyvas, "Civil Wars," 111.

43. Cf. Tetsuro Iji, "Cooperation, Coordination and Complementarity in International Peacemaking: The Tajikistan Experience," *International Peacekeeping* 12, no. 2 (2005): 189–204.

44. Reinhart Koselleck, *Futures past: On the semantics of historical time* (New York: Columbia University Press, 2004), 127. See also Richard Lebow, "Contingency, Catalysts, and International System Change," *Political Science Quarterly* 115, no. 4 (2000): 591–616; David Mandel, "Simulating History: The Problem of Contingency," *Analyses of Social Issues & Public Policy* 3, no. 1 (2003): 177–80. For contingency in the Iranian Revolution 1979 see Charles Kurzman, *The unthinkable revolution in Iran* (Cambridge: Cambridge University Press, 2004), 163–172; In Egyptian uprising 2011 see Killian Clarke, "Unexpected Brokers of Mobilization: Contingency and Networks in the 2011 Egyptian Uprising," *Comparative Politics* 46, no. 4 (2014): 379–97; In the Ukrainian Revolution 2005 see Mark Beissinger, "Mechanisms of Maidan: The Structure of Contingency in the Making of the Orange Revolution," *Mobilization* 16, no. 1 (2011): 25–43.

45. Karim, *Faryodi*, 242.

46. Stathis Kalyvas, *The logic of violence in civil war* (Cambridge: Cambridge University Press, 2009).

47. Cf. Karim, *Faryodi*; Asliddin Sohibnazar, *Subhi sitorakuš.* 2 vols. (Dušanbe: Doniš, 1997 and 2000); Yūsuf, *Tāǧīkistān*.

48. Raewyn Connell, *Masculinities* (Cambridge: Cambridge University Press, 2005).

49. Cf. Laura Adams, "Can We Apply Postcolonial Theory to Central Eurasia?" *Central Eurasian Studies Review* 7, no. 1 (2008): 2–7 and John Heathershaw, "Central Asian Statehood in Post-Colonial Perspective," In *Stable outside, fragile inside? Post-Soviet statehood in central Asia.* Edited by Emilian Kavalski (Farnham: Ashgate, 2010).

50. For a comment on the value of autobiographical accounts see Stéphane Dudoignon and Sayyid A. Qalandar, "They Were All from the Country: The Revival and Politicisation of Islam in the Lower Wakhsh River Valley of the Tajik SSR (1947–1997)," In *Allah's Kolkhozes: Migration, de-stalinisation, privatisation, and the new muslim congregations in the soviet realm (1950s–2000s).* Edited by Stephane A. Dudoignon and Christian Noack (Berlin: Klaus-Schwarz, 2013).

51. The administration of the National Library of Tajikistan, which moved in 2012 to newly constructed premises, has used the relocation to "sort" out "objectionable" material and sources (for instance periodicals from 1991 or 1992).

52. Sadriddin Aynī, *Yoddoštho*, 2 vols. (Dušanbe: Irfon, 1954/55) and Ǧalol Ikromī, *Onči az sar guzašt* (Dušanbe: Irfon, 2009).

53. See Margaretta Jolly, ed., *Encyclopedia of life writing: Autobiographical and biographical forms.* 2 vols. (London: Fitzroy Dearborn, 2001); Winfried Schulze, ed.,

Ego-Dokumente: Annäherung an den Menschen in der Geschichte (Berlin: Akad. Verlag, 1996); James Olney, ed., *Studies in autobiography* (New York: Oxford University Press, 1988).

54. Cf. Charles Taylor, *Modern social imaginaries* (Durham: Duke University Press, 2004).

55. Cf. Pierre Bourdieu, "The Social Space and the Genesis of Groups," *Theory and Society* 14, no. 6 (1985): 723–44.

56. K. von Greyerz, "Ego-Documents: The Last Word?" *German History* 28, no. 3 (2010): 281.

57. M. Fulbrook and U. Rublack. "In Relation: The 'Social Self' and Ego-Documents," *German History* 28, no. 3 (2010): 267.

58. See also Būrī Karim, *Dar girdobi zindagī. Yoddošt, maqolaho, musohibaho* (Možaysk: Terra, 1995).

59. Karim, *Faryodi*, 13–27. Karim referred to the historian Boboğon Ġafurov by declaring that history writing should not be entertaining but above all consultative (*pandomūz*).

60. Karim, *Faryodi*, 26–27.

61. Hikmatulloh Nasriddinov, *Tarkiš* (Dušanbe: Afsona, 1995), 8.

62. In 1998, Nasriddinov established the Agrarian Party of Tajikistan with little success (the party was suspended in 1999).

63. Sohibnazar, *Subhi 1*, 5.

64. For instance Sohibnazar, *Subhi 2*, 52–55.

65. Hoğī Akbar Tūrağonzoda, *Miyoni obu otaš. Tarhi sulh andoxtam, ammo...* (Dušanbe, 1998).

66. Whilst the first volume of Kenğaev's *Tabadduloti Toğikiston* was published in Dushanbe 1993, the other two volumes were published in Uzbekistan (Tashkent) in 1994 and 1995.

67. Dūstov's whereabouts are unknown and he is on the Interpol Warrant list for banditry and abuse of power.

68. Qiyomiddin Sattorī, ed., *HNIT—Zodai ormoni mardum* (Dušanbe: ŠKOS HNIT, 2003).

69. See Saidumar Husaynī, *Xotiraho az naxust ošnoiyam ba Harakati Islomii Toğikiston to rasmiyati on* (Dušanbe: Muattar, 2013); Zubaydulloh Roziq, *HNIT dar masiri ta'rix* (Dušanbe: Muattar, 2013). Additionally, the IRPT's weekly *Nağot* published between 2009 and 2013 numerous shorter memories and articles on the civil war.

70. Tim Epkenhans, "The Islamic Revival Party of Tajikistan: Episodes of Islamic Activism, Postconflict Accommodation, and Political Marginalization," *Central Asian Affairs*, no. 2 (2015), 321–346.

71. Davlat Nazriev and Igor Sattarov, *Respublika Tadžikistan: Istoriya nezavisimosti god 1991-y (Tom I)* (Dušanbe: AK-94, 2002); id., *Respublika Tadžikistan: Istoriya nezavisimosti god 1993-y (Tom III)* (Dušanbe: Irfon, 2006) and id., *Respublika Tadžikistan: Istoriya nezavisimosti god 1992-y (Tom II)* (Dušanbe: Nur, 2005).

72. The term "nomenklatura" was popularized by Mikhail Voslensky, *Nomenklatura. The Soviet ruling class* (New York: Doubleday, 1984).

73. Cf. Teresa Rakowska-Harmstone, *Russia and nationalism in Central Asia: The case of Tadzhikistan* (Baltimore: Hopkins Press, 1970); John Schoeberlein-Engel, "Conflict in Tajikistan and Central Asia: The Myth of Ethnic Animosity," *Harvard Middle Eastern and Islamic Review* 1, no. 2 (1994): 1–55.

74. The Russian term *intelligenciya* is also used in Tajik. In the 1980s the Tajik term *ziyoī* became more frequent.

75. Cf. F. J. M. Feldbrugge, ed., *The Constitutions of the USSR and the union republics: Analysis, texts, reports* (Alphen aan den Rijn: M. Nijhoff Publisher, 1979).

76. TAJSTAT, ed., *Hayati millī, donistani zabonho va šahrvandii aholii ğumhurii Toğikiston*. Dušanbe: RMT MKH, 2010), 7.

77. Cf. Peter G. Mandaville, *Islam and politics* (New York: Routledge, 2014).

78. Marshall G. Hodgson, *The venture of Islam: Conscience and history in a world civilization*, 3 vols. (Chicago: University of Chicago Press, 1974).

79. Please note the following special characters: к/К = q/Q; ғ/Ғ = ġ/Ġ; ч/Ч = ǧ/Ǧ; ъ = ʿ; ӣ = ī and ӯ/Ӯ = ū/Ū.

80. The suffix *–zoda* is the past participle of the Tajik verb *zodan* ("to be born").

81. For toponyms see Nurmuhammad Amiršohī, *Fehristi nomi mahalhoi Toğikiston* (Dušanbe: Ensiklopediyai Millii Toğik, 2013) and Soviet military 1:100,000 maps of the USSR (sheets 10:42: 10–128; 11:42: 105–142; 10:42: 13–110).

Chapter 1

Prelude

A Post-Colonial Moment in Late Soviet Tajikistan

The Brezhnev years (1964–1982) mark the period of "Mature Socialism" in which the Soviet system compared to the Stalinist era became more predictable and socially stable for its citizens as well as the nomenklatura. Brezhnev's dictum of the "stability of cadres" signaled to the local nomenklatura the prospect of an extended tenure as long as they complied with Moscow's expectations. Many cadres who were appointed in the early Brezhnev years remained in office until they passed away or were dismissed in the wake of Gorbachev's Perestroika reforms in the early 1980s. The TaSSR's first secretary, Ğabbor Rasulov, is a good example for this stability of cadres with his 21 years' tenure from 1961 to 1982.[1] While the Central Asian nomenklatura enjoyed a degree of local autonomy, they had limited career opportunities outside their republican constituency and were rarely represented in the union's higher executive committees: except for Kazakhstan's Dinmukhamed Konayev (between 1964 and 1986 the first secretary in the Kazakh SSR), a confidant of Brezhnev, none of the Central Asian CP secretaries had been elected to the Politburo prior to 1990.[2] Perhaps, the limited career options outside Central Asia further promoted the proliferation of patronage networks on the subrepublican level. Although most of the republican ministries and commissions were subordinated to central USSR structures, the local cadres had plenty of opportunity to divert resources to their personal patronage networks—the center had neither the political will nor the capacity to restrict the autonomy and illicit transgression of local cadres during the Brezhnev tenure.[3]

Personal relations and access to resources allowed elites on the republican and local level to establish patrimonial patronage networks along the lines of regional, ethnic or professional affiliation with little interference by the center.[4] Critchlow describes how the republican elites of the UzSSR manipulated imaginations of the respective national culture with serious long-term societal ramifications:

[W]hile cheating the state economy, [Central Asian elites] have also conspired to frustrate the leadership's long-range goals of social integration. In the name of *miras* [Uzbek/Tajik for heritage] they have helped to keep the masses culturally aloof, immobile, and unwilling to relinquish traditional ways of doing things, whether in the realm of spiritual culture (Islam) or material (resistance to mechanized cotton-picking).[5]

Simultaneously, the TaSSR experienced an expansion of the public sector and a period of relative urbanization and industrialization.[6] The interventionist Soviet state mobilized hitherto marginalized parts of the population, for instance among the *muhoğir* communities, changing the composition of the Tajik urban population. The émigrés from Bukhara, Samarqand and Leninobod gradually lost their dominance in the intellectual field. Many of the protagonists in this book benefitted from the social transformation in the 1960s and 1970s and they portray these years as an ideal time, in which the population enjoyed tangible social and economic progress while work discipline and commitment to the socialist society were considered high.[7] Important large scale development projects, such as the hydroelectric power plant (HPP) dam at Norak (built between 1961 and 1980), the Yovon Electro-Chemical Combine, the Vaxš Nitrogen Fertilizer Combine (close to Kalininobod) or the Aluminum Combine (Talco/TadAz) in Regar/Tursunzoda (built between 1965 and 1975) marked the ambitious industrialization plan of the southern TaSSR. But despite the impressive record on paper, the economic realities were desolate: Gosplan's construction projections were far behind schedule (the construction of Norak took 19 years instead of the projected 10 years), the initial budgets massively overspent and the productivity dramatically lower than expected often exceeding the production costs. The industrialization of the southern TaSSR was never sustainable let alone profitable and dependent on substantial subsidies by the center.[8] Although the Soviet media reported critically about the low productivity and economic unsustainability, the Tajik nationalist intelligentsia portrayed the TaSSR as a genuinely affluent country with abundant resources, which was mismanaged and exploited by the center. They raised expectations of an economic future the country's resources could not possibly provide.

Not only the economic field was characterized by inconsistencies and a profound contrariness between appearance and reality. Yurchak observes for the late Soviet society a synchronicity of paradoxes and dichotomies diagnosing its "internal displacement."[9] While the official Soviet system constantly reproduced its ideological principles by mass-mobilization and participation, the population had developed strategies to elude or outwit societal and political constrains as Fürst explains:

Mature socialism [...] was a complicated conglomerate of performative practices, collective habits, individual mechanisms of survival strategies of self-improvement, and segregated spaces for action, all of which were linked and interacted with each other in the person of the Soviet subject and citizen. The mature socialist subject was a multi-tasking individual, embedded in and divorced from the Soviet collective at the same time. One of the very hallmarks of 'mature socialism' was that it provided a fragmented and, at times, contradictory experience. Stagnation, apathy, and cynicism were term frequently employed by observers of the later Soviet Union and by subsequent commentators and analysts.[10]

These two intertwined and contradictory aspects of the Soviet society are important for the portrait of the TaSSR in the late 1980s since the emerging nationalist discourses during Perestroika and Glasnost are directly related to the transformations during Brezhnev's mature socialism. When in February 1982 the terminally ill Ğabbor Rasulov resigned as first secretary, a typical representative of the Brezhnev era secured the succession: Rahmon Nabiev. As a former minister for agriculture and long-term chairman of the Council of Ministers (1973–1982) Nabiev possessed both, favorable relations to Moscow and local patronage networks in the agro-industrial complex. But after Brezhnev's demise and the short tenures of Andropov and Chernenko, the center-periphery relations changed with Gorbachev's election in March 1985 and the introduction of Perestroika. In an unprecedented U-turn Moscow started to employ themes of consumerism, political transparency and reform profoundly changing the political discourse as well as the atmosphere in the USSR. The center unleashed a campaign against regional party elites who were made responsible for widespread corruption, the social and economic decline, the lack of adequate housing, access to health care and basic consumer goods.[11] The Central Asian Soviet republics had been already during Andropov's tenure as chairman of the KGB (1967–1982) subject to occasional campaigns by Moscow denouncing corruption, clientelism and religious traditionalism.[12] Perestroika signaled a fundamental change. The public demotion of high ranking part officials in the early Gorbachev era and public perceptions of accountability and responsiveness of political elites highlighted the transformation of the Soviet society, but what was intended to restructure and invigorate the Communist Party of the Soviet Union (CPSU) eventually undermined its authority since the reforms did not deliver the expected social and economic improvements.

PERESTROIKA IN THE TASSR

On 14 December 1985, the Central Committee of the CPT formally dismissed Rahmon Nabiev on directives from Moscow. A few days later, Moscow also intervened in the Turkmen SSR and ordered the dismissal of Muhammetnazar Gapurow, who had been the first secretary of the CC since 1969, and replaced him with Sapamurat Niyazov "Türkmenbaşy." Moscow intended to disrupt the autonomy of local elites in Central Asia and their sub-state networks of resource allocation. While the dismissal of Gapurow was linked to a cotton-scandal, Nabiev's demotion was related to his personal shortcomings and inner-elite struggles within the nomenklatura from the northern Leninobod province. Gulğahon Bobosodiqova, a Deputy in the USSR Supreme Soviet from Ūroteppa (today Istaravšon), reported confidentially to the Central Committee of the CPSU about Nabiev's alcohol habit after Gorbachev had launched his anti-alcohol campaign in May 1985.[13] While the dismissal of Nabiev was the most visible expression of change, earlier, subtler changes had been implemented gradually shifting the power relations in the TaSSR.[14] Although the intervention by the center disrupted the autonomy of the elites, it reinforced the renationalization of politics since Gorbachev's intervention was interpreted by the non-Russian societies as an indication of Russian chauvinism. Furthermore, in the late 1980s control mechanisms and disciplinary authority of the state rapidly contracted and limited Moscow's ability to influence politics in the periphery. The center increasingly had to react to crisis instead of shaping politics. As Beissinger points out, the republican cadres gradually shifted from mediators of the center's politics to autonomous local elites in the context of rising nationalist sentiment.[15] Nabiev's successor Mahkamov was less able to penetrate and manipulate the patronage networks in the TaSSR ultimately intensifying the rivalries between different elite factions.

Rivalry within the Tajik Elite

The autobiographies narrate Mahkamov's tenure as a time in which the cleavages in the Tajik society deepened. The nomenklatura in all fields—culture, academia, administration and economy—was divided and competition for rents, resources and formal position intensified in a time of economic contraction. Regional-based solidarity groups were frequently identified as constitutive elements in this rivalry. Hikmatullo Nasriddinov maintained that with Mahkamov's appointment three major competing elite groups emerged around individual representatives of the TaSSR's nomenklatura: Ğoibnazar Pallaev (GBAO & Kūlob), Mahkamov (Leninobod) and Nabiev (Leninobod). Nasriddinov considered Mahkamov as a product of this "game of networks (gurūhbozī) and regionalism,"[16] who was not able to play the game himself and increasingly relied on non-Central Asian representatives from the center, such as Lučinskiy (the second secretary of the CC/CPT) and Vladimir Petkel' (chairman of the TaSSR's KGB).[17] Both, Lučinskiy and Petkel', handled the regional balance imprudently alienating important individuals and networks. The discourse on regionalism, the administrative practice of resource allocation and the marginalization of rival regional networks generated tensions within the Tajik nomenklatura. However, individual affiliation with professional networks in the agro-industrial complex, the planning bureaucracy, academia, culture or security as well as individual attitudes toward Perestroika, economic and political reforms frequently undermined regional solidarity. Moreover, personal (contingent) animosities and rivalries were often fought maliciously with anonymous defamations, accusations, proxy conflicts and smear campaigns aggravating the tensions in the political field.[18] The autobiographies narrate these conflicts within the context of regional rivalries, obviously as a strategy to rationalize the divisions within the elite. For example, Nasriddinov reported how the conflict between Pallaev and Nabiev intensified during Nabiev's tenure as first secretary of the CC/CPT. Pallaev had been appointed chairman of the Presidium of the Supreme Soviet in 1984, a position he held until 1990. According to Nasriddinov, Pallaev was not appointed for his qualifications but due to his regional provenance from Badaxšon (the chairman of the Presidium of the Supreme Soviet was supposed to be a cadre from GBAO as part of the regional balance). Pallaev allegedly used his position to provide family members and confederates with lucrative positions and apartments in Dushanbe—a highly contentious issue due to the tense housing situation. Young men in secondary schools, polytechnic institutes or universities of Dushanbe increasingly fought out the conflict between Nabiev and Pallaev. While Nabiev mobilized male youth from Kūlob who had a higher representation in the agricultural university, Pallaev incited young men from Qarotegin, Darvoz and Badaxšon who had a higher representation in the pedagogical university and secondary schools in Dushanbe.[19]

> These simple young men (*ğavononi sodda*) from Kūlob and Badaxšon never understood that two political leaders of the republic jeopardized the future of their own youth out of personal interests and animosities. They did not understand that their leaders savored their lives day and night and forged plans while being drunk which ultimately would draw these young men into their conflicts. They also did not know that at one day these incitements would result in bloodshed and would take the lives of their children.[20]

The conflict between Pallaev and Nabiev originated in the competition for resources and positions to be distributed in their patronage networks. But Nasriddinov, Karim and Sohibnazar were apparently more concerned about youth-related violence in the late Soviet society in which the Soviet state was not able to integrate and "contain" youth anymore. Adolescence and youth violence had long been identified as a serious destabilizing factor for the Soviet society and was widely discussed in the Soviet press. Rivalries between youth from different universities, secondary schools or sports clubs are neither an extraordinary phenomenon in urban areas nor unbeknown to other societies, but Nasriddinov tried to rationalize youth violence by integrating it into his overall narrative on regionalism in Tajikistan. The particular contexts of youth violence—scarcity of commodities and social space for youth, rapid modernization and urbanization, societal indifference, the illicit shadow economy, organized crime, adolescent "rituals" and so forth—are not addressed in the sources.[21]

The Mahkamov Administration

Moscow selected Mahkamov in the context of a determined and public intervention to re-establish authority over the Central Asian republics, limit the autonomy of the local elite and fight corruption as well as nepotism.[22] The intervention aggravated the inner-elite tensions in the TaSSR and simultaneously demographic change and societal transformation disrupted the system that had been informally established in the late 1940s. Mahkamov therefore faced several challenges: First, he "inherited" a political economy with a dominance of patrimonial networks in the agro-industrial complex (*kompleksi agrosanoatī*) down to the local collective farm directors and he had to deal with the idea of a regional balance in resource allocation and political representation between the major regional groupings in the TaSSR including the rivalry between Leninobod/Kūlob and Ġarm/Badaxšon. Second, Mahkamov was born in 1932 in Leninobod; he grew up in a Soviet orphanage and was not recruited from one of the local elite families with ties to the influential agro-industrial complex. The majority of the TaSSR's political leaders, such as Ġabbor Rasulov, Rahmon Nabiev, Izatullo Hayoyev (chairman of the Council of Ministers between 1986 and 1992), Ġoibnazar Pallaev, Qadriddin Aslonov (chairman of the Supreme Soviet in 1990/1991) or the incumbent President Emomalī Rahmonov, were agronomists or directors of collective farms in the important cotton sector. The pedigree in agriculture was extremely important due to the patronage networks and economic opportunities—at least as important as the regional provenance. Mahkamov in contrast was a mining engineer, who had graduated from the mining institute in Leningrad and managed a coalmine close to Isfara before he embarked on a career in the CPT and Gosplan.[23] Thus, without the prestigious social and professional pedigree Mahkamov had only a limited ability to penetrate the sub-state networks. Third, Mahkamov had to negotiate his appointment with competing elite networks in order to win support in Moscow. Bobosodiqova and Hoğiev supported Mahkamov's nomination but increased the split within the larger Leninobodī elite since they alienated Nabiev's networks, predominately mid-ranking cadres in the agrarian sector who had started their career in Nabiev's patronage networks and tenure as minister of agriculture.[24] Fourth, Mahkamov "purged" the Nabiev administration and replaced within a short period of time

26 leading cadres with different regional affiliations. At the same time, he relied on non-Tajik cadres—in times of rising nationalist sentiment a contentious decision. Even Kenğaev, a staunch *homo sovieticus* who ostentatiously hailed internationalism and Peoples' Friendship, criticized the appointment of non-native cadres from the center who have no idea about the "history, conventions and traditions" of the Tajik people. These individuals were not diligent senior officials but they behaved in an "adventurist and chauvinist (*avantyuristiyu šovinistī*) fashion,"[25] which eventually undermined Peoples' Friendship as well as the reputation of Mahkamov among the people.[26]

While Nabiev beyond doubt came to power with Moscow's blessing, he nonetheless was able to present himself as a shrewd politician outsmarting the center and defending the interests of the Tajik people—and his "dedication" eventually led to his dismissal by the center similar to Rašidov in Uzbekistan.

Mahkamov could not plausibly deny his close attachment the Soviet system. As an avowed atheist and internationalist, he did not have the habitual flexibility to present himself at discretion as a nationalist politician rooted in the agrarian society of Tajikistan. Other cadres were also performative atheists and internationalists, but they had obviously a more instrumentalist and flexible approach to ideology and religion if deemed appropriate.[27] Importantly, Mahkamov had only a limited command of Tajik and therefore could not adapt easily to the different contexts in which Tajik was predominately used. In times of rising nationalism and an intense debate about the status of Tajik as an official language, journalists and intellectuals exploited Mahkamov's weak spot and labeled him Moscow's marionette.[28] Shortly after his resignation in September 1991, the Tajik media reviewed Mahkamov's tenure in harsh terms:

> He had a limited personality with a molded ideology, a coward without any principles and without any leadership quality, influenced by a group of CPT demagogues […]. Mahkamov will be remembered in the history of Tajikistan as a person who divided the Tajiks into members of the "Communist Party" and the Others (*digaron*).[29]

Nabiev ruled the TaSSR in a time of relative economic and social stability—Mahkamov in contrast had to deal with a rapidly unfolding social and economic crisis whose magnitude he did not comprehend. Correspondingly, Kenğaev reported about the disappointment among CPT cadres and their desire for a more audacious leadership in the times of rapid change.[30] Sohibnazar found initially some positive words for Mahkamov and considered him as a genuine supporter of Perestroika but not of Glasnost. Mahkamov's mishandling of the February 1990 crisis, however, prompted him to reconsider Mahkamov's personality and he characterized him as educated and diligent, but a coward. His national pride was irreducible and he was completely obedient to the center (*markaz*). Nonetheless, he was committed to regionalism (*mahalgaroī*). He could not speak Tajik well, but his Russian was flawless. However, for using regionalism, you need to be a nationalist. But he could never be a nationalist since for him Internationalism was more sacred than national pride. Judging Mahkamov is not difficult, since he lacks far-sightedness and the ability for a mature political analysis.[31]

Ibrohim Usmonov came to a relatively balanced assessment of Mahkamov's tenure and concluded that Mahkamov and his confidants were unwilling and incapable to reform the system and eventually betrayed the people.[32] For the majority of Tajiks, reform meant above all reform of the economic sector, although the Tajik intelligentsia rather focused on nationalist debates and political change revealing a rather limited understanding of economics.

THE ECONOMY AND FAILED REFORMS

In the late 1980s it became clear, that Perestroika could not reverse the rapid economic and social decline in the Soviet Union. The relative liberalization had created economic opportunities to "privatize" former state property. While few were able to exploit the new opportunities, the vast majority of Soviet citizens experienced the final years of the USSR as a catastrophic economic decline. The statistical data for the Tajikistan indicates a steady macro-economic downward spiral since the 1980s, which dramatically accelerated after 1990 (Tables 1.1 and 1.2). The data collected by the State Committee for Statistics is to some extent deceptive since the system of data collection, the selection of indicators and their analysis were designed to *confirm* the existing system as well as model of economic planning and not to question it. The statistical data and prevalent success stories about the USSR's economic, scientific and cultural accomplishments often concealed the desolate reality.[33] In 1990, the TaSSR had the highest population growth with 2.72% compared with 0.66% average in the USSR[34], the second highest infant mortality rate (43.2 per thousand births), the lowest per-capita income and the lowest rural housing conditions (51% of the USSR average).[35] Although unemployment in the USSR had been officially eliminated in 1930, the analysis of complementary data suggests that the TaSSR had in 1985, with 12.6%, the highest unemployment rate in the USSR; in the agricultural sector even one-third of the workforce was considered unemployed or at least underemployed.[36]

Uneven Development

A common complaint among Tajik cadres and intellectuals was the uneven development in the Soviet Union and the alleged neglect of the industrial development of the Central Asian Soviet Republics. With Perestroika and Glasnost, the debate on the problematic economic development took place increasingly in public and the media. The Perestroika discourse—consumerism, accountability and reform—in the center had changed perceptions regarding the economic system, its centralization and private ownership.

Reformers in Dushanbe recognized the virtuality of the Tajik administrative and economic institutions as well as their dependency on Moscow.[37] Officials, such as Sohibnazar, Abduğabbor or Karim, understood in the late 1980s that Moscow's capacity to interfere in and regulate republican affairs was diminishing and a larger degree of autonomy seemed to be possible. They developed far-reaching reform programs in the agricultural sector, such as the establishment of a land registry office, privatization of collective farms as joint stock companies, a land reform introducing private ownership of agricultural land, abolishment of the five-year plans, deregulation of cotton, tobacco and silk production and so forth. Considering the lack of capital, the prevalent corruption in the system and the political situation, these reform programs were from an economists' perspective highly unrealistic.

Nonetheless, when reading through interviews and memoirs, one can sense the enthusiasm and aspirations of the Tajik reformers. For instance, Būrī Karim explained *Adabiyot va San 'at* in detail that the level of investment in the

Table 1.1   USSR Selected Social Indicators by Republic in 1989

	Average Family Size	Natural Growth Rate (per 1,000)	Infant Mortality Rate (per 1,000)	Life Expectancy at Birth (Years)	Doctors (per 10,000)	Hospital Beds (per 10,000)
USSR	3.5	7.6	22.7	69.5	44.4	133
RSFSR	3.2	3.9	17.8	69.6	47.3	139
Kazakhstan	4.0	15.4	25.9	68.7	40.9	136
Uzbekistan	5.5	27.0	37.7	69.2	35.8	123
Armenia	4.7	15.6	20.4	72.0	42.7	90
Tajikistan	6.1	32.2	43.2	69.4	28.5	105

Source: IMF, Study, Vol. 1, 232

Table 1.2   Income per Capita by Selected Republics, 1975–1988 (USSR = 100)

	1975	1980	1985	1988
RSFSR	109	110	109	110
KaSSR	92	93	91	93
UzSSR	66	67	64	62
Armenia	76	80	82	96
TaSSR	61	58	55	54

Source: IMF, Study, Vol. 1, 231

different economic sectors and in infrastructure and housing construction of the TaSSR has been constantly falling since 1975 while the population growth has accelerated. Karim presented a list of priorities demanding improvements in the irrigation system including the adoption of technologically advanced dry farming he had observed in the United States, the diversification of crops, amelioration of seeds, new standards of housing and industrial construction for areas with seismic activities, the construction of small and micro hydro stations for decentralized electricity production and eventually the protection of the environment.[38] However, the republican leadership hesitated to initiate economic reforms on its own and waited for directives from Moscow, which never came. In an interview with *Argumenty i Fakty* in April 1991, Mahkamov still downplayed the magnitude of the economic problems in the TaSSR: Although he cursory mentioned the problematic economic situation, he nonetheless pointed out to the achievements of his administration and affirmed his confidence in Moscow's determination to support the TaSSR. Apparently, Mahkamov did not comprehend the whole extent of the political, social and economic crisis in the USSR and Moscow's evanescent capacity and willingness to deal with the problems of the Central Asian periphery.[39]

The Tajik reformers did not only complain about the uneven development between the different Soviet republics but also within the TaSSR. In the centralized planned economy of the USSR, the different republics followed an economic specialization and the Central Asian republics were to provide the agricultural basis for the Soviet economy. As for the TaSSR this was cotton. During the Brezhnev era, Moscow increased the responsibilities of local nomenklatura for the agricultural-industrial complex silently tolerating the emergence of patronage networks and patrimonial structures in rural Central Asia. The industrial sector—above all the aluminum smelter in Tursunzoda— was stronger, embedded into the union structures due to the high level of capital investment, supply chains and technical expertise. Reservations, if not downright racist prejudice, about the qualification and work ethic of Central Asian nationalities in industrial labor, but also different employment preferences by ethnic Tajiks or Uzbeks resulted in an uneven ethnic division of labor. While Central Asian nationalities were overrepresented in the agricultural sector, non-Central Asian nationalities dominated industrial management, skilled labor and academic-scientific positions. Several Tajik intellectuals interpreted this imbalance as a Russian strategy to perpetuate the underdevelopment of Tajikistan and secure the exploitation of resources and raw material.[40] Abdulloh Habibov, a MVD general and deputy of the Supreme Soviet, accused the center of systematic discrimination against the ethnic Tajik population: "If they built factories in Tajikistan, they brought people from other republics to work there and gave them good accommodation and livelihood. The place of the local people was always in cotton cultivation."[41] While some Tajik intellectuals and politicians considered the sectorial employment distribution in the TaSSR as a Soviet-Russian plot, complementary Soviet research suggests that the low rural-outmigration and employment preferences in agriculture were an indication for the traditionalism and patriarchy in the Tajik society.[42]

Although the reformist intelligentsia supported a market economy and a vague idea of capitalism, they considered the state as the main actor in the economic sphere. Central to their economic agenda was the diversification of the economy, the establishment of independent financial institutions and the introduction of a national currency. However, the reformers underestimated the enormous challenges of restructuring the centralized and integrated economic system of the Soviet Union and the trajectories of a rapidly changing world economy. Many reformists indulged themselves in serious misperception of economic autarky and the economic achievements and potential of Tajikistan. The discourse of Soviet economic exploitation of Tajikistan's wealth—cotton, precious metals (gold, silver and uranium)—was obviously deceptive and generated unrealizable expectations.[43]

The "Curse of Cotton"[44]

Cotton has always been a highly politicized commodity in the three Central Asian republics of Tajikistan, Turkmenistan and Uzbekistan. Since the creation of Soviet Tajikistan, cotton is displayed on the coat of arms and the white stripe in the today's national flag represents cotton, purity and the snow of the mountains. Cotton cultivation in the collective farms has created dependencies and patronage networks in which a significant percentage of Tajikistan's political elite was socialized. In 1989, 42% of employment in the TaSSR was in the agricultural sector and cotton was by far the most important cash crop cultivated in in the south (Qūrġonteppa, Qubodiyon, Panǧ, Kūlob and Šahrtuz) and north (Xuǧand). In 1926, the Soviet authorities ordered the transformation of the Vaxš valley for large-scale cotton cultivation. Since cotton cultivation heavily relies on irrigation and manual labor, a dense irrigation system was constructed and large parts of the mountainous population were forcibly resettled to the lowlands. The area under cotton cultivation was continuously extended until the 1970s. In the mid-1980s, the TaSSR produced in average more than 900,000 tons of cotton a year (some 10% of the entire USSR cotton production) on approximately one-third of the arable land.[45] The large-scale cotton cultivation came with a price: Desertification, erosion as well as pollution by pesticides and fertilizers had (and have) severe effects on public health and the environment. To fulfill the plan, cotton cultivation was compulsory for collective farms regardless of the environmental and economic consequences. Due to the high level of manual labor in the cotton sector and low degree of mechanization, the per capita net output in the agricultural sector in the TaSSR was almost one-third lower than in the USSR average.[46]

Reformers realized that the collective farms were not competitive in a market economy, aggravated the inequality in the Tajik society and created patrimonial dependencies undermining the development of a democratic political system. Sohibnazar reported about agricultural productivity and planning in an article for the weekly *Saxovat* addressing major deficits in the agricultural system, namely the low per capita productivity, the lack of flexibility and engagement in the collective farms as well as the low output of basic staple food products. After the article had been published, kolkhoz employees complained to Sohibnazar that Perestroika and democracy were actually responsible for the economic decline and not the collective farm system. In a follow-up article he replied with a Marxist approach maintaining that Perestroika only revealed the "miserable life in the kolkhoz and people now understand that life in a kolkhoz is not different from Feudalism in medieval times. The kolkhoz system alienates the farmer from his soil (*az zamin begona kard*)"[47] and the directors of collective farms as well as the local chairmen and CPT cadres treat peasants like slaves. They create dependencies and opaque local networks which resist reform. Unfortunately, the republican structures, in particular the ministry of agriculture and the agricultural university in Dushanbe, act in concert with the local nomenklatura undermining reform and privatization.[48]

Rapid population growth, low rural out-migration, limited availability and increasing degradation of arable land increased local tensions and competition between and within the collective farms. Since the subdivisions in the kolkhoz and sovkhoz were often organized along homogenous ethnic or regional groups, conflicts about private plots, access to markets, water management and distribution of fuel, fertilizers, seeds or pesticides often appeared as ethnically motivated.[49] For instance, in 1988 tensions escalated between Kyrgyz and Tajik communities in the northern Isfara district next to the enclaves of Čorkūh and Batkent in the Fergana Valley. The conflict unfolded between Kyrgyz and Tajik communities in the Oktyabr sovkhoz about water, fertilizers, the local distribution of electricity as well as transport and access to local markets. Although the republican administration tried to mediate in the conflict, the situation further escalated and in May 1989 violent clashes left several dead. While local strongmen appealed to ethnicity and identity, political incompetence and the socio-economic crisis compounded the tensions between the communities.[50] Similar conflicts emerged in 1991 between Tajiks and "Arab Tajiks" in a kolkhoz close to Qubodiyon and between Tajiks and Uzbek Laqay in the southern Kolxozobod.[51] In these conflicts not the land under cotton cultivation was disputed but rather the private "kitchen gardens" and access to water. In rural Tajikistan, small plots adjacent to a house were usually exempt from collectivization and cultivated privately. The private horticulture contributed significantly to the income of rural communities and their resilience during economic crisis.[52] Accordingly, Nasriddinov, Sohibnazar or Yusuf reported the industriousness of the rural population from Ġarm, Qarotegin, Hisor or Kūlob and how they established a thriving horticulture as a romanticized Tajik version of authentic rural life in Central Asia.[53]

Environment

The 1980s saw an increased discussion about the environment in the Soviet Union, particularly after the nuclear catastrophe in Chernobyl 1986. The Chernobyl disaster had an immediate impact on the discussions in the TaSSR, since some 6,000 liquidators from the TaSSR were deployed to the Ukraine and came back with upsetting memories and severe medical problems.[54] Tajik political activists initiated a debate about the environmental impact of Soviet's large-scale development projects. *Adabiyot va San'at* started to publish a regular column on "Perestroika: Economy, Social Affairs and the Environment." Civil associations addressed five central concerns: first, the uranium mining and enrichment by the Industrial Association Eastern Combine for Rare Metals (*Vostokredmet*) in Čkalovsk (close to Xuǧand); second, the impact of the cotton cultivation on public health, salinization and soil contamination by the massive use of pesticides and fertilizers; third, the construction of the Roġun HPP (Vaxš River, close to Obigarm 100 km northeast of Dushanbe)[55]; fourth, the fertilizer factory in Kalininobod (today Tajik Azot) and finally, the aluminum smelter in Tursunzoda/Regar west of Dushanbe.[56] The discussion on the environment was at times ambivalent: The civil society did not reject Industrialization *per se*, but perceived the Soviet Union as a colonial power that was only interested in the exploitation of primary resources and never invested in sustainable processing industry but instead established hazardous industrial complexes in Tajikistan. The nationalist reformers maintained that the Soviets intentionally ruined the TaSSR economically and polluted its pristine environment.[57] Environmental concerns generated public pressure and in July 1991 the Dushanbe city Soviet decided to dismantle the experimental Argus Nuclear Reactor in the city's physical research institute. Next to seismological concerns, reports circulated that nuclear fuel leaked due to repeated flooding of nuclear storage. Similar concerns were voiced regarding a storage facility in Fayzobod (some 25 km east of Dushanbe), where depleted radioisotope thermoelectric generators (RTGs) and other radioactive material were kept.[58]

The construction of hydroelectric power stations was a controversial public issue in Tajikistan. In 1959, Moscow decided to allocate resources for the construction of the Norak Hydroelectric Power Plant (next to other projects to improve the infrastructure of the TaSSR). The construction of Norak should provide the energy for the further industrialization of southern Tajikistan. The construction started in 1961 and finished in 1980, some 10 years behind schedule (electricity was produced since 1972, but the last hydroelectric generating unit was only commissioned in 1979).[59] In the 1970s, two additional large-scale HPPs were projected by the Soviet authorities: Roġun and Daštiġum (in south-eastern Tajikistan, east of Moskowsky close to the Afghan border).[60] According to initial projections, the Roġun HPP's first unit should have been producing electricity already in 1990, but progress in the construction of Roġun was slow due to the lack of capital and increasing concerns for the environment.[61] In the late 1980s, reformers and political activists saw Roġun as a Soviet colonial project and the vice-chairman of the Council of Ministers, Otaxon Latifī, critically evaluated the environmental impact of Roġun for the Vaxš valley and Central Asia.[62] However, the narratives on large-scale development projects in the TaSSR were often inconsistent and contradictory; Ibrohim Usmonov, for instance, insinuated that Roġun was not finished in time, because it would have made TaSSR independent from electricity imports.[63] The image of Roġun as a colonial project has completely changed in recent years: In 2008, President Rahmon announced the resumption of the construction of Roġun. Since Tajikistan could control the water flow of the Vaxš and Amu Daria in case Roġun is constructed, Uzbekistan's government immediately protested against the project and imposed various unofficial and undeclared sanctions on Tajikistan. Uzbekistan's opposition in turn has elevated the Roġun HPP to the central national (re-)construction project of Tajikistan which is supposed to provide energy security, significant revenues from energy export and a splendid future for Tajikistan.[64]

The Oligarchs

The disintegration of state authority and uncontrolled deregulation of the economy facilitated the rise of oligarchs throughout the USSR. Among the better known Tajik oligarchs were Sayfiddin Tūraev (b. 1945 in Istaravšan) and Abdumalik Abdulloġonov (b. 1949 in Leninobod).[65] Tūraev had been minister for consumer industries between 1986 and 1988 until he transformed the ministry into a state-owned stock company called *Širkat* ("Corporation"). In the privatization process, Tūraev accumulated several state holding companies and created the *Hizmat* ("Service") group in 1990. The same year, Tūraev was elected to the Supreme Soviet from the Istaravšan constituency and ran (unsuccessfully) for presidency in the 1991 elections.

Abdulloġonov graduated from the Agricultural University in Odessa and managed several combines in the north of Tajikistan in the 1980s. In 1987 he became the TaSSR's minister of grain products and gradually outsourced the ministry's portfolio and privatized the lucrative parts. He later established the *Suġdiyon* Company with Swiss and Israeli investment. Reportedly, cotton processing and the production of counterfeit jeans counted among *Suġdiyon's* more profitable and lucrative business activities. Abdulloġonov's family was well established in Xuġand; his younger brother, Abduġanī, was mayor of Xuġand and his brother-in-law, Abduġalil Homidov, chairman of the Leninobod *viloyat* Ispolkom between 1990 and 1992.[66] This new generation of businessmen expected a sort of reforms that would support their business activities that were at times downright illegal or part of the expanding shadow economy in the late Soviet Union. They initially supported the more dogmatic and arguably less corrupt Mahkamov but they reconsidered their loyalty due to Mahkamov's indecisiveness and reluctance to implement reforms. More importantly, the Leninobodī elite was less and less disposed to invest in the politics of Dushanbe and eventually kept the north out of the civil war. Additionally, the new economic elites were not anymore habitually linked to the agro-industrial complex—for them cotton was a cash crop and not a politicized symbol of Tajikistan's social fabrics. Eventually the emergence of oligarchs raised the awareness of the widening disparities in income, wealth, and opportunity in the Soviet society.

STRATIFICATION OF THE SOVIET TAJIK INTELLIGENTSIA

The creation of the Tajik Autonomous SSR in 1924 and the TaSSR as a fully-fledged USSR republic in 1929 was a complicated and convoluted affair, which to this day contributes to serious tensions between Uzbekistan and Tajikistan.[67] Today's Tajikistan was a remote territory in eastern Bukhara with inhospitable swampy lowlands in the south (Qūrġonteppa, Kūlob and Šahrtuz) and barren mountain valleys in the east (Qarotegin and the Pamir Mountains) without any major urban center (except for Xuġand, which, however, was only assigned to the TaSSR in 1929). Dushanbe, a conglomerate of small hamlets with a few hundred inhabitants in 1924, was elevated to the republic's capital without any urban tradition so important for the Iranian/Tajik culture.[68] Since the USSR understood itself as a force of liberation and national self-determination, Moscow prioritized the recruitment of indigenous cadres (*korenizaciya*, from Russ.: *koren* = root, "indigenization") in Central Asia. With the recruitment of local cadres, the Soviets intended to demonstrate that the USSR was not an imperialist empire (the "prison of the people" as Lenin called Tsarist Russia) but a force of national emancipation and liberation.[69] In Tajikistan, the Bolshevik authorities could only recruit a few indigenous cadres mostly from Xuġand and the Pamir Mountains—regions, which had been integrated into the Russian colonial administration already between 1866 and 1896. Additionally, the Soviet authorities recruited representatives of the Persian-speaking reformist intelligentsia from Samarqand and Bukhara who formed the kernel of the Tajik intelligentsia. One of the most important representatives of the early Tajik intelligentsia was the writer, poet and lexicographer Sadriddin Aynī (1878–1964), who was one of the leading personalities in the "Tajik emancipation" (Lutz Rzehak). Since the mid-1920s, Aynī invited his "Tajik" students (i.e., those who decided to become Tajik[70]) from Samarqand and Bukhara to Dushanbe. Throughout the 1920s and 1930s, Aynī's men from Bukhara and Samarqand developed the standard Tajik language as well as literature.[71] Importantly, they shaped the establishment of universities and academic institutions in Dushanbe, such as the Academy for Agricultural Pedagogy, the Tajik Pedagogical Institute and the Tajik Academy of Science in 1931/1932. Successively Aynī's men dominated the literary field for the decades to come.

Until the late 1940s the intellectual field in the TaSSR was comparably small in numbers and the frequent Stalinist interventions severely disrupted the nascent academic community by "purging" its ranks or imposing bizarre theories on various disciplines.[72] Nonetheless, in the 1940s the Soviet-Tajik master narrative in important academic disciplines such as history and linguistics had been developed: Within the ideological limits Aynī and his students had created the concept of a distinct standard Tajik language and literature (different from Farsi and Dari) and Boboğon Ğafurov defined with his *The History of the Tajik People* the foundational principles of Tajik historiography.[73]

The structural transformation of the TaSSR's society accelerated in the 1950s and although Tajikistan remained the least urban Soviet republic, urbanization, in particular the development of Dushanbe to a Soviet capital, profoundly transformed the Tajik society.[74] With the growth of Dushanbe, the local administration, health care as well as cultural and educational institutions expanded replicating the structures in the center. A professional Tajik intelligentsia emerged as a cognizable field in the early 1960s with the expansion of universities, research institutes and the academy of science stipulating the dependency of the intellectual field on Soviet institutions. In the 1960s the internally resettled *muhoğir* communities from Ğarm, Zarafšon, Mastčoh and Badaxšon recovered from the disruption of forced resettlement and consolidated their social and economic situation. A younger generation of Tajiks born in the 1950s entered Dushanbe's universities. Regional and professional networks often influenced the students' admission to particular departments: Students from Kūlob were strongly represented in the agricultural university, students from Badaxšon in the pedagogical institute and students from Qarotegin in the humanities departments of the universities. The incumbent elites controlled access to the academic institutions in Dushanbe and assigned to the "new" generation from Tajikistan's *muhoğir* population the literary faculties (such as philosophy, history, Oriental studies, etc.), while the economic and law departments remained in the hands of the established elites.[75] In the applied science departments non-Central Asian academics and scientists were significantly overrepresented until 1991. Thus, the humanities developed as the key disciplines dominated by ethnic Tajiks preoccupied in defining the Tajik history and cultural heritage according to the dictum "National in form, Socialist in content." Since the late 1960s, an increasing number of intellectuals with a *muhoğir* background enrolled in the humanity programs and many considered this time as a period of national recovery and gradual "awakening (*bidorī*)"[76] defined by their (re-)reading of the TaSSR's history. Šodmon Yusuf is a good example for this development. Born in 1949 in the Kommunistī kolkhoz close to Qūrğonteppa into a *muhoğir* family from Ġarm, he benefited from the "affirmative action," studied in Saratov (1968–1974) and graduated from the philosophy department at the academy of science in Moscow. In 1987 he returned to the TaSSR and worked in the academy of science.[77]

During the Brezhnev tenure, the Tajik intelligentsia cultivated similar patronage networks like cadres in the political and agro-industrial fields. Moreover, the political and intellectual nomenklatura of the TaSSR shows interesting intermarriage patterns beyond regional affiliations among the generation born in the 1950s. In conversations, representatives of this cohort emphasize the specific Soviet context: Similar socialization patterns as children of the nomenklatura, social mobility, post-graduate studies in Moscow or Leningrad, the internationalist outlook and confidence as members of the privileged elite.[78] Until the mid-1980s, the Tajik intelligentsia enjoyed a symbiotic relation to the Soviet system as Dudoignon remarks pointedly:

> The fondness felt by many Tajik intellectuals of the apparatus for the institutions and political sphere handed down by the USSR can be explained in part by their awareness that radical political reform would fell the branch on which they were comfortably perched: the intellectual mediocrity prevalent in Dushanbe, as in all the Soviet provincial capitals, precluded any hope for the intelligentsia's survival outside the national Socialism of which it had made itself the official custodian.[79]

One of the key representatives of the TaSSR's intelligentsia since the 1960s was the former minister of education and long-serving president of the academy of science (1965–1988) Muhammad Osimī (Russ.: Asimov). Osimī, born in 1920 in Xuğand, was a powerful and controversial actor within the intellectual field since he was able to control access to academic positions in the TaSSR's institution. Educated in the 1930s in a RabFak (a preparatory college for workers), he started his academic career after the war in 1955 with a degree from Moscow's Communist Party Academy for Social Sciences. Between 1956 and 1962 he was the rector of the newly established polytechnic university in Dushanbe and occupied different administrative positions. During his tenure as president of the academy of science, Osimī acted as editor-in-chief of the eight-volume *Tajik Soviet Encyclopaedia* (modelled after the *Great Soviet Encyclopaedia*) between 1978 and 1988. The *Tajik Soviet Encyclopaedia* is the central hallmark of the Tajik-Soviet academic field since it defined the "idea" of Soviet Tajikistan more than any other publication.[80]

The stability (or better: stagnation) of the intellectual field in the TaSSR came to an end with the economic contraction in the 1980s and the decline of investment in the academic institutions intensified the rivalry and competition among the intellectuals. In the context of Perestroika and rising nationalism academic debates about history, language, culture, religion and "Tajikness" were suddenly discussed in public and became politically relevant. A younger generation of academics and intellectuals, some of them with a *muhoǧir* background, started to challenge the intellectual dominance, social status and complacency of the incumbent intellectual elites. The continuous social mobilization by the Soviet state, the expansion of higher education and its consolidation, as well as the proliferation of numerous professional associations were important preconditions for the development of an urban civil society among the intelligentsia in the TaSSR, although the totalitarian control limited the autonomy of these associations.[81] Unsurprisingly, these younger intellectuals called the "old guard" around Osimī to account for the stagnation in the academic sector, the opaque appointments and their intellectual mediocrity. Yusuf, who was himself a philosophy lecturer in the academy of science, acridly remarked about Osimī:

> This ignorant person has distanced the Academy of Science from any form of science during his long years as president. With Glasnost and Perestroika, a younger generation of academics and scientists emerged and he became afraid of the intellectuals of this time. In particular, he feared the question, in what discipline he was a specialist. He belonged to those Soviet scientists, who actually fought against the intelligentsia and true scientists. For instance, he once turned to Sakharov in a meeting and announced that he is ashamed that Sakharov is also a member of the Academy of Science. He was a political player acting for the Xuǧandī elite and the Communist clan [...]. He divided small Tajikistan in north and south, in the self and the other. He was one of those who colonized the people (*mardom rā esteṣmār mīkardand*).[82]

Although Yusuf gained some notoriousness for his controversial comments, the quote nonetheless points to the central issues in the unfolding conflict, that is, the role of the intelligentsia in the society, the emancipation from Soviet discourses and the redefinition of "authentic" Tajik identity. Moreover, it supports Georgi Arbatov's diagnosis of a virulent cynicism and embitterment among the Soviet intelligentsia, in particular in the social sciences where a strong regression diffused since the 1980s.[83] With Perestroika and Glasnost the political relevance of the Soviet version of social sciences evaporated and Tajik intellectuals embraced nationalism in order to demonstrate their political significance. The reformist intelligentsia in the late 1980s had high rising ambitions and followed a Gramscian ideal about their role in the Tajik society. Paraphrasing Anton Chekhov, the historian Muhammadğon Šukurov (Šakurī, 1925–2012) assertively stated that "the strength of the people derives from its intellectuals (*ziyoiyon*)."[84] Šukurov criticized the transformation of the intellectual field in the 1980s: Now, everyone with a higher education was considered an intellectual. Instead, Šukurov demanded that a "true intellectual" needs extraordinary qualities and values and needs to be engaged with his society and politics and "his own thoughts should be enlightened by the light of the people's culture."[85] However, the meaning of "people's culture" needed to be defined first and the evolving debates contributed to the overall cleavages in the Tajik society. The divides within the intelligentsia, between an older and younger generation of academic cadres, between the émigré families from Samarqand/Bukhara and the "indigenous" intellectuals from the eastern parts of Tajikistan or with a *muhoğir* background, between formally trained academics and those who passed through a rather improvised ideological education during the 1930s and 1940s and eventually between competing patronage networks mirrored the conflict dynamics in the political field.

The Urban and Rural Divide

Despite the Soviet transformation, the large majority of the Tajik population (in 1989, 67%) lived in rural areas dominated by collective farms. Therefore, one of the central divisions in the Tajik society in the late 1980s was between the urban and rural population. The kolkhoz/sovkhoz was place of residence and formed a local social-economic solidarity group with a patrimonial hierarchy epitomized in the *brigadir* (the leader of a *brigada*, a labor division in the kolkhoz) and the kolkhoz director who regulated the interaction with the regional administration. Būrī Karim argued that the majority of Tajiks were villagers (*dehotī*) who did not understand the political discourse on Perestroika, Glasnost and economic reform lead by the urban intelligentsia.[86] He bitterly complained about the isolation of the intelligentsia and their limited outreach to the workers and peasants. For Karim, the workers and peasants were to blame for their ignorance, since they did not understand that the public good (*manfiathoi millī*) should be more important than their individual welfare.[87] The centerpieces of the urban intellectuals' political

agenda—market economy, private property, human rights and democratization—had unfortunately "no meaning for the common people (*omma*)."[88]
Hence, many urban intellectuals had strong reservations toward rural Tajiks,
even if most of them had their roots in rural Tajikistan. After the elections to
the Supreme Soviet in February 1990, Sohibnazar invited deputies to form
a parliamentary group of democratic reformers, but he explicitly excluded
deputies with a rural background. He bluntly stated that the deputies in a
parliament should be urban lawyers and intellectuals, who are able to lead
the country and not farmers and villagers.[89] During the confrontation in 1992,
Sohibnazar labeled the protestors on Ozodī Square as "rural people (*mardumi
dehot*),"[90] who did not understand why reforms were necessary. Yusuf joined
Sohibnazar by concluding that rural Tajiks "are ignorant and common people
who have no idea about the world and the life of educated people."[91] It is
important to notice, that both, Sohibnazar and Yusuf, considered themselves
as the leading democratic politicians of the TaSSR; nonetheless, they adopted
prevalent Soviet discourses on rural Central Asia. For these urban intellectuals, rural Tajiks had no agency; they were sent to the squares and did not
come intentionally, they did not know about the affairs discussed, they did not
understand the original manners and customs of authentic urban Tajiks and
finally they did not even speak proper Tajik.[92] The bitterness of Sohibnazar,
Karim, Yusuf and others is related to their inability to mobilize support
among rural communities (this was done by the IRPT) and their marginalization in spring 1992 by the rise of militias from the Kūlob, exactly from those
areas of the TaSSR they considered as rural, traditional, underdeveloped and
uncultured.

The Tajik Perestroika intelligentsia was far from being united and personal animosities limited their readiness to cooperate and the mounting
political tensions since 1990 deepened these divisions precluding any unity
and solidarity among them. Būrī Karim remarked that the civil society and
intellectuals united the people and promoted inclusive national values in
other USSR republics, the Tajik intellectuals disunited the society. In the
Baltic Republics local reformers and intellectuals were an organic part of
the entire society, in Tajikistan reformers and the intelligentsia were the
main obstacle for progress.[93] Accordingly, Rubin notes "Tajikistan lacked a
cohesive intelligentsia with a common conception of a Tajik nation."[94] Perhaps, this has to be seen more nuanced: There was certainly not a hegemony
of a certain "school" of Tajik intellectuals in the late 1980s, but the Soviet
conceptualization of Tajik history and national identity provided a pervasive
master narrative which was back then only challenged in details but not in
substance—apparently a result of the dependency of Tajik nationalism on
the Soviet nation building in Central Asia. While the political agenda and
details in the interpretation of Tajik history and culture contributed to the

divisions on the performative level, the real matters of contention were often of personal—contingent—nature.

POLITICAL CLUBS AND PARTIES IN THE LATE TASSR

The civil society dimension of Glasnost reached the TaSSR in 1988/1989. Above all, developments in the Baltics shaped the proliferation of civil associations in Central Asia and the first associations, such as Rastoxez, printed their leaflets and newspapers in Lithuania with support of the Sajūdi movement.[95] The early Glasnost figurehead in the TaSSR was the film director, people's deputy to the USSR Supreme Soviet and chairman of the USSR's Union of Cinematographers, Davlat Xudonazar, a well-connected public figure among reformist circles in Moscow and St. Petersburg. Xudonazar's early cinematographic works had been censored and he became an acquaintance of the prominent dissident Sakharov. In 1988, he was elected people's deputy to the Congress of People's Deputies of the Soviet Union from the Šuġnav constituency in GBAO.

The majority of Glasnost activists in the TaSSR were employees and graduates of the local academic and cultural institutions created by the USSR's contradictory social mobilization: Despite the totalitarian control, the state emphasized freedom, emancipation and political participation and notably, it was the Communist Youth Organization Komsomol, which established the first semi-independent political club Rū ba rū (*Face to Face*) in March 1989. Rū ba rū appealed to a younger generation of ethnic Tajik intellectuals and embraced the nascent nationalist sentiment in order to contain the discussion on national history, tradition and language. Central to the agenda of Rū ba rū was the adoption of the language law elevating Tajik as the official state language and environmental protection, in particular the suspension of the construction of the Roġun HPP.[96] When the Komsomol realized it was losing control over Rū ba rū in September 1989, it suspended the association's independence. Rū ba rū immediately disintegrated and other associations, such as Rastoxez, filled the gap.[97] The establishment of Rū ba rū was a signal for the civil society and soon a plethora of associations mushroomed not only in Dushanbe but also in the regions. Many civil associations responded to local issues and complaints, but articulated these grievances in the master narrative of reform, nationalism and independent statehood. The heterogeneity of the nascent civil society in the TaSSR reflects a societal fragmentation but should be also understood as the result of the previous public discourse on mobilization and participation by the Soviet state. In early 1992 Būrī Karim identified more than 70 registered associations and parties in and 9 outside of Tajikistan.[98] Many political associations, such as the Party of Economic Freedom

(*Hizbi ozodii iqtisodī*), the Party of Tajikistan's Patriots (*Hizbi vatanparasti Toğikiston*) or the Democratic Farmers' Party of Tajikistan (*Hizbi demokratii dehqononi Toğikiston*) were centered around one individual and either disappeared during the civil war or were co-opted by the Presidential People's Democratic Party of Tajikistan (PDPT, *Hizbi Xalqii Demokratii Toğikiston*), which was established in December 1994. Other parties split in the 1990s due to personal animosities, conflicting political agendas or external manipulation.

Rastoxez

On 14 September 1989, some 40 Dushanbe-based intellectuals and reformers founded the association Rastoxez (*Resurrection*) in order to renew the discussion on Tajik identity and the Iranian heritage. The term Rastoxez had been popular among Persian-speaking political reformers since the 19th century and the founders of Rastoxez were inspired by Muhammad Iqbal's well-known poem *Az xobi garon xez* (Rise From the Deep Sleep), which became the hymn on Šahidon Square.[99] Initially, Ziyo Abdullo suggested naming the new association in reference to the political developments in the Baltic Republics Popular Front (*Fronti xalqī*) but Abduğabbor and Xoliqzoda preferred Rastoxez as a more explicit reference to the distinct Tajik identity.[100] The founders of Rastoxez followed a romantic, ethnic idea of Tajik nationalism and their agenda focused on political independence, the diversification and reform of the economy and a fundamental cultural re-orientation.[101] Rastoxez' leadership around Tohir Abduğabbor, an economist in the academy of science and Afghan War veteran, was politically more ambitious than many civil society associations or cultural clubs of the Perestroika/Glasnost time. Disappointed CPT reformers joined Rastoxez and transformed the nationalist association into a political platform from which they criticized the political system, in particular the dominance of the Communist Party as well as the relationship between Moscow and the union republics.[102] Rastoxez announced during its first congress on 31 December 1989 that the group would nominate candidates and participate in the forthcoming elections to the Supreme Soviet scheduled for February 1990.[103] Thus, Rastoxez was the first political association that directly challenged the monopoly of the Communist Party prior to the March 1990 amendments of Article 6 of the USSR's constitution, which abolished the monopoly of the CPSU.

The political nomenklatura perceived Rastoxez as a provocation since most of its leading representatives were part of the larger academic and administrative establishment of the TaSSR. Nasriddinov accused the leaders of Rastoxez of adopting a legal nihilism (*nigilizmi huquqī*) since they ignored the laws of the TaSSR (in reference to the national nihilism diagnosed by Rastoxez, see below). Furthermore, he insinuated that Rastoxez was under the influence of reactionary Islam and chauvinist nationalism. While demanding democracy and freedom for themselves, they did not accept that their political opponents enjoy the same rights. Instead of contributing constructively to the political debate, Rastoxez resorted—in the words of Nasriddinov—to defamation campaigns in the media contributing to confrontational tone in the republic.[104]

Rastoxez was not a homogeneous group. Most of its members agreed on the importance of Tajik as the official language and the distinguished position of the Tajik heritage in Central Asia, but were less united on more tangible issues such as economic policy, political participation or the political system. Many Rastoxez members projected their romantic ethnic nationalism on the economic system and envisioned ideas of economic autarky, overstating Tajikistan's natural resources and economic capacity. Others, such as Abduğabbor, instead warned of the economic consequences in case the integrated economy of the USSR would collapse and demanded a gradual reform of the economic system.[105] In general, the nationalist opposition did not comprehend the magnitude of the economic crisis and had only a very short list of economic measures to tackle it: privatization, promotion of international tourism and intensified cooperation with technologically advanced nations. Rastoxez remained a nationalist civil association pre-occupied with the issues of culture, national heritage and language. The association did not transform to a political party and lost its relevance in early 1992, however key members of Rastoxez established in the summer of 1991 the Democratic Party of Tajikistan (DPT); the first full-fledged political party challenging the monopoly of the CPT.

THE DEMOCRATIC PARTY OF TAJIKISTAN

The DPT held its constituent congress on 10 August 1990 in the academy of science in Dushanbe, but the registration process with the ministry of justice took until 21 June 1991. Initially, the DPT attracted a more urban, multi-ethnic and educated electorate, however with a strong representation of members with a *muhoğir* background from Qarotegin.[106] In order to attract non-Central Asian nationalities, Viktor Terletskiy, an ethnic Russian, was elected deputy chairman of the DPT. Terletskiy, however, left the DPT in February 1992 after internal disputes over the legitimacy of the presidential elections.[107] The DPT's founding members, Šodmon Yusuf, Rahim Mosalmoniyon, Daler Imomnazar, Abdunabī Sattorzoda, Oynihol Bobonazarova, Bozor Sobir and Abdullo Očilov were mostly representatives of the Tajik nomenklatura but gradually disassociated themselves from the Communist Party and adopted an anti-colonial discourse on the Soviet past which shaped the DPT's program.[108] The first section of the DPT's program postulated a political, social and moral crisis in Tajikistan induced by Soviet rule, namely the destruction of Tajik culture, the economic exploitation, uneven development and environmental pollution. The DPT defined itself as a conservative-centrist party and demanded unequivocally political, cultural and economic independence of Tajikistan. Furthermore, the DPT expressed its commitment to human rights including the equal rights for national minorities. The program further emphasized the importance of national traditions and language. The advocates of the one-language concept (*yak zabon,* see below) dominated the ranks of the DPT; therefore, the party's program explicitly states that Farsi is the official language in Tajikistan and that the educational system should initiate the transition to the Persian-Arabic script.[109] For a short time, between September 1991 and April 1992, the DPT was the most important opposition party in Tajikistan: Popular poets, journalists, former CPT cadres and political activists supported the party and its political agenda. Erratic decisions by the DPT's leadership, the increasing political polarization of the Tajik society as well as the forceful establishment of the IRPT marginalized the DPT in 1992, as we will see in the following chapters.

La'li Badaxšon

Yuri Slezkine observes that the creation of nations and nationalities in the early USSR "turned into the most extravagant celebration of ethnic diversity that any state had ever financed."[110] With the establishment of the GBAO in 1925, the Soviet authorities recognized the diversity of the population in Tajikistan and Badaxšon in particular: The Pomirī population speaks varieties of eastern Iranian languages, such as Šuġnī, Rošanī, Yazġulāmī or Iškāšmī, and—in case they practice religion—belong to the Ismaili-Nizari branch of Shia Islam and accept Aga Khan as their spiritual leader.[111] Since Tsarist Russia had established its presence in the Pamir Mountains already in 1896, those Pomirīs who spoke Russian, such as Širinšoh Šohtemur (1899–1937), advanced in the early Bolshevist administration in Soviet Tajikistan to leading cadres until the Great Terror. The "celebration of ethnic diversity" ended with the Great Retreat in the mid-1930s. In the 1959 All-Union Census the Pomirī-Badaxšonī people had disappeared as distinct people and were now considered Tajiks. Accordingly, the *Enciklopediyai sovetii Toğik* plainly stated in 1978 that 91.3% of GBAO's population were Tajiks.[112] Despite the re-designation, the Pomirī community remained a distinct social group in the TaSSR and responded readily to the Soviet social mobilization in the 1960s. Out-migration from GBAO established a substantial Pomirī community in Dushanbe.

Perestroika and Glasnost provided the public space to reconsider their identity and relation to the non-Pomirī Tajiks.[113] The Pomirī association Laʿli Badaxšon (*The Ruby of Badaxšon*) was established in late 1990 by the Dushanbe-based Pomirī community around Atobek Amirbek, a mathematics lecturer and deputy dean of the pedagogical institute in Dushanbe. It's constituent congress took place on 4 March 1991 and the registration with the ministry of justice was completed on 30 May 1991. Initially, Amirbek intended to establish a cultural and educational association to support the development in the Pamir region. The status of GBAO as an autonomous region within the TaSSR was not addressed in Laʿli Badaxšon's original charter in 1991. With independence, the situation changed: First, political activists in Badaxšon's capital Xoruġ demanded greater autonomy rights and even discussed a changed status as an Autonomous *Republic* of Badaxšon. Second, the Pomirī Davlat Xudonazar announced his candidacy for the presidential elections in November 1991 ultimately politicizing Laʿli Badaxšon and transforming it from a cultural association to the central Pomirī political representation in Dushanbe.[114] While Pomirī political activists demanded greater autonomy rights and more resources for the development of the mountainous east, politicians in Dushanbe, such as Safaralī Kenġaev, insinuated that the Pomirīs are neither "real" Tajiks nor "real" Muslims.[115] Importantly, Laʿli Badaxšon played a short but significant role in the mobilization of the opposition in March 1992.

Although Laʿli Badaxšon was an exclusively Pomirī association, by far not all Pomirīs supported Laʿli Badaxšon. Some Pomirīs supported the DPT and many had benefited from the "affirmative action" by the Soviets and had made a career in the Soviet system, such as Šodī Šabdolov, the chairman of the CPT since 1991, and were staunch communists.

A POST-COLONIAL MOMENT: THE TASSR 1987–1991

While discussing the Soviet past and the nature of Soviet rule in Central Asia, my Central Asian friends and colleagues usually hesitate to call the Soviet Empire a colonial one. Many commenced their careers in Soviet institutions and did not necessarily experience 1991 as a process of decolonization and liberation but of decline and personal reversal of their social, academic or political status. Some look back to the later USSR with some nostalgia as a time without regional borders in Central Asia, a modest livelihood and predictable opportunities. They consider the TaSSR as an inherent part of the USSR and themselves as Soviet citizens with equal rights and opportunities echoing Martin's concept of the "affirmative action empire."[116] Perhaps, this perception has delayed the introduction of post-colonial theory to the field of Central Asian studies. Recently, John Heathershaw has empathically advocated a stronger integration of post-colonial perspectives theory in Central Asian studies, and over the past years several important contributions have advanced our conceptual thinking about post-colonialism in Central Asia.[117] A substantial debate has evolved about early Soviet rule in Central Asia emphasizing the participation of local elites in the micromanagement of the authoritarian modernization but also the ambivalences in the Soviet modernization project.[118] In her seminal study on Kazakhstan Bhavna Dave demonstrates the potential for a post-colonial perspective in her analysis of how the Soviet system influenced the conceptual understanding of nation, statehood and national narratives.[119]

Moscow's promotion of territorial nations in Central Asia was in its kernel contradictory: On the one hand Tajik intellectuals were well aware that Tajikistan was a Soviet invention, on the other hand Moscow's promotion of exclusive and competing linguistic and territorial nation states (albeit dependent on the Soviet center) reinforced the perception of Moscow's rule as external, foreign or colonial. The following annotations locate a brief post-colonial moment in the final years of the TaSSR. This post-colonial episode ended with the outbreak of the civil war and the fragmentation of the urban intelligentsia.

In the late 1980s a group of Tajik intellectuals, political reformers and writers, among them Šodmon Yusuf, Bozor Sobir, Gulruxsor Safieva, Asliddin Sohibnazar, Būrī Karim, Mirbobo Mirrahim, Otaxon Latifī, Loiq Šeralī or Akbar Tursunov, had no doubts that the Soviet Union was a "colonial system (*soxti iste'morii šūravī*)"[120] and that they—as Tajik intellectuals—were in a subaltern position to the Soviet center. Karim explicated that the majority of Tajik intellectuals were leading a "slave-like life"[121] under Soviet rule and condemned the intellectual dependency on the Communist Party. This dependency induced corruption and opportunism among the intelligentsia in Dushanbe who became mere "Yes-men (*labbī-gū*)"[122] of the center. Moreover, the proximity to the Soviet colonial structures and institutions has undermined the intellectuals' credibility, their ability to build enduring coalitions and to mobilize a larger social support base.[123] Since the communists were only interested in exploiting the TaSSR's resources, they had no interest in the culture or dignity of its people. And to govern and rule, Moscow created colonized native elites, in Yusuf terms "slaves, people who sold their religion, their culture for nothing."[124] Rahim Mosalmoniyon narrated Tajikistan's history in a *longue durée* perspective as a continuous struggle against foreign enemies and occupation since Alexander the Great. The Bolsheviks eventually destroyed the Tajik traditions and its cultural heritage transforming the population to the new Soviet Man "void of spirituality, culture, traditions and customs, without respect or a sentiment of honor (*nomus*)."[125] Worse, the Soviet system turned intellectuals to a guild, which cultivated nepotism and corruption while the ordinary academics lived in precarious conditions.

Tūrağonzoda developed an interesting post-colonial approach to the role of Tajik intellectuals in the USSR echoing Eisenstadt's analysis on the "ideological kernels"[126] of the Soviet intelligentsia and Dudoignon's diagnosis of the mediocrity in the intellectual field. Tūrağonzoda described them as a generation, who grew up with a Soviet *Weltanschauung* and perceived the world exclusively "through Soviet eyes [...]. These young atheists received a carefully filtered knowledge and they were rewarded with academic honors for their works on the *Anti-religious Poetry of Hofizi Šerozī* or their treatise on *Religion as a Relict from the Feudal Age*. This mind-set was imposed from the nursery to the university."[127] Tūrağonzoda ridiculed these colonized intellectuals as academics who merely *know* academically about the national culture (*donandai farhangi millī*) from encyclopedic works and contrasts them with those, who actually *have* national culture (*dorandai farhangi millī*) as part of their inner spiritual self and who consider it as the foundation of their

> *Weltanschauung* (*ğahonbinī*), morals and way of life. The education system of the USSR alienated us [Tajiks] from our genuine national culture and values and produced intellectuals, who pretended to be enlightened, especially those who were raised in Soviet boarding schools based on the materialistic and anti-religious culture of the Soviets and not in the environment of national Tajik families.[128]

He recollected a discussion with Nodir Odilov and Akbar Tursunov. Both, Odilov and Tursunov, complained to him, that "the Tajik people pay more respect to and even more money on a half-educated mullo but never showed any sympathy or support for the intellectuals during the difficult time after the Civil War."[129] Tūrağonzoda replied that these intellectuals *vice versa* also never showed any respect for the "religion, the manners and customs, as well as the culture and values of their own people." Tūrağonzoda's reply is remarkably consistent with Chatterjee's postulate on the nature of colonial nationalism and the separation of the colonial society in a material and spiritual domain.[130]

How long will the water run under the ice?

Chingiz Aitmatov's novel *The Day Lasts More Than a Hundred Years* (1980) is widely seen as an example for a subtle anti-colonial critique.[131] The TaSSR's reformist intelligentsia attentively received Aitmatov's novel and the *Mankurt* motif became a popular synonym for the process of alienation from the Soviet state, which had distorted the authentic local culture and history.[132] The *Mankurt* in Aitmatov's novel were an enslaved tribal group and a *Mankurt* "did not know his name, could not remember his childhood, father or mother—in short, he could not recognize himself as a human being."[133]

Soviet Tajik prose literature does not feature a similar novel like *The Day
Lasts More Than a Hundred Years*. Tajik intellectuals initiated a debate on the
particular Tajik cultural and historical identity in the late 1980s focusing on
language, history and traditions.

This debate evolved gradually and inconsistently, often resembling more
a monologue than a dialogue. The main protagonists were the historian and
academic Muhammadǧon Šukurov, the poet Šeralī Loiq, the historian Akbar
Tursunov, the film director Mirbobo Mirrahim, the journalist Otaxon Latifī,
the poets Gulruxsor Safieva (as one of the very few female protagonists),
Mū'min Qanoat, Bozor Sobir and a few others. The forum for their discussion was mainly the periodical press in the TaSSR, for instance *Adabiyot
va San'at, Toǧikistoni sovetī* or *Ǧavononi Toǧikiston*, but references were
frequently made to union-wide distributed press, such as *Literaturnaya
Gazeta, Družba Narodov* and *Ogonyok*. Already in 1989, a first edited volume
(a second followed in 1991) of contributions to this debate was published by
Mahmadnazar under the title *A Lesson in Self-Awareness* with an impressive
print run of 40,000 copies for the first volume and 80,000 for the second volume indicating the enormous public interest in the discussion.[134] Arguably,
the most frequently cited and influential article was written by the journalist,
documentary film director and Rastoxez activist Mirbobo Mirrahim (b. 1954)
and published under the title "How long will the water run under the ice?" on
27 January 1988 in *Komsomoli Toǧikiston*.[135] In his article, Mirrahim reflected
on the Soviet ideological work in the TaSSR. He criticized the methods and
slogans with which these foundational pillars of Soviet ideology were propagated as "indications of obsolete thinking" which have neither promoted
internationalism nor scientific atheism but instead increased the "national
nihilism (*nigilizmi millī*)" among the population. In Mirrahim's view, the
ideological discourse and authoritative representation (Alexei Yurchak) had
become a pretext for the economic exploitation of Central Asia and Tajikistan
in particular. The pervasive ideological discourse has forced the Central Asian
nations to accept the "compromise of national nihilism, which implies the
rejection and demotion of one's own nation, language, civilization, traditions and historical legacy. This nihilism will not yield a pleasant result."[136]
The ideological premise of internationalism followed, according to Mirrahim,
the rationale of concealing the sycophancy among the political elites toward
Moscow and of discrediting any discussion about nationalism. He explicated
his concerns with examples of Tajik academics, which have dispraised the
pre-Soviet Tajik culture and society as a time of superstition, ignorance and
oppression in order to follow the paradigms of internationalism. He was even
more concerned about deviations in scientific atheism: Instead of "keeping up the values, principles and the intellectualism of scientific atheism,"
Tajik academics resorted to arguments resembling Stalinist times. Notably,

Mirrahim defended scientific atheism and demanded instead a more sophisticated approach including the establishment of a special department at the
academy of science with a focus on Central Asia.[137] Mirrahim's critique of the
ideological foundations of the Soviet society echoes Yurchak's analysis of the
last Soviet generation:

> [I]t became less important to read ideological representations for 'literal' (refer-
> ential) meanings than to reproduce their precise structural forms. This transfor-
> mation of the discursive regime eventually led to a profound shift within Soviet
> culture of the late period, opening up spaces of indeterminacy, creativity and
> unanticipated meanings in the context of strictly formulaic ideological forms,
> rituals, and organizations.[138]

Yurchak's "unanticipated meanings" emerged around the issues of religion,
language, identity and nationalism since they were intrinsically connected to
the intellectual reproduction. For Mirrahim, the simple disrespect for religion
and the freedom of faith undermines the very project of intellectual atheism,
since performative atheism often depreciates at the same time as the national
heritage (*meros*) of the Tajiks. He complained that the "national sentiment
of young Tajik women has been humiliated by the label 'religion' on their
traditional clothes."[139] The simple equitation of religion, national heritage and
national identity has led to an unjustifiable condemnation of the poetry and
works of the Tajik poets and writers such as Bozor Sobir, Muʻmin Qanoat,
Loiq Šeralī and Gulruxsor Safieva as nationalistic (*millatčiona*).[140]

At this point Mirrahim's article departed from his original topic and ventured on an issue he was apparently more concerned about: the relation to
Uzbekistan and the "plight" of the ethnic Tajik population in the UzSSR, who
were exposed to an increasing "Panuzbekism (*panūzbakistī*)" and pressured
to assimilate into the Uzbek culture since several decades. Uzbek historians
were rewriting Tajik history either by claiming Tajik historical figures as
Uzbeks, such as Ibn Sino (Avicenna), or by discrediting them as representatives of a reactionary bourgeoisie, such as the Soviet historian Boboǧon
Ġafurov. Furthermore, Mirrahim stated that in Uzbekistan "an anti-Tajik and
anti-Semitic policy has flourished in recent years and the chauvinist element
of 'Uzbek Greatness' has become visible."[141] He eventually transferred the
post-colonial element of his article to the immediate regional rivalry and the
debate between the subaltern Uzbek and Tajik historians, intellectuals and
academics about the regional cultural "ownership." Mirrahim's post-colonial
attitude eventually remains inconsistent due to the intellectual dependencies
superimposed by an anti-Uzbek revisionism many Tajik intellectuals share(d).
Eventually, he returned to his original subject and concluded his article with a
reference to Aitmatov's *Mankurt* motif:

A person, who does not know his history, will not work for the future. He is a *Mankurt*, who only lives for the moment and only for himself, not for humanity. [...] More than everything, we need to find a possibility to understand the entire heritage (*meros*) of our ancestors in order to be spared from the sickness of «*mankurtī*».[142]

Many urban intellectuals considered Mirrahim's article as a key text and even among the Islamic activists the text created a "revolutionary imagination"[143] despite its endorsement of scientific atheism. Again, Chatterjee's observation that modern anti-colonial nationalisms tend to distinguish between an outer domain of politics and economics dominated by the colonial center and a spiritual domain which bears "the 'essential' marks of cultural identity"[144] is reflected in Mirrahim's comments on the Tajik's spiritual heritage. Additionally, the text reveals a similar perception Bhavna Dave has described for a Kazakh intellectual:

What he [Dave's respondent] conveyed most eloquently was not a disapproval of colonial domination *per se*, but a feeling of disappointment by the failure of the Soviet state to fully deliver its promised goals. The agency and responsibility for the ultimate failure to deliver modernity and progress was attributed to the empire.[145]

As for Mirrahim, he was disappointed by the unsophisticated approach of Soviet scientific atheism and internationalism to the Central Asian population and by the performative character of the center's discourse. The ambiguities in Mirrahim's text echo the "sense of Soviet identity"[146] among representatives of the Tajik intelligentsia who had benefited from the interventionist Soviet state and made a career as public-political intellectuals unprecedented in their society.

In Search of the Self: Episodes, Discourses and Ambiguities

Tajikistan's reformers and political activists—mostly representatives of the urban intelligentsia—considered themselves as advocates for a democratic and independent nation state based on the rule of law, human rights and religious freedom. However, most of these reformers and political activists were not prepared for the sudden and rapid transformation of their society as the popular Russian musician Andrey Makarevič put it: "It had never even occurred to me that in the Soviet Union anything could ever change. Let alone that it could disappear."[147] Perhaps it is no surprise that many representatives of the opposition and intelligentsia had only vague ideas and ambivalent thoughts about the central concepts associated with democracy. The philosopher and director of the Institute of Oriental Studies of the TaSSR, Akbar Tursunov, warned in 1988 of excessive nationalism. He discussed nationalism strictly within the limits of Marxist-Leninist theory and asserted "that on a truly democratic foundation, within the borders of a united social-ist state, the progress of each of our federal Homelands is possible."[148] A democratic society, Tursunov continued, is able to abandon "national nihil-ism (*nigilizmi millī*) as well as nihilism toward our own native language." But simultaneously, he admonished his fellow intellectuals that they should not fall victim to an excessive nationalism but instead promote a Tajik nation-alism "free of nationalist bigotry,"[149] which should not infringe on the rights of minorities.

Central to the discussion in the TaSSR became the term *xudšinosī* for self-awareness. Karim identified the Glasnost years as "a path to conscious-ness (*xudogohī*), self-awareness (*xudšinosī*), religiousness (*xudošinosī*), the religious law (*šariat*), the mystical path (*tariqat*), knowledge (*ma 'rifat*) and truth (*haqiqat*)."[150] Accordingly, the first nationalist civil association Rastoxez chose the slogan *Xudro bišnos! (Know yourself!)* as its motto. Muhammadǧon Šukurov defined *xudšinosī* "as the principle way for humans to acquire culture and civilization."[151] Without hesitation, he quoted the Prophet Muhammad and Karl Marx as authorities for the validity of his statement. *Xudšinosī*, Šukurov concluded solemnly, reflects the entire being and the connection between the individual and the society: "The national Self-Awareness, the historical and cultural Self-Awareness are the origins of the spiritual strength of the individual and the people."[152]

During the brief post-colonial episode, Tajik intellectuals had to demarcate their nationalist project as a sovereign territory without any interference by the colonial power.[153] Since the quintessential and foundational paradigms of Tajik nationalism—race, language and history of the territory—had been already formulated by their Soviet predecessors in the 1950s and 1960s, Tajik reformers were confronted with the difficult and ambivalent task of recon-structing their authentic Tajik self by reconfiguring the Soviet paradigms.

AMBIVALENT AND INVENTED TRADITIONS

Composing national history in the Soviet Union was a delicate affair: Historians had to meet ideological requirements of Marxism-Leninism as well as Stalin's *Marxism and the national Question* and carefully include public affirmations of Internationalism and Peoples' Friendship not to be accused of bourgeois nationalism or chauvinism.[154] Moreover, the history of Central Asia in the pre- and early Islamic periods was not very well docu-mented and many events and the origins or "ethnogenesis" (Russ.: *Ėtnogenez*) of various peoples migrating through and settling in Central Asia were and are contested.[155] In the case of the Tajikistan, matters were complicated and

Tajik national identity was narrated in different, at times contradictory layers. The complexity derived already from the very question of the meaning of the word "Tajik" and their alleged ethnogenesis. Vasily Barthold (1869–1930), the doyen of Russian and Soviet oriental studies, describes the Tajiks as Iranian people who came to Central Asia through

> immigration from Persia: this alone would account for the disappearance of the Soghdian language from the plains of Turkestan. [...] The name *Tāzīk*, or *Tajīk*, which was originally given to the Arabs, is an Iranian derivation from the name of the tribe Tayy, in Northern Arabia. The Turks seem to have understood the term *Tajīk* in the sense of 'Muslim', 'one belonging to Muslim culture', and used it, accordingly, as a designation for the main mass of Muslims known to them, namely for the Iranians, making no distinction between the *Tajīks* and the Arabs. The mountaineers *Gharcha*, or *Ghalcha* (from the word *ghar* 'mountain') differed greatly from the inhabitants of the plains in their language, and especially in their manners and customs.[156]

According to Barthold's postulate, Tajik had been historically not an ethnic but rather sociological term distinguishing settled people occupied with agriculture or an urban trade from transhumant groups in Central Asia *after* the Arab conquest in the 8th century, a version that is today widely seen as plausible—at least outside Tajikistan.[157] Out of nationalist sentiment, Aynī and Ġafurov rejected the derivation of *tāğik/toğik* from *tāzīk* (Middle Persian for "Arab," apparently related to Ṭayyʼ, one of the Arabic tribal groups in the borderlands of the Sassanid Empire) and instead suggested the etymology from "crown" (*tāğ/toğ* plus an adjectival *–ī* and a nominalizating *–k*), thus *toğik* as the "crowned one." While linguists consider the theory as implausible from a morphologic and semantic point of view, contemporary Tajik politicians endorse—unsurprisingly—Aynī's version.[158]

In his *Toğikon*, Boboğon Ġafurov already ignored Barthold's theory and offered an alternative version, which became the master narrative for the Tajik historiography until today: (1) The ethnogenesis of the Tajiks goes back to the arrival of the of the Indo-Aryan people, the immediate ancestors of the Tajiks, in the region, thus centuries *before* the Turkic (= Uzbek) migration to Central Asia. (2) The Somonid dynasty (819–1005 CE) established the first Tajik statehood (*davlat* or *davlatdorī*) of the Tajik people (Taj.: *xalq*, Russ.: *narod*) under Ismoil Somonī (ca. 849–907 CE). (3) Ġafurov asserted that Tajiks and Uzbek—despite the many commonalities in culture and history—are two distinct nationalities.[159]

The Uzbek Other

Arguably, the most contentious issue remained and remains the question of the ethnogenesis of Tajiks and Uzbeks. Ethnogenesis as constructed by

Ġafurov and his colleagues implies a historical continuity over centuries of a particular ethnicity regardless of historical plausibility, migration and interethnic contacts. Tajik intellectuals adopted the postulate of historical continuity and narrated Tajik history as a defiant assertiveness against Turkic intrusion and therefore rationalized the alleged political marginalization of the Tajiks in Central Asia—as for instance Qadriddin Aslonov demonstrates:

> The Gengizides destroyed the thriving cities and villages and killed thousands of people, but the national knowledge and culture, and our alphabet they did not change. Tajik mothers again gave birth to their children. And their descendants again cultivated the devastated land of their forefathers. And our eternal national spirituality again flourished and developed.[160]

Through the lens of Tajik intellectuals, the border delimitation of Soviet Central Asia in 1924/1929 was the last chapter of the continuous marginalization and humiliation of the Tajiks by the Uzbeks. The historical narratives by Ġafurov and his successors on ethnogenesis and statehood postulate the cultural and civilizational ascendency of the Tajiks prior to the Uzbeks, who in contrast only acquired culture and civilization by deceiving the Tajik people and by absorbing the Somonid state. Ġafurov also determined the ethnogenesis of the Uzbeks in the 14th century CE (thus, approximately 2,000 years *after* the Tajiks) writing back a self-reassurance for his Tajik compatriots.[161] Obviously Ġafurov reached the limits of tolerance in Soviet historiography and he concluded in a more conciliatory tone to appease his Soviet and Uzbek colleagues:

> Those racial differences (*tafovuthoi nažodie*), we have talked about here, will never be a source of conflict between different people. In the progress of the human civilization all the people of Central Asia had a great share. Both, the Iranian speaking people as well as the Turkic speaking people, have distinguished men of science and culture, which are the pride of all people in Central Asia.[162]

Ġafurov shaped the master narrative of the early ethnogenesis of the Tajiks, their civilizational ascendency and cultural uniqueness. Simultaneously, he also fixed the stereotype of the Turkic/Uzbek Other: First, they arrived later in Central Asia, thus they have not the same vested rights to the territory of Central Asia. Second, they are related to the Mongols, thus they do not even possess an 'authentic,' pure ethnicity and achieved their tribal identity only by virtue of the Mongols. Third, like the Mongols, the Uzbeks conquered the territory using inhumane violence and destroying thriving civilizations. Finally, they acquired culture and civilization only from the Tajiks and built their statehood parasitically on the Tajik one. Thus, the basic ingredients for the anti-Uzbek sentiment among Tajik intellectuals had been already prepared by Ġafurov and others in the 1950s.

The relationship between Tajik and Uzbek cadres was strained already since the Soviet border demarcation in 1924/1929, which assigned Bukhara and Samarqand to the UzSSR and not to the TaSSR. This "deprivation" had nourished the Tajik intelligentsia's anti-Uzbek sentiment. Ġafurov's assumptions about the early ethnogenesis of the Tajiks and the emergence of Tajik statehood during the glorious Somonid dynasty were contrasted by Uzbekistan's contemporary political influence and cultivated a revisionist anti-Uzbek sentiment which became virulent in the late 1980s. The cultural proximity between Uzbeks and Tajiks, their shared history, literature and religion, did not attenuate the tensions but generated additional disputes about the cultural "ownership" in Central Asia.[163] During Soviet time, the revisionism could be only expressed implicitly and even Ġafurov had been accused of national chauvinism and bourgeois tendencies. In the later TaSSR, however, anti-Uzbek sentiment became prevalent among the Tajik intelligentsia and the construction of the Uzbek Other a constituent element in the imagination of the Tajik Self and nation.[164] While the Tajiks constructed their Self as sedentary, peaceful, sophisticated, urban and cultured, the Uzbek Other was considered nomadic, violent, uncultured, deceptive and destructive.

Mirrahim's article "How long will the water run under the ice?" exhibited this anti-Uzbek sentiment mildly compared to the contributions by members of the Academy of Science which portrayed Uzbek chauvinism and Pan-Turkism as the main reason for Tajikistan's desolate situation. While this historical interpretation was only cautiously expressed during Soviet times, the ethnocentric historical perspective—flavored with a variety of conspiracy theories and a strong revisionism—gained momentum in the late 1980s and had in Rahim Masov its most vocal spokesperson. Masov, born 1937 in Vanǧ/GBAO, had been appointed director of the history and archaeology department of the TaSSR's Academy of Science in 1988. In 1991, he published his controversial but popular *The History of territorial Demarcation* followed in 1995 by *Tajik History with the Seal 'Top Secret'*.[165] In his accounts, Masov described the border delimitation in Central Asia as an Uzbek conspiracy to marginalize the culturally superior Tajiks and to deny the Tajiks the regional preponderance they are historically entitled to. Masov stipulated that Pan-Turkist Uzbek chauvinists manipulated the Russian-Soviet authorities and outpaced lenient Tajik cadres in the negotiations on the future borders. Masov embedded his analysis of the border delimitation in the 1920s into a larger historical narrative in which Turkic/Uzbek tribes were the main antagonists of the settled (cultivated) Tajiks since the 8th century thus nourishing romanticized nationalist ideas of an eternal struggle between the two people. The obvious racist elements (the Tajik Aryans vs. the Turkic Uzbeks) in the interpretation became virulent in the

2000s, when the Tajik government assertively pronounced the Aryan origins of the Tajiks by declaring the year 2006 as the "Year of Aryan Civilization."[166]

In 1991/1992, Masov became entangled in politics and supported the political nomenklatura in Kūlob. His publications (including a recent panegyric on Rahmonov as the *The Architect of Peace*) advanced his career in the academic institutions and for a long time he was considered as one of the most influential academics in Tajikistan controlling access to academic positions.[167]

In many respects, Muhammadǧon Šukurov was—with his more nuanced view on regional history and his emphasis on the common cultural heritage of Tajiks and Uzbeks—Masov's antagonist. In his widely quoted article "An Opinion on History" Šukurov criticized the Soviet-induced national nihilism in a similar way like Mirrahim does in January the same year. But Šukurov also reminded his readers of the common Tajik and Uzbek literary heritage and placed the "Uzbek" poet and polymath Mir Ališer Navoī (1441–1501) on the same level as the Persian poets Hofizi Šerozī (Hafez, 1320–1389) or Sa'dī (1210–1291).[168] Šukurov was more concerned about the development of modern Tajik and he complained that the contemporary Tajiks were not able to preserve the sophistication of their language since Bukhara and Samarqand were excluded from the TaSSR. Quoting the authoritative Lenin who said that cities are always the center of the economic and social strength of the people, Šukurov concluded that the Tajiks lost their "speech culture (*madaniyati suxan*)"[169] due to the loss of their urban centers. Šukurov also shared some of Masov's assumptions: He left no doubts that the Tajiks completed their statehood much earlier than any Turkic/Uzbek polity and he considered the creation of the TaSSR in 1929 as a "societal national injustice."[170] Nonetheless, the strategies of Šukurov and Masov differ considerably: By embracing the cultural diversity in Soviet Tajikistan, Šukurov tried to consolidate the cultural influence of the Bukharan émigré community in Dushanbe. Masov instead intended to undermine the émigrés' reputation by presenting the Tajiks from the mountainous regions as the "true" and "authentic" Tajiks while he depicted the "urban" Tajiks from Bukhara and Samarqand as lenient and effete. Their contact with the Uzbek population had diluted their "Tajikness" and therefore they did not resist the border demarcation in 1924/1929 and accepted the Uzbek "Pan-Turkist" conspiracy. Šukurov depicted the border demarcations as well as a "national injustice," but he concluded that the creation of Soviet Central Asia was a Soviet initiative, which brought suffering to both, the Tajiks and Uzbeks.[171]

Šodmon Yusuf adopted a similar perspective: He asserted that the Uzbek culture had benefited tremendously from the Tajik culture, but the Soviets instigated the Uzbeks to reject the Tajik culture and eventually they turned against "their own culture and against the founders [i.e. the Tajiks] of their culture."[172] Thus Yusuf reproduced the idea of the Tajiks' civilizational superiority and the ingenuous Uzbeks who only acquired culture through contact with the Tajiks. Sohibnazar likewise asserted the distinct Tajik genius in administration, culture and politics. In his brief discussion of Masov's *The History of territorial Demarcation* he argued that the Turks—like the Arabs—failed to destroy the Tajik culture and actually became Tajik through language and social practice. Sohibnazar ventured beyond the fixed political territory of Tajikistan and concluded in reference to the poet Bozor Sobir that the territory of Tajikistan is virtually set by the geographic extent Tajik is spoken and not by political borders. Sohibnazar criticized Masov as an historian who follows "Marxist concepts and the commands of the eternal Lenin"[173] and therefore did not understand the genuine roots of the Tajik culture—language and religion—which they share with the Uzbeks. Eventually, Masov's intellectual dependency on the center deterred him from understanding that both, the Tajiks and Uzbeks, are victims of a malicious conspiracy by the Soviets.

In the early 2000s the dispute between Masov and Šukurov (then Šakurī) flared up again, ostensibly about the location of the Tajik culture in the larger Persianate and regional context. After the civil war, Masov emerged as one of the most influential historians in Tajikistan and contributed to the official historiography of contemporary Tajikistan affirming the statements by President Rahmonov in his *The Tajiks in the Mirror of History*. In several polemic publications Masov and his colleague Sohib Tabarov confirmed the distinctness and originality of the eastern Iranian culture and Tajik language.[174] Again, the dispute was less about the interpretation of history: As in his earlier publications, Masov again "exposed" the Pan-Turkist Uzbek conspiracies and the perfidious collaboration of "urban" Tajiks with their Uzbek enemies.[175] As a Tajik from Vanğ (GBAO), Masov challenged the domination of "lowland" Tajiks from the northern Fergana Valley and from Bukhara or Samarqand— such as Šukurov—in historical and literary studies. Although their influence in the humanities had already diminished since the 1980s, Šukurov still enjoyed popularity and respect among an urban, Soviet generation of intellectuals and academics in Tajikistan and was internationally acknowledged as one of Tajikistan's leading historians.[176]

But also Šukurov had an agenda in his academic activities: While Masov tried to limit the authority of the émigré intellectuals, Šukurov's central concern was the preservation of their position in the larger cultural and academic field.[177] Thus, the question of civilizational affiliation (Iranian, eastern Iranian, Greater Khorasanian and—in a different context—Muslim) had also an immediate domestic political and societal dimension in the late 1980s.

Regional Ownership and the Iranian Heritage

Ġafurov determined that the Tajiks form a distinct and exclusive eastern Iranian ("Greater Khorasan"/*Xorazmi buzurg* and Bactria/*Boxtar*) culture and history within the larger Persianate world, which is different from the history and culture of Iran and Afghanistan.[178] With his master narrative, Ġafurov challenged Soviet historiographical paradigms in Central Asia: By presenting the Tajiks as immediate descendants of the Aryans he was able to reconstruct the "ethnogenesis" of the Tajiks beyond recorded history and to venture beyond the narrowly confined territory of the TaSSR (see Map 1). Ġafurov implicitly disregarded Stalin's dictum of a common territory as a characteristic feature of a nation that was an important paradigm for Soviet historians. Moreover, the postulate of the formation of a Tajik state in the 9th century CE contradicts earlier Russian/Soviet orientalists' versions according to which nationalism in Central Asia only developed with the Russian expansion in the late 19th century.

In the 1980s, Tajik historians and intellectuals scrutinized the paradigms of Soviet-Tajik historiography. Throughout the long stagnant reign of Brezhnev, official identity politics and historiography became increasingly formulaic, ritualized and predictable. The "real" objects of contention, that is, the cleavages within the Tajik-Soviet society, social and ethnic divides, the silent

Figure 1.1   The Somonid State by N. Negmatov in the Soviet Tajik Atlas.

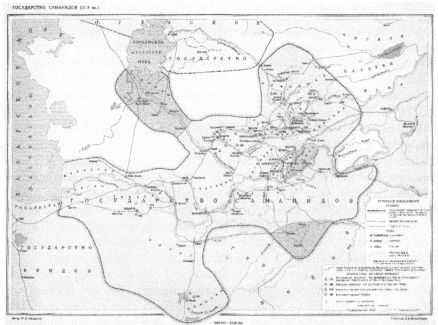

Source: I. Narzikulov and K. Stanyokovič. *Atlas Tadžikskoy sovetskoy socialističeskoy respubliki*. Dušanbe: GUGiK, 1968, 195.

resistance and the "displacement" of the hegemonic system of the Soviet Union were concealed by the virtuality and ritualization of politics in the late USSR.[179] While Perestroika and Glasnost opened the discursive space, two historical events fundamentally influenced the discussion in Tajikistan: First, the 1979 Revolution in Iran and the establishment of the Islamic Republic of Iran with its anti-imperialist revolutionary zeal blending Islam with a distinct Iranian heritage symbolizing an unprecedented historical vitality and relevance—the Islamic element was often neglected by Tajik observers and some saw in Iran the new Great Power they had lost with the collapse of the USSR. Second, the Soviet invasion of Afghanistan in 1979 reconnected Tajik intellectuals with the wider Persianate world. Many intellectuals and activists, such as Tohir Abduǧabbor, Mahmadalī Hait, Ibrohim Usmonov or Xudoberdī Xoliqnazar, were veterans of the Soviet campaign in Afghanistan and served in the Soviet military intelligence GRU as translators or engagement officers in Kabul. Modern Persian literature became suddenly accessible beyond the Soviet censorship and profoundly influenced the motifs and national sentiments in the Tajik debates. Moreover, some intellectuals reconsidered the distinctness and exclusiveness of the Tajik language and culture in favor of a more inclusive idea of an Iranian civilization. The location of the Tajik culture within the broader Persianate civilization became a contentious issue.[180] The discussion on culture and civilization had an immediate analogy in the discussion on the nature of the Tajik language: While Soviet intellectuals insisted on a distinct and separate development of the Tajik language (the *se-zabon*—"three languages"—paradigm, see below) and the exclusive "ethnogenesis" of the Tajiks, advocates of the *yak-zabon* ("one language") theory stressed the common origin and the mutual cultural heritage of Afghans, Iranians and Tajiks. Since the supporters of a separate eastern Iranian origin had an authoritative advocate in Boboǧon Ǧafurov, most of the Tajik historians and intelligentsia *nolens volens* agreed with the doyen of Tajikistan's historical science and did not challenge the central paradigms of ethnogenesis and language until today. When in 1991 the historian Samd Sa'dī postulated in *Adabiyot va San'at* that Tajik statehood actually began with the Achaemenid Empire (550–330 BCE) and had its first revival as a "united and nationally centralized state"[181] during the Somonid dynasty, he was criticized that his theory contradicts Ǧafurov's earlier definition and blurred the demarcation between the Iranian and Tajik statehood.

Although Ǧafurov's general assumptions on Tajik historiography are still valid today, details have been reinterpreted and modified. Šukurov for instance suggested a more inclusive regional concept of culture and civilization in his influential essay *Xuroson ast in ǧo* (Khorasan Is here), which was published in 1997. Šukurov had developed the main ideas already earlier in his works on linguistics and Tajik literature. He became more outspoken in the late 1980s in his contributions for *Adabiyot va San 'at* and his *samizdat* delineating the central ideas of *Xuroson ast in ğo*.[182] Šukurov integrated Tajik history into the wider context of "Greater Khorasan," the idea of a larger historical region comprising today's Iran, Afghanistan, Tajikistan and Uzbekistan where the urban Persianate/Iranian civilization emerged stressing the common origins of the Iranians, Tajiks and Afghans. Many Tajik historians and intellectuals rejected Šukurov's idea since it calls into question central parts of the Soviet-Tajik academic institutional system which was based on the paradigm of a distinct Tajik ethnogenesis, language and culture and therefore legitimized the oversized departments for Tajik literature, history and language. Controversially, Šukurov extended his ideas about a common regional culture and civilization also to the Uzbek neighbor prompting angry reactions from his colleagues in the academy of science.

Beyond the academic discussion, concepts of culture and civilization became relevant on the political level with the emergence of civil associations in the late 1980s. Many civil society associations exhibited a strong sentiment for (eastern) Iranian historical and cultural motifs of the epic Šohnoma by Hakim Abulqosim Firdavsī (940–1020 CE) and the ancient religion of Zoroastrianism. Civil society associations adopted names such as *Dirafši Koviyon* (The Banner of Kova's followers[183]) in Norak, *Boxtar*[184] in Xovaling, *Kuruši kabir* (Cyrus the Great), *Oriyonoi buzurg* (Great Aryana[185]), *Mehri Xatlon* (Sun/Friendship of Xatlon) and *Gangi Xusrav*,[186] to name a few. Motifs of the Iranian mythology were also employed in the political confrontation. In the demonstrations in August/September 1991, President Mahkamov was compared to Zahhok, an evil figure in the Iranian mythology and a symbol for tyranny as well as foreign rule, and the demonstrators called for a Kova, the mythological blacksmith who defeated Zahhok and ended his tyranny.[187] The proliferation of an Iranian cultural sentiment should not be considered as a radical break with the Soviet paradigms. Early Soviet Tajik poets and writers, such as the Stalin Prize Laureate Lohutī, referred with blessings of the CPSU to motifs of the Iranian mythological literature, but Lohutī's *Kovai ohangar* (*Kova the blacksmith*, 1947) is unsurprisingly the prototype of a socialist revolutionary worker.

The distinction between Iranian and eastern Iranian was initially limited to academic debates, but the situation changed in 1990/1991 with Iran's political debut in Central Asia. The pragmatist Rafsanjani administration reached out to the former Soviet republics of Central Asia on the political-diplomatic, economic and cultural level with the intention to rebalance regional relations.[188] While the Tajik government oscillated between high rising expectations of economic investment and political reservations about the intentions of Iran, the reformist intellectuals and academics embraced the new opportunities, travelled on Iranian embassy stipends to Iran and

established closer ties with their Iranian colleagues.[189] The Nabiev administration portrayed the opposition's rapprochement with Iran as an indication
for the "hidden political agenda," namely the establishment of an Islamic
republic in Tajikistan. The frequent insinuations and accusations in the
media prompted Tūrağonzoda to comment on the transfer of Iran's political
system:

> That is impossible for a number of reasons. First, we are Sunni Muslims and in
> contrast to the Shi'ites the Sunni do not have a single imam. Sunni doctrine does
> not recognize leadership by one man. With us each spiritual leader is autono-
> mous. Second, 70 years of anti-Islamic propaganda have done their job. Young
> people have formed liberal views.[190]

Nonetheless, many Tajik politicians and activists exhibited a certain
naiveté regarding Iran's political system and Kenğaev pointedly remarked
that he did not understand the enthusiasm by democratic politicians for Iran
since the Islamic Republic is anything but a democracy.[191]

National Minorities

Next to the relationship with the Uzbek neighbor, the Tajik intelligentsia
controversially argued about the societal and political role of national
minorities. The TaSSR's society was multi-ethnic in which the titular nation-
ality accounted in 1989 for 62% of the population while Uzbeks, Russians,
Tatars, Kyrgyz and various other groups formed significant national
minorities (see Table 1.3). The public assurance of Peoples' Friendship and
Internationalism were central elements of the Soviet ideology which claimed
that the Soviet system liberated the various nations from the Tsarist 'prison
of the peoples' and at the same time overcame chauvinist nationalism or
bourgeois cosmopolitanism. The continuous propaganda only partially concealed the inter-ethnic tensions in the TaSSR particularly in the late 1980s
with the gradual disintegration of the Soviet coercive mechanisms. Publicly,
Tajik intellectuals, politicians and activists emphasized their respect for the
rights and freedoms of all ethnicities in Tajikistan.[192] In their narrative, intellectuals repeatedly referred to an essential Tajik mentality, which depicts
them as peaceful, tolerant, cultured, hospitable and sedentary people who
never did any injustice to other people but who were constantly deceived,
threatened and conquered by intolerant, uncultured and nomadic migrants
or neighbors. As an indication for the Tajiks' tolerance and "culturedness,"
Yusuf and others frequently referred to the alleged exemplary integration
of the Uzbeks into the Tajik society even though the Uzbeks never recipro-
cated the appreciation they have received from the Tajiks. While Uzbekistan
restricted the Tajiks' rights, not a single Uzbek association had been closed
in Tajikistan.[193]

Table 1.3   Nationalities in Tajikistan in 1989 and 2000

Nationalities	Population in 1989	Population in 2000
Tajiks	3,172,420 (62.3%)	4,898,400 (79.9%)
Uzbeks	1,196,900 (23.5%)	936,700 (15.3%)
Russians	388,500 (7.6%)	68,200 (1.1%)
Tatars	72,200 (1.4%)	18,900 (0.3%)
Kyrgyz	66,200 (1.3%)	65,500 (1.1%)
Other	198,600 (3.9%)	139,800 (2.3%)
Total	5,093,000	6,127,500

Source: TAJSTAT, *Hayati millī*, 7

The Tajiks' cultural finesse and their tolerance is (at least in Yusuf's imagination) also accepted by the Kyrgyz, who "look upon the Tajiks as their fathers."[194] Tajik intellectuals saw themselves in a vanguard and pioneering role in the region and "the awakening of the Persian culture of the Tajik has a tremendous influence on the awakening of all other people in Central Asia."[195] Despite the affirmations of tolerance toward ethnic minorities, Uzbeks, Kyrgyz or non-Central Asian nationalities were gradually excluded from the political debates. After the adoption of the Law on the Tajik Language in July 1989 and the February Events 1990, non-Central Asian nationalities started to emigrate from the TaSSR—by November 1990 almost 100,000 had left the country and more than 90% of the remaining expressed their intention to leave.[196] The opposition responded ambiguously to the exodus of the non-Central Asian nationalities. On the one hand they were rhetorically committed to an open society and ethnic pluralism, on the other hand virulent nationalist sentiment erupted in hostile statements against Russians and Uzbeks. Even in the memoirs—which had been edited and sometimes revised—the prejudices and bias regarding ethnicity and religion are palpable. Sohibnazar, for instance, drily commented on the exodus of Russians from Tajikistan:

> The Russians should look after Russia proper and try to cultivate her first ... if you want to leave Tajikistan, it will be only at your own disadvantage. They won't give you housing space in their cities and you will end up in the barren villages your fathers have left 60 years ago.[197]

Yusuf complained that the uneducated Russian peasants were sent to Central Asia to work in the higher echelons of the administration or in the industrial sector displacing Tajiks to the margins of society, excluding them from adequate housing, employment and education.[198] He eventually ascertained that the Tajiks possess an unrivalled culture, while the Russians in contrast "are from the perspective of culture and morals rather destitute"[199]:

> Killing and destruction is an embodiment of the Russian culture. They are without culture, morals and an enemy of the human civilization. The inhuman

culture of the Russians has resulted in the situation that nobody has any sympathy for them anymore. [...] Russia destroyed the culture and religion of Central Asia. The Russians implanted the seed of hatred between the people of Central Asia.[200]

Even centrist and less polarizing figures exposed an ambivalent attitude toward ethnic minorities. For instance, in one of his editorials Adaš Istad, co-editor of the prestigious *Adabiyot va San'at*, reflected on the nature of a "national government":

> In a national government, the main nationality forms the government but guarantees freedom and equality to all other nationalities living in the borders of the nation. The national government allows the participation of national minorities in the general affairs of government, but not in those related to state secrets. Even if representatives of other nationalities have shared their life with us, they nonetheless—from the perspective of their own virtue and soul—will always be loyal to their original nationality. [...] Therefore the armed forces and the national security committee in a national state must exclusively be in the hands of the titular nationality. Once the Somonids established a Turkish guard, they relinquished Tajik statehood for more than a thousand years.[201]

The very notion of "state secrets" reproduces the ambiguous Soviet discourses on confidentiality, secrecy and security which blurred the boundaries between "information" and "secrecy" indicating the intellectual challenges of the transformation and democratization process. Academic or journalistic work could (and can) be easily denounced as subversive and undermining "state security." The Tajik civil society and Glasnost media reproduced these Soviet discourses signifying the persuasiveness of conspiracy theories in the Soviet and post-Soviet context and the absence of a critical public. Moreover, Istad followed the idea of an organic nationalism based on an invariable and categorical ethnic solidarity. In a similar argument Šukurov postulated the existence of distinct and foundational national (ethnic) characteristics:

> Representatives of all nationalities have the right to participate in the national government of the Tajiks; in the economic and financial spheres, in the cultural and spiritual life in the legislature and so forth. But the foundations of the state need to be national. The government—must be a national government. The parliament—a national parliament, the economy—a national economy, the army—a national army, the guard—a national guard. I repeat: In all these affairs representatives of other nationalities are allowed to take part but the foundations of all these institutions, the ideology and the principles must be national. This will guarantee that the government will have the capacity to protect the welfare of the Tajik nation.[202]

The readiness of the democratic opposition to exclude ethnic minorities from "sensitive" domains of the state as well as the historical *longue durée* contextualization of the ethnic Other restricted the opposition and the civil society to reach out to the national minorities in Tajikistan and abandon an ethnic in favor of an inclusive civic nationalism. Remarkably, the Nabiev government and in particular Kenğaev—at least on the rhetorical level— explicitly integrated ethnic minorities in their imagination of Tajikistan as a nation and emphasized the participation of non-Tajik nationalities in their political project.[203]

The Urban Intelligentsia and Islam

The urban intelligentsia who demanded a return to the alleged authentic Tajik cultural roots was divided over the question how to deal with Islam in their reconstruction of Tajikness. Although Islam was considered to be a source for morals and values, many Soviet trained intellectuals were uneasy with integrating Islam into their nationalist imagination. The Soviet intelligentsia had been exposed to the Soviet modernization project and consistent atheist propaganda, which influenced their understanding of religion as a regressive element in the Marxist superstructure concealing the "real" class relations. Many located Islam outside the "modern" Soviet-urban society as a phenomenon of "traditional" rural Tajikistan. Mirrahim reluctantly accepted religion as part of a larger cultural identity and demanded a refined and invigorated Central Asian strategy for promoting scientific atheism with the Marxist expectation that religion would eventually wither in the continuous Soviet modernization process.[204] Several intellectuals cultivated a pre-Islamic Iranian sentiment and portrayed Islam as an alien religion imposed by the Arab conquest of Central Asia, in their reading a catastrophe only surpassed by the Mongol invasion. Instead they rediscovered Zoroastrianism as the truly authentic Tajik religion and popularized the Zoroastrian motto "good deeds, good speech and good thoughts (*raftori nek, guftori nek, pindori nek*)." While the turn to Zoroastrianism remained a marginal phenomenon in Tajikistan,[205] Islam— amalgamated with Tajik nationalism—experienced a forceful "renaissance" since the mid-1980s. Loiq Šeralī conceded that Islam with its 1,400 years of history cannot be removed overnight despite Soviet atheist politics, and he portrays a society divided between the Soviet and the traditional/religious domain. According to Šeralī, the Tajik society was in 1989 at crossroads and had to decide on the essence of its traditions and history:

> Today, fathers and mothers celebrate the graduation from middle school, the school certificates of their children, the membership card for the Komsomol, the draft to and healthy return from the military service and the admission

to university like spiritual festivities. The old traditions of the mountains have disappeared and the new socialist traditions have become enrooted. But unfortunately, there is a deep division between the new and the old traditions. For instance, today bride and groom go to ZAGS [the Soviet registry office] and secretly to the mullo for the *nikoh* [Islamic wedding ceremony]; the dead, if they are members of the Soviet nomenklatura, are buried secretly (or at night) according to the *ǧanoza* [Islamic funeral ceremony] in the cemetery and the loud speaker announces from paper their achievements—willing or unwillingly— their service and the medals they have received; the dead are dressed in their suits but under these suits they are wrapped in the shroud (*kafan*) and as soon as they reach the grave the mourners remove the suit and take the wooden coffin to bury him only with the shroud.[206]

In Šeralī's diagnosis of the contemporary Tajik society, religious traditions and Islam had been imposed on the Tajiks and infiltrated their daily life, in particular the rites de passage, and replaced the original and authentic Tajik culture, which is embedded in the literary heritage:

> Islam in its 1,400 years' history has banned the singing of songs, the construction of statues and busts, i.e. the glorification of all kinds of works, which were done by men. This ban has resulted in the fact that there is no single monument for classical literates of the Tajik and Farsi literature. The Islamic religion has influenced our own people in a way, that they forgot about a mausoleum for Rūdakī and even forgot about the greatness of Rūdakī, but they still venerate the tomb of some sheikh or *imom*. [...] Instead, the cemetery should be like a museum where the youth can develop into humans by reading the verses written in stone on the graves of the literates. In general, the cemetery is not only for the dead, it is for the appreciation of the living.[207]

In many respects, Šeralī defends the concept of a secular, enlightened and cultured (*kulturny*) society and perceives religious practice as superstition and as alien to authentic Tajikness. At the same time, however, many intellectuals realized that Islam through its symbiosis with nationalism had become a forceful cultural, political and social marker in the Tajik society and they tried to integrate Islam in their ideas of Tajik identity. One strategy to accommodate their intrinsically secular worldview with Islam was to conceptualize Islam as one variable in their projection of culture, tradition or civilization—next to language, race and history. Hereby Islam becomes an inconvenient but unavoidable marker for national identity.[208] Šukurov's *An Opinion on History* is a good example for this strategy: Šukurov lectured about the importance of vague "historical spiritual experience and eternal human values" and conceded that religion is part of the people's spiritualty. Šukurov called the atheist campaigns a mistake since it also destroyed the physical (architecture and archaeology) heritage of

Central Asia contributing to the wide spread "spiritual vacuum, a historical nihilism which is eventually also a national nihilism (*nigilizmi millī*)."[209] Sohibnazar depicted Islam as an intrinsic part of Tajik culture, a "complete religious system," which was undermined by Soviet rule and the introduction of "alcoholism, harlotry (*fohišagarī*) and deprivation (*goratgarī*)."[210] The prevalent hostile discourse on Islamic radicalism and simultaneously on the backwardness of Tajik morals and customs had been established by the Soviet center in order to instigate fear among the population and to legitimate Soviet rule.[211] Yusuf wrote that "in the renaissance of Central Asia there is no other way than to rely on its own Islamic culture."[212] Like Sohibnazar, Yusuf discovered the particular anti-colonial element in religion and postulated that Moscow exploited the accusation of Islamism and nationalism to discredit the opposition.[213] However, Yusuf reportedly confided to Sergei Gretsky (an advisor to Tūraǧonzoda) in 1989 that he feels "disgusted that you should link the culture of my nation with Islam."[214] The anecdote about Yusuf's change of opinion should remind us about the particular trajectories of political thought among the opposition in Tajikistan before the civil war. Although Islamic activists in the *harakat*/proto-IRPT forcefully emerged as a popular political movement in Tajikistan, the urban intellectuals thought that they still exerted hegemony over the intellectual field and the definition of Tajik history, customs and language. This rapidly changed in autumn 1991 and within a few weeks, the secular national-democratic dominance among the urban opposition diminished and the IRPT emerged as the central opposition party with the ability to mobilize followers also outside of Dushanbe.

Many secular intellectuals adapted to the changing situation by reconsidering their attitude toward religion. Kenǧaev smugly pointed out that both, Mirrahim and Yusuf, followed in their academic writings the official party policy of scientific atheism but changed their attitude completely with Glasnost. Hence, they followed no principles and had no belief, but sold out long-time friends for their personal gain.[215] Likewise, he rhetorically asked if Gulruxsor Safieva, the «mother of the nation (*modari millat*)», could "live freely in an Islamic state such as Iran."[216] Accordingly he assumed that the secular opposition displayed an Islamic habitus to gain influence:

[T]he «democratic forces», like Mirbobo Mirrahim, Muhammadalī [Mahmadalī] Haitov, Šodmon Yusuf, Otaxon Latifī, Davlat Xudonazarov, Amirbek Atobek, Dodoǧon Atovulloev, Salim Ayubzod and others consider themselves as unselfish followers of the indisputable religion of Islam in order to get an office and they follow Hoǧī Akbar Tūraǧonzoda blindly from mosque to mosque like headless chicken.[217]

Soviet History

The entire Tajik academic establishment of the late 1980s had graduated
from Soviet academic institutions and had to refer in their scholarly treatises
at least pro forma to the Marxist-Leninist principles. Many intellectuals and
academics only gradually reconsidered the nature and history of the Soviet
system and state. Lenin was widely venerated as the revolutionary leader and
the October Revolution of 1917 was associated with liberation and progress.
Sohibnazar quoted a conversation with an elderly communist and veteran of
the Great Patriotic War, "Bobo" Abdurahim:

> Lenin is our leader, he was the father of all people on earth. He gave to the Tajiks
> science and knowledge. He made everyone literate. He created the Tajik state.
> He elevated our culture. I could not read, but we fought against the mullos, the
> *boyho* [owner of large estates], the *bosmači* and drove them out of Tajikistan,
> destroyed them and ruled the country. We fought the war against Hitler and
> conquered Germany. And now, the mullos want to make us *vahhobī* again. They
> brought back the *boyho* and in the kolkhoz they instigate the people to tear down
> the Lenin statues and even curse Lenin. We will not accept this. We have lost
> our patience.[218]

Sohibnazar demonstrated with his quote, that he is generally sympathetic
with the first generation of Bolsheviks and ascertained that the opposition has
to listen to these people and enlighten them about the "truth." But instead of
"enlightening" Bobo Abdurahim on the Bolsheviks and the role of Lenin, he
lectured on the Turkish Other:

> The Tajiks were educated before, but the hand of the Russians and Turks
> destroyed their literary tradition and therefore made them illiterate. [...]
> The Turks, Mongols and thousands of other foreigners (*ağnabiyon*) had piled
> up the heads of dead Tajiks and more than a thousand years, the Turks consid-
> ered themselves as rulers of the Tajik state, however, they governed in the Tajik
> language.[219]

In 1989 Šukurov still hailed the October Revolution as a central event in
Tajik history and Karim considered the revolution as an event of liberation
and the manifestation of independent Tajik statehood similar to the establishment of the Somonid dynasty or independence.[220] Loiq Šeralī asserted that
the modern achievements in the TaSSR, orderly houses, electricity, schools,
a water system, TV and radio, are blessings of the October Revolution and
added that "even the population from the mountainous regions of the country
are literate and educated today."[221] Only in 1989, reformers and activists from
Rastoxez, the DPT or IRPT, started to express their criticism of the Soviet

system more explicitly. Tohir Abduğabbor (Rastoxez) repudiated in an editorial for *Dunyo* the Soviet nation building in Central Asia and remarked that under the label of "progressive Socialism the different nations were torn apart and their language and culture contaminated and destroyed and eventually people were alienated from their own genealogy (*nasab*), their customs and sacred affairs."[222] In a similar approach Yusuf condemned the entire Soviet historiography, which depicted

> Bolshevist aggressors and occupiers as revolutionary and freedom-loving forces, while the heroic Tajik ğavonmard, the martyred patriots and pure descendants of the Islamic culture, who fought against the immoral and uncultured communists, were vilified as enemies of the people or *bāsmāčī*. During the horrible and bloodthirsty years of the [19]20s and 30s, the soldiers of the Red Army [...] killed thousands and thousands of Central Asians. Our older generation still remembers how they killed without remorse children, women and old people and how thousands of Muslim women were raped.[223]

Qadriddin Aslonov compared the Mongol conquest of Central Asia with the enforcement of Soviet rule:

> Genghis Khan destroyed the thriving cities and villages and killed thousands of people, but the national knowledge and civilization, and our alphabet they did not change. Tajik mothers again gave birth to their children. And their descendants again cultivated the devastated land of their forefathers. And our eternal national spirituality again flourished and developed. Lenin did not destroy the villages himself, and perhaps he even wanted to improve them, but Lenin [...] created the Tajik people without culture and he reduced the reputation of Tajiks to those of nomadic tribes (*qabilahoi kūčī*). In human history, there is no shortage of traitors who governed a country and still today traitors are in power [...] and there is no doubt—even if he is called the 'chief of the proletarians of the world', he [Lenin] and his party are criminals.[224]

Aslonov acknowledged the Soviet formation of national identities but pointed out to its ambiguity since the Soviets never adequately understood the spiritual domain of the Tajik people. Notably, in contemporary Tajikistan Rahmonov's academic entourage reassesses the Soviet nation building as the genuine rebirth of Tajik polity after the downfall of the Somonid dynasty. The authors of the history textbook for the 11th grade, Rohat Nabieva and Farhod Zikriyoev,[225] offer an unambiguous interpretation of the Soviet Union, which can be read as a story of colonizing the self:

> The October Revolution provided hope (*umed*) and life for our people. The Tajik people eventually regained their independence a thousand years after the collapse of the Somoniyon dynasty [...]. The revolution gave the Tajiks borders

and liberated them from the oppression of malicious people (*badxohonaš*). However, it was also restrictive for the people, the workplace, production and all other activities were centrally planned. Gradually they [the Tajiks] managed to establish thriving villages and cities in the barren valleys and remote mountains. Quickly, schools and education, sciences and culture were rediscovered. The sons and daughters of the Tajik people achieved with the fraternal support of Russian, Ukrainian and other scientists highest academic merits. But we believe, the most important development in these years was related to the Tajik language, which recovered its position. Through the efforts of academics and intellectuals the Tajik language developed finesse (*sufta*) and complexity. The sentiment for pride and identity of the Tajik nation gained momentum.[226]

The content and form of the historical narrative is characteristic for Tajikistan's contemporary official history writing: The "malicious people" are not explicitly identified, but the authors have confidence that the attentive reader understand the insinuations and identify these "malicious people" according to the prevalent political discourses on Tajikistan's external and internal enemies.

Islamic activists compiled a counter narrative in which they offered a different reading of the Soviet-Tajik history. The centerpiece of their counter narrative was the reference to the late 19th-century *ğadidī* (renewal) movement as an authentic Tajik and Muslim project of modernization and reform in Central Asia.[227] Many secular intellectuals shared the Islamic activists' enthusiasm since the resumption of the *ğadidī* reform project included a return of a didactical discourse on educating or enforcing social discipline among the "common people" in order to implement "progress" in a modern nation-state. Education meant the internalization of a corpus of distinct national-spiritual values and morals.[228] From the perspective of Tajik intellectuals the reference to the *ğadidī* project comprised several important elements for the reconstruction and imagination of the Tajik self: First, the *ğadidī* project could be portrayed as an authentic Tajik modernization project. Second, although some representatives of the *ğadidī* movement collaborated with the Soviet system, leading personalities were executed in the Stalinist purges in 1937/1938, such as Buzurgzoda, Fitrat, Hakim Karim, Abdaššukur Primuhammadzoda and Habib Yusufī. Therefore, the *ğadidīs* could be portrayed as a genuine anti-colonial movement. While the Tajik intelligentsia generally accepted the historical relevance of the *ğadidī* movement, the evaluation of the *bosmačī* resistance was a more contentious issue. The *Enciklopediyai Sovetii Toğik* characterized the *bosmačī* unsurprisingly in negative terms as an "armed nationalist and counterrevolutionary movement in Central Asia (1917–1926), where the fight against Soviet rule was instigated by the feudal class, the *boyho*, *kulakho*, the fanatic mullos (*mullohoi irtiğoī*) and the bourgeois nationalists (*millatčiyoni buržuazī*)."[229] The interpretation of the *bosmačī* was fundamentally different among Islamic activists and descendants of *bosmačī* leaders. For them, the *bosmačī* was a Muslim resistance movement against alien (Soviet) rule and their leaders, such as *qurbašī* Fuzayl Maxsum, were not simple *bosmačī* but *mуǧohid* (lit.: those who struggle / are committed to *jihad*).[230] Even Sangak Safarov referred in his legitimation narrative to the *bosmačī*. Safarov claimed to be related to one of the local *bosmačī* leaders in Darvoz, *ešoni* Sulton.[231] Safarov's anecdote—regardless of its validity—demonstrates the importance of contentious historical narratives and their interpretation in the Tajik conflict. The official state media launched in November 1990 a campaign against the IRPT led by the daily *Toǧikistoni sovetī* insinuating that the IRPT is in fact a Wahhabi group sponsored by Saudi Arabia. The article also made reference to the *bosmačī* uprising in the 1920s and depicted them as Islamists driven by "nothing else than robbery and pillage and the attack on the honor (*taǧovuz ba nomus*) of our women and daughters, a barbarous killing and bloodshed of the Tajik people under the slogan of *ǧihod* and *ǧazo*"[232] implicating a connection to the IRPT. Although the IRPT accentuated their allegiance to the ǧadidī movement, the *bosmačī* episode was likewise important, and several field commanders of the IRPT, such as Mirzo "Ǧaga" Ziyoyev, took over a *bosmačī* habitus and followed the itinerary of *bosmačī* groups in the 1920s.

Language

Glasnost opened the discursive space for public discussions and rising nationalist sentiment in the TaSSR. The status of the titular languages and national symbols became an increasingly controversial issue in the Soviet Union's republics. The three Baltic SSRs in 1998 had already adopted language laws which declared their titular languages as official state languages and referred to Russian as a language of inter-ethnic communication.[233] Influenced by the developments in the Baltic republics, urban intellectuals in the TaSSR initiated a similar discussion and in late 1988 the Tajik Academy of Science held a first conference on the status of the Tajik language reflecting the debates about the "self-awareness of the nation."[234] According to the official statistical data, proficiency in the titular language Tajik was compared to other Soviet republics high, while proficiency in Russian was comparatively low: In 1989 only 36.4% of the TaSSR's population was fluent in Russian compared to 56.7% in the Kyrgyz SSR or 83.1% in the Kazakh SSR.[235]

The discussion evolved along two major themes: the recognition of Tajik as an official state language complementing rather than replacing Russian and the question whether Tajik, Dari and Farsi are three different languages or merely dialect variations of one language. Most of the intellectuals followed a highly functional concept of language, which was considered to be the central marker for the national characteristics and the national self-awareness reflecting "all forms of social, economic, political and cultural progress of the nation."[236] This functional approach was not without ambivalences: Since language was considered to be an authentic representation of a nation's history as well as level of cultural sophistication, linguists and historians had to operate with the category of "progress" (*taqaqqī*) in literary history. A problematic undertaking, since the sublimeness and transcendence of "classical" Persian (= Tajik) poetry were already globally recognized, which in turn reinforced domestic debates on language and history as "exceptional"—not necessarily coinciding with political or social realities. Thus, the Tajik intelligentsia elevated the Tajik language to a timeless (in Nietzsche's terms *überhistorisch*) actor embodying the Tajik genius.[237]

Šukurov contributed frequently and eloquently to the language discussion and was one of the most important advocates of the Language Law. He considered the transformation of Tajik within the context of Soviet modernization and progress: "The history of the contemporary Tajik language reflects the history of the Soviet society like a mirror."[238] The introduction of Perestroika also meant the gradual democratization of the society and therefore the "democratization of the Tajik literary language."[239] While Bukhara and Samarqand played a paramount role in the completion of the Tajik language in the 9th and 10th century, these regions have unfortunately lost their importance for the contemporary "civilization and spirituality of the people, in particular the progress of the language and literature."[240] Šukurov postulated that the gravity of the development of the Tajik language has moved to the east (i.e., to Dushanbe), but he also diagnosed that in recent years the level of spoken Tajik had deteriorated, in particular the "word formation, terminology, the syntactical structure *et al.* as well as the grammatical rules have been destroyed."[241] Šukurov did not identify those who do not speak proper Tajik, but considering the transformation of the Tajik nomenklatura and his intention to preserve the Bukhara/Samarqand émigré influence in the academic field, he certainly had representatives of the nomenklatura from the eastern regions in mind who graduated from Russian-speaking institutions and were never trained in standard literary Tajik. Advancement in the CPT structures required proficiency in Russian and not the titular language. For political cadres, such as Qahhor Mahkamov, Talbak Nazarov, Rahim Masov and Rafiqa Mūsoeva, Tajik was assigned to contacts with the local, "rural" population and therefore remained on a formulaic and colloquial level.[242] Not only in the political field Russian was the more prestigious language, also in academics/humanities Russian was important for professional advancement in the USSR's institutions.

In his discussion of the language law, Šukurov argued within the limits of Marxist-Leninism presenting the official status of Tajik in the TaSSR not as an expression of nationalist chauvinism but as perfectly in line with Lenin's ideas of the "freedom of the native language." The question of national interests and the principles of internationalism do not necessarily oppose each other.[243] The only solution, in Šukurov's words, was the revaluation of Tajik as an official language in the TaSSR. Loiq Šeralī followed a similar argument and stated that Tajik as a national language should not be understood as opposed to the Soviet system but as an indication for its success:

> When the Tajik language is given the status of an official language and at the same time the constitution is amended with [a law on] the national language, only then we can consider the Constitution as complete. The language is the past, present and future of the people, it is the passport of the nation on its path through history.[244]

Šeralī's argumentation soon followed a highly revisionist anti-Uzbek tone: "Panturkists and bourgeois nationalists" undermined the importance of Tajik. They followed a concerted plan to deny a "future for the Tajik language."[245]

In a strategy to contain the nationalist movements, the nomenklatura around Mahkamov submitted the draft "Law on the Tajik Language" to the Supreme Soviet, which adopted the law on 22 July 1989. The law stipulated that Tajik should have the status of the official state language and defined Russian as the language of communication between the nationalities. The law even committed the state to provide assistance for the teaching and disseminating of the Persian-Arabic script.[246] Mahkamov expected to satisfy and contain the nationalist sentiment among the urban intellectuals by this symbolic move. Theoretically the law banned non-Tajik speakers from certain positions and although the law was not consequently implemented, it changed the overall atmosphere in the TaSSR, particularly in Dushanbe, a city where ethnic Tajiks accounted only for 37% of the population in 1989.[247]

The second theme was predominately a contentious issue in intellectual debates and contributed to the ideological disputes among the intelligentsia. The official academic establishment of the TaSSR insisted on the theory of three separate languages (*se-zabon* = Farsi, Dari and Tajik) confirming Tajik as a veritable language and not a dialect variety of Farsi. For the academic establishment the *se-zabon* tenet was an essential part of their legitimation in the intellectual field, in particular against Iranian hegemony in the larger Persianate cultural sphere and as an affirmation of the dominance of the Soviet academic establishment against the challenges of independent intellectuals. Furthermore, the *se-zabon* paradigm legitimized the resource allocation for the oversized academic system and institutions established to research peculiarities of the *Tajik* language and literature. Next to Osimī, Rahim Masov was a vocal apologist of the *se-zabon* paradigm. However, several intellectuals and political activists decidedly rejected the *se-zabon* paradigm and insisted on the dialect variation of one language (*yak zabon*). Academics such as Muhammadǧon Šukurov, Akbar Tursunov and the journalist Mirbobo Mirrahim oriented themselves strongly toward Iranian cultural spheres and exploited the discussion on *se-zabon* and *yak-zabon* for their general critique of the Academy of Science, which they perceived as an instrument of Soviet colonial domination.[248]

Entwined in the *yak* and *se-zabon* dispute was also the question of the appropriate script for Tajik. The TaSSR had adopted for the Tajik language a modified Latin script in 1927 and a modified Cyrillic script in 1940.[249] Within the Persianate context, language reformers repeatedly demanded either a reform of the Arabic-Persian script or its abolition in favor of a modified Latin script. Reformers pointed out—in an anti-Arabic and anti-Islamic sentiment—that due to its ambiguities the Arabic-Persian alphabet is unsuitable for Persian since short vowels are omitted and various consonants have the same phonetic value, difficult to learn and therefore causative for the high level of illiteracy. In Iran the discussion ebbed away already in the 1930s. Iranian intellectuals reconsidered the Arabic-Persian alphabet in the context of authoritarian modernization project of the Pahlavi state and "discovered" the exclusive Persian script variations (such as the popular *nasta'līq* or *šekaste*) as an integral part of Iran's cultural identity. Although Tajik-Soviet intellectuals referred to the 19th-century language and script reformers such as Axundov or Mirza Malkum Khan, the adoption of the Latin and later Cyrillic alphabet was presented as imperative in the socialist reconstruction of the society.[250] In the late 1980s, the status of Tajik initiated a discussion on the question of the proper Tajik script like in other Soviet republics.[251] In August 1989, Tohir Abduǧabbor considered the introduction of the Latin and later Cyrillic alphabet as one of the most serious mistakes by the Bolshevist revolutionaries since it constructed a dam between the past and the present culture of the Tajiks. Interestingly, Abduǧabbor repeated some of the 19th-century reformers' concerns regarding the Persian-Arabic alphabet but now applied his criticism to the Cyrillic alphabet, which allegedly cannot reproduce the specific phonetics of Tajik properly, and does not represent the national characteristics of the Tajiks.[252] The 1989 Language Law did not stipulate a change of alphabet but encouraged the teaching and disseminating of Persian-Arabic language material and several journals and magazines immediately started publishing guidance how to write proper Persian.[253] After independence in September 1991, Article 26 on the state language was included in the constitution and the state was committed to support a change to the Persian-Arabic script. But progress in the implementation was slow and a member of the Academy of Science complained that it would take minimum another 9 to 10 years to reintroduce the Persian-Arabic script.[254] When finally, the post-Soviet constitution of Tajikistan was adopted in 1994, it did not contain any reference to the Persian-Arabic script. Article 2 of the constitution (amended in 1999 and 2003) merely stipulates that Tajik is the state language and Russian the language of international communication and all other ethnic minorities may freely use their native language.[255]

Colonial Spatiality: Bukhara, Samarqand and Dushanbe

The creation of the TaSSR in 1929 happened as a compromise between various regional stakeholders and Moscow. Tajik cadres had successfully described the plight of the Tajiks within the UzSSR and warned in Moscow about the risks of Uzbek hegemony in Soviet Central Asia. As important were Moscow's foreign policy considerations regarding Afghanistan (after the abdication of Amānullāh Khān in 1929) and Iran, which had embarked on a nationalist modernization under Reza Shah. Moscow intended to court the Afghan and Iranian leadership with the establishment of a Persian (= Tajik) speaking Soviet Socialist republic and demonstrate that the USSR was a force of national emancipation and liberation.[256] At the same time, the Communist International supported the Iranian Communist Party and its activists.

Although Stalin decreed the transfer of Xuğand and the surrounding district from the UzSSR to the TaSSR, Bukhara and Samarqand remained within the UzSSR to the dismay of Tajik intellectuals who view both cities as the epicenters of Tajik culture and statehood. In 1929, Xuğand was the only urban center in the TaSSR with some 30,000 inhabitants, but Dushanbe with its population of a few hundred people had already been declared capital of the Autonomous TaSSR in 1924 for political reasons. As Šukurov stated in the TaSSR teachers' journal *Omuzgor* in August 1989:

> The national government of the Tajiks—the autonomous Tajik Republic—was established in a remote corner of their previous historical homeland. The RASS Tajikistan was a Soviet republic, which did not have a city. The centers of social, economic and political life of the Tajiks' civilization—Bukhara, Samarqand and Xuğand—remained outside its borders. This national and societal injustice (*beadolatii iğtimoivu millī*) was only partially compensated after 1929 [with the integration of Xuğand].[257]

Until the late 1920s, Dushanbe was a Soviet garrison in the outer frontier. Predominately built by non-Central Asian Soviet nationalities under dire circumstances, the city lacked most amenities associated with urban life.[258] Despite the enormous difficulties, Dushanbe gradually transformed to a Soviet provincial capital. The Soviet bureaucracy established its branches in the TaSSR's capital and numerous cultural and educational institutions followed. Throughout the Soviet period, Dushanbe remained a "European" city

82 *Chapter 1*

with a majority population of non-Central Asian nationalities and only in the 1980s the ratio changed.[259]

Šukurov reflected on the importance of urbanity for the Tajik civilization, the cultural, economic, societal and political gravity, which was lost with the establishment of Soviet Tajikistan since Bukhara and Samarqand remained outside the Tajik homeland. He conceded that Dushanbe has been transformed into a "beautiful and lovely city"; however, it remained rather an economic and political center and has not attained the same importance for the field of language as the old cities had with their particular influence on the "regulation (*tanzimkorī*) and standardization (*meyorguzorī*) of the language."[260] The diversity of spoken Tajik in Dushanbe and the lack of respect for and acceptance of the standard language has inhibited Dushanbe to attain a more distinguished role. Sohibnazar even claimed that Dushanbe should not be considered as the Tajik capital. The Soviets, by depriving the Tajiks of Bukhara and Samarqand, introduced the Turkic term *qišloq* (village) into the Tajik language and Dushanbe was initially nothing more than a Turkic *qišloq*:

> And even if Dushanbe is in the meantime a thriving and beautiful place, we are still Samarqandīs, Xuǧandīs, Hisorīs, Ġarmīs, Badaxšonīs or Kūlobīs in this village-like-city (*šahri qišloqī*). And every official, who arrives in Dushanbe, is expected to follow his own rural thinking and not the great historical and civilizational thinking of the Tajiks. [...] Today they call us again regionalists. One should understand this by referring to the establishment of a newly established Bolshevik city—Dushanbe. Dushanbe is a village and not a place of the Tajik civilization—like Bukhara, Samarqand, Xuǧand or even Panǧakent and Ūroteppa.[261]

Yusuf equally complained that Dushanbe is rather an internationalist city and not a national capital in which Tajiks had no place (hence, insinuating that the Tajiks were intentionally barred from Dushanbe).[262] Interestingly, Safaralī Kenǧaev—the major antagonist of Sohibnazar and Yusuf—criticized exactly this attitude toward Dushanbe as narrow-minded: Since the nationalist intellectuals did not consider Dushanbe as their "own original place of birth and home,"[263] Dushanbe's urban (and 'restive') youth copied their attitude and lost their moral/spiritual orientation and readiness to integrate in the national urban spatiality of Dushanbe. For Kenǧaev, Dushanbe epitomized the Soviet urban modernity, which allowed him to advance through the Soviet institutions.

Crestfallen Expectations: Values and Morals

The nationalist movements and individuals involved in the late Soviet-Tajik debates referred to opaque "values" (*arzešho*), mostly national, cultural or

Islamic ones. Apparently, there was a common perception that the Soviet system had made the people immoral, uncultured and faithless.[264] The Soviet slogans of Peoples' Friendship or Internationalism were increasingly perceived as hollow, void of any meaning as Yurchak diagnoses for the last Soviet generation.[265] Mirrahim's assessment of the ideological reproduction of the Soviet system was echoed by Sohibnazar's perception of the economic sphere: "Like every year," he reported about a Gosplan meeting in 1988, "posters announced the same old slogans announcing new records and calling on the people to work diligently."[266] However, the realities on the ground were very different Sohibnazar conceded, in particular in the TaSSR's cotton sector (his area of expertise). He concluded, the promises of a socialist society were a "lie, a mendacious and self-deceiving (*xudfireb*) illusion."[267] Sohibnazar and Karim, both veteran Gosplan officials, expressed ambivalence in their validation of the Soviet system characteristic for a post-colonial setting referring to a "contamination" of the spiritual domain by the colonial system. The economic scarcity and decline, Yusuf postulated with a similar argument, had undermined values and morals:

> Life in the USSR was the daily struggle for a place in a nursery, a car, a parking space, a promotion or simply a bottle of vodka. [...] The Communists propagated the vision of a superior culture, but the reality was only the loss of culture and morals. [...] Generations of Tajiks have lost their historical, religious and cultural memory resulting in complacency, a detachment from reality and stagnation among the people.[268]

The "mimicry" of the colonial center too implied that the alternative "values" envisaged by the national Tajik intelligentsia were never defined and often did not correspond with a conventional understanding of values. For instance, the national language, alphabet, independence, or "Samarqand" and "Bukhara" would be listed as values, while democratic principles, justice and the rule of law or ethical values (such as respect, honesty, sincerity and so forth) were often extremely strained in their meaning.

CONCLUSION

The post- or anti-colonial attitude and interpretation of the TaSSR's history, political economy and culture by reformers and intellectuals antagonized communist cadres which claimed "ownership" in the project of Soviet Tajikistan. The conflict between the reformers and the established nomenklatura was concomitantly a generational conflict related to the patterns of social mobilization and resettlement since the late 1950s. The social and economic crisis of the Soviet system compounded the tensions between reformist intellectuals and the "old guard." Beyond their criticism on the academic institutions of the TaSSR, the younger generation expressed their disappointment over the failed Soviet "experiment" and questioned foundational aspects of the Soviet system, however still adhering to its hermeneutical and epistemic categories—similar to what Homi Bhabha describes as ambivalence: the paradoxical attraction and simultaneous repulsion of the center's political and academic culture.[269] This ambivalence significantly shaped the discussions among the Tajik intellectuals in the short post-colonial moment, which was suspended with the outbreak of violence in May 1992. There was arguably a second form of ambivalence among the reformist or democratic opposition related to the overarching political agenda in the late 1980s: Romantic/ethnic nationalism, experiences of marginalization or exclusion as well as exorbitant expectations and aspirations undermined visions about an open, democratic and multi-ethnic society.

NOTES

1. Rasulov (1913–1982) had succeeded Tursun Ūlğaboev in 1961 and resigned from office in February 1982 due to illness. He passed away two months later on 4 April.

2. Only with the 28th Politburo (1990–1991) all Soviet republics had a representative in the Politburo (see John Löwenhardt, John, James R. Ozinga and Erik van Ree, *The rise and fall of the Soviet Politburo* (London: UCL Press, 1992).

3. Cf. Georgij Arbatov, *Das System* (Frankfurt/Main: Fischer, 1993).

4. Cf. James Critchlow, "'Corruption', Nationalism, and the Native Elites in Soviet Central Asia," *The Journal of Communist Studies* 4, no. 2 (1988): 142–61; Mark R. Beissinger, "Elites and Ethnic Identities in Soviet and Post-Soviet Politics," In *The Post Soviet nations: Perspectives on the demise of the USSR*. Edited by Alexander J. Motyl (New York: Columbia University Press, 1992) and Pauline Jones Luong, *Institutional change and political continuity in Post-Soviet Central Asia* (Cambridge: Cambridge University Press, 2002).

5. Critchlow, "Corruption," 150.

6. Cf. TAJSTAT, *Demografiyai*. Urbanization in the TaSSR reached a peak around 1970 (with 37% urban population). Although urban areas still registered a population growth, the growth rates in the rural TaSSR were disproportionately higher.

7. Cf. Karim, *Faryodi*, passim; Safaralī Kenğaev, *Tabadduloti Toğikiston 1* (Dušanbe: Fondi Kenğaev, 1993); Nasriddinov, *Tarkiš*, passim; Sohibnazar, *Subhi 1*, passim.

8. Karim, *Faryodi*, 57–71; Yūsuf, *Tāğīkestān*, 23–52; see Nourzhanov and Bleuer, *Tajikistan*, 150–155.

9. Alexei Yurchak, *Everything was forever, until it was no more: The last Soviet generation* (Princeton: Princeton Univ. Press, 2006), 283.

10. Juliane Fürst, *Stalin's last generation: Soviet post-war youth and the emergence of mature socialism* (Oxford: Oxford University Press, 2010), 26.

11. Cf. Critchlow, "Corruption," 142–150.

12. See Arbatov, *System,* passim and Yegor Ligachev, *Inside Gorbachev's Kremlin* (Boulder: Westview Press, 1996). For the TaSSR see Stéphane Dudoignon, "Political Parties and Forces in Tajikistan, 1989–1993," In *Tajikistan: The trails of independence*. Edited by Mohammad-Reza Djalili, Frédéric Grare and Shirin Akiner (Richmond: Curzon, 1998), 57.

13. Gorbachev's abolition campaign started in May 1985. Reportedly, Bobosodiqova leaked a report of Nabiev's binge drinking with subordinated officials. See Yūsuf, *Tāǧīkestān*, 101; Sohibnazar, *Subhi 1*, 117–118.

14. For the USSR see Arbatov, *System*, passim; Ligachev, *Gorbachev*, passim; for the TaSSR Nasriddinov, *Tarkiš*, passim and Sohibnazar, *Subhi 1*, passim.

15. Beissinger, "Elites," 157.

16. Nasriddinov, *Tarkiš*, 32.

17. Petru Lučinskiy/Lucinschi (b. 1940), a Moldovan CPSU cadre, had been appointed Second Secretary (as Mahkamov's deputy) of the CC/CPT in 1986. He remained in office until 1989 when he was appointed 1st Secretary of the Moldovan SSR. In 1996, Lucinschi won the presidential elections in Moldova. Vladimir Petkelʻ, a career KGB officer, was appointed Chairman of the KGB in 1985 and remained in this position until 28 June 1991. Cf. Vladimir Petkelʻ, *Žiznennye ukhaby ekista* (Donetsk: Astro, 2010).

18. Nasriddinov, *Tarkiš*, 35.

19. Nasriddinov, *Tarkiš*, 26–27. For a similar assessment see Yūsuf, *Tāǧīkestān*, 158.

20. Nasriddinov, *Tarkiš*, 26–27. Karim pointed out, that Kūlobī and Badaxšonī youth fought out proxy conflicts of the political elite already in the 1960s (Karim, *Faryodi*, 457).

21. See the special volume of *Central Asian Survey* on youth (2010); Sophie Roche, *Domesticating youth: Youth bulges and its socio-political implications in Tajikistan* (New York: Berghahn Books, 2014; Richard Dobson, "Youth Problems in the Soviet Union," In *Soviet social problems*. Edited by Anthony Jones, Walter D. Connor and David E. Powell (Boulder: Westview Press, 1991); William Fierman and Martha B. Olcott, "Youth Culture in Crisis," *Soviet Union/Union Soviétique* 15, 2/3 (1988): 245–262; James Riordan, ed., *Soviet youth culture* (Bloomington: Indiana University Press, 1989); Christopher Williams, V. I. Chuprov, and I. Zubok, *Youth, risk, and Russian modernity* (Burlington, VT: Ashgate, 2003).

22. See Ligachev (*Gorbachev*, 210–224) report on the Central Committee Control Commission.

23. Osimī, *Enziklopediyai*, Vol. 4, 289.

24. Nabiev was Minister of Agriculture in 1971–1973 and then Chairman of the Council of Ministers until he was appointed 1st Secretary CC/CPT in 1983.

25. Kenğaev, *Tabadduloti 2*, 196.

26. For a similar assessment see Karim Abdulov, *Rohi behbud* (Dušanbe, 1995), 16.

27. FBIS-SOV-91–063-S, 2 April 1991, 53–55.

28. Sohibnazar, *Subhi 1*, 101.

29. Nizom Qosim, "Farğomi prezidenti bexalq," *Adabiyot va San'at*, September 5, 1991, 36: 11.

30. Kenğaev, *Tabadduloti 2*, 228.

31. Sohibnazar, *Subhi 1*, 101.

32. Ibrohim Usmonov, *Soli Nabiev* (Dušanbe, 1995), 7.

33. Cf. Arbatov, *System*, 235–242.

34. International Monetary Fund (IMF), World Bank, OECD, and EBRD, *A study of the Soviet economy*, Vol. 1 (Paris: OECD, 1991), 206.

35. See IMF, *Study*; Igor Filatochev and Roy Bradshaw, "The Soviet Hyperinflation: Its Origins and Impact throughout the Former Republics," *Soviet Studies* 44, no. 5 (1992): 739–59.

36. I. Adirim, "A Note on the Current Level, Pattern and Trends of Unemployment in the USSR," *Soviet Studies* 41, no. 3 (1989): 454.

37. John Schoeberlein-Engel, "Identity in Central Asia: Construction and contention in the conception of 'Özbek,' 'Tajik,' 'Muslim,' 'Samarquandi' and other groups," (PhD diss., Harvard University, 1994), 290.

38. Karim, *Faryodi*, 83–85.

39. FBIS-SOV-91–063-S, 2 April 1991, 53–55. Sohibnazar, *Subhi 1*, 39 and 121–128. For a similar perception see Ligachev, *Gorbachev* and V. Ponomarev, "Kolokola nadeždy," *Pravda* 131, May 11, 1990, 2.

40. Karim, *Faryodi*, 24–26; Rahīm Mosalmāniyān-Qobādiyānī, *Tağīkestān: āzādī yā marg* (Tehrān: Daftar-e našr-e farhang-e Eslāmī, 1373hš=1994/95), 12. The statistical data (IMF, *Study*, Vol. 1, 219–224) on the sectoral distribution of employment in the TaSSR indicates that only 21% of employment was in industry (compared to 38% in the USSR), but 42% in agriculture (compared to 19% in the USSR). 52% of the workers in the industrial sector were non-Central Asian nationalities, who comprised in 1989 only 15% of the TaSSR's population.

41. Cited from: http://www.nahzat.tj/1/item/7879-yode-az-bahman. Accessed April 2, 2013.

42. See Sergej Poljakov, *Everyday Islam: Religion and tradition in rural Central Asia* (Armonk, NY: Sharpe, 1992); Nikolay Kislyakov, *Tadžiki karategina i darvaza*, 3 vols. (Dušanbe: Doniš, 1966–1976). Cf. Nourzhanov and Bleuer, *Tajikistan*, 77–87.

43. See Yūsuf, *Tağīkestān*, 80 or Adaš Istad, "Sohibi in zamin kist," *Adabiyot va San'at*, August 15, 1991. 33, 4–5. Compare with IMF, *Study*, Vol. 1, 218.

44. The title is borrowed from the report by the International Crisis Group (ICG), *The Curse of Cotton: Central Asia's Destructive Monoculture* (Osh/Brussels, 2005).

45. Don van Atta, "'White Gold' or Fool's Gold? The Political Economy of Cotton in Tajikistan," *Problems of Post-Communism* 56, no. 2 (2009).

46. IMF, *Study*, Vol. 1, 219–224.

47. Sohibnazar, *Subhi 2*, 17.

48. Sohibnazar, *Subhi 2*, 20–28.

49. Roy, *Central Asia*, 1–24.

50. Nasriddinov, *Tarkiš*, 61–66.

51. Karim, *Faryodi*, 47. For the 'Arab Tajiks' see Thomas Barfield, *The Central Asian Arabs of Afghanistan* (Austin: Univ. of Texas Press, 1981).

52. Cf. William Rowe, "Kitchen Gardens in Tajikistan: The Economic and Cultural Importance of Small-Scale Private Property in a Post-Soviet Society," *Human Ecology* 37, no. 6 (2009): 691–703; Dudoignon and Qalandar, "They Were All," 81.

53. Yūsuf, *Tāğīkestān*, 21; Nasriddinov, *Tarkiš*, 77–78; Sohibnazar, *Subhi 2*, 16–20.

54. Cf. http://iwpr.net/report-news/tajik-chernobyl-victims-still-waiting, Accessed July, 27, 2013.

55. G. Košlakov, "Roğun: Čī boyad kard?," *Adabiyot va San'at*, January 5, 1989. 1. See Sohibnazar, *Subhi 1*, 157.

56. Cf. Karim, *Faryodi*; Sohibnazar, *Subhi 1*, 1997; Yusuf 1994/95. See Atkin, "Tajikistan," 367.

57. Karim, *Faryodi*, 24–26; Mosalmāniyān, *Tāğīkestān*, 12; Sohibnazar, *Subhi 2*, 36; Yūsuf, *Tāğīkestān*, 13–15.

58. FBIS-SOV-91–136, 16 July 1991, 102; FBIS-SOV-91–169, 30 August 1991, 128; Richard Stone, "Combating Radioactive Risks and Isolation in Tajikistan," *Science* 309, no. 5731 (2005): 44–45. The construction of the Argus reactor was finished in 1991 but it was never fueled. RTGs (radioisotope thermoelectric generators) are small electric generators used for remote lighthouses or weather stations.

59. Cf. N. G. Savčenkov, *Nurekskaya GĖS: Tadzhikistan ėnergogigant na Vakhshe* (Moskva: Speckniga, 2009).

60. Sohibnazar, *Subhi 2*, 153.

61. Ibrohim Usmonov, *Ta'rixi siyosii Toğikistoni sohibistiqlol* (Xuğand: Nuri ma'rifat, 2003), 54–55.

62. Otaxon Latifī, "Sarband," In *Darsi xeštanšinosī*, Edited by A. Mahmadnazar (Dušanbe: Irfon, 1989), 197–211.

63. Usmonov, *Ta'rixi siyosii*, 54–55.

64. Cf. John Heathershaw, "The Global Performance State," In *Ethnographies of the state in Central Asia: Performing politics*, Edited by Madeleine Reeves, Johan Rasanayagam and Judith Beyer (Bloomington: Indiana University Press, 2013) and Mohira Suyarkulova, "Between National Idea and International Conflict: The Roghun HHP as an Anti-Colonial Endeavor, Body of the Nation, and National Wealth," *Water History* 7, no. 1 (2015): 1–17.

65. Nasriddinov, *Tarkiš*, 181–188; see Nourzhanov and Bleuer, *Tajikistan*, 130.

66. Already in pre-Soviet times, the Abdulloğonov family belonged to the local elite. The grandfather of Abdumalik, Abdurahmon b. aš-Šayx Muhammad Sulton al-Ma'sumī, had fled Central Asia in 1922 and settled in Saudi Arabia where he became a religious scholar with ties to the Ibn Saud family. Abdulloğonov indicated that the wealth of his family is related to a heritage from his Saudi Arabian relatives (See Kamoludin Abdullaev and Shahram Akbarzadeh, *Historical dictionary of Tajikistan* (Lanham, MD: Scarecrow Press, 2002), 1–2; Osimī, *Enziklopediyai*, Vol. 8, 515).

67. Cf. Paul Bergne, *The birth of Tajikistan: national identity and the origins of the Republic* (London: Tauris, 2007); Francine Hirsch, *Empire of nations: Ethnographic knowledge & the making of the Soviet Union* (Ithaca: Cornell Univ. Press,

2005); Adeeb Khalid, *Making Uzbekistan: Nation, empire, and revolution in the early USSR* (Ithaca, London: Cornell University Press, 2015), 291–315.

68. The doyen of Tajik historical studies, Boboğon Ġafurov explicitly connected the ethnogenesis of the Tajiks with sedentism and urban culture. Ġafurov and the majority of Tajik intellectuals thereafter considered sedentary lifestyle as an expression of the cultural sophistication which distinguishes Tajiks from their 'nomadic' (i.e. Uzbek) neighbors, see: Boboğon Ġafurov, *Toğikon* (Dušanbe: Irfon, 1998), 30–37; R. M. Masov, *Istoriya topornogo razdelenija* (Dušanbe: Irfon, 1991). See Bert Fragner, *Die "Persophonie": Regionalität, Identität und Sprachkontakt in der Geschichte Asiens* (Berlin: Das Arab. Buch, 1999) and Hodgson, *Venture*, Vol 2., 12–368.

69. Cf. Yuri Slezkine, "The USSR as a Communal Apartment, or How a Socialist State Promoted Ethnic Particularism," *Slavic Review* 53, no. 2 (1994): 414–52.

70. See Chika Obiya, "When Faizulla Khojaev Decided to Be an Uzbek." In *Islam in politics in Russia and Central Asia*, Edited by Stéphane A. Dudoignon and Hisao Komatsu (London: Kegan Paul, 2001).

71. Lutz Rzehak, *Vom Persischen zum Tadschikischen: Sprachliches Handeln und Sprachplanung in Transoxanien zwischen Tradition, Moderne und Sowjetmacht (1900–1956)* (Wiesbaden: Reichert, 2001), 148–168.

72. See Yuri Slezkine, "N. Ia. Marr and the National Origins of Soviet Ethnogenetics," *Slavic Review* 55, no. 4 (1996): 826–62; Rzehak, *Vom Persischen*, 312–319.

73. Ġafurov (1908–1977) had been a Bolshevik activist and journalist since the 1930s and served as 1st Secretary of the CC/CPT between 1946 and 1956. After his resignation 1956 he was appointed Director of the Institute for Oriental Studies in the Academy of Science of the USSR until his death 1977. The first edition of the Tajik history was published 1949 under the title *Istoriya tadžikskogo naroda* (*The History of the Tajik People*). An extended version appeared between 1963 and 1965 and the final version as *The Tajiks* in 1972 (Russ.: *Tadžiki*, Taj.: *Toğikon*).

74. According to the first Soviet census in 1926, only 10% of the Tajik population lived in cities. In 1959 32% of the population lived in cities and in 1970 37% but gradually declined to 32.6% in 1989. Dushanbe's population increased from 1961–1970 by 60% (from 250,000 to 400,000); in 1979 the population had reached 500,000 and in 1989 600,000). (TAJSTAT, *Demografiyai*).

75. Dudoignon, *Communal*, 21–22.

76. Mosalmāniyān, *Tāğīkestān*, 15.

77. Yūsuf, *Tāğīkestān*, 1–2.

78. This observation is based on conversations in Dushanbe with representatives of this cohort, see also Dudoingnon, "Segmentation" and Dudoignon, *Communal*. Nourzhanov and Bleuer, *Tajikistan*, 121–125.

79. Dudoignon, "Political Parties," 58.

80. H. Borjian, "ĖNTSIKLOPEDIYAI SOVETII TOJIK," In *Encyclopædia Iranica*, Vol. VIII, Fasc. 5, 463–465.

81. S. N. Eisenstadt, "The Breakdown of Communist Regimes and the Vicissitudes of Modernity," *Deadalus* 121, no. 2 (1992): 30.

82. Yūsuf, *Tāğīkestān*, 170–171.

83. Arbatov, *System*, 261; compare with Sohibnazar, *Subhi 1*, 43–46.

84. Muhammadǧon Šukurov, "Du silsilaǧunboni madaniyati Toǧik," In *Darsi xeštanšinosī. Daftari duyum*, Edited by A. Mahmadnazar (Dušanbe: Irfon, 1991), 128. See for a similar Gramscian postulate Mosalmāniyān, *Tāǧīkestān*, 82–91.

85. Adaš Istad, "Musohibai Adaš Istad bo Muhammadǧon Šukurov. Ziyoī ravšangari aqlhost," *Adabiyot va San'at*, September 19, 1991, 38: 5.

86. Karim, *Faryodi*, 243.

87. Karim, *Faryodi*, 461.

88. Karim, *Faryodi*, 239.

89. Sohibnazar, *Subhi 1*, 88. Niyazi comes to the opposite conclusion arguing that the opposition never understood the "city morality," see Aziz Niyazi, "The Year of Tumult: Tajikistan after February 1990," In *State, religion and society in Central Asia: A post-Soviet critique*, Edited by Vitalij V. Naumkin (Reading: Ithaca Press, 1993), 269.

90. Sohibnazar, *Subhi 2*, 8.

91. Yūsuf, *Tāǧīkestān*, 169.

92. Usmonov, *Nabiev*, 7.

93. Karim, *Faryodi*, 21–23; see also Usmonov, *Nabiev*, 74.

94. Barnett Rubin, "Russian Hegemony and State Breakdown in the Periphery: Causes and Consequences of the Civil War in Tajikistan," In *Post-Soviet political order: Conflict and state building*, Edited by Barnett R. Rubin and Jack L. Snyder, (London: Routledge, 1998), 135.

95. Karim, *Faryodi*, 81–82. See Muriel Atkin, "Tajikistan: Reform, Reaction, and Civil War," In *New states, new politics: Building the post-soviet nations*, Edited by Raymond C. Taras and Ian A. Bremmer (Cambridge: Cambridge University Press, 1997), 603.

96. Usmonov, *Ta'rixi siyosii*, 19 and Roziq, *HNIT*, 131.

97. Y. Kul'čik, S. Rumyantsev, and N. Čičerina, *Graždanskie dviženiya v Tadžikistane* (Moskva, 1990), 166–168.

98. Karim, *Faryodi*, 482.

99. The imperative *xez* derives from the verb *xestan* which is also part of the term *rasto-xez*. For Iqbal's poem see the front page of *Adabiyot va San'at* 36 (5 September 1991); Nasriddinov, *Tarkiš*, 67, 78; Kenǧaev, *Tabadduloti 1*, 279.

100. Nationalist movements in the Baltic Soviet Republics used similar terms as 'resurrection' in their titular languages, for instance the newspaper of the Popular Front of Latvia, *Latvijas Tautas fronte*, was called *Atmoda* (Awakening) and movements in Estonia (the Popular Front *Rahvarinne*) and Lithuania (the reform movement *Sąjūdis*) used a similar vocabulary than the Tajik nationalists. See Nuralī Davlat, "Istiqloliyate ki onro xudi deputatho dark nakardand," *Faraǧ*, September 18, 2013, 38.

101. Mosalmāniyān, *Tāǧīkestān*, 19.

102. Kul'čik, Rumyantsev and Čičerina, *Graždanskie dviženiya*, passim.

103. Mosalmāniyān, *Tāǧīkestān*, 19.

104. Nasriddinov, *Tarkiš*, 106–120.

105. Davlat, "Istiqloliyate"; Yūsuf, *Tāǧīkestān*, 81.

106. The DPT had between 3,500 (media reports) and 15,000 (DPT figures) members.

107. Cf. Vladimir Babak, Demian Vaisman, and Aryeh Wasserman, eds., *Political organization in Central Asia and Azerbaijan: Sources and documents* (London: Frank Cass, 2004), 280–282; Abdullaev and Akbarzadeh, *Dictionary*, 53–54. In 1994, the DPT spilt into the DPT Almaty and DPT Tehran Platform. The DPT Tehran Platform led by Yusuf did not join the UTO in 1995, but the DPT Almaty Platform was part of the UTO and participated in the Commission for National Reconciliation.

108. Yūsuf, *Tāǧīkestān*, 78–79.

109. Babak, Vaisman and Wassermann, *Political*, 283–289.

110. Slezkine, "Communal Apartment," 414.

111. Tajik in contrast is a Western Iranian language (like the closely related Farsi and Dari). The Soviet authorities tried to introduce a script system for the Pamir languages, however in vain, and until today, none of the Pamir languages is written (Rüdiger Schmitt, *Die iranischen Sprachen in Geschichte und Gegenwart* [Wiesbaden: Reichert, 2000], 92–96). For the Ismaili religion see Farhad Daftary, *The Ismā'īlīs: Their history and doctrines* (Cambridge: Cambridge University Press, 1999).

112. Osimī, *Enziklopediyai*, Vol. 1, 622–623.

113. Cf. Schoeberlein-Engel, *Identity*, 130–136.

114. Talabšoh Salom, "Amirbek Atobek—Vahdati mellī nadorem," *Naǧot*, June 6, 2012, 23. See Babak, Vaisman and Wassermann, *Political*, 307–308.

115. Kenǧaev, *Tabadduloti 2*, 229 and 289.

116. Terry Martin, *The affirmative action empire: Nations and nationalism in the Soviet Union, 1923–1939* (Ithaca: Cornell University Press, 2001), 19.

117. Heathershaw, *Central Asian*, 87.

118. See for instance Mark Beissinger, "Soviet Empire as 'Family Resemblance'," *Slavic Review* 65, no. 3 (2006): 294–303; Douglas Northrop, *Veiled empire: Gender & power in Stalinist Central Asia* (Ithaca: Cornell University Press, 2004); Deniz Kandiyoti, "The Politics of Gender and the Soviet Paradox: Neither Colonized, nor Modern?," *Central Asian Survey* 26, no. 4 (2007): 601–23; Adeeb Khalid, "Introduction: Locating the (post-) colonial in Soviet history," *Central Asian Survey* 26, no. 4 (2007): 465–73.

119. Bhavna Dave, *Kazakhstan: Ethnicity, language and power* (London: Routledge, 2007), 23–24.

120. Karim, *Faryodi*, 23.

121. Karim, *Faryodi*, 243.

122. Mosalmāniyān, *Tāǧīkestān*, 9.

123. Karim, *Faryodi*, 461.

124. Yūsuf, *Tāǧīkestān*, 86.

125. Mosalmāniyān, *Tāǧīkestān*, 8–9.

126. Eisenstadt, "Breakdown," 30.

127. Hoǧī Akbar Tūraǧonzoda, *Šariat va ǧomea* (Dušanbe: Nodir, 2006), 9.

128. Tūraǧonzoda, *Šariat*, 157.

129. Tūraǧonzoda, *Šariat*, 158.

130. Partha Chatterjee, *The nation and its fragments: Colonial and postcolonial histories* (Princeton: Princeton University Press, 1993).

131. Adams, "Postcolonial," 4.

132. See Mirbobo Mirrahim, *Hamtabaqi Šodmon Yusupov va Xul 'kar Yusupov pūkid* (Dušanbe: Buxoro, 2012); Mosalmāniyān, *Tāǧīkestān*, 8; Sohibnazar, *Subhi 1*, 207; Yūsuf, *Tāǧīkestān*, 38–39. Roziq creates a neologism with the composite adjective "manqurtandeš" (*Mankurt* & the Tajik *andeš* = "manqurt-minded") describing CPT Deputies in the Supreme Soviet, see Roziq, *HNIT*, 141.

133. Chingiz Aitmatov, *The day lasts more than a hundred years* (Bloomington: Indiana University Press, 1983), 126.

134. See A. Mahmadnazar, ed., *Darsi xeštanšinosī* (Dušanbe: Irfon, 1989) and *Darsi xeštanšinosī. Daftari duyum* (Dušanbe: Irfon, 1991).

135. *Komsomoli Toǧikiston*, January 27, 1988. Reprinted in Mirrahim, *Hamtabaqi*, 110–128.

136. Mirrahim, *Hamtabaqi*, 134

137. Mirrahim, *Hamtabaqi*, 150.

138. Yurchak, *Everything*, 14.

139. Mirrahim, *Hamtabaqi*, 137.

140. Mirrahim, *Hamtabaqi*, 138.

141. Mirrahim, *Hamtabaqi*, 141.

142. Mirrahim, *Hamtabaqi*, 151–152.

143. Roziq, *HNIT*, 129. See also Sohibnazar, *Subhi 2*, 38.

144. Chatterjee, *Nation*, 6.

145. Dave, *Kazakhstan*, 2.

146. Heathershaw, "Central Asian," 93.

147. Quoted in Yurchak, *Everything*, 1. Makarevič is member of the band *Mašina vremeni*.

148. Akbar Tursunov, "Padidahoi millatgaroī," In *Darsi xeštanšinosī*, Edited by A. Mahmadnazar (Dušanbe: Irfon, 1989): 56. Tursunov's article was first published in *Pravda*, May 5, 1988, 126: 3 under the title "Fenomen nacionalizma [The Phenomenon of Nationalism]".

149. Tursunov, "Padidahoi," 56.

150. Karim, *Faryodi*, 89. *Xudšinosī* is the compound of *xud* (self) and *šinosī* (recognition/identification).

151. Istad, *Musohibai*, 4.

152. Istad, *Musohibai*, 4.

153. Cf. Chatterjee, *Nation*, 95–115.

154. Stalin considers the nation as a historically constituted, stable community of people, formed on the basis of a common language, territory, economic life, and psychological make-up manifested in a common culture. See Joseph Stalin, *Marxism and the National and Colonial Question* (Moscow: Co-Operative Publishing Society of Foreign Workers in the USSR, 1935). See Eric Hobsbawm, E. J. and T. O. Ranger, eds., *The Invention of tradition* (New York: Cambridge University Press, 1983).

155. Cf. Jürgen Paul, *Zentralasien* (Frankfurt: S. Fischer, 2012), 46–130 and Svatopluk Soucek, *A history of inner Asia* (New York: Cambridge University Press, 2000).

156. V. V. Barthold, *Four Studies on the History of Central Asia*. Vol. 1 (Leiden: Brill, 1962): 15. See also Barthold's entries "Tāḏjīk" and "Sart". In: *Encyclopaedia of Islam, First Edition (1913–1936)*.

157. See Bert Fragner "TĀDJĪK," In *EI2*; John Perry, "TAJIK i. THE ETHN-ONYM: ORIGINS AND APPLICATION," In *Encyclopædia Iranica*, online edition, availabe at http://www.iranicaonline.org/articles/tajik-ii-tajiki-persian. Accessed September 6, 2016.

158. Sadriddin Aynī, " Maʿnoi kalimai «Toǧik»," *Adabiyot va San ʿat*, September 13, 1992, 37 (a reprint of an article published 1942). In his history of the Tajiks, Rahmonov referred to Aynī's theory as well and asserted that "the term Toǧik as 'crowned people' (*mardumi toǧdor*) replaced the previous ethnic designations Iranians (*eroniyonī*) and Aryans (*oriyoī*)" (Rahmonov, *Istiqloliyati*, Vol. 2, 5).

159. Ġafurov, *Toǧikon*, 63–86 and 442–521.

160. Quoted in Sohibnazar, *Subhi 1*, 173.

161. Ġafurov, *Toǧikon*, 33–45.

162. Ġafurov, *Toǧikon*, 45.

163. See Bergne, *Tajikikistan*, 15–43; Hirsch, *Empire*, 145–186; Khalid, *Uzbekistan*, 291–315; Lisa Yountchi, "The politics of scholarship and the scholarship of politics: Imperial, Soviet, and post-Soviet scholars studying Tajikistan," In *The heritage of Soviet Oriental studies*, Edited by Michael Kemper and Stephan Conermann (New York: Routledge, 2011).

164. Anaita Khudonazar, "The Other," Berkeley Program in Soviet and Post-Soviet Studies, Unpublished manuscript, 2004.

165. See Masov, *Istoriya* and *Tadžiki: istoriya c grifom 'sovershenno sekretno'* (Dušanbe: Payvand, 1995).

166. See Marlene Laruelle, "The Return of the Aryan Myth: Tajikistan in Search of a Secularized National Ideology," *Nationalities Papers* 35, no. 1 (2007): 55–57; Tim Epkenhans, "Zwischen Mythos und Minenfeld: Historiographie in Tadschikistan," *Osteuropa* 62, no. 3 (2012): 137–50.

167. Rahim Masov, "Emomali Rahmon: 'The Architect of Peace'," *Diplomatic World*, no. 36 (2012): 64–68. In April 2015, a group of historians and archeologists published an open letter in the weekly *Nigoh* ("Rahim Mastov [sic] kist?," *Nigoh*, April 15, 2015) in which they accused Masov of corruption, violations against academic standards, favoritism and nontransparent employment policy. Apparently, Masov had already fallen from favor during the construction of the new National Museum of Tajikistan (*Osorxonai millii Toǧikiston*) since he reportedly did not agree to transfer some of the invaluable pre-Islamic exhibits from 'his' Museum for Antiquities to the new museum. President Rahmon eventually dismissed him on 21 April 2015.

168. Muhammadǧon Šukurov, "Nazare ba taʿrix," In *Darsi xeštanšinosī*, Edited by A. Mahmadnazar (Dušanbe: Irfon, 1989), 139–140. The assignment of nationalities such as Uzbek, Tajik or Iranian for the above mentioned poets stems from 20th-century nationalism. Navoī, for instance, came from a Uighur (an ethnonym which was only 'invented' in 1924) family and there are only few details known about the biographies of Saʿdī and Hafez (not to mention the influence of Arabic poetry on the Persian poetry).

169. Šukurov, "Madaniyati Toǧik," 121. For the issue of 'speech culture' see also Rzehak, *Vom Persischen*, 411–412.

170. Šukurov, "Madaniyati Toǧik," 123.

171. Yountchi, "Politics," 231.

172. Yūsuf, *Tāǧīkestān*, 96.

173. Sohibnazar, *Subhi 1*, 193–195.

174. R. M. Masov, «Nasledie» Mangytskoy dinastii (Dušanbe, 2002) and Sohib Tabarov, *Spor 'derevenskogo intelligenta' s 'gorodskim intelligentom'* (Dušanbe, 2004). I would like to thank Lutz Rzehak who called my attention to the dispute between Masov and Šakurī in his paper "Auf der Suche nach den Wurzeln des tadschikischen Nationalismus" presented on 12 June 2013 at the Austrian Oriental Society in Vienna.

175. Cf. Masov, *Tadžiki*, passim.

176. See http://www.ozodi.org/content/article/24709185.html. Access September 10, 2014.

177. Eisener, *Spuren*, 29.

178. For instance he refers to Viktor Sarianidi's designation of the Bactria–Margiana Archaeological Complex or Oxus Civilization (2300–1700 BCE); Ġafurov, *Toǧikon*, 38–59.

179. Yurchak, *Everything*, 282–296.

180. Cf. Muriel Atkin, "Tajikistan: ancient heritage, new politics," In *Nation and politics in the Soviet successor states*, Edited by Ian Bremmer and Ray Taras (New York: Cambridge University Press, 1993).

181. Samd Saʿdī, "Bedorii siyosī lozim! Davlati Toǧik či xel bud va či xel xohad šud?," *Adabiyot va Sanʿat*, August 22, 1991, 32: 12.

182. Muhammadǧon Šakurī (Buxoroī), *Xuroson ast in ǧo: Maʿnaviyat, zabon va ehyoi millii Toǧikon* (Dušanbe: Olii Somon, 1997). For the *samizdat* see Reinhard Eisener, *Auf den Spuren des tadschikischen Nationalismus: Aus Texten und Dokumenten zur Tadschikischen SSR* (Berlin: Das Arabische Buch, 1991).

183. Kova (Farsi: Kāve) is a mythological figure in Ferdowsi's epic *Šohnoma* who musters the Iranians under his banner (*dirafš*) and initiated an uprising against the tyrant Zahhok.

184. *Boxtar* is Tajik for Bactria/Bactriana, a historical region in today's Turkmenistan, Uzbekistan, Afghanistan and Tajikistan.

185. *Aryana* is an eastern Iranian term for the Iranian plateau and is derived from the proto-Iranian *aryānām*.

186. *Xusrav* (Khosrau II) was a Sassanid King (reigned 590–628 CE), his epithet was 'Parviz' (the Victorious). *Ganǧ* (treasure) became proverbial in Persian as the wealth of Khosrau Parviz.

187. Karim, *Faryodi*, 126.

188. Cf. Edmund Herzig, "Regionalism, Iran and Central Asia," *International Affairs* 80, no. 3 (2004): 503–17; David Menashri, "Iran's Regional Policy: Between Radicalism and Pragmatism," *Journal of International Affairs* 60, no. 2 (2007): 153–67.

189. Mirrahimov, *Hamtabaqi*; Yūsuf, *Tāǧīkestān*, 9–10. See FBIS-SOV-92–130, 7 July 1992, 59; FBIS-SOV-92–137, 16 July 1992, 70.

190. FBIS-SOV-91–194, 7 October 1991, 81–82.

191. Usmonov, *Nabiev*, 43.

192. Yūsuf, *Tāǧīkestān*, 162.

193. Yūsuf, *Tāǧīkestān*, 10.
194. Yūsuf, *Tāǧīkestān*, 67.
195. Yūsuf, *Tāǧīkestān*, 213.
196. Helsinki Watch, *Conflict in the Soviet Union: Tadzhikistan* (New York: Human Rights Watch, 1991), 62.
197. Sohibnazar, *Subhi 1*, 79.
198. Yūsuf, *Tāǧīkestān*, 46–47.
199. Yūsuf, *Tāǧīkestān*, 45.
200. Yūsuf, *Tāǧīkestān*, 263–264.
201. Adaš Istad, "Davlati millī čī guna boyad?," *Adabiyot va San'at*, July 4, 1992, 23: 6. Istad refers to the Ġaznavid dynasty, whose founder, Sebüktegīn, started his military career as a military slave in the service of the Somonids in the late 10th century CE, but eventually turned against his masters and established the Ġaznavid dynasty, cf. Clifford E. Bosworth, *The Ghaznavids: Their empire in Afghanistan and Eastern Iran 994–1040* (Edinburgh: Edinburgh University Press, 1963).
202. Muhammadǧon Šakurī, "Naǧoti mo az davlati millist!," *Adabiyot va San'at*, June 25, 1992, 26: 4.
203. Cf. Safaralī Kenǧaev, *Tabadduloti Toǧikiston 3* (Toškand: Fondi Kenǧaev, 1995).
204. Mirrahim, *Hamtabaqi*, 137.
205. See Nū'mon Ne'matov, *Ta'rixi xalqi Toǧik. Kitobi yakum. Az insoni oqil to Toǧiki barkamol* (Dušanbe: Sarparast, 2003); Ibrohim Usmonov, *Toǧikon. Surudi ta'rixi xalq va zamin* (Dušanbe: Payvand, 2001).
206. Loiq Šeralī, "Dar duroha," In *Darsi xeštanšinosī*, Edited by A. Mahmadnazar (Dušanbe:Irfon, 1989), 148–149.
207. Šeralī, "Dar duroha," 152–153.
208. S. Gretsky, "Qadi Akbar Turajonzoda," *Central Asia Monitor* 1 (1994): 20.
209. Šukurov, "Nazare," 145–146. A similar view in Karim, *Faryodi*, 278.
210. Sohibnazar, *Subhi 1*, 81.
211. Sohibnazar, *Subhi 1*, 190.
212. Yūsuf, *Tāǧīkestān*, 40.
213. Yūsuf, *Tāǧīkestān*, 65.
214. Gretsky, "Qadi," 20.
215. Kenǧaev, *Tabadduloti 1*, 118.
216. Kenǧaev, *Tabadduloti 1*, 277.
217. Kenǧaev, *Tabadduloti 1*, 69–71 and 116–117.
218. Sohibnazar, *Subhi 1*, 191.
219. Sohibnazar, *Subhi 1*, 192.
220. Šukurov, "Madaniyati Toǧik," 122; Karim, *Faryodi*, 325.
221. Šeralī, "Dar duroha," 148.
222. Quoted in Karim, *Faryodi*, 260.
223. Yūsuf, *Tāǧīkestān*, 31.
224. Sohibnazar, *Subhi 1*, 173. A similar perception in Karim, *Faryodi*, 15–17.
225. Rohat Nabieva (born 1936) was among the first female Soviet-Tajik historians dealing with a gender perspective. Farxod Zikriyoyev (born 1940) is a philologist.

226. Rohat Nabieva and Farhod Zikriyoev, *Taʿrixi xalqi Toğik. Kitobi darsī baroi sinfi 11* (Dušanbe: Sobiriğon, 2006), 67–68.

227. See Sattorī, *HNIT*, 17 and 47. See Adeeb Khalid, *The politics of Muslim cultural reform: Jadidism in Central Asia* (Berkeley: Univ. of California Press, 1998) and Franz Wennberg, *On the edge: The concept of progress in Bukhara during the rule of the later Manghits* (Uppsala: Uppsala University, 2013).

228. See Karim, *Faryodi*, 263

229. Osimī, *Enziklopediyai*, Vol. 1, 492–493.

230. Nasriddinov, *Tarkiš*, 164.

231. Vladimir Medvedev, "Saga o bobo Sangake, voine," *Družba Narodov*, no. 6 (1993): 188.

232. Nuralī Davlat, "Qozikalon dar girdobi siyosat," *Nigoh*, March 5, 2014, 49: 12. *Ġazo* is the Tajik version of the Arabic *ġazwa*, in the Islamic tradition a military expedition lead by the Prophet Muhammad. In the context of imperial and colonial expansion *ġazwa/ġazavat* were used to describe a 'just' resistance against the colonial power (cf. T. Johnstone, "Ghazw," In *EI2*).

233. Michael Kirkwood, "Glasnost', the National Question' and Soviet Language Policy," *Soviet Studies* 43, no. 1 (1991): 61–81.

234. Roziq, *HNIT*, 130.

235. IMF, *Study*, Vol. 1, 205. There is little information on the proficiency of Tajik among non-Tajik ethnicities. Ethnic Uzbeks have often some command of colloquial Tajik, while non-Central Asian nationalities do not speak Tajik.

236. Tohir Abduğabbor, "Muhiti zist va zabon," In *Darsi xeštanšinosī. Daftari duyum*, Edited by A. Mahmadnazar (Dušanbe: Irfon, 1991), 210.

237. Sohibnazar, *Subhi 1*, 192.

238. Muhammadğon Šukurov, "Zaboni millī ğamxorii maxsus xohon ast," In *Darsi xeštanšinosī*, Edited by A. Mahmadnazar (Dušanbe: Irfon, 1989), 3.

239. Šukurov, "Zaboni millī," 4.

240. Šukurov, "Zaboni millī," 8–9.

241. Šukurov, "Zaboni millī," 9.

242. Sohibnazar, *Subhi 2*, 141. See also Muhammadğon Šakurī, *Har suxan ğoevu har nuqta maqome dorad. Čande az masʿalahoi farhangi suxan* (Dušanbe: Irfon, 2005) and Rzehak, *Vom Persischen*, 411–412.

243. Šukurov, "Zaboni millī,"14.

244. Loiq Šeralī, "Šinosnomai millat," In *Darsi xeštanšinosī*, Edited by A. Mahmadnazar (Dušanbe: Irfon, 1989), 28.

245. Šeralī, "Šinosnomai," 22.

246. Cf. Ūktam Xoliqnazar, "Donistani taʿrix vağib ast!," In *Darsi xeštanšinosī. Daftari duyum*, Edited by A. Mahmadnazar (Dušanbe: Irfon, 1991).

247. TAJSTAT, *Hayati millī*, 7.

248. On *se-zabon* and *yak-zabon* see Mirrahim, *Hamtabaqi*, 147; Yūsuf, *Tāğīkestān*, 61–62 and Bert G. Fragner, "'Glasnost' in einem fernen Land: die tadschikische Literaturzeitschrift Adabijot va San'at als Meinungsforum," In *Presse und Öffentlichkeit im Nahen Osten*, Edited by Christoph Herzog, Raoul Motika and Anja Pistor-Hatam (Heidelberg: Heidelberger Orientverlag, 1995), 48.

249. Cf. John Perry, "Script and Scripture: The Three Alphabets of Tajik Persian, 1927–1997," *Journal of Central Asian Studies* 2 (1997): 2–18.

250. Rzehak, *Vom Persischen*, 169–258.

251. Cf. Barbara Kellner-Heinkele and Jacob M. Landau, *Language politics in contemporary Central Asia: National and ethnic identity and the Soviet legacy* (London: I.B. Tauris, 2012).

252. Abduğabbor, "Muhiti," 212–213.

253. For instance a series in *Adabiyot va San'at* throughout 1991. See Perry, "Script," 12–13.

254. Masrur Abdulloh, "Či tavr ba xati millii Toğikī bargardem?," *Adabiyot va San'at*, August 15, 1991, 33: 3.

255. Ğumhurii Toğikiston, *Sarqonuni Ğumhurii Toğikiston* (Dušanbe: Šarqi ozod, 2000).

256. Bergne, *Tajikistan*, 113–114; Hirsch, *Empire*.

257. Šukurov, "Madaniyati millī," 123.

258. See Botakoz Kassymbekova and Christian Teichmann, "The Red Man's Burden: Soviet European Officials in Central Asia in the 1920s and 30s." In *Helpless imperialists: Imperial failure, fear and radicalization*. Edited by Maurus Reinkowski and Gregor Thum (Göttingen: Vandenhoeck & Ruprecht, 2013), 170–174. See the travelogues by Egon E. Kisch, *Asien gründlich verändert* (Berlin: Erich Reiss Verlag, 1932) and Joshua Kunitz, *Dawn over Samarkand: The Rebirth of Central Asia* (London: Lawrence and Wishart, 1936).

259. TAJSTAT, *Hayati millī*, 7.

260. Šukurov, "Madaniyati millī," 126.

261. Sohibnazar, *Subhi 1*, 195.

262. Yūsuf, *Tāğīkestān*, 46.

263. Kenğaev, *Tabadduloti 1*, 281.

264. Yūsuf, *Tāğīkestān*, 80. Similar narratives in Karim, *Faryodi* and Mirrahim, *Hamtabaqi*.

265. Yurchak, *Everything*, passim.

266. Sohibnazar, *Subhi 1*, 35.

267. Sohibnazar, *Subhi 1*, 155.

268. Yūsuf, *Tāğīkestān*, 36.

269. Homi Bhabha, *The location of culture* (London: Routledge, 1994).

Chapter 2

Narrating a House Divided

Regionalism Revisited

Regionalism is widely seen as one of the main reasons for the cleavages in the Tajik society and causative for the outbreak of the civil war. Nourzhanov and Bleuer consider regionalism as the "ultimate cause of social polarisation" in the Tajik society and postulate "that the entire course of Tajik history, both before and after the 1917 revolution, has been conducive to the emergence and survival of distinctive sub-ethnic communities that could never merge effectively into a modern nation."[1] At times regional identities are narrated with a primordial value, but most researchers suggest that regional identities and solidarity groups have emerged and gained political-social meaning in the context of the Soviet system.[2] Pauline Jones Luong considers the Soviet administrative practice as an important agent for the proliferation of regionalist networks and identities in Central Asia. First, the Soviet administrative divisions and the federal structure "fostered regional rather than national cleavages due to its coincidence with very weak (or non-existent) national identities and very strong (pre-existing) local identities."[3] Luong Jones argues that pre-Soviet "tribal" identities were split in the Soviet nation building of the 1920s while region-based "clans" persisted and were gradually redefined by the local nomenklatura. Second, the economic specialization of the different union republics of the USSR reinforced regional patron-client relationships due to the uneven economic development of the Central Asian republics and concomitantly the failure of social and economic modernization. In order to fulfil the center's expectations of economic performance (which in return granted some local autonomy), republican leaders, such as Rasulov and Nabiev, strengthened their patron-client networks with the rural population in those regions with cotton cultivation in order to have direct access to the economic resources. The expansion of national cadres on the republican level facilitated this development:

[R]egional identities in Central Asia can be explained as conscious investments that Central Asian elites and masses alike make in response to the structural incentives created under Soviet rule. [...] The sum result of the Soviet political and economic system in the Central Asian republics was to create, reinforce, and politicize regional socio-political cleavages by restructuring individual identities, group relations, and power asymmetries on the basis of regional affiliation, while at the same time supplanting and depoliticizing pre-existing sociocultural identities.[4]

As for Tajikistan, Roy points out that the collectivization and forced migration gave traditional regional identities a political, social and economic meaning in the Soviet administrative system since these identities were reproduced on the local kolkhoz level.[5] Akiner emphasizes the role of personal networks and Aktin reminds us that there are no fixed or categorical loyalties within these networks.[6] Tunçer-Kılavuz challenges the validity of "clan"-based regional networks and emphasizes factors such as education, professional networks, economic interests and personal interests as well as relationships including patron-client networks.[7]

Collins instead argues that regional identities are inextricably centered on clans. Due to the specific historical context—the late state formation and Soviet administrative practice—clans persisted and adapted to the challenges of the Soviet system. During the Brezhnev era, clan elites consolidated their power and local networks. With the Perestroika reforms of Gorbachev, the regional political economy was disrupted and clans had to negotiate "pacts" with competing groups. The ability to negotiate pacts is for Collins an important indicator for the regime's consolidation and durability in the transformation process in the 1990s. Collins assumes that the center's intervention in 1985 was less intrusive in the TaSSR than in the other Central Asian republics and therefore "the ruling Tajik clan had no incentive to negotiate a pact introducing a more inclusive and stable division of power and resources among competing clan elites."[8] Collins' assumptions, however, disclose several inconsistencies: First, the center's intervention (i.e., the removal of Nabiev and Mahkamov's restructuring) in the Tajik political economy was as intrusive as in other Central Asian republics. Second, Collins hesitates to consider internal frictions in regionally based "clans." Third, her reference to "clans" within the Tajik context becomes a discretionary affair when she classifies the affiliation of Qadriddin Aslonov (born in Hasorčašma/Ġarm) first as a member of the Communist Party and then as "a client of the Khodjenti clans," since "Karateginis had traditionally been client clans of the Kulyabis—hence, subclients of Khodjent."[9] Apparently, Tajik respondents conveyed the idea of different levels of clan-(sub)client-relationships to Collins and the subordination of the "Karateginis" to the "Kulyabis" should be considered a rather idiosyncratic interpretation of Tajikistan's regionalism. Furthermore, fanning out inter-clan and regional relations in such a discretionary way undermines the analytical value of the category "clan," since almost everyone can be included in vague clan relations or hierarchies.

Regional-based identities and solidarity networks in Central Asia are often depicted as exotic, traditional and fundamentally different from "modern" non-Central Asian societies. References to allegedly "exotic" phenomena such as *mahalla* (city district), *avlod* ("clan," extended family), *qavm* ("tribe"), *gap/gaštak* (male village talks) or "Islam" do not necessarily contribute to better understanding of a given society or community. Brubaker and Cooper remind us that

> [w]e should seek to explain the processes and mechanisms through which what has been called the "political fiction" of the "nation"—or of the "ethnic group," "race", or other putative "identity"—can crystallize, at certain moments, as a powerful, compelling reality. But we should avoid unintentionally reproducing or reinforcing such reification by uncritically adopting categories of practice as categories of analysis.[10]

John Schoeberlein offers a convincing anthropological approach to regional and family/clan solidarity in Central Asia embedded in the social and economic context of the later USSR:

> This is in part a consequence of the Soviet bureaucratic system which controls access to positions and allows for a considerable amount of "corruption." Since virtually all property and resources are state-controlled, connections are essential in order to negotiate the extra-legal and unofficial mechanisms that regulate access to the resources necessary for any kind of economic activity: permission to sell goods in the market, provision of raw materials, access to vehicles or buildings—even simply freedom from the legal or illegal interference of "law enforcement" authorities. All of this requires an elaborate and effective network of mutual back-scratching relationships, which is most readily developed within the family framework. Thus the son takes over the network that the father established. However, as each person seeks to maximize the breadth and effectiveness of her network, it is often expedient to draw on criteria of connectedness that extend beyond the immediate family to a larger community.[11]

"Connectedness" includes various forms of group identities, which are modulated continuously by everyday practice and need. The extension of networks could include the local community, kolkhoz brigade, graduating class or university. Simultaneously, the Soviet state gave group identities a social, political or economic meaning by classification or recognition and implemented policies, which were designed to manipulate communities.[12]

The sources reflect regionalism in the Tajik society not as a primordial phenomenon of the Tajik mentality but as a result of the Soviet administration and ultimately as catalysts for the conflict: Tūrağonzoda postulated in his memoirs the "old disease of contentiousness, regionalism and political gamble"[13] as central causes of Tajikistan's civil war. He explicated that the TaSSR's nomenklatura in the 1980s did not maintain anymore the traditional balance (*muvozinat*) of regional representation in the state structures and institutions.[14] Nasriddinov, Sohibnazar and Abdulov also mentioned the importance of a regional balance. Karim considered "regionalism as our worst enemy," but explained that regionalism is not an original feature of the Tajik mentality but manipulated by "clans (*klanho*)" and individuals, in particular by Rahmon Nabiev who deepened the antagonism between Leninobod/Kūlob on the one side and Qarotegin/Badaxšon on the other.

> In fact, the leadership and the members of the opposition were representatives of the entire republic, their place was not the periphery but in the capital of the republic. The agenda, they followed, had no traces of regionalist favors. The opposition's intention was the achievement of national unity, the improvement of the standard of living, the level of culture, economy and social life of all parts of the republic.[15]

Nasriddinov provided one of the most detailed accounts on regionalism. He considered regionalism as the determining factor of the Tajik political economy and devoted his memoirs to identify the "origins of regionalism,"[16] the main curse on the Tajik society dividing the country and its people. He did not consider regionalism as a primordial or inevitable character trait of the Tajiks, but a sentiment manipulated first by the Russian/Soviet colonial intervention and eventually copied by the northern Leninobodī elite, which wrote "regionalism in their script for the puppetry (*teatri lūxtake*) of domestic politics."[17] Nasriddinov postulated that regionalism emerged in the 1930s and described it in reference to the Soviet *korenizaciya* policy of the 1920 and 1930 as "*šimolizaciya*,"[18] embodied in Tursun Ūlğaboev, a corrupt and belligerent cadre who never had the development of the country in mind but his own pleasure and delight (*ayšu išrat*), patronage (*ğūrabozī*) and enrichment. The northern elites manipulated the colonial center and neglected the development of the south.[19]

THE DOMINATION OF LENINOBOD

In the 19th century, between 1936 and 1991 Leninobod, today Suğd, the northern province of Xuğand was already economically more developed and urbanized than southern Tajikistan. Xuğand was not only a historic urban center with some political and economic weight in the 18th century, it was also—unlike other cities in the TaSSR—a hybrid colonial/traditional city with a population of 30,000 (1897) divided between the old town and the new Russian colonial quarter with an emerging colonized native elite. Xuğand's proximity to Tashkent (some 160 km), the Russian colonial capital of Turkestan, influenced this transformation.[20] Since Xuğand featured educational institutions and urban employment opportunities, literacy rates were comparably higher than in southern Tajikistan and eligible local students had access to Russian schooling.[21] For instance, Abdullo Rahimboev (an early Bolshevik activist and chairman of the Soviet of People's Commissars) went to the Russian high school in Xuğand and graduated from a teacher's college in 1917.[22] With the Russian conquest in 1866, Xuğand had been integrated into the Turkestan *oblast'* and as the second largest city after Samarqand firmly embedded in the colonial economy and administration. In contrast, eastern Bukhara was never fully integrated into the colonial administration. The connection of Xuğand and eastern Fergana Valley to the Trans-Caspian Railway in 1898 was a hallmark moment for this integration—the first train arrived in Dushanbe only in 1929. The economic integration concomitantly facilitated opportunities for the native population in the local administration and in 1929, the northern *okrug* of Xuğand had—compared with the southern TaSSR—already a physical infrastructure and a cohort of literate Tajiks.

The Soviet administration did not introduce regionalism to the TaSSR but—in collaboration with local stakeholders—integrated regional provenance to its informal administrative practice and recruitment of qualified local cadres. A regional representation in different administrative domains emerged since the 1920s: Culture and academia went to émigrés from Samarqand, Bukhara and the Fergana Valley, the political field—especially positions in the higher echelon of the Communist Party of the TaSSR—was dominated from the 1950s on by officials from Leninobod. The post-war *korenizaciya* of Tajik cadres is to some extent associated with Boboğon Ğafurov, who initiated the transformation of the TaSSR's administration and political economy. While before 1947, 51 out of 67 districts in Tajikistan were governed by non-Central Asian cadres, Ğafurov successively appointed Tajik and Uzbek officials, although his *korenizaciya* policy was hampered by the few Central Asian specialists available.[23]

With the social mobilization of the 1960s and 1970s, the regional representation in the different professional spheres gradually changed and the apparent domination of cadres from Leninobod in the top tiers of the TaSSR's administration was increasingly criticized by representatives of regional groups, which considered themselves marginalized, in particular from Ğarm, Badaxšon or Kūlob. Nasriddinov described how the tensions between alleged

regional solidarity groups increased in Dushanbe's educational institutions in
the 1970s, when students from Leninobod and Kūlob were establishing alliances against students from Qarotegin and Badaxšon:

> But unfortunately, the ordinary youth (*ǧavononi sodda*) from Kūlob and
> Badaxšon did not understand that two, three leaders of the republic put them
> into harm's way out of their own interests and personal animosities. They had
> no idea that these leaders led a debaucherous life and intrigued intoxicated by
> alcohol how they could draw the youth into their conflict and eventually abed
> them to the looming war.[24]

Nasriddinov considered regionalism rather as "an ordering device"[25] but
not as the genuine origin of the violence among Tajik youth. In Nasriddinov's narrative, personal animosities and rivalry within the political elite
intensified the politics of regionalism from the 1980s on. In particular,
the conflict between Ġoibnazar Pallaev (a Pomirī) and Rahmon Nabiev (a
Xuǧandī) ostensibly divided the country along regionalist solidarity patterns. While the origins of the conflict were personal animosities, regionalism served as a strategy to rationalize the conflict by those involved. In the
political confrontation, the reference to regionalism was an important narrative strategy to denounce the opposition. Yusuf condemned the Leninobodī
elite for the uneven development of the TaSSR eventually "Othering" them
as those who

> sell their nation (*mellatforūš*), their homeland, their culture and their religion.
> This clan (*qoum*) was worse than the Jews, Americans and Britons, since they
> ruined thousands of Tajiks. They were the new Mongols who fought against the
> Iranian race (*Irān-nežat*). [...] The Leninobodī elite received money and advice
> from abroad to colonize (*este 'mār*) the Tajik people.[26]

Xuǧand emerged, Yusuf continues, as the "jewel of Bolshevism" while its
inhabitants do not even speak Tajik properly. The Leninobodī elites "instigated hatred among brothers and provoked one province to wage war against
another province, whilst their own people remained neutral and spectators."[27]
Yusuf's defamations nourished prevalent prejudices and conspiracy theories,
and also indicated the irreconcilability and "Othering" of the political opponent, which contributed to the rapid deterioration of the situation in Tajikistan
in 1992. Eventually, Karim concluded his thoughts on regionalism with the
observation that like in any other country, tensions existed between the different regional and ethnic groups, between the Uzbek and Tajiks, the Badaxšonīs
and Kūlobīs and so forth. However, Nabiev made the serious mistake of organizing his administration by exploiting these tensions and by constructing the
opposition as the regional "Other."[28]

ADMINISTRATIVE DIVISIONS

Between 1931 and 1980, 25 administrative reforms were implemented in the TaSSR reorganizing the administrative entities. In general, the TaSSR (as other Soviet republics) was divided in to three administrative tiers: the national republican level, the province (Taj.: *viloyat*; Russ.: *oblast*ʿ or *okrug*) and finally the district (Taj.: *nohiyya*; Russ.: *rayon*). Additionally, cities (Taj.: *šahr*; Rus.: *gorod*) and agricultural communities (Taj./Rus.: *sel*ʿ*sovety džamoati*) formed separate tiers comparable to the district.[29] In 1929, the TaSSR was divided into the six provinces: Ūroteppa (Istaravšan), Panǧakent, Dushanbe, Ġarm, Kūlob and Qūrġonteppa, a special region around Regar (the Karatagskiy *tyumen*),[30] the region (*okrug*) of Xuǧand and the autonomous *oblast*ʿ of Gorno Badaxšon/Badaxšoni kūhistonī (Mountain Badaxšon, GBAO, established in 1925). The administrative reforms in 1951, 1954 and 1958 reduced the number of *viloyat* to three (Leninobod, Qūrġonteppa and Kūlob), dissolved the Ġarm *viloyat* and placed the districts in central Tajikistan (Hisor, Dushanbe, Ġarm) under republican administration. The autonomous *viloyat* of Badaxšon was enlarged by the Vanǧ and Qalai-Xum districts, which were previously part of Ġarm. Between 1963 and 1971, the *oblast* level was disbanded in the TaSSR and all districts had to answer the republican administration. The administrative reorganization allowed the republican administration to reallocate resources and official positions, at the same time it provided regional networks with a political and social relevance. Between 1971 and 1977 the *viloyat* tier was reintroduced with three provinces and directly administered districts.[31] In the 1980s—within the context of Perestroika—further administrative reforms were implemented.

A highly contentious issue was the administrative division in the south between Qūrġonteppa and Kūlob. In a session of the Supreme Soviet on 2 April 1988, the merger of Kūlob and Qūrġonteppa to the Xatlon *viloyat* was controversially discussed as Nasriddinov recollected in detail: Hayoyev (the chairman of the Council of Ministers from Dehqonobod south of Qūrġonteppa) endorsed the merger of Qūrġonteppa and Kūlob to one province as an attempt to restructure the allocation of resources as well as transport capacities. With the administrative reform, Mahkamov intended to break up the local patronage networks. The reform had the approval of Moscow but had not been negotiated with the local population. The local elites in both regions decidedly objected the merger since both regions were dominated by agriculture, unevenly developed and competed for the same resources.[32] In an unprecedented move, the local Kūlobī elite, led by Qurbon Zardakov and Safarmuhammad Ayubī, fiercely opposed the administrative reform in a public meeting with the republican leadership in Kūlob 1988. Pallaev, Hayoyev and Mahkamov faced an angry audience. Zardakov (a local strongman, popular musician and chairman of the Housing and Sport Facilities Combine in Kūlob[33]) attacked the republican leadership in harsh terms. As Nasriddinov recollected, Zardakov cried out:

> 'You are the leadership of the TaSSR. Do you have an independent opinion or not? Do you know that Kūlob is an ancient cultivated region and nonetheless our young men (ğavonmardon) and girls are unemployed? [...] You have merged our *viloyat* three times in recent decades. Billions of Rubles were wasted this way. Have you done the same only once with Leninobod? For more than 70 years, the Leninobodīs have built their *viloyat* at the expenses of Kūlob and our budget. The city of Isfara [a city some 100 km southeast of Xuğand] today has more industrial enterprises than the entire south of Tajikistan. Your regionalism has made our lives miserable!' The audience was agitated and shouted 'Are you Tajik, Mahkamov?' Eventually Hayoyev had to intervene: 'Hey, you were impolite! What is this talk about!'[34]

Nasriddinov might have dramatized the meeting in Kūlob, but the failure of the republican nomenklatura to communicate the terms of the administrative reforms with the local population had sparked public protest. Local officials showed open hostility toward the republican leadership. And Nasriddinov vividly illustrated Mahkamov's limited empathy in dealing with the local population. The decision to merge Kūlob and Qūrġonteppa was finally revoked, but the issue remained contentious and the 16th Session of the Supreme Soviet decided to merge the two provinces to the Xatlon province with Qūrġonteppa as the administrative center in November 1992.[35]

LANDSCAPE, RESETTLEMENT AND THE
SHAPING OF REGIONAL IDENTITIES

In some accounts, the geographical landscape of the mountainous country is considered an important factor for the emergence of regional identities[36]: The dividing mountain range of the Alay Mountains extending from the Tien Shan, the rugged Pamir with its numerous isolated valleys and the lowlands of the south naturally divides the various regions of Tajikistan. Furthermore, the Soviet creation of the TaSSR politically merged regions, which never had been integrated before. Xuğand had been part of the Fergana Valley/Tashkent region, Panğakent virtually a suburb of Samarqand, Hisor administratively a part of the Emirate of Bukhara but economically stronger, oriented toward the southeast, and throughout the 19th century Kūlob looked south to Kunduz and Taloqan.[37] However, the emphasis of geographic divides underestimates inter- and intra-regional trade, cultural and religious exchange as well as migration.[38] *Longue durée* regional in- and out-migration as well as the (not always peaceful) coexistence between the sedentary and nomadic population including intermarriage continuously changed the composition of the local population even in regions considered as "remote" or "isolated."

Since the 1920s, the Soviet resettlement campaign and the migration from other regions of the USSR to the TaSSR changed the population distribution and composition in Tajikistan. These changes are associated with the development of Dushanbe and the transformation of the Vaxš River basin. Although the rationale behind the resettlement policy was primarily to provide manpower for the cotton cultivation, there were other motives as well, such as extending the control over the traditionally elusive mountainous regions and concerns about natural disasters such as earthquakes, mud slides and so forth. Prior to the 1920s the lower Vaxš River valley was relatively sparsely populated and large parts of the population were Uzbek semi-nomadic tribal groups, such the Laqay or Qataġan, and a few Turkmen and Kazakh groups. Already in pre-Soviet times cotton was cultivated around Qūrġonteppa on a small scale, but in 1931 the Soviet authorities initiated with the *Vaxšstroy* the complete transformation of the region for cotton cultivation. Large kolkhoz complexes with dense irrigation networks were built around Qūrġonteppa, Šahrtuz and Kūlob. Simultaneously, the forced resettlement of large parts of the population in mountainous regions to the lowlands of the Vaxš valley accelerated and changed the regional composition of the population lastingly.[39] The resettlement did not undermine regional or local identities but strengthened or even created them. In cases where the entire population of a village or valley was resettled to one kolkhoz/sovkhoz, the resettled *muhoğir* were often numerous enough to reproduce their village community in their new environment. Soviet political discourses of participation and mobilization, resource allocation and the organization of collective farms and the collective experience of resettlement eventually gave regional identity or origin a political and social meaning.[40] Resettlement, as Ibrohim Usmonov observed, fostered a distinctive idea of origin and provenance and undermined the development of new concepts of local identities: "It became clear that the second generation of *muhoğir* from Ġarm who were born in the Vaxš valley never became Vaxšī but remained Ġarmīs."[41] Even during the 1960s and the accelerated urbanization and expansion of Dushanbe, people with common origins would move into one particular apartment block or micro-district thus reproducing their *mahalla* in an urban context.[42] Resettlement also meant that a population, which previously lived in mountain valleys predominately occupied with horticulture and animal husbandry, had to adapt to cotton cultivation in specialized kolkhoz brigades under harsh climatic conditions. The experience of forced resettlement became an important marker for identity and personal narratives usually do not try to rationalize the resettlement in terms of the Soviet transformation and modernization, but describe the tragedy and the suffering, which the resettlement caused to them. Šodmon

Yusuf, whose family was resettled from the Ġarm Valley to Qūrġonteppa in
the 1930s, considered the entire resettlement as a mass murder of the Ġarmī
population by the Soviet authorities (who in Yusuf's narrative were subalterns
to their Uzbek masters).[43] In no less dramatic terms but without the conspiracy theories did Hoǧī Akbar describe the resettlement of his grandfather *ešoni*
Xalifa Abdulkarim from the mountainous Pičef (close to Romit northeast of
Dushanbe) to the southern cotton areas. After two years in the inhospitable
hot climate of the southern lowlands, several family members had died and
eventually *ešoni* Xalifa Abdulkarim was invited to stay clandestinely with one
of his Uzbek *murids*, Ahmad Hoǧī Ibrohim, in Turkobod (today Vahdatobod)
in the Kofarnihon district. But the resettlement had distressed *ešoni* Xalifa
Abdulkarim and he died a few months later.[44]

Paradoxically, the resettlement and cultivation of the Vaxš valley was
also a source of pride for the *muhoǧir*. Mosalmoniyon, for instance, portrayed the Ġarmī population as the "genuine Tajiks," who work diligently
and industriously as farmers, who cultivated barren land and transformed it
into affluent communities. Islam occupied a central role in their life and the
Ġarmī population has preserved a special esoteric knowledge of the religion
even throughout the Soviet Union. Ġarmī wives and mothers were the best
teachers for the younger generation, Ġarmī communities have a special sense
of solidarity and are well connected by trade with the wider Islamic world.
However, despite their outstanding qualities, the Ġarmī population has been
continuously excluded from political representation—a result of the Uzbek
Pan-Turkism (*turkestongaroī*) that tried to expel the Iranian race from Central
Asia.[45] Sohibnazar narrated the Ġarmī population too as the original Tajiks
who were forced into exile and who cultivated the Vaxš valley due to their
unrivalled skills in farming and trade. The Kūlobī population, in contrast,
was not able to resist the Turkish race (*turknažod*) and was replaced by them:
"Eventually, the Tajiks whose grandfathers have cultivated the land with their
own hands, have to cede their land to strangers and return to the mountains of
Qarotegin, the Hisor range, the desert of Danġara and the hills of Qarotov."[46]
Sohibnazar narrated the internal deportation as a Soviet campaign to destroy
the Tajik culture. At the same time, he romanticizes the pristine origins of
the *muhoǧir*, for instance in a recollection of a conversation with Nuriddin, a
70-year-old *mūysafed* in a kolkhoz close to Qūrġonteppa, who was deported
with his family in the 1940s from Tavildara:

> From our conversation I [Sohibnazar] got the impression that Nuriddin was well
> versed in our thousand years old literature. He was reciting couplets from every
> period of our classical poets. All his recitations dealt with the Homeland and
> the thought of being separated from the homeland [...]. The time they deported
> Uncle Nuriddin, his family counted 20 people. They deported them to a place

where there was no tree and no shade. There was no housing and they had to live in makeshift huts. The heat of the sun relentlessly blinded everyone and made even breathing hard. Most of the time, the *muhoğir* took water from the inner yard, although they knew that in this heat standing water was harmful for the health. But there was no alternative. [...] A few months after the deportation, Nuriddin's mother could not endure the life conditions there, got sick and passed away. A few months later his sister-in-law and her son also died. Eventually, less than a year after the deportation, only nine members of his large family were still alive.[47]

Sohibnazar narrated the mountainous region of Tajikistan as the authentic spiritual homeland of the Tajik with clear water, pleasantly cool mountain valleys and a pristine nature.[48] During increasing tensions in Dushanbe, Sohibnazar frequently retreated to this unspoiled and authentic Tajik land-scape, as he described (or better romanticized) his home village of Kūhdara some 20 km east of Dushanbe: In Kūhdara, the people were "literate not in the modern disciplines but in the old ones (*savodi kūhna*)"[49] with a deep spirituality and ethical-moral orientation embedded in the rich Persian literary tradition epitomized in "classical" works such as the *Čor Darveš* ("The four Dervishes" by the 13th-century poet, mystic and polymath Amir Khusrow), the collection of animal fables *Kalila va Dimma* or the *Ğavome' al-Hikoyot* (a 13th-century collection of Persian anecdotes by Sadiduddin Muhammad Aufī).[50] In Soviet academic discourses and the politics of the center, however, the population in the mountainous regions was portrayed differently: As intellectually limited and without culture, unable to govern their own affairs, therefore the cadres from the north decided that the south and the mountain regions should remain agricultural regions without indus-trial development.[51]

CONCLUDING REMARKS

The authors discussed here mention regionalism as one of the most important factors for the political conflicts and eventually the outbreak of the civil war in Tajikistan. But the discussion of regionalism remains cursory, vague and imprecise. Alleged regional solidarity networks are introduced, but in the evolving narrative on the political and social dynamics often entirely dropped as a subject. Instead the economic crisis, organized crime, the absence of the rule of law, contingent personal interests or external influences are presented as the immediate factors determining the conflict in Tajikistan. The issue of regionalism is often not presented as a compelling argument—thus as an original source of conflict—but rather as an ambiguous feature of the Tajik society which is cited in order to rationalize the cause of events. Importantly, the Tajik sources agree that affiliation based on regional provenance did not generate categorical loyalties: Būrī, Kenğaev, Nasriddinov, Sohibnazar, Tūrağonzoda or Yusuf can hardly conceal the deep divisions and conflicts *within* regional solidarity groups and Schoeberlein concluded already in 1994 that neither Leninobod nor Kūlob represent "clans" or "indeed unified constituencies of any kind."[52] Representatives of his own northern constituency initiated Nabiev's dismissal in 1985 and continued to conspire against him after his election in 1991.[53] Mahkamov likewise plotted with support of Badaxšonī elites (Moyonšo Nazaršoev) against both, networks from Leninobod (Nabiev) and from Badaxšon (Pallaev). Eventually, the "alliance" between Kūlob and Leninobod did not evolve out of regionalist solidarity, but personal interests and contingent considerations by elite representatives.[54] During his short and bloody reign as commander of the Popular Front from October 1992 to March 1993, Sangak Safarov, the infamous field commander and ex-convict from Kūlob, first and foremost eliminated or marginalized his *local* rivals among the political nomenklatura of Kūlob before he turned against the opposition. The fearsome field commander Fayzalī Saidov equally did not take up arms because of a regional sentiment, but in order to take revenge for the murder of his father. The deviation between the master narrative and the actual contingent dynamics on the local level reveals

> disjunction between identities and actions at the central or elite level, on the one hand, and the local or mass level, on the other. This disjunction takes two forms: first, actions 'on the ground' often seem more related to local or private issues than to the war's driving (or 'master') cleavage; second, individual and local actors take advantage of the war to settle local or private conflicts often bearing little or no relation to the causes of the war or the goals of the belligerents.[55]

The appeal to a regional sentiment *was* important to recruit and rally support and due to the polarization and prevalent discourses on dependencies and uneven development regionalism became a popular "ordering device."[56]

Nasriddinov lengthily elaborated on regionalism in Tajikistan, but when he analyzed the major grievances in the Tajik society, he first and foremost referred to the social and economic situation in the republic: unemployment, the deteriorating gender equality, the rise of Islamic activism, the structural weakness of the opposition and its inability to articulate a common ideological platform, corruption, the dismantling of state structures, the weakness of the CPT's ideological work or the split within the intelligentsia. Only at the very end of his list, Nasriddinov concludes that all these previously mentioned factors have somehow generated regionalism in Tajikistan and not *vice versa*.[57] Eventually Nasriddinov adopted a more post-colonial attitude toward the issue of regionalism in the TaSSR and the discrimination against the population of Kūlob (his home region). The mountain people always had been slaves and with the assertion of Soviet rule, the Bolsheviks started to oppress the people of Kūlob in a concerted strategy, executing their intellectuals and religious leaders. Notably, Nasriddinov considered the funeral of Sangi Kulūlo, an influential Naqšbandiyya *sheikh* in 1968, as one of the central manifestations of Kūlob's resistance to Soviet rule and part of the spiritual domain important in generating a regional identity.[58] In a similar approach, Sohibnazar and Yusuf conceded that regionalism was not central to Nabiev's administration: Nabiev did not consider the regional background in his appointment of officials, but the bribes (*pešakī*) paid in advance; likewise, in the presidential election campaign, regionalism was only a secondary issue.[59]

Muriel Atkin, Shirin Akiner and İdil Tunçer-Kılavuz emphasize the importance of professional networks in the Tajik society for the mobilization in the early conflict.[60] For the late TaSSR one can identify various ideal types of professional networks: first, the agro-industrial complex, in particular the cotton sector with its extensive network of collective farms, specialized brigades and administration in rural Tajikistan; second, the transport sector with the local *avtobaza* (motor depots) throughout the country (an astounding number of field commanders, combatants and politicians had professional relations to the *avtobaza*)[61]; third, the security sector, that is, the MVD, KGB, DOSAAF and the military; fourth, the Communist Party and its sub-organizations in the regions; fifth, the academia, writers and artists organized in the expansive educational and cultural sector; sixth, the sports clubs (martial arts, football); finally, the vast shadow economy and organized crime. Affiliation to these professional networks gave access to the informal resource allocation in an economy of scarcity. Common experience, socialization and professional interests often prevailed over regional identities.[62]

Finally, Tajik intellectuals identified regionalism as the major impediment for the development of a unifying Tajik nationalism in the Perestroika years. While Šarof Rašidov revitalized Uzbek culture and united the Uzbeks, Tajikistan's intelligentsia immersed in an ideological struggle in which regional sentiment and the "game of regionalism by the regionalists"[63] inhibited the development of an inclusive Tajik nationalism. Even worse, the best intellectuals, Nasriddinov ascertained, were excluded by discourses labelling them as *vahhobī* or *vovčik*. This view has also been forwarded by scholars who maintain that strong regionalist sentiment constrained the development of a unified Tajik nationalism.[64] Perhaps, this interpretation gives too much credit to nationalism as a force of cohesion in the tumultuous period of independence and too much weight to regionalist cleavages for the outbreak of the conflict. The general parameters of

Tajik nationalism were fixed and widely accepted even among the opposition. The disputes over the nature of the Tajik language and the location of
the Tajik culture in the wider Persianate context were academic debates.
Moreover, none of the larger regional factions (with the exception of
Badaxšon[65]) questioned the borders of Tajikistan or envisioned a secession
and independence from the republic. In fact, some opponents were even
united in a revisionist aspiration for Bukhara and Samarqand. Therefore,
regionalism in the Tajik Civil War was—like ethnicity in the Yugoslav Civil
Wars—predominately an

> ordering device than as an impelling force [which] proved essentially to be
> simply the characteristic around which the perpetrators and the politicians who
> recruited and encouraged them happened to array themselves. It was important
> as an ordering device or principle, not as a crucial motivating force.[66]

This assumption does not deny the influence of imagined regional communities but invites us to consider the often contingent and confusing local
issues which are often disconcerting in their banality, a deviation from the
master narrative and—from an empirical perspective—bewilderingly complex and at times unsatisfying.

NOTES

1. Nourzhanov and Bleuer, *Tajikistan*, 89–90.
2. See Teresa Rakowska-Harmstone, "The dialectics of nationalism in the
USSR," *Problems of Communism* 23, no. 1 (1974), 1–22.
3. Jones Luong, *Institutional change*, 64.
4. Jones Luong, *Institutional change*, 63.
5. Roy, *Central Asia*, 1–24 and 85–100. Roy calls the Tajik conflict a "war of the
kolkhoz" (94).
6. Akiner *Tajikistan*, 24; Atkin, "Tajikistan."
7. Tunçer-Kılavuz, "Understanding," 324.
8. Collins, *Clan politics,* 133.
9. Collins, *Clan politics*, 200.
10. Rogers Brubaker and Frederick Cooper "Beyond 'Identity'," *Theory and Society* 29, no. 1 (2000): 5.
11. Schoeberlein-Engel, *Identity*, 268–269.
12. Schoeberlein-Engel, *Identity*, 269–274.
13. Tūrağonzoda, *Miyoni*, 4.
14. Tūrağonzoda, *Miyoni*, 9 and 18.
15. Karim, *Faryodi*, 552.
16. Nasriddinov, *Tarkiš*, 8.
17. Nasriddinov, *Tarkiš*, 8. For a similar assessment see Abdulov, *Rohi*, 19.

18. Nasriddinov, *Tarkiš*, 11. *šimol* in Tajik means "north," thus the term *šimolizaciya* could be translated as "northernization."

19. Nasriddinov, *Tarkiš*, 6–15.

20. Cf. Keith Hitchins, "KHUJAND," In *Encyclopædia Iranica*, online edition, avialable at http://www.iranicaonline.org/articles/khujand-city-in-northwestern-tajikistan. Aaccessed September 6, 2016. In 1897 Tashkent had a population of 155,680 and Samarqand 55,130, see Henning Bauer, Andreas Kappeler, and Brigitte Roth, eds., *Die Nationalitäten des russischen Reiches in der Volkszählung von 1897* (Stuttgart: F. Steiner, 1991), 537.

21. According to the Russian census in1897, the average literary rate in Tsarist Central Asia stood at 7.9% for the male and 2.2% for the female population with significant regional/ethnic differences.

22. Osimī, *Enziklopediyai*, Vol. 6, 229.

23. Sohibnazar, *Subhi 1*, 95. Cf. Rakowska-Harmstone, *Russia and Nationalism*, 95–110. In 1959 13% of the TaSSR's population were Slavs but they constituted 40% of all party members in the CPT. This ratio gradually changed in the 1960s.

24. Nasriddinov, *Tarkiš*, 26; Sohibnazar, *Subhi 1*, 92.

25. Mueller, "Ethnic War," 62.

26. Yūsuf, *Tāǧīkestān*, 116.

27. Yūsuf, *Tāǧīkestān*, 134–135.

28. Karim, *Faryodi*, 552.

29. Cf. Ašūrboy Imomov, *Administrativno-territorial'noe ustroystvo Tadžikistana* (Dušanbe: Ofset Imperiya, 2013).

30. The Karatagskiy *tyumen* was a concession to the majority Uzbek population living in the region.

31. Imomov, *Administrativno,* 181. Cf. Mukhammad Asimov, ed., *Tadžikskaya sovetskaya socialističeskaya respubika* (Dušanbe: SIEST, 1984).

32. Nasriddinov, *Tarkiš*, 53–58. See also Markowitz, *State erosion*, 56–57.

33. Y. Yaʿqubov, ed., *Kūlob Ensiklopediia* (Dušanbe: Ensiklopediyai millii Tojik, 2006), 184.

34. Nasriddinov, *Tarkiš*, 58–59.

35. FBIS-SOV-92–233, 3 December 1992, 31.

36. Nourzhanov and Bleuer, *Tajikistan*, 91.

37. Cf. H. Borjian, "KULĀB," In *EIr*.

38. Religious students would travel to important religious authorities to be admitted to their teaching circle. Furthermore, the visit (*ziyorat*) to shrines (*mazar*) of prominent religious figures is an important religious practice in Central Asia.

39. Kurbanova, *Pereselenie*; Dudoignon and Qalandar, "They Were All," 67–74.

40. Roy, *Central Asia*, 1–24.

41. Usmonov, *Nabiev*, 83. Cf. Sohibnazar, *Subhi 1*, 93.

42. Davlat Khudonazar, "The Conflict in Tajikistan: Questions of Regionalism," In *Central Asia: Conflict, resolution, and change*, Edited by Roald Sagdeev and Susan Eisenhower (Washington, DC: The Eisenhower Institute, 1995), 256.

43. Yūsuf, *Tāǧīkestān*, 32.

44. See http://turajon.org/imam/cat.php?imam_id=8 Accessed March 21, 2013.

45. Mosalmāniyān, *Tāǧīkestān*, 69–70.

46. Sohibnazar, *Subhi 2*, 93.

47. Sohibnazar, *Subhi 2*, 95–96.

48. Sohibnazar, *Subhi 2*, 98–101.

49. Sohibnazar, *Subhi 2*, 230.

50. Sohibnazar, *Subhi 2*, 229–232.

51. Nasriddinov, *Tarkiš*, 41–42. See Kislyakov, *Tadžiki*, passim.

52. Schoeberlein-Engel, *Identity*, 334.

53. Sohibnazar, *Subhi 1*, 213; Nasriddinov, *Tarkiš*, 29.

54. Nasriddinov, *Tarkiš*, 249.

55. Kalyvas, "Ontology," 475–6.

56. Sohibnazar, *Subhi 2*, 79. Cf. Mueller, "Ethnic War," 42–70.

57. Nasriddinov, *Tarkiš*, 85–86.

58. Nasriddinov, *Tarkiš,* 296. Several thousand followers of Sangi Kulūla attended the funeral, including some 200 CPT officials whose membership was suspended.

59. Sohibnazar, *Subhi 1*, 130 and 212; Yūsuf, *Tāǧīkestān*, 147.

60. İdil Tunçer-Kılavuz, "The Role of Networks in Tajikistan›s Civil War: Network Activation and Violence Specialists," *Nationalities Papers* 37, no. 5 (2009): 693–717.

61. For instance Narzullo Dūstov, Davlat Usmon, Rizvon Sodirov (see chapter 7).

62. Sohibnazar, *Subhi 1*, 130.

63. Nasriddinov, *Tarkiš*, 13–14. For the term *vovčik* see chapter 5.

64. Shahram Akbarzadeh, "Why Did Nationalism Fail in Tajikistan?" *Europe-Asia Studies* 48, no. 7 (1996): 1105–29; Lynch, "Tajik Civil War," 52–5; Nourzhanov and Bleuer, *Tajikistan*, 27–49.

65. A few intellectuals and activists contemplated independence of GBAO after Davlat Xudonazar lost against Nabiev in the presidential elections in November 1991. A call for independence, however, was revoked (FBIS-SOV-91–240; 13 December 1991, 90; FBIS-SOV-91–241, 16 December 1991, 81–82).

66. Mueller, "Ethnic War," 62.

Chapter 3

"Bloody Bahman"

Имсол…
Дар интихоботи намояндагон
Ба ҷои халқ,
Тир дод овоз,
Ки ҳизби Коммунист,
Ба курсии хунини худ нишинад боз.
Имсол…
Соли дурӯғгӯии шоир,
Соли дурӯғгӯии олим,
Соли дурӯғгӯии ҳоким буд.
Пайкарнамои шаҳр, ки рӯяш сиёҳ бод,
Ҷуз пайкари дурӯғ,
Ба мо наменамуд…

Bozor Sobir[1]

The final years of the Soviet Union saw increasing social and political unrest among the population. The authorities were unable to contain, suppress or divert the tensions and a series of violent confrontations erupted in the USSR's periphery, such as the 9 April Tragedy in the Georgian SSR, the pogrom against the Meskhetian Turks in Uzbekistan's Fergana Valley in 1989, the Osh riots a year later, the continuous violence in the Azeri SSR since 1988 culminating in the "Black January" in 1990 and finally the February riots in Dushanbe the same year. Tajikistan's civil war did not start with the February riots, but the dynamics of the confrontation and the involvement of different types of actors illustrate a set of important factors relevant for the evolving conflict in 1992: First, the riots erupted shortly before the 1990 elections to the Supreme Soviet highlighting the political dimension and the limited ability of the incumbent nomenklatura to negotiate the terms of the rapid political, social and economic change with a population demanding to have a voice in the process. Second, violent non-state actors, such as racketeers, criminals and youth gangs, contributed to the escalation of violence and exploited the anarchy and disorder (perhaps even with the silent approval of parts of the political elite)—a pattern symptomatic for the civil war in 1992/1993. Third, the gradual corrosion of the security forces—due to their complicity with networks of organized crime, corruption and shifting loyalties—had significantly reduced the government's latitude and efficiency in dealing with the unfolding crisis. Fourth, the political nomenklatura was fragmented in several rivalling groups divided along political orientations, professional affiliations, ideology and regional origin. Finally, the events in 1990 and 1992 have produced master narratives on the cleavages and the origins of violence in the Tajik society, but a closer examination of the events reveal significant deviations from the master narrative and the inexorable contingency in the events. The following chapter starts with a closer look at the sequence of the events in the February riots in Dushanbe. Since both, the February 1990 events and the civil war, are frequently explained and understood as manifestations of conspiracies by foreign powers or hidden forces against the Tajik people and their independent statehood, a short excursus summarizes the most prevalent conspiracy theories surrounding the origins of the Tajik Civil War.

THE SEQUENCE OF EVENTS

In early 1990, tensions between the Armenian and Azeri population in Baku escalated into a violent pogrom against the Armenian population, which was eventually suppressed by a Soviet military intervention on 19 and 20 January. The pogrom resulted in the exodus of Armenians from Baku to other Soviet Republics. On 17 January, the USSR's Council of Ministers appealed for support from the union republics to provide housing for the Armenian refugees.[2] In early February, unconfirmed reports spread in Tajikistan, that Dushanbe would provide shelter for up to 3,000 refugees. While only a few dozen refugees actually came to Dushanbe and were in most cases hosted by their relatives, rumors spread quickly and were enriched with insinuations, suspicions and conspiracy theories. The accommodation of refugees was a highly contentious issue, in particular since adequate housing was in short supply in Dushanbe.[3] Neither the Central Committee nor the Council of Ministers deemed it necessary to inform the public in Dushanbe about the decree of the USSR's Council of Ministers on the refugee issue. This failure to communicate is widely considered a major catalyst for the unfolding events. Whether parts of the nomenklatura *intentionally* misinformed the public and manipulated civil associations, political activists and organized crime networks, however, remains a contentious question. Several sources report that representatives of the political elite intended to discredit rivals and the opposition on the eve of the elections to the Supreme Soviet scheduled for 25 February: "They intimidated the population, not to vote for those, who searched for a new path and who said something new."[4] Other versions, however, point out that the course of events damaged the reputation of Mahkamov, therefore his political adversaries were behind the unrest in Dushanbe. The following accounts look at the sequence of events, the main protagonists and the contingency that shaped the dynamics of the conflict.

Sunday, 11 February

In early February the atmosphere in Dushanbe got tense and the people were in anticipation of "something to happen."[5] The MVD reportedly concentrated OMON units in the city center and the KGB operatives were on high alert. In the early afternoon of February 11, a group of approximately 200–300 demonstrators gathered in front of the building of the Central Committee at the T-crossing of Lenin/Putovsky in central Dushanbe and demanded information concerning the Armenian refugees crisis.[6] Although Mahkamov's office announced to inform the demonstrators, nothing happened until the early evening and eventually Tūrağonzoda, whose *qoziyot* was not far from the square, spoke to the crowd and calmed down the situation. The protestors dispersed after a follow-up meeting was announced for the next day. Neither the memoirs nor the media coverage disclosed who actually organized the rally and called for a continuation of the protests fueling rumors about an involvement of the KGB.[7] None of the better known reformers and political activists, such as Būrī Karim, Otaxon Latifī, Mirbobo Mirrahim, Tohir Abduğabbor, Bozor Sobir and Nur Tabarov, were involved or took part in the first protests on 11 February.

Monday, 12 February

Despite an unusual cold weather, a few hundred protestors gathered from 10 am on at the crossing of Putovsky Street and Lenin Prospect. The number of demonstrators increased over the next hours and in the early afternoon several thousand people demanded accountability from Mahkamov on the Armenian refugee issue. The demonstration on 11 February had obviously mobilized political activists, university students and citizens of Dushanbe who now joined the rally in force.[8] The crowd waited for more than two hours in the cold for Mahkamov. Around 3:30 pm random skirmishes broke out between youth and MVD troops who fired warning shots into the air. Around 4 pm Mahkamov finally came out on the square surrounded by his KGB security detail. He briefly addressed the demonstrators but his appeal went unheard since there were no loud speakers. When the demonstrators showed increasing hostility, Mahkamov was immediately escorted back into the CC/CPT building.[9] After his retreat, OMON/MVD units surrounded the square and the situation escalated when they tried to disperse the protestors. Despite shots fired into the air, the crowd remained defiant and did not withdraw. At 5 pm, the security forces opened direct fire with life ammunition killing 6 and wounding 70.[10] Many eyewitnesses maintained that snipers on the surrounding buildings deliberately targeted the protestors with the intention to kill. Others remarked that the Dushanbe based OMON/MVD were neither equipped nor trained for containing a demonstration of this size and with the participation of violent protestors who exploited the situation and challenged the MVD.[11]

In the early evening, the situation deteriorated when criminal gangs—in many accounts intoxicated youth, racketeers (*reket*), hooligans, criminals or extremists—took to the streets depredating some 50 commercial shops, administrative buildings and two cinemas in central Dushanbe.[12] Rauf Saliev and his henchman Yaqub Salimov, who ran a criminal gang in the northern Vodasavod area of Dushanbe, exploited the situation or—as some assume— acted on behalf of elite representatives (either Nabiev, Huvaydulloev or Kenğaev) in order to undermine the reputation of Mahkamov. Saliev and Salimov selectively targeted emergency rooms in hospitals and stole the equipment.[13] At this point, the political demonstrators became "hostages of criminal elements"[14] as the Tajik media reported. The riots soon spread over the entire city and rioters targeted the small Armenian community in Dushanbe's western Zarafšon and No. 102 districts where several houses were burned down.[15]

The MVD was caught off guard and not able to suppress the disorder and at 6 pm the Politburo imposed emergency rule over Dushanbe. Since the commanding officer of 201st Motor Rifle Division (MRD) deployed in Dushanbe announced that the division would not interfere in the urban riots and remain neutral, Moscow decided to fly in reinforcements. Reportedly the Slavic officers of the 201st MRD had doubts about the loyalty of their Tajik rank and file.[16] Facing the decomposition of the local MVD, the distressed Politburo sanctioned the set-up of "internationalist" vigilante groups in Dushanbe's city districts to take "security" in their own hands—an unprecedented privatization of violence indicating the dramatic disintegration of the state in the Soviet periphery. Throughout the night, fighting and looting continued in several districts in Dushanbe. Although the militia arrested around 60 people including some "ringleaders," most were released the next day. Navğuvonov, the minister of interior, told TASS, that he was ordered to release them in order to calm down the situation; criminal proceedings, however, had been initiated by the prosecutor's office. The swift release of the perpetrators fueled the conspiracy theories regarding the complicity between the political leadership, the security forces and organized crime.[17]

Tuesday, 13 February

In the morning of 13 February, some 1,000 additional troops from the 103rd Guards Airborne Division arrived in Dushanbe with parts of the 15th KGB Special Forces Team from Tashkent. Moreover, Moscow dispatched Boris Pugo, the chairman of the CPSU's Internal Control Commission, to Dushanbe to advise the Central Committee on the handling of the crisis. Despite the state of emergency, thousands of demonstrators gathered again on the square in front of the Central Committee around 10 am in the morning. The military and MVD cordoned off administrative buildings in the center and tried to disperse the protestors. The protestors, however, remained defiant and gathered again on the square at 1:30 pm, this time to commemorate those who were killed and to protest against the government's indiscriminate use of force. The unprecedented violence had changed the nature of the demonstration and eclipsed the question of the Armenian refugees. Now reformist cadres and intellectuals joined the protest and demanded the resignation of Mahkamov, Pallaev and Hayoyev, the establishment of an investigative commission into the violence, the lift of the curfew, the withdrawal of the military and the release of those protestors held in custody.[18] The heterogeneous opposition realized the significance of the events and articulated their frustration over the political and social development. The agenda of the protestors varied and some called for the shutdown of industrial enterprises polluting the environment or demanded to tackle the unemployment in the TaSSR.[19] In the early afternoon, a group of 17 intellectuals, journalists and artists—among them Mehmon Baxtī, Olim Zarobekov, Bozor Sobir, Mirbobo Mirrahim, Tohir Abduğabbor, Askar Hakim, Safar Mastonzod, Mavčigul Ibodulloeva (the only woman in the group) and Būrī Karim—formed the 'People's Committee' to represent the interests of the protestors in negotiations with Mahkamov.[20] In the early evening, a meeting took place between Karim, who had been appointed chairman of the People's Committee, and Mahkamov, Pallaev, Hayoyev, Pugo and Vladimir Petkel', the chairman of the TaSSR's KGB. Emotions ran high during the negotiations but eventually the Politburo gave in and signed a protocol in which Mahkamov, Pallaev and Hayoyev agreed to resign. The 15th, 16th and 17th of February were declared days of public mourning and the MVD was ordered to re-establish security in Dushanbe. In return, the People's Committee suspended the demonstrations.[21] The protocol's content was immediately announced by sound trucks on the square, but Mahkamov, Pallaev and Hayoyev prohibited a TV and radio broadcast since they insisted that—in accordance with the TaSSR's constitution—the Plenum of the CC/CPT should accept their resignation first. Mahkamov obviously wanted to gain time and unintentionally Karim had maneuvered himself to a precarious situation: As the deputy chairman of the Council of Ministers, he would become de jure acting chairman of the Council of Ministers after Hayoyev's resignation—and therefore the head of the Tajik government.[22] The CC/CPT as well as the state media immediately portrayed the events in the Soviet elocution as a coup d'état instigated by the "careerist" Būrī Karim.

Wednesday, 14 February

Throughout the night and during the day, the security forces and the neighborhood vigilante groups were able to re-establish order over central parts of Dushanbe. Only in western districts sporadic violence flared up. As agreed in the protocol, no further demonstration took place and in the afternoon, the 16th extraordinary Plenum of the CC/CPT convened in Dushanbe. Unsurprisingly, the Plenum rejected the resignation of Mahkamov, Pallaev and Hayoyev without any discussion and instead formally approved all decisions taken by Mahkamov during the crisis as justified and appropriate. The 'People's Committee' was disbanded and Karim was to be subpoenaed by the disciplinary committee of the CPT.[23] Pallaev ordered the establishment of an inquiry commission of 15 members who should investigate the events in Dushanbe between 11 and 14 February.

Thursday, 15 February

On the morning of 15 February the Plenum continued and the nomenklatura had apparently recovered from the unexpected events. In the session, the CPT's leadership unleashed their wrath on the "People's Committee" calling them a group of extremists, bandits, riff-raff or aggressive rabble. Only three CC/CPT members, Hikmatullo Nasriddinov, Abdullo Očilov and Saidmurod Taġoev, spoke out in favor of the "Committee of the 17" and lauded their efforts to calm down the situation.[24] Nasriddinov criticized the many violations against the constitution by both, the government and the opposition, during the confrontation in the last days and called on a return to the rule of law. He criticized those who claimed to knew about the impending crisis or were informed by the KGB that they did not act to prevent he events from happening.[25] Nonetheless, the government portrayed the burgeoning opposition as accomplices of criminals and hooligans who were ultimately responsible for the disorder and violence.[26]

The Aftermath

According to the MVD, 24 people had been killed (21 by bullet wounds), 74 people had received gunshot wounds and 590 people had been hospitalized during the riots on 12 and 13 February 1990.[27] The General Procurator brought charges against 300 individuals of whom 105 were eventually sentenced to prison terms. Moreover, the General Procurator opened criminal proceedings against 20 "ringleaders" of the riots, but most of the charges were later dismissed.[28] Despite the malicious media campaign and the crackdown on reformist cadres, the Soviet leadership could not disregard the popular outrage. On 17 February, Boris Pugo met with representatives of the intelligentsia, the civil associations and the *qoziyot*. In an interview with Radio Dushanbe Pugo conceded: "A great deal has to be changed in the development of the economy. A lot has to be improved in the ecological sphere. We have to have considerably greater respect and understanding for culture."[29] The discussion with the civil society and reformist CPT cadres turned out to be cosmetic and Mahkamov was not ready for substantial reforms.

Since Mahkamov did not assume the political responsibility for the events, many urban mid-ranking cadres turned away from the CPT. Roziq remarked that "in case Mahkamov ordered to open fire, he had no right to remain in office, and even if Petkel' ordered to open fire, Mahkamov still had the political responsibility and forfeited his right to rule."[30]

For now, Mahkamov could rely on the conservativeness of the Communist Party. With its political monopoly and access to the state's resources, the CPT was able to manipulate the Supreme Soviet elections in February and convene a parliament in which the majority of deputies came from conservative rural constituencies. These deputies were overwhelmingly hostile toward Gorbachev's Glasnost reforms. Many CPT Deputies, however, did not genuinely support Mahkamov and instead preferred his indecisiveness and defensive political maneuvers to a more vigorous and audacious reformist alternative.[31]

The urban intelligentsia and civil associations were not so easily to intimidate. On 18 February, Gulruxsor Safieva, Bozor Sobir, Būrī Karim, Hoğī Akbar Tūrağonzoda and Davlat Xudonazar organized a rally with some 15,000 participants at the Koxi Borbat in Dushanbe.[32] The opposition and civil society made a concerted effort to counter the Politburo's defamation campaign. Davlat Xudonazar, who had just returned from the Berlin International Film Festival and who was well connected with the Moscow/St. Petersburg Glasnost and dissident circles, emerged as a figurehead of the urban opposition asserting the opposition's commitment to democracy and Glasnost under the Soviet slogan of Peoples' Friendship.[33] Tūrağonzoda, who had briefly appeared on the Putovsky/Lenin Prospect on 11 February but was not a member of the "Committee of the 17," distinguished himself not only as a religious authority but a veritable Tajik intellectual-cum-nationalist. In a pointed speech he addressed the contentious religious question with an anti-colonial tone:

> The Politburo even said: we should build instead of 60 mosques 30 theatres (as Maryam Isoeva[34] did so many times), while now the three theatres we have [in Dushanbe] have no visitors due to the non-existing program. Muslim brothers! Our youth! The moment you return to your own language and to your own Persian-Arabic alphabet, that moment you regain your pride and you will be rewarded. And then you will enjoy the spiritedness, the education and the instruction from the mosques. [...] But I do not want to enter politics. Politics are dirty (*iflosī*), politics are lying! The Caliph Umar said the politics are dirty. These are historical words.[35]

With his speech on 18 February, Tūraǧonzoda reached out to the secular intelligentsia and the reformist cadres in the CPT and established himself as a key political figure—including the coquetry regarding the "dirty politics" he does not want to enter—and eventually he shaped Tajikistan's politics in this tumultuous time more than many other politicians.[36]

The February events marginalized and divided the small group of reformist cadres. Nur Tabarov, the minister of education and a close associate of Būrī Karim, cooperated with the Procurator's office and incriminated Karim by confirming that the latter had indeed prepared for a coup d'état prior to the February events.[37] Karim expressed his deep disappointment in a very personal tone and concluded that "politics are dirty, there is no place in politics for friendship and companionship."[38] As a result, both reformers withdrew from politics and in the evolving crisis of 1991/92 neither Karim nor Tabarov should play a decisive role. Although Moscow did not reprimand the incumbent nomenklatura, the center also did not express its unconditional support for the Tajik leadership. For Sohibnazar and others it became clear that Moscow was not capable and—importantly—not *willing* anymore to intervene and invest in the restructuring of domestic politics in the TaSSR.[39]

After the elections in February, the Presidium of the Supreme Soviet established an inquiry commission headed by Safaralī Kenǧaev, Bedilxon Odinaev (Procurator at the Juvenile Court in Dushanbe), and Yusifxon Ishoqī (the Rector of the Medical University in Dushanbe). The 15 members of the commission were distinguished members of the CPT, some of them deputies in the Supreme Soviet of the Soviet Union or the TaSSR and represented the "ideal" composition of the Soviet society, including women, national minorities, blue-collar workers, kolkhoz brigadiers and intellectuals.[40] Then, Kenǧaev was considered a promising politician who aptly mastered the different discourses of reform, nationalism, Glasnost and Perestroika. Even democratic deputies in the Supreme Soviet, such as Sohibnazar, supported Kenğaev: "We all thought that Kenğaev was the right person for the commission since he was a lawyer and an honest person... indeed, he knew the law well, but he had his own agenda."[41] The commission eventually came to the conclusion that the Armenian refugee issue was only a pretext for the protests:

> The events of February 12 through 14 were not spontaneous. They were pre-saged by serious economic and ecological difficulties, a low living standard, scarcity of land and residential facilities, inequitable development of regions, lack of attention to the needs of the people and to the preparation of local cadres, parochialism and inadequate use of cadres, increasing unemployment, violation of human rights laws. One can also state with certainty that these conditions were deftly exploited by politically ambitious elements, religious leaders, infor-mal organizations, as well hooligans and criminal elements, This was clearly shown by the attempt to use unconstitutional methods to unseat the head of government and replace him with B[ūrī].B. Karim[ov].[42]

The report insinuated complicity between radical Islamists and the nascent nationalist movement of Rastoxez. Various *imom-xatib* were implicated in instigating the local population against the Armenians.[43] The commission also explicitly addressed the inefficiency of the MVD and KGB insinuating a compliance with networks of organized crime. The report called on the exten-sion of competences for the procurator's office and a renewed ideological campaign diminishing the influence of religious authorities in the Tajik soci-ety. While drafting the report, Kenğaev certainly had his own career in mind by applying a mixture of Perestroika/Glasnost demands (rule of law, control of KGB and MVD) with Soviet techniques of self-incrimination.

Although none of the eyewitness statements and memoirs mentioned the involvement of Islamic activists, the Soviet media readily adopted the CPT's narrative: The news agency Interfax reported about Islamists who harassed unveiled women and Moscow's Television Service depicted the riots as an indication for the "Central Asian Syndrome," namely "Islam, or, more accurately, what sort of influence the religion has on social processes in Tajikistan."[44] In fact, none of the *harakat* activists, such as Nurī, Usmon, Qiyomiddin or Himmatzoda took part in the protest. Only Tūrağonzoda briefly addressed the protestors on 11 February in order to calm them down. Apparently, the Communist Party nomenklatura adopted the Islamist narra-tive *after* the events. Sohibnazar, for instance, expressed his astonishment after a conversation with Ġoibnazar Pallaev in late March 1990 who suddenly blamed the "mullos" for the February events.[45]

The February 1990 riots in Dushanbe took place in the context of increas-ing political and social tensions in the later USSR. The TaSSR's unpopular and unimaginative nomenklatura faced growing opposition from within the CPT and by civil-society associations with a nationalist agenda focusing on language and culture, uneven development, colonial dependencies and democratic reform. Certainly the developments in the Baltic Republics were a clarion call for the Tajik civil society. Simultaneously, inner-elite conflicts and contingent personal animosities compounded the complex political and societal situation. The social and economic crisis aggravated the grievances in the Tajik society. Adolescents—graduates from universities and polytechnic institutes—were disproportionately affected by the economic contraction and the rumors about the Armenian refugees finally provided the pretense for public protest and violence. Urban criminal gangs exploited the situation and contributed to the dramatic escalation on 12 February while the republican law enforcement agencies were not able to control the demonstration and defuse the situation without violence. The incompetence of the political nomenklatura and their rejection of any political responsibility for the events deepened the political divides and made the different factions—communists, reformers, democrats and Islamic activists—increasingly intransigent and irreconcilable. Finally, the February events highlight a pervasive feature of Tajik political and historical narratives: Almost all memoirs and recollections of the February events operate with conspiracies by the omnipotent Soviet state, an ominous "third force" or agents of a foreign power.

"BLOODY BAHMAN" AND THE CIVIL WAR AS A CONSPIRACY

Conspiracy theories are ubiquitous in contemporary Tajikistan and many Tajik politicians, intellectuals and academics refer to conspiracies (in Tajik *dasisa* or *tavtea*) in explaining the trials and tribulations of modern Tajik history. Without exception, all autobiographies under consideration blame foreign powers for the outbreak of the civil war and the official Tajik historiography comes to the conclusion that "it is unconcealable, that foreign forces were involved in these events, as they contributed to the outbreak of the Civil War."[46] While research on form, function as well as political and societal implications of conspiracy theories in the United States and the Middle East has significantly increased in recent years, the related discussion in the post-Soviet and Soviet space has only recently commenced.[47]

Sunstein and Vermeule conclude in their widely recognized definition that "a conspiracy theory can generally be counted as such if it is *an effort to explain some event or practice by reference to the machinations of powerful people, who attempt to conceal their role (at least until their aims are accomplished)*."[48] Mark Fenster points out that conspiracy theories should not be merely considered as pathology or paranoia, but understood in their particular political and social context "as a form of hyperactive semiosis in which history and politics serve as reservoirs of signs that demand (over) interpretation, and that signify, for the interpreter, far more than their conventional meaning."[49] Drawing on Fenster and others, John Heathershaw postulates, "conspiracy theories should be understood as a form of performance. The concept of performativity suggests two functions of conspiracy theorizing: *constative* (or instrumental) and *performative* (or constitutive)."[50] According to Heathershaw, conspiracy theories "serve as means to rally support [...] and to condemn opponents as part of a conspiracy [...] and in turn, to delegitimate the opposition by branding *their* beliefs as paranoid. In this respect, both conspiracy and conspiracy theory frequently serve as political strategies, not pathologies."[51]

The conspiracy theories prevalent in Tajikistan owe their origins to Russian and Soviet narratives, however many Tajik politicians have been exposed to conspiracy theories omnipresent in the Islamic Republic of Iran. Tūrağonzoda, Yusuf and several others spent years of exile in Iran and wrote parts of their memoirs there. In contrast to Soviet narratives, Iranian conspiracy theories—in particular those nourished by the Islamic government—focus less on the "deep state," but through a post-colonial lens on foreign powers, their "real" sovereigns, the Freemasons and Zionists, and above all their local agents labeled as "servants of imperialism" (*noukarān-e este'mar*) or the "Fifth Column" (*sontūn-e pangom*).[52] Iranian conspiracy theories have influenced Tūrağonzoda, who reproduced a conspiracy narrative, which had been prominently proliferated by Ayatollah Khomeini. According to Khomeini, the colonial powers established the discipline of Oriental studies with the intention to subvert Islam. Western Orientalists and their colonized henchmen in the Orient henceforth misinterpreted the Koran and misrepresented Islam in the Middle East undermining the intellectual and spiritual consistency of Islam by introducing alien religious and political concepts to the Muslim Middle Eastern societies.[53] In a similar narrative, Tūrağonzoda maintained that Western Orientalists and their Freemason/Zionist accomplices "invented" the radical Islamic movement Hizb ut-Tahrir in order to defame Islam.[54]

However, a more thorough and comparative approach to conspiracy theories in the Middle East and post-Soviet Central Asia—as suggested by Ortmann and Heathershaw—is beyond the scope of the following discussion, which intends to provide an initial inventory of the main narratives and tropes in the context of the Tajik Civil War.[55]

"We All Know..."—Conspiracy Theories in Tajikistan

Most of the memoirs and interviews depicted the February events as carefully planned in advance and as a conspiracy either against the TaSSR's nomenklatura, the nascent civil society, the political opposition, the Islamic activists or the entire Tajik nation and statehood.[56] Qahhor Mahkamov described the February riots vaguely as instigated by a "conspiracy (*tavtea*) of a special group that benefited from the cause of the events,"[57] but neither specified the identity of the group's members nor how they actually benefited from the course of events. Davlat Usmon merely spoke about a "civil strife and revolt, which was instigated from above."[58]

Būrī Karim narrated the events as a meticulously planned conspiracy (*dasisa*) by the hardline CPT leadership to discredit the civil associations such as Rastoxez, the *harakat* or DPT in the run-up to the Supreme Soviet elections on 25 February 1990.[59] Karim was far from consistent in his narrative since he also related the events to rivalries within the CC/CPT, in particular between Hayoyev and Pallaev who competed for access to formal positions and resource allocation. Accordingly, Hayoyev and Pallaev orchestrated the demonstrations and the escalation in order to undermine Mahkamov's position within the TaSSR's political economy and to impair his relation with Moscow. At the same time, the "supporters of Glasnost and Tajikistan's true independence"[60] were too weak and too easy to manipulate in 1990 and therefore were made scapegoats in the unfolding elite conflict. Buškov and Mikul'skiy assumed in their account on criminal networks that Kenğaev (on behalf of Rahmon Nabiev) instructed the criminal gang of Rauf Saliev to exploit the situation and undermine the position of Mahkamov, however they did not provide any evidence for their assumptions.[61] Asliddin Sohibnazar and Rahim Mosalmoniyon depicted the February riots of 1990 in Dushanbe as a plot by the KGB against the Tajik opposition and not as an inner-elite rivalry: The KGB was concerned, that Rastoxez and the intellectual young *ulamo* could win the forthcoming election. Therefore the KGB circulated rumors about the Armenian refugees and orchestrated the riots for which they blamed the opposition.[62]

Even the official statement by the Central Committee of the Communist Party referred to "conspiracies of various political gamblers, adventures, riff-raff and criminals" which instigated the "horrible tragedy."[63] Even the Soviet press hinted at a KGB involvement in the riots.[64] An often-quoted source for the validity of the various conspiracies is the former KGB officer Abdullo Nazarov, a rather controversial figure in Tajikistan's recent history.[65] Nazarov reported that the KGB knew in advance about the demonstration and that plainclothes agents provocateur infiltrated the ranks of the protestors on 12 February chanting slogans such as "'down with Mahkamov' or 'long live Islam.'"[66] The involvement of the security structures in the riots has been adopted by the academic analysis as well; for instance, Niyazi concluded:

> Nevertheless there is evidence that the scenario had been planned by corrupt and ambitious apparatchiks in collaboration with operators of the underground

economy who were connected with criminal mafia groups. The leaders of the conspiracy recruited the help of a few radical *mullas* and secular opposition leaders.[67]

The role of the KGB, corrupt nomenklatura, Islamists or the "mafia" in the February events has been frequently reproduced by the Tajik media in the past years and is widely accepted by today's urban civil society. Many intellectuals and activists recognize the history of Tajikistan's national awakening and the political aspirations of the Glasnost period as fundamentally legitimate and positive. However, this perception is profoundly depreciated by the ambiguous interpretations of the February events and the outbreak of the civil war. To assume a carefully planned conspiracy behind the February riots provides a rationale behind the events and "explains" the lack of agency by the civil society activists in the events and why "things went wrong." Remarkably, these narratives simultaneously deny mullos, adolescents, and organized crime networks any agency—they are *sent, ordered* or *recruited* by the state/KGB/nomenklatura/foreign powers.[68] The reports and stories about KGB involvement often reflect very personal experiences of state surveillance and intrusion, which many Soviet citizens had made—therefore conspiracy theories are considered as plausible and often fall on fertile soil. The post-conflict government of Tajikistan has carefully cultivated prevalent conspiracy theories insinuating that the civil associations in the early 1990s were not prepared for the political change, did not respect the societal order and therefore "accidentally" contributed to the outbreak of the civil war.[69] This performative dimension corroborates Heathershaw's hypothesis that conspiracy theories constitute and reconstitute the patriarchal order in the Tajik society.[70]

A popular strategy of discussing the civil war in Tajikistan's media and public are insinuations and allusions pretending that there is a hidden "truth" behind the origins of the conflict. Phrases such as "we all know…" are frequently used insinuating a commonly shared knowledge without explicitly disclosing it. A good example is an article by S. Xaliliyon in the newspaper *Farağ* 2011. Xaliliyon analyzed the activities of Sangak Safarov describing his contingent role in the origins of the civil war, but suddenly he interrupted his balanced reflections and concluded that "the reasons for the Civil War were entirely different and all of us know the reasons and there is no need to further elaborate on this."[71] Post-conflict societies often prefer to suppress the commemoration of violence and the horrors of civil war—instead, peace and stability is conjured in the post-conflict rehabilitation—as in the case of post-conflict Tajikistan.[72]

Conspiracy theories have become pervasive to such an extent that Tajik politicians assume a hidden agenda behind almost every political issue. For instance, Sohibnazar, after rationally analyzing the reasons for adopting the "Law on the Tajik Language" in 1989, nonetheless concluded that "there is possibly another secrecy (*sirri digar*) behind it"[73] insinuating that the language law was a plot by the (Uzbek) KGB to divide the Tajiks and defame the Tajiks as xenophobic nationalists.

...the World According to Safaralī Kenğaev

Safaralī Kenğaev cultivated a multitude of different, often contradictory conspiracy theories and entire chapters in his memoirs are entitled with an alarming "conspiracy" (*dasisa*).[74] Kenğaev was an ideal type of the *homo sovieticus* who could quickly and performatively assimilate to changing discourses within the Soviet system—his mastery of different conspiracy theories indicates his flexibility as well.[75] Kenğaev did not only compose lengthily

Figure 3.1   Safaralī Kenğaev's Formula About the Origins of the Civil War in Tajikistan.

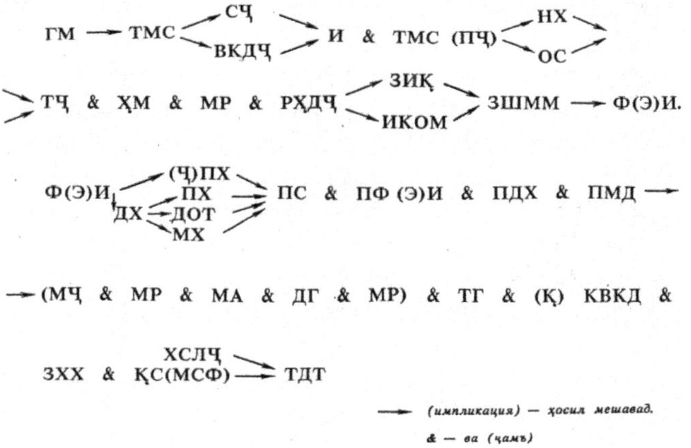

Note: Kenğaev maintains that there is a group of position seeking people (GM), who establish the political mafia (TMS) in order to control the state structure. They bring the state economy (SĞ) and the Ministry of Interior (VKDĞ) under their control. The Ministry of Interior reaches an agreement with the economic structures (I), by the uneven development and corruption, the people become dissatisfied (NX). The dissatisfaction leads to the establishment of civil associations (TĞ), political parties (HS), people's movements (HM) whilst political leaders are under the influence of the political mafia and racketeers (MR & RHDĞ). The situation weakens the law and officials (who are not corrupt) are dismissed (ZIQ & IKOM). Unregistered religious schools and mosques (ZŠMM) multiply in the country and fundamentalism (F) spreads. Supported by foreign countries (PX), foreign groups and experts actively working for a coup (DOTD & MX) and with access to domestic and foreign economic resources (PS, PF & PDX) as well as financial resources of the domestic mafia (PMD), the criminal mafia (MĞ), the journalist mafia (MR) and so forth in cooperation with the forces of the Ministry of Internal Affairs (KVKD) and Vahhobī groups, which had access to military equipment (XSLĞ), execute a Coup d'état (TDT).
Source: Kenğaev 1994: 200–201.

narratives on conspiracies, he also offered a mathematical formula on the origins of the civil war. The formula does not only indicate his disturbingly paranoid world-view, it also possesses a compelling simplicity, which fits into the socio-psychological analysis of conspiracy theories.[76]

The KGB and the "Deep State"

The conspiracy theories cultivated by Tajik politicians, intellectuals and journalists regarding the Tajik Civil War are often centered on the Soviet Union, Russia or Uzbekistan, which they portray as malicious and omnipotent actors undermining the sovereignty of Tajikistan in order to preserve the economic, political and social dependency and to preclude that the Tajiks regain their predetermined historical, cultural and political supremacy. Unsurprisingly, the Soviet KGB plays a prominent role in these conspiracy theories.

Sohibnazar offered the most detailed and elaborated background story on the omnipotent KGB and its role in the February events and the civil war: On an official trip for Gosplan to Moscow in 1989, Sohibnazar visited his acquaintances Irina and Andrej, who had left Dushanbe due to the increasing Tajik nationalism. Andrej insinuated that he is a KGB officer and told Sohibnazar, that he will send one of his former subordinates called "Mūso" (whose family, as it turned out, Sohibnazar knew well and who later becomes a well-known figure in Tajikistan) in order to warn Sohibnazar about negative developments in the TaSSR.[77] And indeed, Mūso visited Sohibnazar in late January 1990 and told him about the preparations and instructions he has received by unnamed superiors for the demonstrations:

> I know my duty. I need to come on 11 February with 15–20 young Mullo-faced villagers (*ǧavoni mullosurati dehotiro*) to the city [Dushanbe]. The majority of them need to be born in the Qarotegin Valley. They have to demand, that Mahkamov comes [from the building of the Supreme Soviet] out to them. [...] Somebody wants to incite the people from Qarotegin against the people from Kūlob and Leninobod in order to scare the Russians.[78]

The overall plot, Sohibnazar maintained, was designed to prevent free and fair elections to the Supreme Soviet and to provoke a Soviet (Russian) intervention. For Sohibnazar, 150 years of Russian colonial domination of Tajikistan was only part of a larger Russian plot to control other territories inhabited by Persian speakers, in particular Afghanistan and Iran. The Russians "feared the intellectual empire of the Tajik language,"[79] therefore they transformed the Tajiks to farmers and excluded the urban Tajik centers, Samarqand and Bukhara, from the TaSSR. "Mūso" visited him a second time on 10 February (a day before the first protests) with more details on the forthcoming events:

The big guys (*kalonho*) want something but it did not happen yet. [...] Perhaps a mullo is going to be killed, or a mullo kills somebody ... there will be a change. A coup! Mr. Asliddin, in case you know Tūraġonzoda, tell him not to come out tomorrow. Būrī Karim as well—the head of Gosplan. He should not join any group, he should not assume any function and he should not talk to anybody. [...] One guy gathers a group of prizefighters (*muštzūrho*) in Dushanbe. Some of them I saw yesterday. Rauf [Saliev] and Yaqub [Salimov], Halim and a few other guys were there. Yesterday they demanded that no Armenian refugee should come to Dushanbe, and there was something else I heard. The guys say that the wife of Ġoibnazar Pallaev is Armenian and that he hides Armenian refugees in his home. [...] It's a secret provocation. It's difficult to understand. The same day they [i.e Rauf Saliev & Yaqub Salimov] have brought a group of young men from Avul, Afġonī and Ispečak [western micro-districts of Dushanbe] to Putovsky market. They returned quickly but they [i.e. Saliev and Salimov] said they should come back tomorrow. They also gave them orders. They have to be ready tomorrow at the square close to the Central Committee. Tomorrow I have to go by car to the square but I have no idea what they want. [...] Everything is ready, booze and food, and other provisions, we even got money.[80]

Regardless of the validity, Sohibnazar's account is remarkably consistent and generates the imagination of authenticity: He imitated a colloquial spoken variation of Tajik, he mentioned key actors who were involved in the February events and he reflected self-critically on his decisions. In the course of his memoirs, he frequently returned to the KGB motif, mostly on the eve of important events. Thus the reference to the KGB provides an external authoritative discourse and verification: A few days before the presidential elections in November 1991, Sohibnazar traveled to Moscow and met his KGB informant who reviewed and explained—as an authoritative Russian colonial voice—the center's perception of the events in Tajikistan: First, the CPT's negative media campaign against Islamism and nationalism in Tajikistan had been successful and influenced Yeltsin's assessment of the situation (i.e., Yeltsin assumed Islamist forces behind the events in Tajikistan and therefore decided to support Nabiev); second, the democratic forces made a serious mistake by appointing a politician from Badaxšon (Xudonazar) since he alienated the population of Kūlob and ethnic Uzbeks; third, Nabiev had already agreed with Moscow and Tashkent on the shares in the aluminum smelter in Tursunzoda, the uranium enrichment plant in Xuġand and the HPP project of Roġun (thus indicating the "real" interests in Tajikistan); fourth, Xudonazar and the democratic opposition made a mistake by negotiating a Dushanbe-Karachi highway with Pakistan, since Russia considered Tajikistan in its immediate zone of economic and political influence and would not accept interference by a Muslim country. Finally, Sohibnazar's informant precisely predicted the outcome of the forthcoming presidential elections insinuating that the omnipotent KGB meticulously orchestrates political processes in Tajikistan.[81`]

Even activists in the *harakat* cultivated an ambivalent mystification of the KGB as an omnipresent and powerful organization. Zubaydullo Roziq stated that the KGB was powerful enough to intentionally dilute the normative teaching of Islam by introducing unlawful innovations (*bid'at*) undermining the intellectual consistency of the religion and disuniting the Muslim community in Tajikistan.[82] The implicit admiration for the KGB—a malignant organization of coercion and repression—is related to the ambivalence in a post-colonial setting: Despite the dominance of non-Central Asian nationalities among the KGB operatives, many Tajiks served in the KGB or the military GRU; therefore, both organizations were—equal to the technological, cultural and political "achievements" of the USSR—a source of pride and "ownership."

The Foreign Conspirer

Already during the civil war, the government in Dushanbe and the opposition in exile cultivated a narrative on the essential qualities of the Tajik people as cultivated, settled, sophisticated and—above all—peaceful.[83] Therefore it was considered impossible that Tajiks were responsible for the outbreak of violence. Instead, the war was portrayed as "imposed" (*tahmilī*) on the Tajik people by a malicious Other. Abdullo Nurī, the chairman of the UTO, unambiguously stated, "The insurgents who started the Civil War in our country were not Tajiks. The war was imposed on the people of Tajikistan from outside (*az birun tahmil šud*). Those who instigated the war have planned and prepared for it for years [...] they just waited for the right moment."[84] Tūrağonzoda likewise postulated in 1998 that the outbreak of the civil war was the result of "political conspiracies instigated by circles of foreign spies."[85] In 2013 he elaborated further on the origin of the foreign spies and asserted: "Our neighboring country understood that in case there would be democratic elections in Tajikistan, the results would not be to its satisfaction. I do not point out to Kyrgyzstan, Kazakhstan and Turkmenistan—they were not involved in the events in Tajikistan."[86] Tūrağonzoda explicated, that the Uzbek intelligence service knew about the deep division within the Tajik society in the late 1980s and manipulated individuals such as Haydar Šarifov or Safaralī Kenğaev who escalated the political conflict. Similar to Nurī or Tūrağonzoda, Kenğaev suspected foreign spies who taught the Tajiks the "killing of unarmed civilians, the cutting of a mother's belly, the crushing of children's heads, the skinning, the cutting of noses and ears, the pulling of fingernails and toenails, the cutting of eyes of living people, the filling of mouths with hot way [...], the killing and the merciless torture of people."[87]

Kenğaev's forceful Othering of his opponents—even dehumanizing them—is a pervasive feature of the conspiracy discourse and contributed to the vicious circle of irreconcilable violence and revenge. Sohibnazar—in the context of the Iranian Revolution in 1979 and the Soviet occupation of Afghanistan—tried to rationalize the perceived intervention by "foreign powers" and diagnosed a deep rooted fear among the United States and Russia of the "Empire of the Persian Language." The US policy toward Iran after 1979 and the Soviet/Russian ideas of Internationalism further divided the solidarity among the Persian-speaking people. The water resources of Tajikistan and the country's economic potential were the central reason for the Russian/US fears and secret plots in the region to undermine Tajikistan's independence and unity with Iran as well as Afghanistan.[88]

The Enemy within: The "Third Force"

Worse than conspiracies by foreign powers are conspiracies set in motion by local agents of foreign powers. Conspiracy theories often refer to an ominous "fifth column" (a term coined in the Spanish Civil War) as a clandestine group that is covertly operating against its "own" people on behalf of a foreign power. In Iran, the Farsi equivalent of the "fifth column," *sotūn-e panğom*, is widely used in conspiracy theories. In the Tajik context many refer in complex and contingent situations to an ominous "Third Force" (*quvvai seyum*). The Third Force is mostly characterized as local agents of a foreign/colonial power and therefore omnipotent and able to manipulate any event or actor. The "true" intentions of the Third Force remain vague but its activities intend to destabilize the political situation and undermine Tajikistan's independent statehood.[89] Yusuf frequently referred to a Third Force operating in Tajikistan, which was either supported by the Soviet KGB or by the USA.[90] For instance, he accused the US Embassy in Dushanbe of "running" the Abdulloğonov brothers Abdumalik and Abduğanī as US spies, albeit he failed to explain the USA's motivation for "running" them.[91] Likewise, he considered the presence of US and Russian diplomats at the 16th Session in Xuğand as clear evidence for their interference into internal affairs and concluded that the civil war in Tajikistan was a proxy war led by the USA and Russia against Islam and Iran.[92] Also Yusuf's antagonist, Kenğaev, insinuated that his enemies, Yusuf, Iskandarov and Tūrağonzoda were agents of the "Third Force" supported by the USA, who "blew the smoke of their Marlboro cigarettes (*dudi sigori 'Mal'boro'*) [...] into the face of their enemies."[93] Eventually, the exposure of secret plots and agents run by foreign powers becomes a convoluted affair in which the mere insinuation is sufficient to discredit opponents as the trope with the Marlboro cigarette demonstrates.

Causes and Consequences

Conspiracy theories profoundly influence the way the origins of the civil war in Tajikistan are addressed by Tajik political activists, the government, academia, journalists and religious authorities. What has not yet been explored sufficiently is how the public in Tajikistan perceives conspiracy theories in the post-conflict political economy of Tajikistan.[94] Incidental evidence—interviews and personal conversations—suggests that conspiracies fall on fertile ground and are part of the daily discursive reproduction of what is perceived as "reality." The tensions in the Qarotegin Valley between 2008 and 2010, the conflict in GBAO 2012, the conflict in the Ukraine 2014 and the ban of the IRPT in the wake of Hoǧī Holim's defection in 2015 are often portrayed by the government as parts of a larger conspiracy. Heathershaw's hypothesis on the performative dimension of conspiracy points out to an important function:

> Conspiracy theories are a form of political discourse which purportedly subverts the existing order in the constative sense (making specific claims against the establishment) while, in reality, normalizing the status quo in the performative sense (deploying and reproducing the prevailing political ideas).[95]

As for the Tajik Civil War, the prevalent conspiracy theories have contributed to the irreconcilable polarization of the society. Abrahamian concluded for Iran that conspiracy theories have created paranoia and mistrust in the political field and severely undermined the development of political pluralism in Iran and the ability to compromise and build coalitions.[96] As for Tajikistan, conspiracy theories, in particular tropes such as the "Third Force" and the Othering of the opponent (and sometimes even allies), have contributed to a climate of mistrust: Throughout 1992 none of the opposing fractions, the Popular Front, the Government of National Reconciliation or the National Salvation Staff could built lasting coalitions, instead they were permanently disrupted by infighting and discord. In the context of the Tajik Civil War, conspiracy theories are discourses, which try to reduce the contingency in the developments and provide a structure as well as determinism for the events. Most of the conspiracy theories were narrated by activists and politicians who had at some point of the evolving conflict lost influence on the rapid political disintegration. Therefore, conspiracy theories are a narrative strategy to rationalize their authors' failure (and their agency panic) and to acquit them of any responsibility for the outbreak of the civil war. Not their personal shortcomings or mistakes were responsible for the failure, but omnipresent and omnipotent hidden forces.

THE ELECTIONS TO THE SUPREME
SOVIET 25 FEBRUARY 1990

Until 1990, elections to the Supreme Soviet for a five-year legislative period had been a carefully orchestrated affair: The CPT would appoint one loyal candidate per constituency and the elections would not result in any unpleasant surprises. The 1989 draft Election Law intended to change the system gradually in order to familiarize the "common people (*mardumi oddī*) with politics and introduce justice and democracy"[97]—that is, a genuine participation and political competition. If this law was implemented thoroughly, Sohibnazar concluded, the best representatives of the people were elected. However, the Politburo did not approve the draft and passed a restrictive law benefitting the incumbent elites and the people faced again the usual candidates from the administrative and economic institutions. And even Pallaev reminded Sohibnazar, that he should not forget "that it was the party [CPT] that made us human (*moro odam kardaast*), and the party decides whom she will give the bridle of the state."[98]

The elections to the 12th Convocation of the Supreme Soviet of the TaSSR were nonetheless the first somehow competitive elections with 1,043 candidates running for the 230 seats. While in some constituencies only one candidate registered, in other constituencies up to 17 candidates competed against each other.[99] Only 12 days after the Dushanbe riots, the campaign and elections were conducted under the state of emergency and the CPT resorted to its administrative resources and concerted propaganda campaign discrediting the nascent opposition. The KGB summoned opposition candidates and intimidated them with fabricated accusations.[100] Unsurprisingly, CPT cadres won 223 out of 230 seats. Three seats went to representatives of the registered religious personnel, Hoğī Akbar Tūrağonzoda (Kofarnihon), Hadyatulloh Odilov (Čorkūh/Isfara) and Haydar Šarifov (Kūlob). Only four democratic reformers entered the Supreme Soviet: Asliddin Sohibnazar, Tohir Abduğabbor, Gulruxsor Safī and Bozor Sobir. The democratic candidates portrayed themselves as nationalist politicians who know about the daily grievance of the "common" people, that is, the failing infrastructure, the non-transparent privatization of public property, scarcity of supplies and food, and the rule of law.[101] Some 20 deputies, among them Safaralī Kenğaev, Abdulloh Habibov, Xolmahmad Azimov, Nurulloh Huvaydulloev, Nurališoh Nazarov and Narzulloh Dūstov, were considered as reformist deputies with some respect for political rights and a multiparty system.[102] The marginal representation of reformist and democratic candidates in the Supreme Soviet was not the only significant outcome of the elections: The gender ratio and ethnic composition dramatically shifted to a predominately male-Tajik representation: In the 12th Convocation, only 9 deputies (or 4%) were women compared to 36% in the 11th Convocation (1985–1990) and only 15% of the deputies were non-Tajiks (29 Uzbeks, 5 Russians and one Kyrgyz). The male and ethnic Tajik dominance had a significant impact on the parliamentary debates and the political agenda in the Supreme Soviet, as we shall see in the following chapters.

Finally, the Supreme Soviet had not been transformed into a professional parliament. The elected deputies received an expense allowance but remained in their previous occupation, mostly positions in the government, administration and collective farms or combines. This system reinforced the deputies' dependencies on the Soviet institutions. The opposition repeatedly demanded the introduction of a full-time professional parliament increasing independence of the elected deputies and enabling candidates outside the administrative structures to run for office. After independence in September 1991, the Supreme Soviet unexpectedly emerged as the key political institution to facilitate the transition to an independent nation state. Eventually, the composition of the Supreme Soviet contributed to the failure of this transition, the polarization of the Tajik society and descent into violence in 1992. Nonetheless, Ibrohim Usmonov is regrettably right when he concludes that the February 1990 elections were the most democratic parliamentary elections in Tajikistan yet.[103]

The 12th Convocation of the Supreme Soviet

The first session of the 12th convocation of the TaSSR's Supreme Soviet did not contribute to a stabilization of the political situation, in particular since Mahkamov and the CC/CPT were not ready to assume responsibility for the February events. Prior to the first session, Mahkamov had a modified regional representation in the top echelons of the TaSSR in mind: The Communist Party's first secretary (Mahkamov himself) was traditional from Leninobod, the chairman of the Council of Ministers from Kūlob and the ministry of interior would be given to a representative from Badaxšon. Additionally, the Leninobodī faction would appoint the mayor of Dushanbe as the deputy chairman of the KGB.[104] Already in 1989, Tūraǧonzoda had been appointed *qozikalon*, the highest office among the registered *ulamo*. Traditionally, the *qozikalon* had been from the Fergana Valley and affiliated to the Naqšbandiyya order; Tūraǧonzoda instead was from the Hisor valley and affiliated to the Qaderiyya (see below). However, Tūraǧonzoda's appointment in 1989 was less controversial, since nobody expected that the young *qozikalon* would transform the office and emerge as one of the key political figures in 1991.

In early 1990 the appointment of the Supreme Soviet's chairman, formally the second highest office, became a contentious issue. Since 1984, Ġoibnazar Pallaev (GBAO) had been chairman of the Supreme Soviet and he apparently expected to be re-elected on the first session of the Supreme Soviet. But Mahkamov intended to replace him with Qadriddin Aslonov, a CPT deputy from Ġarm. Mahkamov's initiative soon caused wider disruptions since several deputies of the CPT, among them general prosecutor Huvaydulloev and Kenġaev, temporarily supported the small democratic group of deputies in their demand for a radical change of the leadership (including the resignation of Mahkamov). But in March 1990 the majority of deputies did not want to destabilize the situation further and blocked any substantial discussion. Pallaev—reportedly caught by surprise by the initiative of Mahkamov—was not ready to resign without a fight. He challenged Mahkamov's plans in the Supreme Soviet and announced his candidacy for re-election to the post of chairman of the Supreme Soviet against Mahkamov's candidate Qadriddin Aslonov. Apparently, several deputies, such as Kenġaev, Huvaydulloev and Sohibnazar had encouraged him to declare his candidacy.[105]

When Šarof Mahmudov, the chairman of the Central Election Committee, inaugurated the first session of the 12th Convocation on 12 April 1990, the atmosphere in the Supreme Soviet had changed significantly after decades of totalitarian rule by the CPT. However, as Sohibnazar explicated, it was not the atmosphere of a democratic change or transparency, but of tense confrontation as if "wolf and lamb were put in one place but it was not clear who would eat whom. Deceit and tricks, provocation and conspiracy dominated the Supreme Soviet."[106] Mahkamov's election to the chairman of the Presidium was supposed to pass without any discussion, but the opposition took the opportunity to address the February events and accused Mahkamov of not taking over the political responsibility. Many CPT deputies were outraged by Sobir's accusation and protested loudly against the accusations but Sobir remained defiant and retorted:

> If you do not have the strength to listen to me, a deputy of the Supreme Soviet, how will you be able to listen to the workers and farmers? How will you behave yourself among them? You, as students of Lenin, do you think you act in the way of Lenin, if you protect Q. Mahkamov, who is the main person responsible for the February events, and who has not the truth on his side?[107]

Sohibnazar supported Sobir in the discussion, citing Sobir's poem *Imsol* adding that "the martyrs of Šahidon Square will not forgive you."[108] Sohibnazar reserved his intervention in the Supreme Soviet session for a harsh validation of the dramatic economic situation in the TaSSR. Over decades, Sohibnazar pointed out, Moscow had spent billions of rubles subsidies for the TaSSR and still villages are without water and electricity, schools and hospitals are in disrepair. As the former head of Gosplan and first secretary of the CC/CPT, Mahkamov had been more than 20 years in leading positions and should therefore assume the responsibility for the situation. Eventually Sohibnazar nominated Pallaev as candidate for the chairman of the Supreme Soviet against Aslonov. In the crucial vote, Pallaev reached a succès d'estime with 73 (out of 230) votes.[109] The majority of deputies were not ready for substantial changes yet and Kenğaev observed that

> [t]he deputies in the Supreme Soviet were divided into two groups regardless of their ethnicity (*millat*), region (*mahal*) or networks (*mansubiyat*). First, those who supported Mahkamov—CPT cadres and senior administration officials. Second, deputies from the democratic block (Democratic Party, *qoziyot*, the people's association "Rastoxez") and deputies who had been members of the CPT and occupied administrative positions as well, but who did not respect the Q. Mahkamov administration and who supported democratic ideas, a democratic and secular system of the state as well the rule of law, and who supported R. Nabiev even if they had no relationship with the DPT, the *qoziyot* or Rastoxez. I [Kenğaev] considered myself as a supporter of the second group. But I have to repeat that I and many of the people's deputies had no idea about the revolutionary plans of the opposition.[110]

Mahkamov eventually prevailed and prepared the stage for the next chapter.

THE PRESIDENTIAL APPOINTMENT

The February 1990 constitutional amendments, which abolished the monopoly of the Communist Party, changed the architecture of political institutions in the TaSSR and necessitated a formal change to a presidential system. The first secretary of the CC/CPT was now (at least theoretically) only an office in one of the political parties and the office of the president was established ostensibly independent from the CPT.[111] After the contested election of the chairman of the Supreme Soviet, Mahkamov and his supporters were concerned that Mahkamov would not win nation-wide elections and therefore preferred his discreet appointment or acclamation by the Supreme Soviet.[112] Mahkamov's manipulations in the Pallaev affair had provoked frictions within the CPT, in particular deputies and cadres from the influential agro-industrial complex had been alienated by the dismissal of Pallaev.[113] Unexpectedly Mahkamov faced a rival in the competition for the presidential appointment from his own regional constituency Leninobod: Rahmon Nabiev. Encouraged by an odd

informal alliance of his networks in the agro-industrial complex, Perestroika
supporters, and the fledging DPT, a campaign unfolded prior to the scheduled session of the Supreme Soviet portraying Nabiev as a genuine reformer
and advocate of Tajik nationalism.[114] Yusuf and Sobir even campaigned for
Nabiev in the south and were briefly arrested in Qūrġonteppa. Mahkamov's
allies initiated a smear campaign portraying Nabiev as an adventurer with
dubious intentions. On 22 November 1990 a heated discussion unfolded in
the Central Committee and among the deputies of the Supreme Soviet on the
question whether the president should be either elected by Presidium of the
Supreme Soviet, by the 230 deputies of the Supreme Soviet or by the people
in nation-wide elections. The debate on the presidential appointment got even
more passionate with the discussion on the candidates. Senior CPT deputies,
such as Moyonšo Nazaršoev, called for an acclamation of Mahkamov without
a vote since Mahkamov epitomizes

> honesty and honor (*nangu namus*), commitment for economic progress, science
> and civilization, knowledge and art. He relentlessly strives to improve the liv-
> ing conditions of our people observing the principles of internationalism to the
> benefit of all nationalities. [...] A president should be compassionate with the
> common people, humble, confident, a sanguine person and internationalist, in
> short: Qahhor Mahkamovič Mahkamov.[115]

Those who favored nation-wide elections formed a rather unusual alliance of deputies particularly in the light of the later events: Bozor Sobir,
Tohir Abduġabbor, Narzullo Dūstov, Tūraġonzoda, Sohibnazar, Kenġaev and
Haydar Šarifov—archenemies less than a year later—were all calling for
nation-wide elections of the president regardless of regional provenance or
professional affiliation.

The first critical intervention against Mahkamov came from the popular
people's artist of the TaSSR, the singer and composer Ġūrabek Murodov, who
criticized Mahkamov for his incompetent handling of the February events.
Sohibnazar remarked that the February events cannot be undone and that
Mahkamov is not the person who can bring peace for the nation. Nasriddinov
similarly asked Mahkamov why he had never assumed the political responsibility for the February events and continued with a highly critical analysis
of Mahkamov's economic policy.[116] Narzullo Dūstov (who later became
Nabiev's vice president) expressed his regret that there were no nation-wide
presidential elections, which clearly shows the deputies' fear of the people's
will. The president should be the unifying symbol of the nation, like Niyazov
in Turkmenistan or Karimov in Uzbekistan, who united their nations through
the process of elections in March 1990.[117]

The question, *who* should elect the first president, remained contested.
While the opposition and CPT officials from rural Tajikistan demanded a

popular vote, the majority of deputies in the Supreme Soviet eventually decided on an election by the Supreme Soviet: Out of 220 deputies present 206 voted for the election of the president by the deputies on the Supreme Soviet, 3 abstained from voting and 11 deputies favored general elections.[118] Mahkamov had closed his ranks and was elected president of the TaSSR and retained his position as first secretary of the CC/CPT. In the crucial vote in the early evening of 22 November, Nabiev received respectably 89 votes while Mahkamov was elected with 131 votes.[119] The heated debate in the Supreme Soviet revealed serious discordance among the CPT deputies in the Supreme Soviet. Moreover, the competences of the presidential office were only tenuously specified in the amendments to the 1978 TaSSR's constitution generating further tensions in the months to come.

While the deputies in the Supreme Soviet were elected in a process, which required some public mobilization and was to a limited extent competitive, Mahkamov's accession was considered by Dushanbe's Glasnost circles as orchestrated by the CPT to preserve its power. Since the Supreme Soviet gained political weight in1991, the competition for and legitimacy of political positions further strained the inner-elite relations.[120] According to Nasriddinov, the creation of the presidential office and the coeval suspension of Article 6 of the TaSSR's constitution—abolishing the monopoly of the CPT—accelerated the dismantling of the state structures, Mahkamov and his entourage systematically weakened the state and bypassed the political institutions.[121] Nasriddinov considered the precipitant appointment of Mahkamov for president as "the first reversal for the establishment of Tajikistan's statehood (*davlatdorī*)."[122] The opposition, the DPT and Rastoxez, reacted with a ten days hunger strike—an unprecedented political statement in Tajikistan.[123] Nabiev's defeat against the unpopular and colorless Mahkamov paradoxically increased his reputation among the urban intelligentsia (who fiercely opposed him a year later). In early 1991, Nabiev—mostly through Dūstov and Kenǧaev—cultivated ties to the opposition *and* disgruntled CPT cadres who disapproved of Mahkamov's administration until August 1991 preparing his "return."[124]

NOTES

1. Translation from Tajik: "This year... / In the elections to the people's deputies / instead of the people, / bullets casted the vote, / which made the Communist Party / remain on its bloody seat. / This year... / the year of mendacious poets, / the year of mendacious academics, / the year of mendacious rulers. / The image of the city, in its face a black wind, / except for the image of a lie, / nothing stays with us..." Sobir's poetry is cited by Š. Suhayl, "Bahmanmoh—oǧozi šikasti režimi pūsida?

[Bahmanmoh—the Beginning of the Collapse of the rotten Regime?]." On: http://www.faraj.tj/life/1890-ba1203manmo1203-o1171ozi-shikasti-rezhimi-p1263sida.html, Accessed February 4, 2014. Bozor Sobir kindly gave his permission to reproduce his poetry here.

    2. See Michael Croissant, *The Armenia-Azerbaijan conflict: Causes and implications* (Westport: Praeger, 1998), 25–56.

    3. Sohibnazar, *Subhi 1*, 76; Karim, *Faryodi*, 92–93. According to the statistical data, the housing situation in the TaSSR was worst among the 15 union republics of the USSR, in 1989 only 58% of the USSR average standard (IMF, *Study*, Vol. 1, 233).

    4. Karim, *Faryodi*, 150.

    5. Sohibnazar, *Subhi 1*, 73–76.

    6. Yūsuf, *Tāǧīkestān*, 67; Nasriddinov, *Tarkiš*, 68.

    7. Karim, *Faryodi*, 95.

    8. Usmonov, *Ta'rixi siyosii*, 29.

    9. Karim, *Faryodi*, 96; Yūsuf, *Tāǧīkestān*, 71.

    10. Karim, *Faryodi*, 95; Helsinki Watch, *Conflict*, 42.

    11. FBIS-SOV-90–032, 15 February 1990, 67–69.

    12. FBIS-SOV-90–032, 15 February 1990, 65–73; FBIS-SOV-90–033, 16 February 1990, 53–62.

    13. FBIS-SOV-90–32, 15 February 1990, 72.

    14. FBIS-SOV-90–034, 20 February 1990, 74.

    15. Yūsuf, *Tāǧīkestān*, 71.

    16. FBIS-SOV-90–034, 20 February 1990, 71; Karim, *Faryodi*, 96.

    17. FBIS-SOV-90–033, 16 February 1990, 60–61.

    18. Karim, *Faryodi*, 99; FBIS-SOV-90–032, 15 February 1990, 65–73.

    19. FBIS-SOV-90–032, 15 February 1990, 69.

    20. Karim, *Faryodi*, 100 and 106–107; Nasriddinov, *Tarkiš*, 71–74. The committee was named "People's Association (*sozmoni mardumī*)," however in the press and other accounts the committee was also labelled "Committee of the 17" or "Provisional Committee."

    21. Karim, *Faryodi*, 106–107.

    22. See Osimī, *Enziklopediyai*, Vol. 8, 583–584.

    23. Karim, *Faryodi*, 109–112; FBIS-SOV-90–034, 20 February 1990, 55, 63.

    24. Karim, *Faryodi*, 118.

    25. Nasriddinov, *Tarkiš*, 88–89.

    26. FBIS-SOV-90–033, 16 February 1990, 57.

    27. FBIS-SOV-90–034, 20 February 1990, 62. Karim (*Faryodi*, 90–91 and 130–131) lists 24 fatalities, Ayubzod maintains 30 civilians were killed, S. Ayubzod, *Sad rangi sad sol. Toǧikiston dar qarni bistum* (Prague: Post Skriptum Imprimatur, 2002), 241.

    28. FBIS-SOV-90–034, 20 February 1990, 78.

    29. FBIS-SOV-90–034, 20 February 1990, 57.

    30. Roziq, *HNIT*, 148.

    31. Usmonov, *Nabiev*, 4–7.

    32. FBIS-SOV-90–034, 20 February 1990, 59.

33. Karim, *Faryodi*, 123. See also Roziq, *HNIT*, 152.

34. Maryam Isoeva was a popular Soviet actress and CPT member (Osimī, *Enziklopediyai*, Vol. 3, 33).

35. Quoted by Karim, *Faryodi*, 171.

36. Tūrağonzoda's dictum of 'dirty/filthy politics' was repeatedly reproduced in the Tajik media (FBIS-SOV-91–138, 18 July 1991, 89–90).

37. Nur Tabarov, "Nilufare rūi gūri orzu," *Adabiyot va San 'at*, February 13, 1992, 7: 6; Karim, *Faryodi*, 139–144.

38. Karim, *Faryodi*, 146.

39. Sohibnazar, *Subhi 1*, 18–19.

40. Karim, *Faryodi*, 153–154. Among the commission member were Vladimir Giro (a TU-154 pilot and people's deputy), Elizavetta Dedova (an operator in Dushanbe's central heating plant and people's deputy) or Ne'mat Yaqubov (an operator in Dushanbe's railway depot).

41. Sohibnazar, *Subhi 1*, 90.

42. Helsinki Watch, *Conflict*, 69. A reproduction of parts of the report in Karim, *Faryodi*, 130–132. See FBIS-SOV-90–171, 4 September 1990, 118 and Nasriddinov, *Tarkiš*, 94.

43. Nasriddinov, *Tarkiš*, 95–97.

44. FBIS-SOV-90–032, 15 February 1990, 72–73; FBIS-SOV-90–034, 20 February 1990, 74.

45. Sohibnazar, *Subhi 1*, 85–86.; Roziq, *HNIT*, 155.

46. Nabieva and Zikriyoyev, *Ta 'rixi 11*, 91. For similar statements see Abdugani Mamadazimov, *Političeskaya istoriya Tadžikskogo naroda* (Dušanbe: Doniš, 2000).

47. For the USA see Mark Fenster, *Conspiracy theories: Secrecy and power in American culture* (Minneapolis: University of Minnesota Press, 2008); for the Middle East see Matthew Gray, *Conspiracy theories in the Arab world: Sources and politics* (London: Routledge, 2010); for Iran see Ervand Abrahamian, *Khomeinism: Essays on the Islamic Republic* (Berkeley: University of California Press, 1993), 111–131. For Central Asia see S. Ortmann and J. Heathershaw, "Conspiracy Theories in the Post-Soviet Space," *Russian Review* 71, no. 4 (2012): 551–64 and John Heathershaw, "Of National Fathers and Russian Elder Brothers: Conspiracy Theories and Political Ideas in Post-Soviet Central Asia," *Russian Review* 71, no. 4 (2012): 610–29.

48. Cass R. Sunstein and Adrian Vermeule, "Conspiracy Theories: Causes and Cures," *Journal of Political Philosophy* 17, no. 2 (2009): 205 (Italics in the original text).

49. Fenster, *Conspiracy Theories*, 18.

50. Heathershaw, "National Fathers," 611.

51. Fenster, *Conspiracy Theories*, 10.

52. Abrahamian, *Khomeinism*, 111–131.

53. In 1980 Khomeini elaborated on the Orientalists' conspiracy in a speech to students, see "Čegūne 'alaye enqelāb-e Irān touṭe'e mīkonand," *Eṭṭelā 'āt*, 23 Dey 1358hš = January 13, 1980, 1 and 12.

54. Tūrağonzoda, *Šariat*, 124. See Tim Epkenhans, "Defining normative Islam: some remarks on contemporary Islamic thought in Tajikistan - Hoji Akbar Turajonzoda's Sharia and society," *Central Asian Survey* 30, no. 1 (2011): 89–91.

55. Ortmann and Heathershaw, "Conspiracy," 563–4.

56. See the summary by Rahmatkarim Davlat, "Bahmanmoh: Hadaf—ğangi šimolu ğanub," *Millat*, February 17, 2011.

57. Cf. http://tojnews.org/jgozi-mahfili-guftugi-tamaddunho-bo-makhkamov, Accessed May 22, 2014.

58. Sattorī, *HNIT*, 154; Roziq, *HNIT*, 148; FBIS-SOV-90–032, 15 February 1990, 66–69.

59. Karim, *Faryodi*, 19. Similar perception in Yūsuf, *Tāğīkestān*, 66; Nasriddinov, *Tarkiš*, 80.

60. Karim, *Faryodi*, 119–123. For a similar narrative see Narzullo Dūstov, *Zaxm bar ğismi vatan* (Dušanbe: Irfon, 1994), 28.

61. Cf. Buškov and Mikul'skiy, *Anatimiya*, passim.

62. Mosalmāniyān, *Tāğīkestān*, 20.

63. Quoted by Karim, *Faryodi*, 151.

64. FBIS-SOV-90–032, 15 February 1990, 67.

65. Abdullo Nazarov, who joined the KGB in 1981, appears frequently as a 'witness' for the February 1990 events or the escalating tensions in May 1992. In the Tajik Civil War he fought on the side of the UTO. After the General Peace Accord in 1997 he was appointed to Major-General and served as head of the GKNB in Badaxšon. He was reportedly involved in various illicit activities and was assassinated on July 21, 2012 by a former field commander in GBAO. The assassination caused a military intervention and violent clashes that left some 50 people dead.

66. Quoted in Yūsuf, *Tāğīkestān*, 70. See Karim, *Faryodi*, 165–169.

67. Niyazi, "Year of Tumult," 266. See Nourzhanov and Bleuer (*Tajikistan*, 179) who refer to the February events as a plot by parts of the political nomenklatura from the south.

68. Conversation with a former Rastoxez/DPT member, Dushanbe, March 2004. For 'agency' and 'agency panic' in conspiracy theories see Fenster, *Conspiracy*, 18.

69. See Nabieva and Zikriyoyev, *Ta'rixi 11*, 91.

70. Heatherhaw, "National Fathers," 629.

71. S. Xaliliyon, "Se xatoi Sangak Safarov. Musohiba bo sobiq komandiri gordi millii Kūlob Ismoil Ibrohimov," *Farağ*, August 22, 2011, 34.

72. Cf. Meier, *Gebot*, passim and Anderson, *Imagined*, 191–210. For the peace talks see: Iji, "Cooperation," 184–201 and Ibrohim Usmonov, *Sulhnoma* (Dušanbe: Matbuot, 2001).

73. Sohibnazar, *Subhi 1*, 51.

74. Kenğaev, *Tabadduloti 1*, 28.

75. Usmonov, *Nabiev*, 25.

76. Richard Hofstadter, *The paranoid style in American politics and other essays* (New York: Vintage Books, 1967).

77. Sohibnazar, *Subhi 1*, 55.

78. Sohibnazar, *Subhi 1*, 74.

79. Sohibnazar, *Subhi 2*, 161.

80. Sohibnazar, *Subhi 1*, 76–77.

81. Sohibnazar, *Subhi 1*, 232–236 and *Subhi 2*, 123.

82. Roziq, *HNIT*, 75.

83. Cf. Karim, *Faryodi*; Kenğaev, *Tabadduloti 1*; Sohibnazar, *Subhi 1*.

84. Sattorī, *HNIT*, 23.

85. Tūrağonzoda, *Miyoni*, 1998, 51.

86. Tūrağonzoda, "Ivazšavii hokim," 9.

87. Kenğaev, *Tabadduloti 1*, 257.

88. Sohibnazar, *Subhi 2*, 161–163.

89. See Kenğaev, *Tabadduloti 1*, 107 and 129; Sohibnazar, *Subhi 1*, 27, 120; cf. also to an interview with the lawyer Oynihol Bobonazarova in *Adolat* 34 (August 1992), reproduced in Karim, *Faryodi*, 450–451.

90. FBIS-SOV-92–121, 23 June 1992, 63–64; Yūsuf, *Tāğīkestān*, 261.

91. Yūsuf, *Tāğīkestān*, 307.

92. Yūsuf, *Tāğīkestān*, 309–321.

93. Kenğaev, *Tabadduloti 2*, 210.

94. Ortmann and Heathershaw, "Conspiracy," 563–4.

95. Heathershaw, "National Fathers," 611.

96. Abrahamian, *Khomeinism*, 130–131.

97. Sohibnazar, *Subhi 1*, 61.

98. Sohibnazar, *Subhi 1*, 61.

99. FBIS-SOV-90–040, 28 February 1990, 97.

100. Yūsuf, *Tāğīkestān*, 66. FBIS-SOV-90–032, 15 February 1990, 69–73; Sohibnazar, *Subhi 1*, 65–67.

101. Sohibnazar, *Subhi 1*, 62–67.

102. Sohibnazar, *Subhi 1*, 18; Mosalmāniyān, *Tāğīkestān*, 22.

103. Usmonov, *Ta'rixi siyosii*, 32. See also Nourzhanov and Bleuer, *Tajikistan*, 227.

104. Sohibnazar, *Subhi 1*, 93; Tūrağonzoda, *Miyoni*, 9.

105. Sohibnazar, *Subhi 1*, 92–98.

106. Sohibnazar, *Subhi 1*, 99.

107. Quoted in Sohibnazar, *Subhi 1*, 102–103.

108. Sohibnazar, *Subhi 1*, 107.

109. Sohibnazar, *Subhi 1*, 108.

110. Kenğaev, *Tabadduloti 2*, 227.

111. The office of the President of the USSR had been created in 15 March 1990 with the election of Mikhail Gorbachev by the Congress of People's Deputies of the Soviet Union.

112. Usmonov, *Nabiev*, 6.

113. Sohibnazar, *Subhi 1*, 59–61, 92.

114. Nasriddinov, *Tarkiš*, 123–124.

115. Nasriddinov, *Tarkiš*, 126–127.v

116. Nasriddinov, *Tarkiš*, 134.

117. Nasriddinov, *Tarkiš*, 127–132. However, Niyazov in Turkmenistan and Karimov in Uzbekistan were elected by the Supreme Soviet and not in nation-wide elections.

118. Sohibnazar, *Subhi 1*, 132.
119. Karim, *Faryodi*, 238; Usmonov, *Ta'rixi siyosii*, 34.
120. Usmonov, *Nabiev,* 6.
121. Nasriddinov, *Tarkiš*, 50–51.
122. Nasriddinov, *Tarkiš*, 49.
123. Mosalmāniyān, *Tāǧīkestān*, 24.
124. Sohibnazar, *Subhi 1*, 133–134.

Chapter 4

Independence

In the early morning hours of 19 August 1991, a group of senior hardline CPSU officials undertook a Coup d'état and formed the State Committee for State Emergency (GKČP) in order to preserve the USSR and prevent the new Union Treaty Gorbachev was supposed to sign on 20 August. After Gorbachev was placed under house arrest on the Crimea, the GKČP consisting of Gennady Yanayev, Valentin Pavlov, and Boris Pugo declared the state of emergency in Moscow, suspended the independent media, issued a curfew and deployed armored troops in Moscow. However, the Russian president Boris Yeltsin avoided detention by the GKČP and organized resistance that resulted in the failure of the coup on 21 August and eventually the collapse of the USSR.[1]

The Tajik nomenklatura was not involved in the coup but like his colleagues Karimov (Uzbek SSR), Nazarbayev (Kazakh SSR) and Niyazov (Turkmen SSR), Mahkamov silently welcomed the coup and expected the restoration of the CPSU's political monopoly as well as the end of the Glasnost politics and decided to await the outcome.[2] Šaforat Usmonova, then secretary for ideological affairs, reported that only fragmentary information reached Dushanbe on 19 and 20 August. Mahkamov and the Politburo were waiting in the administration for directives from Moscow, which never came. Usmonova remarked that "Mahkamov did not even have the courage to talk [to Otaxon Latifī] and seemed to be lost completely." Nonetheless, the sympathies among the nomenklatura and the "common" people in Dushanbe were according to her perception unanimously with the GKČP:

> It was reported that the GKČP wanted to restore order. At that time, as you know, disorder and confusion had reached a point where people were longing for a strong government and order. This is what the people (and in my opinion

also the senior leadership) associated with the GKČP. Since there was talk about order, the leadership of the cities and districts as well as the common people supported them. They sent letters and telegrams. That's why we should not condemn them for supporting order, I mean if a strong government emerged, there would be order.[3]

Although no arrests of opposition politicians took place, the KGB exerted pressure on the media to suspend their publication on 19 and 20 August. After the coup failed, Mahkamov obviously did not have a Plan B and reluctantly prepared for independence. In the meantime, the urban opposition, sensing that the tide has turned, put their feet down and organized the first rally in support of the Russian Duma and Boris Yeltsin on 25 August 1991. Under the impression of the protests against the Communist Party throughout the USSR, Mahkamov decreed the liquidation of CPT structures in the government and the confiscation of the party's property on 27 August.

With the Coup d'état in Moscow Nabiev's moment arrived: He instinctively decided to oppose the coup while Mahkamov appeared double-minded and indecisive. After initial demonstrations in support of Yeltsin, the opposition— the DPT, Rastoxez and the (still not registered) IRPT—called on their supporters to demonstrate against the TaSSR's leadership, in particular President Mahkamov, demanding his resignation. Several ten thousand demonstrators gathered for a peaceful demonstration in front of the Supreme Soviet.

On the emergency plenum of the Communist Party of Tajikistan on 29 August 1991, the CPT declared its break from the CPSU and Mahkamov maintained he did not yield to the demands of the GKČP.[4] Mahkamov's ambivalent decision to break with the CPSU further damaged his already diminished reputation and neither the opposition nor the conservative CPT deputies honored his move. With his inconsistent handling of the crisis, Mahkamov disappointed the nomenklatura who expected a conservation of their position (like in neighboring Central Asia) and they ultimately withdrew their support for him.

The rallies encouraged moderate and reformist deputies in the Supreme Soviet who raised their voice and Mahkamov suddenly faced stiff opposition. Kenğaev opened the extraordinary session of the Supreme Soviet on 31 August lauding Mahkamov for his achievements but eventually he concluded that Mahkamov had lost control over the situation. In a populist turn Kenğaev pretended to take sides with the demonstrators and issued an ultimatum that he and 28 other deputies of the Supreme Soviet would immediately leave the session, in case Mahkamov would not submit his resignation.[5] Kenğaev initiated a no-confidence vote in which 124 of the 172 deputies present in the Supreme Soviet (53 deputies were absent) expressed their lack of confidence in Mahkamov who resigned in the early afternoon. His resignation was accepted with 170 out of 172 votes (on 4 September, Mahkamov also resigned from the office of the first secretary). In the evening of 31 August the Supreme Soviet decided to rename the TaSSR as Republic of Tajikistan and the chairman of the Supreme Soviet, Qadriddin Aslonov, took over the responsibilities of an interim president until presidential elections scheduled for October.[6] With the organization of the vote of no confidence against Mahkamov, Kenğaev emerged as one of the major political actors in Tajikistan—albeit his political agenda remained obscure for many observers. Yusuf, for instance, assumed that Kenğaev was a communist and intended to preserve the Communist Party, but Kenğaev did not make any serious efforts to reinvigorate the Communist Party, instead he pushed forward his opportunistic and populist agenda without any cognizable political ideology or constrains of party discipline.[7]

Mahkamov's resignation (the only resignation among Soviet Central Asian presidents in 1991) had a paradoxical outcome: With the office of the president vacant, the highest legislative body, the Supreme Soviet, which had a rather ceremonial function in Soviet times, emerged as the most powerful political institution in Tajikistan. The deputies in the Supreme represented in majority conservative male functionaries entrenched in rural Tajikistan with its paternalistically governed collective farms who had little experience in legislative processes and a limited understanding for the enormous challenges of independence. Thus, on the eve of independence the legislature was deeply divided between a vocal minority of reformist deputies, a small group of populist opportunists and a majority of conservative deputies who wanted to preserve the Soviet system (but not necessarily the Communist Party), their privileges and local authority. But even within these three factions there was little homogeneity or commonality—intrigues, bitter rivalries and personal enmity were all too common. Loyalties were fluid and never categorical regardless of the regional origin, professional background or political agenda.

The Communist Party disintegrated and its former nomenklatura failed to transform the party into a presidential caucus with a "democratic" agenda. During the tumultuous days in August and September some 20 deputies in Supreme Soviet resigned from the CPT and joined the parliamentary opposition or became independent deputies.[8] Among the reformist deputies were politicians such as Sohibnazar (with a democratic/Glasnost agenda), Tūrağonzoda (conservative Islamic statism) and Kenğaev (Andropov-era authoritarian-populist). The democratic reformers had ties to the extra-parliamentary opposition, such as the DPT or IRPT, and could mobilize a significant number of supporters in Dushanbe.

One of the most urgent issues was the restructuring of the government. With independence, authority transferred from the union to the republican level and entire ministries had to be established from scratch. The adjustment process to the new realities in the Supreme Soviet was slow and inconsistent reflecting the lack of administrative capacity, experience and political vision. In none of the vital sectors, economy, security or foreign affairs, substantial reforms were implemented. A lengthy debate evolved instead around the procedure *how* to select the new president. Some deputies favored a swift appointment of a new president by the Supreme Soviet (as they did with Mahkamov). The democratic deputies and the extra-parliamentary opposition fiercely criticized this proposition and demanded presidential elections by popular vote.[9] At this time, Nabiev apparently favored an appointment by the Supreme Soviet instead of nation-wide elections as well. But in autumn 1991, the times they are a-changin' and a wave of protests made nation-wide elections inevitable.

SEPTEMBER 1991: THE EMERGENCE OF THE RADICAL-RELIGIOUS ALLIANCE[10]

In his memoirs, Karim cited the poem *Maydoni Ozodī* by Bozor Sobir describing the demonstrations in autumn 1991. Sobir conjured an electrified atmosphere on Ozodī Square, which he elevates to the nation's place of prayer. The protestors experience the demonstration as an internal/external ablution (*tohorat*), but at the same time they are aware that only the martyrs (*šahid*) of February events achieved independence. Remembering their suffering, the protestors shed the tears of Rustam's mother.[11] The mixture of religious and Iranian mythological motifs in Sobir's poem indicate one of the most remarkable developments in this tumultuous time: The emergence of the nationalist-religious alliance or movement (*ǧunbiši millī-mazhabī*) with the IRPT supporting the secular democratic opposition of DPT, La'li Badaxšon and Rastoxez. After the collapse of the GKČP, the IRPT leadership met with the leaders of Rastoxez and the DPT in order to coordinate the demonstrations against Mahkamov.[12] Usmon, Himmatzoda and Nurī realized that the cooperation with the secular opposition would increase the political relevance of the IRPT. Likewise, their strategic decision *not* to nominate an own candidate for the presidential elections was an equally momentous decision for the Islamist party underlining its readiness for political compromise and commitment to accept coalitions with other political groups. The IRPT agreed to support the candidacy of Davlat Xudonazar in accord with the DPT and La'li Badaxšon. Although the decision was not without controversy within the party, the leadership of the IRPT wanted to show its commitment to political reform and democratization.[13]

A Leap in the Dark: Independence

In early September, the declaration of independence was inescapable. After 7 of the 15 USSR republics had already declared their independence, the Supreme Soviet of the TaSSR eventually adopted the declaration of independence during an extraordinary session on 9 and 10 September 1991. The deputies made several amendments to the 1978 constitution stipulating that the president should be elected by popular vote. The deputies renamed Lenin Square as Ozodī ("freedom"), Lenin *prospect* as Rūdakī, *ulica* Putovsky as Ismoil Somonī and finally Putovsky Square as Šahidon ("martyrs"). Additionally, the Supreme Soviet declared 9 September the official independence day of the Republic of Tajikistan, adopted a law on a general amnesty, annulled the ban of the IRPT and ordered the construction of a monument on Šahidon Square commemorating the victims of the February 1990 events. Qadriddin Aslonov announced that Tajikistan would apply for membership in the United Nations and establish a ministry of defense including a national guard.[14] A substantial uneasiness with the sudden independence overshadowed the nationalist enthusiasm. Aslonov cautiously remarked that he could not imagine Tajikistan outside the union and demanded swift negotiations for a treaty establishing a union of sovereign states.[15] Otherwise, Aslonov moved quickly, resigned his membership in the CPT and withdrew from the Politburo.

The Fall of Lenin

The extraordinary party congress of the CPT convened on 21 September 1991 in the House for Political Education (today Kohi Vahdat) in a tense atmosphere. Since the early morning, some 4,000 protestors, among them several former CPT officials such as Abdunabī Sattorzoda, Šodmon Yusuf or Rahim Mosalmoniyon, gathered on Šahidon Square (500 m south of the convention center) demanding the CPT's ban and the confiscation of its property.[16] The CPT congress started defensively with Sulton Mirzošoev (first secretary of the CPT in Kūlob) accepting the confiscation of the party's property. The newly elected Chairman, Šodī Šabdolov, announced plans to rename the CPT to *Socialist Party of Tajikistan* and promised a new beginning.[17] But the formerly omnipotent CPT was unable to cope with the rapid change and was paralyzed and outpaced by the opposition.[18] The protestors on Šahidon Square were unimpressed by the CPT's announcements and turned against the central icon of Soviet rule in Tajikistan: the Lenin statue on Ozodī Square (the former Lenin Square). In the evening of 21 September, the protestors moved from Šahidon to Ozodī Square chanting slogans against the CPT and citing Muhammad Iqbal's poem "Awake From the Deep Sleep." Sobir, Mirrahim,

Aslonov, Abduğabbor, Tūrağonzoda and others were among the speakers at
Ozodī. Aslonov announced the CPT's ban and the confiscation of its property, which was enthusiastically celebrated by the demonstrators.[19] He and
Dushanbe's mayor Maqsud Ikromov burned their CPT membership cards and
gave order to dismantle the Lenin statue. A group of protestors—allegedly led
by Mullo Abduġaffur Xudoydodov who should emerge in May 1992 as one of
the Dushanbe based violent non-state actors—started immediately to demol-
ish the Lenin statue with a ZIL-130 truck and a crane eventually beheading
the statue. The unsubtle destruction of Lenin's statue was broadcasted on TV
profoundly alienating parts of Dushanbe's population.[20] Ibrohim Usmonov
recalled his thoughts while watching the unfolding events on TV:

> They beheaded and demolished the statue in the tradition of the Afri-
> cans (*an'anavii afrikoiyon*). [...] I felt pity with the intellectuals such as
> T. Abduğabbor, Bozor Sobir or Šodmon Yusuf. [...] The CPT suffered defeat.
> But it was its own mistake, the CPT suffered defeat from its own ignorance,
> from its own self-deception. In its decline those intellectuals I just mentioned
> had no particular role. It was Mahkamov, Ikromov, Aslonov and others who
> provoked the suicide of the CPT. The way the people celebrated the ban of the
> CPT was perceived—I assume—by the intellectuals, who called themselves
> democrats, as the awakening of a noble consciousness. [...] But I saw the fear
> in Aslonov's eyes [...] as he realized that he accepted the wrong advice of
> S. Abdullo [Nurī] and other mullos.[21]

Also Tūrağonzoda described the mixed emotions by some of the witnesses
when the statue was beheaded and broke into pieces. He commented that
he was "an open opponent to the Communist ideology," but "violence and
repression against any party was not to the benefit of the society." While he
assumed that the demolition of the statue was a foreign plot, he conceded that
he never regretted the demolition of the statue since it merely symbolized
the "heritage of Communist idolatry (*merosi butparastī*)."[22] He continued
that Aslonov, Ikromov and many DPT/Rastoxez activists underestimated
the sentiments of the multi-ethnic population of Dushanbe and deputies of
the Supreme Soviet, who were predominately CPT members from rural
Tajikistan. The dismantling of the Lenin statue eventually caused "many divisions and polarized the society [...] making friends to enemies and enemies
to friends."[23] Even god-fearing individuals were shocked by the destruction.

Lenin was still associated with the "positive" achievements of the October
Revolution and the early Soviet Union while Stalin was portrayed as his
antagonist who corrupted and destroyed the values of Leninism. Lenin's function as a "master signifier"[24] in the authoritative discourse of the Soviet Union
was pervasive beyond the existence of the USSR and in particular the imperial periphery. The state TV (which was still controlled by the staunch CPT

cadre Otaxon Sayfulloev) showed a montage of the events, which portrayed the demonstrators as an uncivilized mob (like Usmonov intended with his racist and derogative comment on alleged "African" traditions) and arranged a group of veteran CPT members with tears in their eyes complaining about the remorseless Islamic fundamentalists.[25] In later narratives, the opposition portrayed the dismantling of the Lenin statue as a decoy, conspiracy and manipulation of the CPT to discredit the opposition and demonstrators in the eyes of the Russian government and the urban population of Dushanbe.[26] Even 20 years later, the removal of one of the ubiquitous Lenin statues in Tajikistan is considered to be a precarious political issue. When in May 2011 the authorities decided to remove the Lenin statue in Xuğand—erected in 1974 and with 24 m the largest in Central Asia—the demolition team dismantled the statue in the dead of night with the escort of the militia.[27]

Outraged by the destruction of the Lenin statue, the Communist Party (officially now the Socialist Party) organized a counter-demonstration on 23 September, but only a few protestors attended the rally indicating a dramatic disintegration of the former omnipotent party. Communist deputies, such as Adolat Rahmonova from Kūlob, demanded the prosecution of those responsible for the destruction of the Lenin statue. But even CPT officials conceded that the speakers were without esprit, tedious and ineloquent. All of them addressed the rally in Russian—still the most prestigious language within the CPT, but rather inappropriate in the nationalist enthusiasm of independence. Moreover, the non-Central Asian nationalities in Dushanbe did not attend the rally fearing rising nationalist sentiment.[28] The demise of the Communist Party indicated the dramatic shift of the center of political gravity from the CPT to the Supreme Soviet as Zürcher postulates for the post-Soviet space in general:

> As the central institutions of the Soviet Union unravelled, as a result of the political reforms at the center and of the pressure from oppositional elites, these parliaments became the locus of political power within the republics, which were now rapidly moving towards independence. In the midst of the collapsing Soviet Union, the political arena had shrunk, and so, too, had the time horizon for actors. Strategic interaction now mainly took place within the republic or within the autonomous region and was largely determined by local actor constellations and local political aspirations, as well as by the perception that the window of opportunity was wide open.[29]

In the meantime, Kenğaev was not idle and presented the opposition in the Supreme Soviet with a *fait accompli* on 23 September: With the support of Nabiev, he rallied the support of 147 deputies for an extraordinary session in which 182 of the 230 deputies took part.[30] Kenğaev opened the session with an aggressive intervention accusing a "group of mullos" for the "crime" of demolishing the Lenin statue and threatening them with serious repercussions.[31] He mobilized the majority of deputies to declare the state of emergency and ban all demonstrations from the following day on. In a quasi-coup d'état Kenǧaev forced Aslonov to resign as chairman of the Supreme Soviet and arranged a vote for Rahmon Nabiev electing him with a majority of 182 deputies as the new chairman (and acting president). One hundred and sixty-eight deputies voted for nullification of the CPT's ban and ordered investigations against Dushanbe's mayor Ikromov for his role in the destruction of the Lenin statue.[32] Moreover, Kenǧaev demanded investigations into Ikromov's contacts with Tehran's mayor Gholamhossein Karbaschi (a pragmatist and prominent reformer in Iran), who had offered support for Dushanbe's city administration. Kenǧaev used these working level contacts with the Iranian government as a pretext for accusing Ikromov's city administration of sympathizing with Islamism and treason.[33] With Nabiev elected, some hardline deputies stood up in the Supreme Soviet and shouted:

> Oh, unfailing Lenin, why did you pass away so untimely? If you were not killed by these unmanly persons (*nomardho*), these mullos and democrats, your society would have flourished. Gorbachev, Yeltsin and all the supporters of Perestroika, these democrats, who do not understand your genius, be cursed![34]

The opposition quickly responded to Kenǧaev's provocation and organized protests against what Karim called in reference to the August Coup d'état in Moscow (GKČP) the "Coup d'état by Kenǧaev (*Kenǧa-ČP*) or Nabiev (*Nabiev-ČP*)."[35] Yusuf remarked that Kenǧaev and Nabiev's strategy opened the pandora's box: anybody could now act outside the law and violate against the constitution, eventually the society lost respect for the political elites.[36]

Many considered Nabiev's appointment objectionable since he left no doubts that he would run for president. The opposition worried that he would use the advantage of incumbency and government resources for his campaign. After the debate in the Supreme Soviet several deputies renounced their membership in the CPT and joined the opposition.[37] In a joint statement, Gulruxsor, Bozor Sobir, Abduǧabbor, Tūraǧonzoda and Sohibnazar protested against the Supreme Soviet's decisions and Davlat Xudonazar even warned of an imminent civil war.[38] The opposition called for a rally on Ozodī Square for 24 September (defying the ban on demonstrations) and, led by Gulruxsor, several protestors started a public hunger strike. The following day, Xudonazar, Yusuf, Sohibnazar and Abduǧabbor entered negotiations with Nabiev and urged him to resign as chairman of the Supreme Soviet in order to facilitate an orderly and transparent election campaign for the presidential elections.

On 26 September, Hoǧī Akbar's father, *ešoni* Tūraǧon, a respected Qaderiyya *sheikh*, and his oldest son, *ešoni* Nuriddinǧon, joined the hunger strike with a group of *ulamo* from the Qarotegin Valley. Tūraǧonzoda followed a day later, after the public Friday prayer. At the end of the month, 129 people held hunger strike on Ozodī Square, where the *qoziyot* had provided tents for the protestors.[39] The opposition issued a list of demands, including the suspension of the state of emergency, the reinstatement of Aslonov as chairman of the Supreme Soviet, the resignation of Nabiev, Kenğaev, Huvaydulloev and Sayfulloev, the suspension of criminal proceedings against Dushanbe's mayor Ikromov and finally the official registration of the IRPT.[40]

The peaceful conduct of the demonstration and the awareness of being part of a historical moment lifted the spirits of many protestors and made them forget about the enormous economic and social challenges of independence.[41] Yusuf idealized the September demonstrations as a time of intense political mobilization and openness when "Ozodī Square transformed into a university, where representatives of all nationalities met and the intelligentsia lectured about politics, the meaning of Islam, freedom and the Self."[42] Muhammad Iqbal's poem became the anthem of the Ozodī Square and the symbol of freedom and revolutionary spirit.[43]

POLARIZATION AND PROTEST

Nabiev and Kenğaev were unperturbed by the protests and not ready to back down or compromise. Nabiev could still count on a majority in the Supreme Soviet and many deputies rallied behind him hoping for a restoration of the CPT. Initially, pragmatic deputies in the Supreme Soviet and even some representatives of the opposition had considered Nabiev as a "reformist," a genuine nationalist and popular politician grounded in rural Tajikistan. The deposition of Aslonov, however, was a game-changer and Nabiev lost the support among the opposition. In his memoirs, Tūrağonzoda claimed that he had warned Nabiev not to assume the office of the chairman of the Supreme Soviet ad interim, since the people would have anyway elected him in the presidential elections.[44] Nasriddinov, Sohibnazar and Yusuf assumed that Nabiev had been manipulated by Kenğaev and did not fully understand the consequences of his decision.[45] Interviews with Nabiev from this time suggest that he had indeed difficulties to understand the momentousness of the challenges of independence and rather expected to govern in a similar fashion he did as first secretary of the CC/CPT between 1982 and 1985.[46] Eventually, it was less Nabiev's return as such, which polarized the society, but *how* he returned.

The autumn protests signify a shift of paradigms from the perspective of political performance with the assertive intervention by registered as well as unregistered religious authorities on Ozodī Square. While Hoğī Akbar was already an established political figure, the intervention by unregistered senior religious figures was a novelty and proliferated "Islam" as a central marker in the political debate. There had been a continuous hostile campaign by the state-controlled media against the *harakat*/IRPT activists since the mid-1980s and the participation of representative of the Tajik *ulamo* (who were neither IRPT supporters nor even well-disposed toward an Islamic party as such) intensified the conflict with performative atheists who portrayed the opposition as Islamists struggling to transform Tajikistan into an Islamic state.[47] The opposition blamed the chairman of the TV and Radio Committee, Otaxon Sayfulloev, for the hostile media coverage and the constant insinuations of complicity between radical Islamists and the opposition. The hostile media coverage forced the opposition to repeated affirmations on their support for a democratic transition and the rule of law.[48] Nonetheless, the secular-religious divide proliferated to the central master narrative of the political conflict in Tajikistan. In late September, the protests intensified and Aslonov even warned in an interview with the German daily *Die Welt* of a civil war.[49] Since 23 September more than 10,000 protestors gathered every day on Ozodī Square, several hundred camped on the square and some 130 were holding a hunger strike continuously for 13 days giving a foretaste of the demonstrations the following year.

The Sobčak Mission

On 4 October 1991, Boris Yeltsin—after an appeal by Xudonazar—dispatched Anatoly Sobčak (the popular mayor of St. Petersburg) and Yevgeniy Velikhov (from the academy of science), both members of his Political Consultative Council, to Dushanbe in order to mediate between the government and the opposition.[50] Sobčak and Velikhov met with representatives of the political leadership (except for Nabiev who excused his absence with illness) and the opposition. Kenğaev was uncompromising in the talks and demanded an immediate suspension of the demonstrations and a harsh punishment of the demonstrators, even execution or exile of the ringleaders.[51] Sohibnazar recollected that Kenğaev told Sobčak, that "the demonstrators are basically Islamists who support *vahhobizm*"[52] and that the alliance between the population from Ġarm and the *vovčik* (= Wahhabi Islamists) poses a serious threat to Moscow's interests. Sobčak finally excluded Kenğaev from further talks due to his belligerent and uncompromising rhetoric. In a press conference, Sobčak clearly spoke out for a legalization of the IRPT. In turn Tūrağonzoda assured that the opposition had no intention to establish an Islamic state.[53] Unsurprisingly, Kenğaev covered the Sobčak mission only briefly in his memoirs and considered the initiative as a foreign intervention and an "undemocratic action in the name of 'democracy' [...] eventually undermining Tajik statehood."[54]

Sobčak's mediation diffused the tensions for four reasons: First, Russia still had influence on the Tajik leadership and Nabiev could not ignore

Yeltsin's initiative. Second, Sobčak recognized the opposition—including the IRPT—as dialogue partners and therefore defined the parameters for a political solution. Third, the forthcoming presidential election offered the different political factions theoretically an option for political participation. Fourth, the enthusiasm of independence and the sense of a historical moment raised the spirits and pushed aside a more realistic assessment of the enormity of the economic and political challenges of independence.

On 5 October, the Supreme Soviet convened to an extraordinary session and the next day Nabiev resigned as interim chairman. In spite of his resignation, the compromise was inexpensive for Nabiev and he still kept the hold of the reins himself: Kenǧaev's fait accompli had demonstrated that he could mobilize a majority in the Supreme Soviet. Moreover, the political unrest was largely limited to Dushanbe—in the populous rural Tajikistan (where two-thirds of the population lived). Nabiev's patronage networks of collective farm directors were still able to manipulate political mobilization and rig elections.

The Supreme Soviet elected Akbaršo Iskandarov as interim chairman and the Presidium issued an 11-point resolution on the democratization of public life in Tajikistan. The resolution was based on the negotiations between Sobčak the DPT, Rastoxez, *qoziyot*, IRPT and envisaged (a) a review of the law on political parties, allowing the registration of the IRPT; (b) the postponement the presidential elections to 24 November; (c) equal access by all political parties and candidates to the Radio and TV during the election campaign; (d) a general amnesty for participants of the protests; (e) the suspension of criminal proceedings against Dushanbe's major Ikromov; (f) the suspension of demonstrations during the election campaign and finally the invitation of international observers to monitor the elections.[55]

A MOMENT OF CONTINGENCY:
THE RETURN OF RAHMON NABIEV

In September 1991 Rahmon Nabievič Nabiev could look back to a typical Brezhnev era career in Soviet Tajikistan—including its suspension by Gorbachev's abolition campaign in 1985. Since Mahkamov and his administration were in 1991 as unpopular as Gorbachev's reforms, Nabiev could now present his removal from office as an intervention by the "colonial" center, thus portraying himself as an upright nationalist with roots in Tajikistan's agro-industrial complex of collective farms and their patriarchic milieu, who defied Moscow and who floated above the prevalent regionalism and daily political debates. Senior administration officials of the kolkhoz and agricultural combines were part of Nabiev's professional networks and overwhelmingly ethnic Tajiks (with a few Uzbeks). For many former Communist cadres and deputies in the Supreme Soviet Nabiev personified a welcomed contrast to the "spineless regime of Q. Mahkamov"[56] and Nabiev's return reinvigorated the influence of the rural, agricultural political sphere in Tajikistan, which was already strongly represented in the Supreme Soviet. Nabiev's habitus (in the sense of Pierre Bourdieu[57]) responded to the expectations of the patriarchal milieu of collective farms in rural Tajikistan and reproduced the social and gendered hierarchies. Abdulov, Sohibnazar, Nasriddinov, Kenğaev, Usmonov and Tūrağonzoda described Nabiev's ability to adapt to these situations, hierarchies and social imaginaries on various levels and initially, he was even able to rally the support of the opposition—regardless of "regionalist" sentiments.

Notably, the Xuğandī elite considered in September 1991 Nabiev as a "goner (*šaxsi tamomšuda*)" and they had lost faith in him, therefore ironically "Rastoxez and the DPT carried his flag (*bayraq*)."[58] Since Nabiev faced stiff opposition from his own northern constituency, he needed to expand his power base and reach out to deputies from the south.[59] Many cadres from southern Tajikistan saw in him less a representative of the Leninobodī elite, but a politician who served their interests of preserving the status quo and who could potentially unite Tajikistan—a quasi-reverse *mahalgaroī*.[60] While the deputies from southern Tajikistan saw in Nabiev a man with their own professional and social background, the urban intellectuals and reform-minded CPT officials—especially those who knew Nabiev from his term in office as first secretary—were less enthusiastic about his return to politics. The opposition saw him with ambiguity: on the one hand, they considered Nabiev as a representative of the stagnant Brezhnev era, on the other hand, he could present himself as a genuinely nationalist politician who was able to outwit Moscow. Tūrağonzoda pointedly summarized the opposition's perception of Nabiev in an interview with the *Komsomolskaya Pravda* on 4 October 1991:

I was among those who helped Nabiyev to return to political life. I also supported him during the elections of deputies to the Supreme Soviet. At that time, when his present entourage was slinging mud at Nabiyev, it was the democratic newspapers which helped him to defend himself. I was ready to join his team at the presidential elections. But on two conditions: If he were to leave the party (I cannot support a Communist) and if he took Davlat Khudonazarov as vice president. Why this combination? If the radical Khudonazarov comes to power alone, he will come up against powerful resistance from the conservatives. And Nabiyev alone will not be able to implement reforms. [...] He thinks in the categories of the eighties. It seems to him that he will be able to use the old methods to introduce order in the republic. [...] Relations between the north and the south of the republic are already strained. But he did not have the courage to take a decision and renounce the alliance with the nomenklatura. He has proved a weak politician. And he will no longer be able in the future to become a symbol uniting the republic. [...] I explained to him that Gosplan [...] no longer exists. We are advancing toward the market. Tajikistan needs investment and an influx of capital from outside.[61]

While Usmonov and Nasriddinov pointed out that the urban democratic associations paved the way for Nabiev, Karim remarked, that Nabiev's return was contingent (*tasadufi*), since the CPT could not agree on another more suitable and popular candidate: The CPT cadres retaliated upon Mahkamov for his "betrayal" of the CPT, Qadriddin Aslonov distanced himself from the CPT after independence and no alternative candidate from the northern constituency was ready to assume the leadership at that time.[62]

Nabiev's political agenda was remarkably flexible; he was not a dogmatic communist and for some time he was able to negotiate political coalitions. Moreover, he could play the populist card and connect to the rural electorate of Tajikistan. But at the same time, Nabiev had serious personal limitations, in particular his alcohol habit and many sources refer to him as an alcoholic.[63] Even sympathetic authors pointed to his various personal shortcomings and insinuated that he had an alcohol problem, although Sohibnazar remarked cynically, that half of the Central Committee had an alcohol problem.[64] The reports and memoirs suggest that Nabiev's comprehension of the political situation, his capacity to discernment and judgment was often severely restricted. Plenty of anecdotes corroborate this perception: In his first press conference after his appointment as chairman of the Supreme Soviet on 23 September 1991, a journalist bluntly asked Nabiev when he had his last vodka. When further question regarding his alcohol habit and health came up, Nabiev harum-scarum stormed out of the press conference and thereupon avoided interviews without questions submitted in advance.[65] Throughout his term in office from November 1991 to September 1992 he frequently "disappeared" for several days, even in times of impending crisis (for instance during the Supreme Soviet Session on 20 and 21 April 1992 or during the negotiations on the Government of National Reconciliation in early May 1992) and his wife had to fend off phone calls and visits by government officials or deputies.[66] Nabiev's absenteeism aggravated the political stalemate and officials in the presidential administration complained that Nabiev could only be addressed for two or three hours a day due to his increasing derangement under the influence of alcohol.[67] Even the otherwise benevolent Usmonov comes to an ambiguous assessment of Nabiev's behavior in office:

> Nabiev was a strange president with an irregular work schedule, a man who could not say "no" (perhaps out of fear). [...] But in general, he was decent, a great human being, an experienced leader and a problem solver (*muškilkušo*)."[68]

Nabiev's return to power was in many ways a contingent development, which can be only to some extent explained with the political economy in Soviet and post-Soviet Tajikistan. While in Kazakhstan, Kyrgyzstan,

Uzbekistan and Turkmenistan Communist Party cadres retained their power after independence (Kyrgyzstan's Askar Akayev was arguably an exception), Mahkamov had to resign upon independence due to his already damaged reputation and his irresoluteness. Instead of uniting the nomenklatura and the deputies of the Supreme Soviet under a new political platform (for instance a presidential nationalist party with a "democratic" bias), he further divided the nomenklatura. His handling of the February events and the peripheral location of the TaSSR in the Soviet Union had undermined the coercive options of the TaSSR's nomenklatura. Mahkamov never assumed political responsibility for the February events and never expressed unequivocally his confidence in and support for the KGB and MVD.

Nabiev's return as the only serious contender of Mahkamov was likewise embedded in a contingent situation. The local nomenklatura in Xuğand was divided and perhaps too pre-occupied with the economic privatization in order to seriously engage in republican politics and therefore "allowed Nabiev to happen."[69] For reasons that need to be explored in greater detail, the Xuğandī elite did not "invest" in Dushanbe's politics after independence and rapidly lost influence on the affairs in the capital. Paradoxically, Nabiev's Brezhnevite background and personal shortcomings facilitated his return: The 1990 Supreme Soviet in its 12th Convocation was not an urban "intellectual" parliament (as Sohibnazar envisioned), but literarily "manned" with representatives of the conservative rural Tajikistan which—from an ideological and habitual perspective—had much more in common with Nabiev than with Mahkamov (or alternatively with the urban intellectuals and the versatile oligarchs).

REGISTRATION OF THE IRPT

After the compromise on 5 October, the ban on parties with a religious program was lifted and the IRPT proceeded with its official registration, which was finalized with the Ministry of Justice on 4 December 1991.[70] Muhammadšarif Himmatzoda and his deputy Davlat Usmon—Nurī remained intentionally in the background—organized the first official party congress and the IRPT was now forcefully entering politics in Tajikistan. However, the majority of Supreme Soviet deputies still opposed the registration of an Islamic party. Even Tūrağonzoda remarked in the parliamentary discussion that "Islam does no need a political party (*Islom ba hizbi siyosī niyoz nadorad*)."[71] He furthermore explicated that if the IRPT has 10,000 members it does not mean that there are only 10,000 Muslims in Tajikistan. Eventually he supported the registration of the IRPT since Tajikistan should transform into a democratic country committed to human rights and civil freedom. After Tūrağonzoda's intervention, Haydar Šarifov vocally rejected the registration of the IRPT referring to his reading of the Islamic tradition: "Neither Amir Said Hamadonī nor Mavlono Yaʿqub Čarxī had a membership card of a party, nonetheless they are famous worldwide."[72] Reportedly, Tūrağonzoda immediately responded to Šarifov with a diversion maneuver accusing him of embezzling funds reserved for the *qoziyot's* administration in Kūlob (which continued to be a contentious issue).

The discussion on the registration of the IRPT turned into a general debate on the *qoziyot* and Islam in the public sphere of Tajikistan. Emomalī Rahmonov, the deputy of the Danġara constituency, intervened and demanded that the people should elect the *qozikalon* in the future. But Tūrağonzoda replied with a remarkable consistent strategy demonstrating his intellectual agility arguing that the office of the *qozikalon* is neither a political office nor a general religious one but affiliated to a specific faith (Hanafi Sunni Islam) and only administers the mosques and institutions, which acknowledge the *qoziyot's* authority. Rahmonov's suggestion would transform Islam to a state religion and the office of the *qoziyot* to a state office abolishing the separation of religion and the state—the basic constitutional principle in Tajikistan.[73]

Ultimately, a narrow majority of deputies of the Supreme Soviet passed the law, which lifted the ban on religious parties on 22 October 1991, and four days later the IRPT convened its first official congress in Dushanbe. In October 1991, the heterogeneous opposition of urban Glasnost intellectuals, Perestroika reformist and Islamic activists won the day—for a brief moment. Karim celebrated this victory as a result of the

> coalition between the religious (*dinī*) and secular (*dunyavī*) intellectuals, the ability to find a single and unifying hymn, the language law and the resurrection of the Persian alphabet, the unification of the official Islam (*islomi rasmī*) with the reformist Islam (*islomi islohotxoh*) represented by the *Qoziyot* and the IRPT was an important element in the unification of the Tajik people. [...] As patriotism was cultivated in the soul of the Tajik people, regionalism was weakened.[74]

A HOLLOW VICTORY: VALIDATING PERESTROIKA AND GLASNOST

The shock waves of the sudden implosion of the Soviet Union in late August 1991 left Tajikistan's political elite largely unprepared. Even those who had aspired toward independence soon realized that the Tajik society faced an abysmal economic and social crisis with the suspension of Moscow's subsidies and the collapse of the integrated centrally planned economic system. While parts of the Tajik political elite initially ignored the consequences and the enormous challenges of independence, a few reformers reflected critically on the recent events. Karim concluded that Perestroika resulted in the direct opposite of the initial intentions (i.e., the reform of the system). He realized that the centrally planned economy could not be reformed and that the communist ideology was based on fundamentally wrong principles. Nonetheless, he radically misjudged the economic resources of Tajikistan as well as the local capacity to implement structural reforms.[75]

Nasriddinov remarked that neither the population nor the nomenklatura were prepared for the political and economic transformation initiated by Perestroika and Glasnost. In an ambivalent post-colonial disappointment, Nasriddinov blamed the center for the failed transition: "Moscow decreed democracy but did not offer the right mechanism to implement it. No one among the political leadership had an idea how to guide the process of developing statehood (*davlatdorī*) in Tajikistan."[76] Furthermore he complained that the opposition was not ready to work within the institutions and instead of reforming the state, they undermined the state structures and in particular the law enforcement and other executive branches of the government: "Many did not realize that democracy does not only mean liberal laws and freedom but also order and organization (*taškilotčigī*). Eventually, respect for the law is a fundamental condition for the rule of law; it is its sword and shield."[77] Likewise, he criticized the CPT and Mahkamov for the manipulation of the political institutions and the rampant corruption: Mahkamov had understood already in the late 1980s that the economy was on the verge of collapse and that the Perestroika reforms came too late. Simultaneously, chairmen of combines and collective farms also realized that the situation was uncontrollable and as a reaction started to depredate the state. Nobody was anymore committed to Perestroika and the reconstruction of the Tajik nation. The exodus of capital, the depletion of the state and corruption led to the impoverishment of large parts of the population, who at the same time witnessed the enrichment of the elites and therefore also resorted to illicit activities. Tajikistan's society moved toward an unknown and dangerous abyss and none of the politicians had the courage or power to stop this development.[78]

In a similar approach, Sohibnazar made the political elites responsible for the increasing disillusionment and disappointment of large parts of the population who had listened to the political slogans of Perestroika, market economy, private property, transparency and democracy for more than six years. These slogans did not yield any tangible results for large parts of the population who turned their back on the political elite.[79]

Yusuf narrated independence as the dramatic end of a chapter, which started in the mid-1980s with Glasnost and Perestroika. Although Yusuf's memoirs are in large parts a bitter polemic, his reflections on the 1980s resonates with a certain nostalgia expressing his understanding for those people who wanted to restore the pre-Perestroika Soviet society, which provided stability and predictability.[80]

Unsurprisingly, the Rahmonov government narrates the dissolution of the USSR and Tajikistan's independence not primarily in terms of Glasnost, democratization and sovereign statehood, but in terms of disorder, anarchy and disintegration. The concept of a national rebirth and restoration of Tajik statehood in 1924 by the Soviet authorities was too pervasive and narratively fixed by Tajik academics and historians to be fundamentally overturned. The depiction of the Coup d'état against Gorbachev on 19 August 1991 in the current history textbook for the 11th grade illustrates the official interpretation of the events of 1991/1992: "On 19 August 1991 the President of the USSR, M. S. Gorbachev, was perhaps due to a deterioration of his health relieved from his duties. A group of civil servants declared a state of emergency for six months."[81] The authors' narrative of the coup d'état as a benevolent intervention by concerned civil servants underlines that the science of history in post-conflict Tajikistan is still a highly contentious issue and that neither the political elite nor the post-conflict intelligentsia have come to terms with the Tajikistan's contemporary history and independence.

THE PRESIDENTIAL ELECTIONS

Initially the presidential elections were scheduled for 27 October 1992 but after the agreement between Nabiev and the opposition, the elections were postponed to 24 November. The campaign for the first nation-wide presidential elections in the TaSSR was unprecedented with regard to the degree of political mobilization and participation by large parts of the population. Ten candidates and their running mates registered with the Central Election Committee: Qadriddin Aslonov (Ġarm) with Mahmadġon Holiqov (Leninobod), Ismoil Davlatov (Badaxšon) with Abdumaġid Dostiev (Qūrġonteppa), Akbar Maxsumov (Ġarm) with Nuriddin Qayumov (Leninobod), Rahmon Nabiev (Leninobod) with Narzullo Dūstov (Darvoz), Hikmatullo Nasriddinov (Kūlob-Mūʿminobod) with Abdurasul Habibov (Leninobod), Būrixon Salimov (Kūlob-Xovaling) with Xušbaxt Ġafurov (Voseʿ), Sayfiddin Tūraev (Istaravšon) with Mūso Dinošoev (Dushanbe), Davlat Xudonazar (Badaxšon) with Asliddin Sohibnazar (Dushanbe) and Bobišo Šoev (Dushanbe/Fayzobod) with Qurbon Hūġamūrodov (Qūrġonteppa).[82] Although Aslonov, Nasriddinov and Tūraev were public figures and enjoyed some public support, the campaign soon focused on Rahmon Nabiev and Davlat Xudonazar.

Nabiev's campaign tried to respond to the tumultuous developments after the declaration of independence and his brief tenure as chairman of the Supreme Soviet, which had caused much opposition. He portrayed his "timely" resignation as a thoughtful strategy to avoid tension and to "manage" the difficult transitional time between independence and the presidential elections. The former transportation procurator and deputy of the Supreme Soviet Safaralī Kenğaev managed Nabiev's election campaign. He should controversially shape Tajikistan's domestic politics for the months to come. As his running mate, Nabiev chose the rather unknown Narzullo Dūstov, an *avtobaza* director from Qal'ay Xumb (Darvoz) and deputy in the Supreme Soviet, who was regarded among the opposition (and not only there) as a less sophisticated person with limited knowledge "in politics and in particular about human culture, since he had never read a book in his life,"[83] but with the right pedigree for Nabiev's campaign with regard to his regional provenance from Ġarm and professional networks in the transport sector. Remarkably, Nabiev did not pick a running mate from Kūlob, which was conjured in regionalist discourses as Leninobod's natural ally and "brother-city" (*barodaršahr*).

In order to portray Nabiev as floating above daily politics and to distance him from the Communist Party (then formally the Socialist Party, which *vice versa* did not support Nabiev), Kenğaev orchestrated the grassroots support of some 270 institutions, combines, kolkhoz and sovkhoz throughout Tajikistan. At the same time, Nabiev announced that he would work together with all political parties and associations in case he is elected president. Habitually, he corresponded to the expectation by the rural electorate employed in Tajikistan's agricultural sector as an "experienced person who knows about the past and the present of the republic [...], a leader"[84]—as Ibrohim Usmonov observed. Accordingly, Nabiev's campaign team addressed in particular the rural elites in the kolkhoz and village communities, whom he promised a continuation of the Soviet system of formal and informal resource allocation. The campaign team avoided public meetings with speeches by Nabiev due to his unpredictable behavior; instead they organized closed meetings with the local grandees.[85] Kenğaev employed state institutions and structures for the election campaign: The militia and procurator's office intimidated rival candidates and their campaign teams. Nabiev's campaign team even recruited criminal networks and local racketeers. Sohibnazar remembered how he met Sangak Safarov the first time in Mū'minobod supporting Nabiev's election campaign.[86] The increasing polarization changed the perception of the Xuğandī/Leninobodī elite toward Nabiev and transformed the "goner (*šaxsi tamomšuda*) again to a person of trust"[87] as Karim wrote in his memoirs.

The Opposition

Dushanbe's public considered Hoğī Akbar Tūrağonzoda as a popular candidate for the presidency, but he ruled out his candidacy in early September 1991.[88] In an interview with *Adabiyot va San'at*, he pointed out that the future president should be a senior figure, not affiliated with any party and able to unite the different political groups in the country. Although Tūraǧonzoda added that he would like to see a Muslim as the future president, he conceded that general morality and opposition to regionalism and chauvinist nationalism are more important.[89] Some 20 years later, in an interview with the weekly *Nigoh*, Tūraǧonzoda reflected again on the question of his candidacy:

> I personally never felt the need for getting an office. In the presidential elections 1991 many people ask me to register, I declined. Rahmon Nabiev asked me to be his vice president, but I refused. I consider the responsibility, which I bore at that time day and night, higher than any state or government office. [...] I was in the service of Islam and the Muslims.[90]

In his memoirs Tūraǧonzoda depicted himself as a courted politician in the center of Tajikistan's political gravity influencing the decision-making process but nonetheless floating above the granular daily political issues.[91]

The IRPT, DPT and Laʿli Badaxšon finally agreed on 16 October to back Davlat Xudonazar as their joint candidate for the presidential elections (with Sohibnazar as his running mate).[92] Xudonazar's campaign faced permanent obstruction from all tiers of the administration and had only limited access to the state media. Furthermore, Xudonazar represented a particular stratum of the Tajik society: the urban intelligentsia which shared his Perestroika/Glasnost visions of a political future. But Xudonazar had tremendous difficulties to connect with the rural communities in Tajikistan and—as Karim remarked—he did not "understand the peculiarities and the characteristics of our people."[93]

Sohibnazar conceded that—despite his long friendship with Xudonazar—he finally realized that he was the wrong candidate: As a devout atheist, Xudonazar was suspicious about the intentions of Tūraǧonzoda and the IRPT and his reservations ultimately impaired the cooperation among the opposition groups. As an intellectual with contacts to the Glasnost and former dissident circles in Moscow and St. Petersburg, he had a rather ambivalent perception of rural Tajikistan. Apparently, he was easy to manipulate and to impress by the offensive behavior of local strongmen such as Sangak Safarov.[94]

The most perfidious strategy of his opponents, however, hinted at Xudonazar's religious background as an Ismaili Muslim insinuating that the Ismailis are neither "real" Muslims nor Tajiks. According to Kenǧaev, Xudonazar was a problematic candidate for the opposition due to his religious affiliation (or the lack of it), he was a Shiite from a "red" atheist family, "a son of a communist (*kommunistzoda*) who in my opinion does not believe in Islam"[95] and "until today he has not fulfilled even one of the five pillars [of Islam] and he should know that I have my doubts how he practices them."[96] Kenğaev's comments on Xudonazar are typical for his defamations and utterly conflicting statements (a few pages earlier he demanded a secular, religiously indifferent state). The discussion on the status of Ismailis as Muslims eventually prompted Tūrağonzoda to clarify that they are considered Muslims by the Hanafi law school.[97] Nonetheless, the debate on Xudonazar's religious affiliation and his alleged atheism influenced the electorate in the rural areas of Tajikistan where "Islam" was part of daily practice and the imagination of morality.

Elections

The voter turnout on 24 November 1992 was 84.6% with significant regional differences.[98] According to the Central Election Committee Nabiev won 56.9% and Xudonazar a remarkable 30.7% of the votes. Xudonazar immediately challenged the results citing invalid votes and the illicit use of state resources by Nabiev. The Central Election Commission rejected his claims and confirmed that the elections were held under regular conditions and in compliance with the republic's electoral law. Observers from Kazakhstan, Kyrgyzstan, Latvia, Ukraine, Uzbekistan, Russia and Georgia affirmed the commission's view.[99] Xudonazar had little leverage except the public opinions of Dushanbe, Ġarm and Badaxšon. The large majority of deputies in the Supreme Soviet supported Nabiev. Since Xudonazar left Tajikistan for Moscow a few days later, he obstructed a more decisive response by the opposition and his supporters. Xudonazar's defeat increased separatist sentiments in Badaxšon and on 9 December 1991 La'li Badaxšon organized a meeting in Xoruġ demanding quasi independence of GBAO.[100]

The discussion of the election results abated when Tūrağonzoda publicly congratulated Nabiev to his election and the opposition accepted—though grudgingly—Nabiev's victory. Sadly, the presidential elections in November 1991 came up closest to democratic, free and fair presidential elections in independent Tajikistan. In the next presidential elections in 1994 during the civil war and without participation of the opposition, Emomalī Rahmonov prevailed with some 60% of the votes against Abdumalik Abdulloğonov. In the elections after the General Peace Accord (1997) Rahmonov claimed 98% (1999) and 80% (2006) and 83% (2013) respectively.

NABIEV IN OFFICE: NOVEMBER 1991 TO MARCH 1992

Nabiev was inaugurated into office at the 10th Session of the Supreme Soviet on 2 December 1991.[101] For a brief period between October 1991 and February 1992 the political situation in Tajikistan apparently calmed down.

Despite doubts about Nabiev's commitment to a democratic transition, there were expectations that he would tackle the enormous economic problems, initiate reforms (above all in the agricultural sector) and conclude an agreement with Moscow on the future of the bilateral relations. However, Nabiev obviously expected to "reign" like he did during his tenure as first secretary of the CC/CPT between 1982 and 1985 with the CPT in control over the political institutions and economic resources of the TaSSR. But now, he had to negotiate majorities in the Supreme Soviet with different parties and self-confident independent deputies. At the same time, his presidential administration was insufficiently funded and Nabiev could only rely on a small staff of some 30 secretaries and officials. According to his office manager, Karim Abdulov, Nabiev preferred an informal management of the daily affairs with little discipline in the administration.[102] Furthermore, Nabiev surrounded himself with people, such as Kenğaev and Dūstov, who followed their own agenda and were gradually able to manipulate Nabiev at their discretion.[103] Nabiev's appointment of Narzullo Dūstov as vice president was seen as part of a strategy to accommodate networks of Dushanbe's shadow economy, in particular the *avtobaza* with its extensive networks in the regions of Tajikistan and beyond. Dūstov's erratic behavior caused some consternation among the public in Dushanbe and the IRPT's chairman Himmatzoda remarked that Dūstov's actions severely undermined Nabiev's reputation and authority.[104]

Ibrohim Usmonov agreed that Dūstov was not a good choice for the vice-presidency, but considered Akbar Mirzoev as chairman of the Council of Ministers as Nabiev's worst miscast: According to Usmonov, Mirzoev avoided any confrontational decision and frequently "disappeared" in difficult situations simulating sickness. He did not discuss cabinet appointments with Nabiev (who was obviously not too interested anyway) and imposed no formal discipline in the cabinet.[105] Reportedly, Mirzoev was a compromise candidate. Nabiev initially kept Izzatullo Hayoyev, Mahkamov's long serving chairman of the Council of Ministers (since 1986), but Hayoyev resigned on 9 January 1992 due to irreconcilable differences with the president.[106] After Nabiev's inauguration, Kenğaev and Dūstov emerged as the most powerful actors in Nabiev's administration dramatically contributing to the rising tensions and increasing polarization in the country. Both did not consult with Nabiev, often undermined his decisions and relied on their informal networks.[107]

Nabiev as the Unpartisan Mediator?

The IRPT accepted Nabiev's electoral victory since the party's leadership publicly declared the elections as free and fair. The IRPT had not nominated its own candidate and notwithstanding contrary public assurances, the party's support for Xudonazar had been only lukewarm. The IRPT had just finalized its official registration process transforming the former clandestine movement to a fully fledged registered political party with reasonable prospects in the next parliamentary elections. Although elections to the Supreme Soviet were only scheduled for 1995 (the formal end of the legislative period), the opposition and civil society thought that snap elections to the Supreme Soviet were inevitable after independence and expected them for 1992. Therefore, the IRPT accepted Nabiev's election and presented itself as a conciliatory political force, which contributed to the consolidation of the political and social situation—in contrast to the defamation campaign, which depicted the IRPT as a group of merciless Islamists who only strive for an Islamic state.[108]

Although Nabiev had repeatedly announced his readiness to cooperate with all political parties in Tajikistan, he eventually refused to establish any meaningful dialogue with the opposition after his inauguration.[109] Worse, he could not even rely on the former CPT as his power base:

> It is true that he [Nabiev] believed in the ideas of the Communist Party, but due to the political crisis, which abolished the Socialist Republic, he could neither be a member of the CPT nor even cooperate with the CPT openly. [...] Perhaps it was one of the tragedies of Nabiev's presidency that he did not have a strong party support. The IRPT, the *qoziyot*, the DPT, Rastoxez and other groups, which generally did not have the right to interfere into politics, decided to work against him. Only the CPT could not do this until the end.[110]

In January 1992, the former Communist Party reversed the decisions taken at the extraordinary party congress in September 1991, reaffirmed its adherence to orthodox Marxism-Leninism and restored its official designation as Communist Party of Tajikistan.[111] Nabiev tried in vain to convince the CPT's chairman Šabdollov to adopt a different name like Islam Karimov had ordered in Uzbekistan where the Communist Party was resurrected on 1 November 1991 as the *O'zbekiston Xalq Demokratik Partiyasi* (People's Democratic Party of Uzbekistan), or in Turkmenistan, where Sapamurat Niyazov decreed, that the Communist Party should resurface as the *Türkmenistaň Demokratik partiýasy* (Democratic Party of Turkmenistan) on 16 December 1991. Šabdollov instead resisted Nabiev's attempts and agitated against "opportunists" who did not adhere to the orthodox communist ideology.[112] After Nabiev failed to embrace the Communist Party, his presidential administration tried to establish a loyal presidential party, but he had neither sufficient resources nor the vigor to form a nationalist "democratic" presidential party.[113]

The Alliance between Leninobod and Kūlob

Since Nabiev could not rely on fixed factions or parties in the Supreme Soviet, he tried to establish informal alliances with deputies from the southern constituencies. Already during his election campaign, Nabiev had approached the nomenklatura from Kūlob, such as Haydar Šarifov or Qurbonalī Mirzoaliev, and offered them a stronger representation in the republican administration: Šarifov should replace Tūrağonzoda as *qozikalon* and by rearrangement of the southern administrative structures Nabiev promised to establish a larger Kūlob province at the expense of Qūrġonteppa.[114] With the support of the southern deputies, Nabiev and Kenğaev were able to secure majorities in the Supreme Soviet and in the rising tensions, deputies from Kūlob and Xuğand would conjure the inseparable solidarity of the two brother cities (*barodaršahr*). The alleged alliance between Leninobod and Kūlob during Nabiev's term in office, however, did not generate categorical loyalties between the elites from Leninobod and Kūlob (let alone between "the people" of Leninobod and Kūlob), but were rather part of personal considerations by individual politicians and contingent dynamics. During the increasing polarization in 1992, these tactical maneuvers were suddenly perceived as fixed regional loyalties or alliances.[115]

ECONOMIC CRISIS

Nabiev won the November 1991 elections also due to his alleged competences as an economist with a deep understanding of Tajikistan's agricultural sector. In this respect, Nabiev was a disastrous choice. His erratic economic and financial policies originated in the pre-Perestroika USSR planned economy. Admittedly, he faced an unprecedented and catastrophic economic downturn after independence: The GDP fell in 1992 by 29%, in 1993 by 11% and in 1994 by 18.9%. In 1994 the GDP was only one-third of the level in 1990, while the consumer prices rose by staggering 1,157% in 1992 and 2,195% in 1993. Construction and agriculture were severely affected by the economic downturn.[116] In 1990 the Presidium of the Supreme Soviet and the Council of Ministers had adopted a series of decisions regarding the rapidly deteriorating economic situation in the TaSSR. But the government's strategy was conservative, contradictory and did not tackle the central problems. By 1992, the industrial sector did not receive basic materials and pre-assembled parts as the union economy disintegrated and collapsed entirely.[117] Any economic liberalization was rejected and Nabiev even imposed a moratorium on land tenure which restricted the private usage of arable land. The government furthermore hesitated to implement reforms in the cotton sector with its high employment rates and abundant possibilities of embezzlement.[118] In 1990 the economic crisis hit the agro-industrial enterprises, which faced increasing difficulties to get the necessary capital for their operations. A year later, the lack of fertilizers, seeds, pesticides, diesel and spare parts severely affected operations on the cotton farms. Still, Nabiev hesitated to implement a fully fledged land reform. Only in February 1992 he issued a decree encouraging free enterprise and new leasing (but not ownership) terms for agricultural land in Tajikistan.[119] However, a week later the government implemented a law, which was already drafted in 1991 by Mahkamov's administration and introduced fixed state purchasing prices for 70% of the products from collective farms, while allowing them to withhold 30% of the products for sales or barter deals.[120] This law eventually endorsed the status quo in rural areas and reconfirmed the position of collective farm directors.

As Mahkamov before, Nabiev hoped to retain the Soviet integrated economy after independence and defiantly announced a new five year plan although Gosplan had been already dismantled and only the statistical committee was left from the former planning bureaucracy.[121] Even the more thoughtful reformers, such as Karim, Abduğabbor or Sohibnazar, did not seriously called Tajikistan's integration into the Soviet economy into question.[122]

The fiscal policy was equally contradictory and inconsistent: In January 1992 the Supreme Soviet adopted a stifling 28% value-added tax to generate desparately needed revenues; the profit tax for industrial and agricultural companies was temporarily calculated on the basis of the absolute turnover (the more turnover, the less profit tax) penalizing smaller businesses and accelerating the economic downturn.[123] In March 1992, the IMF predicted a budget deficit of 50% and urged the government to raise prices (for instance for flour by eight times) and cut subsidies for housing rent, electricity and heating.[124]

In January 1992 the deregulation of consumer prices resulted in a rapid rise in prices and above all the urban population faced increasing difficulties to afford staple food. The situation in Dushanbe deteriorated quickly and in February the US Embassy commenced humanitarian food aid to the population.[125] Nabiev tried to tackle the problem less with tangible measures but with appeals for the unity among the population. The rapid economic decline forced Nabiev to demonstratively visit Dushanbe's Šohmansur market and to address the population in a radio message in which he defended his policy but laconically stated "Life, however, is life."[126] Nabiev envisioned an unrealistic re-industrialization of Tajikistan with new cotton processing plants and an extension of the aluminum plant at Tursunzoda, which, however, had never been profitable and could not operate with its normal capacity as the bauxite supply had collapsed. Nabiev even announced that Tajikistan would reach self-sufficiency in the supply of gas and oil by intensifying explorations—an entirely unrealistic plan. Between January and April 1992, the government launched various but largely uncoordinated activities to attract external aid or investment, however without tangible results.

The unprecedented economic decline in the wake of the USSR's disintegration deeply unsettled the Tajik society and statistical data does not sufficiently reflect the traumatic experience on the micro-economic/household level. Although the USSR's economy was an economy of scarcity and the violent disruptions of the 1930s were not forgotten, life had been fairly predictable since the 1960s and the first Tajik post-Stalin baby boomer generation had grown up in relative prosperity. The modest certainties of the Soviet system disappeared overnight and left a deeply distressed population. Even a more audacious president and government would have not been able to avert the dramatic economic collapse in 1991/1992. But Nabiev with his erratic work schedule and Brezhnevite economic policies aggravated the crisis—incompetence, negligence and vicious rivalries among the nomenklatura further contributed to the rapid economic decline and escalation of the tensions in 1992.

INDEPENDENCE AND THE QUESTION
OF A NATIONAL ARMY

In Soviet times, the TaSSR was part of the Central Asian Military District with its headquarters in Tashkent. In 1991 the 201st Motor Rifle Division (MRD), a standard Soviet mechanized infantry division, was deployed in Tajikistan. After the division's participation in the invasion and military occupation of Afghanistan between 1979 and 1989, the 201st MRD was deployed in the TaSSR since February 1989 with units in Dushanbe (the 92nd Motor Rifle Regiment, logistical support and air defense units, a military hospital, department store and headquarters), Qūrġonteppa (the 191st Motor Rifle Regiment) and Kūlob (the 149th Guards Motor Rifle Regiment). The nominal strength of the 201st MRD was 12,000 servicemen, 120 battle tanks and 300 APCs, but already in 1990 the 201st MRD was significantly understrength. With independence, Tajik recruits did not follow the conscription calls and the (mostly Slavic) career officers applied for redeployment in Russia proper.[127] In May 1991 Major General Muhriddin Ašurov, an ethnic Tajik, was appointed commander of the 201st MRD, obviously in a move to demonstrate the integration of Tajiks in the Soviet Armed Forces. Ašurov, born 1950 in Dushanbe, was a Soviet career officer with no notable nationalist sentiments for Tajikistan.[128] Together with the KGB Border Troops, the 201st MRD was the only noteworthy military formation in the TaSSR on the eve of independence. The deployment of the 201st MRD became more complicated with independence and with the mounting violence in May 1992 servicemen of the 201st MRD became gradually entangled in the conflict.

Upon independence, Tajikistan had no general staff, no department of defense and no funds allocated for the establishment of national armed forces.

The few Tajik officers from DOSAAF and the Soviet Armed Forces had only a limited lobby among the political nomenklatura. The National Defense Committee under the president (formally the commander-in-chief) and the cabinet of Ministers discussed defense-related issues only reluctantly.[129] While in the other newly independent republics units of the former Soviet Army, Navy and Air Force were either nationalized or disbanded, Tajikistan's government deferred the decision on the military forces on its territory and eventually abstained from nationalizing the 201st MRD. In September 1991 the commander of the Central Asian Military District, Colonel General Fuženko, ruled out an intervention by the 201st MRD into domestic affairs in Tajikistan—similar to the February 1990 events.[130] In the presidential election campaign, the candidates did not address the question of national armed forces. After his election, Nabiev deferred the decision on the nationalization of the former Soviet military forces in Tajikistan.[131] Also in other former Soviet republics it took time for the governments to decide on the nationalization and restructuring of the armed forces. In neighboring Kyrgyzstan (which was in a similar economic situation as Tajikistan), President Akayev decreed only in June 1992 that all former Soviet forces in Kyrgyzstan would be taken under Kyrgyz jurisdiction and therefore nationalized.[132] Nabiev cautioned against the nationalization, citing budgetary constraints. While his reluctance was perhaps based on a realistic assessment of Tajikistan's financial capacity, it bereaved the government of establishing armed forces under its command. With the disintegration of the MVD and KGB, Nabiev and his government soon lost the monopoly on coercion and had to negotiate "security" with various violent non-state actors.

CONTINGENCY: THE RISE (AND FALL) OF SAFARALĪ KENǦAEV

At Nabiev's inauguration on 2 December 1991, the Supreme Soviet also had to elect a new chairman. Three candidates competed for the position: Akbaršo Iskandarov, Madumar Karimov and Safaralī Kenǧaev. Although Nabiev backed Kenǧaev's candidacy, he was a controversial candidate and only 55% of the deputies eventually voted for him.[133] Tūraǧonzoda reported that Nabiev had initially even contemplated to choose Kenǧaev as his running mate, but eventually selected Dūstov due to Kenǧaev's divisive character. According to Usmonov, Kenǧaev's appointment was even more controversial than previous decisions by Nabiev, since the position of the chairman of the Supreme Soviet was traditionally reserved for a politician from the Qarotegin Valley and with Kenǧaev's appointment Nabiev poured "oil into the fire of regional sentiment."[134] But the reference to regionalism should be considered as a pretense in this context: Kenǧaev's appointment did not generate tensions because of his regional affiliation but because he was a divisive, populist and opportunistic politician who did not hesitate to demonize his opponents.

In the tumultuous Perestroika years, where the social and economic expectations of large parts of the population had failed, corruption was omnipresent and the inequalities in the Soviet society widened, Safaralī Kenǧaevič Kenǧaev emerged as a populist and polarizing politician. He performatively mastered the Perestroika/Glasnost discourse on reform, democracy, human rights and transparency; therefore, representatives of the opposition saw in Kenǧaev initially the embodiment of political reform and the rule of law. As a former prosecutor, Kenǧaev was influenced by Andropov's reform politics and he campaigned against corruption and published on the question of human rights and civil liberties.[135] In September 1991, he demonstrated his tactical political skills by organizing a majority in the Supreme Soviet to oust Aslonov and appoint Nabiev as chairman—against the opposition of key representatives of the former Soviet nomenklatura and the opposition. Kenǧaev presented himself as a reformer in the Communist Party who shared the nationalist and "democratic" agenda of the opposition—at the same time he showed only muted commitment to reform the Communist Party.[136]

Kenǧaev ostensibly floated above the prevalent discourses on regionalism due to his regional background from the Zarafšon/Yaǧnob valley. Muhammad Farzod, who introduced the first volume of Kenǧaev's memoirs, even characterized him as a "foreigner to Tajikistan's political field, who came out of the Soviet Union just with the membership card of Lenin's party, his sense of responsibility and his thinking as well as his sound humanist ideas."[137] The motif of being a "foreigner" to politics reflects a wider public perception of politics in the Tajik society as "dirty business."

Usmonov characterized Kenǧaev pointedly as someone who combined the "old and new traits of thought,"[138] but was too impatient and inexperienced. Where diplomacy was needed, Kenǧaev's aggressive language polarized; where a drawback was appropriate, he obstinately insisted on his position. In unison, Kenǧaev is portrayed in the memoirs as an intriguer who continuously conspired (*dasisaboz*) against friends and enemies as well. Sohibnazar concluded that "Kenǧaev was responsible for the turn of events in Tajikistan. While the Tajiks were on their way of Self-awareness, freedom, on their return to their traditional roots and old civilization, he drew them into a bloody maelstrom. [...] I made a serious mistake by supporting Kenǧaev."[139]

Aslonov remarked about Kenǧaev, "as soon as he is in the Supreme Soviet, there is no peace (*tinǧī*) anymore"[140] and Yusuf considered him as a hateful person, an enemy of freedom and Islam and a Stalinist who had sold himself to the Uzbeks and Russians.[141] Tūraǧonzoda described Kenǧaev as a duplicitous character without any loyalty plotting even against his associates.[142]

Likewise, Sohibnazar remarked that Kenğaev and Dūstov publicly agreed with Nabiev's policy and directives, but acted diametrically opposed to his orders. Both obviously established parallel structures in which their cronies and supporters managed state affairs bypassing the Supreme Soviet and the government.[143] Iraj Bashiri, in contrast, portrayed Kenğaev in a radically different way that would have certainly pleased the latter:

> Kenjaev's politics combined his deep knowledge of the Soviet law, especially as it is applied to the republics of Central Asia (Tajikistan in particular), with a thorough understanding of Soviet government. His objections to illegal acts committed by those who operated outside the law indicated his commitment to and reverence for that law. In addition, he was proficient in the Islamic Shari'a law and had a deep understanding of the differences between the teachings of Imam Hanafiyyah and the edicts followed by the *Wahhabiyyah*. Furthermore, Kenjaev was fully familiar with the Soviet military, and tried to use this knowledge to harness the energies of the youth of the republic for the common good. His organization of the Popular Front of Tajikistan, created and made operational within a short period of time, was indicative of the depth of his knowledge about military affairs and about attracting the youth of the nation around a single cause—liberation.[144]

Bashiri's partisan portrayal of Kenğaev has probably been dictated by Kenğaev's ardent admirers in Dushanbe. Nonetheless, Kenğaev's biography illustrates how complex Soviet and post-Soviet biographical narratives are, in particular since Kenğaev had a distinctive impulse for complex (and often contradictory) manifestations of the self.

Kenğaev was born in 1942 in Čor'yakkoron, a western suburb of Dushanbe, into a Yağnobī family, which originally came from Tağob (Aynī *nohiyya*). His parents, Qimat Šarifova (mother) and Kenğa Rağabov (father), had moved in 1936 to Dushanbe and worked on a nearby kolkhoz.[145] Kenğaev grew up in Čor'yakkoron, graduated from school and was admitted to the law department at Dushanbe's State University in 1960. He graduated in 1965 and worked in various positions in the prosecutor's office. In the mid-1980s, he became general prosecutor in the Railway Transport Department and in 1989 chairman of the Internal Oversight Committee of the CC/CPT. In February 1990, he was elected deputy of the Supreme Soviet for the Ğūybodom constituency in the Lenin district.[146]

"Milk brothers"? Kenğaev and Tūrağonzoda

Kenğaev and Tūrağonzoda had a complex relationship and rumors circulated (and still circulate) that Kenğaev's father was a *murid* (follower) of *ešoni* Tūrağon and that Safaralī grew up in the household of *ešoni* Tūrağon as a milk brother of Hoǧī Akbar establishing a "milk kinship."[147] Kenǧaev frequently claimed that he was virtually a family member and had a special relationship with Hoǧī Akbar addressing him several times as one of his only "true friends."[148] Simultaneously, however, Kenǧaev portrayed Tūraǧonzoda as a duplicitous character, a "jackal (Russ.: *šakal*)" and "conspirator (*dasisaboz*) who ultimately betrayed their friendship."[149] Kenǧaev invited Tūraǧonzoda several times in his memoirs to reconsider who his real friends are, since the representatives of the opposition "will finally sell out each other as they will betray the religion of Islam and you, esteemed Hoǧī Akbar."[150] Kenǧaev pretended to be surprised by Tūraǧonzoda's sudden hostility toward him:

> One point is until today [1993] a puzzle for me. Compared to others, I was very close to the *qozikalon* of the republic, Hoǧī Akbar Tūraǧonzoda, our families and we ourselves had frequent contact and through bad times and good times we were companions. He often said to me: "We are like finger-tip and nail." But the moment the government was seized by the opposition [in May 1992], he did not invite me to stay in my hometown Dushanbe.[151]

Apparently, the rumors prompted Kenǧaev to comment more explicitly on his relationship with Tūraǧonzoda. As a peg on which to hang the matter on, Kenǧaev quoted a report by the Iranian weekly *Kayhān-e havā'ī* about the relationship between him and Tūraǧonzoda (indirectly insinuating a special interest of Iran in Tūraǧonzoda). According to *Kayhān*, Kenǧaev and Hoǧī Akbar "consider each other as brothers. Kenǧaev was an orphan and the father of Tūraǧonzoda took him out of an orphanage into his own family and looked after him like his own son."[152] In his response to *Kayhān*, Kenǧaev pointed out that his mother, Qimat Šarifova, passed away in 1957 and his father, Kenǧa Raǧabov, 10 years later (when Kenǧaev was 25). Both came from Taǧob and worked for the "Pobeda" kolkhoz close to Dushanbe. He explicitly pointed out that he had never been to any orphanage and that Tūraǧonzoda's father is only 15–18 years older than Kenǧaev himself (in fact *ešoni* Tūraǧon was only 8 years senior to him), therefore the rumors are entirely unfounded.

Kenǧaev the Populist Anti-Politician and Tajik "Commissar Cattani"

In his memoirs Kenǧaev called politics in a characteristic populist tone "dirty" and professional politicians as incompetent, malicious, unprincipled and so forth (echoing his antagonist Tūraǧonzoda and several other politicians). Interestingly, Kenǧaev never explicitly referred to his regional provenance. Instead, he performatively acted as a Soviet official who entered public service at an early age and did not owe his career to regionalist networks but to his intelligence, diligence and principle of equal opportunity in the Soviet system.[153] Although he conceded that he was a member of the CPT, he nonetheless portrayed himself as floating above daily politics and emphasized his commitment to humanity, the rule of law, independence, elections, democracy and equality.[154] Importantly, he presented himself as a truly nationalist politician, who at the same time did never resort to nationalist chauvinism or regionalism like the opposition but included all ethnicities and nationalities in Tajikistan into his political vision.[155] In one of his speeches on Ozodī Square he addressed the protestors in a solemn programmatic and populist speech: "I have never defied the will of the people and I will never do this. All of you who came out to offer me protection (*himoya*), actually stood up to protect the constitution, justice, truth and the rule of law. Before you I bow my head."[156]

Kenǧaev was far from consistent in expressing his political visions and loyalties. In frequent erratic twists he either hailed or disapproved Russian involvement in Tajikistan's affairs and although he readily conceded that he is supported by Uzbekistan, he nonetheless considered any other external involvement as a betrayal.[157] Although he had only a few genuine supporters among the political elite, he enjoyed popularity among the deputies in the Supreme Soviet, who benefited from Kenǧaev's term as chairman, and among young men in Dushanbe who originally came from the northern (Zarafšon) as well as western (Hisor) parts of Tajikistan and were less represented in the capital's informal networks.[158] While the deputies fought a rearguard action after Kenǧaev's dismissal in May 1992, young men hailed Kenǧaev as the "Tajik *Komissar Kattani*." Commissar Corrado Cattani was the main protagonist in the Italian mafia TV series *La Piovra* (The Octopus) starring Michele Placido. The series was broadcasted in the USSR under the Russian title *Sprut* (Russ. for Octopus, in Tajik *haštpo*) from 1986 on and became a blockbuster. The term "Kommissar Kattani" became a saw in the late Soviet Union and a symbol for the society's struggle against organized crime and corruption.[159]

Kenǧaev the Religious Specialist

Kenǧaev did not only portray himself as an ideal *homo sovieticus*, but also as a devout Muslim adept in religious practice and thought.[160] In his memoirs, Kenǧaev frequently lectured about Islam, its religious dogma, practice and history. Although he conceded, that he was not a trained religious specialist, he nonetheless provided the reader with his reading of Islam. For instance, he reflected on the nature of *ǧihod* as a "just war" which was only rarely declared in history.[161] In a similar attitude, he criticized the demonstrators on Šahidon Square for transgressing the "proper" Islamic practices by singing, dancing and other forms of *"ekstaz"* (= ecstasy).[162] After the occupation of Qūrǧonteppa, Kenǧaev reported how he visited the mosques of IRPT/*vahhobī* mullos and gauged the direction of the *qibla* (the direction for the ritual prayer, facing Mecca) discovering that in *vahhobī* mosques the *qibla* did not face Mecca but the mausoleum (*oromgoh*) of Muḥammad b. ʿAbd al-Wahhāb, the founder of the Wahhabiyya.[163] This anecdote illustrates how Kenğaev works with insinuations, allusions and absurd fabrications: The Wahhabiyya is known for its radical rejection of any form of "saint" veneration or ecstasy, Wahhabi mosques have the same *qibla* as mosques operated by other Islamic denominations and eventually Muḥammad ʿAbd al-Wahhāb is buried like all other representatives of the Saudi Arabian political and religious elite in an unmarked grave, therefore there is no *oromgoh* to adjust the *qibla* to.

Kenğaev further informed his readers that Islam in the Hanafi-Sunni varia- tion is "tolerant" religion and Hanafi Muslims would immediately recognize deceit and treason. Therefore, Tūrağonzoda would be punished on the Last Judgment for the civil strife he has instigated among the people: "But the destiny of our Muslims is the hand of God and not of an errant and fake *qozikalon*, *ešon* or son of an *ešon*."[164] In a similar tone, he depicted the nature of the IRPT leaders: While the religion of Islam "is pure and has no sin," the leaders of the IRPT are "a group of bloodthirsty riff-raff (*avboš*) and gangsters (*rohzan*) [...] who have covered the walls of the Hoğī Yaqub Čarxī Mosque with the blood of the true believers."[165] His alleged knowledge on Islamic affairs allowed Kenğaev eventually to assess the opposition's "true" religious sentiments: Mirrahim, Hait, Yusuf, Latifī, Xudonazar, Amirbek and Ayubzod "have all declared their altruistic commitment for the Islamic cause," however published throughout their career in the USSR academic essays based on the principles of atheism, Marxism and Leninism, eventually, these people are "neither complete unbelievers nor true Muslims but only a clan (*toifa*) of criminals."[166]

In an interview with *Komsomolskaya Pravda* during his brief occupation of Dushanbe on 24 October 1992, he referred several times to the Koran as his guidance—next to Persian *andarz* literature.[167] Finally, Kenğaev maintained that Islam should be exclusively considered as part of the spiritual realm without any political dimension:

> History taught us that every time people did not implement the commands of the Koran and placed their own abject intentions over the verses of the Koran, the ignorant people lost their path and God subjected them to a test [...]. Politics are entirely secular (*dunyavī*) and not religious. Islam is guidance for the After- world and every Muslim who wants to enter the Afterworld and to whom Islam was revealed, will distance himself from any transgression. Islam is not only separated from politics, it is opposed politics. This World and the Afterworld are like East and West, and each time you come close to one, you depart further from the other.[168]

In the end, Kenğaev's pretended deep knowledge on the Islamic tradition consists of a biased reading of Soviet literature on Islam enriched with motifs from KGB defamation campaigns.

In the context of the rapid transformation of the later Soviet society, Kenğaev nonetheless opportunistically "performed" different, often contradictory identities: Firstly, the ideal *homo sovieticus* who made a career in the security structures due to his work ethics and self-discipline; secondly, the Perestroika/Glasnost reformer who easily adapted to the prevalent discourses on transparency, democracy and human rights; thirdly, the nationalist Tajik politician embedded in the local culture; fourthly, the populist anti-politician with a deep understanding of the common people's grievances and morality and finally the educated, "authentic" Tajik Muslim. The rise of Kenğaev was in many respects contingent and not explicable by referring to regionalism, "clan" loyalties or the politics of elite networks. As a Yağnobī born in Dushanbe, he did not belong to one of the major regionalist groups and he had no immediate ties to the agro-industrial complex. However, his career as a procurator in the transport sector connected him with local strongmen in the motor depots (who became field commanders in 1992) and the expanding shadow economy of the later USSR/TaSSR. These contacts, his opportunism and populism perhaps explain the puzzle of Kenğaev's fateful rise and fall.

NOTES

1. Cf. Ignaz Lozo, *Der Putsch gegen Gorbatschow und das Ende der Sowjetunion* (Köln: Böhlau, 2014).

2. Sohibnazar, *Subhi 1*, 136–138; Usmonov, *Nabiev*, 6; FBIS-SOV-91-167, 28 August 1991, 118.

3. Interview with Mirzo Salimpur on: http://www.ozodi.mobi/a/606249.html, accessed October 10, 2015.

4. FBIS-SOV-91-169, 30 August 1991, 128.

5. Karim, *Faryodi*, 300; Yūsuf, *Tāğīkestān*, 102.

6. FBIS-SOV-91-170, 3 September 1991, 114.

7. Yūsuf, *Tāğīkestān*, 102. In 1996 Kenğaev founded the Socialist Party of Tajikistan, which remained a marginal opposition party in Tajikistan.

8. Nuralī Davlat, "Qozī," *Nigoh*, February 25, 2014, 48: 5.

9. Sohibnazar, *Subhi 1*, 141.

10. The title is a reference to Nikki Keddie, "The Origins of the Religious-Radical Alliance in Iran," *Past and Present* 34, no. 34 (1966): 70–80.

11. Quoted in Karim, *Faryodi*, 390. In the *Shahname* the hero Rustam is the son of Zal and Rudaba. The tears of Rudaba are related to her prolonged labour giving birth to Rustam. Zal has to summon the mythical flying creature Simurgh who instructs Zal how to perform a caesarean section saving Rudabah and the child (cf. S. Shahbazī, "RUDĀBA," In *EIr*).

12. Sattorī, *HNIT*, 160; Karim, *Faryodi*, 461; Roziq, *HNIT*, 201–202.

13. Conversation with a former IRPT member (Dushanbe, March 2010). See Karim, *Faryodi*, 365.

14. Karim, *Faryodi*, 335–336. The monument was never built and today not even a street sign remembers the changeful history of the square.

15. FBIS-SOV-91-180, 17 September 1991, 71.

16. Usmonov, *Nabiev*, 8.

17. Alternative versions were discussed as well such as Socialist People's Party (*Hizibi socialistii mardumi Toğikiston*), People's Unity Party (*Hizbi vahdati mardum*) or People's Party (*Hizbi xalq*). See Usmonov, *Nabiev*, 8.

18. Davlat Usmon on http://www.ozodi.mobi/a/25044882.html, accessed October 17, 2013.

19. Karim, *Faryodi*, 336; Kenğaev, *Tabadduloti 1*, 23; Roziq, *HNIT*, 200; Usmonov, *Nabiev*, 11.

20. Tūrağonzoda, *Miyoni*, 12 and Usmonov, *Nabiev*, 9–12.

21. Usmonov, *Nabiev*, 12. For a similar assessment see Nasriddinov, *Tarkiš*, 143–144.

22. Tūrağonzoda, *Miyoni*, 13.

23. Tūrağonzoda, *Miyoni*, 14.

24. Yurchak, *Everything*, 73.

25. Tūrağonzoda (*Miyoni*, 15) considered Otaxon Sayfulloev, the Chairman of the State Radio & TV Commission, because of the TV coverage of the demolition of the Lenin statue as one of the "faces of the conspiracy [...] and a principal initiator of the later catastrophe of our beloved homeland."

26. Yūsuf, *Tāğīkestān*, 111.

27. See http://www.bbc.co.uk/tajik/institutional/2011/05/110531_ea_aa_lenin_khujand.shtml, accessed September 25, 2014.

28. Usmonov, *Nabiev*, 13; Karim, *Faryodi*, 338.

29. Christoph Zürcher, *The post-Soviet wars: Rebellion, ethnic conflict, and nationhood in the Caucasus* (New York: New York Univ. Press, 2007), 211.

30. Kenğaev, *Tabadduloti 1*, 24.

31. Sohibnazar, *Subhi 1*, 169–171.

32. Usmonov, *Ta'rixi siyosii*, 37; FBIS-SOV-91-186, 25 September 1991, 84; FBIS-SOV-91-189, 30 September 1991, 96.

33. Karim, *Faryodi*, 337–339; Mosalmāniyān, *Tāğīkestān*, 28.

34. Sohibnazar, *Subhi 1*, 181.

35. Karim, *Faryodi*, 338.

36. Yūsuf, *Tāğīkestān*, 114–115.

37. Yūsuf, *Tāğīkestān*, 114.

38. Usmonov, *Nabiev*, 14.

39. FBIS-SOV-91-189, 30 September 1991, 93; FBIS-SOV-91-190, 1 October 1991, 75. See Yūsuf, *Tāğīkestān*, 123; Karim, *Faryodi*, 341.

40. Karim, *Faryodi*, 341.

41. Interviews and conversation with former DPT and Rastoxez members (Dushanbe, October 2003).

42. Yūsuf, *Tāğīkestān*, 121.

43. Yūsuf, *Tāğīkestān*, 125.

44. Tūrağonzoda, *Miyoni*, 16–18.
45. Karim, *Faryodi*, 354–359; Sohibnazar, *Subhi 1*, 171–174; Yūsuf, *Tāğīkestān*, 112–124.
46. Cf. FBIS-SOV-91-187, 26 September 1991, 87–88; FBIS-SOV-91-189, 30 September 1991, 92–93.
47. Sohibnazar, *Subhi 1*, 188–192.
48. FBIS-SOV-91-186, 25 September 1991, 86–87; FBIS-SOV-91-187, 26 September 1991, 86; FBIS-SOV-91-189, 30 September 1991, 94.
49. *Die Welt*, September, 25 1991, 5.
50. Karim, *Faryodi*, 342; Sohibnazar, *Subhi 1*, 196.
51. Yūsuf, *Tāğīkestān*, 129.
52. Sohibnazar, *Subhi 1*, 196–197.
53. Yūsuf, *Tāğīkestān*, 126–128; see also FBIS-SOV-91-194, 7 October 1991, 81.
54. Kenğaev, *Tabadduloti 1*, 25.
55. The complete text is reproduced in Karim, *Faryodi*, 343–345.
56. Kenğaev, *Tabadduloti 2*, 228.
57. Pierre Bourdieu, *The logic of practice* (Cambridge: Polity Press, 1990), 52–66.
58. Usmonov, *Nabiev*, 5. For a similar analysis see: Nasriddinov, *Tarkiš*, 145 and Sohibnazar, *Subhi 1*, 118.
59. Karim, *Faryodi*, 302; Sohibnazar, *Subhi 1*, 118–119, 199.
60. Karim, *Faryodi*, 351.
61. FBIS-SOV-91-194, 7 October 1991, 81–82.
62. Karim, *Faryodi*, 352.
63. Yūsuf, *Tāğīkestān*, 117. See also Kenğaev, *Tabadduloti 2*, 225; Sohibnazar, *Subhi 2*, 35.
64. Sohibnazar, *Subhi 1*, 117–118.
65. FBIS-SOV-91-189, 30 September 1991, 92–93. See Usmonov, *Nabiev*, 16; Yūsuf, *Tāğīkestān*, 140.
66. Kenğaev, *Tabadduloti 1*, 46; Nasriddinov, *Tarkiš*, 145; Sohibnazar, *Subhi 2*, 35; Usmonov, *Nabiev*, 3–4; FBIS-SOV-92-082, 28 April 1992, 61; FBIS-URS-92-062, 27 May 1992, 104; FBIS-SOV-92-122, 24 June 1992, 68.
67. Yūsuf, *Tāğīkestān*, 153 and 274.
68. Usmonov, *Nabiev*, 48.
69. Paraphrase of a conversation with a former official in the Xuğand *viloyat* Ispolkom (Xuğand, May 2004).
70. Abdulloev and Akbarzadeh, *Dictionary*, 97–99.
71. Davlat, "Qozī," 5.
72. Davlat, "Qozī," 5. Mīr Sayyid ʿAlī Šahāb ad-Dīn Hamadānī (Hamadonī) (1314–1384 CE) was a Kubrawiya mystic, Persian poet and scholar from Hamadān, whose mausoleum is an important *mazar* (shrine) in Kūlob. Mavlono Yaʿqub Čarxī (1360–1447 CE) was a Naqšbandī mystic, whose *mazar* is the most important Islamic sanctuary in Dushanbe.
73. Davlat, "Qozī," 5. The separation of religious organization and the state is stipulated in Article 8 of the Tajikistan's Constitution. See Ğumhurii Toğikiston, *Sarqonuni*, 2.

Independence 177

74. Karim, *Faryodi*, 351.
75. Karim, *Faryodi*, 330–333.
76. Nasriddinov, *Tarkiš*, 92.
77. Nasriddinov, *Tarkiš*, 121–122.
78. Nasriddinov, *Tarkiš*, 136. See Venelin Ganev, "Post-communism as an episode of state building: A reversed Tillyan perspective," *Communist and Post-Communist Studies* 38 (2005): 425–45.
79. Sohibnazar, *Subhi 1*, 141.
80. Yūsuf, *Tāǧīkestān*, 77.
81. Nabieva and Zikriyoev, *Ta'rixi 11*, 81.
82. Yusufǧon Ahmadov (Konibodom) registered but suspended his campaign. The complete list of registered candidates was published in *Adabiyot va San'at*, October 10, 1991, 41 and its special edition on October 24, 1991, 43: 3; see also: Karim, *Faryodi*, 336 and 364; Nasriddinov, *Tarkiš*, 149.
83. Yūsuf, *Tāǧīkestān*, 146.
84. Usmonov, *Nabiev*, 19.
85. Yūsuf, *Tāǧīkestān*, 141.
86. Karim, *Faryodi*, 365; Sohibnazar, *Subhi 1*, 211; Yūsuf, *Tāǧīkestān*, 138.
87. Karim, *Faryodi*, 355.
88. FBIS-SOV-91-175, 10 September 1991, 101.
89. S. Qiyompur and P. Ǧahongir, "Raisi ǧumhur čī kase bošad?," *Adabiyot va San'at*, September 12, 1991, 37: 7.
90. Tūraǧonzoda, "Ivazšavii," 9.
91. Tūraǧonzoda, *Miyoni*, 11.
92. Yūsuf, *Tāǧīkestān*, 136–137.
93. Karim, *Faryodi*, 365.
94. Sohibnazar, *Subhi 1*, 201–211.
95. Kenǧaev, *Tabadduloti 3*, 289.
96. Kenǧaev, *Tabadduloti 2*, 229.
97. Tūraǧonzoda, *Miyoni*, 51.
98. In Badaxšon the turnout was reportedly 98.7%, in Leninobod 93% and in Dushanbe 63.8% (FBIS-SOV-91-228, 26 November 1991, 89).
99. FBIS-SOV-91-229, 27 November 1991, 72.
100. FBIS-SOV-91-240, 13 December 1991, 90.
101. Yūsuf, *Tāǧīkestān*, 146.
102. Abdulov, *Rohi*, 84–86.
103. Sattorī, *HNIT*, 161–162.
104. A. Qayumzod, "Xudo bo most, pirūzī niz," *Čaroǧi rūz*, 1992. 24: 3.
105. Usmonov, *Nabiev*, 21.
106. Nasriddinov, *Tarkiš*, 150.
107. Karim, *Faryodi*, 369.
108. See the interview with Davlat Usmon in Sattorī, *HNIT*, 161–162.
109. Nasriddinov, *Tarkiš*, 150.
110. Usmonov, *Nabiev*, 21.
111. Abdullaev and Akbarzadeh, *Dictionary*, 45.

112. FBIS-SOV-92-013, 21 January 1992, 84.

113. Only in December 1994, Rahmonov's associate Abdumağid Dostiev established the People's Democratic Party of Tajikistan (PDPT, *Hizbi xalqi demokratii Toğikiston*) as the presidential party. Rahmonov assumed the PDPT's Chairmanship in 1998. Abdullaev and Akbarzadeh, *Dictionary*, 164–165; Usmonov, *Nabiev*, 22; Karim, *Faryodi*, 369; FBIS-SOV-92-003, 6 January 1992, 62.

114. Karim, *Faryodi*, 356.

115. Nasriddinov, *Tarkiš*, 160–162.

116. EBRD, *Tajikistan: 2000 Country Investment Profile* (London: EBRD), 6–7; FBIS-SOV-92-118, 18 June 1992, 61; FBIS-SOV-92-148, 31 July 1992, 46.

117. Nasriddinov, *Tarkiš*, 88.

118. Mosalmāniyān, *Tāğīkestān*, 24.

119. FBIS-SOV-92-042, 3 March 1992, 71.

120. FBIS-SOV-92-047, 10 March 1992, 43.

121. FBIS-SOV-92-017, 27 January 1992, 65–66.

122. Davlat, "Istiqloliyate," 8.

123. FBIS-SOV-92-004, 7 January 1991, 73; FBIS-SOV-92-119, 19 June 1992, 69.

124. FBIS-SOV-92-047, 10 March 1992, 44.

125. FBIS-SOV-92-030, 13 February 1992, 88.

126. FBIS-SOV-92-013, 21 January 1992, 85; FBIS-SOV-92-017, 27 January 1992, 65–67.

127. Originally, a second MRD, the 134th, had been deployed in the TaSSR but the unit was disbanded in 1989.

128. Ašurov had enlisted in the age of 18 with the Soviet Armed Forces. He had been deployed to Afghanistan and the GDR. From 1991 to 1993 he was commander of the 201st MRD. After his return to Russia, he served in various General Staff position in the Russian Armed Forces and between 2002 and 2004 he was the official Russian advisor to the Syrian Chief of Staff. In 2005 he retired and passed away in 2007 (see the obituary in the internet newspaper *Soldat Rosii* on www.soldatrossii.com).

129. Kenğaev, *Tabadduloti 1*, 109.

130. FBIS-SOV-91-185, 24 September 1991, 90; FBIS-SOV-91-186, 25 September 1991, 86.

131. Cf. the special edition of *Adabiyot va San'at*, October 24, 1991, 43: 2–11.

132. FBIS-SOV-90-106, 2 June 1992, 33.

133. FBIS-SOV-91-233, 4 December 1991, 82.

134. Usmonov, *Nabiev*, 24.

135. See Safaralī Kenğaev, *Huquq va ozodihoi graždaninho* (Dušanbe: Irfon, 1988) and Safarali Kendžaev and Kutfiniso Mirzoeva, *Očerk istorii prokuratury Tadžikistana* (Dušanbe: Fondi Kendžaeva, 1995).

136. Cf. http://www.ozodi.org/content/article/606495.html, accessed June, 13, 2014.

137. Kenğaev, *Tabadduloti 1*, 9.

138. Usmonov, *Nabiev*, 25

139. Sohibnazar, *Subhi 1*, 89.

140. Karim, *Faryodi*, 353.

141. Yūsuf, *Tāğīkestān*, 149–150.

142. Tūrağonzoda, *Miyoni*, 24.

143. Sohibnazar, *Subhi 1*, 256–266.

144. Iraj Bashiri, *Prominent Tajik Figures of the Twentieth Century* (Dushanbe, 2002), 143.

145. Kenğaev does not explicitly refer to his Yağnobī origin and only cursory mentions his family (Kenğaev, *Tabadduloti 1*, 177).

146. Kenğaev, *Tabadduloti 1*, 17; Abdulmağid Dostiev, *Toğikiston—šikastanho va bastanho* (Dušanbe: Irfon, 2005).

147. See for instance Nasriddinov, *Tarkiš*, 287; Yūsuf, *Tāğīkestān*, 103–104, 157; Roy, *Central Asia*, 139–140 and Monica Whitlock, *Land beyond the river: The untold story of Central Asia* (New York: Thomas Dunne Books, 2003), 155. As for milk kinship see Peter Parkes, "Milk kinship in Islam. Substance, structure, history," *Social Anthropology* 13, no. 3 (2005).

148. Kenğaev, *Tabadduloti 1*, 119.

149. Kenğaev, *Tabadduloti 1*, 38.

150. Kenğaev, *Tabadduloti 1*, 119.

151. Kenğaev, *Tabadduloti 1*, 227.

152. *Kayhān-e havā'ī*, November 11, 1992, 1004: 32.

153. See Yūsuf, *Tāğīkestān*, 103.

154. Kenğaev, *Tabadduloti 1*, 13–15.

155. Kenğaev, *Tabadduloti 1*, 79.

156. Kenğaev, *Tabadduloti 1*, 83.

157. Kenğaev, *Tabadduloti 1*, 74.

158. Sohibnazar, *Subhi 2*, 288.

159. Nasriddinov, *Tarkiš*, 287; Sohibnazar, *Subhi 1*, 287 and *Subhi 2*, 266; FBIS-SOV-92-085, 1 May 1992, 47. Placido starred in the 1990 Russian-Italian coproduction *Afghan Breakdown* (*Afganskiy izlom*) playing a Soviet officer in the Afghan campaign. Parts of the Leninfilm production were scheduled to be filmed in Tajikistan, but when the cameraman Matrosov was killed during the February 1990 Events, Leninfilm suspended the shooting in Tajikistan and finalized the production in Syria. The Tajik actor and wrestler Mūso Iso[ev] played the Afghan Adil in *Afghan Breakdown* (see Chapter 7).

160. Kenğaev, *Tabadduloti 1*, 116.

161. Kenğaev, *Tabadduloti 1*, 30–31.

162. Kenğaev, *Tabadduloti 1*, 280.

163. Kenğaev, *Tabadduloti 3*, 56.

164. Kenğaev, *Tabadduloti 1*, 71.

165. Kenğaev, *Tabadduloti 1*, 177–178.

166. Kenğaev, *Tabadduloti 1*, 117–118.

167. FBIS-SOV-92-210, 29 October 1992, 61.

168. Kenğaev, *Tabadduloti 1*, 73.

Chapter 5

Islam

The Soviet Union understood itself as a secular state in which the society and the state needed to be protected from the negative influence of religion. Religion and religious belief were considered as irrational, obscurant and diametrically opposed to the holistic modernization project of the USSR. During the 1920s and 1930s, the Soviet authorities systematically destroyed religious institutions and arrested religious specialists throughout the Soviet Union. In Soviet Central Asia the anti-religious campaign commenced with the abolishment of religious institutions such as the *šari'a* courts and religious endowments (*vaqf*) depriving religious specialists of their income and social-economic status. Since the late 1920s, mosques, religious schools (*madrasa*), shrines (*mazar*) and convents were closed, destroyed, desecrated and transformed into "socially useful" buildings. Many representatives of the established *ulamo* either migrated from Soviet Central Asia or they were arrested, deported and often executed, dramatically changing the composition of the religious field. Within less than a decade, the fierce anti-religious propaganda stigmatized the observance of religious practice and excluded Islam from the public space. Political campaigns, such as the emancipation of women in Central Asia, known as *huğum* (Arabic for "attack") with its focus on the un-veiling of women in Central Asia, demonstrated the determination of the Bolsheviks to eradicate religion.[1]

The anti-religious campaign in Central Asia was compounded by the suppression of the *bosmačī* resistance, which was classified by the Soviet authorities as an "armed nationalist and counterrevolutionary movement in Central Asia (1917–1926), where the fight against Soviet rule was instigated by the feudal class, the *boyho*, *kulakho*, the fanatic *mullos* (*mullohoi irtiğoī*) and the bourgeois nationalists (*millatčiyoni buržuazī*)."[2] Despite the aggressive anti-religious campaign, religious belief and practice persisted among the population and transformed, less regulated by normative guidelines and scriptural sources, but embedded in the reconstruction of an (alleged) authentic culture and as a moral orientation.[3]

While the majority of scholars associate the Perestroika years with the Islamic revival in Central Asia,[4] Stéphane Dudoignon identifies earlier periods of Islamic revival with the establishment of official religious institutions in 1943 followed by the general amnesty 1953 after Stalin's death.[5] In 1943, the Soviet authorities changed their religious policies, established official religious institutions and adopted legal provisions designed to regulate and appropriate religion. As for Central Asia, the central institution was the Spiritual Administration of the Muslims of Central Asia and Kazakhstan (SADUM = Russ.: *Dukhovnoe upravlenie musul'man Sredney Azii i Kazakhstana*) in Tashkent, which administered, regulated and appropriated "Islam" in the region. The SADUM, chaired by a senior religious specialists (usually from the Naqšbandiyya order), organized the registration of mosques, appointed loyal religious specialists, monitored the religious personnel and issued its expertise (*fatvo*) on religious questions. Furthermore the SADUM represented the USSR's Muslims abroad and organized the yearly hajj for Central Asian Muslims (albeit only for a limited number of loyal and merited communists). Unsurprisingly, the Soviet authorities, in particular the state Committee for Religious Affairs (CRA) and the KGB, tightly controlled the SADUM.[6] In 1946, the SADUM reopened the Miri Arab *madrasa* in Bukhara for elementary religious education and in 1971 it established the Imam al-Bukhari Institute in Tashkent for graduate religious studies.[7]

The establishment of "official" Islamic institutions facilitated the emergence of a particular analytical and instrumentalist framework developed by Soviet scholarship to categorize Islam and Muslims in the USSR, in particular the dichotomy between a scriptural, normative "pure" Islam as represented by the SADUM and an unregulated "traditional," "popular" or "parallel" Islam practiced outside the SADUM and the socialist society.[8] The Communist Party, the SADUM and the Soviet academia were accomplices in the endeavor of adopting "a 'rigorist' interpretation of what constituted 'real' Islam."[9] At the same time, the SADUM and academia operated in a contradictory environment: While the general ideological premise of the Communist Party was still the creation of an atheist society and the repression of religion, the SADUM and academia actively aspired to define an Islamic normativity and the "correct" religious practice and doctrine against a traditional, superstitious "popular" Islam. This "traditionalist" Islam was portrayed by Soviet ethnographers and Orientalists as refractory to the Soviet modernization process and entangled in pre- or un-Islamic customs—following the argument that the "correct" Islamic practice was defined by the SADUM.[10] The Soviet administrative practice of appropriation and control was legitimized and facilitated by an academic discourse on Islam. One of the most influential academics was Lucian Klimovič (1907–1989), an "ideological Orientalist *par excellence*" as Eren Tasar points out:

> Klimovich's contribution was the transformation of this dichotomy into that of partially respectable versus uncontrolled, anarchic Islam. This set the stage for the crystallization of the normative (official) / folk (popular) Islam dichotomy that became a hallmark of all studies dealing with Muslims in the Soviet Union [...]. Thus, the SADUM / non-SADUM and registered / un-registered dichotomies carried meaning on an administrative, not religious, level, and the mosque / social and normative / folk dichotomies which they spawned had their roots entirely in Soviet administrative realities rather than a sound and sincere study of Muslim life.[11]

The validity of these categories and their epistemology have been repeatedly questioned. Tasar points out that the notion of "popular Islam" was an important analytical category for both, the SADUM portraying itself as the legitimate representation of a normative Islam, and the USSR bureaucracy as a categorization for allegedly uncontrollable religious activities outside the limits of the SADUM. Thus, the label "popular" Islam emerged as an essentialist concept to summarize the very heterogenous religious field not registered with the SADUM. Mark Saroyan questions the rationality of the dichotomy between representatives of the registered religious personnel and their unregistered counterparts. Saroyan portrays the registered *ulamo*'s efforts to reconcile the communist ideology with religion not primarily as a strategy of accommodation but as a subtle Muslim version of the "Soviet man" in which religion was not anymore perceived as an anti-modern phenomenon that would eventually wither away with Soviet modernity but as an alternative variation.[12]

The categorization of "official," "un-official" or "parallel" reveals little about the religious agenda and neglects the interaction, dynamics and commonalities among religious specialists within the religious field. This is not to deny the importance of official registration or the ostentatious refusal to register, respectively the denial of registration with the Soviet authorities. The categorization of religious authorities as "official," "parallel" or "popular" refers first of all to Soviet administrative and not religious practice among the Muslim population. For Tajikistan, Abdullo Rahnamo applies similar categories as his Soviet predecessors and distinguishes between three types of religious specialists in Tajikistan: the official *ulamo* (*rūhaniyoni rasmī*) who are integrated into the official, state-sponsored institutions, the traditional *ulamo* (*rūhaniyoni sunnatī*), who are quietist and apolitical, and finally the political (*siyosī*) or reformist (*islohtalab*) *ulamo*.[13] And like his Soviet predecessors, Rahnamo is directly involved in the administration of religion, for instance in the attestation of *imom-xatibs* for the Committee of religious Affairs and the Council of Tajikistan's *ulamo* echoing DeWeese's statement on the complicity between the state, academia and registered *ulamo*.[14] Eventually, the categories of "official," "parallel" or "popular" possess an ambiguity and refer to very different constituents of a religious specialist's interaction with the wider social space. For instance, the religious agenda of the overwhelming majority of the TaSSR/Tajikistan's religious specialists is rooted in the larger Hanafi Sunni Islamic "tradition" while discourses of an Islamic "reform" were (and are) limited to a very few lay religious intellectuals. Religious specialists, such as the Tūraǧon family, are both "traditional" and "reformist" since they struggle to re-establish a more normative understanding of the Hanafi Sunni religious tradition as well as to reform the institutional structure regulating Islam in the TaSSR/Tajikistan. Simultaneously, lay religious communities expect religious specialists to provide "authentic" religious advice to very tangible daily problems and grievances, which often implies a flexible (or *reformist*) approach to the larger religious tradition.[15]

An equally contentious issue is the significance of the Islamic mystical tradition—*tasavvuf* or Sufism—in Soviet and post-Soviet Central Asia. The majority of religious specialists in Tajikistan claim affiliation to a Sufi order, mostly from a descent, influential Sufi lineage such as the Naqšbandiyya or Qaderiyya. The use of honorific titles such as *ešon, pir, maxsum* and *šayx/sheikh* locates a religious specialist in a specific *silsila*, a mystical genealogy of important spiritual predecessors. The persecution by the Soviet authorities and the social transformation of the Soviet society changed the social landscapes of Central Asia and reduced the social relevance and importance of Sufism. Especially the influential Naqšbandiyya with its elaborated internal regulations and complex interaction with the larger social field (politics, religion and economy) experienced a catastrophic disintegration. Soviet rule deprived the Naqšbandiyya of its economic fundament and undermined its extensive networks of *murids* by resettlement campaigns, persecution and collectivization.

Since the religious revival in the 1950s, Sufism in Tajikistan has not been re-institutionalized and is only tenuously associated with particular religious practices (for instance the *zikr*), but predominately rooted in local genealogies and their social environment. The genealogy and the relationship between the spiritual teacher (*muršid*) and his student (*murid*) are important for the transmission of religious knowledge and therefore constituents for an individual's symbolic religious capital next to memorizing the Koran, mastery of the foundational religious sources, knowledge of Arabic and the canon of classical Persian poetry. Importantly, the *muršid-murid* relation facilitates the establishment of patronage networks by integrating important businessmen or politicians with the *muršid* mediating between the different constituents among his followers.[16]

The protagonists in the TaSSR's religious field considered the reference to a specific local/regional genealogical mystical tradition and the student-teacher relation in small teaching circles *huğra* (lit.: small cell, room) or *halqa* (lit.: circle) as important constituents of their religious capital. Although Islamic activists of the *harakat*/IRPT were affiliated to important Sufi masters, for instance Muhammadšarif Himmatzoda was a *murid* of the imminent Naqšbandī *ešoni* Abdurahmonğon (1920–1991), there was little public discussion among the activists on the mystical traditions and practices.[17]

One of the central concerns of the registered as well as unregistered *ulamo* between the 1950s and 1970s was a re-establishment of a normative Hanafi Sunni understanding of Islam and the education of a younger generation of *ulamo*. After Stalin's death, the religious field in the TaSSR gradually recovered and two major directions proliferated until the mid-1970s: The SADUM and its few registered religious authorities, such as the former *qozīkalon* Mūsobekzoda (1883–1978), represented a normative and regulated Hanafi Islam embedded in the Soviet idea of the regional Central Asian heritage, while unregistered circles, for instance around *qorī* Muhammadğon Hindustonī, propagated a neo-traditionalist interpretation of Islam. Although there were disagreements on the normativity of ritual practice among the registered and unregistered *ulamo*, there were apparently only minor disputes about theology and religious thought. Importantly, there was a constant interaction between representatives of the two spheres.[18] Furthermore, the personnel within the religious field were relatively small. Zubaydulloh Roziq identifies for the early 1980s only 96 religious specialists who actively spread Islamic knowledge in the TaSSR and some 36 younger activists and 13 Sufi *sheikhs* who also preserved the "customary knowledge and practices (*urfu odat*), the national traditions, the national language, culture and civilization."[19] The *ulamo* active between the 1950s and 70s shared the memory of the tremendous disruptions since the 1920s, the destruction of their religious institutions and structures, the arbitrary violence during Stalinism, the imprisonment and execution of many religious authorities, the forced resettlement of their communities as well as the fundamental social change creating an urban Soviet communist society in which religion was largely excluded. Hindustonī (who had been arrested several times) as well as other *ulamo* of his generation therefore adopted a quietist, non-interventionist attitude toward the political field and admonished their students not to interfere with politics.[20] Thus, one can draw an analogy with the Brezhnevite era of mature socialism and "stability of cadres" in the religious field and like in the political field, this stability came to end in the 1980s.

REFORMISM, RENEWAL AND THE POLITICAL

The social transformation in the TaSSR, urbanization and industrialization, profoundly changed the social, economic and political context in which Islam was practiced and negotiated.[21] This is particularly valid for the southern lowlands of Tajikistan, where the *muhoğir* communities gradually recovered from resettlement and consolidated their social position in the large collective farms since the 1960s. The younger *muhoğir* generation benefited from the social mobilization and intervention of the Soviet state, although their access to higher echelons of administration, academia or politics was limited. Soviet discourses on the alleged traditionalism of the Qarotegin population converged with the experience of (real or imagined) marginalization. The embeddedness in a specific local Islamic context created societal conditions which made the younger *muhoğir* generation apparently more perceptive for an alternative social-interventionist understanding of Islam and political activism promoting concepts of an Islamic order. In the early 1970s, clandestine circles of Muslim activists emerged and the Revolution in Iran 1979 as well as the Soviet Invasion of Afghanistan (where many Tajik conscripts had to serve) triggered an unprecedented politicization of Muslims in Soviet Central Asia. Simultaneously, an increasing number of foreign Muslims students from "friendly" Muslim countries such as Yemen, Syria or Iraq, who studied in the USSR, introduced the Central Asian activists to the "classic" reading of Islamist literature (such as Qutb or Mawdudi) and therefore facilitated their politicization. Stéphane Dudoignon considers this development as a "mutation" from the previous periods of "revival." While the revival of the 1950s and 1960s took place within the larger Hanafi-Sunni tradition of Central Asia, the developments in the 1980s were "a completely different phenomenon of mutation led by actors with new profiles, new backgrounds, new techniques of communication and new audiences, with a rapidly changing geopolitical, social and institutional framework."[22] Although I share Dudoignon's ideas on the early revival, I am hesitant to use the pathological term "mutation" for the transformation of Tajikistan's religious field in the 1980s. The developments and shifts within the religious field since then were related to Central Asia's reconnection with the wider Islamicate world and therefore embedded within the transformation of political Islam since the 1970s.[23] In the TaSSR, this transformation—or mutation—is above all associated with students of *qorī* Muhammadğon Hindustonī.

qorī Muhammadğon Hindustonī: The Central Asian Neo-Traditionalist

qorī (or *mavlavī* or *domullo*) Muhammadğon Hindustonī Qūqandī (1892–1989)[24] was one of the most influential religious scholars in the Islamic revival in Central Asia due to his extensive network of students including several of the leading Islamic activists in Tajikistan and Uzbekistan. Hindustonī's biography mirrors the transformation of Central Asian societies and the religious field since the 1920s and defies general categorizations: Hindustonī was born in 1892 in the village Čorboġ close to Kokand and joined a religious seminar in Bukhara in 1908. Around 1914/1915 he left for Balkh and became a student of Muhammad Ġafs Saidzoda, whom he followed to Bukhara, Tashkent and Jalalabad (in Afghanistan). After Ġafs passed away in 1921, Hindustonī continued his education in Ajmer (in India's state of Rajasthan). Only in 1929, Hindustonī returned to his native Kokand where he was employed in a kolkhoz. He soon came in conflict with the Soviet authorities and he was arrested for the first time in the early 1930s. The NKVD arrested Hindustonī a second time in 1937 as a religious agitator and sent him for three years to a Gulag in Sverdlovsk. Even though almost fifty, he was drafted to the Soviet Army in 1943 and severely wounded in a combat close to Minsk in 1944. After his recuperation, he went to Tashkent in 1945/1946, where he was contacted by the SADUM and appointed *imom-xatib* of the Yaʿqub Čarxī Mosque in Dushanbe in 1947. His tenure as a registered *imom-xatib* lasted only two years. In 1949, he was again denounced as "enemy of the people" and sentenced to 25 years in a labor camp. Hindustonī served four years of his sentence in Karaganda (Kazakhstan) and was finally released in the general amnesty after Stalin's death. After his return to Dushanbe, he did not continue his career as a registered *imom-xatib*; instead, he was employed as a translator for Urdu, Arabic and Farsi in the Institute for Oriental Studies at the academy of science until his retirement in 1955. At the same time, Hindustonī was occupied with private scholarly work and teaching. Hindustonī composed a six-volume *tafsīr* of the Koran in Uzbek and translated Hanafi-Sunni text collections from Arabic to Tajik and Uzbek. He taught small clandestine circles (called *huġra*, *davra* or *halqa*) of young Uzbeks and Tajiks and among his students were several prominent Islamic activists, such as Abdullo Nurī (who was introduced to Hindustonī by his grandfather in 1965), Qiyomiddin Ġozī, Muhammadšarif Himmatzoda, *mavlavī* Abdulhay, *domullo* Hikmatullo Toġikobodī, *maxsumi* Burhoniddin Ešonġon, Nuriddinġon and Mahmudġon Tūraġon and Alloma Rahmatullo (an influential Uzbek activist who died in 1981 in a car accident). Hindustonī was very selective with his students and accepted only some 150 students throughout the 30 years of his clandestine scholarly career. He organized different *huġra*s, smaller circles with up to five senior students (such as Nurī or Ġozī) and larger circles with up to 25 students in which he conveyed more basic knowledge on Islamic practices and doctrines.[25] Apparently, the local KGB tolerated Hindustonī's activities, but KGB operatives frequently visited his teaching circles, took the names of the students and inspected the textbooks. Sulton Hamad (himself a former KGB

officer) described the KGB intrusions as distressing and sometimes students
were dismissed from the university for their religious studies.[26]

Hindustonī was not only an important religious authority in the TaSSR but,
due to his extensive networks and complex biography, an important "intermediary between the demographically limited 'registered' religious personnel of the Tajik SSR and a wider variety of 'non-registered' protagonists of
the religious field."[27] Locating Hindustonī and his religious-societal agenda
in the religious field encounters some ambivalent narratives and controversies, which are related to the academic and political discourses on Islam
and Islamic activism in Central Asia. Since many Islamist activists attended
Hindustonī's teaching circles, he is often portrayed as the intellectual mentor of Islamist activism in Soviet Central Asia and associated with the (albeit
heterogenous) Deobandi network. Conspicuously, Hoǧī Akbar maintained
that Hindustonī graduated from a Deobandi *madrasa* in Ajmer—an assumption, which has been repeatedly questioned and which is not supported by
Hindustonī's autobiographical writings.[28] Arguably, the Deobandi designation
was above all a signifier in the political struggle and an effort to appropriate
the highly respected Hindustonī as a genuine representative of the IRPT and
their political as well as societal objectives with the ulterior intention to reach
out to the established *ulamo* whose sympathies for the IRPT were muted.
Eventually, the categorization and location of Hindustonī in a fixed religious
"tradition" (such as the Deobandi) is not necessarily constructive: After
his return to Soviet Central Asia, Hindustonī had to operate in a social and
political environment in which religious institutions and structures had been
destroyed and public religious practice banned. Therefore, Hindustonī's main
objectives were the conservation and—in his later years—the rehabilitation of
the pre-Soviet Hanafi-Sunni societal order and not the introduction of "new"
reformist political trends of Islamic thought.[29] However, a satisfying analysis
of Hindustonī's religious writings is beyond the scope of this manuscript and
here more research has to be conducted.

Dissent and Politicization

The increasing politicization of Central Asian Muslims in the 1970s and
1980s nurtured dissent among Hindustonī's students who refused to con-
strain themselves to the promotion of quietist normative Hanafi Sunni Islam.
Remarkably, the most contentious disputes between the established *ulamo*
and the younger activists were not related to political issues, Islamic jurispru-
dence or theology, but to religious practice, in particular those rituals, which
were silently tolerated by the Soviet authorities, such as funerals (*ǧanoza*)
or the visit to local shrines (*ziyorat*).[30] Roziq reports, that with the post-
Stalinist revival of religious communities, the "correct" religious practice

was increasingly undermined by unacceptable "innovations (*bid'atho*) [...] local conventions and customs as well as superstitions (*urfu odatho va xurofot*)."[31] Activists criticized that local mullos had transformed religious rituals to a lucrative business and invented additional rituals and practices not within the *harakat*'s normative understanding of Islam. Individual religious scholars disapproved these practices, and Abdullo Nurī—after his father had passed away—declined to arrange a *ğanoza* with the obligatory *oš* expected by the population in the Turkmenistan sovkhoz.[32] The disputes over the "correct" religious practice and "innovations" between the local population, the local (registered or unregistered) mullos and adolescent activists triggered fierce debates damaging the reputation of the *harakat* and later the IRPT among traditionally minded religious circles.[33]

THE RISE OF THE ISLAMIC RENAISSANCE PARTY OF TAJIKISTAN (IRPT)

According to its official history, the group which was to become the IRPT was formed in Qūrġonteppa on 20 April 1973 by a group of five Islamic activists: Hoğī Qalandar Sadriddin, Ne'matulloh Ešon, Odinabek Abdusalom, *qorī* Muhammadğon Muhiddin and last but not least Abdulloh Nurī. Initially, Nurī and his associates did not adopt a name for their group and simply called it *harakat* (Tajik for movement). Only some years later, the *harakat* became the "Revival of the Islamic Youth of Tajikistan" (*Nahzati Ğavononi Islomii Toğikiston* with the acronym *Nağot* = salvation). In the words of Nurī the *harakat* was a "group of freedom-loving (*ozodī-xo*) and reformist (*islohtalab*) youth"[34] who were concerned about the withering knowledge on normative Hanafi Islam in the Tajik society. The name was apparently a retrospective adoption to provide the IRPT with a historical panache and tradition as one could observe in 2013 when the IRPT celebrated its 40th anniversary.[35] Due to the heterogeneity of the movement until the early 1990s, the term *harakat* is much more suitable for the movement in these early years.[36]

The undisputed leader of the *harakat*/IRPT until his death in 2006 was "Sayid" Abdullo[h] Nurī, who was born on 15 March 1947 in Oštiyon, a small village in the Sangvor/Tavildara *nohiyya*.[37] The family was resettled in 1953 in the Turkmenistan sovkhoz in the Vaxš district south of Qūrġonteppa, where his father and brother, Nuriddin and Ato Saidov, worked in the administration of a collective farm. After graduation from school in 1964, Nurī studied geodesy in Qūrġonteppa's technical college.

Nurī and Himmatzoda located the establishment of the proto-IRPT movement within the particular regional context: The movement arose among the people of the Qarotegin Valley since they were pious and devout Muslims

deeply rooted in the culture of the mountain valleys. The *harakat* emerged
therefore in an authentic local context entrenched in the culture of the Qarotegin
Valley without any influence by "foreign" movements.[38] Nurī's attention to the
genuine origins of his movement is related to the official discourses delineating
Islamic activism and political Islam as "foreign," alien and non-Tajik.

The devotion of the Qarotegin population to traditional Islamic education
has produced many important religious scholars (like Nurī and Himmatzoda
themselves). Furthermore, the local horticulture combined with Qarotegin
work ethics has made local communities prosperous and allowed them to
send their sons and daughters to the centers of Islamic civilization. Finally,
Himmatzoda and Nurī located the movement firmly within the larger Central
Asian Hanafi-Sunni tradition as a continuation of the regional *ğadidī* movement after the enforced hiatus of 50 years Soviet rule. However, the reference
to the *ğadidī* movement remained vague—neither Himmatzoda nor Nurī
explicated what the *ğadidī* movement (in their imagination) actually stands
for. Apparently, the *ğadidī* movement served as a marker for an authentic
Central Asian project of an autochthonous modernization. Related to the
issue of authenticity, the *harakat* nourished a strong anti-colonial perception
of Soviet rule.[39]

Tūrağonzoda, for instance, observed that the political nomenklatura feared
the *harakat*/IRPT since they posed "a serious threat to their own colonizing
project."[40] Hoğī Qalandar Sadriddin, one of the *harakat*'s founding members, elaborated that they stood for a reintroduction of Islamic culture and
teaching in the Tajik society, the fight against unlawful novelties (*bid'at*) and
superstitions (*xurofot*) and eventually the end of the *ulamo*'s silence with the
resumption of a public "Command Right and Forbid Wrong."[41] Therefore,
the early activists in unison mentioned the spread of Islamic knowledge and
morals (*axloqi islomī*) among the younger generation as their central concern.[42] The *harakat*'s agenda and their activism gradually generated tensions
with the established religious authorities. Next to the issue of "innovations"
and the "correct" religious practice, *harakat* members criticized the political
quietism and lack of social intervention by the *ulamo*.[43]

The majority of *harakat* activists were well-adjusted members of the
Soviet society with inconspicuous careers. Several leading activists graduated in applied sciences, economics or related subjects. Nurī studied geodesy
and worked in the Qūrğonteppa land survey department, Gadoev graduated
in mechanical engineering (therefore his nickname *inžener*—engineer) and
Usmon has a law degree. Some activists looked for occupational niches,
which offered them time for private studies but allowed them to formally
integrate into the Soviet society with a modest income and the important *propiska* (the local registration/residence permit).[44] At the same time, the activists emphasized their rigid self-discipline, their abstinence from alcohol and

cigarettes, propagating a particular Islamic morality disapproving of sexual liberty and extramarital relationships.[45] Nurī and his followers thus located themselves (and their habitus) outside the mainstream milieus in the later Soviet Union projecting an alternative lifestyle neglecting the system's career patterns and forms of social recognition.

The *harakat* carefully expanded beyond Qūrġonteppa since the late 1970s. In 1977 Davlat Usmon and a year later Muhammadšarif Himmatzoda became involved in the group and soon advanced to be the leading activists next to Nurī.[46] The expansion of the *harakat* eventually attracted the attention of the republican KGB and Sulton Hamad, an early *harakat* activist *and* KGB officer in Qūrġonteppa, who remembered that the first reports about the group were collected in 1977, but then local networks and family relations provided protection.[47]

Ibrohim Usmonov pointed out that until the 1980s the *harakat* resembled more a regional cultural club with vague political ambitions than a political party. This might be related to the origins of the *harakat* in rural Tajikistan and among the *muhoğir* from the Qarotegin Valley—social groups, which were arguably less receptive to political Islamism compared with the "classical" social origins of Islamism in the industrial (sub-)urban areas. Internal resettlement and the emergence of the agro-industrial complex shaped the social transformation since the 1950s replicating social milieus and hierarchies of rural Tajikistan.[48] Ultimately, the emergence of the IRPT in rural Tajikistan accounts for the lack of versatile Soviet intellectuals in its ranks bridging the IRPT to the urban Soviet electorate in the TaSSR. This, however, changed gradually with the inclusion of new members and abruptly due to political events on the global level: The Iranian Revolution in February and the Soviet invasion of Afghanistan in December 1979. Both events accelerated the politicization of the movement and its leadership. While the activists perceived the revolution in Iran an groundbreaking event for political Islamism, the invasion of Afghanistan violated the very "Honor of Islam" (*nomusi islomī*) and the *harakat* decided that they could not remain neutral confronted with this "merciless aggression."[49] With the politicization, the *harakat*'s leadership—Nurī and Himmatzoda—agreed on a division of labor: While Nurī served as the spiritual and religious authority, Himmatzoda took over the political organization of the *harakat* and invited the various clandestine operating activists to a meeting close to Kofarnihon for a discussion on the political agenda in 1985.[50]

In the late 1980s the *harakat* became popular among students and a more formal structure emerged with a central committee as well as subdivisions for women, education, finances and security. But in 1989 there was only a tentative coordination between regional branches of the *harakat* when Davlat Usmon eventually travelled to the northern district of Isfara and Čorkūh, where he invited local activists to join the southern movement. At the same time, the *harakat* reached out to Muslim activists in other parts of the USSR.[51] Of particular importance were contacts to foreign students, in particular from Arab countries who studied in the USSR. Roziq and Davlat Usmon recall their acquaintance with the Yemenite student Muhammad ʿAlī Valī, who studied at Moscow's Patrice Lumumba University but changed to the Medical University in Dushanbe in the early 1980s. There, Valī organized a study circle for five activists of the *harakat* reading of the "mandatory" texts of political Islam by Hasan al-Banna (the founder of the Muslim Brotherhood in Egypt), the brothers Sayyid and Muhammad Qutb (the main ideologists of the Muslim Brotherhood) and Sayyid Abul Ala Mawdudi. Introductory works on Islamic theology, history, morals and Arabic language/grammar (*nahv*) were part of the reading list as well.[52] These key texts of political Islamist thinking, however, only had a limited impact on the *harakat*/IRPT's political agenda, which was dominated by Glasnost discourses, national sovereignty and democratic transformation.

Since the mid-1980s the KGB started eavesdropping meetings of the *harakat* and on 22 June 1986 the KGB launched a major operation under the codename *Sahar* (Dawn) against the group. Some 50 sympathizers of the *harakat* were arrested in Dushanbe, Qūrġonteppa, Yovon and Vaxš, among them *domullo* Muhammadqosim Rahim, *domullo* Muhammadšarif Qalandarov and Zubaydullo Roziq. The KGB arrested Nurī, who worked at that time as topographic surveyor in Qūrġonteppa, two days later on his way to Yovon.[53] The KGB applied a double strategy: On the one hand, they accused the activists of illegal propaganda against the structures of the Soviet state, on the other hand they tried to discredit the activists' moral reputation by planting drugs (cannabis) as evidence. Nurī's arrest and subsequent trial mobilized his supporters and family in the Turkmenistan sovkhoz to organize a demonstration of some 300 people on 14 August 1986 in front of the CPT building in Qūrġonteppa. The demonstration continued throughout the night and was only suspended when Nurī's family was able to talk with him on the phone. Nurī was eventually charged with propaganda against the Soviet state as well as illicit drug abuse and sentenced to 18 months in a correction camp in Siberia.[54] Several of Nurī's accomplices, such as "Bobo" Sang, "Bobo" Avġon or Šamsiddin Šamsiddin, were sentenced to short prison terms. Others suspended their activities or went into reclusion such as Himmatzoda, who hid in the remote Romit Valley for some time. Davlat Usmon was interrogated several times but neither arrested nor expelled from university.[55] Eventually, the Soviet authorities reached the opposite of their initial intentions with Nurī's arrest: His prison term increased his credibility (or symbolic capital) among the activists as a religious dissident who defied the system and remained true to his principles.[56]

When Nurī was released in 1988, the society and politics in the Soviet Union had further changed: Secular civil associations proliferated and the KGB gradually lost its coercive power. The *harakat* operated more assertively and started to distribute its own periodical *Islamizdat* under the title *Haqiqati Islom* (The Truth of Islam) in 1988. The following year, the activists organized the secret duplication of a thousand copies of an *Islamizdat* written by *qorī* Qiyomiddin Ġozī with the title *Zaruriyoti dinī* (The religious exigencies) in a state-printing house.[57] With the growing politicization and arrest of several of its members, the *harakat* attracted followers outside of their initial constituency. Šamsiddin Šamsiddin, an activist from Mastčohi kūhistonī, reported how a small circle of youth emerged in his home region discussing politics, religion and culture in the late 1980s. In order to connect with kindred spirits, Šamsiddin contacted Nurī in Dushanbe and established the first branch of the *harakat* in Leninobod *viloyat* in 1989.[58] Although the legal registration of a religious party was still unthinkable that year, Nurī and *ešoni* Saidašraf registered as independent candidates in the elections for the Supreme Soviet in February 1990 (however, without being elected in their constituencies).[59]

Throughout 1990, the *harakat* increased its political activities and published openly a monthly magazine *Hidoyat* (Guidance) with a print run of a thousand copies.[60] Despite the emergence of more formalized structures, the *harakat*'s membership remained heterogenous. Nurī followed a modest reformist idea of Islam in reference to the ǧadidī movement with a special emphasis on the social and political relevance of Islamic morals and economics. The *harakat* demanded the privatization and promotion of small and medium businesses meeting expectations of their electorate. Eventually the *harakat* stood for a post-colonial understanding of Soviet rule and its founding members positioned themselves outside the Soviet system of social mobilization and recognition. The leading activists were not former cadres in the Soviet institutions and portrayed the *harakat* as an uncompromising break with the Soviet system, which aroused additional suspicion—if not outright hostility—among the Soviet nomenklatura.

The centerpiece of their religious agenda was the restoration of the Hanafi-Sunni normativity and the authoritative "Commanding Right and Forbidding Wrong" recognizing the social and political transformations of everyday life since the 1980s. By stressing the social relevance of Islam, the *harakat* offered "common" Muslims a religious moral guidance embedded in the idea of an authentic Tajik/Central Asian Islamicate civilization. The social-political implications could be interpreted ambiguously, both by the *harakat*'s supporters (some of them embarking on a Salafist reading) and the TaSSR's government, which quickly adopted a belligerent discourse on Islamist activism.

The Vahhobī Label

Since the early 1980s, after the revolution in Iran and the Soviet occupation of Afghanistan, the analysis of Islam in the USSR both by Soviet and Western

researchers has been since dominated by concerns of Islamic extremism sub-
verting the stability of the USSR and today's post-Soviet Central Asia. This
analysis and political discourse has become increasingly instrumental for
legitimizing a narrow security driven and authoritarian approach to Islam.[61]
In Soviet Tajikistan, the discussion on the emergence of clandestine Islamist
activist circles and the increasing return to religious practice transformed
into a hostile discourse depicting any form of public religiosity outside the
SADUM as a manifestation of extremism or "fundamentalism" instigated
from abroad.[62] Rarely, the alleged Islamist "threat" was used for self-reflection
and self-criticism: Nasriddinov, for instance, concluded that the proliferation
of Islamic extremism was a reaction to the increasing decadence of the CPT
and its local cadres who devoted themselves "to luxuriousness and the sleep
of ignorance not paying attention to the changes in society."[63] Kenğaev criticized the Soviet security agencies that they did not take the threat posed by
the Islamist activists seriously enough and insinuated complicity between the
KGB and Islamic activists.[64]

In the mid-1980s the term *vahhobī* emerged as a central designation for
the opposition in the unfolding conflict. Although the term refers to the Saudi
Arabian variation of the Hanbali law school in Sunni Islam (the Wahhabiyya),
those who employed the term were less concerned about its religious or
historical meaning but realized its potential for defamation. Popularized by
the Soviet press, the KGB and established religious authorities used the term
to denounce unregistered Islamist activists who followed "non-traditional"
forms of religious practice not sanctioned by the SADUM. Bakhtiyar Babajanov asserts that the alleged *vahhobī*s in late Soviet Central Asia had nothing
in common with the Saudi Arabian Wahhabiyya but were labeled *vahhobī*
due to their non-compliance with the narrowly defined religious normativity
of the SADUM.[65] Notably, the introduction of the politicized term *vahhobī*
in Soviet Central Asia is associated with Hindustonī, who reportedly used
the label the first time for a group of dissident students. Roziq concedes that
"it is a reason for sadness, however, that the term was first used by Mavlavī
Qorī Muhammadğon Hindustonī"[66] in disputes with younger Islamic activists. Hindustonī's fierce criticism and denunciation of his students as *vahhobī*
contributed to an increasing polarization between the old established religious
specialists (born between the 1890s and 1930s) and their younger contenders (born since the late 1940s). The term *vahhobī* was eventually plagiarized
by the KGB as a "seal (*tamğo*)"[67] for Muslim activists in their defamation
campaigns in the public and media and constructed—as Johan Rasanayagam
points out—a local Otherness.[68] The term *vahhobī* soon entered the public
political discourse and on 30 November 1990 *Toğikistoni sovetī* published
an article under the title "The Vahhobiya and the Islamic party." Since the
author of the article, a certain Sunnatullo Ibrohimzoda, was unknown among

Tajikistan's journalists and intelligentsia, it was widely believed that the KGB had launched the article in order to discredit the IRPT.[69] The article described the conflict between foreign-inspired *vahhobī* adherents and the established (national-Tajik) *ulamo* about "Commanding Right (*amri ma'ruf*) in the sphere of religious ceremonies."[70] The article in *Toǧikistoni sovetī* illustrates that the distinction between a benign local/traditional Islam regulated by the registered *ulamo* and a malign foreign/non-traditional Islam (*vahhobī*) practiced by unregistered "extremists" was already an important divisive strategy by the authorities during Soviet times.

In particular Kenǧaev utilized the discourse on Islamism and Wahhabism in his philippic attacks on political adversaries. During the mediation between the demonstrators on Ozodī Square and Nabiev on 4 October 1991, Kenǧaev told Gorbachev's special envoy, Anatoly Sobčak, that the demonstrators are "basically Islamists (*islamiho*) who support *vahhobizm*."[71] The label *vahhobī* simultaneously entered the Western academic occupation with Islam in Central Asia/Tajikistan.[72] Only a few reports tried to balance the media coverage on the Wahhabiyya: *Adabiyot va San'at* published in July 1992 an interview with Qahhor Rasuliyon from the academy of science who—in sober terms—explained the origins of the Wahhabiyya in the 18th century. To the question if there are any *vahhobī* groups in Tajikistan, he evasively replied that possibly there are a few.[73] In the public discussion the meaning of the term *vahhobī* remained vague, elusive and a political instrument. Kenǧaev insinuated that *vahhobī* is in general alien to the Tajik culture and nation, therefore essentially a foreign Other.[74] In a polemic against Tūraǧonzoda and the IRPT, Kenǧaev subsumed the Egyptian Muslim Brotherhood, Hasan al-Banna, Sayyid Qutb, Mawdudi and the *harakat*/IRPT as *vahhobī* without differentiation, demonstrating the ahistorical and discretionary application of the term.[75]

The opposition consistently repudiated the notion of *vahhobizm*. Būrī Karim categorically rejected the existence of *vahhobī* sympathizers in Tajikistan and concluded that Kenǧaev's campaign was similar to "Don Quixote's war against wind mills."[76]

Until the early 1990s, the *harakat* was a movement, which encompassed diverse groups of Islamist activists who adhered to a broad religious agenda striving to re-establish their idea of a Hanafi-Sunni normativity among the Muslims in the TaSSR. Nurī and Himmatzoda merged the normative Hanafi Sunni Islam of the pre-Soviet Central Asian tradition with the political interventionist teachings of Qutb or Mawdudi and a variation of anti-colonial Tajik nationalism. However, the label *vahhobī* for the movement was intentionally misleading: The *harakat* did not embrace the narrow Wahhabi-understanding of the Islamic tradition, instead, Nurī and his followers revered or even followed the regional mystical tradition and practiced religious rituals not accepted by the Wahhabiyya, such as the *mavlud* (birthday of the Prophet Muhammad), *ğanozat* (funeral) or the *ziyorat* to a local shrine. The term *vahhobī*—in the Russified variation *vovčik*—nonetheless became one of the central markers for Otherness in the early stages of the civil war in Tajikistan.

Perestroika, Glasnost and Islam

From the perspective of religious associations and communities, Gorbachev's Perestroika reforms initially meant a setback since Soviet authorities stepped up their atheism campaign throughout the USSR.[77] In late November 1986, Gorbachev held a speech in Tashkent demanding "a determined and pitiless combat against religious manifestations."[78] The Central Asian nomenklatura immediately increased the regional atheism campaigns. Already in late August, Qahhor Mahkamov had published a feature article in *Kommunisti Tadžikistana* announcing a renewed atheism campaign in the TaSSR. Mirrahim's article "How Long Will the Water Run Under the Ice" was likewise a response to these renewed efforts. However, government policies regarding the regulation and appropriation of Islam remained inconsistent, ambivalent and contradictory, and Mirrahim's article adumbrated the increasing exhaustion of the constant ideological mobilization of the Soviet regime.[79]

Islam became entwined with Tajik nationalism and the idea of a distinct Tajik cultural heritage. Even representatives of the Soviet nomenklatura reconsidered their former atheist habitus. Moyonšo Nazaršoev, a senior cadre from Badaxšon and former chairman of the ideology department of the CC/CPT, for instance, blended in a speech to the Supreme Soviet in late August 1991 concerns about religion with the alleged national heritage:

> Regarding religion and devout people, we have engaged in a policy which even did not allow printing the Koran in Tajik. This was an unfortunate mistake, since religion is one element in the cultural orientation of the people. In the 1930s, the Bolsheviks have burnt the Koran and the literary works of the Tajik classics (Mavlono Rumī and Xisrav), but today we need to bring all forces into service for the republic—religion as well.[80]

The political nomenklatura responded inconsistently to the increasing importance of Islam in nationalist debates and public practice. Mahkamov demonstrated his limited empathy and understanding of the late Soviet Tajik society as well as the role of religion when he called himself an unshaken atheist and internationalist in an interview with *Argumenty i Fakty*.[81] In contrast, Rahmon Nabiev had a better understanding of conservative rural communities in Tajikistan and included Islam in his political performance. On the diplomatic stage, he played the religious card aptly affirming Tajikistan's commitment to the freedom of religion and its determination to fight Islamic fundamentalism and extremism. Domestically, Nabiev avoided all too controversial statements on religion.[82]

Kenğaev likewise mastered a more subtle approach to Islam. In a publication on Human Rights and Soviet Constitutional Law, Kenğaev discussed the freedom of religion and the rights of religious associations in Soviet Tajikistan and concluded that the relationship between the government and religious associations is characterized by tolerance and the spirit of cooperation. The Muslim population of the TaSSR supports the constitution since it reflects human rights and guarantees

> that in our republic independent Muslim and Christian associations work. Only in Dushanbe, four mosques (Hoğī Yaqub, Sariosiyo, Šohmansur and Qaramiršikor) operate. In these mosques, not only the prayer is performed, but also the basics of religion are taught and guests find shelter in them.[83]

Kenğaev adopted prevalent Soviet discourses on religion and particularly Islam and gradually developed the dichotomy between a religious Self which was embedded in the normative regional Hanafi tradition represented by the state-controlled institution of the SADUM and a malign Other, adherents of a foreign "distortion" of Islam, the *vahhobī* opposition. In contrast to his memoirs, however, he insisted in his early writings that the religious communities in Tajikistan followed a moderate (*mū 'tadil*) interpretation. Instead he accused the Western media of a distorted representation of Islam in Central Asia as radical, extremist and dangerous.

Kenğaev consistently presented himself as a concerned, devout and knowledgeable Muslim with a religious agenda in politics.[84] In March 1992, Kenğaev requested from the Presidium of the Supreme Soviet to ban the sale of alcohol on *Eid al-Fitr* (celebrating the end of Ramadan on 4 April that year) and ordered the local administration to prepare slogans and banners for the celebration emphasizing the particular national traditions related to *Eid al-Fitr*.[85] At the same time, Kenğaev resorted in his attacks against Islamist activists to the Soviet psychiatric discourses on dissidents and diagnosed Mullo Abdurahim with a "sluggish schizophrenia"—a form of schizophrenia exclusively diagnosed by Soviet psychiatric institutions for "asocial" elements and political dissidents.[86]

Episode: The Union Islamic Revival Party

The Mahkamov administration prohibited the official registration of the IRPT in Soviet Tajikistan, but activists from other union republics proceeded with the formation of an all-union Islamic Renaissance Party (Russ.: *Partiya islamskogo vozroždeniya*). On 23 May 1990, the first party congress was held in Astrakhan. Initially, the congress was scheduled for three days in the local DOSAAF building, but the municipality administration ordered the suspension of the congress already after the first day. Among the participants, Tatars and Muslims from the Caucasus formed the largest regional group while Central Asian Muslims were underrepresented. Davlat Usmon, Muhammadšarif Himmatzoda, Sayidibrohim Gadoev (Muhammadnazar), Sayidumar Husaynī and Zubaydullo Roziq took part in the congress on behalf of the Tajik *harakat*. The delegates elected the Daghestani Ahmed Qazi Akhtayev as chairman and Gadoev as one of his deputies. Davlat Usmon became member of the Presidium. However, there was little enthusiasm among the Tajik participants for an all-union party and the delegation of authority to a Moscow-based association. Reportedly, Akhtayev had to urge Davlat Usmon to join the Presidium in order to balance the regional representation. The *harakat* had previously positioned itself as a pronounced nationalist Tajik movement (in order to counter allegations of "Pan-Islamist" tendencies) and adopted a decidedly anti-colonial agenda. The movement's leadership expressed therefore its skepticism about the prospects of an all-union association. The Tajik activists saw in the union IRP a vehicle to advance their objectives in the TaSSR, namely the registration of a local Tajik branch of the IRPT.[87]

The all-union IRP remained an intellectual and idealistic episode too dependent on Soviet perceptions, institutions and structures. Commitment to all-union projects withered with the accelerating disintegration of the USSR and Islamist movements in the periphery of the empire followed a nationalist agenda. With the collapse of the USSR, the all-union IRP lost its political relevance.

The Čortut Party Congress and the Registration of the IRPT

Throughout 1990, the *harakat* leadership advanced the formal registration of the Tajik IRP. On 6 October 1990, Gadoev and Usmon submitted their request for registration to the Supreme Soviet and asked for permission to convene a party congress. They presented their case to the deputies of the Supreme Soviet and a short discussion evolved, but the majority of the deputies rejected their request.[88] Kenğaev allegedly told Mahkamov that the IRPT's program was mendacious and "there is no need to establish the IRP in our republic since it violates against the constitution. In our republic state and religion are separated as well as education and religion."[89] However, the *harakat* ignored the decision of the Supreme Soviet and organized its first informal congress clandestinely on 5 October 1990 in the mosque of Čortut in the Lenin district close to Dushanbe. With the experience from the congress in Astrakhan in mind, Himmatzoda decided to convene at the middle of the night. Usmon drafted the agenda of the meeting and Himmatzoda gave a lecture to the 500 people present on the necessity to establish a party with Islamic values and the "intention to build a society based on Islamic principles."[90] Although the local *mahalla* administration wanted to suspend the meeting, the activists were defiant and elected a Presidium (*riyosati olī*) with Himmatzoda as chairman and Usmon as his deputy. Abdullo Nurī, in Roziq's terms the founder and principal ideologist of the *harakat*, did not occupy any formal position because of security concerns. In 1990, Nurī and his associates considered Glasnost a reversible process and decided to follow a double strategy: Himmatzoda—as an able and trusted organizer—would lead the party while Nurī would continue to head the "hidden wing."[91]

According to Ibrohim Usmonov, the Čortut congress marked an important transition from the *harakat* to the IRPT, which operated from October 1990 as a semi-legal political association.[92] While other civil associations and political parties, such as Rastoxez, the DPT and La'li Badaxšon, were established largely by former CPT members and state employees, the leading *harakat* members had not been affiliated with the CPT and were unknown to the TaSSR's urban public. The Tajik nomenklatura therefore had difficulties to assess their political opponents—next to the general concerns regarding the IRPT's political orientation. Their relative anonymity, however, allowed IRPT members to present themselves as a credible political alternative and not as turncoats of the old system.

Shortly after the Čortut congress, the Supreme Soviet adopted on its 4th Session on 14 December a resolution "On restricting the activity of the party and socio-political organization banned by the TaSSR legislation" prohibiting the registration of the IRPT.[93] The political nomenklatura insinuated that the movement had been responsible for the February riots and the KGB stepped up its surveillance and intimidation of the IRPT's activities. Roziq recalled a conversation with a KGB official in Qūrġonteppa who told him: "Didn't I tell you, that they are fanatics? You want to build Islam? Go to the forests and build Islam there, or to Iran."[94]

The Tajik intelligentsia and media were divided over the role of religion in independent Tajikistan. While the government press was hostile toward the IRPT, independent journalists offered a more balanced view on the IRPT. Umed Babaxanov (today the director of the independent media group ASIA-Plus) published a sympathetic feature on the IRPT in the *Komsomolskaya Pravda* on 23 March 1991 criticizing its ban and predicting increasing tensions in case the Supreme Soviet continues its restrictive policies. Babaxanov pointed out

> the use of force would meet with an answering response. It would then once again be possible to play the national card, covering the Islamic Party in the blood of innocent people and win prestige as the defender of the "indigenous population's" interests and fighters of extremism.[95]

The events in September 1991 eventually paved the way for the official registration of the IRPT. Although the majority of deputies in the Supreme Soviet remained skeptical about the intentions of the IRPT, the protests and the mediation by Sobčak pressured the deputies to reconsider the IRPT's status. The Supreme Soviet lifted the ban on religious parties and the Ministry of Justice accepted the registration of the IRPT on 9 December 1991. Perhaps the IRPT's decision *not* to nominate an own candidate for the presidential elections appeased the political nomenklatura around Nabiev. On 26 October 1991, 657 members of the IRPT and some 300 guests took part in the foundational congress of the IRPT in the House of political Education.[96] The congress also adopted a party program in which the IRPT defines itself as a

> social-political entity for the Muslims of the Republic of Tajikistan, based on Islamic principles (*aqidai islomī*) which is based on the belief in the one God and on the prophet Muhammad (s). [...] The Islamic Revival Party of Tajikistan is a parliamentary party and participates in elections and suggests its own candidates as people's candidates. [...] The aims of the IRPT are: Spiritual revitalization of the citizens of Tajikistan / economic and political independence of the republic / political and legal awakening with the aim to implement the foundations of Islam in the life of Muslims in Tajikistan.[97]

Islam as a Signifier: Politics, Tradition, Moral and Cultural Authenticity

Representatives of the IRPT expressed at times diverging and ambivalent views on the preferred future political system in Tajikistan. Although the leading representatives of the IRPT carefully avoided radical statements and stressed their commitment to democratic institutions, the ambiguity remained. Himmatzoda and Usmon, for example, repeatedly proclaimed that they would respect the "will of the people," insinuating—in analogy to the Iranian Revolution's referendum in March 1979 on the establishment of an Islamic government—that an Islamic system could be established with majority support of the population.[98] In an interview with *Izvestiya* on 8 May 1992, Himmatzoda explained that the IRPT has

> no plans to create an Islamic state by force. Unlike the communists, we have no intention of imposing our ideology and system on the country. Of course, if the people favor an Islamic state in a referendum, they will have the right to choose that path. But, even if that happens, we will remain committed to human rights.[99]

Consequently, Himmatzoda, Nurī and Usmon emphasized their commitment to democratic principles and during a press conference on the occasion of the official registration of the IRPT, they remarked that the IRPT attempts to come to political power constitutionally and intends to create a democratic state based on Islamic values and principles.[100] At the same time, the activists referred to a short reading list with titles by the Qutb brothers and Mawdudi, or they mentioned political role models such as Imam Khomeini or Burhanuddin Rabbani. The Islamic utopia, the momentary enthusiasm of independence and the political transformation inspired them to articulate more ambitious objectives: Usmon and Himmatzoda announced after the establishment of the Government of national Reconciliation (GNR) and Usmon's appointment to the position of a deputy prime minister in May 1992, that the IRPT's ultimate objective is the creation of an Islamic state, however in a democratically legitimized process.[101] Himmatzoda put his view on the all-encompassing claim of Islam strait: "Islam does not only consist of the ritual obligations. Islam is religion, state, politics, Islam concerns this world as well as the afterlife."[102]

Tūrağonzoda commented on the issue less ambiguously and repeatedly rejected the very idea of establishing an Islamic state in Tajikistan. Instead, he maintained that strengthening belief and ethics in Tajikistan was his central concern. Politically he referred to three central issues: democracy, human rights and market economy.[103] In an interview with *Komsomolskaya Pravda* on 4 October 1992, Tūrağonzoda explained:

I do not want to say that I am a 100 percent democrat but I am a supporter of radical changes. And I adhere to opposition views not because I am a *qadi* but because I have that world outlook. [...] There is no unity among the leaders of the Islamic Rebirth Party, some of them are stating their reluctance to build an Islamic society. My credo is a democratic secular state in which religion will be separated from the state. Perhaps I will begin to have serious differences with them [the IRPT]. But I hope that they understand that building an Islamic state in the 20th century means dooming the republic to isolation.[104]

Many observers nonetheless remained skeptical of Tūrağonzoda's intentions and Ibrohim Usmonov commented: "In his speeches he was against a government based on Islam, but in his activities he struggled for one and that removed the curtain from his language."[105]

In 1991 the IRPT was a heterogeneous movement and although IRPT publications portray Nurī as its undisputed leader, there were many activists—such as Ġozī, Rizvon, Mullo Abdurahim—who exploited the ambiguity and ambivalence of the Islamic political discourse and advanced more radical political positions only tenuously following Nurī's strategy of political accommodation. In an interview in 2003, Nurī maintained that the original members of the IRPT never wanted violence and bloodshed. Although he did not mention the Islamist field commanders, he conceded that the IRPT activists lacked the political experience and could not control or contain the more radical elements.[106]

The secular opposition and independent media had—as already mentioned—ambivalent views on the IRPT. At least in their memoirs, representatives of the secular opposition are generally sympathetic toward the IRPT. Būrī Karim, for instance, positions the IRPT in the tradition of important Muslim thinkers such as Sayyid Jamal ad-Din al-Afghani (1837–1897), the Bukharan scholar Ahmad Doniš (1827–1897), Muhammad Abduh, al-Kawakibi, Muhammad Iqbal, Sayyid Qutb, Ayatollah Khomeini, Ali Shariati and Ayatollah Motahhari as intellectuals who "reconstructed their faith"[107] but did not strive for an Islamic state.

Nasriddinov assumed that the particular Islamic ideology was less important for the IRPT's success and instead emphasized the ability of the IRPT to portray Islam as an exclusive part of Tajik identity and the IRPT as a genuine nationalist movement.[108] Many secular reformers and democrats believed that the IRPT with its (albeit ambiguous) model of a society based on Islamic values was in general supportive of a capitalist economy with respect for private property.[109] Journalists were in general divided over the question of the role of Islam and the IRPT in the Tajik society. Two editorials in *Adabiyot va San 'at* demonstrate this ambivalence: In the first editorial from May 1992, shortly after the GNR had been established, Adaš Istad reflected on the sources of statehood next to the Persian/Iranian civilization and carefully embraced the idea that "Islam is a foundational pillar of the national civilization." Istad endorsed a secular nation-state instead of an Islamic state since the nation-state would provide favorable conditions for all religions. An Islamic state would only be based on laws derived from its foundational sources.[110] A second article followed some six weeks later and reflected the crestfallen expectations of the GNR: Now Istad explicitly warned about an Islamic state since it would result in the "dictatorship of the Islamic sciences and the Islamic sword [...] and nobody can guarantee that this sword will not be raised against secular intellectuals."[111]

Nonetheless, Islam with its strong appeal to justice and the rule of law crystallized in the politically and morally charged concept of *šari 'a* as the quintessential idea of a legitimate Islamic social order offered a strong alternative to official narratives of Tajik national identity, polity and culture. Islam in this context emerged as a signifier for cultural authenticity and genuine morality transcending the Soviet legacy as well as the complex post-Soviet disorder.[112] Sohibnazar, for instance, considered Islam as a morally and ethically consistent concept of life, which fundamentally differs from the Soviet system, in which "alcoholism, harlotry, and pillage are protected by state law."[113] Islam, instead, is a central part of the national customs and has the potential to overcome the cleavages in the country. Eventually, Islam signifies the authentic spiritual dimension of the Self, which could not be appropriated by the colonial center:

> They [the TaSSR's nomenklatura] wanted to reconcile Muslims with Lenin's party, but they wanted to keep Islam separated from Lenin's party. The activities of Lenin's party and Islam can certainly be separated, but you cannot separate Muslims from Islam. A person who considers himself a Muslim has the religion of Islam in his mind, not Lenin's party.[114]

THE QOZIYOT IN THE TASSR AND TAJIKISTAN

Until 1989 the republican representative of the SADUM administered registered Muslim affairs in the TaSSR. After the SADUM's establishment in 1943, the TaSSR representatives used to be appointed among the *ulamo* of the Fergana Valley, such as *qorī* Abdulmağid, *ešoni* Abdusattor or *ešoni* Abdurašid, who were educated prior to the October Revolution. Throughout the Brezhnev era and even beyond, from 1965 to 1988, the Leninobodī Abdulloh Kalonzoda was the SADUM's *qozikalon* in the TaSSR mirroring the Brezhnevite stability of cadres in the religious field. Kalonzoda (1906–1988) was a quietist and loyalist *qozī* who experienced the establishment of Soviet power and the horrors of Stalinism as a young man. The registered *ulamo* administered the few registered mosques and trained small numbers of successors between the 1960s and 1980s.[115] Although Islamist activists reported that the *qoziyot* was widely considered an extension of the KGB by the Muslim population, the reality was more complex as Dudoignon, Saroyan and Tasar have pointed out.[116]

When Kalonzoda passed away in 1988, a much younger and independent representative of the registered *ulamo* was appointed his successor: Hoğī Akbar Tūrağonzoda (b. 1954). In 1988/1989, the republican *qoziyot* in the TaSSR was formally still subordinated to the Central Asian *muftiyot* in Tashkent. The *mufti* in Tashkent, Muhammad Sodiq Muhammad Yusuf (1952–2015), had been appointed in 1989 and represented—like Tūrağonzoda—a generational shift (both were well under 40 when they assumed their positions) in the administration of Islamic affairs in Central Asia. Tūrağonzoda and Muhammad Sodiq studied in the Miri Arab in Bukhara and the Imam al-Bukhari Institute in Tashkent, both were among the few religious specialists who were allowed to pursue their post-graduate Islamic education abroad, Tūrağonzoda in Amman (Jordan) and Muhammad Sodiq in Tripoli (Libya). Eventually, both were unconventional representatives of the Soviet religious establishment with an interventionist social and political agenda in the age of Perestroika and Glasnost.[117]

The *qoziyot* in Dushanbe had an ethnic dimension since it oversaw the religious affairs of ethnic Tajik Muslims in Central Asia including the Tajik Muslims in the Kyrgyz SSR and UzSSR while the *muftiyot* in Tashkent regulated the affairs of ethnic Uzbek Muslims including those in the TaSSR. Initially, Tūrağonzoda considered the particular arrangement useful since it protected the *qoziyot* from direct interference by the TaSSR's government. In the wake of rising nationalist sentiment, the Supreme Soviet decided in autumn 1989 to establish an independent *qoziyot* in the TaSSR, obviously with the ulterior motive to control the institution without interference by Tashkent. Furthermore, the appointment of Tūrağonzoda in 1988 marked an important shift in the regional representation from the Fergana Valley to southern Tajikistan.

Hoǧī Akbar Tūrağonzoda as Qozikalon

Hoǧī Akbar Tūrağonzoda (or Akbar Turaevič Qah[h]orov/ Kakh[kh]arov) was born in 1954 in Vahdatobod (Kofarnihon/Vahdat) into the family of *ešoni* Muhammadrafi', better known as *ešoni* Tūrağon, an imminent *sheikh* (or *pir*) of the regional Qaderiyya *tariqa*. *ešoni* Tūrağon was born in 1934 in Pičef, a small remote village in the mountainous Romit Valley some 50 km north of district center Romit, but the family traces back its ancestry to the Samarqand region. *ešoni* Tūrağon's father, *ešoni* Xalifa Abdulkarim, was the son of Mullo Gulmuhammad from the family (*zurriya*) of Xoǧa Zarrin of the *xoǧagoni* Dahbedī from Samarqand. The *xoǧagoni* Dahbedī have their origin in the circle around the influential and prominent mystic Ahmad Kasanī Hazrati Maxdumi A'zam (1461–1542), a *sheikh* in the Naqšbandiyya *silsila* who acted in Samarkand and Bukhara.[118]

ešoni Xalifa Abdulkarim became a *murid* of Said Qalandaršoh b. Šohsohib, better known as *mavlavī* Ğununī, who was originally from Qandahar in Afghanistan but went for his religious education to Bukhara in the mid-19th century. He eventually settled in the Hisor valley and spent the rest of his life occupied with teaching and horticulture in Rohatī (some 25 km east of today's Dushanbe and some 50 km west of Romit). *ešoni* Xalifa Abdulkarim followed *mavlavī* Ğununī as a local religious authority in the 1920s but was arrested in the 1930s and spent some four years in a Siberian Gulag. His son, Muhammadrafi' was born in 1934. In 1950, Soviet authorities forcibly resettled ešoni Abdulkarim, his family and some *murids* from the Romit Valley in the Vaxš valley. With the support of one of his Uzbek *murids*, Ahmad Hoǧī Ibrohim, *ešoni* Abdulkarim was able to return with his family to the Kofarnihon area and the family eventually settled in Turkobod (south of Kofarnihon/Vahdat), where they established a large Friday mosque complex called Xalifa Abdulkarim.

After *ešoni* Xalifa Abdulkarim passed away in 1957, his son *ešoni* Tūrağon took over the spiritual duties of his father at an unusually young age of 23. *ešoni* Tūrağon lived a reclusive life rarely leaving his home where he instructed a small circle of *murid*s. He only became a more public figure in the early 1991 during the public protests in Dushanbe.[119] Among the 10 sons of *ešoni* Tūrağon, 3 became important religious specialists in Tajikistan: *ešoni* Nuriddinğon (b. 1953), *ešoni* Mahmudğon (b. 1960) and Hoğī Akbar (b. 1954). While Nuriddinğon and Mahmudğon were educated in clandestine circles including the one of *domullo* Hindustonī, Hoğī Akbar enrolled in the registered Soviet Islamic institutions administered by SADUM. From 1972 to 1977 he studied in the Miri Arab *madrasa* in Bukhara and in 1980 he graduated from the Imam al-Bukhari Islamic Institute in Tashkent, the official higher education institution for registered religious personnel in the USSR.[120] After a two-year term in the international relations department of the SADUM, Hoğī Akbar went—as one of the few selected religious specialists from the USSR—to the Islamic University in Amman, where he graduated in 1987 with a law degree. Tūrağonzoda was neither a religious dissident nor Islamic activists, but integral part of the Soviet system. With his background in the official structures of the Soviet Union, his education abroad and as a descendant from a respected religious lineage, Tūrağonzoda represented a new generation of religious specialists within the particular context of the late Soviet Union. He presented himself by his habitus and symbolic capital as a versatile religious specialist with an impeccable knowledge in theology and Arabic, but also as somebody who is concerned about profane life-worlds, such as economics, health and social relations. Furthermore, he knew how to interact with the political nomenklatura and cultivated personal relations with them.[121]

In 1988 the TaSSR's Council of Ministers and the head of 5th Directorate of the KGB in the TaSSR, Sirogiddinov, named three candidates for the office of the *qozikalon* in the TaSSR: Hoğī Habibullo A'zamxon, the *imom-xatib* of the Sari Osiyo Friday Mosque in Dushanbe (who withdrew his candidacy), Hoğī Muslihiddin, the SADUM representative in Leninobod *viloyat*, and Hoğī Akbar Tūrağonzoda who was then working in the SADUM's external relations department. Tūrağonzoda seemed to be the perfect candidate for the position of the *qozikalon*: Although not from the Fergana Valley (as the previous *qozikalon*), he came from a respected Tajik family of religious authorities; he had graduated from the Soviet institutions and—sanctioned by the authorities—studied abroad. But Tūrağonzoda faced stiff resistance by the KGB (which reportedly backed Hoğī Muslihiddin) and only the support from the political nomenklatura secured his appointment as *qozikalon*. Reportedly, the political leadership intended to disrupt the autonomy of the Fergana religious personnel and saw in Tūrağonzoda a suitable candidate with the right Soviet pedigree to change the balance in the religious field.[122]

Tūrağonzoda modernized the *qoziyot* and increased its legitimacy by introducing a formalized participation of *imom-xatibs* in the *qoziyot*'s affairs (bylaws and elections) and by embracing the prevalent discourses on political reform.[123] By increasing the political and social relevance of the institution, Tūrağonzoda consolidated the "Islamic awakening (*bidorii islomī*) in Tajikistan"[124] against the opposition of the communist nomenklatura. Simultaneously he intended to contain the Islamist activism and the emerging *harakat* by absorbing their agenda. Apparently, the nomenklatura expected exactly this containment of the Islamist networks from Hoğī Akbar and therefore accepted his appointment. In November 1990, the state media even announced that the CPT shares the general values, morals and culture of Islam and supports the registered religious authorities (*rūhoniyoni rasmī*) who oppose the Islamic movement and support the establishment of a democratic system based on the rule of law.[125]

Tūrağonzoda's religious and political agenda was (and still is) based on three central elements: First, he envisages a more interventionist and public role for the *ulamo* in the society. The "Commanding Right" (*amr ba maʿruf*) should be done in public and consider beyond religious guidance the everyday social and political contexts in which Muslims interact with each other. Tūrağonzoda—like many Islamic activists—has a strong didactical impetus and campaigns for the extension of normative Islamic teaching and its social relevance for the "common people." Second, Tūrağonzoda is not a reformist Muslim scholar in the sense that he advances the interpretation of the religious sources or tradition. However, he is a reformist in the sense that he promotes a normative but simultaneously *flexible* Hanafi-Sunni concept of religious practice and dogma within the context of everyday life. Third, Tūrağonzoda's perspective on religion and politics is influenced by statism; he strongly believes that the state should regulate and control social and economic politics. Finally, beyond considerations of spiritualty and the transcendent, Tūrağonzoda considers Islam (in its normative Sunni-Hanafi variant) as a central element in the imagination of the Tajik nation, civilization and culture generating social cohesion and a sense of unity.[126]

Eventually, he was widely considered as an unusually charismatic and intellectually agile religious scholar. As Monica Whitlock, the BBC correspondent in Tashkent recalls, Tūrağonzoda

> was a young, vigorous official cleric of a kind never seen before. [...] He had éclat and confidence and said what he thought. He talked openly about the Muftiat of the past had been rotten with spies. He joked with journalists where others shied away; he was witty, trenchant and a natural public speaker.[127]

Hoǧī Akbar is not as altruistic as some of his supporters claim and he portrays himself. He and his extended family unfolded various business activities (cotton processing, trade, agriculture[128]) and Tūraǧonzoda appointed several family members to influential positions in the *qoziyot* fostering the influence of the southern Tajik religious networks: His father, *ešoni* Tūraǧon, became a member of the *qoziyot*'s steering committee, the council of *ulamo* (*Šūroi ulamo*), and his older brother, *ešoni* Nuriddinǧon, was a senior lecturer in the Islamic Institute and his younger brother, Mahmudǧon, became the editor of the *qoziyot*'s newspaper *Minbari Islom*.[129]

Although Tūraǧonzoda was well connected with the leading representatives of the *harakat* (his brothers Nuriddinǧon and Mahmudǧon were fellow students of Nurī in the teaching circle of Hindustonī) and he even hired Nurī after his release to co-edit the *qoziyot*'s newspaper, he unequivocally expressed his reservations regarding the establishment of an Islamic party. In September 1990 Tūraǧonzoda invited all registered *imom-xatibs* for a discussion on political activities and legal issues. The meeting and discussion was related to the establishment of an all-Union Islamic Revival Party in Astrakhan and Tūraǧonzoda called on the *imom-xatib*s to remain neutral in times of political and social upheaval.[130] He urged all officials in the *qoziyot* to sign a statement that they are not members of the IRPT and will not join the party thereafter.[131] Tūraǧonzoda certainly saw the IRPT as a major challenge to the *qoziyot*'s (and his) authority; therefore, he adopted a two-fold, to some extent contradictory, strategy: As a deputy in the Supreme Soviet he publicly spoke out against the official registration of the IRPT since the society was allegedly unprepared for an Islamic party. At the same time he opened the *qoziyot* to the IRPT, employed Abdullo Nurī and cooperated with local IRPT sympathizers against his opponents. He even appointed IRPT members, such as *mavlavī* Muhammadalī Fayzmuhammad in Panǧ or Mullo Abdurahim in Kūlob, to the position of *imom-xatib* of registered Friday mosques under the jurisdiction of the *qoziyot*.

In 1991 Tūraǧonzoda faced increasing pressure by the government and the opposition to suspend his "neutrality" and position the *qoziyot* in the evolving political struggle. In September and October 1991 the *qoziyot* supported the demonstrations against Nabiev and even *ešoni* Tūraǧon abandoned his reclusive and quietist life to assume a public role by joining the hunger strike of the opposition and resuming the public *amri ma'ruf* in September/October 1991.[132] Since late 1991, Nabiev and Kenǧaev tried to increase government control over the *qoziyot* and replace Tūraǧonzoda with his antagonist Haydar Šarifov. However, Tūraǧonzoda—also with the support of his disciplined family—was able to deflect the pressure and rally the support of the majority of registered *ulamo* behind him.[133]

Although Tūraǧonzoda and his *qoziyot* supported the opposition, his relation to the IRPT remained complex and strained by his rivalry with Abdullo

Nurī—both, on the religious as well as the political level. After the protests on Šahidon Square had commenced in September 1991, Tūraġonzoda hesitated to join the demonstrations and only after disputes with communist deputies in the Supreme Soviet, he joined the protests on the Square, however without ceding his autonomy. In November, he relinquished his reservations over the legal registration of the party and urged the deputies in the Supreme Soviet to pass the law that finally established the IRPT as a political party in Tajikistan. However, he maintained his independence and in the April 1992 protocol between representatives of the presidential administration, the Supreme Soviet, the Council of Ministers and the opposition on Šahidon, the *qoziyot* was still listed as an autonomous party to the negotiations.[134] Tūraġonzoda vividly described the increasing polarization in Dushanbe and estrangement between the political actors and he realized that he could not steer the *qoziyot* as an independent institution through the mounting tensions. The increasingly belligerent rhetoric by Kenġaev, Dūstov and their supporters in and outside the Supreme Soviet against him personally ("down with Tūraġonzoda"[135]) as well as the political polarization between the supporters of Šahidon Square and Ozodī Square prompted him to ally with the opposition.[136]

Tūraġonzoda and the Soviet State

Since Tūraġonzoda was educated in the Soviet system, his relation to the KGB has been frequently discussed in Tajikistan's media, often as a defamation portraying him as a KGB informant who reported on his fellow students, colleagues and even family. The defamation campaign has flared up several times in recent years obviously with the intention to tarnish the reputation Tūraġonzoda enjoys as a public religious figure in contemporary Tajikistan.[137] Already Kenġaev addressed Tūraġonzoda's alleged complicity with the KGB. During his short appointment as Chairman of the KGB/NSC in April 1992, Kenġaev claimed that he had access to Tūraġonzoda's voluminous KGB files with the alleged pseudonyms "Abdukarimov" and "Tohir."[138]

In 2009 the government mouthpiece *Ġumhuriyat* launched hitherto the most vicious smear campaign with the reproduction of an online article by the journalist Farrux Mamadšoev with the title "Tūraġonzoda—an agent of the KGB?" implicating that not only Tūraġonzoda himself but also his father were KGB agents.[139] According to Mamadšoev, *ešoni* Tūraġon was a local informant of the KGB under the alias "Sobit" who arranged his son's enrolment with the Miri Arab *madrasa* in Bukhara (which is portrayed as a KGB outfit) and established contacts with the Uzbek KGB. Mamadšoev based his report on alleged KGB files in Tashkent and Moscow and provided a narrative with numerous anecdotal details (which, however, suspiciously resemble Kenġaev's account) in an effort to corroborate the authenticity and validity of his allegations. Mamadšoev reproduced an (alleged) interview between Hoǧī Akbar and his KGB case officer in Tashkent discussing his alias. Initially, the KGB suggested "Maksim" as his alias since it does not hint at a Muslim identity, but Tūraǧonzoda (allegedly) insisted on the "Muslim" alias "Abdukarimov" (his uncle's name).[140] After graduating from the Miri Arab, Tūraǧonzoda entered the Uzbek KGB and prepared reports in Uzbek "and eventually lost command of his mother tongue."[141] According to Mamadšoev, Tūraǧonzoda was a diligent agent spying on his fellow students, friends and family and rising quickly through the ranks of the Uzbek KGB. His studies in Amman's Islamic University were only a pretense since his actual assignment was to spy on his fellow students. In particular his close contacts to a "famous" Chechen Muslim KGB agent (whose identity is not disclosed) made Tūraǧonzoda a valuable agent in the KGB and eventually Moscow installed him as *qozikalon* in the TaSSR.[142] Under his alias "Abdulkarim" Hoǧī Akbar became Vladimir Petkel''s most valuable informant on Islamists in the TaSSR, Afghanistan and Pakistan.[143] Mamadšoev's narrative has all the ingredients of a defamation campaign within the particular context of independent Tajikistan: First, the allegation that the entire Tūraǧon family were informants of the KGB, thus portraying religious authorities as immoral, duplicitous and dishonest; second, Hoǧī Akbar's choice of his alias "Abdukarimov" insinuates that he disdains his own family's name and reputation but also "Muslimness" and "Tajikness" as such; third, the cooperation with the Uzbek authorities—Tajikistan's regional antagonist—and the abandonment of his mother tongue in favor of Uzbek and Russian portrays Tūraǧonzoda as a hideous traitor of the nation.

The question whether Tūraǧonzoda was a KGB informant or not cannot be determined here. More important is how ambiguously officials and the wider public refer to the Soviet KGB—sometimes proudly as a spy agency, which outwitted the enemies of the USSR, sometimes as an oppressive tool of a foreign or colonial power instigating Tajiks to forget their national identity and even language. Considering the biography of Tūraǧonzoda, his studies abroad and service for the Soviet institutions regulating Islam, in all probability the KGB closely monitored him. In a different context Davlat Usmon remarked that in Soviet times invariably *all* registered *ulamo* had to maintain close contacts with the KGB since operating a mosque was considered an issue of national security. Usmon pointed out that these contacts with the KGB should not imply that the *ulamo* acted on behalf of the KGB or were informants.[144] Tūraǧonzoda openly addressed the infiltration of the religious structures by the KGB in his memoirs. He recalled his stay in Jordan where the KGB closely monitored the Soviet student groups and everybody knew the identity of the informants in the group. He also recollected a conversation with Kenǧaev who threatened him in April 1992 with the words: "Don't think that all Mullos are your people. Among them are Mullos, who are in fact our agents. We know everything you do."[145]

Most of the authors described how the KGB manipulated the civil associations and opposition parties since the late 1980s. However, the narratives also indicate that the perception of the KGB as an omnipotent and terrifying organization changed. Individual activists and politicians openly challenged the authority of the KGB and refused to comply with its orders. Family relations, professional and private networks protected individuals through the *murid-muršid* relationship, common interests and business opportunities as well as the high level of corruption in the later Soviet society—and the Tūrağon family was in the center of one of these patronage networks.[146]

Tūrağonzoda as a Politician

After his appointment as *qozikalon*, Hoğī Akbar soon interfered in politics. Since the *qoziyot* office was close to the CC/CPT building, he came out on the square to appease the demonstrators on 12 February. A few days later, on 18 February, Tūrağonzoda was one of the key speakers next to the urban intelligentsia on the pro-Glasnost demonstration at Koxi Borbat.[147] As the *qozikalon*, he was supposed to become a deputy in the Supreme Soviet and was dutifully elected in his constituency in Kofarnihon in 1990 as one of the three religious authorities in the Supreme Soviet—next to Haydar Šarifov (Kūlob) and Hadyatulloh Odilov (Čorkūh/Isfara in Leninobod *viloyat*). Tūrağonzoda was soon recognized as an intellectually agile and independent deputy, who defied appropriation by the CPT. Unsurprisingly, the (re-) introduction of "Islam" in public featured high on his agenda: In early 1991 Tūrağonzoda suggested in a Supreme Soviet session to recognize the central Islamic feasts (*Idi Qurbon* and *Idi Fitr*) as official holidays and the weekly holiday should be moved from Sunday to Friday.[148] He further demanded that the state meat combines should slaughter livestock according to Islamic law and finally that religious institutions should be generally tax exempt. When the CPT deputies rejected the proposal, the *qoziyot* circulated a *fatvo* (legal opinion) prohibiting the registered religious specialists to hold funeral services (ğanoza) for deceased CPT cadres.[149] Tūrağonzoda's confrontational policy was not unanimously welcomed by all registered *ulamo* and deepened the divisions within the *qoziyot*.

As a deputy of the Supreme Soviet, Tūrağonzoda remained until 1991/1992 a remarkably independent figure and even his antagonist Kenğaev conceded that he could not classify Tūrağonzoda into one of the political factions. In September/October 1991, Tūrağonzoda obviously tried to identify some common ground with Nabiev's accomplices such as Kenğaev and Dūstov. He adopted a pragmatist policy realizing that the former CPT networks would not disintegrate overnight and that the opposition was at that time not strong enough to seriously challenge the political system.[150] As already mentioned, he consistently argued that he does not intend to establish an Islamic state and that he considers the ideal political system a secular democracy based on the rule of law.[151] Similarly, in his memoirs he depicted himself as an anti-communist and advocate of a pluralist and democratic society:

> I was an open opponent of the communist ideology and I am against any coercion or limitation of political parties and groups which are not against the common good since this is the fundament of democratic freedom.[152]

A careful reading of his statements, however, allows the interpretation that he considered a democratic system only as transitional. Likewise, he maintained that the *qoziyot* would stay outside politics—but he could hardly conceal the intrinsic political character of his office.[153] And Tūrağonzoda obviously enjoyed his influential political position as his numerous references to informal conversations with the political elite demonstrate. He frequently mentioned confidential "back room" talks in which political decisions with far reaching consequences were taken on his advice.[154] Although Tūrağonzoda portrays himself as a mediator in the unfolding conflict, his capacity as mediator was certainly limited due to his undeniable sympathies for the opposition.[155]

For many representatives of the "old" system, Tūrağonzoda was the main villain in the events of 1992. Usmonov described him as the main instigator of the opposition and its main financier, who divided not only the religious elites but also the entire country with his acrimonious propaganda.[156] Indeed, Tūrağonzoda's increasing political weight generated tensions within the religious field. The Leninobodī *ulamo*, in particular the Mūsozoda and Kalonov (Kalonzoda) families, moved out of the *qoziyot*'s orbit and the *imom-xatib* of Kūlob; Haydar Šarifov challenged Tūrağonzoda's authority eventually splitting the *qoziyot* into a northern (Leninobod), central (Dushanbe and Qarotegin) and southern (Kūlob) part.[157]

Haydar Šarifov and Tūrağonzoda

The rivalry between Haydar Šarifov and Tūrağonzoda unfolded in 1988 when both applied for the succession of the late *qozikalon* Abdullo Kalonzoda. While Šarifov was not even considered on the short list, Tūrağonzoda won the recognition of the registered *ulamo* and the political leadership.[158] Šarifov did not accept his defeat and started to organize religious affairs in Kūlob independently from the *qoziyot*, insisting that he was formally still subordinated to the Central Asian department in Tashkent. The conflict between Šarifov and Tūrağonzoda intensified throughout 1990/1991. First, Tūrağonzoda organized his re-election to increase his legitimacy and in March 1991 tried to convince the deputies of the Supreme Soviet to (re-)introduce Islamic customs to the Tajik society. Šarifov publicly opposed Tūrağonzoda on this issue as well as on the question of the registration of the IRPT. Additionally, there was also a very local dimension to their rivalry: Šarifov competed with a younger religious specialist, Abdurahim Karimov (aka Mullo Abdurahim or *mavlavī* Abdurahim), over influence in Kūlob. Mullo Abdurahim was associated with the IRPT and a politically ambitious, religious specialist who was actively supported by Tūrağonzoda. Tūrağonzoda tried to marginalize Šarifov and remove him from the position of *imom-xatib* on charges of embezzlement of funds and to replace him with Mullo Abdurahim.[159] Šarifov had allegedly used some 30 million rubles (at that time some 1.5 million USD) for the refurbishment of his Friday mosque. Since Tūrağonzoda did not succeed to replace Šarifov, he—without further ado—upgraded Mullo Abdurahim's mosque to a fully fledged Friday mosque. At the same time, Šarifov had a dispute with Mullo Abdurahim over the important *mazar* (shrine) of Mir Sayid Alī Hamadonī, a 14th-century Kubrāwiyya Sufi master, in central Kūlob. Hamadonī's *mazar* had been transformed during Soviet times into a museum and was an important destination for local *ziyorat* and source of prestige and income.[160]

Nasriddinov considered the IRPT representatives, in particular Šayx Kamol (an associate of Mullo Abdurahim), as shrewd individuals who intellectually outpaced Haydar Šarifov and who enjoyed genuine support among Muslims in Kūlob. Therefore Šarifov had to look for external allies (Nabiev) and local strongmen (Sangak Safarov) who were able to consolidate his position in Kūlob.[161] At the same time the "urban" Tajik intellectuals-cum-politicians such as Tūrağonzoda or Sohibnazar derided Šarifov. Sohibnazar portrayed Šarifov as a "Leninist Muslim" or "Red Mullo," a simpleton and an advocate of Soviet rule who was responsible for the outbreak of the civil war and who never understood "the reformist Islam in the understanding of Hoğī Akbar"[162]: Šarifov subordinated Islam under his personal interests and those of the Communist Party while Tūrağonzoda understood Islam as an integral part of the Tajik nation. Similarly, Yusuf used the example of Šarifov to contrast two ideal types of religious scholars in Tajikistan: the enlightened Self and the obscurant Other. He depicted Haydar Šarifov as an uneducated, selfish pseudo Muslim who "resembled more a KGB spy than a Muslim mullo."[163] The opponent of Šarifov, Mullo Abdurahim, in contrast was a representative of the national *qoziyot* and in the diction of Yusuf a young and well-educated religious leader, an altruistic Muslim, who was especially popular among the younger generation.[164]

The "urban" and "cultured" Tūrağonzoda ridiculed Haydar Šarifov in his memoirs and presented him as an ignorant rural mullo who could not articulate himself properly. In a meeting between the opposition, deputies from Kūlob and Nabiev, on 25 April 1992, Tūrağonzoda recalled an intervention by Šarifov and reproduced his language with a thick local accent:

> *Ata*[165], they [pointing to Abduğabbor and Sohibnazar] destroyed the republic, they ruined the USSR (*SSSR-a ay bayn burdand*). They are capturing the government, don't you understand (*hukumata girifta istodaand hečī mefahmī*)!? Even our mother tongue they ruined (*hatto zaboni modariamona ay bayn burdand*)! When Tohir [Abduğabbor] speaks, you don't understand a word (*gap mezana hečiša namefahmī*). *Ata*, this should not happen (*ita nameša*), do something (*yak kor kunen*), the people are worried (*mardum ba šur omaday*).[166]

On listening Šarifov's complaint, Tūrağonzoda and other "urban" and "cultured" attendees could only hardly manage to suppress their laughter (in Tūrağonzoda's narrative) which infuriated Šarifov even more, again addressing Nabiev "with a childish gaze (*nigohi kudakvor*) seeking help (*iltiğoomezona*)": "*Ata*, look at this, even in your presence they wink at each other and ridicule [us] (*Ata, o, ata, ira bin, dar peši xudut boz ba ham čašmak zada masxara meknan*). Here (*Mana*)! Xayrulloev and the *Qozī* are winking at each other."[167]

The bitter rivalry (or as Roziq calls it: *fitna*—civil strife) soon became a violent conflict in Kūlob since both could mobilize young men in their neighborhood to fight out a proxy war, which had—according to Roziq—rather a personal character than a religious or regionalist background. Šarifov could rely on the support of the local political elites and security structures and consequently moved against Mullo Abdurahim who was branded with the "*vahhobī*" seal (*tamğa*) while Abdurahim called Haydar Šarifov a hypocrite (*munofiq*), a corrupt person and an advocate of illegal innovations."[168] As many observers agree, Tūrağonzoda was by far the more versatile and intellectually alert of the two contenders, but he likewise contributed to the increasing confrontation.

On 24 April—after the resignation of Kenğaev–Šarifov was one of the leading local actors who called on the march on Dushanbe and demanded the resignation of Tūrağonzoda and the election of the next *qozikalon* by a popular vote. Šarifov established a parallel institution to the *qoziyot* with the "Independent Board of Muslims of the Kūlob *viloyat*." He also moved personally against Tūrağonzoda's subordinates: in Dangara Šarifov's accomplices drove out the *imom-xatib* with his family and in Kūlob violent clashes continued in late April 1992 between the congregations of two mosques including the one administered by Mullo Abdurahim.[169] Šarifov denounced Mullo Abdurahim and other IRPT supporters as *vahhobī* as he did with Tūrağonzoda and 17 IRPT members in Kūlob *viloyat* were arrested in May and later executed. After Šarifov had expelled Mullo Abdurahim, he

transformed the latter's mosque into a museum of *vahhobī* "mechanizations."
On exhibition were fabricated evidence, such as a table the *vahhobīs* used to
cut off their opponents' head, sport facilities and boxes of hemp seeds allegedly grown in the mosque's yard (however, a journalist and trained botanist
from a Russian magazine identified the "hemp" as tomato seeds).[170] Šarifov
provided the political nomenklatura and local strongmen with a lacquer of
religious legitimacy and was the driving force in the early mobilization of the
local population.[171]

In the summer of 1992 Sangak Safarov gradually marginalized Šarifov.
Safarov had begun to invent his own polycentric legitimation narrative and
did not need Šarifov anymore. After its appointment in November 1992, the
Rahmonov government quickly dismantled the *qoziyot* as an independent
institution demoting it to a Islamic Center (*Markazi Islomī*) and its High
Council as Tajikistan's *ulamo* (*Šūroi olii ulamoi Toğikiston*, sometimes also
called *muftiyot*). Remarkably, Rahmonov did not appoint Šarifov as the new
qozīkalon, but Fathulloh Šarifzoda Hisorī.[172] Apparently Šarifov, like many
other protagonists in the early stages of the conflict, was not considered anymore a suitable candidate for Rahmonov's project of post-conflict legitimation and state building.

CONCLUSION: THE RISE OF ISLAMISM IN THE TASSR

Islamism emerged the spatial and social context of the rural Qarotegin and
Vaxš valley in Soviet Tajikistan among a post-Stalin generation of men, predominately with a *muhoğir* background who repudiated the Soviet system
and intentionally remained at the margins of the Soviet society by relin-
quishing Soviet career patterns. They developed a conservative Hanafi-Sunni
religious agenda, which aimed at (re-)establishing a *public* and *normative*
religious practice as well as social-political relevance of Islam in the Tajik
society. Their religious agenda merged the neo-traditionalist teachings of
Hindustonī with the political interventionism of "classical" Islamism (such as
the Muslim Brotherhood) and manifests parallels to Islamism in other parts
of the wider Islamicate world: The *harakat* activists challenged the authority
of the established *ulamo* in religious and social affairs which correlated with
a generational conflict and embarked on a post-colonial critique of the Soviet
system claiming a moral superiority. Importantly, the *harakat* members presented their idea of Islam as authentic and embedded in the national culture
of the Tajiks and the wider regional civilization of Central Asia. Their political agenda responded to Perestroika and Glasnost discourses in the USSR
(i.e., transparency, the rule of law, democracy, freedom of faith) as well as to
developments in the wider Islamicate world, above all the revolution in Iran

in 1979 with its merger of "Islamic" politics, post-colonial nationalism and a modern political system. The *harakat*/IRPT considered Islam in general compatible with a democratic political system but capitalized on the ambiguity in the debate on Islamic politics. Despite the ambiguousness, the *harakat* has never been a *vahhobī* or jihadist movement as the government propaganda constantly claimed. The *harakat* was a heterogenous movement and since the late 1980s individual violent non-state actors claimed affiliation to the movement with a very different agenda and at times without the approval of the leadership around Nurī or Himmatzoda, who had only limited possibilities to enforce their decisions. Imaginations of an Islamic political and social order apparently became popular among local strongmen and youth gangs legitimizing hierarchies, protection rackets and other illicit or semi-illicit activities (like Mullo Abduġaffur in Dushanbe or Rizvon Sodirov in Kofarnihon). Arguably, the nomenklatura's belligerent discourse against the Islamic activists denouncing them as *vahhobī*, fundamentalists and radicals further elevated Islam to a social imaginary of a rebellious youth movement diametrically opposed to the (post-)Soviet societal model.

In a time of rising nationalist sentiment Islam emerged as an authentic Tajik and Central Asian alternative to the Soviet order undermining the legitimacy of the incumbent Soviet elites, which to some extent explains the aggressive campaign against the *harakat*. Eventually, the dominant elite's exclusive understanding of state security and the disproportionately hostile and intransigent campaign of "Othering" the Islamist activists considerably contributed to the immense confrontation and polarization of the Tajik society.

NOTES

1. Cf. Shoshana Keller, *To Moscow, not Mecca: The Soviet campaign against Islam in Central Asia, 1917—1941* (Westport: Praeger, 2001); Northrop, *Veiled,* 69–101; Niccolò Pianciola and Paolo Sartori, "Waqf in Turkestan: The Colonial Legacy and the Fate of an Islamic Institution in Early Soviet Central Asia, 1917–1924," *Central Asian Survey* 26, no. 4 (2007).

2. Osimī, *Enziklopediyai,* Vol. 1, 492–493.

3. I understand normativity in this context as constructed, often based on the interpretation of scriptural sources and enforced by actors in the Islamic religious field against alternative and competing interpretations. In general see Maria E. Louw, *Everyday Islam in post-Soviet Central Asia* (London: Routledge, 2007); Adeeb Khalid, *Islam after communism: Religion and politics in Central Asia* (Berkeley: Univ. of California Press, 2007) and Johan Rasanayagam, *Islam in post-Soviet Uzbekistan: The morality of experience* (Cambridge: Cambridge University Press, 2010).

4. See for instance Alexandre Bennigsen, ed., *Soviet strategy and Islam* (Basingstoke: Macmillan, 1989); Vitaliy Naumkin, *Radical Islam in Central Asia:*

Between pen and rifle. (Lanham: Rowman & Littlefield, 2005) or Galina Yeme-lianova, ed., *Radical Islam in the former Soviet Union* (London: Routledge, 2010).

5. Stéphane A. Dudoignon, "From revival to mutation: the religious personnel of Islam in Tajikistan, from de-Stalinization to Independence (1955–91)," *Central Asian Survey* 30, no. 1 (2011): 59. Islamic activists considered the Brezhnev years as an important transitional time in which religious practice and debates fundamentally changed. However, the IRPT usually holds on to the idea of an Islamic revival in the 1970s, which is intrinsically tied to the activities of the IRPT's founder Nurī. See Sattorī, *HNIT*, 151.

6. Yaacov Ro'i, *Islam in the Soviet Union: From the Second World War to Gorbachev* (London: Hurst, 2000), 11–53.

7. Cf. Eren Tasar, "Soviet and Muslim: The Institutionalization of Islam in Central Asia, 1943–1991," Dissertation, Harvard University, 2010.

8. See Lyucian Klimovič, *Islam* (Moskva: Nauka, 1965) and the transfer into the Western discourse by Alexandre Bennigsen and Chantal Lemercier-Quelquejay, "'Official' Islam in the Soviet Union," *Religion in Communist Lands*, no. 7 (1979): 148–59. See Michael Kemper, "Ljucian Klimovič: Der ideologische Bluthund der sowjetischen Islamkunde und Zentralasienliteratur," *Asiatische Studien/Études Asiatiques* 63, no. 1 (2009): 93–133; Mark Saroyan and Edward W. Walker, *Minorities, mullahs, and modernity: Reshaping community in the former Soviet Union* (Berkeley: Univ. of California, 1997).

9. Devin DeWeese, "Islam and the legacy of Sovietology: a review essay on Yaacov Ro'i's Islam in the Soviet Union," *Journal of Islamic Studies* 13, no. 3 (2002): 310.

10. See Mark Saroyan, "Rethinking Islam in the Soviet Union," In *Beyond Sovietology: Essays in politics and history*, Edited by Susan G. Solomon (Armonk: M.E. Sharpe, 1993).

11. Eren M. Tasar, "Muslim Life in Central Asia, 1943–1985," Social Research Center/AUCA, 2007: 46.

12. Saroyan, "Rethinking," 44.

13. Abdullo Rahnamo, *Ulamoi Islomī dar Toǧikiston* (Dušanbe: Irfon, 2009), 195–208.

14. DeWeese, "Islam," 310.

15. Cf. Shahnoza Nozimova and Tim Epkenhans, "Negotiating Islam in emerging public Spheres in contemporary Tajikistan," *Asiatische Studien/Études Asiatiques* 67, no. 3 (2013); Epkenhans, "Defining," 88–92. For the general theoretical implications see Pierre Bourdieu, *Religion* (Berlin: Suhrkamp, 2011).

16. For a historical perspective see Hamid Algar, "The Naqshbandi Order: A Preliminary Survey of Its History and Significance," *Studia Islamica* 44 (1976) and Jürgen Paul, *Die politische und soziale Bedeutung der Naqsbandiyya in Mittelasien im 15. Jahrhundert* (Berlin: de Gruyter, 1991).

17. See Sattorī, *HNIT*, 48.

18. Tasar, "Soviet," 139–172.

19. Roziq, *HNIT*, 39.

20. Sattorī, *HNIT*, 30.

21. Dudoignon, "Revival," 70–72.

22. Dudoignon, "Revival," 59.
23. Cf. Mandaville, *Islam and Politics*, 65–202.
24. The Russian version of Hindustonī's name is Muhammadžon Rustamov. Hindustonī is often addressed with the honorific title *mavlavī* ('scholar of the Islamic sciences') or *damullo/domullo*.
25. Husaynī, *Xotiraho*, 8–17.
26. Sulton Hamad, *Dar payrahai nur* (Dušanbe: Muattar, 2013), 22–25. Cf. Hindustonī's biography in: B. Babadjanov and M. Kamilov, "Muhammadjan Hindustani (1892–1989) and the Beginning of the 'Great Schism' among the Muslims of Uzbekistan." In *Islam in politics in Russia and Central Asia*, Edited by Stéphane A. Dudoignon and Hisao Komatsu (London: Kegan Paul, 2001), 197–200. See also Naumkin, *Pen and Rifle*, 44–51.
27. Dudoignon, "Revival," 68.
28. Akbar Turajonzoda, "Religion: The Pillar of Society," In *Central Asia: conflict, resolution, and change*, Edited by Roald Sagdeev and Susan Eisenhower (Washington, DC: The Eisenhower Institute, 1995), 268. See also Whitlock, *Beyond the River*, 34–35 and Dudoignon and Qalandar, "They Were All," 86–88 (they call Hindustonī a Deobandi neo-traditionalist). For Hindustonī's autobiographical writings see Ğamoliddin Tošmatov (ed.), *Yodnoma. Hazrati Mavlono Muhammadğon Qūqondī* (Dušanbe: Ilhom, 2003). For the Deobandi school see Barbara Metcalf, "The Madrasa at Deoband: A Model for Religious Education in Modern India," *Modern Asian Studies* 12, no. 1 (1978); Muhammad Zaman, *The ulama in contemporary Islam: Custodians of change* (Princeton: Princeton University Press, 2002), 68–69. See also Khalid, *Islam*, 218. Nourzhanov and Bleuer (*Tajikistan*, 258) have identified the Dar ul-Usmaniya *madrasa* in Ajmer as an outlet by the South-Asian *tariqa* of the Čistiya (however, their URL link does not function anymore). I am additionally grateful to PD Dr. Dietrich Reetz (ZMO Berlin), who pointed out in a personal conversation (Berlin, 13 November 2015) that the Barelvī *tariqa* apparently organized the Dar ul-Usmaniya *madrasa* during Hindustonī's studies in Ajmer. Considering his determined struggle for the re-establishment of a Hanafi-Sunni normativity and his apparent tolerance for Sufi orders—many of his students, such as the brothers of Tūrağonzoda, were representatives of popular Sufi circles following religious practices decidedly rejected by Deobandi networks—a Barelvī influence on Hindustonī is likely.
29. Tim Epkenhans, "The Islamic Revival Party of Tajikistan: Episodes of Islamic Activism, post-conflict Accommodation and political Marginalization," *Central Asian Affairs* 2, 2015, 312–46.
30. Cf. Dudoignon and Qalandar, "They Were all," 89 and Tūrağonzoda, *Šariat*, 29–38.
31. Roziq, *HNIT*, 70–71.
32. Roziq, *HNIT*, 74–76. See also Dudoignon and Qalandar, "They Were all," 91.
33. Roziq, *HNIT*, 75; Epkenhans, "Islamic Revival Party," 329–334.
34. See the interview with Nurī in Sattorī, *HNIT*, 14.
35. The IRPT published in 2003 (on the occasion of its 30th anniversary) and in 2013 (on the occasion of its 40th anniversary) several publications commemorating

the party's development since 1973, see Muhammad Orzu, ed., *40 soli Nahzat. Xotira, andeša, didgoh* (Dušanbe: Muattar, 2013); and the special edition of *Nağot* 17, 26 April 2013.

36. Dudoignon and Qalandar, "They Were All," 49–50.

37. In some *harakat* and IRPT documents Nurī is addressed as *sayid* Abdullo[h] Nurī (Arabic: *sayyid*), an honorific title which denotes males accepted as descendants of the Prophet Muhammad. According to my knowledge, Nurī never claimed officially descent from the Prophet's family.

38. Sattorī, *HNIT*, 16.

39. Sattorī, *HNIT*, 17 and 47. See Epkenhans, "Islamic Revival Party," 326–327.

40. Tūrağonzoda, *Miyoni*, 50.

41. Roziq, *HNIT*, 45. The Arabic/Persian term *amri ma'rufu nahyi munkar* (Command Right and Forbid Wrong) refers to a central tenet of the Islamic tradition, see Michael Cook, *Commanding right and forbidding wrong in Islamic thought* (Cambridge: Cambridge University Press, 2000). For the interview with Qalandar Sardiddin see: http://www.ozodi.org/content/tajik-islamic-party-turns-40-from-underground-to-parliament/24968279.html, accessed December 20, 2013.

42. See Husaynī, *Xotiraho*, 17–18; 39–42; A. Qayumzod, "Xudo bo most, pirūzī niz," *Čaroği rūz*, 1992, 45: 3.

43. Roziq, *HNIT*, 46–49.

44. Conversation with an Islamic activist (Dushanbe September 2008) and Husaynī 2013: 19–30.

45. Husaynī, *Xotiraho*, 33.

46. Sattorī, *HNIT*, 48; Roziq, *HNIT*, 46–47.

47. Husaynī, *Xotiraho*, 27. In general, IRPT representatives are relatively unexcited about their relationship to the Soviet state. Hait, for instance, was an officer in the GRU (military intelligence) during the occupation of Afghanistan.

48. Dudoignon, "Political Parties," 67. Cf. Diego Gambetta and Steffen Hertog, "Why are there so many Engineers among Islamic Radicals?," *A.E.S.* 50, no. 2 (2009).

49. Roziq, *HNIT*, 50–51.

50. Roziq, *HNIT*, 53.

51. Roziq, *HNIT*, 54–58.

52. Roziq, *HNIT*, 61–66.

53. Roziq, *HNIT*, 109–110.

54. Husaynī, *Xotiraho*, 54; Roziq, *HNIT*, 116.

55. Sattorī, *HNIT*, 153.

56. Roziq, *HNIT*, 124–125.

57. Sattorī, *HNIT*, 400.

58. Sattorī, *HNIT*, 89–90.

59. Roziq, *HNIT*, 139–141. According to the IRPT lore, the KGB manipulated the local elections otherwise both would have won their constituencies.

60. Roziq, *HNIT*, 170.

61. See for instance Bennigsen, *Soviet Strategy*, passim; A. Bennigsen and S. E. Wimbush, *Mystics and commissars: Sufism in the Soviet Union* (London: Hurst, 1985); T. Saidbaev, *Islam i obščestvo. Opyt istoriko-sotsiologičeskogo issledovaniya*

(Moskva: Nauka, 1978); Naumkin, *Pen*, passim. For an evaluation see Heathershaw and Montgomery, *Myth*, 4–5; Saroyan, "Rethinking," 24–26.

62. Epkenhans, "Islamic Revival Party," 329–334.

63. Nasriddinov, *Tarkiš*, 24–25.

64. Kenğaev, *Tabadduloti 1*, 343–344.

65. Babadjanov and Kamilov, "Hindustani," 200–204; B. M. Babajanov, A. Muminov, and A. von Kügelgen, *Disputes on Muslim Authority in Central Asia in 20th Century* (Almaty: Daik-Press, 2007), 126–130.

66. Roziq, *HNIT*, 77.

67. Roziq, *HNIT*, 78. *Tamğa* is originally a Mongol term. In Farsi *tamğā* means 'stamp' or 'stamp-tax' associated with the (non-Islamic) Mongol tax system.

68. Rasanayagam, *Islam*, 122, 144–153. See also Roziq, *HNIT*, 104; Rahnamo, *Ulamoi*, 173–182.

69. Until today, the government mouthpiece *Ğumhuriyat* launched defamation campaigns with op-eds whose authors are unknown and have neither published before nor after the publication of the op-ed.

70. Cited in Davlat, "Qozikalon," 12. See also Roziq, *HNIT*, 178.

71. Sohibnazar, *Subhi 1*, 196.

72. See Muriel Atkin, *The subtlest battle: Islam in Soviet Tajikistan* (Philadelphia: Foreign Policy Research Institute, 1989), 35 and Alexandre Bennigsen, "Unrest in the World of Soviet Islam," *Third World Quarterly* 10, no. 2 (1988): 778–779.

73. Qahhor Rasuliyon, "Vahhobiho kistand?," *Adabiyot va San'at*, July 2, 1992, 27: 6.

74. Kenğaev, *Tabadduloti 1*, 140.

75. Kenğaev, *Tabadduloti 1*, 259.

76. Karim, *Faryodi*, 459.

77. John Anderson, *Religion, state and politics in the Soviet Union and successor states* (Cambridge: Cambridge University Press, 1994), 200–205.

78. FBIS-SOV-86–230, 1 December 1986, R6.

79. Mirrahim, *Hamatabaqi*, 150. In general Yurchak, *Everything*, 5–10.

80. Cited in Nasriddinov, *Tarkiš*, 140–141. Ğalāl ad-Dīn Rūmī (1207–1273) and Amīr Xosrav (1254–1325) were prominent poets of the mystical tradition. While Xosrav was from Samarqand, Rūmī was either from Balx today Afghanistan or Vaxš in southern Tajikistan.

81. Karim, *Faryodi*, 278. For the interview see FBIS-SOV-91–063-S, 2 April 1991, 53–55.

82. FBIS-SOV-92–047, 10 March 1992, 44–45; FBIS-USR-02–050, 1 May 1992, 103.

83. Kenğaev, *Huquq*, 151–152.

84. For instance: Kenğaev, *Tabadduloti 1*, 115–120.

85. FBIS-SOV-91–061, 30 March 1992, 43–44.

86. Kenğaev, *Tabadduloti 2*, 66. According to Kenğaev, Mullo Abdurahim was discharged from the military service and spent some years in psychiatry. His low work ethics, Kenğaev continues, was also related to the alleged 'sluggish schizophrenia'. For the function of psychiatric diagnosis in the USSR see Eric Stover and Elena

O. Nightingale, eds., *The Breaking of bodies and minds: Torture, psychiatric abuse, and the health professions* (New York: Freeman, 1985).

87. Roziq, *HNIT*, 164; Sattorī, *HNIT*, 156–157.
88. Sattorī, *HNIT*, 158–159, 400.
89. The conversation is quoted in Keṇğaev, *Tabadduloti 1*, 16.
90. Roziq, *HNIT*, 173.
91. Roziq, *HNIT*, 189. Cf. also Sattorī, *HNIT*, 20, 160.
92. Usmonov, *Ta'rixi siyosii*, 39.
93. FBIS-SOV-91–063-S, 2 April 1991, 56.
94. Roziq, *HNIT*, 175
95. FBIS-SOV-91–063-S, 2 April 1991, 57.
96. Roziq, *HNIT*, 204; Orzu, *40 soli*, 428, 438; FBIS-SOV-91–209, 29 October 1991, 73.
97. See the copy of the program in Orzu, *40 soli*, 438.
98. FBIS-SOV-92–083, 29 April 1992, 61.
99. FBIS-SOV-92–097, 19 May 1992, 43.
100. FBIS-SOV-91–237, 10 December 1991, 74.
101. FBIS-SOV-92–096, 15 May 1992, 62–63.
102. Qayumzod, "Xudo," 3.
103. FBIS-SOV-91–229, 27 November 1991, 73–74; FBIS-SOV-92–156, 12 August 1992, 56; FBIS-SOV-92–195, 7 October 1992, 51–52;
104. FBIS-SOV-91–194, 7 October 1991, 81–82.
105. Usmonov, *Nabiev*, 81.
106. Sattorī, *HNIT*, 23.
107. Karim, *Faryodi*, 459.
108. Nasriddinov, *Tarkiš*, 25.
109. See for instance Sohibnazar, *Subhi 1*, 82.
110. Adaš Istad, "Davlati millī," *Adabiyot va San'at*, May 21, 1992. 21: 6.
111. Istad, "Davlati," 6.
112. Cf. Wael B. Hallaq, *Shari'a: Theory, practice, transformations* (Cambridge: Cambridge Univ. Press, 2009); Peter G. Mandaville, *Transnational Muslim politics: Reimagining the umma* (London: Routledge, 2001).
113. Sohibnazar, *Subhi 1*, 81.
114. Sohibnazar, *Subhi 2*, 62.
115. Cf. for instance Ro'i, *Islam*, passim.
116. Roziq, *HNIT*, 127. Cf. Dudoignon, "Revival," passim; Tasar, "Soviet," passim; Saroyan, *Minorities*, passim.
117. Atkin, "Survival," 608. The previous *mufti* in Tashkent, Šamsuddin Babaxan, had been removed through public protests by Muslims from the Fergana Valley, the home region of Muhammad Sodiq, see Martha B. Olcott, *A Face of Islam: Muhammad-Sodiq Muhammad-Yusuf* (Washington: Carnegie, 2007).
118. *Xoğa* (Pers.: *ḫvāğa*, plural *xoğagon*) is an honorific title for religious authorities of the Naqšbandiyya in Turkestan. See Frank J. Allen, *Dictionary of Central Asian islamic terms* (Springfield: Dunwoody Press, 2002).
119. See Nuralī Davlat, "Qozikalon. Kommuniston boyad ğanoza našavand?," *Nigoh*, March 11, 2014, 50: 5.

120. Mark Saroyan, "Authority and Community in Soviet Islam." In *Accounting for fundamentalisms: The dynamic character of movements*, Edited by Martin E. Marty and R. S. Appleby (Chicago: University of Chicago Press, 1994).

121. Yūsuf, *Tāğīkestān*, 129; Tūrağonzoda, *Miyoni*, 14; Usmonov, *Nabiev*, 81. Epkenhans, "Defining," 85–92; Nozimova and Epkenhans, "Negotiating," 971–985.

122. Davlat, "Qozī," 5.

123. FBIS-SOV-92–139, 20 July 1992, 62. Davlat Nazriev and Igor Sattarov, *Respublika Tadžikistan: Istoriya nezavisimosti god 1992-y (Tom II)* (Dušanbe: Nur, 2005), 141.

124. Tūrağonzoda, *Miyoni*, 50.

125. Karim, *Faryodi*, 362.

126. Cf. Tūrağonzoda, *Šariat*, 141; 154–156.

127. Whitlock, *Beyond the River*, 143.

128. Cf. Epkenhans, "Defining," 85–86.

129. Buškov and Mikul'skiy, *Anatimiya*, 74–77; Roziq, *HNIT*, 183. Himmatzoda wrote the editorial for the first issue of *Minbari Islom* (see Sattorī, HNIT, 19). Due to the lack of funds, only 8 issues of *Minbari Islom* were published (see Gretsky, "Qadi," 18).

130. FBIS-SOV-90–192, 3 October 1990, 88.

131. Roziq, *HNIT*, 181–182.

132. Sohibnazar, *Subhi 1*, 275.

133. FBIS-SOV-92–085, 1 May 1992, 46–49.

134. Karim, *Faryodi*, 397.

135. Karim, *Faryodi* 405; FBIS-SOV-92–082, 28 April 1992, 60.

136. Tūrağonzoda, *Miyoni*, 23.

137. Nozimova and Epkenhans, "Negotiating," 971–76.

138. Kenğaev, *Tabadduloti 1*, 52–53. See also the following chapter on Kenğaev's appointment as Chairman of the NSC/KGB in April 1992.

139. Farrux Mamadšoev, "Tūrağonzoda—agenti KGB?," Ğumhuriyat, March 15, 2009.

140. Xalifa Abdulkarim (in the spelling of the Tūrağon family), however, was Tūrağonzoda's grandfather and not his uncle.

141. Mamadšoev, "Tūrağonzoda".

142. Davlat, "Qozī," 5.

143. See Petkelʻ, *Žiznennye*, 141. He reports in his short memoirs about the agent "Abdurahman" and his family, but the details he gives do not match with the Tūrağon family.

144. FBIS-SOV-90–032, 15 February 1990, 65.

145. Tūrağonzoda, *Miyoni*, 23.

146. See Sohibnazar, *Subhi 1*, 66–67, 83–84.

147. Karim, *Faryodi*, 95.

148. *Idi Qurbon* (in Arabic ʻĪd al-aḍḥā), the Feast of the Sacrifice, falls on 10th of the Islamic Dhu al-Hijjah month, *Idi Ramazon* (or *Idi Fitr*, in Arabic ʻĪd al-Fiṭr) concludes the month of Ramadan.

149. Davlat, "Qozikalon Kommuniston," 5.

150. Kenğaev, *Tabadduloti 1*, 26; Tūrağonzoda, *Miyoni*, 8–11; FBIS-SOV-92–085, 1 May 1992, 46.

151. FBIS-SOV-92–131, 8 July 1992, 73; FBIS-SOV-92–139, 20 July 1992, 61; FBIS-SOV-92–156, 12 August 1992, 56; FBIS-SOV-92–178, 14 September 1992, 34–35.

152. Tūrağonzoda, *Miyoni*, 13.

153. FBIS-SOV-92–139, 20 July 1992, 61.

154. See Tūrağonzoda, *Miyoni*, 9 (conversation with Nabiev), 10 (conversation with Kenğaev), 12 (conversation with Himmatzoda, Abduğabbor, Šabdolov, Yusuf, Usmonova), 16–19 (conversations with Kenğaev and Nabiev), 24–26 (conversation with Nurī, Kenğaev and Nabiev). 30 (as an informal mediator between the deputies in the Supreme Soviet)

155. Tūrağonzoda, *Miyoni*, 20–21.

156. Usmonov, *Nabiev*, 109.

157. Usmonov, *Nabiev*, 109.

158. Roziq, *HNIT*, 141. In a conversation in Dushanbe (March 2010), a Tajik respondent maintained that the enmity between Tūrağonzoda and Šarifov was going back to a feud between two regional groups of religious scholars in the Hisor-Kūlob-Qarotegin area. Pre-Soviet migration patterns, inter- and intra-regional contacts as well as religious affiliation reportedly shaped the conflict already in the 19th century.

159. Gretsky, "Qadi," 18.

160. Davlat, "Qozikalon Kommuniston," 5

161. Nasriddinov, *Tarkiš*, 147–148.

162. Sohibnazar, *Subhi 2*, 104 and *Subhi 1*, 203–205.

163. Yūsuf, *Tāğīkestān*, 166.

164. Yūsuf, *Tāğīkestān*, 166–168.

165. *Ata* is originally an Uzbek word for father but widely used in Tajik as well. The transcription reproduces the original text by Tūrağonzoda.

166. Tūrağonzoda, *Miyoni*, 45.

167. Tūrağonzoda, *Miyoni*, 45.

168. Roziq, *HNIT*, 144.

169. FBIS-SOV-92–086, 4 May 1992, 52.

170. FBIS-USR-92–076, 22 June 1992, 105.

171. FBIS-SOV-92–081, 27 April 1992, 60.

172. FBIS-SOV-93–012, 21 January 1993, 71–72; FBIS-SOV-96–015, 23 January 1996, 65–66.

Chapter 6

Tensions Rising

The Tale of Two Squares (March and April 1992)

On 25 March 1992, the Tajik state television broadcasted two hours of a joint session of the Presidium of the Supreme Soviet and the Council of Ministers chaired by Safaralī Kenğaev. In this session Kenğaev accused Mamadayoz Navğuvonov, the minister of interior, of incompetence, negligence toward the needs of the MVD, corruption, nepotism and illicit transgression of his competences.[1] Kenğaev had organized the denunciation of Navğuvonov carefully in advance: He informed the Presidium only shortly in advance and caught Navğuvonov by surprise. In his response, Navğuvonov did not answer to the allegations, but immediately accused Kenğaev of discrimination against the Pomirī minority (to whom he belonged) and warned that Kenğaev's agitation would increase the separatist tendencies in GBAO.[2] But Kenğaev had already committed the Presidium to issue a resolution of no confidence asking Nabiev to dismiss Navğuvonov. Due to Navğuvonov's dubious role in the February events, the opposition would have even welcomed his dismissal, if not Kenğaev's comments on the Pomirī community as well as his tone and aggressive language violated against the "general conventions on which statehood should be based on."[3] Sohibnazar remarked that Kenğaev talked to Navğuvonov in a way "the chairman of a kolkhoz or a *brigadir* would talk to his subordinates"[4] and criticized that Kenğaev emphasized Navğuvonov's regional background. Similarly, Nasriddinov called Kenğaev an irresponsible provocateur and concluded "if this session did not happen, the people would have not been so furious and the situation would have not deteriorated to such an extent."[5] Although Kenğaev—through the arrest of Ikromov and his relentless defamation—had already increased the pressure on the opposition, his public denunciation of Navğuvonov antagonized the opposition and resulted in an unprecedented mobilization of opposition supporters in Dushanbe. Many regard 25 March 1992 as the pivotal date and catalyst for the unfolding conflict. Keṅğaev's intentions behind the attack on Navğuvonov are contested and interpreted from different perspectives: Keṅğaev himself portrayed his decision to confront Navğuvonov with his advocacy for the "rule of law" and "truth" and not personal animosities. Navğuvonov was responsible for the disintegration of the MVD and deterioration of public order in Dushanbe due to his inefficiency, personal shortcomings and nepotism. Navğuvonov, Keṅğaev concluded, had antagonized veteran and merited MVD officials and replaced them by incompetent officials from his native GBAO.[6]

Yusuf instead assumed frictions within the government and maintained that Keṅğaev acted on behalf of Nabiev who wanted to dismiss Navğuvonov, but did not want to be implicated in the dismissal himself. According to Yusuf's narrative, Nabiev wanted to get rid of Navğuvonov since he had already "sold" his position to one of his confidants. Simultaneously, Nabiev wanted to discredit Keṅğaev whom he considered as a potential rival. Nabiev was well aware of Keṅğaev's unsettled temperament and immoral behavior; therefore, he expected that Keṅğaev's authority would be undermined by the confrontation with Navğuvonov and he (Nabiev) could eventually replace both of them with more amenable candidates.[7]

Sohibnazar analyzed Keṅğaev's intention from a slightly different perspective: Within the larger Leninobodī elite, Keṅğaev was a controversial figure and some, for instance Rif'at Hoğiev and the Abdulloğonov brothers, considered him as a rural *mastčohī* and not a "true" (i.e., lowland/urban) Leninobodī.[8] With his polarizing confrontation of Navğuvonov, Keṅğaev intended to consolidate his position, since the Leninobodī nomenklatura would almost certainly support him against any political attacks by the opposition. Additionally, the Leninobodī faction lacked a charismatic and unifying political personality—a deficit Keṅğaev obviously tried to exploit. Since Nabiev did nothing to defuse the situation ("he remained neutral in the unfolding drama"[9]), Sohibnazar assumed that Nabiev ultimately wanted to sideline both, Navğuvonov and Keṅğaev. Tūrağonzoda recalled that Keṅğaev informed members of the presidium telling them that he did not understand why Nabiev gave him the *order* to confront Navğuvonov.[10] Nasriddinov concluded that Nabiev lost his balance in leadership and politics in Tajikistan degenerated to a

> clownery (*masxarabozī*) in which three incompetent leaders occupied the highest offices, forgot about the people and entertained themselves with personal hostilities. [...] Is there any worse treason than this? Today we accuse other countries of destroying our nation and our people, but the main criminals who are responsible for all the agony is the leadership of that time.[11]

To some extent Keṅğaev supported Nasriddinov's version by claiming that he (Keṅğaev) had to act preventively in order to stop the "unmanly perfidiousness (*xiyonati noğovonmardona*)."[12] He blamed that the opposition and so-called intellectuals were responsible for the deteriorating tone in the political debate. For instance, he reported how Akbar Maxsumov, the director of the Dushanbe Botanical Garden and son of Nusratullo Maxsum, announced full of hatred that in less than two months there will be an explosion (Rus.: *vzryv*) in the political situation and the people will decide about the fate of the alcoholic Rahmon Nabiev. "I [Kenğaev] said to myself: By God, what kind of opinion was this, what terror came out of the mouth of this experienced intellectual, this well-known Tajik scholar and skilled politician? [...] Was he not pouring oil into the fire?"[13]

Ibrohim Usmonov remarked, that although some of the allegations—such as the lack of efficiency in the ministry as well as the shortcomings of the minister himself—needed to be addressed, it should have never been broadcasted on TV especially since Navğuvonov (and not Kenğaev) irresponsibly played the regional card and mobilized his networks in Badaxšon.[14] Unintentionally, Kenğaev made Navğuvonov a public figure uniting the opposition—a rather unusual role for a career MVD officer.[15]

The elaborated narratives on Kenğaev's alleged intentions should not conceal, that he severely disrupted the fragile political equilibrium after the presidential elections. Kenğaev had a rather short-term objective, that is, to assume direct control over the MVD, and he perhaps did not expect that the assault on Navğuvonov would generate solidarity and a sense of unity among the heterogeneous opposition.

THE LOCATION

The Lenin Prospect in Dushanbe was the central boulevard epitomizing the Soviet model of urban modernization in the TaSSR. Shaded by lines of trees, the prospect runs in a north-south direction for several kilometers passing by the main representative administrative and residential buildings built in the 1930s. On the southern edge (where the Lenin Prospect turns south-east for a few kilometers until it reaches Aynī Prospect) was Lenin Square with the Lenin monument opposite the building of the Supreme Soviet. On Lenin Square the Soviet authorities celebrated public holidays, such as International Labor Day (1 May), Victory Day (9 May) or Revolution Day (7 November), with parades and the patronizing nomenklatura on a stage below the Lenin statue. A trolleybus station north, less than a kilometer from Lenin Square, at the T-crossing of *ulica* Putovsky (today Ismoil Somonī) and Prospect Lenin (Rūdakī) was the main building of the Central Committee of the CPT (today the presidential administration), where in February 1990 the demonstrations took place and 21 demonstrators were shot—therefore the opposition renamed the place Šahidon (Martyrs) Square. With the declaration of independence on 9 September 1991, the Supreme Soviet renamed Lenin Prospect after the poet Abuabdulloh Rūdakī (858–941) and *ulica* Putovsky after Ismoil Somoni (reigned 892–907); on the same day Lenin Square eventually became Ozodī (freedom) Square. The escalation of tensions in 1992 is associated with these two squares (*maydon*) in central Dushanbe. In September 1991, Ozodī Square had been the venue for protests for consecutive 14 days, but the demonstration on Šahidon Square, which commenced on 26 March 1992 and took 52 days until 14 May 1992, eclipsed the previous protests.

Kenǧaev's provocation mobilized in particular the opposition from Badaxšon and on 26 March a small group of perhaps 150 Pomirī youth started to demonstrate on Šahidon Square despite heavy snowfall demanding an apology from Kenǧaev and his resignation. Organized by La'li Badaxšon, the demonstration attracted a few more participants during the day. Although a militia detachment tried to block access to the square on the morning of 27 March, they did not enforce the blockade and eventually the commanding officer gave order to return to the barracks. Some militiamen reportedly even joined the protestors on the square.[16] After consultations, the DPT and Rastoxez called on their supporters to join the protests. According to Himmatzoda, the IRPT leadership initially hesitated to join the demonstration since "we were a political party, and we should not risk the reputation (*obrū*) of our association in order to provide someone with a position or to dismiss him from one. [...] Unfortunately, however, on the initiative of some of our friends, in particular Davlat Usmon, our party eventually entered the stage [on Šahidon Square]."[17]

In an interview 20 years later, Davlat Usmon still considered the IRPT's participation as a matter of course: "Since we permanently coordinated our activities with the democratic forces and were united with them, I thought that we had to join the demonstration to reinforce them."[18] In the same interview, however, he conceded: "Today I think, that the participation in the demonstrations was a grave and serious mistake, but at that time and in that situation we had no alternative than to join the other democratic forces on the square with the results we all know."[19]

The participation of other opposition groups than La'li Badaxšon broadened the agenda and the DPT and IRPT pressed for the dissolution of the Supreme Soviet and snap elections. The Supreme Soviet in its 12th Convocation had been elected in 1990 under emergency law and its deputies were overwhelmingly functionaries of the former Soviet administration. Furthermore, the opposition demanded the release of Dushanbe's former mayor Maqsud Ikromov, who had been arrested earlier for his involvement in the demolition of the Lenin statue in 1991 and the alleged embezzlement of municipality funds. Remarkably, none of the opposition groups demanded the resignation of President Nabiev at this point.[20]

Next to Kenğaev's resignation, the dissolution of the Supreme Soviet became the most controversial issue in the evolving political confrontation. The opposition was confident that in case of elections they would gain a significant representation and change the composition of the Supreme Soviet and therefore the political landscape in Tajikistan as such. Although many deputies who were elected in February 1990 had left the Communist Party, had joined the opposition or claimed to be independent deputies, the conservative, anti-reformist and anti-democratic group still formed the majority. Kenğaev was confident that he could rely on this majority and rejected the demands by the opposition referring to Tajikistan's constitution, which did not contain legal provisions for the dissolution of the Supreme Soviet.[21]

Since both, the government and the opposition presented themselves as advocates of the rule of law and a constitutional order, legal arguments carried some weight in the political discussion: The opposition dropped the demand for the dissolution of the Supreme Soviet due to the constitutional constraints, instead they focused on the resignation of Kenğaev and the Presidium of the Supreme Soviet.

Figure 6.1 The Center of Soviet Dushanbe—the Upper Circle Marks Šahidon Square, the Lower Circle Ozodī Square.

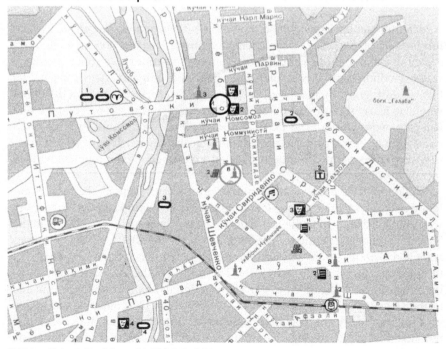

Source: Osimī, *Enziklopediyai*, Vol. 2, 336.

Kenğaev and Dūstov handled the situation inconsistently. Usmonov recalled a meeting with representatives of Tajikistan's print media on 31 March, where Dūstov first referred to the "amicable" relationship between Navğuvonov and Kenğaev. The latter instead acidly remarked that those responsible for the negative coverage in the press should be—as the people behind the crisis—considered as criminals. He (Kenğaev) only acts according to the law and his conviction.[22] Nabiev did not intervene to reduce the tensions and the increasing polarization. Instead he announced his neutrality (*betarafī*) in the unfolding drama, called Navğuvonov an able official and told the media that Kenğaev acted on his own.[23]

Although the presidential administration issued constant flow of decrees, Nabiev rarely participated in government meetings and became more and more elusive.[24] Observers agree that during the first five, six days of the demonstration on Šahidon Square, the tensions and polarization could have been reduced by an intervention of Nabiev or some sort of apology by Kenğaev. However, the latter even poured oil into the fire by his relentless rhetoric denouncing the opposition as Islamists and criminals.[25]

RAMADAN 1992: THE IRPT TAKES THE HELM

Apparently Nabiev expected the protests to attenuate after *Eid al-Fitr*, which fell in 1992 on Saturday, 4 April. The demonstrations had continued uninterrupted day and night for 10 days and the government expected that the harsh weather conditions—it was unusually cold and rainy for April, the public fasting during daylight as well as the high level of political mobilization would exhaust the opposition and weaken its determination.[26] Nabiev and Kenğaev were wrong. The IRPT skillfully blended religious with nationalist sentiment generating a sense of unity on the square. Even avowed atheists were overwhelmed by the particular atmosphere of the moment as they recalled later.[27]

While the IRPT was able to mobilize their followers among the rural population and in particular among Ġarmī *muhoğir*, the party lacked a personality who could also appeal to the urban audience with a stronger rootedness in the Soviet intellectual traditions. The three leaders of the IRPT—Nurī, Himmatzoda and Usmon—were all born into *muhoğir* families, which were resettled to Qūrġonteppa region in the 1950s. The rural, kolkhoz background was an important constituent of their symbolic (religious) capital which originated in the spatiality of the Qarotegin Valley as well as Qūrġonteppa and which was influenced by the social consolidation, transformation and eventually mobilization of the *muhoğir* communities since the 1960s.[28] Arguably, one of the few personalities that could bridge the divide between the rural IRPT and an urban electorate was Tūrağonzoda. As the son of a respected *ešon* and graduate of a veritable Islamic university with an impeccable knowledge of Arabic, he possessed a symbolic capital important for a "traditional" religious constituency. As an elected deputy of the Supreme Soviet and graduate of the Soviet educational institutions, he could habitually also reach out to a more urban Soviet constituency.

Nurī approached Tūrağonzoda shortly before the end Ramadan and invited him to join the protests on the square and demonstrate his allegiance to the democratic Islamic cause.[29] Initially, Tūrağonzoda rejected the invitation and declared that the *qozikalon* needs to remain independent and any political involvement would infringe on the reputation and nature of his office.[30] In mid-April he offered Nurī and Himmatzoda to join the opposition under two conditions: First, the opposition should demand the dissolution of the Supreme Soviet and snap elections and second, they should insist on the adoption of a new constitution by the newly elected Supreme Soviet.[31] Since the opposition had already contemplated on these questions, they immediately agreed and on 11 April 1992, Tūrağonzoda joined the opposition. In an address shortly afterwards, he nonetheless portrayed himself as floating above the political disputes: "You know and God is my witness, I did not invite you to come to this square, you came yourself. But those inside [the government] do not believe me. [...] Since I did not invite you, I can't tell you to leave. You have the right to stay if you want or to leave."[32]

The opposition, in particular the chairman of the Constitutional Control Commission Ašurboy Imomov, had already addressed the issue of a new constitution earlier. Shortly after Tūrağonzoda had joined the opposition, Himmatzoda demanded the immediate drafting of the new constitution and the transformation of the Supreme Soviet to a professional parliament. He issued an ultimatum threatening to convene a "national congress" as a parallel legislature dominated by the democratic opposition.[33] Early April 1992 marked a significant shift in the equilibrium of oppositional forces with the IRPT mobilizing its supporters in rural Tajikistan. In particular the celebration of *Eid al-Fitr* was a demonstration of the IRPT's capacity to mobilize several ten thousand of its sympathizers performing collectively the prayers and breaking fast on Šahidon Square.[34] Abduğabbor conceded that the IRPT emerged as the dominant faction within the opposition.[35] The secular opposition only hesitatingly embraced the coalition with the IRPT and Yusuf was anything but enthusiastic about the growing influence of the IRPT and the *qoziyot* in the opposition. Paradoxically, he even warned Dushanbe's public of the rise of the IRPT in March 1992 and criticized the government's strategy of discrediting the secular democratic opposition as being conductive for the IRPT and the radicalization of the opposition.[36]

While the IRPT became the most influential political party in the opposition, Tūraġonzoda emerged as the most popular oppositional figures upstaging Yusuf, Abduġabbor, Himmatzoda, Usmon and others.[37] The rise of the IRPT and its successful mobilization of their supporters and the popularity of the *qozikalon* in the highly symbolic month of Ramadan changed the parameters of the political conflict gradually marginalizing the secular Glasnost intelligentsia in the DPT and other civil associations.

THE CHANGING NATURE OF THE CONFLICT

The rise of the IRPT changed the political confrontation in the regions of Tajikistan as well. IRPT members in Kūlob and Qūrġonteppa advanced their views and challenged the authority of incumbent authorities. Simultaneously, local strong men in the shadow economy and organized crime, such as Sangak Safarov (Kūlob), Yaqub Salimov (Dushanbe/Kūlob) or Mullo Abduġaffur (southern Dushanbe), became more assertive with the accelerating disintegration of the former Soviet coercive structures and defied the authorities with which they previously had well-established contacts. The catastrophic economic decline further eroded the authority and reputation of the incumbent administration and political elites accelerating the rise of racketeers who offered "protection" and who identified new "business" opportunities. On the inter-regional level competition over the limited resources increased and in particular in Qūrġonteppa divisions among the local population were often understood in terms of the regionalist master narratives forged in Dushanbe. There, Kenġaev and Dūstov described the struggle as an ideological conflict between secularism (= *yurčik*) and Islamism (= *vovčik*), between Ġarm/Badaxšon and Leninobod/Kūlob or between an inclusive Iranian identity and exclusive Tajikness.

At this point the communication between the opposition and the government had not completely collapsed and several confidential meetings between the main protagonists took place: Kenġaev mentioned six meetings with the opposition only during late March and early April.[38] Sohibnazar and Tūraġonzoda hoped to convince Kenġaev to resign and offered him as a face-saving compensation various positions in the administration, but the latter rejected to resign since he considered this move as "unmanly (*nomardī*)."[39] Kenġaev instead demonstrated his questionable tactical capability by offering his resignation on two conditions: First, the opposition should withdraw from the square *prior* to the session of the Supreme Soviet and second, the Supreme Soviet should accept his resignation by majority vote.[40] Kenġaev sensed that it was highly unlikely that one of his conditions would be met: The opposition would not withdraw after organizing more than three weeks of continuous day and night demonstrations on his promise to resign and he was confident that the majority of the Supreme Soviet detested the opposition even more than him and would not approve his resignation. Ultimately, Kenğaev's tactical maneuvering decisively contributed to aggravation of tensions compounded by Nabiev's reluctance or inability to act. Throughout April, Nabiev followed the dangerous strategy oscillating between accommodation, "neutrality" and inner resignation. He announced his readiness for dialogue even offering government positions to the opposition, promising to accelerate the draft process for a new constitution or inviting CSCE or UN mediators to Tajikistan, but told opposition representatives that he had no influence on Kenğaev.[41]

Ultimately, Nabiev avoided contentious decisions and worse, he even did not attend important sessions of the Presidium or Supreme Soviet.[42] Only in mid-April 1992, he showed some readiness to discuss the opposition's demands in a more conciliatory way: He lengthily elaborated on the new draft constitution and the dissolution of the Supreme Soviet. While he indicated that the constitution would be drafted by his experts and without consultation of the civil society or the opposition, he emphasized the national character of the new constitution that would be written in Tajik and even renamed the Supreme Soviet to *Mağlisi millī* (National Assembly). Obviously, he hoped the opposition would accept his nationalistic decoy and overlook the more important issue: Nabiev demanded that the new constitution should be adopted by the *incumbent* Supreme Soviet, which was elected in February 1990 and in its majority hostile toward the opposition and the political transformation to a more inclusive and democratic society.[43]

TENSIONS RISING: THE 13TH SESSION OF THE SUPREME SOVIET

On 17 April, the general prosecutor's office instituted proceedings against the opposition on Šahidon Square for violations against the law for convening rallies and demonstrations. The prosecutor demanded that the opposition should compensate for the costs accumulated for tents, the premises of the Rohat Café next to the Šahidon Square and the rerouting of trolleybuses bypassing Šahidon Square.[44] The opposition, however, remained defiant and even extended the demonstrations to the TV & Radio Committee building and several traffic junctions in central Dushanbe paralyzing public transport in the capital. Thereupon, Nabiev issued an ultimatum to the demonstrators demanding the clearing of Šahidon Square until 10 am the next morning before the 13th Session of the Supreme Soviet was scheduled to commence. Nabiev offered a general amnesty to the demonstrators, but had no means to enforce his ultimatum.[45] Yusuf further contributed to the escalation of tensions with ambiguous comments on an impending civil war and Islamic revolution.[46]

On 20 April 1992, the 13th Session convened despite the on-going demonstrations on Šahidon Square. As a concession to the opposition, the Presidium of the Supreme Soviet issued a modified agenda for the session with eight discussion points: (1) a presentation by Narzullo Dūstov of the president's report on the social and economic situation; (2) the resignation of Kenğaev; (3) the enlargement of the Presidium by opposition deputies[47]; (4) the reinstatement of the right to demonstrate; (5) the suspension of criminal proceedings against the protestors; (6) the schedule for parliamentary elections in December 1992; (7) the reconsideration of the autonomy status of GBAO; and finally (8) the appointment of an inquiry commission for the Ikromov case.[48] Nabiev did not take part in the session, which observers interpreted as a signal that he wanted to get rid of Kenğaev but not get involved personally.[49] Instead, a group of moderate deputies—democrats and independents—tried (in vain) to convince Kenğaev to resign. Šūhrat Sultonov (a CPT deputy from Dushanbe) criticized the serious malpractice by Kenğaev who violated against the separation of powers by acting like a prosecutor while being chairman of the Supreme Soviet. Emomalī Rahmonov criticized (the absent) Nabiev for his inactivity and demanded from him to address the people to defuse the tense situation.[50]

But Kenğaev had secured his majority of deputies and ended the conciliatory tone. In the crucial vote, the majority of deputies decided that the demonstration on Šahidon violated against the constitution and the organizers should be prosecuted. Enraged, Usmon, Himmatzoda and Yusuf immediately left the Supreme Soviet and issued an ultimatum to the Supreme Soviet to meet all demands of the opposition by 21 April 1992.[51] This time the Supreme Soviet ignored the opposition's ultimatum and continued the session the following morning.

The resignation of Kenğaev remained on the agenda and Sohibnazar warned the deputies that in case Kenğaev does not resign, he would tear apart the country.[52] Kenğaev reacted evasively and referred to his record of 600 passed laws in the Supreme Soviet while the opposition did not submit a single substantial draft law. The demonstrators had no idea about the current situation, his outstanding work ethics and idea of duty—he has only one principle (*princip*) in his work, and that is the "struggle for truth and the service for the people."[53] After the outcome of the debate the day before, he was confident that the majority of the deputies would never support his resignation. Defiantly he arranged a vote on his resignation and as expected, the majority of 131 against 54 deputies expressed their confidence in him.[54] The vote of confidence incensed the opposition on Šahidon even more and in

the early evening *ešoni* Qiyomiddin Ġozī stormed with his men the building
of the Supreme Soviet taking 18 deputies hostages.[55] Tūraġonzoda described
the situation as extremely tense and hinted to frictions within the opposition:
qorī Muhammadġon and Qiyomiddin Ġozī, the latter in military fatigues living up to his title as "General of the People," incited young men and intimidated even members of the opposition, such as Tūraġonzoda and Sohibnazar.
In his memoirs Tūraġonzoda described the tumultuous situation and how representatives of the opposition—among them the poet Bozor Sobir—verbally
assaulted the kidnapped deputies further exacerbating the situation.[56] In the
turmoil, Adolat Rahmonova, a deputy from Danġara (Kūlob), was allegedly attacked and during the mobilization campaigns in Kūlob, she publicly
claimed that she had been sexually assaulted that night and that the opposition
had violated the collective *nomus* (honor) of the people of Kūlob.[57]

The hostage taking of deputies seriously strained the relationship between
the *qoziyot*, the IRPT and the secular opposition. In a confidential meeting
on 21 April Tūraġonzoda reportedly warned Nurī about the consequences.
In case the deputies are not released, Tūraġonzoda would address the demonstration on Šahidon and call on the demonstrators to leave the square. Nurī
asked Tūraġonzoda for patience and both agreed that Himmatzoda should
formally address the Supreme Soviet and offer an excuse for the hostage
taking. In his memoirs, Hoġī Akbar expressed his regrets that he did not
distance himself from Šahidon Square that day.[58] Nasriddinov remarked, that
the hostage taking changed the parameters of the conflict: The radicalization
of the opposition and the intransigence of the government undermined any
reconciliation.[59]

Simultaneously, the KGB and MVD further disintegrated and on 21 April
the chairman of the National Security Committee (NSC), Stroykin, categorically ruled out an intervention by the security forces. Throughout the
night, Kenġaev and Dūstov tried to rally support, but finally, at around 4
am on 22 April, Kenġaev submitted his resignation. Kenġaev's decision
was not only determined by the increasing tensions and the defection of the
security forces—importantly, Nabiev offered him the position of the NSC/
KGB Chairman. In late April, Nabiev suddenly became active. In hectically
arranged confidential meetings he entered negotiations with the opposition
on a political solution of the crisis, however without including Kenġaev (see
below). Nabiev's tactical move briefly diffused the tensions and appeased
Kenġaev with a face-saving exit. But he failed to inform the opposition about
the castling and Kenġaev remained an antagonizing key figure in the political field. Eventually, his appointment enraged the opposition even more and
further destabilized the situation.

Kenġaev submitted his resignation in the early morning of 22 April and in
an emergency session the Supreme Soviet accepted the resignation without

discussion. In the same session, the deputies fulfilled most of the demands by the opposition: Nation-wide elections were scheduled for December 1992, restrictions on the media abolished and opposition representatives included to the Presidium of the Supreme Soviet as well as to the Constitutional Commission. Furthermore, the deputies agreed on a general amnesty for the protestors on Šahidon Square, ordered the release of Dushanbe's former mayor Ikromov and held out the prospect of a discussion on the future status of Badaxšon (either as an autonomous republic or autonomous province). In turn, the opposition announced the suspension of the demonstration for 24 April.[60] During the session of the Supreme Soviet, Tūrağonzoda suggested that Kenğaev should remain a member of the Presidium of the Supreme Soviet, but Kenğaev declined and resigned from the Presidium as well.[61] After the results of the emergency session of the Supreme Soviet were announced on Šahidon Square, the demonstrators celebrated their success with a public feast (*oš*) and Nurī announced that the forthcoming Friday prayer on 24 April would be conducted on Šahidon Square.[62] Tūrağonzoda later commented on the events:

> In fact, the people on Šahidon felt like having achieved victory, since the path for important political reforms was eventually open. This was a very important achievement for all the people of Tajikistan. Unfortunately, the positive change for the nation was opposed by the CPT nomenklatura and the leadership of the republic. Foreign analysts came to the conclusion that in case Tajikistan would hold free parliamentary elections and a referendum on the constitution, the national and Islamic forces would win the majority and this would be an example for other countries in the region.[63]

In late April the situation got more confused with the "Youth of Dushanbe (*Ğavononi Dušanbe*)" proliferating as an intransigent splinter group on Šahidon Square. The "Youth of Dushanbe" consisted of some 18 local youth gangs, which were loosely coordinated by Mullo Abduğaffur Xudoydodov, the *imom-xatib* of the Yužniy Mosque in Dushanbe.[64] Based around Spartak Stadium with its sports facilities and the Šohmansur bazar, the "Youth of Dushanbe" controlled central parts of Dushanbe and contributed to the rapid privatization of violence in spring 1992.

Major General Kenğaev

Kenğaev's exit from politics only lasted a few hours, which he spent according to his memoirs reading classical Persian Mirrors for Princes literature reflecting on the nature of manliness, politics and statehood.[65] In the evening of 23 April, the radio program announced his appointment as chairman of the NSC/KGB.[66] Kenğaev expressed his gratitude to those deputies of the

Supreme Soviet and honorable citizens, who had supported him over the last weeks. With his resignation, the unity of the nation should be preserved, the constitution honored and the bloodshed avoided: "truth will be with those who legitimately claim the truth."[67]

After his appointment, he ordered the KGB files of Mirbobo Mirrahim, Tohir Abduğabbor, Dūstmuhammad Dūstī, Muhammadšarif Himmatzoda, Davlat Usmon and Hoğī Akbar Tūrağonzoda. Although Kenğaev usually insisted on his professional work ethics and observance of the law, he nonetheless informed the reader about his "discoveries" in these confidential files: All of the personal KGB files had either an annotation that all the persons in questions were "agents" or "informants" of the KGB. The file of Tūrağonzoda consisted of two volumes with more than 400 pages each containing "reports" by Tūrağonzoda in which he "betrayed his fellow Muslims of the Hanafi school [...]. Such a person, who has betrayed his fellow Muslims, will never be forgiven—neither in this world nor in the Afterworld."[68] Ultimately Kenğaev's insinuations were far from cogent and his reading of Mirbobo Mirrahim's diaries reveals similar discrepancies. Mirrahim was arrested in Ashgabat in January 1993 and extradited to Tajikistan, where he was imprisoned until an exchange of prisoners in November 1994. Kenğaev apparently got access to Mirrahim's confiscated diaries covering the period between February 1992 and March 1993 and lengthily quoted from the diary in his memoirs.[69] Kenğaev presented extracts from Mirrahim's diary without any contextualization "exposing" Mirrahim as a narrow-minded, divisive nationalist—however, he never presented any substantial compromising "secrets" from Mirrahim's diary or Tūrağonzoda's KGB files. Eventually, Kenğaev's insinuations and suspicions were part of a malicious defamation campaign nourishing conspiracy theories and exhibiting his ambiguous perception of the rule of law, integrity and ethical standards. Unsurprisingly, Kenğaev's appointment infuriated the opposition and instead of suspending the demonstration, the protests continued. Then, news from Kūlob heralded a further escalation of the conflict in Dushanbe.

OZODĪ SQUARE AND THE ECHO IN THE REGIONS

On 24 April, Haydar Šarifov, Qurbon Zardakov, Sangak Safarov (an ex-convict and local strongman), Rustam Abdurahimov (an ex-convict, popular folk musician and English teacher[70]), Adolat Rahmanova and Qurbonalī Mirzoaliev (the chairman of the Kūlob *viloyat* Ispolkom) organized a rally of some 6,000 demonstrators in central Kūlob in support of Nabiev and the government demanding the reinstatement of Kenğaev as well as the dismissal of Tūrağonzoda, Tūraev and Sohibnazar from the Presidium of the Supreme

Soviet. Šarifov, Abdurahimov and Rahmonova instigated the protestors and
announced a march on Dushanbe.[71] Šarifov conjured that the motherland
is in danger of being taken over by Tūraǧonzoda's *vahhobī* Islamists and
Adolat Rahmonova insinuated in her speech that the Islamists on Šahidon
Square sexually assaulted her a few days earlier. In tears, she called for the
"*ǧavonmard* of Kūlob to defend the dignity and honor (*nāmūs*) of their own
women."[72] The rally and the march on Dushanbe were not spontaneous but
planned in advance. The local administration and collective farms in Kūlob
provided 38 busses and several automobiles including fuel and additional
supplies. In the afternoon of 24 April some 500 men and a few women left
Kūlob and reached Dushanbe in the night. Vice-president Dūstov welcomed
the women and men from Kūlob and handed out supplies as well as posters
with slogans in support of Nabiev and Kenǧaev.

The protestors appointed Abdullo Očilov as head of a paramilitary staff
(Russ.: *štab*) and set up a camp in the early morning of 25 April on Ozodī
Square, a trolleybus station—or less than a kilometer—down from Šahidon
Square (see Map 2).[73] Simultaneously rumors circulated in Dushanbe that
supporters of Kenǧaev from Panǧakent, Zafarobod, Aynī and Xuǧand were
leaving for Dushanbe as well.[74] Throughout the night, Kenǧaev, Dūstov,
Huvaydulloev and Major General Niyazov (Nabiev's chairman of the
National Defense Committee) met with Oǧilov, Safarov and Abdurahimov
to coordinate their activities. Reportedly, the establishment of a "presidential
guard" was discussed then and Niyazov promised to allocate 700 automatic
weapons for this purpose.[75]

The opposition immediately assumed that Nabiev, Dūstov, Kenǧaev were
the actual leaders on the "backstage of Ozodī."[76] However, Šarifov and
Mirzoaliev had their own vested political interests, which they could not
effectively claim or defend in Kūlob. Likewise, the protests in Dushanbe and
the mobilization in Kūlob offered new opportunities for local strongmen such
as Safarov (providing protection, "organizing" supplies etc.) and Sohibnazar
assumed that Nabiev was not even involved in the mobilization recalling a
conversation with him in early May 1992:

> [Nabiev:] Kenǧaev instigated the guys from Kūlobī (*bačahoi Kūlob*). He brought
> them to Dushanbe. I didn't expect this from him. You did not advise him, Aslid-
> din. You did not tell him that this behavior is wrong. I gave him a position. He
> became Chairman of the Security Committee. […] Thus, why did they call Kūlob
> and invited all these people? I did not understand why he always tried to hide
> the apparent. What did he want from me? Actually, I didn't notice anything.[77]

When Sohibnazar asked Nabiev why he did not ask Haydar Šarifov to
suspend the demonstration and instead even encouraged the protestors in

his speech on Ozodī Square, Nabiev replied: "What should I do? N[arzullo]. Dūstov and S[afaralī]. Kenğaev acted on my behalf. Nobody asked me. They didn't ask for my approval. They simply put me there. Whom I addressed, I don't know."[78] Sohibnazar's impression of a disoriented and helpless Nabiev might be anecdotal, but similar accounts by Tūrağonzoda and Abdulov (Nabiev's chief of staff) confirm Sohibnazar's version.[79]

While the IRPT, DPT and La'li Badaxšon organized the rally on Šahidon Square, local strongmen in complicity with several deputies organized the protests on Ozodī Square. Although some of the organizers on Ozodī Square were deputies or members of the CPT, its chairman, Šodī Šabdolov, initially expressed his disapproval of the protests and only reluctantly decided to address the protestors on Ozodī Square in early May.[80] Kenğaev claimed that the demonstration on Ozodī represented all regions, religious groups and ethnicities in Tajikistan; though most observers and eyewitnesses agreed that non-Central Asian nationalities—a significant percentage of Dushanbe's population—did not participate in any of the rallies.[81] Tūrağonzoda reported that among the protestors from Badaxšon and Qarotegin a sense of insecurity had increased with the public humiliation of Navğuvonov and Aslonov. Importantly, the religious authorities from the Qarotegin Valley, the imminent Sufi authorities (*ešonho va ahli tasavvuf*) decided to support the protests on Šahidon Square. In contrast to the criminals and riff-raff on Ozodī, these people represented—in the words of Tūrağonzoda—the truly authentic Tajik Self.[82]

The protests on Ozodī Square gave Kenğaev and Nabiev the opportunity to regain influence on the developments and they convened an emergency meeting in the presidential office with representatives of both squares in the afternoon of 25 April. Both sides agreed on the establishment of two committees, which should persuade the protestors to suspend the demonstrations. Reportedly, Tūrağonzoda convinced the Šahidon protestors to leave the square in the afternoon of 25 April; however, public speeches on Ozodī by Kenğaev and others increased the tensions and the opposition on Šahidon refused to suspend their rally.[83] On Sunday, April 26, several thousand demonstrators gathered on the two squares and sporadic violence flared up with youth gangs exploiting the confusing situation. On 27 April, some 20,000 people gathered on Ozodī and 15,000 on Šahidon. A day later more than 100,000 came to Šahidon from the rural areas marginalizing the urban representation in the protests.[84] The polarization between Šahidon and Ozodī was compounded by mutual recrimination and both sides considered their concerns and protests as legitimate and just. The opposition on Šahidon portrayed the protestors from Kūlob as uncultured and "less organized, they were the mob (*avom*) compared with the aristocrats (*ašrofon*) on Šahidon"[85]:

In one city, on one road, on two squares which were only 500 paces in distance, the citizens of one people, one nation and one home country and one state were divided in two groups by barricades and trenches. On one square [were] the communists and incumbent office-holders, on the other square the toilers. Both were strong and armed, but with the Šahidon Square was truth and with the Ozodī Square the government. [...] On Ozodī were the criminals around Sangak Safarov, Mullo Haydar and Rustam Abdurahimov, on Šahidon the *litterateurs* and *ulamo*.[86]

"Nest bod Islom—nest bod Tūraǧonzoda"[87]

On 28 April, Šarifov and Mirzoaliev issued an ultimatum demanding the immediate suspension of the opposition's demonstration—otherwise their supporters on Ozodī would clear Šahidon Square by force. Most sources agree, that the protestors on Ozodī took comparatively more drastic measures than their opponents on Šahidon: Books by oppositional writers and poets, such as Bozor Sobir, Gulruxsor or Loiq Šeralī, were publicly burned and the slogans became increasingly belligerent accusing the opposition leaders as traitors of the nation, hailing Kenǧaev and rejecting democracy (*nest bod demokratiya*) as well as Islam.[88] In his address to the protestors on Ozodī Square, Kenǧaev presented himself as a political reformer who antagonized the opposition because of his relentless fight against the "mafia" and corruption. The successful mobilization in Kūlob and organization of a counterdemonstration (which for a few days even outnumbered the opposition) obviously multiplied Kenǧaev's already abundant assertiveness and he categorically rejected any negotiation with the opposition.[89] The protestors on Ozodī were celebrating Kenǧaev as a Tajik Andropov and "Commissar Cattani."[90] Kenǧaev affirmed that on Ozodī Square the "toilers" stood up against the *vahhobiyon* on Šahidon Square and presented Tūraǧonzoda as the main villain.[91] The derogatory slogans against Islam (*nest bod Islom*), however, were criticized by a small group of demonstrators on Ozodī Square, who abandoned the protests. Also urban intellectuals, such as Yusuf Akbarzoda criticized the turn against Islam, since they realized that Islam has become a powerful signifier for an authentic Tajik identity:

> We have absorbed Islam with our mother's milk [...]. Our entire ancient history and civilization, our knowledge and culture are intimately connected with Islam. Those who say *Down with Islam!* spurn the Tajiks, their knowledge and their Persian culture.[92]

Prominent representatives of the opposition, such as Bobonazarova, Sohibnazar and Sattorzoda, tried to address the demonstrators on Ozodī Square but emotions were running high and the group had to leave the square before they could speak. A mediation attempt by *ešoni* Tūraǧon was rejected as well and reportedly Rustam Abdurahimov organized a violent assault on a group of opposition protestors, who were on their way to Šahidon Square. On the evening of 27 April, Davlat Usmon warned of an impending civil war in Tajikistan should the belligerent propaganda on Ozodī Square continue.[93] The same evening, the protestors on Ozodī Square rendered their demands: An emergency session of the Supreme Soviet should immediately reinstate Kenǧaev as chairman, the resolutions and laws adopted on 23 April should be annulled and the opposition representatives dismissed from the Presidium. Tūraǧonzoda should resign as *qozikalon* and the chairman of the state TV and Radio Committee, Otaxon Sayfulloev, reinstated. The ministry of justice should consider a ban of the IRPT and finally the deputies should discuss amendments to the constitution introducing general elections to the position of the chairman of the Supreme Soviet.[94]

With the last issue, Kenǧaev intended to enhance the legitimation and importance of the position he had occupied since November 1991 and eventually eclipse the position of President Nabiev. Kenǧaev obviously thought he could manipulate the incumbent Supreme Soviet with its strong majority of former CPT cadres and re-establish a more authoritarian rule. However, his strategy alienated his political mentor and patron, President Nabiev, and induced the latter to negotiate confidentially a solution with the opposition that eventually led to the establishment of the Government of National Reconciliation (GNR) on 7 May. In the meantime, the confrontation between the opposition and the nomenklatura in Kūlob escalated to violent clashes on 29 April leaving several people wounded.[95]

THE 14TH SESSION OF THE SUPREME SOVIET

The demonstration on Ozodī Square restored the confidence of Dūstov and Kenǧaev and they regained the initiative by inviting the Supreme Soviet to its 14th Session on 28 April. Thuggish vigilantes from the local *avtobaza* secured the premises of the Supreme Soviet creating an intimidating atmosphere and Kenǧaev carefully prepared the session's agenda.[96]

The most important topic on the agenda was the bill on "presidential rule," which extended the constitutional rights of the president to control legislative, executive and judicial branches of the government including the right to suspend any political party or movement and to impose a ban on public protests including the authority to declare martial law.[97] The Law on Presidential Rule was a thinly disguised annulment of the constitution resulting in a (self-) disempowerment of the Supreme Soviet, which even Kenǧaev—who had prepared the draft—could only legitimate with an alleged impending danger to Tajikistan's statehood. The Law on Presidential Rule was one element in Kenğaev's strategy of consolidating authoritarian rule and a legal smoke-screen for the "solution" of the political confrontation by force. Eventually it allowed him (in Nabiev's name) to impose martial law and recruit an ad hoc presidential guard which eventually resulted in a privatization of violence in early May.[98]

On 28 April, the 14th Session of the Supreme Soviet convened with 170 out of 230 deputies present. Kenğaev had closed his ranks among the deputies from Xuğand and Kūlob while oppositional deputies boycotted the session. The remaining deputies discussed the amendments to the constitution includ-ing the Law on Presidential Rule but postponed the vote to the following day. At the same time, Nabiev addressed the demonstration on Ozodī Square for the first time expressing his support for their cause and announcing the estab-lishment of a presidential guard.[99] In the afternoon the government organized negotiations between the two squares. According to Kenğaev, Sangak Safarov addressed the opposition with an ostensibly reasonable appeal to peace and reconciliation:

> Brothers, for God's sake, please be righteous! For more than a month you are demonstrating on Šahidon Square. You should have been able to tell the Tajik people as well as the foreign countries what you had on your mind. [...] Nobody has tried to interfere or prohibit the demonstrations, but now the normal people (*mardumi oddī*) have come and demand from you [i.e. the opposition on Šahidon] to calm down that we can go back to work. But you reject this. The demonstrators on Ozodī Square do not want war; they did not come for a fight but for justice.[100]

Sohibnazar, Usmonov and Yusuf did not remember such a balanced inter-vention by Safarov. Instead they expressed their consternation that an ex-convict like Safarov was present at these high level political talks.[101]

Tūrağonzoda suggested to appoint Kenğaev as an ambassador to an embassy abroad—a popular procedure that time—but Nabiev refused to discuss Kenğaev's dismissal at all.[102] The atmosphere in the negotiations was irreconcilable and eventually the talks broke down. Supported by the dem-onstrations on Ozodī Square, Kenğaev and the majority of deputies in the Supreme Soviet thought to have regained the upper hand in Dushanbe and were not ready to compromise.

The 14th Session of the Supreme Soviet continued throughout the first days of May amidst increasing tensions. After adopting the Law on Presidential Rule (for a duration of six months) on 30 April, the deputies annulled the decisions taken on the 13th Session (20–22 April 1992). With 132 votes (3 dissenting votes and 25 abstentions) they reinstated Kenğaev as chairman of the Supreme Soviet.[103] In his memoirs Kenğaev described his reinstatement as an initiative by the working people: "I never defied the will of the people and I will never do this. All of you who came out to offer me protection (*himoya*), actually stood up to protect the state constitution, justice, truth and the rule of law. Before you I bow my head."[104]

Acting on behalf of Nabiev, Kenğaev decreed the increase of the monthly minimum wage to 700 rubles and the multiplication of the salary of state employees by the factor 2.5.[105] The deputies demanded the arrest of Tūrağonzoda and the closedown of the major oppositional newspapers *Adolat* (DPT), *Suxan* (published by the Union of Journalists), *Ğavononi Toğikiston* (published by the former Komsomol Youth Organization), *Čaroği rūz* (a private paper edited by Dodoğon Atovulloev) and the Russian *Tadžik-Press*. Moreover, the deputies asked the ministry of justice to consider a ban on the IRPT. Since 38 deputies (including Tūrağonzoda, Sohibnazar and Bozor Sobir) did not take part in the session without notifying the chairman, Kenğaev's faction demanded to unseat them.[106] The opposition responded to the aggressive tactic with equally aggressive ripostes: On 29 April, the protestors occupied the Radio and TV station and the presidential administration taking 41 staff-members hostage for 48 hours.[107]

On 2 May Qiyomiddin Ğozī poured oil into the fire by telling *Ğumhuriyat* that the opposition had mobilized 27,000 armed men.[108] Although Ğozī's statement was a fabrication, it dramatically escalated the tensions: Dūstov and Kenğaev consistently legitimized the disastrous decision to establish a presidential guard among the protestors on Ozodī with the reference to Ğozī's statement. However the complementary sources suggest a converse sequence of events and that Ğozī's statement was only published *after* the fateful decision to arm the protestors on Ozodī Square.[109]

With the distribution of weapons among civilian protestors on Ozodī the state monopoly on violence (Max Weber's *Gewaltmonopol*) disintegrated and the use of violence was privatized resulting in a complete state failure.[110] The dissolution of Tajikistan's security forces, the MVD's militia and the KGB/NSC, had been a gradual process which begun in the late 1980s and dramatically accelerated with independence—Nabiev's cataclysmic decision to arm untrained civilians on Ozodī Square was therefore only the culmination of a longer development.

'NEUTRALITY' AND THE DISINTEGRATION OF THE SECURITY STRUCTURES

After the February 1990 Events, Qahhor Mahkamov never assumed the political responsibility for the operations by the state security forces, namely the

KGB and the militia. This refusal had a lasting negative impact on loyalty and operational readiness of the security forces. Besides, the Supreme Soviet Inquiry Commission on the February events severely criticized the MVD and KGB for their incompetence and insinuated complicity with networks of organized crime further undermining the authority and reputation of the security forces.[111] The disengagement of the security services in Tajikistan followed patterns observed elsewhere in the later Soviet Union. During the Baku pogroms against the Armenians in January 1990, the MVD troops did not intervene and the Soviet Armed Forces deployed in Baku did not leave their barracks, either pointing out its neutrality or missing orders from Moscow. Facing the assertive ethnic nationalism and the rapid decomposition of the Soviet ideological assertions, the continuous high level of ideological mobilization among the security forces now recoiled and resulted in an inner resignation and revocation of loyalty. Simultaneously, the economic meltdown and the inability of the state to pay the salaries in time undermined the allegiance of the security structures and contributed to the privatization of violence. In the late 1980s, while nationalist sentiment in the TaSSR became more assertive, funding for the security structures contracted and in particular non-Central Asian nationalities that were overrepresented among the officer corps, resigned or looked for redeployment in the Russian Federation realizing that their career options in an independent Tajikistan were henceforth limited.[112] Furthermore, prevalent discourses on the attribution of specific employment sectors or occupations, such as MVD, KGB, organized crime, industrial labor as well as agriculture to a particular regional provenance undermined the authority and reputation of the KGB and MVD. For instance, Navğuvonov's alleged nepotism and favoritism toward his Pomirī networks was (and is) frequently mentioned in the relevant literature, and persistent rumors maintain that he changed the staff of the MVD with officers and servicemen from Badaxšon after his appointment in 1989 transforming the MVD into a Badaxšonī bastion.[113] The relevant sources and interviews with former and current MVD officials indeed suggest that Pomirīs were overrepresented in the MVD since the 1970s due to the reforms implemented by Andropov who considered minorities in the Soviet periphery as particularly loyal to the Soviet cause. However there is to my knowledge no accessible data on the composition of the TaSSR's MVD in the late 1980s and the alleged overrepresentations might be part of the discourse on national minorities and regionalism in Tajikistan.[114] With the tumultuous events in 1991/1992 and the spread of ad hoc recruited units the composition of the MVD changed substantially and the alleged overrepresentation of officers and servicemen from Badaxšon came to an end.[115] The disintegration of the security forces was a general phenomenon throughout the Soviet Union as Eisenstadt observes:

Of special interest, certainly, is the fact that the middle echelons of the security forces of the armies no longer protected the rulers or the regimes. They surrendered power quickly, and not because they had lost a war. This is intriguing, especially when one recalls that many of these middle echelons benefited greatly from the regimes—that the security organizations and the armies were major avenues of social mobility.[116]

While the ranks of Tajikistan's MVD and KGB were depleted by migration and resignation, the disintegration of the USSR and the political crisis since September 1991 further undermined the loyalty of the remaining officials. MVD and KGB officers publicly declared their "neutrality" and refused to follow orders while reserve officers and reservists in the armed forces did not observe their service obligation and ignored the draft call.[117] Until April 1992, the KGB's chairman had traditionally been an ethnic Slav appointed by Moscow (between 1985 and 1991 Vladimir Petkel' served as the KGB's chairman; his successor, Anatoly Stroykin, was dismissed on 23 April 1992), therefore the KGB was widely perceived as the center's agency, which further hampered a reform or nationalization of the security structures. In an interview with Interfax in March 1992, Stroykin pointed out to the significant structural changes in the service: The nominal strength was down by 27% in total while 32% of the senior officers had left the service. As for the ethnic composition of the KGB in March 1992, 54% were Tajiks, 30% Russians and 16% other nationalities.[118] Stroykin had little support in the government and was replaced on 23 April 1992 by Kenğaev. Vice president Dūstov justified the dismissal of Stroykin with the inability of the KGB to protect the deputies of the Supreme Soviet.[119] After a few days in office, Nabiev replaced Kenğaev with the enigmatic Rizo Tursunov. The political leadership (or better the lack of it) accelerated the disintegration of the security services and Navğuvonov signaled in September 1991 that he would not order an intervention by OMON forces to break up the opposition's demonstration.[120] In April/May 1992, Tajikistan's internal security forces had largely disintegrated whilst the 201st MRD remained under Russian command and did not intervene in the internal political conflict. Kenğaev assumed that Nabiev understood

that the two central supporting pillars of the state (VKD [MVD], KAM [KGB]) had entirely denounced their support for him and the government; they had announced their neutrality but were actually dancing after the rhythm of the opposition's kettledrum. The third pillar—the national republican army had not been established due to the fault of the state leadership. That means, that the state was without any pillars and the authority of the president of the republic was nothing more than a balloon.[121]

Keṇǧaev's narrative is far from consistent: After his assumption of the position of the chairman of the NSC/KGB, he suddenly considered the security forces as "a capable, serious and competent force, which could prevent the decent into violence."[122] Related to prevalent Soviet discourses, the political nomenklatura and civil society had at times a naïve and inconsistent perceptions about the societal role of the militia and KGB as "non-political" despite their intrinsically political function.[123]

In general, the role of individual KGB officers remains dubious and the various sources do not necessarily contribute to a clarification and many narratives contribute to the prevalent conspiracy theories.[124] In late April 1992, the KGB and MVD had largely disintegrated as centralized and hierarchical institutions. Individual officers had publicly declared their "neutrality" or joined one of the two factions accelerating the privatization of violence. The random and uncoordinated recruitment of presidential or national guards illustrates this development as well.

Presidential and National Guards

After independence, the Tajik government hesitated to nationalize the Soviet armed forces on its territory, namely the 201st MRD and the KGB Border Guards. Instead, Nabiev commissioned the establishment of a National/Presidential Guard as a motorized infantry unit with similar responsibilities as the MVD's Special Purpose Mobility Unit OMON. On 28 December 1991, Nabiev appointed Major General Bahrom Rahmonov, the former chairman of DOSAAF, as his security advisor and commander of the National Guard. The National Guard would be directly subordinated to the president and not the Supreme Soviet or the Council of Ministers.[125] The recruitment of guardsmen progressed only slowly—mostly by transferring men from the MVD's OMON to the guard—and not even a company-sized unit (less than 80 men) took their oath of allegiance on 12 January 1992.[126] The shortage of trained military personnel and the reluctance of the population to follow draft calls seriously hampered the establishment of the guard. When the Nabiev administration purchased 37 BTRs (APCs) from the Russian Federation, no qualified personnel could be recruited to maintain and operate the APCs, therefore they were stored in Qaratoġ.[127]

In January 1992, Nabiev appointed Major General Farrux Niyazov from Xuǧand, a former officer in the USSR Strategic Missile Forces and since 1985 chief of staff of the TaSSR's Civil Defense Department, as chairman of the National Defense Committee (equivalent to a Ministry of Defense). Niyazov announced that Tajikistan would not create its own armed forces but coordinate external security with the partners in the CIS.[128]

MAY 1992: STATE FAILURE AND THE
PRIVATIZATION OF VIOLENCE

The situation in late April and early May 1992 was confusing and complex since the conflict was not limited to two homogenous factions but many individuals and splinter groups: The opposition on Šahidon Square consisted of an uneasy coalition between the IRPT, DPT and La'li Badaxšon, three associations with very different constituencies and objectives. Individual actors, such as Yusuf, Gozī or Mullo Abduġaffur, and different groups, such as the "Youth of Dushanbe" or the criminal gangs of Rauf Saliev, Yaqub Salimov and Ġum'axon Būydoqov, had their own agenda and agency. Even among Dūstov, Kenğaev and Nabiev there was less consensus than demonstrated in public. While Kenğaev relentlessly pursued his agenda in the Supreme Soviet, Nabiev confidentially negotiated a compromise with representatives of the opposition, which later resulted in the establishment of the Government of National Reconciliation. Kenğaev—who was excluded from the negotiations and the government—had to realize that he was not the only conspirer and manipulator:

> Among the representatives of the government were traitors who abandoned and sold the people. There was no unity among them, they only lied, deceived each other, incited each other to wage war and betrayed each other, there was only peculation and corruption. The state was in complete stagnation.[129]

Despite the tense situation, the government adhered to the Soviet performative conventions and celebrated May Day or International Workers' Day on Ozodī Square. Prominent members of the CPT and former Soviet nomenklatura addressed the protestors and public on Ozodī Square: Kenğaev, Dūstov, Nabiev, Huvaydulloev, Sayfulloev, Mirzoaliev and the historian Masov addressed the protestors.[130] In the evening Tūraġonzoda responded with an opposition meeting in the office of the *qoziyot*. In the following press conference, the opposition demanded the resignation of President Nabiev since he had become partisan and violated the constitution by introducing presidential rule.[131]

After the adoption of the Law on Presidential Rule in the afternoon, Nabiev ordered Major General Niyazov and Major General Mahmadğonov to form a National Guard within the next two weeks. Instead of a regular recruitment process, Niyazov appointed one of the leaders on Ozodī Square, Būrixon Ġobirov (a mid-ranking MVD officer from Kūlob who was promoted overnight to the rank of a colonel), as commanding officer of the guard and ordered the distribution small arms among the protestors on Ozodī

Square. Ğobirov should answer only to Kenğaev, who organized equipment and supplies.[132] Kenğaev, Niyazov, Oğilov and Safarov had discussed the recruitment of a "guard" already upon the Kūlobīs' arrival in Dushanbe 24 April. Instead of two weeks, the guard was levied among the demonstrators on Ozodī overnight and equipped with some 1,700 automatic rifles on 2 May.[133] The establishment of the presidential guard is at times portrayed as the result of a security dilemma spiraling out of control with the increasing militarization of both sides.[134] The organizers on Ozodī insisted that the set-up of the guard was only a response to the armament on Šahidon Square and skirmishes provoked the opposition. Safarov claimed in February 1993, that he convinced Nabiev personally to set up the National Guard only on 5 May.[135] Likewise, Kenğaev depicted the establishment of the National Guard as an immediate response to the threats by *qorī* Qiyomiddin and the defection of Bahrom Rahmonov. Kenğaev referred to the broadcasting of the state TV and Radio Commission, which fueled rumors about weapons being distributed on Ozodī Square and Afghan *mujahidin* approaching Dushanbe.[136] Since the government controlled the TV and Radio Commission, Kenğaev reproduced his own fabrications as a self-fulfilling prophecy. Instead, he insisted that the establishment of the guard did not violate against the constitution since it was an official order by Nabiev who had after the adoption of the "Law on Presidential Rule" the authority to do so.[137] Davlat Usmon reported that the opposition on Šahidon Square only started to equip some 50 men in late April after rumors circulated that the government was considering the establishment of a guard. Although the organizers on Šahidon could muster more men and several youth gangs with a better knowledge on the place, they were poorly equipped, mostly with hunting rifles and self-made Molotov cocktails.[138]

The distribution of arms on Ozodī Square changed the balance between the two squares and marked an unprecedented privatization of violence: Despite the formal appointment of Ğobirov as commanding officer of the guard, the "servicemen" were ad hoc recruited among the civilian protestors on Ozodī Square. With the protestors on Ozodī Square armed, Kenğaev felt confident enough to finalize the 14th Supreme Soviet Session and arrange his reinstatement.

Kenğaev's advantage, however, was short lived: On 5 May, the commander of the National Guard and Chairman of the National Defense Committee, Bahrom Rahmonov, suddenly appeared on Šahidon Square in the late evening and announced his defection to the opposition. With Rahmonov some 200 trained servicemen joined the opposition with 450 small arms and 7 APCs.[139] In a brief speech on the square, Rahmonov justified his defection with his family background as the grandson of an imminent religious authority whose family was "purged" in 1937. Kenğaev acidly commented, that Rahmonov in fact was an "coward (*noğavonmard*) who could not even recite a single verse from the Koran."[140] Rahmonov's defection shifted the balance in favor of the opposition but now both squares had modern assault rifles and APCs at their disposal. Within a few days in early May 1992, Tajikistan spiraled down to complete state failure: The security forces had either disintegrated or declared their "neutrality," and the everyday life in Dushanbe came to a standstill. State combines were closed, food supplies limited and opportunistic individuals and groups relentlessly exploited the unfolding disorder.

NOTES

1. Kenğaev, *Tabadduloti 1*, 101–103. Kenğaev accused Navğuvonov of selling illegally 139 MVD automobiles and trucks and of appropriating several apartments and dachas in Dushanbe for himself and his extended family.
2. FBIS-USR-92–046, 24 April 1992, 80–81.
3. Usmonov, *Nabiev*, 31.
4. Sohibnazar, *Subhi 1*, 272.
5. Nasriddinov, *Tarkiš*, 152.
6. Kenğaev, *Tabadduloti 1*, 102.
7. Yūsuf, *Tāğīkestān*, 157–158.
8. Sohibnazar, *Subhi 1*, 272.
9. Sohibnazar, *Subhi 1*, 273.
10. Tūrağonzoda, "Ivazšavii," 9.
11. Nasriddinov, *Tarkiš*, 154.
12. Kenğaev, *Tabadduloti 1*, 28.
13. Kenğaev, *Tabadduloti 1*, 335.
14. Usmonov, *Nabiev*, 31.
15. Sohibnazar, *Subhi 1*, 270.
16. FBIS-SOV-92–061, 30 March 1992, 40.
17. Sattorī, *HNIT*, 51.
18. Sattorī, *HNIT*, 162.
19. Sattorī, *HNIT*, 163.
20. Karim, *Faryodi*, 413.
21. See Osimī, *Enziklopediyai*, Vol. 8, 575–587. The Constitutional Committee issued a statement on 7 April 1992 that the Supreme Soviet has the right to decide on its dissolution without violating against the constitution (FBIS-SOV-92–068, 8 April 1992, 58).
22. Usmonov, *Nabiev*, 42.
23. Sohibnazar, *Subhi 1*, 273.
24. Abdulov, *Rohi*.
25. Sohibnazar, *Subhi 1*, 276–278.
26. FBIS-SOV-92–065, 3 April 1992, 64.
27. Conversation with former DPT members (Dushanbe, May 2004).

Chapter 6

28. Dudoignon and Qalandar, "They Were All," 49–51.
29. Tūrağonzoda, *Miyoni*, 21–22.
30. Tūrağonzoda, *Miyoni*, 22–23.
31. Nuralī Davlat, "Qozikalon. Siyosati mustaqili Hoğī Akbar," *Nigoh*, March 26, 2014. 1: 5.
32. Usmonov, *Nabiev*, 47.
33. FBIS-SOV-92–065, 3 April 1992, 63.
34. FBIS-SOV-92–066, 6 April 1992, 68.
35. FBIS-SOV-92–083, 29 April 1992, 59.
36. FBIS-SOV-92–047, 10 March 1992, 43.
37. FBIS-SOV-92–085, 1 May 1992, 47.
38. Kenğaev, *Tabadduloti 1*.
39. Kenğaev, *Tabadduloti 1*, 43.
40. FBIS-SOV-92–074, 16 April 1992, 63.
41. Sohibnazar, *Subhi 1*, 277.
42. Sohibnazar, *Subhi 1*, 290. FBIS-SOV-92–069, 9 April 1992, 60–61; FBIS-SOV-92–071, 13 April 1992, 57–58; FBIS-SOV-92–072, 14 April 1992, 59–60; FBIS-SOV-92–074, 16 April 1992, 63.
43. FBIS-SOV-92–075, 17 April 1992, 59–62.
44. FBIS-SOV-92–079, 23 April 1992, 46–47. Šahidon/Putovskiy Square was an important public transport hub for trolley busses running down Rūdakī/Lenin Prospect and to the western parts of Dushanbe.
45. Nazriev and Sattorov, *Respublika Tadžikistan II*, 124–127.
46. FBIS-SOV-92–079, 23 April 1992, 46–47.
47. The opposition demanded that Qahhorov, Sohibnazar, Tūraev and Tūrağonzoda should be included in the Presidium of the Supreme Soviet.
48. Karim, *Faryodi*, 396–396; Kenğaev, *Tabadduloti 1*, 44–45.
49. Usmonov, *Nabiev*, 51; Tūrağonzoda, *Miyoni*, 25–26.
50. Nasriddinov, *Tarkiš*, 154–157; Tūrağonzoda, *Miyoni*, 30.
51. Usmonov, *Nabiev*, 53–55; FBIS-SOV-92–077, 21 April 1992, 43.
52. Sohibnazar, *Subhi 1*, 277.
53. Nasriddinov, *Tarkiš*, 157–158.
54. Usmonov, *Nabiev*, 49–50; Nazriev and Sattorov, *Respublika Tadžikistan II*, 126–127.
55. Nasriddinov, *Tarkiš*, 163–164; Usmonov, *Nabiev*, 56.
56. Tūrağonzoda, *Miyoni*, 32–33.
57. In a 2011 interview with the Tajik service of the BBC, Rahmonova denied her earlier statements: http://www.bbc.co.uk/tajik/institutional/2011/08/110810_sq_adalat_rahmonova.shtml. Accessed February, 2 2014]. See also Usmonov, *Nabiev*, 56.
58. Tūrağonzoda, *Miyoni*, 33–37.
59. Nasriddinov, *Tarkiš*, 164.
60. Karim, *Faryodi*, 396; Usmonov, *Nabiev*, 56–57; FBIS-SOV-92–078, 22 April 1992, 43–44.
61. Tūrağonzoda, *Miyoni*, 39.
62. Tūrağonzoda, *Miyoni*, 42; Usmonov, *Nabiev*, 57.

63. Tūrağonzoda, "Ivazšavii," 8.

64. Usmonov, *Nabiev*, 62. Abduġaffur Xudoydodov was born 1954 in Ġarm and grew up in the Vaxš Valley. Since the mid-1980s, he was a religious activist in Dushanbe.

65. Kenğaev, *Tabadduloti 1*, 51.

66. FBIS-SOV-92–081, 27 April 1992, 60.

67. Kenğaev, *Tabadduloti 1*, 49.

68. Kenğaev, *Tabadduloti 1*, 52–53.

69. Kenğaev, *Tabadduloti 2*, 151 and *Tabadduloti 3*, 261–269. See also Mirrahim, *Hamtabaqi*, 247.

70. Karim, *Faryodi*, 439.

71. Nasriddinov, *Tarkiš*, 165.

72. Karim, *Faryodi*, 439–444; Yūsuf, *Tāğīkestān*, 168; Sohibnazar, *Subhi 1*, 284–285. Rahmonova's version on the events on http://www.bbc.co.uk/tajik/institutional/2011/08/110810_sq_adalat_rahmonova.shtml Access February, 2 2014. The narratives of the event differ in wording but not in substance.

73. Karim, *Faryodi*, 400, 444.

74. Usmonov, *Nabiev*, 59–60.

75. Karim (*Faryodi*, 440) citing from the interrogation protocols of Safarov.

76. Karim, *Faryodi*, 406.

77. Sohibnazar, *Subhi 2*, 40.

78. Sohibnazar, *Subhi 2*, 40.

79. Abdulov, *Rohi*, passim; Tūrağonzoda, *Miyoni*, passim.

80. Usmonov, *Nabiev*, 61.

81. FBIS-SOV-92–079, 23 April 1992, 47; Medvedev, "Saga," 197.

82. Tūrağonzoda, *Miyoni*, 49.

83. Tūrağonzoda, *Miyoni*, 45–47.

84. FBIS-SOV-92–083, 29 April 1992, 60.

85. Usmonov, *Nabiev*, 61.

86. Mosalmāniyān, *Tāğīkestān*, 30–31.

87. Tajik for: "Down with Islam, down with Tūrağonzoda".

88. Karim, *Faryodi*, 408.

89. FBIS-SOV-92–083, 29 April 1992, 59–62.

90. See Nasriddinov, *Tarkiš*, 287; Sohibnazar, *Subhi 1*, 287 and *Subhi 2*, 266.

91. Kenğaev, *Tabadduloti 1*, 54; Karim, *Faryodi*, 405; Yūsuf, *Tāğīkestān*, 172; FBIS-SOV-92–082, 28 April 1992, 60.

92. Quoted in Karim, *Faryodi*, 408.

93. Yūsuf, *Tāğīkestān*, 173–174.

94. FBIS-SOV-92–082, 28 April 1992, 61; FBIS-SOV-92–085, 1 May 1992, 47.

95. FBIS-SOV-92–085, 1 May 1992, 46.

96. Cf. Kenğaev, *Tabadduloti 1*, passim; Usmonov, *Nabiev*, passim.

97. Nazriev and Sattorov, *Respublika Tadžikistan II*, 142.

98. Kenğaev, *Tabadduloti 1*, 61; see also the assessment by Yūsuf, *Tāğīkestān*, 176.

99. FBIS-SOV-92–085, 1 May 1992, 49.

100. Kenğaev, *Tabadduloti 1*, 56.

101. Sohibnazar, *Subhi 1*, 201; Usmonov, *Nabiev*, 61; Yūsuf, *Tāǧīkestān*, 185.

102. Kenǧaev, *Tabadduloti 1*, 57.

103. Nazriev and Sattorov, *Respublika Tadžikistan II*, 143, 152.

104. Kenǧaev, *Tabadduloti 1*, 83.

105. FBIS-SOV-92–087, 5 May 1992, 55.

106. Karim, *Faryodi*, 415; FBIS-SOV-92–086, 4 May 1992, 54–55; FBIS-SOV-92–087, 5 May 1992, 54.

107. FBIS-SOV-02–083, 29 April 1992, 60; FBIS-SOV-92–085, 1 May 1992, 49.

108. Karim, *Faryodi*, 414, 440; Nazriev and Sattorov, *Respublika Tadžikistan II*, 149. See also the open letter by Salomiddin Mirzorahmatov, "Šumo kisted?," Ǧumhuriyat 94 (17 July 2012).

109. Kenǧaev, *Tabadduloti 1*, 270; FBIS-SOV-92–085, 1 May 1992, 47–50.

110. Max Weber, *Wirtschaft und Gesellschaft* (Tübingen: Mohr, 1990), 19–30.

111. See Sohibnazar, *Subhi 1*, 50–76; Kenǧaev, *Tabadduloti 1*, 40.

112. Usmonov, *Nabiev*, 110; Sohibnazar, *Subhi 1*, 50–76.

113. See Dūstov, *Zahm*, 24; Kenǧaev, *Tabadduloti 1*, 42. Nasriddinov (*Tarkiš*, 190) quoted a conversation with Akbaršo Iskandarov, who maintained in early 1992 that 90% of the MVD staff were Pomirī. Cf. Nourzhanov and Bleuer, *Tajikistan*, 167; Schoeberlein-Engel, *Identity*, 37.

114. Cf. Dudoignon, *Communal*, 4 and "Political," 57. Kenǧaev (*Tabadduloti 1*, 42 and *Tabadduloti 2*, 226) claimed that the Pomirī 'take over' of the MVD started with Pallaev's term in office 1985.

115. Conversation with a retired MVD colonel (Dushanbe, May 2003), who maintained that perhaps 10% of the MVD servicemen in Dushanbe were in the late 1980s originally from Badaxšon.

116. Eisenstadt, "Breakdown," 24.

117. Kenǧaev, *Tabadduloti 1*, 39–40.

118. FBIS-SOV-92–049, 12 March 1992, 63.

119. FBIS-SOV-92–081, 27 April 1992, 60.

120. FBIS-SOV-91–187, 26 September 1991, 87.

121. Kenǧaev, *Tabadduloti 1*, 146.

122. Kenǧaev, *Tabadduloti 1*, 81.

123. Sohibnazar, *Subhi 2*, 119.

124. Kenǧaev, *Tabadduloti 1*, 112, 139; Karim, *Faryodi*, 375–376.

125. FBIS-SOV-92–003, 6 January 1992, 61.

126. FBIS-SOV-92–010, 15 January 1992, 73.

127. Kenǧaev, *Tabadduloti 1*, 41.

128. FBIS-SOV-92–006, 9 January 1992, 67.

129. Kenǧaev, *Tabadduloti 1*, 78.

130. Yūsuf, *Tāǧīkestān*, 176.

131. FBIS-SOV-92–086, 4 May 1992, 52; Kenǧaev, *Tabadduloti 1*, 139.

132. FBIS-SOV-92–086, 4 May 1992, 52.

133. Karim, *Faryodi*, 414. Usmonov (*Nabiev*, 64) reported about 1,700 AK-74 handed out to the demonstrators; FBIS-SOV-92–086, 4 May 1992, 51–56. Safarov (in

the interrogation protocols cited by Karim, *Faryodi*, 440) spoke about 700 AK-74 and Dūstov (*Zahm*, 239) about 870.

134. Nourzhanov and Bleuer, *Tajikistan*, 316.

135. Medvedev, "Saga," 197.

136. FBIS-SOV-92–087, 5 May 1992, 56.

137. Kenğaev, *Tabadduloti 1*, 69, 167–168. The coverage of the events in the press suggests that the distribution of weapons on Ozodī Square happened clearly prior to the defection of Bahrom Rahmonov (FBIS-SOV-92–086, 4 May 1992, 52–56). The statement of *qorī* Qiyomiddin was published on 2 May, thus after the distribution of arms on Ozodī. For the sequence of events see Nazriev and Sattorov, *Respublika Tadžikistan II*, 137–150 and FBIS-SOV-92–115, 15 June 1992, 48.

138. Henry Dunant Centre for Humanitarian Dialogue, ed., *Humanitarian engagement with armed groups: The Central Asian Islamic opposition movements* (Geneva, 2003), 13.

139. Kenğaev, *Tabadduloti 1*, 59; Nazriev and Sattorov, *Respublika Tadžikistan II*, 152. The numbers on the men, automatic rifles and APCs vary in the sources.

140. Kenğaev, *Tabadduloti 1*, 65.

Chapter 7

Men of Disorder

Masculinity, Crime and Violent Conflict[1]

In late Soviet Tajikistan various competing and complementary "concepts of masculinity" circulated in public.[2] Official Soviet discourses praised the "cultured" Soviet men while the media published sensational reports on "uncultured" male youth and networks of organized crime.[3] In academia an aspiring intelligentsia rediscovered and reconstructed the ideal of Persian/ Tajik manliness (*ǧavonmardī*) since pre-Islamic times—usually under the Zoroastrian dictum of "good deeds, good speech and good thoughts," which was also the motto of the civil associations Rastoxez and Oškoro. The Tajik actor and wrestler Mūso Iso, the "Lion of Mastčoh (*šeri Mastčoh*)," personi- fied the pre-Islamic Iranian mythological heroes of the *Šohnoma* in several Toǧikfilm productions and was hailed by the intelligentsia and media as a true *pahlavon* (Tajik for champion, athlete or hero), but at the same time Mūso Iso was a racketeer who led a local youth gang in the Šohmansur district of Dushanbe practicing a very different idea of *ǧavonmardī*, which often legiti- mized the transgression of formal laws in a local context as a male "custom" or "tradition." Finally, in the religious field registered as well as unregistered *ulamo* formulated in the context of "Commanding Right" or the Naqšbandī tenet "The Heart with God and the Hand at Work" (*dil ba yoru dast ba kor*) concepts of manliness that borrowed from the Islamic (*futuwwa*) and Persian- ate (*ǧavonmardī*) tradition conveying ideas of a male morality, ethics and work discipline.[4] These concepts were not just public discourses but transcended into social practice and determined strategies of legitimation in the context of the increasing political confrontation, mobilization and violence in 1992.

Ǧavonmard and Ǧavonmardī

In Tajik the compound *ǧavonmard* and its deduction *ǧavonmardī* are argu- ably the most widely used terms for categorizing "manliness." In the classical Persian Islamicate tradition, in particular in the Mirrors for Princes literature, the ideal *ğavonmard* combines various characteristics such as courage, decency, modesty, fidelity, hospitality, generosity (with food, such as the *ṣofre-dārī* in Iran or the *oš* in Tajikistan), decency, good conduct and honor. A *ğavonmard* defends the weak, leads an ascetic life and follows a moral codex. Although the various attributes of *ğavonmardī* seem to have a long-term historical constancy in the Persianate context, their meaning and social practice in different historical and social contexts varied and varies covering very diverse and often ambivalent aspects of masculinity. Some of these ideal concepts were transmitted as part of the national culture and taught in Soviet Tajik schools and universities in literature, history or Oriental studies. The curriculum was usually based on carefully selected and filtered excerpts of classical Persian literature.[5] Kenğaev, for instance, frequently referred to the Persian *andarz* literature (comparable to the European mirrors for princes): After his resignation as chairman of the Supreme Soviet he ostensibly withdrew from public to the Varzob Gorge (north of Dushanbe) discussing his future plans with a small circle of male confidants followed by an intensive reading of the classical *andarz* literature such as Košifī's *Axloqi muhsinī* or *Futuvvatnomai sultonī*. For Kenğaev, the *andarz* literature was a marker for political and cultural authenticity and he portrayed himself as the epitomization of the *ğavonmard* depicted in these texts.[6] In the second volume of his memoirs, Kenğaev included a portrait of himself in military fatigues with the motto: "For me a *ğavonmard* is a person, whose lowest deed is the sacrifice of his life."[7] He offered a more elaborate definition of *ğavonmard* referring to the Islamic tradition of consultation and participation:

> A *ğavonmard* is a person who does not fight with a weapon but with the intellect and who achieves his objectives through negotiation as the Prophet Mohammad has pointed out in the *hadith*: "Muslims, do consult with each other. There is need to discuss issues within the community. In case differences and disputes appear, solve them by majority opinion."[8]

The Soviet transformation, social intervention and modernization in Central Asia fundamentally changed the society as well as their social imaginaries. While the term "honor" (*nomus*) recurs frequently as an attribute of a *ğavonmard*, the meaning of honor among professional networks, Communist Party cadres, kolkhoz employees, the urban intelligentsia, Islamic activists or criminal networks varied. The Soviet transformation introduced alternative concepts of masculinity, both as positive role models such as the new Soviet man contributing to the creation of the Socialist Soviet society, which carried a particular idea of "culturedness," abstinence from alcohol, physical fitness and so forth, but also as the negative model embodied in the *vor v zakone* ("thief in law") or *sportsmen* (in the martial arts):

The masculine ideal, described in Russian as *ku'lturnyi* or "cultured," was juxtaposed in the sports press to a much criticized antithesis, *nekul'turniyi* or "uncultured" male behavior. Uncultured masculinity valorized self-indulgence (typically expressed in smoking, drinking, and sexual adventures) and aggressive physical self-assertion both in relation to other men and to women.[9]

While Soviet concepts of masculinity were prevalent in the state media, the Soviet-Tajik academic establishment carefully scrutinized traditional ideas of masculinity regarding their contribution to Soviet-Tajik history. Soviet anthropological research exoticized concepts of masculinity or male crime/solidarity networks in Central Asia and portrayed them in an Orientalist fashion.[10] In their account on the civil war, Buškov and Mikul'skiy for instance consider criminal networks and youth groups as a manifestation of a specific "traditional character (Russ.: *tradicionalistskiy kharakter*) of a primitive society (*primitivnykh obšestv*) in the East"[11] with historical roots in the 10th century. The cruelty and violence in the Tajik Civil War is explained with the particular characteristics of "the Orient." To support their argument, they quote a Soviet work on the 12th-century Arabic Caliphate and provisions in the Islamic law, which allow a particular cruel punishment. Eventually they assert a historical continuity locating criminal networks in the pre-Soviet traditional "oriental" bazars, such as Dushanbe's Šohmansur bazar.[12] Buškov and Mikul'skiy are only one example of many similar publications. The Soviet discourse on Tajik culture and history was also reproduced by the Soviet-Tajik academia, which emerged in the decades after the Great Patriotic War.

As pointed out earlier, political activists of the later Perestroika years were confronted with a difficult and ambivalent task of reconstructing an authentic Tajik Self, whose quintessential and foundational paradigms—race, language, history and territory—were already formulated during Soviet times. Būrī Karim asserted that the majority of Tajik intellectuals were leading a "slave-like life (*zindagii ġulamona*)"[13] under Soviet Rule and condemned the intellectual dependency on the Communist Party. Karim also offered a postcolonial reading of the term *ġavonmard* and masculinity:

We are a nation ruled by oppressors we idolize as false gods and we forget those of our true *ġavonmard* who sacrifice themselves on the path of truth. We are a nation who gives flowers to its murderers and even bows to them. We are a nation who declares those men 'people's heroes' who conquer our streets with tanks and weapons, whilst we consider those, who revolt against the tanks, as riff-raff and extremists [...]. We are a nation who embraces the history, the past, the literature, the culture of other nations but we do not know our Self.[14]

According to Karim, a *ġavonmard* is first of all a male Tajik political activist who is aware of his Self, his culture, language and history and who

defies the Soviet imposed national nihilism. Thus, the *ğavonmard* becomes
a representative of a post-colonial authentic Tajik culture and the opposite of
the Soviet man.

Ğavonmardī and Honor (nomus) of the Colonized

Tajik has a variety of terms, which can be broadly translated as "honor,"
such as *šaraf*, *viğdon*, *izzat*, *obrū*, *ehtirom* or *nomus*.[15] Drawing on various
anthropological accounts, *šaraf* and *obrū* can be best translated as individual
"social prestige," which can be acquired, lost and retrieved. *Nomus* has a
different dimension and is usually attributed to men who are able to protect
the sexual integrity of the female members of a household/family, that is,
regulating their social contacts outside the family and giving females into
acceptable marriages (from an Islamic legal and/or a personal local/family
perspective). King describes *nomus* pointedly as "patrilineal sovereignty,
particularly reproductive sovereignty."[16] Harris adds, that a man's *nomus* is
not violated in case *he* sexually assaults women—an important aspect in the
context of Tajikistan's civil war, where those who "defended" *nomus* were
celebrated while those who violated *nomus* were rarely punished. The collection of obituaries of Kūlobī militiamen by Rağab Munkī and Amiršoh Xatlonī
under the title *Nomus* implicates that Kūlobī men successfully defended the
honor (*nomus*) of the population of Kūlob and insinuates vice versa that their
opponents were not successful in defending theirs.[17]

In nationalist discourses, *nomus* is often assigned to a feminized homeland
whose honor has to be defended by the nation's men.[18] Representatives of the
Tajik intelligentsia followed a similar projection, for instance, Yusuf considers the violation of honor as the central indicator for the Soviet colonization
of the Tajik nation and the erosion of its "pure morals":

> Alcoholism, harlotry and sodomy became commonplace [in Soviet Tajikistan].
> We have plenty of historical evidence showing that Muslim-Tajik women had to
> prove their commitment to the communist ideology by drinking wine. Even in
> newspapers it was reported that a woman drank vodka in front of witnesses to
> demonstrate her freedom and independence. The more a woman drank alcohol,
> or the more she betrayed her own husband, this was a sign of her freedom, the
> higher she could rise in the echelons of the Communist Party. This means, that
> the more a human (woman) abandoned herself to morally unsuitable behavior,
> the more she loathed the traditions of her ancestors, she was rewarded.[19]

Yusuf's portrayal of women who deliberately relinquish their morality in
order to rise in the Communist Party hierarchies points out to the problematic
gender relations in late Soviet Tajikistan, where local representatives of the
male intelligentsia and political cadres were unsettled by officially advocated

Soviet gender models and by Tajik women, who demonstrated their social mobility, intellectual adaptability and often preponderance in many aspects of daily life. Representatives of the male Tajik intelligentsia, such as Yusuf, were obviously afraid of losing control over women in the Tajik society (as well as their own marginalization) and reacted with malicious insinuations and suspicions. In his critique of the Soviet system, he gave Nizorahmoh Zarifova, a CPT official from Vose' (Kūlob), as an example for the colonized women: After her father, allegedly a prominent religious scholar, had been executed by the Soviet authorities, Zarifova was raised in an orphanage as a devout communist disdaining her father and therefore the Tajik heritage and ultimately nation.[20] Yusuf launched a similar assault on Adolat Rahmonova, a CPT Deputy from Kūlob who was—as one of the few female politicians— actively involved in the rallies and protests in April and May 1992:

Rahmonova played a central role in outbreak of the fratricidal war in Tajikistan. In the Supreme Soviet, she always talked about the destitute Tajik mothers and cried whilst she insulted the national democrats. She frightened the people of Islam and she accused us [the DPT] of making Tajikistan a part of Iran and oppressing women like in Iran (without knowing their situation). In the entire history of Tajikistan, there has never been a woman who was so immoral, mendacious and corrupt. She justified the Coup d'état in August and she insinuated on TV that Islamists had attacked her. [...] She was the daughter of the devil.[21]

The intelligentsia's response to the transformation consists of the reconstruction of alleged authentic gender roles which envisaged a rather secluded role for women in the society (and which corresponded to some extent to concepts promoted by Islamist activists from rural Tajikistan).[22] Importantly, these perceptions indicate that the disintegration of Soviet gender equality in Central Asia had already started in the Perestroika/Glasnost era, in which the Soviet intelligentsia employed themes such as transparency, democratic reform or human rights. In Soviet Tajikistan, Perestroika/Glasnost revealed strong patriarchic and hierarchical imaginations of a society even shared by the reformist intelligentsia. The elections to the Supreme Soviet in February 1990 dramatically documented this tendency: While in the 11th Convocation (1985–1990) 36% of the deputies were female, in the 12th Convocation only 4% (or 9 out of 230) deputies were female—although (or because) the 1990 elections were the first somehow competitive elections with more than 1,000 candidates.[23]

One should not over-interpret the application of terms such as *ğavonmardī* or *nomus* among representatives of Tajikistan's intelligentsia—these terms were certainly often used randomly or contingently without the implications mentioned here. However, the outbreak of Tajikistan's civil war was in many

ways contingent and local field commanders adopted an assertively masculine
habitus.

MEN OF DISORDER: RACKETS ("REKET") AND AGENCY

The dynamics and violence of the Tajik conflict were—as often in civil
wars—significantly influenced by violent non-state actors who were not integrated into official state institutions and who often emerged in a contingent
local context.[24] These "men of disorder," the field commanders of the different militias, representatives of organized crime and criminal groups, such as
Yaqub Salimov, Rauf Saliev, Sangak Safarov, Rizvon Sodirov, Gumaʿxon
Būydoqov, Ibodullo Boymatov or Mullo Abduġaffur are often portrayed
as subalterns without agency in the political economy of the TaSSR and
independent Tajikistan who were "activated" by the dominant elites in the
evolving political confrontation.[25] Beyond controversy, these men of disorder
closely collaborated with representatives of the political elites due to convergent interests or as an exchange of favors/obligingness in the informal
economy of the TaSSR (as well as in other parts of the former USSR[26]).
In general, networks and individuals in the TaSSR's organized crime are
poorly documented and most of the information is based on hearsay and
rumors. Many men of disorder were reclusive and neither wrote their memoirs nor gave extensive interviews—perhaps with the important exception of
Sangak Safarov (see below).

In the 1980s, Glasnost removed the restriction to discuss crime in the
Soviet society. The Marxist tenet that crime would recede in a socialist society and disappear in a communist society (which effectively restricted any
discussion on crime and its nature in the USSR) was relinquished and the
political nomenklatura expressed their concerns about the increasing crime
problem. The MVD statistics were declassified and the media reported extensively and often with a sensational tone about the "mafia," spectacular corruption cases, the abuse of authority, fraud, drug trafficking, alcohol abuse and
above all youth violence.[27] The late Soviet press frequently featured articles
and op-eds on networks of organized crime in Tajikistan and the former
Soviet Union. In December 1991, for instance, the *Komsomolʿskaya Pravda*
reported under the title *Mafiya u vlast* (Russ.: "The Mafia and Power") about
the influence of organized crime networks and criminal youth in the February 1990 events.[28] Buškov and Mikulʾskiy reproduce various rumors about
the relationship between the political nomenklatura and organized crime in
the TaSSR.[29] According to these reports, criminal groups led by individual
racketeers had established themselves in various districts of Dushanbe in
the 1980s, for instance at the Barakat (Putovskiy) bazar, the Šohmansur

(Rohi Ohan/Railway) district or in the northern Vodonasos district. Some of the groups were recruited exclusively among young men with a particular regional provenance, for instance from Ispečak, Avul and Qazokon, that is, western districts of Dushanbe with significant *muhoğir* communities. The scattered narratives report about redistributions among various individuals and groups until the 1960s followed by a consolidation of domestic organized crime networks. According to these narratives, non-Tajiks, above all Chechens deported during the Second World War to Central Asia, initially dominated organized crime in the TaSSR. In the 1960s, local crime groups from Kūlob made inroads into the organized crime business, but competitors from Ġarm and Badaxšon soon challenged the groups from Kūlob and reportedly dislodged them from Dushanbe in the 1970s. In 1989/1990 Rauf Saliev (or Soliev), an Ossetian from Samarqand, was considered to be one of the most influential racketeers in Dushanbe. Saliev and his henchman Yaqub Salimov (born in 1958 in Vaxš into a family from Kūlob) operated a criminal group of male youth in Dushanbe and organized illegal betting, cockfights, boxing events, illicit drugs, alcohol and goods in short supply and, importantly, they offered "protection" for private businesses and local communities. Both, Saliev and Salimov are often implicated in the February 1990 events and reportedly Salimov had to leave the TaSSR for several months until he resurfaced in May 1992.

Discussing the Dushanbe-based criminal networks, Ibrohim Usmonov concluded that the civil war was provoked by organized crime, youth gangs and racketeers.[30] The term *racket* was popularized in Russian and Tajik (*reket*) with Perestroika and the expanding private, often semi-legal, business in the 1980s. Businessmen relied on rackets and racketeers for protection and to enforce their business interests. Max Horkheimer and Charles Tilly refer to the intrinsic relation between protection rackets and crime in the emergence of political order. Tilly moreover reflects on the ambivalence in the meaning of "protection":

> With one tone, "protection" calls up images of the shelter against danger provided by a powerful friend, a large insurance policy, or a sturdy roof. With the other, it evokes the racket in which a local strong man forces merchants to pay tribute in order to avoid damage—damage the strong man himself threatens to deliver. The difference, to be sure, is a matter of degree. [...] Someone who produces both the danger and, at a price, the shield against it is a racketeer. Someone who provides a needed shield but has little control over the danger's appearance qualifies as a legitimate protector, especially if his price is no higher than his competitors.[31]

Kenğaev used the term *reket* to describe the protection (*himoya*) networks of the political nomenklatura for their private business activities and he described how *rekets* infiltrated the MVD/KGB and offered protection or applied extortion as representatives of the system. The complicity between the security forces and organized crime/racketeers is widely acknowledged.[32] In the civil war, *reket* was a common term for combatants, for instance an infamous accomplice of Fayzalī Saidov, Tohir Tešaev (b. 1974/1975 in Qūrġonteppa) took the nom du guerre "Tohir-Reket." Although Saidov's militia was notorious for its cruelty and destructiveness, they simultaneously "governed" in areas under their control and provided protection or took revenge for injustices done to local communities under their protection.[33] Racketeers were recruited among the male urban youth in martial arts or billiard clubs and local mosques.[34] Furthermore, the popular culture, above all Western crime movies (such as *The Godfather* or the TV series *La piovra*), often featured male heroes who violated against social as well as legal norms and formed a distinct habitus of masculinity (Kenġaev's self-stylization as the Tajik Commissar Cattani is a good example). Based on ethnographic observation in Tajikistan, Greta Uehling comes to the conclusion that "quasi-legal activities were fundamentally gendered, having as much to do with reinforcing constructions of masculinity as filling a vacuum left by the collapse of state structures."[35]

Spatial and Political Contexts of Rackets and Racketeers

Racketeers and organized crime had a distinct spatial context in the TaSSR. Most important were the central markets/bazars in urban areas, such as Šohmansur or Barakat bazar in Dushanbe. Racketeers controlled access to markets, offered protection, stored contraband and provided their subalterns with formal positions, such as guards or porters, which made them eligible for the *propiska* (residence permit). Due to the central role of the bazar not only for the daily supply of the population but also the urban intermediary trade, racketeers could extend their influence beyond the immediate bazar location. Various networks with contacts to the nomenklatura could additionally gain access to the expansive Soviet infrastructure, such as combines, collective farms, sanatoriums, youth camps and motor depots.[36] The TaSSR had a relatively small rail network and private ownership of a car was uncommon, therefore commercial and private transport rested upon road transport: Cars, trucks and busses were the most important means of inter- and intra-regional transport in the TaSSR, in particular for agricultural products, contraband, spare parts and people. To provide transport, the republican ministry for transport and roads maintained motor depots (Russ.: *avtobaza*) throughout the TaSSR. The depots operated busses, trucks and passenger cars, provided drivers and maintenance including spare parts and fuel in short supply and therefore became important hubs in the Soviet informal economy and *blat* networks.[37] Crime networks smuggled contraband through the motor depots and the ministry for transport and roads was widely perceived as corrupt and controlled by organized crime.[38] Notably, a significant number of combatants and field commanders in the civil war had been involved in the transport sector and motor depots in Tajikistan: Kenğaev was general procurator of the republican transport sector, Šeralī Xoliqov (a commander in Kenğaev's Popular Front) was director of the *avtobaza* No. 15 in Tursunzoda, Sūhrob Qosimov (an influential field commander of the Popular Front) and Narzullo Dūstov were both directors of *avtobaza*s, Ibod[ullo] Boymatov (a commander in Hisor/Tursunzoda) was an *avtobaza* bus driver on the important route Dushanbe-Tursunzoda-Denav-Samarqand, Ğu'maxon Būydokov (an opposition commander) worked at the *avtobaza* No. 3 in Dushanbe's Šohmansur district, Ğaffur "Sedoī" Mirzoev (a field commander from Kūlob and later commander of the presidential guard) was in the mid-1980s a driver in an *avtobaza* in Kūlob, Rizvon Sodirov (an opposition field commander) worked at an *avtobaza* in Kofarnihon and Mirzoxūğa Mirzoğonov (an IRPT activist) was the director of the *avtobaza* No. 50 in Qubodiyon—just to name a few better known field commanders of the civil war. The profession of a driver or mechanic in the motor depots was an assertive male occupation and enabled the establishment of professional networks beyond the immediate local context with ample possibility for semi-legal or illegal activities.[39] Apparently, Kenğaev became acquainted with Dūstov, Xoliqov and Boymatov during his tenure as transport procurator and was able to recruit/mobilize his militia through these networks. Access to vehicles, fuel, mechanical expertise and spare parts was a significant advantage for militias in the early civil war.

Equally important were sports facilities as recruiting grounds for local strongmen and a substantial number of violent non-state actors in Tajikistan's civil war were trainers of Karate or Sambo (a mixture of several disciplines such as Judo or various forms of wrestling trained in the armed forces) or managed sports facilities.[40] The sports ethos could—as in the case of *ğavonmardī*—implicate a variation of contextual meanings, from the Soviet idea of the athlete competing in the Olympic Games or the Spartakiad to the traditional Tajik *pahlavon* in wrestling and eventually thuggish sportsmen protecting their *biznesmen*.[41] The martial arts disciplines were at the same time closely monitored by the KGB/MVD indicating the interaction between the two spheres.[42] Since the late 1980s, local businessmen and their racketeers often took over local sport facilities and sponsored martial arts or billiard clubs for male youth, which served as recruitment grounds for their networks and ad hoc mobilization.[43]

Eventually, mosques were an important location for male networks as well. Both, the registered mosque and the unregistered mosques or teahouses (*čayxona*) were often located close to the bazar and financed by local "businessmen" (like billiard parlors or martial arts clubs, which were often

sponsored by the same local strongman and situated in adjacent buildings).
Mullo Abduġaffur Xudoydodov, for instance, established himself as a racketeer
and the *imom-xatib* of the "Yužniy" mosque in a southern Dushanbe suburb.
His youth gang emerged as an important armed militia in the summer of 1992.[44]

In late April 1992, various informal youth groups started to coordinate
their illegal activities around the Spartak Stadium and Aynī Square under
the label "Youth of Dushanbe (*ğavononi Dušanbe*)." The Youth of Dushanbe
were reportedly 18 gangs who were loosely affiliated with the demonstration
on Šahidon Square. Some of these groups around the Šohmansur bazar and
the *avtobaza* No. 3 and their strongmen, such as Ismat Habibulloev, Mullo
Abduġaffur, Ruslan Muborakqadamov or Rizvon Sodirov, looked back to
a dubious career as local criminals or as sportsmen, such as Alī "Boksyor"
(Alī "the Boxer"), in the 1980s.[45] Although some referred to the prevalent
political motifs of the conflict's master narrative, their activities were often
of a predatory character. The Youth of Dushanbe were united in their rivalry
with established criminal groups, in particular the one of Rauf Saliev and
Yaqub Salimov (who eventually sided with the militias from Kūlob). The
Youth of Dushanbe therefore saw in the cooperation with the opposition
on Šahidon Square and the Government of national Reconciliation a possibility to dislodge Saliev and take over his share of the shadow economy,
contraband, drug trafficking, and other "services," such as protection, extortion, intimidation or hostage taking in Dushanbe. The Youth of Dushanbe
consisted of various intransigent groups which did not simply follow orders,
although some of the groups claimed allegiance to an important representative of the Tajik political elite, for instance to Tūraġonzoda, Huvaydulloev,
Pallaev or Nabiev. However, it is deceptive to conclude a particular hierarchy
or subordination, which presumably allowed the nomenklatura to "activate"
or "deactivate" these groups ad libitum.[46] The developments since May 1992
demonstrate that the political leadership had only very limited control over
the different youth gangs and the government had to negotiate "security" in
Dushanbe with several individual actors and groups often shifting loyalties.
Ibrohim Usmonov stipulated that not the Government of National Reconciliation controlled Dushanbe between May and December 1992, but the Youth
of Dushanbe.[47] After Nabiev's resignation in September 1992, they dislodged
rival informal groups, which were close to Nabiev. Abduġaffur, Ismat Avulī
and Rizvon turned against the established networks of Rauf Saliev and even
burned down Saliev's residence. Saliev and his henchman Yaqub Salimov
eventually sided with the Popular Front against the Youth of Dushanbe.
For Kenğaev, the Youth of Dushanbe were—in contrast to the *ğavonmard*
from Hisor or Kūlob—simply criminals without any honor and orientation
since they did not consider Dushanbe as their home due to the prevalent discourses that depicted Dushanbe not as a Tajik but Soviet-internationalist city:

If the Youth of Dushanbe were like the *ğavonmard* of Kūlob, Hisor, Xuğand, Ūroteppa [Istaravšon], Panğakent or Isfara a generation of *ğavonmard*, they would have honesty and honor (*nangu namus*), they would consider Dushanbe as their own home and would respect their mother as well as their cradle [i.e. Dushanbe]. Under these conditions, Dushanbe would have not turned into a zone of war and terror, of riots and demonstrations [...] instigated by the dissentious people of Badaxšon and a group of *vahhobī* from Qarotegin and Qūrģonteppa.[48]

"BOBO" SANGAK SAFAROV—A CASE STUDY

One of the most controversial violent non-state actors in the early civil war was "Bobo" Sangak Safarov, an ex-convict and *bufetčik* (waiter) in a café in the southern city of Kūlob. Safarov, born in 1928 in Farq-Šodī (Šuģnav district) into a family from Vaxiyo (Xovaling district), grew up in Kūlob. His father and older brother were arrested during the Stalinist purges in the 1930s and died in a Gulag. Safarov, who grew up with his mother and two younger brothers, came into conflict with the authorities in 1951, however not as a political dissident but as an ordinary criminal. His first prison term for car theft between 1952/1953 was soon followed by a second term from 1957 until 1959 for vehicular homicide and a third term in 1961 for hooliganism. In 1961, Safarov was sentenced a fourth time for seven years, reportedly for killing a Chechen criminal in self-defense. His sentence was extended several times since Safarov (according to his own narrative) led a revolt against the prison administration due to the inhumane conditions in the labor camp. He was finally released in 1976 and returned to Kūlob where he married the then 17-year-old Davlatmoh Xoğaeva in an arranged marriage (which changed his status as a *ğavonmard*). Safarov worked as a *bufetčik* in a local café and established himself as a local criminal or, perhaps more pointedly, as a local racketeer offering "protection" and regulating local affairs informally. In an interview with *Radioi Ozodī*, his widow portrayed Safarov as a local mediator whom neighbors in the *mahalla* used to ask for advice in case their boys violated against the law or local customs. Safarov would admonish them and get them back on the straight and narrow. He mediated in conflicts with other communities and always had the *nomus* of his community in mind. Although Safarov served in his *Lazzat* café alcohol, he never encouraged its abuse and "if there was a place without conflict and trouble in Kūlob it was his workplace."[49]

In the tumultuous summer of 1991 Safarov became entangled in local politics supporting Nabiev's campaign for presidency in the Kūlob *viloyat*. In April/May 1992, he suddenly emerged as one of the leaders of the public protests against the democratic Islamic opposition in Dushanbe—to the surprise of many politicians and activists who considered him an "accidental (*tasodufī*) person"[50] and not part of the established local elite networks. Ibrohim Usmonov remarked, the name Safarov was virtually "unknown to the population of Dushanbe"[51] and Yusuf likewise expressed his astonishment when Safarov was introduced as one of the leaders of the government delegation: "We were aghast! How could it be possible that a person who was a murderer and criminal for his entire life now leads a government committee?"[52]

Why "Bobo" Sangak?

The puzzle of "Bobo" Sangak's rise has to be seen in the context of the complexity of civil wars as Kalyvas points out: "civil wars are not binary conflicts but complex and ambiguous processes that foster an apparently massive, though variable, mix of identities and actions."[53] Kalyvas furthermore observes a disjunction

> between identities and actions at the central or elite level, on the one hand, and the local or mass level, on the other. This disjunction takes two forms: first, actions "on the ground" often seem more related to local or private issues than to the war's driving (or "master") cleavage; second, individual and local actors take advantage of the war to settle local or private conflicts often bearing little or no relation to the causes of the war or the goals of the belligerents.[54]

Sangak Safarov became entangled in the unfolding conflict on various levels: First, he supported Nabiev's presidential campaign in Kūlob intimidating Nabiev's contenders and contributing to the confrontational tone in the local political competition. The population in Kūlob were not in unison supporters of Nabiev. The DPT had a determined local representation led by Šamsuddin Sobir (a philosophy professor at the local university) and the Kūlob branch of the IRPT became more active after the party's registration.[55] Second, Safarov interfered in the local conflict between Šarifov and "Mullo" Abdurahim. The conflict between Abdurahim and Šarifov had a national dimension through the interference of the *qoziyot* in the appointments in Kūlob and Šarifov's personal rivalry with Tūragonzoda. Both conflicts had a national dimension, which could be easily explained in terms of the political master narrative in Dushanbe. The implications and motivations, however, were local, namely the political competition over public support in Kūlob and access to important religious institutions which generated legitimacy and revenues. The political nomenklatura considered Safarov initially as a subaltern, an expedient racketeer, who could—if deemed necessary—apply physical pressure on local rivals without the constraints officials might face. Safarov offered his "services" selectively and expanded his protection racket beyond

Kūlob. He aptly responded to the changing dynamics in the unfolding conflict, distanced himself from the political nomenklatura in Kūlob and eventually eliminated some of its key representatives. In autumn 1992, his Popular Front (*Fronti xalqī*) had become the most powerful militia in the early civil war. After he had consolidated his position in Kūlob, he conquered Qūrġonteppa and the southern Šahrtuz. Eventually he established with Emomalī Rahmonov a new political leadership on the national level in November and captured the capital Dushanbe in December 1992 virtually deciding the civil war.

In his public appearance, Safarov exhibited a multi-faceted habitus as the "traditional" Tajik *ǧavonmard* (being just and generous, protecting the weak), the intimidating (Russian/Soviet) *vor v zakonye* ("Thief in law"), the astute politician/diplomat and eventually a "man of order" floating above mundane ideological and political conflicts.[56] Remarkably, Safarov formulated a narrative of legitimation based on these habitual configurations. The demonstrated masculinity and the self-expression by Safarov and other field commanders suggest that they tried to generate legitimacy by implementing a specific hierarchy and code of conduct in their militias that were perceived as "authentic," "just" and "traditional" by their followers.[57]

Narratives of Legitimation

In April/May 1992, Bobo Sangak gradually changed his role from a local racketeer, ex-convict, henchman of local elites and *buffetčī* to a politician with a regionalist agenda and nationalist sentiment. He was able to assert himself as one of the leaders on Ozodī Square next to established local elites such as Mirzoaliev (politics), Šarifov (religion) or Abdurahimov (civil society). With his new role as a political representative of Kūlob, Safarov gradually developed a political narrative and legitimation project.[58] His transformation from a local criminal to a politician was, however, interrupted by his brief arrest in May 1992. The arrest apparently increased his determination to oppose the Government of National Reconciliation *and* the political elite in Kūlob, which—in Safarov's view—had abandoned him and his brother in Dushanbe. Safarov returned reinvigorated to Kūlob and established himself as a leading field commander in the summer of 1992. In late July 1992, at the Xoruġ Peace Talks, Safarov was still considered as one among several field commanders from Kūlob,[59] but within four months, until November 1992, he conquered most parts of southern Tajikistan, marginalized or eliminated his rivals in Kūlob and installed a new political leadership on the national level before he seized Dushanbe. In early 1993, Bobo Sangak confided in the Dushanbe born historian and journalist Vladimir Medvedev and reconsidered his past, his role in the recent events and his vision of the future political landscape of Tajikistan in an extensive interview.[60]

While Safarov's initial legitimation rested in the unrestrained violence he himself and his militia resorted to, he now started to reformulate his political project and broaden his legitimation. Veit and Schlichte point out that legitimacy of violent non-state actors is central to their ability to mobilize support and eventually accomplish their objectives. Violence, however, produces counter narratives of de-legitimation and therefore the violent non-state actors refer at some point of their "career" to alternative forms of legitimation.[61] Likewise, Korf and Raeymaekers point out that warlords have to develop a political project and narrative, which legitimizes their actions among their supporters.[62] The attention by the international media, such as *Der Spiegel* or *The New York Times*, perhaps contributed to Safarov's transformation as well.[63]

In his conversation with Vladimir Medvedev, Safarov embedded his narrative in a complex historical context referring to various layers of *ǧavonmardī* and honor: Namely as (1) a Russian/Soviet *vor v zakone*—"a thief in law"— who defied the Soviet (penitentiary) system and became an *avtoritet* in the organized crime;[64] (2) a locally entrenched Islamic identity by claiming matrilineal descent from an important Sayyid and Sufi family in the upper Qarotegin Valley; (3) an historical/cultural identity describing his "clan" (Russ.: *rod*) as the original (eastern Iranian) inhabitants of south-eastern Tajikistan; and finally as (4) a conciliatory politician, who advocates a secular government, opposes radical Islam and cooperates with the UN in the repatriation of IDPs and refugees under his protection.[65] In discussing Safarov's legitimation narratives, I am less interested in the validity or historicity of his claims—most likely, he was neither related to a Sayyid family nor a true *vor v zakone* in the criminal hierarchies of the USSR.[66] Instead, I consider Safarov's self-description as an important indication for his perception of masculinity and symbolic capital, that is, he reconstructed his identity by emphasizing important forms of symbolic capital in the social space. My general assumption is that Safarov did this intentionally and with the knowledge of the social imaginaries and hierarchies in the larger social space. Certainly, this analysis does not provide any insights to the *reception* of Safarov's legitimation narrative or his political project by his subordinates or followers. Here, the analysis of oral history sources as well as ethnographic research might contribute to a better understanding of the popularization of Safarov's performance.

"Vor v zakone": Authority and Violence

Safarov spent some 23 years in various labor camps and in his interview he laconically states, "I was in prison for deeds my father and my people (Russ.: *rod*) were repressed for, it was not politics, but life made me to lead my people."[67] Although he conceded that he was not a dissident, he nonetheless referred to Stalinist suppression insinuating a political substrate in his ambitions and a general injustice not only against his family but his entire *rod* (which is best translated as extended family or clan with the Tajik equivalent *avlod* or *qavm*). Safarov emphasized several elements in his narrative, which are important for the reconstruction of his concepts of symbolic capital. Initially, Safarov had cultivated a demonstratively intimidating male behavior, which was embedded in the Soviet sub-culture of criminal networks and their complex relation to the security structures as well as concepts of *ğavonmardī* in the local context of southern Tajikistan. As several activists report, he addressed people usually in a mixture of Tajik and Russian, using the second person singular (*tu* instead of the appropriate *šumo*). Sohibnazar remembered Safarov as a person with a face "distant to any wisdom (*az xirad farsaxho dur*)" and how Safarov addressed him in a hostile and intimidating mixture of Russian and Tajik:

> You (*tu*), brother (Russ.: *brat*), don't know Sangak [here with a Russian genitive ending –*a*]? [...] I am Nabiev's man, brother. [...] Brother, you should not play together with those Pomirīs and Ğarmīs. You do not have enough strength. The Vahhobis do not provide any protection. I will kill all of them (*sarbur mekunam*).[68]

Safarov obviously symbolized for representatives of the Tajik intelligentsia an ambivalent Other and his intimidating behavior strangely appealed to them: After a meeting with Safarov, Davlat Xudonazar was apparently impressed by Safarov and suddenly declared that he is an "advocator of truth and he fought his entire life for truth."[69] Xudonazar's unexpected sympathies for an ex-convict and brutal field commander might be related to his antipathies toward the IRPT, but his perception of Safarov as an upright democrat can be perhaps qualified as a subordinate masculinity while Safarov symbolized a dominant configuration of masculinity. In the tumultuous disintegration of the USSR, Xudonazar realized that the "official" Soviet configurations of dominant masculinities, that is, the cultured intelligentsia or the austere state official, withered away and were replaced by masculinities embodied by individuals from the fringes of the Soviet society.[70]

Safarov's performative resilience and defiance of established customs as well as his violent language contributed to his authenticity. His credibility was further enhanced by the fact that Safarov personally and in public resorted to unrestrained violence by executing several rivals, such as Ğahonxon Rizoev, Qurbon Zardakov, Talab Kuznets and Qadriddin Aslonov.[71] At the same time he always claimed to adhere as a fighter (*voyne*) to a specific code of conduct rooted in the Soviet penitentiary system and criminal sub-culture. He claimed that he protected the weak among the inmates (for instance a Baptist religious dissident) and occupied himself with *kulturny* activities such as reading, writing poetry and playing chess.[72] Similar, Yaqub Salimov—Rauf Saliev's henchman and racketeer who was implicated in the February events and had been convicted for a sexual assault in the 1980s—initially appeared as reputable "man of order" to Tajikistan's intelligentsia due to his male code of conduct.[73] Only much later, Sohibnazar conceded, he found out that Salimov is just a "gambler (*qartaboz*) for whom the national welfare was actually only a regional issue and most important, his personal welfare ranked highest for him."[74] The ambivalent attraction of racketeers and "men of disorder" among representatives of Tajikistan's urban, 'cultured' intelligentsia might be also related to the lack of assertiveness of the political leadership as well as ambivalent imaginaries of a Tajik *ğavonmard* or *pahlavon*.

The Religious Narrative

Although Safarov is sometimes portrayed as a "neo-communist" and the main opponent of the Islamist opposition, he integrated a religious narrative to his political legitimation as well: "The Islamists accuse me that I am against Islam, but that's not true. I am a Muslim and I received religion with my mother's milk."[75] Safarov's narrative is surprisingly sophisticated and embedded in the complex historical context of Tajikistan and the wider region since the 18th century: He claims that his maternal grandfather was *ešoni* Sultan, a local religious authority with Sufi affiliation in the upper Qarotegin Valley who opposed the foreign (Turkish) infiltration of the *bosmačī* movement by Enver Pasha and his local intermediary Fuzayl Maxsum in the early 1920s. Safarov portrayed his grandfather *ešoni* Sulton as a descendant from the first generation of Arab conquerors and from a Sayyid family claiming direct lineage to the family of the Prophet Muhammad. *ešoni* Sultan was not only a religious authority with more than 1,000 *murids* (followers), but also a local political authority in pre-Soviet times. Although *ešoni* Sulton defied Soviet rule in the beginning, he finally cooperated with the Bolsheviks, who appointed him in 1921 chairman of the RevKom in Ġarm and bestowed him, in Safarov's rich narrative, with a "magic" bulletproof overcoat. He accepted the appointment in order to organize the resistance against the Turkish infiltration of the Qarotegin Valley. However, Fuzayl Maxsum successfully mobilized the local elites in Tavildara and Ġarm against *ešoni* Sulton. The family estate in Yozgand (close to Tavildara) was depredated and *ešoni* Sulton and his brother Sulayman were captured and publicly hanged in Darvoz in the summer of 1921.[76] There are two interwoven and recurrent elements in Safarov's narrative, which are important to him: The Sufi/Sayyid lineage of *ešoni* Sultan and the authority/resistance *ešoni* Sultan personified in the particular historical context. Safarov portrayed his grandfather's cooperation with the Bolshevik as rational decision since their support should enable him to protect his people from Turkish suzerainty (a worse predicament than Soviet/Russian rule). Implicitly, Safarov hereby also legitimized his own shifting alliances in 1992/1993 as inevitable to preserve the unity of the nation.

The Cultural-Iranian and Historical Narrative

The cultural-Iranian narrative refers to his paternal grandfather and father, Safar Pirnazarov, who had been executed during the Stalinist purges. In Safarov's narrative, his grandfather and father were gold miners and metallurgists in the Pamir who worked and transformed metal (with allusions to an Iranian *magi*) with a tradition and continuity in Xuttalān (today's Xatlon) since pre-Islamic time, which was only interrupted by the Mongol invasion.[77] The cultural-Iranian and historical narrative is partly intertwined with the religious one, in particular by the introduction of *ešoni* Sulton's son and uncle of Safarov, Mullo Abdulhaq, whom Safarov presented as his role model: Mullo Abdulhaq resembled Kova or Fereydun of the *Šohnoma*, who fought for their people and Mullo Abdulhaq equally combined religious charisma with the Iranian mythological panache. Finally, Safarov integrated a revenge narrative (for his grandfather *ešoni* Sulton and his entire *rod/avlod/qavm*) referring to the regional enmity between Ġarm and Kūlob, which is today one of the master narratives for Tajikistan's civil war. Thus, Safarov presented the civil war in terms of an unfinished history, since Soviet rule prevented between the 1924 and 1991 that Safarov's *rod* could take revenge and retrieve their historical position. The developments in 1992 only mirror the events in the 1920s.[78]

"Bobo" Sangak, the Statesman

Eventually, Sangak presented himself as an altruistic "man of order" and veritable politician who has re-established order (Russ.: *poryadok*) in the regions under his control: Safarov supported the reconstruction of local administration, secured the return of the more than 500,000 internally displaced people in winter 1992/93 and negotiated aid with foreign governments (Kazakhstan, Kyrgyzstan, Russia and Uzbekistan) and international organizations (UNHCR).[79] In late 1992, Safarov refrained from unrestrained violence and even tried to discipline subordinate or rival field commanders. Eventually, he started to articulate an independent political narrative by distancing himself from the old Soviet cadres whom he called "rotten careerists (Russ.: *prognivšikh kar'eristov*)." He adopted a more nationalist and inclusive idea of the motherland (*rodina*), copying prevalent nationalist discourses by indicating that he had a conversation with Islam Karimov about the future of Samarqand and Bukhara demanding the cities' return to Tajikistan.[80]

Apparently, Safarov's legitimation strategy was to some extent successful and even his declared enemies conceded, that he adapted to the role of
a statesman and diplomat in late 1992.[81] His role as a statesman, however,
intensified the conflict with a rival field commander and ultimately took his
life: On 29 March 1993, Safarov invited Fayzalī Saidov for negotiations on
the refugee issue to Boxtar (a small town close to Qūrġonteppa). The repatriation of refugees to Qūrġonteppa had generated tensions between the two field
commanders: Whilst Safarov cooperated with UNHCR, Saidov remained the
locally entrenched field commander and opposed any reconciliation including violent attacks on refugee convoys under Safarov's protection. Reportedly, Safarov tried to convince Saidov to accept his new policy in a personal
meeting, but disputes over the future strategy escalated and—accidently or
not—an exchange of fire killed both.[82]

The Puzzle of Mobilization

In late October/early November Safarov re-designated his militia as the Popular Front in order to gain some formal recognition and legitimacy. The recruitment followed certain patterns: First, fragmentary sources and reports suggest
that many of the combatants were part of criminal networks who had been
imprisoned during Soviet times. With the collapse of the USSR, Tajikistan
could not maintain the penitentiary system and several facilities were closed.
Numerous inmates were released in the early civil war regardless of the nature
of their criminal offense. Unsurprisingly, many ex-convicts had no economic
perspectives and readily joined the ranks of the militias of Mullo Abduġaffur,
Sangak Safarov, Yaqub Salimov and Langarī Langariev.[83] In equal measure,
former MVD officers commanded or joined militias in 1992. For instance,
Langariev—who was one of the most respected commanders until he was
fatally wounded in October 1992—had been a MVD guard in the penitentiary
colony in Dushanbe and his father "Bobo" Salmon Langariev was a retired
militia officer in Kūlob. Two other sons, Fayzalī and Baxtiyor Langariev,
served also in the MVD and military.[84] Second, a number of *afgancy*—veterans of the Soviet occupation of Afghanistan between 1979 and 1989—
joined the militias, some as mercenaries—Kenġaev called them "war experts
(*mutaxassisoni harbī*),"[85] while others romanticized the comradeship and
solidarity during the Afghan war and never re-adopted to a civilian life. Third,
with the disintegration of the state security agencies, protection on the individual and collective (*avlod* or *mahalla*) level became an important incentive
to join a militia. The code of conduct within the militias integrated individuals into protection rackets including their families and *mahallas*. Moreover,
membership in a militia could enable combatants to take revenge for previous
"injustices." Fourth, militias offered protection for financial compensation
and resorted to extortion. The profits from protection and extortion enabled

militia commanders such as Safarov to offer his men a substantial financial compensation for their service.[86] Finally, concepts of masculinities influenced the mobilization, since they offered orientation in the complex transitional period in which new role models proliferated. In conversations I had between 2002 and 2013, former field commanders and militia men often expressed a nostalgia regarding their time in the mountains, a life of a "real man" only restrained by a male code of honor and conduct perceived as "authentic" Tajik/Muslim/Central Asian or Soviet.

"Bobo" Sangak's Legacy

Safarov was not the only popular field commander in the civil war who adopted a narrative of legitimation which resorted to concepts of masculinity: Safarov's accomplice Fayzalī Saidov legitimized his relentless campaign in and around Qūrġonteppa in terms of revenge and the restoration of his family's honor. According to the few sources available, Fayzalī Saidov was born in 1963 into a Laqay family in the Boxtar. He graduated from a technical college in Qūrġonteppa and was drafted to the Soviet Army in the early 1980s. Reportedly, he served a prison sentence for homicide committed during his military service until 1991. On the eve of the civil war he worked as a night guard in a Dushanbe cotton mill. Saidov was active in one of the local Laqay/Kūlob "self-defense" groups in mid-July 1992, when his 65-year-old father, "Bobo" Qurbon, was abducted by one of his neighbors called "Ğangī" (*Warrior*), taken with other hostages to the Turkmenistan sovkhoz, tortured and brutally killed despite Saidov's readiness to pay ransom. The mutilated body of "Bobo" Qurbon was dropped in the center of Qūrġonteppa and Saidov reportedly made the IRPT responsible (since "Ğangī" was an alleged IRPT sympathizer).[87] After the brutal murder of his father, Saidov embarked on a merciless revenge campaign until his death in March 1993.

Mirzo "Ğaga" Ziyoyev, one of the most successful UTO/IRPT field commanders from the Tavildara region, likewise resorted to a particular male habitus. Ziyoyev had not been involved in the political struggle in 1991/92 but later coordinated the UTO's military operations in the Qarotegin Valley. Reportedly, the founders of the Islamic Movement of Uzbekistan, Tohir Yoldošev and Ğumʿa Namangonī, fought with Ziyoyev's militia until 1997. However, Ziyoyev did not adopt his nom du guerre "Ğaga/Jagga" by borrowing from the Islamic tradition, but Indian movies popular in Soviet Central Asia since the 1950s. Ziyoyev's namesake was Jagga Jatt (or Dakoo), a Punjabi outlaw and Robin Hood figure who rebelled against the colonial system in the early 20th century. His story was the plot for at least four popular Indian movies produced between 1940 and 1991.[88] These Indian movies were shown in the TaSSR even in remote villages and apparently induced Ziyoyev to adopt Ğaga as his nom du guerre. A more detailed account on the different field commanders as well as combatants in the civil war would be desirable and deserves additional scholarly attention beyond this manuscript.

CONCLUSION

Terms, such as *ğavonmard*, *ğavonmardī* or *nomus* are used as markers for an authentic male Tajik identity. The idea of authenticity was in a time of pervasive national sentiment of paramount importance, while references to the Soviet system—for instance to internationalism or Peoples' Friendship with their particular concepts and ideals—were increasingly perceived as alien, Russian and colonial. Authenticity was consequently important for the legitimation, both of status as well as of action. The analysis of the different and changing concepts of masculinity in the Tajik Civil War might contribute to a better understanding of the mobilization of militias, legitimation strategies and loyalties. A closer analysis of individual field commanders and combatants might reveal important deviations from the established conceptualizations of the Tajik Civil War. With the reference to the importance of criminal networks I do not intend to qualify the Tajik conflict exclusively as a "new" civil war characterized as "criminal, depoliticized, private, and predatory"[89] as opposed to "old" civil wars, which were fought with an ideological and political intention. Kalyvas critically evaluates this distinction and reminds us that it "is highly possible that interpretations of recent civil wars that stress their de-politicization and criminalization are attributable more to the demise of the conceptual categories generated by the cold war than to the end of the cold war per se."[90] Furthermore, the violent non-state actors in the case of the Tajik Civil War are often portrayed as subalterns without agency in the unfolding events, to some extent in order to rationalize the outbreak of the civil war as politically motivated and to reduce the contingency. The short account on Safarov and other field commanders indicate that these field commanders had agency and sometimes even articulated a legitimation narrative, but for a better understanding of the particular dynamics in civil wars, further research is needed.

NOTES

1. The title of this chapter is a variation of Touraj Atabaki and Erik J. Zürcher, eds., *Men of order: Authoritarian modernization under Atatürk and Reza Shah* (London: I.B. Tauris, 2004) and the title of a comparative research project on concepts of masculinity among violent non state actors in Iran and Tajikistan at the University of Freiburg.
2. Cf. R. W. Connell and James W. Messerschmidt, "Hegemonic Masculinity: Rethinking the Concept," *Gender & Society* 19, no. 6 (2005).

3. See Ponomarev, "Kolokola," 3; Dobson, "Youth Problems," 227–251; Fierman and Olcott, "Youth Culture," 245–262.

4. On 'male associations' (*Männerbünde*) in the Islamic world see Axel Havemann, "Männerbünde im islamischen Orient: Soziale Bewegungen in Iran, Irak und Syrien," In *Geregeltes Ungestüm: Bruderschaften und Jugendbünde bei indogermanischen Völkern*. Edited by Rahul P. Das and Gerhard Meiser (Bremen: Hempen, 2002) and Franz Taeschner, *Zünfte und Bruderschaften im Islam: Texte zur Geschichte der futuwwa* (Zürich: Artemis-Verlag, 1979).

5. See the compilation by Qurbon Voseʿ, *Adabiyoti ğavonmardii Toğiku Fors*, 2 vols. (Dušanbe: Doniš, 2007).

6. Kenğaev, *Tabadduloti 1*, 51–52 and *Tabadduloti 2*, 141. Kamāl ad.-Dīn Ḥoseyn Vāʿeẓ Kāšefī (1436–1505) completed his essay on ethics and statecraft *Aḫlāq-e moḥsenī* around 1501/2, his authorship of the *Fotovvatnāme-ye solṭānī* is disputed, see Maria Subtelny, "Husayn Vaʾiz-i Kashifi: Polymath, Popularizer, and Preserver," *Iranian Studies* 36, no. 4 (2003), for the importance of Persian Mirror for Princes literature see Patricia Crone, *God's rule: Government and Islam* (New York: Columbia University Press, 2004), 148–164.

7. Kenğaev, *Tabadduloti 2*, 64 ("peši man ğavonmard on buvad, kamtarin koraš fidoi ğon buvad").

8. Kenğaev, *Tabadduloti 1*, 367.

9. Julie Gilmour and Barbara E. Clements, "'If You Want to Be like Me: Train!': Contradictions of Soviet Masculinity," In *Russian masculinities in history and culture*, Edited by Barbara E. Clements, Rebecca Friedman and Dan Healey (New York: Palgrave, 2002), 210.

10. Cf. Kislyakov, *Tadžiki* or R. Raximov, *'Mužskie doma' v tradicionnoy kul'ture tadžikov* (Leningrad: Nauka, 1990).

11. Buškov and Mikul'skiy, *Anatimiya*, 80.

12. Buškov and Mikul'skiy, *Anatimiya*, 82.

13. Karim, *Faryodi*, 243.

14. Karim, *Faryodi*, 188.

15. See S. Nazarzoda, *Farhangi tafsirii zaboni Toğikī* (Dushanbe: Pažūhišgohi zabon va adabiyot ba nomi Rūdakī, 2008).

16. Diane E. King, "The Personal is Patrilineal: Namus as Sovereignty," *Identities* 15, no. 3 (2008): 317. For *nomus* in Tajikistan and Central Asia see Colette Harris, *Muslim youth: Tensions and transitions in Tajikistan* (Boulder: Westview Press, 2006), 71; Madeleine Reeves, "Staying Put? Towards a Relational Politics Of Mobility at a Time of Migration," *Central Asian Survey* 30, 3–4 (2011): 563–566. On *nomus* and şeref (šaraf) see Werner Schiffauer, *Die Bauern von Subay: Das Leben in einem türkischen Dorf* (Stuttgart: Klett-Cotta, 1987).

17. Rağab Munkī and Amiršoh Xatlonī, *Nomus* (Dušanbe: Paik, 1994).

18. For Iran see Afsaneh Najmabadi, "The Erotic Vaṭan [Homeland] as Beloved and Mother: To Love, To Possess, and To Protect," *Comparative Studies in Society and History* 39, no. 3 (1997).

19. Yūsuf, *Tāğīkestān*, 33.

20. Yūsuf (*Tāğīkestān*, 74) depicted the story of Zarifova with insinuation to the Pavel Morozov case in 1932. See Orlando Figes, *The whisperers: Private life in*

Stalin's Russia (New York: Metropolitan Books, 2007), 122–126 and the biographical entry in Osimī, *Enziklopediyai*, Vol. 2, 469.

21. Yūsuf, *Tāǧīkestān*, 116.

22. To some extent, Sohibnazar (*Subhi 1*, 187) acknowledges this development.

23. Dostiev, *Toǧikiston*, 148–158.

24. Cf. Kalyvas, *Logic*; Koselleck, *Futures past*, 115–127.

25. See the narratives of Būrī, Nasriddinov and Sohibnazar. Cf. Tunçer-Kılavuz, *Power*, 107–129.

26. Cf. Ganev, "Post-communism"; for Kyrgyzstan see Scott Radnitz, *Weapons of the wealthy: Predatory regimes and elite-led protests in Central Asia* (New York: Cornell University Press, 2010) and Alexander Kupatadze, *Organized crime, political transitions and state formation in post-Soviet Eurasia* (New York: Palgrave Macmillan, 2012).

27. See: Akiner, *Tajikistan*, 25–26; Dobson, "Youth Problems," 227–251; Riordan, *Soviet youth* or Lousie Shelley, "Crime in the Soviet Union." In *Soviet social problems*, Edited by Anthony Jones, Walter D. Connor and David E. Powell (Boulder: Westview Press, 1991).

28. Quoted in Sohibnazar, *Subhi 1*, 295–299.

29. Buškov and Mikul'skiy, *Anatimiya*, 81; Nourzhanov and Bleuer, *Tajikistan*, 302–304.

30. Usmonov, *Nabiev*, 82.

31. Charles Tilly, "War Making and State Making as Organized Crime." In *Bringing the state back in*, Edited by Peter B. Evans, Dietrich Rueschemeyer and Theda Skocpol (New York: Cambridge University Press, 1985), 170–171. Max Horkheimer, *Gesammelte Schriften* (Frankfurt am Main: Fischer, 1985), Vol. 12, 287–291.

32. Kenǧaev, *Tabadduloti 2*, 193–194. Cf. Janine R. Wedel, "Corruption and Organized Crime in post-communist States: New Ways of Manifesting old Patterns," *Trends in Organized Crime* 7, no. 1 (2001).

33. For Saidov's self-stylization see the video on http://www.youtube.com/watch?v=J04qUtpDs_s Accessed October, 5 2014.

34. The term *rėket* was already used by Varlam Šalamov (a writer and Gulag survivor) in his *Kolyma Tales* (written between 1954 and 1973). See Caroline Humphrey, "Russian Protection Rackets and the Appropriation of Law and Order," In *States and illegal practices*, Edited by Josiah M. Heyman (New York: Berg, 1999) and A. Gurov, *Professional'naja prestupnost': Prošloe i sovremennost'* (Moskva: Juridičeskaja literatura, 1990); Kenǧaev, *Tabadduloti 1*, 62; Nasriddinov, *Tarkiš*, 180.

35. Greta Uehling, "Dinner with Akhmet," In *Everyday life in Central Asia: Past and present*, Edited by Jeff Sahadeo and Russell G. Zanca (Bloomington: Indiana Univ. Press, 2007), 128.

36. Sohibnazar, *Subhi 2*, 281.

37. For *blat* (cronyism) see Sheila Fitzpatrick, *Everyday Stalinism: Ordinary life in extraordinary times. Soviet Russia in the 1930s* (Oxford: Oxford Univ. Press, 2000), 62–65 and Alena Ledeneva, *Russia's economy of favours: Blat, networking, and informal exchange* (New York: Cambridge University Press, 1998).

38. Yūsuf, *Tāǧīkestān*, 207.

39. Conversations with a former driver from a motor depot in Qūrǧonteppa (Dushanbe, May 2004). See also Kenǧaev, *Tabadduloti 3*, 19 and 76.

40. Qurbon Zardakov (an organizer on Ozodī Square) was the director of the stadium and central sports facilities in Kūlob, Sūhrob Qosimov, Ġaffur Mirzoev, Mirzoxuġo Nizomov (IRPT), Maġnun Pallaev (field commander in Badaxšon) and Ibodullo Būydoqov (a criminal in Dushanbe) were Karate/Sambo teachers. Mūso Iso graduated from Dushanbe's Sports University and was a prominent ringer and Karate champion.

41. Cf. James Riordan, *Sport, politics, and communism* (Manchester: Manchester University Press, 1991); for the post-Soviet context see Kupatadze, *Organized crime*, 140–180.

42. Kenġaev, *Tabadduloti 1*, 340.

43. Observations by the author in Xuġand and Dušanbe in 2003 and 2004.

44. Kenġaev, *Tabadduloti 1*, 62; Sohibnazar, *Subhi 2*, 180.

45. Sohibnazar, *Subhi 2*, 223.

46. Nasriddinov, *Tarkiš*, 200–204.

47. Usmonov, *Nabiev*, 62–63.

48. Kenġaev, *Tabadduloti 1*, 281.

49 See the interview with Davlatmoh Xoġaeva on Radioi Ozodī (http://www. ozodi.org/content/article/24626789.html Accessed November 5, 2015.

50. Sohibnazar, *Subhi 1*, 201.

51. Usmonov, *Nabiev*, 61.

52. Yūsuf, *Tāġīkestān*, 185.

53. Kalyvas, "Ontology," 475.

54. Kalyvas, "Ontology," 475–6.

55. Sohibnazar, *Subhi 1*, 211; Yūsuf, *Tāġīkestān*, 186.

56. Nasriddinov, *Tarkiš*, 198–209.

57. As observed by Christopher Clapham, "Introduction: Analysing African Insurgencies," In *African guerrillas*, Edited by Christopher S. Clapham (Bloomington: Indiana University Press, 1998) and Alex Veit and Klaus Schlichte, "Zur Legitimierung bewaffneter Gruppen," In *Bürgerkriege erzählen: Zum Verlauf unziviler Konflikte*, Edited by Sabina Ferhadbegović and Brigitte Weiffen (Paderborn: Konstanz University Press, 2011).

58. Nasriddinov, *Tarkiš*, 286–293.

59. In the Xoruġ Protocol, Safarov was mentioned as "deputy commander of the national guard of the Kūlob *viloyat*" in a handwritten insertion. See the reproduction of the protocol in Kenġaev, *Tabadduloti 2*, 21–23.

60. Medvedev, "Saga," 202–204.

61. Veit and Schlichte, "Legitimierung," 153.

62. Benedickt Korf and Timothy Raeymaekers, "Geographie der Gewalt," *Geographische Rundschau* 64, no. 2 (2012): 8.

63. See (Der Spiegel), "Tadschikistan: Stalins Blut," *Der Spiegel*, no. 4 (1993): 143–50; Serge Schmemann, "War Bleeds Ex-Soviet Land at Central Asia's Heart," *The New York Times*, February 21, 1993: 1 & 12.

64. Whilst Safarov was certainly not a *vor v zakone*, he perhaps was an *avtoritet* in the periphery of the Soviet organized crime. *Avtoritet* is considered a lower rank in the hierarchies of Russian/Soviet organized crime comparable to a *capo* in Mafia structures.

65. Medvedev, "Saga," 204.

---

276 Chapter 7

66. My Tajik respondents decidedly rejected Safarov's claims and Medvedev ("Saga," 188) is also skeptical about the Safarov's narrative.

67. Medvedev, "Saga," 188.

68. Sohibnazar, *Subhi 1*, 211. Cf. also Yūsuf, *Tāğīkestān*, 186. Conversation with Davlat Usmon, Mirbobo Mirrahimov and Ibrohim Usmonov, Bishkek, September 2013.

69. Quoted in Karim, *Faryodi*, 477.

70. Sohibnazar, *Subhi 1*, 201–202; see also Connell and Messerschmidt, "Hegemonic," 848.

71. FBIS-SOV-92-221, 16 November 1992, 83; Medvedev, "Saga," 202–203; Nasriddinov, *Tarkiš*, 167 and Xaliliyon, "Se xatoi."

72. Medvedev, "Saga," 189–90.

73. Sohibnazar, *Subhi 2*, 80–81.

74. Sohibnazar, *Subhi 2*, 84.

75. Medvedev, "Saga," 188.

76. Safarov cites the ballade of *ešoni* Sulton which was sung by the local population in the area: "400 armed *ğigit* [a Kyrgyz term for 'young man'] captured the *ešon* and enchained him / Entire Darvoz gathered and kneed down in front of Maxsum they cried out / Release him, release him / All armed men from Vahyo were at the town gates / whilst it was silent around / *ešon* Sulayman said / There is no truth in this world / Our Destiny is on Judgement Day / And went directly into the Fire" (Medvedev, "Saga," 194).

77. Medvedev, "Saga," 188–190, 195.

78. Medvedev, "Saga," 195.

79. FBIS-SOV-93-005, 8 January 1993, 33; Nasriddinov, *Tarkiš*, 287–293.

80. Medvedev, "Saga," 203.

81. Karim, *Faryodi*, 476.

82. Conspiracy theories circulated about a Russian/Uzbek or government involvement. See Karim, *Faryodi*, 642; Kenğaev, *Tabadduloti 3*, 142; Sohibnazar, *Subhi 2*, 209–211; FBIS-SOV-93-060, 31 March 1993, 73–74.

83. Sohibnazar, *Subhi 2*, 253–254.

84. The official newspaper of the Tajik MVD, *Qonun va ğomea* (Law and Society), frequently publishes obituaries of MVD officers who were killed during the Civil War under the caption "They will not be forgotten (*Onho faromūš nameăvand*)!" At times, the obituaries indicate that the deceased officer fought in a militia and not in the MVD. See for instance Nosir Nazarzoda, "Fayzullo Saidov (1959–1992)," *Qonun va ğomea*, January 14, 2016, 2:13.

85. Kenğaev, *Tabadduloti 3*, 93 & 97.

86. Sohibnazar, *Subhi 2*, 253–254.

87. Yūsuf, *Tāğīkestān*, 260; Kenğaev, *Tabadduloti 1*, 351–353.

88. For the various movies on Jagga Jatt see: http://www.imdb.com/title/tt0231809/. On his biography see: http://www.jattworld.com/online/tale-jagat-singh-jagga-jatt-robinhood-punjab Access August 10, 2012.

89. Kalyvas, "New and Old," 100.

90. Kalyvas, "New and Old," 117.

Chapter 8

Civil War

In the morning of 5 May, a group of protestors from Šahidon Square occupied the TV and Radio Station and Rahim Mosalmoniyon (DPT) went on air with an idealistic but naïve appeal (considering the illegal seizure of the station):

> We need to have a democratic society from tomorrow on. This is either the moment of building (ğomeasoz) or of burning the society (ğomeasūz). All depends now on the government, either it dresses in camouflage fatigues or it resigns from its positions. Truth is with the people, truth is with Šahidon Square.[1]

At the same time the appeal was broadcasted, the first fatal clashes were reported from Olii Sovet, a southern suburb of Dushanbe. Although the sequence of events is contested, a conflict between two youth gangs from Kūlob and Dushanbe turned violent leaving three men dead including the head of the local militia of the Leninsky district, who tried to mediate between the two sides.[2] Violence reached the center of Dushanbe a few hours later when Muradullo Šeralizoda, the editor of the government newspaper *Sadoi Mardum*, was shot at the back entrance of the Supreme Soviet.[3] The violence prompted Nabiev to declare the state of emergency in the evening. After a phone conversation between Nabiev and Yeltsin, the 201st MRD was deployed to guard sensitive facilities in Dushanbe but did not intervene in the violent confrontation. Major General Mahmadğonov was appointed commander of the Dushanbe garrison and ordered to set up check-points and to disarm civilians, however he had virtually no troops under his command to enforce the state of emergency. The announcement was only broadcasted on radio since the opposition had already taken over the TV station and refused to air Nabiev's order.[4] Worse, Nabiev's administration was not even able to contact the MVD and convey the orders for the state of emergency since the minister (Navğuvonov) and leading officers did not respond to calls indicating that the MVD had disintegrated or become partial in the conflict. Realizing his powerlessness, Mahmadğonov resigned on 6 May and Nabiev decided not to reappoint another garrison commander.[5] At this point—in the early morning hours of 6 May 1992—the situation for the demonstrators on Ozodī Square deteriorated: Parts of the MVD sided with the protestors on Šahidon Square and youth gangs from the southern and western parts of Dushanbe attacked the protestors on Ozodī Square. Previous conflicts and competition within Dushanbe's criminal milieu contributed to the confrontation.[6] During the day, sporadic fighting between the supporters of Ozodī and Šahidon took place, in which the combatants from Šahidon prevailed. Youth gangs, who knew the city terrain better than the demonstrators on Ozodī, applied permanent pressure with a hit-and-run tactic using small side alleys and blocking access to supplies. In the early evening hours Olim Zarobek, a founding member of Rastoxez, and Širin Amirğon, a journalist, were fatally wounded by gunshots close to the Radio and TV studio.[7] Conflicts and serious differences had appeared among the leaders on Ozodī, in particular between Safarov, Abdurahimov, Mirzoaliev and Šarifov: Without consulting with the other leading figures, Šarifov had reportedly offered a ceasefire including their withdrawal to Kūlob—he even announced to respect Tūrağonzoda's authority as *qozikalon*.[8]

GOVERNMENT OF RECONCILIATION OR COUP D'ÉTAT?

In late April, Nabiev realized that Kenğaev played a duplicitous game and that he could neither rely on the Leninobodī elites nor the protestors on Ozodī Square. Therefore, he entered confidential negotiations with the opposition. Without consulting Kenğaev, he offered the opposition the inclusion to the government.[9] Reportedly Rizo Tursunov, who had just returned to Tajikistan after two years of absence succeeding Kenğaev as chairman of the NSC/KGB, organized the secret talks. Initially, Nabiev favored the establishment of a special "state council" with opposition representation instead of a formal inclusion of the opposition into the government. But the opposition insisted on its formal inclusion and Tursunov advised Nabiev with acquiescence of the Yeltsin administration to accept their demands.[10] In the early morning hours of 7 May 1992, Nabiev agreed with representatives of the IRPT, DPT, Rastoxez, La'li Badaxšon and Nasiri Xusrav on the formation of the Government of National Reconciliation (GNR, *Hukumati musolahi millī* or *Hukumati murosoi millī*, Russ.: *Pravitel'stvo nacional'nogo primireniya*). Although not involved in the negotiations, Kenğaev and Dūstov were summoned to Nabiev's office to sign the protocol.[11] As a quid quo pro Nabiev would stay in office—a compromise, which was severely criticized by Bozor Sobir and

Davlat Usmon, who demanded the formation of an entirely new government without Nabiev. Tūrağonzoda, Sohibnazar and Iskandarov, however, called for reconciliation and argued that Nabiev was the legally elected president. Reportedly, the commanding officer of the 201st MRD, Major General Ašurov, and the commanding officer of the KGB Border Guards, Major General Martovitsky, had urged the opposition to accept Nabiev's offer.[12]

The GNR's Charta

The next morning, Radio Dushanbe announced the agenda of the Government of National Reconciliation: The GNR vowed to work for the common good (*salohiyat*) and re-establish the rule of law in Tajikistan (*huquqbunyod*). The prevention of violence and disarmament of irregular militias ranked high on the agenda: The GNR announced the dissolution of the Presidential Guard and the subordination of the National Defense Committee (the former KGB) under the GNR (and not anymore under the president). Likewise, the GNR dismissed Otaxon Sayfulloev, the chairman of the state Radio and TV Committee, and assumed control over the committee. The protocol agreed on the dismissal of Dūstov and Niyazov, but postponed the decision on the resignation of Kenğaev and Huvaydulloev. Finally, it was agreed that the property of the CPT was transformed into public ownership and 8 May was declared a day of public mourning.[13] Nabiev, Kenğaev, Dūstov and Niyasov signed the protocol on behalf of the government, Himmatzoda, Yusuf, Abduğabbor, Xudonazar and Amirbek on behalf of the opposition. Akbar Tursunov, Abdurašid Rahimov and Otaxon Latifī signed the protocol as witnesses. Tūrağonzoda did not sign the protocol insisting that the *qoziyot* was not a political institution.[14]

The agreement on 7 May left several issues untouched, in particular the representation of the IRPT in the interim government. The GNR was formed on 11 May mostly with representatives of the "ancient regime" in central functions: Nabiev as president, Akbar Mirzoev as chairman of the Council of Ministers and Akbaršo Iskandarov as chairman of the Supreme Soviet replacing Kenğaev. Mirzoev, the former chairman of the Kūlob and Qūrğonteppa Ispolkom between 1987 and 1992, had been appointed chairman of the Council of Ministers in January was considered a compromise candidate. Mamadayoz Navğuvonov remained minister of interior.[15]

The opposition occupied only a few positions: Mirbobo Mirrahim became the chairman of the state TV and Radio Committee, Xudoberdy Xoliqnazarov minister of foreign affairs and Davlat Usmon (IRPT) vice-chairman of the Council of Ministers. Importantly, the members of Presidium of the Supreme Soviet changed. With the inclusion of Tūrağonzoda and Sohibnazar the composition and political weight in the Presidium shifted in favor of the opposition. For the next months, the Presidium became the central political institution in Dushanbe while the Supreme Soviet—the legislature—was paralyzed and convened only once for the 15th Session.

The inclusion of the IRPT in the GNR was certainly the most contentious issue and on the initial cabinet list distributed on 11 May, no IRPT representative was included. Himmatzoda and Nurī had demanded that Davlat Usmon should be appointed vice-president, which Nabiev rejected categorically. Eventually, the IRPT agreed on a compromise, which left the office of the vice president vacant and Nabiev appointed Usmon to the position of the deputy chairman of the Council of Ministers.

The secular opposition, in particular the DPT, hesitated to support Usmon's appointment. Yusuf considered him in his memoirs as too inexperienced and a too controversial choice for the position.[16] Sohibnazar raised similar concerns: Although he considered Usmon as an able politician, he worried that his appointment would further polarize the public and play right into their opponents' hands.[17] Unsurprisingly, Kenğaev echoed these concerns in his comment on Usmon's appointment:

> See, let us judge, who is the opposition: The IRPT, the *qoziyot*, DPT and the people's associations Rastoxez and La'li Badaxšon. They came to power by exerting pressure and by bloodshed [...]. But look, whom they appointed Deputy Prime Minister of the Republic responsible for the law enforcement agencies fighting criminality and providing security for the state [...]. Davlat Ismon [Usmon], born 1952, «higher» education, graduated with agony and many problems in 1990 from the law faculty of Tajikistan's State University. He earns his life as a sunflower seeds' vendor, meaning he buys sunflower seeds from somebody and sells them with some *tin* profit. He has neither the slightest idea nor minimal experience to be responsible for the law enforcement, national security or the protection of the law.[18]

Kenğaev reminded his readers that Usmon was responsible for the hostage taking of the 18 deputies of the Supreme Soviet during the 13th Session on 21 April 1992 which triggered the "bloody events of May."[19] He concluded: "For the leaders of the opposition, the protocol was only a sly deception, which gave them time for gathering weapons and deploying their forces. Their words had nothing in common with their deeds."[20]

Gravediggers of the Constitutional Order?

The establishment of the GNR increased the centrifugal forces in the country: On 14 May, the Leninobod provincial Soviet discussed the political situation and Huvaydulloev called the establishment of the GNR a coup d'état. The Leninobod Soviet demanded the restoration of the constitution and a statement by Nabiev against the activities of the opposition.[21] Kenğaev

concluded that Nabiev and the GNR bypassed the Supreme Soviet and violated the constitution by subordinating the NSC under the GNR, whom he
called "gravediggers of the constitutional state (*gūrqovi davlati qonunī*)."[22]
He accused the opposition of establishing parallel structures and in particular
the *qoziyot* acted "as a state within the state."[23] At the same time Kenğaev
criticized his mentor Nabiev for his indecisiveness, which eventually paralyzed the entire government and allowed the GNR to happen: "Both, the government and the presidential administration watched the opposition violating
against the constitution without interfering and declaring their neutrality.
[...] Everybody was waiting for orders from the President or another senior
administration official, but nobody gave orders."[24]

Although Ašūrboy Imomov, the chairman of the Constitutional Control
Commission, evaluated the GNR's protocol as constitutionally acceptable,
the interpretation of the constitution remained contentious for months to
come.[25]

Nabiev's Political Survival Strategy: Neutrality

Nabiev's political survival did not come as a surprise: The opposition claimed
to be champions of the rule of law and Nabiev was the legally elected president. Importantly, external actors, such as Russia and the USA, considered
Nabiev as the legitimate president as well.[26] Since Kenğaev and Dūstov had
been excluded from the negotiations, the opposition was optimistic about
a more meaningful cooperation with Nabiev—or they thought they could
at least manipulate him as Kenğaev had done before.[27] Sohibnazar and
Usmonov pointedly remarked that the opposition paradoxically saved Nabiev,
since they expected that Kenğaev and the northern elites would have deposed
Nabiev the moment they deemed appropriate.[28]

Nabiev portrayed himself in a noncommittal way as "neutral" and floating
above the mundane conflicts between Kenğaev and the opposition. Sohibnazar
concluded that Nabiev's frequent declarations of neutrality "were the reason
for the increasing powerlessness of the government [...] and the neutrality
of the President was certainly a reason for the outbreak of the Civil War."[29]
Sohibnazar did not only criticize Nabiev for his noncommittal behavior, but
other representatives of the political elite as well, such as Navğuvonov:

> The same Navğuvonov whose honor was defended by Šahidon Square less than
> two months ago has now decided in the moment of confrontation to become
> neutral [...]. [W]e have repeatedly made clear that these declarations of neutral-
> ity by the president, the Chairman of the Supreme Soviet, the Prime Minister,
> the Minister of Interior, the Chairman of the KGB or the General Persecu-
> tor—as well as the non-recognition of the GNR by the governors of Kūlob and
> Leninobod—will not extinct the flames of war.[30]

Nabiev or Navğuvonov referred to their ostensible neutrality as if they were not involved in the developments and Kenğaev came to a similar assessment as Sohibnazar:

> Neutrality was considered by a significant number of ministers, officials as well as the republican intelligentsia as the right way, whilst they were closely observing the daily situation. They were bystanders, people with no backbone, they were and they are double-mined and two-faced, since their soul is afflicted by the same infectious disease of regionalism; they were hypocrites.[31]

EVACUATION OF OZODĪ SQUARE AND THE ARREST OF SANGAK SAFAROV

After the protocol between the opposition and Nabiev had been signed, Abdulloh Habibov, a deputy in the Supreme Soviet and MVD general, mediated between the two squares and reached an agreement: The protestors on Ozodī would clear the square and enjoy safe conduct for their return to Kūlob. Servicemen of the 201st MRD escorted the protestors to busses and Davlat Xudonazar accompanied them to the Šar-Šar Pass (the provincial border with Kūlob).[32] However, not all demonstrators from Ozodī Square had left Dushanbe: In the afternoon of May 7, the opposition arrested Sangak Safarov, his brother Davlatalī and Rustam Abdurahimov in the headquarters of the Border Troops behind the Ğomī Cinema on Ozodī Square. Different narratives have emerged about their arrest, confinement and eventually, on 12 May, their release. Most of the reports agree that Safarov and his companions were kept for five days in the basement of the presidential administration where they were interrogated, beaten and exhibited on TV "confessing" their crimes and misdeeds.[33] At the same time, the state TV—now under GNR control—aired features on the deserted Ozodī Square showing broken bottles of vodka, used heroine syringes, condoms, torn women's clothing and garbage apparently left behind by protestors from Kūlob defaming them as "uncivilized," "primitive" and "uncultured."[34]

In his version of the events Safarov reported how he trusted the assurance of the opposition and stayed behind to organize the orderly return of the demonstrators to Kūlob. He soon realized that the opposition had different plans when Tūrağonzoda ordered (in Safarov's narrative) that the deserted square should be "prepared." When rumors circulated that the body of a young woman had been found in a ditch close to Ozodī Square, Safarov and his companions decided to take refuge in the headquarters of the Russian Border Forces. After a brief confrontation, the Border Forces handed Safarov over to the opposition. Tūrağonzoda then ordered his criminal henchmen to interrogate and torture them. The arrest and exhibition on TV of Safarov and

Abdurahimov was an affront and public humiliation of Kūlob nourishing demands for revenge and retaliation.[35]

Remarkably, the opposition indeed released Safarov and his companions a few days later. Several opposition representatives considered Safarov's arrest as a violation of the protocol and Davlat Xudonazar actively campaigned for their release. IRPT and DPT members from Kūlob likewise insisted on Safarov's release since they were concerned about reprisals against their families and followers in Kūlob.[36] Usmonov remarked, that in early May 1992 "the wave of inhumanity had not reached its peak."[37] The opposition portrayed the release of Safarov as a manifestation of their peaceful intentions and willingness to compromise and reconciliation.[38] Importantly, at this time Safarov was not yet considered to be such a central actor in the Kūlobī faction. Obviously, the opposition in Dushanbe considered the incumbent political nomenklatura in Kūlob, such as Mirzoaliev or Šarifov, as the key players and Safarov only as their subaltern henchman and therefore not important enough for making an example for the opposition's resoluteness by—for instance—executing him.[39]

In his interview with Vladimir Medvedev, Sangak Safarov offered an additional explanation for his release, namely the solidarity among the criminal authorities in Tajikistan regardless of their regional or political affiliation: Rahim[bek] Nurullobekov, a criminal *avtoritet* from Badaxšon, who had sided with the opposition on Šahidon, extended his "protection" according to the criminal code of conduct to a rival but fellow criminal *avtoritet*, Sangak Safarov, prohibiting physical torture and eventually securing his release.[40]

Perhaps, there was another reason for the opposition to release Safarov and send him back to Kūlob: The interrogation disclosed divisions and conflicts among the different local actors in Kūlob, in particular between the political office holders, local security officials and informal strongmen (or violent non-state actors) such as Safarov. With his release and return, the opposition apparently expected to increase the tensions in Kūlob. The Safarov brothers and Abdurahimov were released on 12 May and Davlat Usmon drove them to the Šar-Šar Pass and handed them over to Muhammadloiq Fazilov, one of the IRPT members in Kūlob. Fazilov accompanied them to Kūlob but—contrary to the agreement—was arrested and five months later executed.[41]

THE FAILURE OF THE GOVERNMENT
OF NATIONAL RECONCILIATION

There is only a muted debate and no research about the period of the GNR in Tajikistan between May and November 1992. Monica Whitlock, then the regional BBC correspondent, maintains that the GNR was the "most radical political experiment by any state of the former Soviet Union. It faced enormous odds. The men in charge of the country [...] had no reason to trust one another, and had no experience of managing public affairs."[42] Contemporary Tajik history textbooks do not share Whitlock's appraisal of the GNR and portray it as an unconstitutional or Islamist government, which was finally removed by Emomalī Rahmonov restoring order, the rule of law and "peace."[43]

In May 1992, the formation of the GNR created further tensions in Tajikistan due to its weak legitimation: it was neither elected by the people nor approved by the Supreme Soviet and Kenǧaev's verdict of a coup d'état cannot be dismissed categorically.[44] Revealingly, Sohibnazar (himself a member of the GNR) remarked that nobody in the GNR actually wanted general elections to the Supreme Soviet since the IRPT and DPT were far from sure to reach a majority.[45] The opposition again exhibited contradictions between their political ideals and actual political performance. These contradictions were not only reflected in the way the GNR was established but also in its composition: Not a single non-Tajik was appointed to a higher position and only two women were represented in secondary positions.[46] Throughout its tenure from May to November 1992 the GNR frequently bypassed the legislature and ruled with presidential decrees. Various political initiatives, such the establishment of a "national assembly" or the subordination of the security forces under the government, violated against the constitution and undermined the legitimacy of the GNR even among oppositional politicians.

The political conflict should not conceal the catastrophic economic and social crisis in Tajikistan aggravating the political tensions and diminishing the government's room to maneuver. The economic decline dramatically accelerated in 1992 with an unprecedented GDP contraction of 30% and an inflation of staggering 1,150% (according to conservative assessments).[47] Sohibnazar, who briefly chaired the National Bank in May, calculated that the Tajik government needed around 600–700 million rubles a month (at that time approximately 108–126 million USD) for paying its employees but had virtually no income from taxation. The severe economic downturn had a dramatic impact on people's life and the situation rapidly deteriorated after the dissolution of the USSR and its integrated centrally planned economy. Since December 1991, the central heating facility in Dushanbe did not receive sufficient fuel supplies to meet the demand resulting in electricity blackouts as well as insufficient heating. The situation in the rural regions of Tajikistan was even worse, since the demand for coal could not be met due to insufficient imports and the collapse of the transport system.[48] Simultaneously, many of the non-Central Asian nationalities who were overrepresented among the technical staff in heating facilities, electricity station, sewage and water treatment plants and so forth were emigrating from Tajikistan leaving behind a public administration that could not cope with the situation.

In 1991/92 the food supply in Dushanbe was on the verge of collapse since the collective farms in the Qarotegin Valley, Qūrġonteppa and Kūlob did not fulfil their quotas for food production and suspended their deliveries to Dushanbe.[49] On 21 January 1992 the government introduced a rationing system for butter (40g/month), sugar (200g/month) and vegetable oil (200g/month). A month later the US embassy commenced humanitarian aid for Tajikistan.[50] Although the population in Tajikistan had endured the social and economic crisis since the late 1980s with resilience and adaptability, the situation worsened during spring and summer 1992 adumbrating the catastrophe to come. The struggle for commodities intensified conflicts among local communities and neighborhoods.

Centrifugal Forces

The political nomenklatura in Leninobod and Kūlob immediately repudiated the GNR: On 12 May, the Kūlob Ispolkom declared Nabiev's decrees on the establishment of the GNR as unconstitutional and two days later the deputies in Leninobod followed suit. The GNR's influence was from the beginning limited to Dushanbe, the eastern Hisor valley, Qarotegin and parts of Qūrġonteppa.[51] For Nasriddinov, Nabiev became a marionette (*lūxtake*) in the hands of Tūraġonzoda and the GNR was like puppetry in which the various incompetent politicians fought for power and influence.[52] Even representatives of the GNR, such as Sohibnazar, conceded that the GNR was crippled from the very beginning for three reasons: First, the political elites in Leninobod and Kūlob did not recognize the interim government; second, Nabiev did not mediate—as expected by some—between the different groups but remained inactive; third, the other leading office-holders, in particular Iskandarov and Mirzoev, never took a clear position and assumed a neutral position in the unfolding conflict.[53]

An important impediment to the work of the GNR was the ambivalent commitment of key opposition representatives. Their commitment was muted to such an extent that both its representatives *and* adversaries labelled the GNR as "opposition."[54] Yusuf, for instance, refused to accept a government position and rejected a ministerial portfolio with ostentation claiming that he never wanted a position portraying himself as a person with integrity floating above daily politics of deceit and duplicity.[55] Sohibnazar resigned as chairman of the National Bank after a few days in office, but remained a member of the Supreme Soviet's Presidium.[56]

While Nurī, Himmatzoda and Usmon managed to uphold discipline and unity within the IRPT, the secular opposition—in particular the DPT gradually disintegrated. In April, the popular poet Bozor Sobir had a falling out with Šodmon Yusuf about the strategy of the DPT and quitted the

party—others followed soon. Deep mistrust prevailed between the opposition and Nabiev. In a press conference on 22 June 1992 Yusuf announced
the establishment of the National Salvation Staff (*Sitodi naǧoti millī*) and
accused Nabiev of indecisiveness, complicity with criminal elements calling him a destabilizing factor in Tajikistan.[57] Himmatzoda remarked in an
interview with *Čaroǧi rūz* that Nabiev did not understand his duties and
obligations:

> He only talked about the plan, cotton and so forth. This is basically the portfolio
> of the government, the Council of Ministers and the Prime Minister. The Presi-
> dent should think about domestic and international politics, the relation with
> other countries, as well as the long-term political and economic perspectives.
> [...] [Nabiev] does not understand his role. He does not have any political expe-
> rience. Certainly, he had some leadership experience, but that time it was from
> another viewpoint, since Tajikistan was then only a province, a district [in the
> USSR], where his duty was simply to implement the orders of the center.[58]

The opposition-controlled media described Nabiev as a duplicitous personality and circulated rumors about his secret contacts with Kenǧaev, Dūstov,
Huvaydulloev and others.[59] *Vice versa*, Nabiev harshly criticized the performance of opposition representatives in the government. In an interview with
Krasnaya Zvezda in July 1992 he described the confrontational atmosphere
in the GNR and announced that he would rather resign than to continue to
work with Mirzoev.[60] He did not resign however, but circumvented cabinet
decisions or reshuffled government positions without consulting Mirzoev.

Last but not least, the GNR did not control any significant security forces
except for a few MVD units. Instead, the government had to negotiate support
with local strongmen and Islamist activists, such as Mullo Abduǧaffur (Yužniy
district in Dushanbe), Rizvon (Kofarnihon), *qorī* Qiyomiddin (Ǧozimalik),
qorī Saidašraf (Qūrǧonteppa) and *qorī* Muhammadī (Kolxozobod). Criminal groups, such as Rauf Saliev or Yaqub Salimov, likewise did not follow
categorical loyalties but changed sides according to personal and contingent
considerations.

Although the opposition—among them several journalists—understood the
importance of favorable media coverage and therefore engaged actively with
the Dushanbe-based press corps, erratic comments by key opposition politicians soon turned the public opinion against the GNR[61]: Yusuf threatened to
take Dushanbe's Russian population hostage and his deputy, Mosalmoniyon,
added demands for the dissolution of the parliament with *Marg bar Amriko*
("Death to America"), a slogan, which was all too well-known from demonstrations in the Islamic Republic of Iran.[62]

Finally, the domestic TV and radio broadcasting was blocked in the regions. Due to the mountainous terrain, radio and TV had to be transmitted through local relay stations, which at the same time aired local radio programs. In summer 1992, the militias targeted some of the relay stations and eventually the Radio and TV Committee in Dushanbe could only transmit its program in Dushanbe, parts of the Hisor valley and Qarotegin.[63] Kūlobī forces occupied the relay stations at the Guliston kolkhoz (close to Sangtuda) and in Tošrabot in mid-May 1992 and renamed the local radio station in Kūlob *Radioi Ozodī* ("Freedom Radio," not to be mistaken with today's Tajik branch of Radio Free Europe/Radio Liberty), which played an important role in the counter-mobilization by broadcasting fabricated "news" on atrocities committed by the opposition.[64]

The National Assembly

Theoretically the GNR had an ambitious political agenda including the reconciliation between the conflicting factions and the preparations for general elections to the Supreme Soviet. Facing an intractable legislature—the Supreme Soviet in its 12th Convocation—with opaque and shifting majorities and insubordinate regions, the GNR envisaged strategies to bypass the legislature. One of the central initiatives was the establishment of an 80-seat national assembly, which should act as an interim legislature until the adoption of a new constitution (scheduled for August) and general elections (scheduled for December 1992).[65] Half of the members of the national assembly were supposed to be deputies from the Supreme Soviet elected in 1990, whilst the other half were to be appointed among the opposition. Notably, the opposition was silent on *who* should select these representatives in the national assembly and *how* the appointment should be organized.[66] The political elite in Dushanbe, however, was either at odds with each other or not overly enthusiastic about the establishment of a national assembly and until the dissolution of the GNR on 25 October 1992, the assembly remained a phantom and never met for a constitutive meeting. Likewise, the GNR never presented a draft for the new constitution.

Most of the Tajik accounts agree that the Government of National Reconciliation failed. The memoirs are usually silent about the controversial nature of some of the decisions such as the establishment of the national assembly. Even after the GNR failed to convene the national assembly, Yusuf continued to demand an ad hoc convocation of a state council, the suspension of the presidential office or the dissolution of the Supreme Soviet without any electoral process. The establishment of the National Salvation Staff was a comparable initiative to circumvent existing institutions.[67]

The inclusion of the IRPT isolated the GNR in the region, but the erratic behavior of key politicians, like Yusuf, who operated with conspiracy theories aspersing any external involvement, exacerbated the already tense situation. Usmonov concluded that Yusuf was "a politician who had no idea about politics"[68] and that the key personalities in the opposition were only "theatre actors in a noise instigated by the democrats whilst the puppet master was Tūrağonzoda."[69] Kenğaev stated that the Government of national Reconciliation never gained "influence, reputation and respect"[70] among the people, since it was dominated by some intellectuals who had no idea how to tackle Tajikistan's problems—in particular, they neglected the rural communities, and there the civil war raged with unprecedented violence and brutality.

The Relation to the Russian Federation

The relationship between Tajikistan and the Russian Federation after the dissolution of the USSR was as expected complex and developed far from linear. The Yeltsin administration was domestically absorbed by the tremendous transformation in Russia and had only limited capacity to influence the Tajik developments let alone to formulate a consistent Central Asian strategy in 1991/92. For the Tajik government, the relations to the Russian Federation were of paramount importance: Tajikistan's public service and economy depended on the former Soviet institutions and the 201st MRD as well as the KGB border guards continued their service under Russian command. Despite these dependencies, the Tajik government agreed on the bilateral treaty with the Russian Federation only on 21 July 1992 (most of the other former Soviet republics had signed similar agreements earlier). The treaty addressed political, economic and humanitarian issues, including the formal subordination of the Border Guards in Tajikistan under Russian jurisdiction.[71] Pressured by Russia, Nabiev demanded from the Presidium and the cabinet of ministers an additional legislative act guaranteeing the rights of national minorities in Tajikistan.[72]

The vital relationship with the neighboring republics of Central Asia—in particular Uzbekistan—remained strained since they did not acknowledge the GNR as Tajikistan's legitimate government. When the GNR requested military hardware in the summer and autumn of 1992, none of the CIS states declared its readiness to provide supplies for the government in Dushanbe. Instead, many reports confirm that the Uzbek air force provided airlift capacity and supplies to the Popular Front while Russia deployed GRU commandos operating with the militias from Kūlob.[73]

THE 201ST MRD IN THE ESCALATING VIOLENCE

After the establishment of the GNR, the discussion about the nationalization of the 201st MRD flared up again. Nabiev had adopted an ambiguous and inconsistent policy adjourning the decision on the 201st MRD. He still contemplated the recruitment of a national or presidential guard, despite the disastrous mobilization of a "guard" on Ozodī Square on 1 May. On 12 June 1992 he again decreed the establishment of a National Guard—the third initiative within less than six months followed by a fourth decree on 14 August 1992. But the government could neither allocate the resources nor muster sufficient servicemen.[74] The opposition instead demanded the nationalization of the 201st MRD and complained that its deployment undermined Tajikistan's sovereignty. The division should be nationalized and become the basis for Tajikistan's armed forces. Yusuf brushed aside budgetary and financial constraints and assured that Tajikistan would be able to mobilize sufficient financial resources to support both, the National Army and the Border Guards.[75] In their memoirs, Kenğaev and Sohibnazar likewise considered Nabiev's unwillingness to nationalize the 201st MRD as one of his most serious mistakes.[76]

Since May 1992, the 201st MRD became more and more entangled in the conflict. On 6 May, an official car of the 201st MRD was attacked killing an officer and his driver. On 10 May, an armored combat team with several tanks and APCs blocked access to the KGB headquarters after prolonged fighting between militias from Šahidon Square and KGB operatives. The 201st MRD suppressed the fighting and secured an apartment block close to the KGB building in which officers and their families were living. Presumably, the military intervention allowed the KGB operatives to destroy the archive, evacuate the building and escape from Dushanbe (see below). Throughout the next months, different militias raided installations of the 201st MRD in Dushanbe, Qūrġonteppa and Kūlob in order to seize weapons, ammunition and military hardware.

Since 1990 the personnel strength of the 201st MRD had been continuously reduced by redeployment of the non-Central Asian officers, desertion and insufficient conscription levels (conscription calls were ignored by the local population), and the composition of the division changed substantially. In the summer of 1992, the division could only muster some 750 servicemen. Ninety six percent of the officers were Russian, Ukrainian and Byelorussian, and only a few servicemen were conscripts from Tajikistan and the Turkestan Military District.[77]

In May, Mirzoev addressed the status of the 201st MRD at the Tashkent CIS Summit. Although his government did not consider the nationalization of the division, he urged the Russian government to allow the 201st MRD a more interventionist role. In late May the commanding officer agreed to back up MVD units at checkpoints in Dushanbe with the 92nd MRR.[78] With increasing violence and further deterioration of security in the south, the Tajik government requested additional support by the 201st MRD to guard the sensitive facilities such as the Norak Hydroelectric Dam, the Yovon Electro-Chemical Plant and the Vaxš Nitrogen Fertilizer Plant in Kalininobod. On 2 July 1992 the Russian minister of defense Pavel Gračev and the CIS Joint Armed Forces commander-in-chief Yevgeniy Šapošnikov agreed with Nabiev on an extended support by the 201st MRD taking over the security at the above mentioned facilities including patrols at the Čormaġzak and Šar-Šar Passes northwest of Norak on the vital road connecting Dushanbe with Kūlob.[79] In return the Tajik government pledged to supply the 201st MRD but already in mid-September Major General Ašurov ordered the withdrawal of the 201st MRD units from Yovon, Vaxš and the Čormaġzak Pass since the troops did not receive sufficient supplies. At the same time, Safarov's militias threatened 201st MRD servicemen and occupied the Šar-Šar and Čormaġzak Passes as well as (albeit briefly) the city of Norak in September.[80]

Throughout the summer and autumn, officers as well as rank-and-file servicemen of the 201st MRD were increasingly caught in the crossfire between the conflicting factions. In most of the cases, local combatants tried to seize light weapons, small arms and ammunition, at times even APCs or tanks.[81] The IRPT and DPT suspected complicity between officers of the 201st MRD and the field commanders in Kūlob (see below).[82] Yusuf insisted that servicemen of the 201st MRD were implicated in the incident at Sari Pul close to Kuybišev in the Boxtar district. On 27 July 1992, a group of civilians from Sari Pul came under fire leaving several dead and wounded. In divergent narratives, either servicemen of the 201st MRD or militias of the IRPT were accused of atrocity. Yusuf demanded the immediate withdrawal of the 201st MRD from Tajikistan in a populist tone blaming Russia and the Russian military for the continuous violence and insinuating Uzbekistan's hidden hand in the events.[83] The editor of *Čaroġi rūz*, Dodoġon Atovulloev, issued a similar statement accusing the 201st MRD of interfering in Tajikistan's domestic affairs and cooperating with anti-democratic forces against the GNR.[84] Sohibnazar related an anecdote about Supreme Soviet deputies visiting the barracks in Qūrġonteppa: A Russian officer allegedly addressed him with the words: "You Tajiks threaten us. But we made you humans (*mo šumoro odam kardem*). You were like animals before. And now you (*tu*) are dressed with a suit, you even wear a tie, from whom did you learn this?"[85] The Russian officer threatened Sohibnazar to hand him over to Safarov's militia if he does not pay ransom: "In case you do not pay USD 10,000, Sangak will buy you. Now, this is all business (*biznes*). What are we? We are like calves which either serve you or Sangak. The war is yours, but the weapons are ours."[86] Sohibnazar's story is difficult to verify but other respondents likewise reported about corrupt officers offering their "services" and his portrayal of the officer as a rude, racist and corrupt Russian highlights the anti-colonial sentiment among opposition politicians.

While the DPT and IRPT implicated the 201st MRD in the atrocities against civilians, Safarov, Abdurahimov and Kenğaev supported its deployment as the last line of defense against Islamist militias and Iranian espionage. Major General Ašurov asserted that none of the division's outfits was involved in the conflict and that none of the factions received any support by the 201st MRD.[87] However, most of the sources report that the equipment of the 201st MRD was an important source for weapons procurement in summer and autumn 1992, in particular for the militias from Kūlob. Sohibnazar concluded that the "civil war was not anymore fought between the people from Ġarm and Kūlob, but was organized by groups who were interested in positions and in particular the profits from dealing with arms."[88]

The Slavic officers in Kūlob and Qūrġonteppa were exposed to intimidations and extortion. The disintegration of the USSR disrupted supply, replacements and remuneration. The deteriorating situation demoralized the servicemen, undermining discipline and the officers' authority. Among the non-Tajik officers there was little readiness to get involved in a local conflict; most of them did not understand and the illicit sale of military equipment became a profitable business in the south. Official statements usually downplayed the involvement of the division in the conflict, but several officers conceded their involvement in the conflict. The commander of the 149th Guards MRR in Kūlob, Colonel Laktionov, cooperated closely with the Kūlobī militia and provided substantial logistical support to them. The field commander Ismoil Ibrohimov (Kūlob) conceded that most of the military equipment his militia used in 1992 had been provided by the 149th Guards MRR and Sangak Safarov boasted to a correspondent from the German weekly *Der Spiegel* in January 1993 that the local garrison in Kūlob only takes his orders.[89] Langarī Langariev, a former MVD officer, was well connected among the former Soviet security institutions providing access to arms and ammunition. On 27 September 1992 Langariev's militia raided the barracks of the 191st MRR in Qūrġonteppa taking 5 officers hostage and seizing three tanks and one APC. According to one version of the events, deserted Tajik and Uzbek servicemen supported Langariev.[90]

After heavy fighting in Qūrġonteppa and an increasing number of desertions, the Russian ministry of defense decided to reinforce the 201st MRD with 800 additional troops in September 1992.[91] Although substantial reinforcement came only in 1993 with the establishment of the CIS peacekeeping force, GRU/Spetcnaz commandos were sent to Tajikistan and the accounts by some of the officers, such as Kolosov, Kvačkov and Sukholesskiy, of their deployment to Tajikistan in 1992 leave little doubts about their involvement in the civil war.[92] Although officially sent as reinforcements for the 201st MRD, the GRU/Spetcnaz immediately provided logistical and tactical support for the militias from Kūlob. Kolosov reported how he closely operated together with the militias of Safarov and Saidov. Sukholesskiy, who labeled his group of GRU/Spetcnaz as "informal advisors (*neoficial'nym sovetnikam*) to the [Popular] Front's leader Sangak,"[93] described in detail the heavy fighting at the Šar-Šar Pass in autumn 1992. Although details are often exaggerated and it is difficult to tell fact from fiction, Kolosov's fragmentary report on the difficult cooperation with the erratic Fayzalī Saidov and duplicitous Sangak Safarov in Qūrġonteppa is credible and supported by complementary sources. Considering the deviance, contingency as well as confusion in civil wars and the complex situation after the disintegration of the USSR, the GRU/Spetcnaz operatives might have decided without formal orders to fight with the militias from Kūlob against the "Islamists."[94] The Russian GRU/Spetcnaz operatives did not mention any support for Kenġaev's militia. But Kenġaev insinuated that he received external support by referring to "Boris" and "Sergey," whom he labeled as "experts in the art of war."[95] The Tajik Civil War—as well as other conflicts in the wake of the USSR's dissolution—attracted (former) servicemen of the Soviet Armed Forces to offer their skills as mercenaries, many of them *afgancy*, veterans from the Soviet war in Afghanistan, who had difficulties to re-integrate into civilian life, compounded by the social and economic crisis of the 1980s, and often romanticized their military service in Afghanistan as a time of male solidarity.

The distrust between non-Central Asian officers and the Central Asian rank-and-file aggravated throughout the summer and Major General Ašurov decided to disarm the remaining Tajik servicemen in September.[96] At that time, the 191st MRR in Qūrġonteppa, which had a nominal strength of 2,000 men, was down to 52 servicemen, 49 of them officers. A similar situation was reported from the 149th Guards MRR in Kūlob.[97] During his visit in August, the commander-in-chief of the CIS Armed Forces, Marshal Yevgeni Šapošnikov, discussed with Nabiev the deployment of a CIS Peace Keeping force after a general cease-fire agreement. With Šapošnikov, a delegation of some 30 CIS military observers travelled to Tajikistan in order to familiarize with the situation.[98]

In autumn, Kyrgyzstan's President Akayev launched a first regional initiative to mediate in the Tajik conflict ahead of the CIS Head of State Summit in Bishkek scheduled for 10 October. Akayev sent his Vice President, Feliks Kulov, to Tajikistan in mid-September in order to facilitate negotiations between the Kūlobī commanders and acting President Iskandarov.[99] Following Kulov's mission, Akayev ordered the deployment of a battalion of volunteers (80 servicemen, later to be extended to 400) as a peacekeeping force to Tajikistan, however the Kyrgyz Parliament vetoed the deployment.[100] The Yeltsin administration considered a more robust mandate for the 201st MRD, but the final agreement signed on 6 November between Iskandarov and Lieutenant General Vorobyov affirmed the 201st MRD's neutrality in the conflict and only sanctioned the use force in self-defense or in case civilians are under immediate threat.[101]

The Situation at the Afghan Border

The situation at the border with Afghanistan became increasingly volatile throughout 1992. Trespassers from and to Afghanistan infiltrated the border area and clashed with border troops.[102] Shortly after the outbreak of violence in May, the Border Guards reported multiple violations of the border to Afghanistan by Tajiks crossing into Afghanistan to purchase weapons and ammunition. In particular Guldbuddin Hekmatyar's *Ḥezb-e Eslāmī* was said to supply IRPT militias.[103] After a serious incident on 30 June 1992, Himmatzoda conceded contacts to Rabbanī government but repudiated claims the IRPT would purchase weapons in Afghanistan.[104] Although IRPT representatives always stressed their cordial relationship with the iconic and popular field commander Ahmad Shah Massoud of the Northern Alliance, a high-ranking field commander admitted in a personal conversation, that the IRPT first contacted Hekmatyar in search for weapons in 1992.[105] Also self-defense groups crossed into Afghanistan and made contact with local Afghan field commanders to purchase ammunition, small arms and light weapons. Fragmented reports suggest, that relatively little money was involved and an AK-74 could be bought for 30–40 USD.[106] Since early 1992, the guards had detained more than 4,000 illegal trespassers and confiscated some 70 weapons and goods worth 5 million rubles (albeit adding that this was only an evanescent percentage of the actual contraband volume). Two border guards were killed in firefights with trespassers.[107] The border guards remained deployed at the border throughout the conflict until 2004. With the opposition's withdrawal to Afghanistan, the border guards were repeatedly attacked by opposition insurgents, one of the worst attacks was led by Mullo Abdurahim on 13 July 1993 on a border guard outpost in the Šūroobod *nohiyya* which left 25 Russian border guards dead.[108]

ARSON ATTACK ON THE KGB AND SECRET PARTY ARCHIVE

On 10 May 1992, opposition protestors from Šahidon Square marched toward the KGB headquarters south of Ozodī Square demanding the dissolution of the agency. According to an *Izvestiya* correspondent the armed protestors suddenly came under fire and a ferocious gun battle broke out which was only ended by intervention of the 201st MRD, which had been dispatched to evacuate the families of KGB and military officers in a near-by apartment complex.[109] The fighting in front of the KGB headquarters left 8 people dead and 11 severely wounded. During the attack, arson destroyed large parts of the republican KGB archive including the Secret Communist Party archive. The opposition immediately implicated Rizo Tursunov in the arson. Tursunov was a veteran KGB officer who had served as deputy KGB chairman during the February 1990 events. After the events he had silently transferred to a position outside the TaSSR, but in May he returned to Tajikistan to replace Kenğaev as chairman of the National Security Commit-tee and advise Nabiev.[110] During the negotiations on the composition of the GNR, the opposition demanded the dismissal of Tursunov for his role in the February events, who was noticed of his dismissal on 10 May. On the same day, he allegedly ordered the arson on the KGB archive in order to destroy incriminating files on KGB operations (and his role in the February events). After the arson, Tursunov immediately left Tajikistan for Russia where he made a career as one of Putin's *siloviki* and vice-president of *Rosneft*, the Russian state oil company.[111]

However, there are alternative narratives on the motifs and persons behind the arson: Since the fire did not only destroy the documents dealing with the February events but also the files of informants among the Islamist activists, some believe that archive was destroyed by IRPT activists who intended to conceal their duplicitous role as KGB informants and now feared the political takeover by the opposition and the exposure of their identities.[112] Although both narratives are in general plausible, the first version is more likely for two reasons: First, the IRPT leadership knew very well that the KGB had infiltrated their ranks since the early 1980s. Nurī's own brother reported to the KGB and several activists, such as Sultan Hamad or Mahmadalī Hait served in the security structures of the USSR. Second, one could easily conjecture that translations and copies of selected KGB files were forwarded to Moscow or Tashkent since there was a continuous coming and going of Islamic activ-ists between the UzSSR and the TaSSR.

CONTINGENCY, CONFUSION AND COMPLEXITY IN CIVIL WAR

Although some political actors had sensed the increasing confrontation in April 1992, most of them described the immediate outbreak of violence as an unforeseen "accident," an escalation that was not planned or expected to happen.[113] In the first months of the civil war there were no clearly delineated fronts and when in the summer of 1992 a multiplicity of local militias emerged, they were usually gathered and held together by a local strongman with connections to the political nomenklatura, organized crime and/or the security forces. Though the political agenda generated some perfunctory unity or cohesion, it did not prevent serious and at times fatal power struggles. In summer the media and government identified militias according to their field commanders and not necessarily a political faction: Among the better known were Langarī Langariev (Kūlob), Sangak Safarov (Kūlob), Fayzalī Saidov (Kūlob), Ġaffur "Sedoy" (the Grey) Mirzoev (Šar-Šar)[114], Yaqub Salimov (Kūlob and Dushanbe), Sūhrob Qosimov (Kūlob and Dushanbe), Mullo Abdurahim (Kūlob), Ġumʿaxon Būydoqov (Dushanbe), Mullo Abduġaffur (Dushanbe) and Rizvon Sodirov (Kofarnihon/Dushanbe).[115] Most of these field commanders and their militias were initially not firmly aligned to a particular regional or political faction but acted out of very personal motivations and Nasriddinov remarked, that there was no "genuine solidarity (*hambastagii fitrī*)"[116] among the militias. Sometimes combatants claimed to represent a political party but suddenly defected to the opposite side. In the early violence in Kūlob individual combatants claimed to be members of the IRPT, but Himmatzoda conceded that he had no information about these individuals and their affiliation with the IRPT.[117]

The former first secretary of the CPT in Qūrġonteppa, Odilbek Qurbonbekov, reported about a complete breakdown of public order in September 1992. Local youth gangs, intoxicated with alcohol and armed with hunting rifles and self-made explosives, were fighting against each other indiscriminately assailing and abducting civilians for ransom. The political crisis in Dushanbe, the deterioration of public security and law enforcement accelerated the societal fragmentation of the Tajik society. The motivations, intentions and background for the mobilization and the outbreak of violence on the local level were manifold, but often local actors referred the master narrative of Tajikistan's civil war—regionalism, the disintegration of the Soviet state, ideological cleavages including Islam and the severe economic crisis. The collapse of state institutions allowed individuals to take revenge for alleged injustice suffered in the past, to proliferate as local racketeers offering "protection" filling the void left behind by the dissipated MVD or simply to secure access to resources. Qurbonbekov's narrative does not indicate fixed regional solidarities or political/ideological affiliation in the fighting but mostly confusion, contingency and rapidly changing circumstances.[118]

In the early stage of local mobilization in May/June 1992, there is little evidence that Nabiev intentionally "activated" his local networks. Not even Safarov, Abdurahimov, Šarifov or Mirzoaliev seemed to have control beyond the city limits of Kūlob. Loyalties shifted and local contenders suddenly marginalized the established Soviet elites—arguably most dramatically in Kūlob.

The breakdown of the security structures facilitated the emergence of local self-defense groups throughout Tajikistan.[119] According to many accounts, individuals—sometimes in the name of a larger family or local neighborhood—purchased small arms and light weapons, set up road blocks and formed vigilante groups generating or increasing the local security dilemma ultimately prompting neighboring communities to follow suit.[120] A relative of Sohibnazar from Qūrġonteppa described the confusing situation:

> Now I own two automatic rifles. I have no idea what to do. I need to go to Qūrġonteppa, but I have no idea what will be the result of this mischief. What should I do with these rifles? With whom I should join sides? For me [the distinction between] a Ġarmī and a Kūlobī does not exist. In my village, perhaps 60 to 70 families are originally from Kūlob and about the same number from Ġarm live there. Additionally, there are families from Samarqand and Bukhara as well as Uzbeks. How can I be at war with them?[121]

Kenġaev and the (former Soviet) security establishment maintained that Afghanistan's Islamist militias provided the IRPT with weapons and ammunition conjuring a continuity of the Afghan War. Most reports indeed indicate that Afghanistan's vast and uncontrolled market for second hand weapons became indeed an important source of supply for the Tajik conflict. But in September 1992 the National Security Committee issued an assessment that only 10–15% of the weapons in the Tajik conflict were contraband weapons and ammunition from Afghanistan; most of the military hardware came from within Tajikistan.[122] In rural areas, hunting rifles and self-made explosives were widespread. In some collective farms tractors (such as the tracked DT-54) were refitted to makeshift tanks.[123] Although Kenġaev described the establishment of the Popular Front as a coordinated military operation, he conceded that the more important development was the establishment of local self-defense groups, organized in the collective farms without any subordination to a higher-ranking command.[124]

It is difficult to estimate the size of the various militias in the early period of the civil war due to the general confusion and conflicting sources. In interviews and memoirs relatively small numbers are provided: The militias of Langariev, Saidov, Safarov, Abduġaffur and others reportedly consisted only of few men. Kenġaev reported that "his" Popular Front in Hisor set up local commands of 10–20 men (obviously at the same time local defense groups) while he was training some 500 men in the Fan Mountains north of Hisor. Langariev, one of the most popular field commanders in the early civil war, only commanded 40 men when he was ambushed and fatally wounded close

to Norak in October 1992. A Russian Spetcnaz officer reported that Fayzalī
Saidov's militia numbered some 300 men in September 1992.[125]

In autumn, several larger militias proliferated and claimed more formal
structures such as the National Guard of Kūlob (*Gordi millii Kūlob*), the
National Salvation Guard of Vaxš (*Gordi Millii Naǧoti Vaxš*), the National
Salvation Staff (*Sitodi Naǧoti Vatan*) in Dushanbe or the Popular Front
(*Fronti Xalqī*) in Hisor. In Kūlob, Sangak Safarov was able to incorpo-
rate or eliminate some of the smaller armed groups, Langariev's militia
dissolved after he was fatally wounded in October and Fayzalī Saidov
remained an independent field commander and rival to Safarov only
occasionally coordinating affairs with him until they killed each other in
March 1993. In order to institutionalize his militia as part of the government forces, Safarov labeled his militia since October/November as the
Popular Front.

DUSHANBE MAY–OCTOBER 1992

Although the situation in Tajikistan's capital Dushanbe calmed down after
10 May, the atmosphere remained tense and an "unspecific fear and danger
loomed over the city."[126] On 23 May 1992, Nabiev addressed the nation in a
TV speech and appealed for the unity of the Tajik nation. But according to
Usmonov, nobody was listening to him anymore since the situation in the
south deteriorated rapidly. There was no joint public appearance of key GNR
representatives and no unified call for peace.[127] The GNR had only a limited
capacity to enforce public security in the city. Rival youth gangs and local
self-defense groups from different districts such as Ispečak, Avūl, Yužni and
Šohmansur competed with the understaffed and demoralized MVD over control and the GNR had to negotiate "security" with different local strongmen.
The 201st MRD guarded a few sensitive facilities in the capital including
its own premises but did not intervene in the conflict throughout the summer. Disorder and insecurity prevailed including random exchanges of fire,
abductions, extortion, sexual violence against women and assassinations.
On 24 August 1992, Procurator General Nurullo Huvaydulloev was intercepted in the early morning on Rūdakī Prospect and executed by gunmen.
The group of Rahimbek Nurullobekov, a criminal from Badaxšon, was widely
implicated in the assassination. Nurullobekov was arrested and transferred to
a detention facility in Xuǧand. But shortly after his arrest, his accomplices,
Ǧum'axon Būydokov, Ismat Habibulloev and Mullo Abduǧaffur, occupied
the presidential administration and demanded Nurullobekov's immediate
release in the last day of August shortly before Nabiev's resignation—political issues became inextricably entangled with criminal activities.[128]

The insecurity, disorder and violence forced thousands of people in the south to flee from their homes. Many fled to neighboring Afghanistan, Kyrgyzstan and Uzbekistan but in the early months of the conflict the majority of refugees fled to Dushanbe where the municipality accommodated them in the city's hotels and surrounding sanatoriums. In June/July, more than 150,000 people had fled the fighting in Qūrġonteppa area and in October 1992 Sohibnazar estimated the number of IDPs at 200,000.[129] A few weeks later—after Sangak Safarov's militia had attacked Qubodiyon and Šahrtuz— the number of IDPs had risen to 430,000.[130] In December 1992 UNHCR commenced its assistance to Tajik refugees in northern Afghanistan counting some 62,000 refugees in the Taloqan area on 8 December.[131]

The violence and disorder dramatically accelerated the exodus of non-Central Asian nationalities from Dushanbe substantially changing the composition of the capital's population. While until 1991 70,000 out of 390,000 Russians had left Tajikistan (plus several thousand Germans, Byelorussians and Ukrainians), more than 100,000 Russians emigrated from Tajikistan in the first months of 1992. In May 1992, the Central Asian Railway container freight capacity from Tajikistan to destinations in Russia was occupied until 1994 and black market prices for a single container (70,000 rubles) almost matched the price for a three-room apartment in Dushanbe (100,000 rubles). The emigration of Russians and other non-Central Asian nationalities resulted in an atypical development of the labor market—while unemployment in less skilled professions multiplied, an acute shortage of trained workforce was reported in vital technical fields such as maintenance of central heating stations, electricity generation and so forth. In an interview with *Pravda* on 9 April 1992, Nabiev remarked that the most skilled workers and specialists had left Tajikistan, which accounted for the sharp decline in industrial production and endangered the electricity and water supply of the capital.[132] But not only non-Tajik nationalities were leaving the country as a journalist for *Nezavisimaya Gazeta* reported in his bleak outlook for Tajikistan:

> The loss of intellectual potential is compounded by the fact that almost all of the Tajiks who have left or are planning to leave the republic are skilled specialists with a fairly high level of education. If the political system in Tajikistan continues to move in the opposite direction from the "civil society," the severe regression of this state as a result of pervasive brain drain will be unavoidable.[133]

The "National Salvation Staff"

On 20 June 1992, 14 representatives of the IRPT, DPT and La'li Badaxšon, among them Yusuf, Nurī, Abduġabbor, Sohibnazar, Karim, Himmatzoda and Bobonazarova, established the "National Salvation Staff (*Sitodi naġoti millī*)" as an umbrella organization to unite all "patriotic forces" in Tajikistan. The National Salvation Staff demanded the transfer of military authority to its headquarters and the recruitment of a defense battalion supporting the official security forces.[134] With the National Salvation Staff the opposition intended to bypass Nabiev, his government and the Supreme Soviet. Karim, Abduğabbor and Bobonazarova were well aware that Tajikistan's constitution did not provide any legal provision for the establishment of a parallel government institution and their reformulation could not conceal the violation against the constitution.[135] The National Salvation Staff could not prevent the further disintegration of the GNR as well as the opposition's military defeat and remained a marginal episode.

KŪLOB MAY–JULY 1992

After the events in early May in Dushanbe, the violence moved south to Kūlob and Qūrġonteppa. The GNR announced a general amnesty until 10 May for those from both squares who would surrender their weapons. But neither the protestors on Šahidon nor on Ozodī complied with the request. The deadline was extended to 20 May, but only a few outdated weapons were submitted.[136]

The protestors from Ozodī Square returned to Kūlob on 8 May and on the following day, Haydar Šarifov invited for a meeting in his mosque to discuss the developments. The tone was belligerent and the assembly decided to establish a National Guard under the command of Langarī Langariev and Said Salimov.

Šarifov first turned against representatives of the *qoziyot*, such as Mullo Abdurahim (Karimov), and sympathizers of the IRPT in Kūlob. Langariev's militia went from city district to city district expulsing suspected opposition sympathizers and their families. The IRPT leadership reported on 15 May, that 10 of their members had been killed and many wounded in Kūlob. The Polytechnic Institute No. 38 was transformed into a prison where alleged IRPT sympathizers were tortured and killed.[137] Yusuf graphically reported on the situation, where "the blood of the youth, the intellectuals and the Muslims was spilled in the alleys of Kūlob."[138] According to his account, dozens of people were brutally tortured and killed, extended families were collectively punished and property depredated.[139]

When Safarov and Abdurahimov returned to Kūlob on 12 May, divisions within the regional faction became obvious. Safarov wanted to make some-body responsible for his personal humiliation. In a blunt move he turned against the political nomenklatura in Kūlob and announced that Qurbon Mirzoaliev, the chairman of the Kūlob Ispolkom, should be removed from his position. In a public meeting, Safarov appointed Habibullo Tabarov, a CPT cadre from Xovaling, to replace Mirzoaliev.[140] But he miscalculated his influence and he failed to mobilize sufficient support to depose Mirzoaliev. According to a fellow field commander, Safarov was even briefly arrested in Kūlob and held in the Šayx Kamol Mosque before he left for Kalininobod 50 km west of Kūlob in the eastern Qūrġonteppa area, where he set up his headquarters. With his move to Kalininobod, Safarov distanced himself from the official political leadership in Kūlob and established himself as an independent field commander. At this time, Safarov did not have a cognizable political project—instead he destroyed the old order.[141]

The defeat on Ozodī Square had divided the Kūlobī elite and on the local level competing groups emerged: Safarov united the criminal networks and youth gangs from the region behind him, whilst Abdurahimov and Haydar Šarifov maintained the former Soviet institutions and established their militia with the support of the local MVD under the command of Langariev. Safarov accused Šarifov of cowardice since he had allegedly fled Ozodī Square dressed as a woman among a group of female demonstrators during the evacuation on 7 May. Furthermore, Safarov suspected that Šarifov had embezzled funds donated for the demonstrations on Ozodī—both accusations Šarifov repeatedly denied. Additionally, the relation between Abdurahimov and Safarov was obviously strained after their imprisonment. Reportedly, Safarov had been told during his detention that Abdurahimov was in fact a KGB informant with the alias "Richard."[142] Rumors, insinuations and suspicions fall on fertile soil and Safarov distanced himself from the political nomenklatura in Kūlob and eventually turned against them dramatically highlighting the deep divisions within the Kūlobī faction. He politically marginalized Haydar Šarifov and personally executed Qurbon Zardakov (a rival strongman) and the Ispolkom chairman Rizoev. In fierce fighting, he annihilated the rival militia of Ġomī Mizonov in Danġara and later deceived Kenġaev in the attack in Dushanbe.

Similarly, Kenġaev's establishment of the Popular Front was more divisive than unifying underlining the fragmentation of the factions into various armed groups led by individual field commanders. This fragmentation complicated any attempt to mediate in the conflict. Not anymore the "traditional" Soviet nomenklatura controlled the terms of negotiation and bargaining but individual actors from the margins of the Soviet society, that is, racketeers, criminals, thuggish martial arts trainers or directors of *avtobaza*.

In June 1992, Langariev had consolidated his position in Kūlob and attacked the eastern part of Qūrġonteppa. He ordered the Uzbek and Kūlobī population of the area to leave since the Ġarmī population allegedly planned to expel them. Some 10,000–15,000 people actually followed their orders and left for Danġara.[143] In the Kalininobod district, Safarov's militia was implicated in widespread looting and robbery. Reportedly, Safarov occupied a gold mine in Šuġnov/Darvaz (where his father had worked in the 1920s) in August 1992 and seized some 170 kg of gold, which allowed him to purchase weapons and vehicles from Russian officers. In any case, Safarov was able to compensate military losses (according to some estimations he lost 47 APCs between June and September 1992).[144]

In June 1992, militias from Qūrġonteppa were able to blockade the main road between Dushanbe and Kūlob at the Šar-Šar Pass and—in only five-kilometer distance—the Čormaġzak Pass.[145] Both passes allow armed groups to control the access and transport to the Kūlob region. Throughout the summer the area saw intense fighting which interrupted transport to the south and aggravated the overall shortage of supplies in the region. In 2012 the weekly *Millat* conducted several interviews with the local population who considered the blockade as the "oil that fueled the Civil War."[146] Since the major road connection passed through Kofarnihon, Tūraġonzoda's home region, the *qozikalon* was accused of ordering the blockade.[147] In late August 1992 the militias of Safarov, Langariev and Saidov occupied Šar-Šar and Čormaġzak and extended their control over Yovon and Norak. Although the Kūlob Ispolkom chairman Mirzoaliev conceded in September that the Kūlobī militias had lifted the blockade, he nonetheless complained that the central government in Dushanbe (which the Kūlob Ispolkom did not recognize) failed to provide the necessary supplies for more than a month resulting in widespread shortages and even the death of 10–15 children each day. According to Mirzoaliev more than 30,000 refugees—mostly ethnic Uzbeks—had fled to Kūlob from Qūrġonteppa resulting in a severe shortage of food and medical supplies.[148] While the suffering of the population was certainly real, some of the reports were exaggerated. Since early September Uzbekistan flew in supplies by helicopter once or twice a day from Termez (sometimes via Tursunzoda in the Hisor valley). The garrison of the 149th Guards MRR had a landing facility and local field commanders used the helicopter service as well.[149] Despite the blockade, planes bound from Dushanbe to Kūlob were still dispatched and flew to Kūlob throughout the summer and autumn 1992, therefore some observers consider the "blockade" of Kūlob as a justification for the following military assaults on Qūrġonteppa and Dushanbe.[150]

QŪRĠONTEPPA JUNE–OCTOBER 1992

While in Kūlob the political nomenklatura was challenged by violent non-state actors, the provincial authority in Qūrġonteppa disintegrated along regional and professional lines in the different districts and collective farms.[151] The densely populated lower Vaxš valley—from Sarband (then Kalinino-bod) over Qūrġonteppa to Ġilikūl in the south—witnessed intense fighting and widespread destruction. As often in civil wars, the situation and fault lines were much more complex than the conflict's master narrative. Militias of Kūlob, Ġarm and Dushanbe, criminal groups, MVD detachments from Dushanbe, neighborhood self-defense groups from the surrounding collective farms, mercenaries and Russian servicemen fought a confusing war with shifting loyalties and changing alliances. The composition of the population of the Qūrġonteppa region contributed to the complexity as well: Large *muhoğir* communities from Ġarm, Badaxšon and Kūlob lived next to the significant Uzbek minority population. In the subunits of collective farms, the population was relatively homogenous. High population growth, low rural out-migration and a deteriorating social and economic situation compounded the local and regional tensions. Local self-defense groups and the security structures in Qūrġonteppa were divided, some recognized the GNR in Dushanbe others sided with the militias from Kūlob.[152] The IRPT was particularly strong in the Yakumi May/Turkmenistan sovkhoz (the home of Abdullo Nurī's family close to Vaxš), in Kalininobod (Saidašraf Abdulahadov), in Kuybišev, Kolxozobod, Kumsangir and Ġilikūl. In late June, IRPT militias organized an attack on the nearby Leningrad kolkhoz. The assault left more than 100 people dead and resulted in a wave of internal displaced persons fleeing from the fighting. The GNR in Dushanbe denied any military involvement or control of the armed groups operating in the area.[153] In July, fighting intensified in the districts of Boxtar, Vaxš, Kalininobod and Qūrġonteppa. The acting chairman of the Qūrġonteppa province, Nurullo Qurbonbov, urged Nabiev to declare the state of emergency in the province and reported that some 200 people had been killed or abducted by the opposing forces, entire villages had been abandoned by the population whilst the number of refugees reached more than 150,000. The agricultural areas had been deserted and the irrigation systems destroyed.[154] Between June and September, the IRPT militias prevailed in Qūrġonteppa and were able to arrest the advance of Langariev and Safarov.

On 25 July 1992, leading DPT and IRPT members, such as Nurī, Usmon, Qiyomiddin and Himmatzoda, Aslonov, Yusuf, Xudonazar, *qorī* Muhammadğon, *ešoni* Saidašraf met in the Turkmenistan sovkhoz and organized a meeting of the "Mountain People" (*mardumi kūhistonī*) under the slogan "From Vanğ to Panğ"[155] in order to coordinate their activities and in preparation of the forthcoming peace talks in Xoruġ (see below). However, the military situation soon deteriorated.

On 24 August 1992, fighting between the different groups sharply increased in and around the Kuybišev sovkhoz north of Qūrġonteppa. Although the MVD tried to intervene, Navğuvonov had to admit that his forces were not able to enforce the state of emergency in the region.[156] On 2 September, the militias of Langariev, Safarov and Saidov launched heavy attacks on opposition militias under the command of Muhammad Salomov (IRPT) in Qūrġonteppa.[157] Safarov led a surprise incursion into the city center where he addressed an intimidated public on the main square—but this time local militias fought back and expulsed Safarov from the city after heavy fighting.[158]

The militias from Kūlob had suffered significant losses during the fighting in Qūrġonteppa including most of their APCs. Therefore, they suspended their campaign and local militias were able to restore order in the city.[159] In the meantime, Safarov's militia briefly occupied Norak and the nearby HPP, but he withdrew after the 201st MRD prepared to intervene and secure the HPP.[160] Obviously, Safarov did not want to risk a serious confrontation with Russian military at this point—and the Russian military did not want a dubious local field commander to control such a sensitive target as the world's highest dam with a reservoir capacity of 10.5 km³ water. The military course of events, the many skirmishes, attacks and counter-attacks, are poorly (if at all) documented. Several contingent coups de main are frequently narrated in the sources as sudden unexpected developments, which changed the military situation suddenly.[161]

It took the militias from Kūlob until mid-October 1992 to occupy Qūrġonteppa and dislodge the opposition.[162] Until then, the fighting in the south killed approximately 20,000–30,000 people and displaced more than 150,000 refugees from the Qūrġonteppa *viloyat* alone. However, the data on the casualties are fragmented, contradictory and unreliable.[163]

Vovčik and Yurčik: Constructing Antagonisms

In the unfolding conflict, two central terms—*vovčik* and *yurčik*—emerged subsuming the antagonist parties.[164] The *vahhobī* label circulated already in the 1980s and Sohibnazar attributed the term to the anti-opposition campaign by the nomenklatura since 1990. The term *vovčik* (or *vahhobovčik*) as a variation of *vahhobī* popularized in 1992, while the term *yurčik* for "Russified" Tajiks developed as self-designation.[165] According to Karim, the terms became increasingly important in the conflict, and the meaning of *vovčik* transformed:

> First, a *vovčik* was essentially a member of the IRPT, later also a member of the DPT or Rastoxez. Eventually, all the people of Kofarnihon, Rašt as well as Badaxšon and as a whole those who supported the nationalist and religious movements, the liberals and the intellectuals were considered to be *vovčik*. *Yurčik* were essentially the people from Kūlob, the opponents of the nationalist movements, the supporters of Communism and the devotees of the Soviet Union (*sovetiparaston*).[166]

Kenġaev, Šarifov and Safarov used the term *vovčik* indiscriminately for any of their opponents. Šarifov addressed the mourners during a funeral service for Sayfiddin Sangov (who had been killed by Mullo Abduġaffur) with the words: "My Muslim brothers, see what the *vohhobiyon* truly are.

We all, young and old, have to unite behind Bobo Sangak in order to free the Tajiks from this sort of people." [167] The Russian Spetcnaz officer Kolosov reported about the shortest briefing in his military career by an officer of the 201st MRD after his arrival in Qūrġonteppa in September 1992: "Remember, the Tajiks are divided into *vovčikov* and *yurčikov*. *Vovčiki*—are fags (Russ.: *pidory*), *yurčik*—ours (*za našikh*). Everything else you will find out yourself."[168]

In an elaborated comment, Kenğaev distinguished between *vahhobī* as pseudo Muslims and genuine believers:

> The people of our republic saw the injustice and the oppression [by the Islamists] with their own eyes and realized that the intention of the *vahhobiyon* was the annihilation of the entire population and the creation of a fundamentalist state. However, the real Muslims know very well what the true religion of Islam demands from its believers and that the central ideas of the *Vahhobī* sect are against the principles of Islam and the blessed Koran. That is why today, all people of the republic, Tajiks, Uzbeks, Kyrgyz, Turkmens, Arabs and Russian speakers have risen against Islamic fundamentalism and the *Vahhobī* school and they are currently purging the provinces of Kūlob, Qūrġonteppa, Leninobod, the cities of Norak and Tursunzoda, the districts of Hisor, Šahrinav, Varzob and Yovon from these *Vahhobī*s.[169]

Kenğaev further "retold" the story of a young man from Kūlob who had been sexually abused by the *vahhobī* Mullo Abdurahim as a minor depicting him as a pedophile homosexual rapist:

> One day, we came to Mullo Abdurahim, he reminded us what it means to swear an oath and told us that the words and orders of a teacher (*muallim*) are law and that this should not be forgotten. After this, he sent everyone home but held me back. After all had left, he locked the door from inside and told me to undress. "What for, *domullo*?" I asked. As an answer he cursed vilely and out of fear I undressed. The *mullo* turned to me and raped me (*taġovuz kard*). When he brought me home with, his car, he put his hand on my throat and told me, in case I would tell anyone, death would select me. My mother asked me why my eyes were so red and I told her that I was hit badly and that it hurt. Several days I stayed home and slept. After some time, I realized that all my classmates had experienced the same.[170]

Kenğaev de-humanized his alleged *vahhobī* opponents and his relentless strategy of Othering the opposition generated an atmosphere of irreconcilability ultimately contributing to the cycle of unrestrained violence. But also the opposition used narratives of sexual violence to de-humanize their opponents. Yusuf, for instance, characterized Fayzalī Saidov as a bloodthirsty Uzbek Laqay hangman just released from prison. In a perfidious narrative, he describes the Laqay as a "relict of the Mongols (*bāzmāndegān-e moġūl*)," who were instigated "to rape the underage girls of their Tajik neighbors in the presence of their parents."[171] "They gave alcohol and drugs to the [Laqay] militia. And there were agitators among them who told the militias that the Islamists and Iran-idolizers (*Iranparast*) were destroying the government. They told them that the Islamists will close the schools and will make the girls their slaves."[172] Yusuf combines the motif of sexual violence with explicit racist stereotypes Othering the Uzbek minority in Tajikistan mirroring Kenğaev's defamation of the *vahhobīs*.

THE VALLEY OF BLOOD AND DEATH (*VODII XUN VA MARG*)

> If war is hell, then civil war belongs to hell's deepest and most infernal regions.[173]

Stathis Kalyvas presents four central theoretical assumptions explaining the sources of unrestrained violence and atrocities in civil wars: *breakdown*, *transgression*, *polarization* and the *technology of warfare*. For the Tajik Civil War, at least two of these explanations provide thoughtful theoretical insights in the dynamics of the conflict: First, the *breakdown* of political order and institutionalized justice removing the constraints to use violence revealing the human nature as naturally violent. The breakdown of political order lowers the costs of violent activities, can activate violent non-state actors at the former margins of society, provide the opportunity for revenge which "gives civil war violence its irrational and anomic glow"[174] or generates a security dilemma where individuals and communities (re-)align with local strongmen out of security fears. Second, *polarization* refers to the antagonisms and divisions between the conflicting groups and factions in a civil war. The motifs might stem from an imagined ideological, religious or ethnic antipathy but the enemy in a civil war is usually portrayed as the essential and categorical "Other." Kalyvas argues, that the link between violence in civil war and *polarization*

> lies at the core of most macro historical accounts of civil wars that generally subsume violence under the theory of deep group rivalry that precedes and causes the war; hence, this is really a theory of *ex ante* or *prewar* conflict.[175]

The reference to *polarization* rationalizes the outbreak and violence in a civil war with a (political/ideological) master narrative, at times not recognizing sufficiently the local deviances and contingencies in civil war as Mueller asserts for the conflicts in Rwanda and the former Yugoslavia:

Rather than reflecting deep, historic passions and hatreds, the violence seems to have been the result of a situation in which common, opportunistic, sadistic, and often distinctly nonideological marauders were recruited and permitted free rein by political authorities.[176]

The fighting in Qūrġonteppa erupted between neighboring communities and often the combatants knew each other personally. The personal and local level of the conflict triggered a vicious cycle of revenge and counter revenge (Fayzalī Saidov's rise to one of the most fearsome warlords is related to such a revenge narrative). Šodmon Yusuf provided one of the most graphic accounts on the fighting in the lower Vaxš River valley, in particular the attack by Safarov's militias on the kolkhozes Dūstī, Moscow, Leningrad and Turkmeniston. According to Yusuf, the male population was humiliated and executed, the female population raped in front of their families: "The savage militias from Kūlob turned the Vaxš valley, which had been cultivated by the *muhoġir* population from Ġarm at great sacrifice, into a valley of blood and death."[177] Yusuf reported about many individual fates, for instance of Fayzullo Xunġar who was tied to an APC and dragged to death,[178] or of the ordeal of 70 women and their minors from Boxtar, who fled the advancing militias into the southern marshes at the Afghan border hiding under appalling conditions until the opposition saved them.[179] In another report, a local community in the south was called together in their mosque under the false pretext of meeting Davlat Xudonazar. Safarov's militia humiliated the women and executed the men. In a village close to Qūrġonteppa, 18 men were shot during their prayer and their bodies thrown into the nearby river.[180] A field commander reported to Yusuf:

I have seen how they killed in Kalininobod 46 Tajik *ġavonmard*. I knew many of them; no one had ever been politically active. They were captured because they were Muslims. The militiamen poured gasoline over them and burned them alive. One of the commanders could not stand what he saw and cried: "What are you doing? Why do you burn your own brothers? Who will be responsible for this crime?" They burned him as well. Those who participated in this atrocity were given a lot of vodka. And the more they drunk, the more they forgot about what they have witnessed. Mother, father, sister, brother, relatives and neighbors, culture, religion and tradition … we are all humans without future.[181]

The memoirs are often inaccurate and at times exaggerated, but the extreme and unrestrained violence perpetrated by militias on both sides in the civil war has been documented in various reports, interviews and oral history accounts.[182] Kalyvas assumes that unrestrained violence is related to the "degree of insecurity faced by armed actors"[183] in the initial months of a civil conflict and concludes that violence can "be either selective or indiscriminate, and there is no definitive logic by which to adjudicate whether an increase in security would lead to an increased proportion of one or the other type. The operationalization of "vulnerability" remains, obviously, a key issue."[184] As for the Tajik Civil War, the worst violence is indeed reported for the first months of the conflict where frontlines were blurred and violent non-state actors exploited the disintegration of public order. The political polarization of the Tajik society since the late 1980s provided a macro-template for ratio-nalizing the conflict, but on the local level competition for resources, revenge or a real or imagined security dilemma might explain the extreme violence in the early months of the conflict.

Sexual Violence

In the patriarchic Tajik society sexuality is a widely tabooed topic. And although the memoirs and interviews frequently refer to forms of sexual violence in the civil war, the topic has never been addressed adequately in the post-conflict Tajik society. Surviving victims are often shunned by their communities and left alone with their dreadful memories and experiences.[185] In her definition, Janie Leatherman points out to the dimensions of sexual violence in armed conflict

> Sexual violence in armed conflict happens in a *place*, and involves *violent acts*, *perpetrators*, *victims*, *survivors* and *impacts* ranging from health to a broad array of social consequences. Sexual violence is also a tool or strategy of war that encompasses the *pre-conflict*, *conflict escalation* and *post-conflict* phases. It *breaks taboos*, thereby violating rules and crossing thresholds that society sets on acceptable conduct. Sexual violence in war is a runaway norm for these rea-sons, and also because it causes the subversion of traditional sexual hierarchies and social order through its political economy of violence.[186]

Leatherman's definition contains some important implications for under-standing sexual violence the Tajik conflict. Concepts of honor, such as *nomus*, contributed to the cycle of violence and revenge but also subverted gender hierarchies in the post-conflict context. Elisabeth Wood establishes a link between sexual violence in civil wars and societal concepts of honor: "where armed groups understand sexual violence as a violation of the family's and community's honor, they are likely to engage in sexual violence as a weapon of war."[187] As the fragmented memories, interviews and reports suggest, sexual violence was systemically used in the Tajik Civil War and shaped the local dynamics of the conflict.

In the following translation of a transcript from the Oral History Project Tajikistan a young woman from the central Qarotegin Valley reported how she was forced into a marriage with a combatant of the Popular Front in spring 1993 after the Popular Front had occupied her village. In many respects, her account is symptomatic for the experience of many women:

> There were other women staying there, but they [the Popular Front militia] noticed me among them. I could not run away and escape. They asked all children in the street, found out that I was a single girl and learnt everything about me. In the evening, they came to our house demanding that "you [i.e. her father] should give us your daughter"; otherwise, they will take me by force. They told my father that they have a young man among them and that they liked him and wanted me to marry him. During those days, everybody was frightened and you could not resist either opposition side or the Government side. They were free in their actions. That time we did not understand anything and were scared very much. Therefore, they could do with you whatever they wanted.[188]

She recalled the negotiation between the combatants and her father indicating the shame and the black despair among the local community:

> They demanded [from my father] that "you have to agree and give your daughter to that young soldier" and that they would arrange a wedding, otherwise they could take me without asking my people. We understood the situation, as they were several soldiers altogether. My people did not give their consent; instead they kept silent all the time in their presence, bowing their heads down. Eventually they decided that they would come on a certain day, arrange the wedding and take me with them. As for me, I was completely frightened and shocked, not realizing whether this was real or not. I was entirely lost. Different thoughts came to my mind. I was thinking that they are going to take me to some unknown place and kill me there. [...] The *nikoh* was by force [...]. Some of my relatives were sent to me to ask my consent, but I did not say "Yes" [...]. At that moment, I was in the kitchen preparing food for them. Nobody, none of the neighbors were there. All of them cowered away since they were afraid. Nobody was with me, I was alone, preparing food and weeping all the time. In short, I did not give them my consent.[189]

There is no question that sexual violence was a strategy in the Tajik Civil War with appalling consequences for the victims during the conflict escalation but also in post-conflict settings. The reports indicate that sexual violence was systematically applied in the civil war to humiliate individuals and entire communities. At the same time, both (as representatives of the opposition and Popular Front) used perfidious narratives de-humanizing their opponents by referring to racist, religious or ideological stereotypes. The victimization of women furthermore reinforced configurations of a hegemonic masculinity and gender inequality in the Tajik society.[190]

NEGOTIATIONS AND ARMISTICE TALKS

Despite the malicious propaganda and the vicious fighting in the south, the fault lines of the conflict in the early months were often blurred and confusing with shifting loyalties. Among the key actors in Dushanbe and Kūlob communication had not completely broken down and they frequently met to negotiate armistices, "peace" or at least the exchange of prisoners.[191] Civil associations, such as *Zarafšon, Xatlon, Vatan, Payvand* or the *Congress of national Unity* tried to mediate between the conflicting parties as well, but with the violent escalation in May 1992, the civil society's voice in Tajikistan became silent.[192] Local communities organized reconciliation and ceasefire meetings and conjured alleged Tajik traditions of reconciliation, such as the public feasts (Taj.: *oši oštī*, literarily "meal of reconciliation"). In most cases the ceasefire agreements broke down after a few hours due to the fragmentation of the conflicting parties, shifting alliances or mere deception. For instance, after Sangak Safarov suffered substantial losses in his unsuccessful assault on Qūrġonteppa on 20 June, he suspended the attack and regrouped his militia in Kalininobod. To win time, he agreed to meet with representatives of the government in Dushanbe at the airport in Qūrġonteppa and both sides agreed on a temporary ceasefire. However, Safarov already broke the ceasefire the next morning with a major assault on the militia of *qorī* Muhammadğon.[193] The peace talks in Xoruġ likewise allowed the warring parties to regroup their forces.

The Xoruġ Accord (26 and 27 July 1992)

In June, Davlat Xudonazar and Būrī Karim, who had left for Moscow after the presidential elections, returned to Tajikistan.[194] They visited Qūrġonteppa and Kūlob in late June and early July 1992 to mediate between the conflicting factions. On 26 June, Xudonazar addressed a meeting in Kūlob appealing to the local leaders including Sangak Safarov for a political settlement of the disputes. A few days later, he announced in Danġara the removal of roadblocks to Kūlob and the exchange of prisoners.[195] Xudonazar suggested convening peace talks and negotiations in GBAO's capital Xoruġ with participation of all parties to the conflict. The Russian government supported Xudonazar's plan, which gave the initiative some weight.[196] Navğuvonov and Iskandarov formally invited the different parties to Xoruġ for 26 and 27 July. The talks in Xoruġ resulted in a reconciliation accord comprising 16 points: The signatories agreed on a cease fire from 10 am 28 July 1992 on, the release of hostages within 24 hours (including the suspension of further hostage taking) and the surrender of small arms and light weapons. Political parties, associations, local executive committees and the *qoziyot* pledged to disband their self-defense groups. A joint commission should monitor the implementation of the disarming process and all parties and associations assured that they would respect the constitution and refrain from further violence in the political process. Importantly, the signatories announced their support for the IDPs and their right to return to their places of residence without fear. At the same time, however, the influence of violent non-state actors was acknowledged by an amendment sanctioning "private" armed security details.[197]

The protocol was signed by 86 participants, among them Iskandarov, Davlat Usmon, Navğuvonov, Yusuf, Sohibnazar, Mirzoaliev (Ispolkom Chairman of the Kūlob *viloyat*), Haydar Šarifov, Said Salimov (a field commander), Tūraev, Sattorzoda (DPT), Sangak Safarov (his name and title as deputy commander of the National Guard in Kūlob added in handwritten to the document), Šabdolov, Amirbek Atobek as well as "representatives of informal groups (*predstavitel' neformal'noy gruppy*)" such as Ğum'axon Būydokov and Rahimbek Nurullobekov.[198] Perhaps, more important was, who did *not* attend the meeting in Xoruğ: Tūrağonzoda and Nabiev. Reportedly, Tūrağonzoda did not attend the negotiations due to his discord with Xudonazar and concerns about his security. Nabiev did not go to Xoruğ since he had not been officially invited to chair the talks—instead he ostentatiously attended a session of the Cabinet of Ministers, met with a Swiss delegation and businessman from Pakistan.[199] Although Iskandarov claimed that he was in permanent contact with Nabiev, the president's nonattendance was heavily criticized by the participants and interpreted as a sign of indifference to the situation and his inaction since the outbreak of violence in May.[200]

The implementation of the Xoruğ Accord proceeded only in a few districts and skirmishes already flared up around the Turkmenistan sovkhoz while the negotiations in Xoruğ were still continuing.[201] On 5 August Usmon Davlat was still optimistic about the Xoruğ Accord and he pointed out, that since 27 July the cease fire had been largely respected and some 300 hostages had been released. However, the collection of small arms did not proceed as projected and on 11 August; the number of collected weapons stood at 40 out of an estimated 15,000 in circulation.[202] A few days later, heavy fighting around the Kuybišev sovkhoz erupted and put an end to optimistic expectations—the Xoruğ Accord had failed.[203]

No Peace

The various armistice agreements were short-lived and none of the negotiations resulted in a lasting settlement of the armed conflict. Sohibnazar concluded that in the summer of 1992 the local elites were not genuinely committed to peace since they still expected to improve their position by continuing the fighting. The meeting in Xoruğ was therefore only a "political gamble, nothing else."[204] The failure to reach a settlement was related to a set of reasons: First, in the summer of 1992, a multiplicity of local actors—self-defense groups, militias and criminal networks—operated independently without coordination and in shifting local alliances. Safarov, for instance, emerged only in October as one the central field commanders, but he was then still contested by rival militia commanders and the former Soviet nomenklatura. The fragmentation, confusion and complexity in the early stages of the civil war made meaningful negotiations—the consideration of costs and benefits of a possible peace deal—extremely difficult. Second, the peace negotiations, such as the Xoruġ Accord, were for all involved parties convenient since they allowed the field commanders to regroup and resupply their militias. Third, none of the fragmented factions had gained a significant advantage in the fighting yet, thus no one was ready to end the conflict at this stage. Finally, the international context did not facilitate meaningful negotiations: Russia and the neighboring countries in Central Asia were preoccupied with the enormous challenges of the collapse of the USSR and independence whilst the UN, CSCE or the USA only slowly adapted to the new realities.[205]

15TH SESSION OF THE SUPREME SOVIET (11–14 AUGUST 1992)

According to Tajikistan's constitution, the Supreme Soviet was still the highest legislative body in the summer of 1992.[206] Although the Presidium of the Supreme Soviet had far-reaching competences, all laws had to be discussed and adopted by a session of the Supreme Soviet. A session needed to be either convened by a formal invitation of the Presidium of the Supreme Soviet or on demand by at least one-third of the deputies.[207] Since 1990 the political affiliation of the deputies in the Supreme Soviet underwent significant changes: While in February 1990, 223 out of the 230 deputies were members of the CPT, only 54 CPT-deputies were left in August 1992.[208] Most deputies were now independent and a few had joined the DPT. Nabiev had not managed to transform the former Communist Party into a new "democratic" or "nationalist" presidential party and therefore could not rely on a fixed political faction in the Supreme Soviet. Instead, majorities had to be negotiated. Since May, the GNR obviated the convention of regular session of the Supreme Soviet since they could not expect to secure majorities on important decisions. However, most politicians realized that a regular session of the Supreme Soviet could offer a way out of the political impasse. The Yeltsin administration repeatedly endorsed the formal convention of the Supreme Soviet and urged the GNR in Dushanbe to convene one. In early August, the Presidium finally agreed and invited the deputies for the 15th Session. The first session on 10

August had to be adjourned since the quorum had not been fulfilled and several deputies expressed concerns about their security. After Iskandarov and Navġuvonov had guaranteed the safety of all deputies, the session convened on 11 August with 165 deputies present.[209] Remarkably, even representatives from Kūlob, such as Qurbonalī Mirzoaliev, Mahmadsaid Ubaydulloev and Sangak Safarov (who were not elected deputies but arrived in Dushanbe to "protect" their deputies) travelled to Dushanbe.[210] Kenġaev followed the invitation as well and was asked (as the former Chairman) to open the session, which was supposed to decide on his resignation. The opposition—that is, the GNR—had secured a majority to approve his resignation and the 131 deputies voted for his dismissal, 30 against and 4 abstained from voting.[211] Akbaršo Iskandarov's appointment as chairman of the Supreme Soviet was confirmed with a 68% majority. Finally, the deputies suspended the "presidential rule" revoking Nabiev's additional powers granted to him in April. The President was fiercely criticized by various deputies who accused Nabiev of indecisiveness and complacency amidst a rapidly disintegrating social and economic situation spiraling down to a civil war.[212] Some deputies, such as Aslonov, Sohibnazar and Tūraġonzoda, demanded Nabiev's resignation and even the abolition of the presidential office, which they wanted to replace with a republican committee. A majority of deputies, however, did not approve a discussion on Nabiev's future and the political system, but the 15th Session showed in the words of Karim that the "reputation (*obrū*) of Nabiev hit rock bottom."[213]

DEFECTION AND DISINTEGRATION OF THE GOVERNMENT OF NATIONAL RECONCILIATION

Remarkably, until September 1992 neither the GNR nor the deputies in the Supreme Soviet were ready to commit "regicide." As the elected president, Nabiev provided the GNR with pretense of constitutional legality, but in the final days of his presidency, Nabiev was largely isolated without any support and amidst mounting criticism.[214] Since August, politicians and senior administration officials insisted on his resignation and discussed the temporarily suspension of the presidential office—a modus operandi finally implemented on the 16th Session in November 1992, when Rahmonov was elected chairman of the Supreme Soviet and the presidential office remained vacant until 1994.

On 28 August 1992, Mullo Abduġaffur and other local strongmen such as Būydoqov, Rizvon, Ismat 'Avulī' and reportedly Yaqub Salimov occupied the presidential administration demanding Nabiev's resignation and—importantly—the release of their criminal accomplice Rahim Nurullobekov (who had been arrested for the murder of Huvaydulloev).[215] Although Nabiev was able to escape to the headquarters of the 201st MRD, several ministers and administrative staff were held hostage by Mullo Abduġaffur who also resumed with some 300 armed men the protests on Šahidon Square.[216] Rizvon took some of the hostages to the Sputnik Resort in Romit and Mullo Abduġaffur held the Supreme Soviet deputy Ğamšed Karimov hostage in his premises in southern Dushanbe. Sohibnazar and Usmon tried to mediate with limited success indicating the autonomy of armed groups in Dushanbe.[217]

On 31 August Akbar Mirzoev resigned as Chairman of the Council of Ministers, a position he held since 9 January 1992, and Nabiev appointed him plenipotentiary to Germany (where he served until 2001). The enigmatic businessman Abdumalik Abdulloġonov from Leninobod followed Mirzoev as chairman of the Council of Ministers.[218]

The Presidium of the Supreme Soviet discussed the situation in an emergency meeting on 2 September. The members of the Presidium were divided between those who preferred a compromise and those who ultimately demanded Nabiev's resignation. The latter group—among them Tūraġonzoda, Aslonov and Sohibnazar—suggested to replace the presidential office with a state council, the compromising faction suggested to keep Nabiev in office but curtailing his authority and transferring his competences to a state council or cooperative committee (*organi kollegialī*). The Presidium's members maintained that "the president of the republic is alienated from the people and their worries are unknown to him."[219] In a subsequent radio address, the Presidium accused Nabiev of complacency and inaction amidst the deepening crisis:

> It is felt that the president of Tajikistan is irresponsible, without authority, and an alien person to his state. [...] President Nabiev has failed to organize solidarity and unity among the various political parties and organizations in the society, and is constantly violating the oath he took in the Supreme Soviet. The Presidium of the Supreme Soviet of Tajikistan and the Cabinet of Ministers, in view of the existing situation, resolutely express their lack of confidence in President Rakhman Nabiyev and consider that he has in fact been removed from power, noting also that it is impossible for him to perform his duty.[220]

On the same day, Navġuvonov—who had been on sick leave for weeks—rendered his resignation as minister of interior heralding the GNR's final disintegration. Other ministers followed suit, among them Davron Ašūrov (culture), Moyonšoh Nazaršoev (youth and education) and Nasriddinov. Other senior administration officials resigned their office as well and urged Nabiev to do the same. Representatives of the Leninobodī political elite publicly distanced themselves from the president but Nabiev obstinately rejected all demands and asserted his intention to stay in office.[221]

Exit Nabiev

Nabiev, either due to ill health or realizing the hopelessness of the situation, decided to leave Dushanbe for Xuğand on 7 September. Upon arrival at Dushanbe Airport, he and his small entourage were intercepted by a group of armed men under the command of Mullo Abduğaffur and Ismat Avulī Habibulloev. Nasriddinov insinuated that the Presidium and Russian officers actually ordered Nabiev's arrest since neither the MVD nor the 201st MRD controlled the roads to the airport that day.[222] The president was confined to the deputies' lounge in a tense and intimidating atmosphere and Mullo Abduğaffur forced Nabiev at gunpoint to sign his resignation.[223] Mullo Abduğaffur's intentions remain obscure: As the memoirs suggest, he had—despite his Islamist habitus—no sympathies for the IRPT and did not coordinate Nabiev's arrest with the Dushanbe government. Reportedly, he was driven by a personal vendetta against Tūrağonzoda and intended to demonstrate his power in Dushanbe by forcing Nabiev to resign.[224] For Nasriddinov, Nabiev's resignation at gunpoint marked the final disintegration of the government in Tajikistan, from "now on, the capital was in the hands of thieves, marauders and racketeers (*reketho*) who divided the city among themselves."[225] Mullo Abduğaffur triumphantly presented the resignation of Nabiev crying out that "with the resignation of Nabiev, the war will end" while Sohibnazar—who recollected the scene in his memoirs—dryly replied that "now the war only starts."[226]

Without much discussion, the Presidium of the Supreme Soviet accepted Nabiev's resignation in the afternoon.[227] The Presidium briefly debated the appointment of Xudonazar or Tūrağonzoda as interim presidents, but after some discussions they decided on a less controversial candidate: Akbaršo Iskandarov.[228] Iskandarov, born 1951 in Darvoz (GBAO), had been acting Chairman of the Supreme Soviet since May 1992, but did not enjoy the full support of the Presidium. Yusuf instead favored the establishment of a state council as the central governing body, bypassing both, the Supreme Soviet as well as the office of the president. The state council should calm down the situation and restore order, only then—perhaps after one year—the council should organize presidential and parliamentary elections. However, Tūraev, Sohibnazar, Tūrağonzoda and Usmon were against the establishment of another parallel governing body and pushed through the appointment of Iskandarov.[229]

With Iskandarov's assumption of office, the situation did not improve since he did not enjoy genuine legitimacy limiting his room for maneuver. Iskandarov had no means to stop the continuous violence in the south or change the precautious situation of his government in Dushanbe. Although the Russian administration accepted Iskandarov as a dialogue partner, they nonetheless insisted on the regular convention of the Supreme Soviet. Also within the GNR Iskandarov faced stiff opposition. Yusuf depicted Iskandarov as "extremely anxious, ignorant and inexperienced"[230] concluding that "the appointment of Iskandarov was a cataclysmal mistake for the democratic movement and the end of the GNR."[231]

From a constitutional point of view, Nabiev's resignation had to be approved not only by the Presidium but also by a simple majority of the Supreme Soviet. Fayzullo Abdulloev (Minister of Justice) and Ašūrboy Imomov, who were both present during Nabiev's resignation, issued a disputable legal opinion concluding that there were no violations against the constitution and no pressure applied on Nabiev indicating the exasperation among the former reformers and democrats.[232] Davlat Usmon conceded several years later that Nabiev's resignation indeed did not happen according to the constitution and was politically motivated. Nonetheless, he saw a conspiracy behind the resignation:

I think it [the resignation] had a political mark. If the resignation was conducted according to the law, a session of the parliament should have voted on the resignation. According to the constitution, only the parliament has the authority to dismiss the president due to inaptitude or by a no-confidence vote. But the situation at that time was in such a way, that the convention of a regular session of the parliament was almost impossible. The country was in a critical situation and it was a political decision, but the events at the airport were a provocation. [...] It was done to denigrate the reputation of the opposition.[233]

Not only the various domestic stakeholders welcomed Nabiev's resignation, there was also no diplomatic intervention by Uzbekistan, Russia or the USA in favor of Nabiev. The different memoirs reflect the relief at Nabiev's exit as well and Sohibnazar concluded:

What kind of president he was? He chatted with other state leaders, who sent him military support, about the fate of his nation and still claimed to be neutral (*betaraf*)? Who is this person, who hands out weapons to his own children on the square to kill each other while he is watching it? A president without any sagacity and competence.[234]

Also Kenǧaev balanced his accounts with his former mentor: Nabiev had not been ready for the "politics of Perestroika and democracy" and—as the majority of Tajikistan's political elite—he did not understand "the teachings from the *Siyosatnoma*, the issues of moral, behavior and conduct, attitude and aptitude."[235] He did not govern proactively but reacted belatedly to challenges. He could not distinguish enemies from friends and relied on advisors "behind the curtain who were miles away from any modern thought and who had only their personal gain in mind."[236] Nabiev simply did not understand the mechanism of modern politics.[237] Finally, Kenǧaev concluded that Nabiev's worst mistake was his negligence toward the rise of militant Islamism in Central Asia. Only Islam Karimov understood the imminent danger of Islamism and consistently as well as successfully opposed radical groups in Uzbekistan.[238]

After his resignation, Nabiev was escorted from the Airport and placed under house arrest in Dushanbe for a few days. Although rumors surround his departure from Dushanbe, he was free to leave for Xuğand in mid-September. Apparently, Kenğaev intended to use the deposed president for his political manoeuvers and immediately went to Xuğand. But the northern elite considered Kenğaev as a destabilizing person and asked him to leave the city. He nonetheless managed to meet Nabiev on 13 September with Dūstov and Azimov in Nabiev's residence in Xuğand.[239] Kenğaev described Nabiev as an embittered man who had lost touch with reality and who was largely isolated by the Leninobodī elite, in particular Abdulloğonov, who had his own political aspirations and even refused to meet with the former president.[240]

Kenğaev tried to depart with Nabiev from the airport in Xuğand on a plane bound to Kūlob, however the chairman of the Leninobod Ispolkom, Abduğalil Homidov (the brother-in-law of Abdulloğonov), intercepted their small entourage and prevented their departure. Kenğaev reportedly slipped away and escaped, but Nabiev was placed under house arrest.[241] A week later, Nabiev presented himself in a defiant mood and told a *Pravda* journalist that he considered himself still president of Tajikistan since his resignation violated the constitution. He announced his readiness to return to Dushanbe in order to build a secular democratic state and insisted that he is the only legitimate representative of the Tajik government to negotiate with.[242] His appeal went unheard and six weeks later, Nabiev had to appear on the 16th Session of the Supreme Soviet and confirm his resignation. After a public *oši oštī* with several field commanders in Xuğand, Nabiev disappeared from public and died a few months later, on 11 April 1993, of a myocardial infarction in Xuğand.[243]

After less than a year, Nabiev's inauspicious presidency came to an end. As a Brezhnevite cadre with serious personal weaknesses who had been already marginalized at the beginning of Gorbachev's Perestroika reforms, he was a disastrous choice for president in November 1991. Nabiev expected that he could govern Tajikistan with his Soviet patronage networks in the agro-industrial sector and populist behavior resembling the chairman of a large kolkhoz rather than the president of a newly independent country with insurmountable challenges. His irresoluteness, frequent absence in times of crisis, erratic appointments and inconsistent policies were divisive and contributed to the political confrontation and impasse as well as the proliferation of centrifugal forces and violent non-state actors.

Aslonov and Rizoev

In the summer of 1992 the former Soviet nomenklatura and the Perestroika/ Glasnost opposition lost rapidly influence on the contingent developments in Tajikistan. Local field commanders from the fringes of the Soviet society marginalized the former political elites. At the time, militias from Kūlob wreaked havoc in Qūrġonteppa, the nomenklatura in Kūlob tried to regain the political initiative and escape the logic of violence. On 28 September, the deputies of the Kūlob Soviet met in an emergency session and replaced Qurbonalī Mirzoaliev with Ġahonxon Rizoev as chairman of the Kūlob Ispolkom. Rizoev had been a senior officer in the Kūlob branch of the MVD and had offered to resume talks with the government in Dushanbe.[244] To give political negotiations between Kūlob and Qūrġonteppa some weight, Iskandarov appointed the veteran politician Qadriddin Aslonov chairman of the Qūrġonteppa Ispolkom on 8 October. Rizoev and Aslonov agreed to meet personally in Panġ in late October/early November.[245]

Rizoev's consent to enter negotiations should not be misunderstood as his readiness to acknowledge the GNR or settle the conflict. Instead he co-operated with Safaralī Kenġaev in the Hisor region planning a coordinated assault on Dushanbe for October 1992. As representatives of the former Soviet system, Rizoev and Kenġaev obviously wanted to regain the initiative and re-establish the hierarchies between the former security structures and networks of organized crime assigning to the latter a subordinate position. Safarov learned about the negotiations, which he considered as a subversion of his authority. He decided to act, withdrew his support from Kenġaev (who started the assault on Dushanbe on 24 October) and on 28 October Safarov personally shot Rizoev in Kūlob. A day later, Safarov's militia intercepted Aslonov and took him hostage on his way to Panġ.

SAFAROV, KENĠAEV AND THE POPULAR FRONT (*FRONTI XALQĪ*)

In contemporary Tajik history textbooks, the establishment of the Popular Front (*Fronti xalqī*) is portrayed as a joint initiative by Safarov, Langariev, Abdurahimov and Kenġaev in autumn 1992 to coordinate the military operations against the opposition, to recapture the state and convene the 16th Session of the Supreme.[246] As always, the reality was far more complex and there are conflicting narratives who established the Popular Front and when. Kenġaev claimed to have formally registered the Popular Front on 28 August 1992 in Xuġand and Muhammad Farzod, who wrote the introduction to Kenġaev's memoirs, remarked, "the founder of the Popular Front of

Chapter 8

Tajikistan was S. Kenğaev and nobody else."[247] Other sources identify Sangak Safarov as the one who established the Popular Front in October.[248] Amirqul Azimov—an associate of Kenğaev who survived him and continued his career in post-conflict Tajikistan—told the Tajik newspaper *Millat* in 2012 that *he* actually established the Popular Front on 13 October 1992 in Tursunzoda without Kenğaev's involvement.[249]

Kenğaev's Version

After his dismissal in May, Kenğaev intended to stay in Dushanbe. However, with the evacuation of Ozodī Square, his position became precarious and decided to leave Dushanbe, however, in a defiant mood as he records in his memoirs:

> Until now, nobody has released me from my duties as Chairman of the Supreme Soviet, isn't it?! [...] The leaders of the Democratic Party and other groups who pretend to act in the name of "the people" need to understand, that the road they have taken, i.e. inviting the people to a fratricidal war, will never calm down the country and will never find the support of the people.[250]

Kenğaev first went to Tashkent and then proceeded to Xuğand where he tried unsuccessfully to mobilize support among the local elites. Kenğaev portrayed himself as unrelenting, a man of integrity above the mean business of daily politics who had a mission but did not aspire toward formal positions or power. He decided to "spit on everything (*ba hamaaš tuf*) and to start again as a simple worker since life is a fight (*muboriza*) and you need to be a fighter in life."[251] He left Xuğand for the Zarafšon/Mastčoh valley where he was (in his narrative) offered the position of the manager in the Aynī Mining Combine. Immediately after he had settled in Aynī, "innocent *ğavonmard* with pure hearts"[252] from all over Tajikistan travelled to Aynī in order to join him in his struggle against the Islamist opposition. Kenğaev's self-portrayal as a modest, unyielding *ğavonmard* departed considerably from reality: After he left Dushanbe in May, Kenğaev used his contacts in Tashkent and received substantial financial and military aid from Uzbekistan. In his memories he concedes that he visited Tashkent several times to "solve urgent issues."[253] The Uzbek support allowed him to train and equip some 500 (according to other sources up to 2,000) men   between May and October 1992 in former Soviet military installations at Qaratoğ and Almosī in the Fan Mountains.[254] In times of rising anti-Uzbek sentiment in Tajikistan, Kenğaev did not conceal his admiration for Islam Karimov and sung his highest praises in terms of a true ğavonmard:

Indeed, intelligence and wisdom, reputation and honor (*nangu nomus*) as well as political capability is only natural for I[slom]. A. Karimov. The Lord Above has blessed his soul with justice and equity, compassion and grandeur, gentleness and love for the people and in particular people in need.[255]

Kengaev negotiated the establishment of a united front with various field commanders and politicians shortly after the funeral of Huvaydulloev on 25 August 1992 in Xugand and he registered the Popular Front on 28 August.[256] The first meeting took place on 8 September—shortly after the resignation of Nabiev when he convened a group of commanders in Sarvoda (close to Aynī), among them Amirqul Azimov, Tagoyxon Šukurov, Ibodullo Boymatov, Abdumalik Solehov, Rahmatgon Xolmatov, Qutfniso Mirzoeva, Davlat Murodov, Šeralī Fayzaliev, Botur Ishoqovmand a few others. Kengaev claimed that he made an effort to coordinate the establishment of the Popular Front with the field commanders in the south, namely Langariev, Safarov, Saidov and Salimov but obviously with limited success since they all insisted to operate in separate militias: Safarov and Langariev commanded the National Guard of Kūlob (*Gordi millii Kūlob*), Yaqub Salimov the Guard of Salvation (*Gordi Nagot*), and Saidov the National Guard of Qūrgonteppa.[257]

Kengaev provided an elaborate legitimation and rationale for the establishment of the Popular Front: He discussed his plans with the major stakeholders and drafted a charter defining the objectives of the Popular Front in a preamble as the "defense of truth, the unity of the people, the indivisibility of the homeland, the honor of each individual and the splendid future for Tajikistan." The Popular Front intended to establish a "truly democratic society based on the rule of law in which social justice is prevailing."[258] As an immediate action program, the Popular Front demanded the convention of the 15th Session of the Supreme Soviet in Leninobod. The agenda for the session should be prepared exclusively by the deputies and not the GNR. The resignation of Nabiev should be declared illegal and invalid. The government as well as senior officials in the MVD and NSC/KGB should be immediately replaced by individuals chosen for their competence and not their regional affiliation. The Popular Front intended to re-establish the constitutional order and demanded the disbanding of the oppositional armed forces.[259] Finally, Kengaev insisted that the establishment of the Popular Front was a reaction to the formation of the Salvation of the Homeland Front by the opposition and its military prevalence in the summer of 1992 (the Salvation of the Homeland Front, however, was established two weeks later than Kengaev claimed to have registered the Popular Front).[260]

In his effort to portray the Popular Front as a legitimate military organization under a central command, Kengaev delineated the command structure

with militias under the command of Fayzalī Saidov, Sangak Safarov, Yaqub
Salimov, Tošmat Kavrakov, Mahkamboy Šarifov, Azim Ġaniev, Būrixon
Ġobirov, Saidšoh Šamolov and Šeralī Mirzoev in Kūlob and Qūrġonteppa.
In the south and west, Bekboy-*pahlavon* and Marqa-*pahlavon* commanded
the Popular Front in Panǧ while Kenǧaev shared the command with Taǧoyxon
Šukurov in Hisor.[261] Unsurprisingly, the realities departed from Kenǧaev's
narrative: His Popular Front militia was an incoherent group of local commanders—many of them criminals and local strongmen—with individual
interests and shifting loyalties. In particular, Kenǧaev's alliance with Safarov
never existed as such as we shall see.

KENǦAEV'S ASSAULT ON DUSHANBE

Since late May, Kenǧaev trained his militia in the Fan Mountains for an
assault on Dushanbe. From the available sources it appears that Kenǧaev
organized the assault with the approval of the Uzbek government. As a representative of the former nomenklatura, he had contacts and access to the
political establishment in Tashkent and Uzbekistan had vital interests in the
developments in Tajikistan. Historically, the Uzbek nomenklatura had closer
contacts with the Tajik elites from Leninobod but in the evolving conflict
Leninobod lost rapidly military and political weight. As a former prosecutor,
deputy and chairman of the Supreme Soviet, the Uzbek government obviously considered Kenǧaev as a sufficiently trustworthy representative of the
Tajik nomenklatura to back in the unfolding conflict.

Kenǧaev narrated his assault on Dushanbe as a concerted military operation meticulously coordinated by his Popular Front involving all major field
commanders from Hisor and Kūlob.[262] However, there was little unity among
Kenǧaev, the political elites and the field commanders. Sohibnazar conjec-
tured that Kenǧaev intentionally concealed the preparations for the assault
on Dushanbe from Safarov. His claim that he discussed everything in detail
with Safarov is in Sohibnazar's reading an *ex post* legitimation of his actions.
By capturing Dushanbe, Kenǧaev wanted to assume the military-political
leadership and marginalize Safarov.[263] While the coordination and recon-
cilement with other field commanders perhaps never happened in the way
Kenǧaev reported, he did meet several times with the political nomenklatura
in Kūlob. On 12 October, a meeting between Kenǧaev, Rizoev and Abdurahimov took place in Tursunzoda. Kenǧaev carefully insinuated disagreements
within the Kūlobī elite but not between him and the Kūlobī commanders.[264]
Their next meeting took place two days later with local commanders presenting situation reports. Amirqul Azimov (Hisor) portrayed the situation
in Dushanbe as extremely tense with IRPT and *qoziyot* militias attacking

the civilian population. In order to protect Dushanbe's civilian population, Kenğaev's alliance of commanders agreed to "liberate" Dushanbe in an assault on 17 October. Rizoev and Abdurahimov claimed to act in the name of all Kūlobī commanders with whom they coordinated the attack:

> Dear Safaralī, believe us, all affairs are discussed with Sangak Safarov. But on the one hand, he does not want to go to Dushanbe as long as the situation in Qūrğonteppa is unstable and he beliefs that an attack by the opposition is imminent. On the other hand, we should consider the opinions of the military experts. Finally, we are not each other's enemies, aren't we?! We have the same intentions, haven't we!?[265]

A few days later Rizoev informed Kenğaev that the attack had to be postponed since the Kūlobī militias needed more time to prepare. Finally, he postponed the second date on 23 October. The "reliable" and "unshaken" Kenğaev instead insisted on the participation of Safarov since he wanted to avoid any visible sign of rivalry (*raqobat*) within the Popular Front. Rizoev—apparently disgruntled by Kenğaev's insistence—angrily responded:

> Safaralī, we do not understand you. Do you think that only Sangak Safarov is a Kūlobī and all others, such as Langarī Langariev, Rustam Abdurahimov, Fayzalī Saidov, Yaqub Salimov, I, Pir Husaynov, who have not been less courageous than he [Sangak], are not from Kūlob? Sir, the Kūlobīs wage war in your name. We ask you not to talk in this way anymore.[266]

Kenğaev trusted in Rizoev's assurance and continued with his preparations. He drew up the plan that Langariev should attack via the Šar-Šar Pass (south-east), Saidov via Kofarnihon (east) and Kenğaev from Hisor (west). Abdurahimov would accompany Kenğaev with a team of radio engineers and presenters from Kūlob who should restart radio and TV broadcasting immediately after the occupation of the state Radio and TV Company in Dushanbe. Abdurahimov flew on 23 October to Tursunzoda, however without the radio and TV team. Reportedly, Safarov had ordered them to his headquarters in Kalininobod and decided that the radio team would accompany Langariev's militia and join them in Dushanbe.[267]

Kenğaev maintained that he had discussed his plans with officers of the 201st MRD and Lieutenant General Eduard Vorobyov, then the deputy commander of the Russian ground forces, who was present in Dushanbe between September and November 1992 to explore the deployment of CIS forces in Tajikistan. Vorobyov took part in the coordination meetings between Kenğaev, Abdurahimov and Rizoev and he insinuated that he had approval of the Russian military for their assault on Dushanbe. Some 20 years later, Kenğaev's version still circulates in Dushanbe implying a Russian conspiracy: The Russians wanted to exclude the unpredictable Sangak Safarov from the operation and since Kenğaev was not an experienced politician he did not realize that external forces took advantage of him.

The Assault on Dushanbe

Kenğaev commenced his assault on Dushanbe in the early morning hours of Saturday, 24 October 1992. His militia, some 500 men supported by a few APCs, entered the western suburbs of Dushanbe meeting no resistance.[268] They moved quickly into the city center and occupied the Supreme Soviet, the presidential residence, the *qoziyot* and the radio station. However, they soon realized that neither Langariev nor Safarov were approaching Dushanbe.[269] In his memoirs, Kenğaev commented on the situation elliptically:

> Those who betray us will be eventually punished by God. I truly do not believe that Langarī Langariev or Fayzalī [Saidov] betrayed us. They were my closest brothers and gave their souls for me and they were searching for truth. They will always be counted as exceptional people of our country.[270]

Kenğaev's militia was able to occupy Dushanbe's radio station, but servicemen of the 201st MRD blocked access to the TV facilities (which indicates that the Russian support for the assault was made-up by Kenğaev). Kenğaev and Abdurahimov were only able to dispatch their appeal on radio and not on TV as initially planned. In the radio address, Kenğaev announced his intention to restore the previous government with Nabiev as president and himself as chairman of the Supreme Soviet. He demanded the immediate convention of the 16th Session of the Supreme Soviet and justified the assault on Dushanbe with the restoration of the legitimate order and the suspension of Islamists' puppet government. Kenğaev appealed to the non-Central Asian nationalities in the capital pledging to preserve the multi-ethnic composition of Tajikistan's population.[271]

However, their performance went awry from the beginning: The nervous (or intoxicated) Abdurahimov made some unthoughtful comments and introduced Kenğaev as president and himself as chairman of the Supreme Soviet. Abdurahimov's mistake caused some consternation. Even three years later, Kenğaev still felt compelled to comment on the affair warning his audience that the opposition was looking for positions, not he himself.[272] In the end, the radio announcement turned into a public relations disaster revealing the inadequate preparations and many personal shortcomings of the people involved.

The assault on Dushanbe did not come as a surprise and the Iskandarov administration was well aware of the looming attack. Xudonazar had even asked the Russian government to urge the Uzbek government to suspend its support for Kenğaev.[273] A curfew had been issued the day before and Iskandarov had asked the 201st MRD to guard access to Dushanbe's airport and the TV station.[274] But Kenğaev was not defeated by the GNR. Instead, it was the Youth of Dushanbe, which fought back: After midday, the Youth of Dushanbe organized a counter-attack and restricted Kenğaev's militia to the city center. Yaqub Salimov and Rauf Saliev, who had reportedly pledged to support Kenğaev, hesitated to commit their criminal group and awaited the outcome of the assault.[275]

At forenoon Abdurahimov contacted Rizoev in Kūlob to inquire about the reinforcements. Rizoev informed him that Safarov blocked the reinforcements and Kenğaev sensed that Safarov had betrayed him.[276] The news from Kūlob prompted Kenğaev to reconsider his strategy and he agreed to enter negotiations with Iskandarov in the afternoon of 24 October. In the talks, Iskandarov promised to convene the 16th Session of the Supreme Soviet in Xuğand with only one topic on the agenda: the resignation of the Presidium and the GNR.[277] In the afternoon, local militias—Mullo Abduğaffur from the south, Rizvon from the east—advanced to the city center and heavy fighting left several combatants dead and wounded on the streets of Dushanbe. In the early evening, news broke that Langariev had been severely wounded in an ambush at the Šar-Šar pass. The disaster that befell Langariev was the official pretext for Safarov to withhold his militia from advancing to Dushanbe and reinforce Kenğaev.[278]

In the evening of 24 October, Kenğaev's men were almost encircled and Abdurahimov disappeared under mysterious circumstances. In Kenğaev memoirs, however, Dushanbe was calm and he even decided to drive back to Tursunzoda to spend the night in his headquarters.[279] The next morning, no reinforcements arrived. Instead, the Youth of Dushanbe and militias from Kofarnihon gained the upper hand. Losses were high and Kenğaev's militia was bogged down in the city center. In the afternoon, their position got increasingly awkward when the Youth of Dushanbe occupied Putovsky Bridge and closed the western exit from Dushanbe to Hisor.

As if he was still able to set the conditions, Kenğaev "agreed" to enter a new round of negotiations with Iskandarov—at least according to the narrative in his memoirs. He threatened a fully fledged assault on Dushanbe with his Popular Front, but in order to prevent further bloodshed he expressed his readiness to withdraw his militia in case Iskandarov invited the deputies for the 16th Session of the Supreme Soviet on 26 October in Xuğand. Iskandarov again approved the demands and Kenğaev agreed to withdraw. In the evening of 25 October the 201st MRD escorted him with his remaining men out of Dushanbe.[280] What Kenğaev narrated as a military triumph, was in fact a disastrous defeat. The fighting in Dushanbe left several hundred

dead and soon rumors about atrocities circulated in the capital.[281] Kenğaev
reported that 63 men of his Popular Front were killed in the fighting, however he only cursory mentioned the death of his accomplice Abdurahimov.[282]
The ex-convict, folk musician, schoolteacher and ideologist of *Oškoro* had
been captured by Mullo Abduġaffur in an apartment in Dushanbe, reportedly
drunk and in a compromising situation. Initially, Mullo Abduġaffur wanted
to exhibit Abdurahimov on TV as the perfidious ideologist from Kūlob, KGB
agent and Uzbek spy, but he expected a rescue mission by Kenğaev's forces
and decided in a "tense and difficult situation" (Yusuf) to execute him in the
evening of 25 October.[283] Reportedly, he was beheaded on the premises of the
avtobaza No. 3 and his severed head shown around as a trophy.[284] Kenğaev
was largely silent about Abdurahimov's fate; He called him a historical person and expressed his regrets that their joint venture was so short.[285]

Kenğaev and Safarov

Despite alleged convergent interests and political objectives, Safarov systematically undermined Kenğaev's plans and claimed that he had not been
informed in time.[286] Considering the lengthy negotiations and the fact that
even the Iskandarov government knew about the attack makes it highly
unlikely that Safarov was indeed unaware of Kenğaev's plans. Apparently,
Safarov reconsidered his options and decided against Kenğaev for several
reasons: First, on 17 October 1992, Abdulloġonov, Major General Ašurov,
Lieutenant General Vorobyov and Safarov had entered negotiations resulting
in a withdrawal of his militia from the Čormaġzak Pass and a suspension of
the fighting in the south allowing the distribution of humanitarian aid to the
population of Qūrġonteppa and Kūlob.[287] These negotiations with official
representatives of the Russian armed forces were an important affirmation
of Safarov's position and legitimacy to act on behalf of Kūlob. He obviously
did not want to risk his newly gained reputation in a controversial assault on
Dushanbe with an uncertain outcome. Second, Kenğaev had staged himself
as the chairman of the Popular Front and Safarov certainly did not want to
appear as one of Kenğaev's subordinated commanders. Nasriddinov assumed
that Safarov tolerated Kenğaev as long as the latter controlled Hisor and
tied up forces in central Tajikistan while Safarov was operating in the south.
Eventually he realized Kenğaev's duplicitous personality and terminated
their cooperation.[288] Third, in mid-October, Safarov, Langariev and Saidov
had been able to seize Qūrġonteppa and suppress the resistance in the area.
After two months of intense fighting and heavy losses, the men under their
command were exhausted. Rather than risking an assault on Dushanbe with
many uncertainties, he decided to consolidate his position in the south by

advancing to Šahritus and Ğilikūl where he met little resistance.[289] Finally, the most important conflict between Safarov and Kenğaev was their political agenda. Kenğaev legitimized his assault on Dushanbe with the restoration of the constitutional government and President Nabiev. At this point, Safarov did not want to reinstate Nabiev and throughout the summer of 1992, he had successfully destroyed exactly the "old" political economy of Tajikistan Kenğaev intended to restore. Now, in autumn, Safarov claimed to re-establish *order*, but certainly not under the leadership of the previous Soviet nomenklatura, such as Nabiev, Kenğaev or the officials from Kūlob, but with a person of *his* choice. Sohibnazar remarked ambiguously that the return of Nabiev "was not in the economic interest of those who fought the war."[290] However, Safarov realized that he needed an acceptable political representative to negotiate with the important external actors. Uzbekistan and Russia would not consider a former convict and warlord as a suitable negotiation partner; therefore, he chose Rahmonov as his political proxy.

In his memoirs, Kenğaev insinuated that he sensed the conflict between the political nomenklatura and Safarov, but conceded that did not realize the extent of divisions.[291] He extensively quoted Ğahonxon Rizoev's assurances (five days before Safarov shot him):

> We have one objective, there must not be any confusion that we have started to change things seriously. We will not accept any shortcomings. We have talked to all the commanders and our word is law for them [...] you [Kenğaev] should believe the political officials of the *viloyat*. Between the field commanders and the Ispolkom leaders of Kūlob does not exist any amenity. All of them respect you like a prophet (*payğambar*) and they stand up for you against the opposition.[292]

After the failed assault on Dushanbe, Kenğaev conceded: "I did not talk to him [Sangak Safarov] anymore since there is no common interest between the Popular Front of Tajikistan [i.e. Kenğaev] and the Staff (*sitod*) of the Qūrğonteppa *viloyat*."[293]

Yusuf offered a third version on the background of Kenğaev's failed attack on Dushanbe: Rizoev intentionally did not inform Safarov about Kenğaev's plans since he was a MVD General who wanted to end the fratricidal war. For saving Dushanbe, Yusuf concluded, Rizoev gave his life.[294] According to this narrative, Kenğaev and Rizoev—as representatives of the Soviet professional security structures—had serious reservations concerning Safarov's future political role in Tajikistan. They considered the ex-convict as an uneducated criminal who was habitually an antipode to them despite their constant affirmations of their respect for "Bobo" Sangak. They represented a particular Soviet dominant masculinity rooted in the security structures, which had been challenged since the disintegration of the USSR and was gradually replaced by new concepts of masculinity, the field commanders from the margins of the Soviet society. Kenğaev and Rizoev considered the assault on and capture of Dushanbe without Safarov's involvement as a chance to exclude or at least marginalize Safarov in the forthcoming political negotiations such as the 16th Session of the Supreme Soviet.

CONCLUDING REMARKS

Kenğaev's assault on Dushanbe ended in a fiasco, which isolated and marginalized him. Iskandarov remarked plainly that the assault on Dushanbe excluded Kenğaev from the circles of Tajikistan's political elite and from October 1992 on he was "no key personality (*figurai kalidī*)"[295] anymore. The attack was widely condemned and Nasriddinov called the attack unjustifiable resulting in further tragedies.[296] Defiantly, Kenğaev flew on 27 October 1992 to Xuğand to open the 16th Session of the Supreme Soviet (which Iskandarov had promised him in their negotiations). But after his withdrawal, Iskandarov revoked the invitation and instead announced the convention of a national assembly with a broader representation for November. Finally, the government announced to open criminal proceedings against Kenğaev.[297] Apparently, he still enjoyed some support among the deputies in the Supreme Soviet and despite the official cancellation, some 100 deputies met on 28 October in Xuğand ready to convene the session (however, not fulfilling the quorum).[298] Kenğaev returned to Tursunzoda in a defiant mood: He ordered a rail blockade of Dushanbe and circulated his version of the events:

> The Popular Front of Tajikistan hereby announces that on 7 May 1992 Islamic fundamentalists with support of the *Vahhobī* sect of Islam and some Islamic countries have staged a coup d'état in Tajikistan, which eventually resulted in a fratricidal war. As a consequence, the blood of innocent people was spilled and several ten thousand people have been killed. Responsible for this senseless (*bema 'nī*) war are the Islamic fundamentalists, the position-seeking democrats, and the group of bloodthirsty criminals from the autonomous Mountain Badaxšon with the intention to establish an Islamic state in Tajikistan. Their militant activities are directed against innocent people and other nationalities under the flag of slogans such as "In the name of God," "Allahu Akbar," "Ğihod" or "kill the unbelievers."[299]

Although Kenğaev had been considered a maverick before, the failed assault on Dushanbe finally discredited him among the Tajik nomenklatura and his Uzbek ally.

Aslonov's Execution and Safarov's Military Triumph

After the seizure of Qūrġonteppa and Kenğaev's failure in Dushanbe, "Bobo" Sangak emerged as the most powerful field commander in the Tajik Civil War in October 1992. And he was not willing to compromise and took drastic action to consolidate his position: On 28 October Safarov personally shot the Kūlob Ispolkom chairman Ğahonxon Rizoev. Safarov executed Rizoev not for the failed assault on Dushanbe (as the media reported), but out of rivalry on the local level and his attempt to bypass Safarov in the talks with Aslonov.[300] A day later, on 29 October, the militia of an Uzbek accomplice of Safarov abducted Aslonov on his way to Panğ and incarcerated him in a kolkhoz nearby. Although Kyrgyzstan's President Akayev dispatched his Vice President Kulov to negotiate Aslonov's release, Safarov was not willing to compromise and portrayed the former secretary of the CPT's Central Committee and chairman of the Supreme Soviet as an Islamist with contacts to Hekmatyar's *Ḥezb-e Islāmī*. Aslonov was exposed to torture for more than two months and finally executed.[301]

After Kenğaev's failed assault on Dushanbe, Safarov started to use the label Popular Front for his militia. In November Safarov advanced in the south conquering one district after the other and within a few months, he had transformed from a local racketeer to Tajikistan's most powerful militia commander.[302] He single-handedly eliminated the political leadership of Kūlob and installed a man of his choice (Emomalī Rahmonov) who only three weeks later became the leader of Tajikistan (and has remained so until today). With Rahmonov appointed, Safarov could "afford" to remain in the background during the important 16th Session of the Supreme Soviet in Xuğand.

Since October, the IRPT militias were on the defense or retreat. Local groups, such as the Youth of Dushanbe, disintegrated, defected or were defeated by rival militias. An increasing number of refugees from the south fled to Dushanbe. The situation worsened in November when Kenğaev blocked the railway transport to Dushanbe.[303]

NOTES

1. Cited in Usmonov, *Nabiev*, 66.
2. Mosalmāniyān, *Tāğīkestān*, 37.
3. Karim, *Faryodi*, 422; Usmonov, *Nabiev*, 66.
4. Kenğaev, *Tabadduloti 1*, 108–110; Nazriev and Sattorov, *Respublika Tadžikistan II*, 153; FBIS-SOV-92–088, 6 May 1992, 53.
5. Kenğaev, *Tabadduloti 1*, 121, 150.

6. The sequence of events is contested, Kenğaev (*Tabadduloti 1*, 149) maintained that the leaders on Šahidon had distributed weapons earlier than on Ozodī but got caught up in contradictions.

7. Karim, *Faryodi*, 423; Oleg Panfilov, *Tadžikistan: Žurnalisty na graždanskoy voyne (1992–1997)* (Moskva: Izd-vo "Prava cheloveka," 2003), 44.

8. Kenğaev, *Tabadduloti 1*, 123; Yūsuf, *Tāğīkestān*, 190.

9. Cf. Dūstov, *Zahm*, passim; Kenğaev, *Tabadduloti 1–3*, passim.

10. Usmonov, *Nabiev*, 70.

11. Kenğaev, *Tabadduloti 1*, 155 and Usmonov, *Nabiev*, 70.

12. Yūsuf, *Tāğīkestān*, 204.

13. Reproduced in Karim, *Faryodi*, 427–431; Kenğaev, *Tabadduloti 1*, 160–163 & 180–182. FBIS-SOV-92–089, 7 May 1992, 53–54.

14. FBIS-SOV-92–089, 7 May 1992, 53–54. Karim, *Faryodi*, 429–431.

15. Yūsuf, *Tāğīkestān*, 206.

16. Yūsuf, *Tāğīkestān*, 211.

17. Sohibnazar, *Subhi 2*, 44.

18. Kenğaev, *Tabadduloti 1*, 213–214. *Tin* is equivalent to kopecks.

19. Kenğaev, *Tabadduloti 1*, 216–217.

20. Kenğaev, *Tabadduloti 1*, 170.

21. Karim, *Faryodi*, 492–494; Kenğaev, *Tabadduloti 1*, 319.

22. Kenğaev, *Tabadduloti 1*, 155 (quote), 182–211, 293.

23. Kenğaev, *Tabadduloti 1*, 147.

24. Kenğaev, *Tabadduloti 1*, 60.

25. See Kenğaev, *Tabadduloti 1*, 196.

26. T. Friedman, "Tajikistan agrees to curbs on arms," *The New York Times*, February 14, 1992.

27. Conversation with a former opposition member, Bishkek, 4 September 2012.

28. See Sohibnazar, *Subhi 2*, 56.

29. Sohibnazar, *Subhi 2*, 35–36.

30. Sohibnazar, *Subhi 2*, 119.

31. Kenğaev, *Tabadduloti 1*, 286.

32. Abdullo Habibov, *Vaqte amr qonunro ivaz mekunad...* (Dušanbe: Vatanparvar, 2009); Karim, *Faryodi*, 438.

33. See Nuralī Davlat, "'Hameša zinda'-e, ki faramūš šud," *Nigoh*, January 8, 2014, 41: 11; Medvedev, "Saga," 198–200; Nazriev and Sattorov, *Respublika Tadžikistan II*, 166.

34. Sohibnazar, *Subhi 2*, 52; Usmonov, *Nabiev*, 74; Davlat, "Hameša," 11.

35. Medvedev, "Saga," 198–200.

36. Qayumzod, "Xudo," 3.

37. Usmonov, *Nabiev*, 73; see also Medvedev, "Saga," 199.

38. Karim, *Faryodi*, 491; Mosalmāniyān, *Tāğīkestān*, 34; Yūsuf, *Tāğīkestān*, 198.

39. Sohibnazar, *Subhi 1*, 201; Tūrağonzoda, *Miyoni*, 52. For a similar assessment see Yūsuf, *Tāğīkestān*, 185; Usmonov, *Nabiev*, 61.

40. Medvedev, "Saga," 200.

41. Yūsuf, *Tāğīkestān*, 197. Fazilov is commemorated as the IRPT's first *šahid* (martyr) in the Civil War (in the words of the IRPT Fazilov became "the first martyr

on the road to peace"), see the campaign video of the IRPT (http://nahzat.tj/14049-onch-dar-borai-nit-boyad-bidonem.html Accessed February 10, 2015. The website of the IRPT has been shut down after the party's ban in September 2015.

42. Whitlock, *Beyond the River*, 164.

43. Nabieva and Zikriyoyev, *Ta'rixi 11*, 94.

44. Usmonov, *Nabiev*, 78.

45. Sohibnazar, *Subhi 2*, 225.

46. Nazriev and Sattorov, *Respublika Tadžikistan II*, 164. Muhabbat Abdurahmonova served in the GNR as Minister for Social Welfare and Zebuniso Rustamova as the Chairwoman for the State Committee for Physical Education, Sports and Tourism.

47. ERBD, *Tajikistan*, 6–7; FBIS-SOV-92–118, 18 June 1992, 61; FBIS-SOV-92–148, 31 July 1992, 46.

48. Sohibnazar, *Subhi 2*, 19–26; FBIS-SOV-91–251, 31 December 1991, 70.

49. FBIS-SOV-92–002, 3 January 1992, 66.

50. FBIS-SOV-92–015, 23 January 1992, 100.

51. Sohibnazar, *Subhi 2*, 60. See also Nazriev and Sattorov, *Respublika Tadžikistan II*, 169–170.

52. Nasriddinov, *Tarkiš*, 170.

53. Sohibnazar, *Subhi 2*, 56–57.

54. Kenǧaev, *Tabadduloti 2*; Sohibnazar, *Subhi 2*; see also Usmon's remarks on the oppositional character of the GNR: http://www.ozodi.org/articleprintview/24319139.html Accessed June 10, 2014.

55. Yūsuf, *Tāǧīkestān*, 204; Sohibnazar, *Subhi 2*, 44, 53–55.

56. Sohibnazar, *Subhi 2*, 53.

57. FBIS-SOV-92–126, 30 June 1992, 48.

58. Qayumzod, "Xudo," 3.

59. FBIS-SOV-92–115, 15 June 1992, 48; FBIS-SOV-92–116, 16 June 1992, 55.

60. FBIS-SOV-92–137, 16 July 1992, 67–70.

61. FBIS-URS-92–062, 27 May 1992, 104–105.

62. Nasriddinov, *Tarkiš*, 169; FBIS-URS-92–076, 22 June 1992, 108; FBIS-SOV-92–063, 1 April 1992, 59.

63. Sohibnazar, *Subhi 2*, 269.

64. Nasriddinov, *Tarkiš*, 171; Sohibnazar, *Subhi 2*, 203; FBIS-SOV-92–133, 10 July 1992, 84.

65. FBIS-SOV-92–094, 14 May 1992, 55.

66. Qayumzod, "Xudo," 3.

67. Yūsuf, *Tāǧīkestān*, 204–239; FBIS-SOV-92–150, 4 August 1992, 74.

68. Usmonov, *Nabiev*, 78; see Gretsky, "Qadi," 23; FBIS-URS-92–062, 27 May 1992, 104.

69. Usmonov, *Nabiev*, 80.

70. Kenǧaev, *Tabadduloti 1*, 208.

71. FBIS-SOV-92–141, 22 July 1992, 72.

72. FBIS-SOV-92–139, 20 July 1992, 60.

73. See S. Kolosov, "Vostok - delo tonkoe," In *Spetcnaz GRU: Pyat'desyat let istorii, dvadcat' let voyny*, Edited by Sergey N. Kozlov (Moskva: Russkaya panorama, 2001), 300–14; FBIS-SOV-92–195, 7 October 1992, 51–52; A. Sukholesskiy,

"Perebal Šar-Šar," In *Spetcnaz GRU: Pyat'desyat let istorii, dvadcat' let voyny*, Edited by Sergey N. Kozlov (Moskva: Russkaya panorama, 2001), 315–329.

74. FBIS-SOV-92–115, 15 June 1992, 48; FBIS-SOV-92–161, 19 August 1992, 61; Kenğaev, *Tabadduloti 3*, 57.

75. FBIS-SOV-92–147, 30 July 1992, 49. FBIS-SOV-92–136, 15 July 1992, 61; FBIS-SOV-92–137, 16 July 1992, 69–70.

76. Nasriddinov, *Tarkiš*, 172; Sohibnazar, *Subhi 1*, 156–157; FBIS-SOV-92–137, 16 July 1992, 69–70.

77. According to the commander of the 201st MRD 90% of the rank and file were from Tajikistan in mid-1992, the majority ethnic Tajiks (FBIS-SOV-92–152, 6 August 1992, 70), but only 4% of the officers were ethnic Tajiks (FBIS-SOV-92–155, 11 August 1992, 55).

78. FBIS-SOV-92–094, 14 May 1992, 56 and FBIS-URS-92–062, 27 May 1992, 104.

79. FBIS-SOV-92–131, 8 July 1992, 72.

80. FBIS-SOV-92–184, 22 September 1992, 53–54.

81. FBIS-SOV-92–196, 8 October 1992, 49.

82. Kolosov, "Vostok," 300–14; Sukholesskiy, "Perebal," 315–19.

83. Yūsuf, *Tāğīkestān*, 248–249, 262–263; FBIS-SOV-92–151, 5 August 1992, 73–74.

84. FBIS-SOV-92–206, 23 October 1992, 62–63.

85. Sohibnazar, *Subhi 2*, 128.

86. Sohibnazar, *Subhi 2*, 129.

87. FBIS-SOV-92–148, 31 July 1992, 45–46.

88. Sohibnazar, *Subhi 2*, 265.

89. Xaliliyon, "Se xatoi," 11; [Der Spiegel], "Stalins Blut," 147.

90. FBIS-SOV-92–189, 29 September 1992, 41; Yūsuf, *Tāğīkestān*, 250.

91. FBIS-SOV-92–189, 29 September 1992, 42.

92. See Kolosov, "Vostok," 300–14 and Sukholesskiy, "Perebal," 315–19. Likewise Vladimir Kvačkov, a former GRU Colonel, reported about his deployment to Tajikistan (cf. http://lenta.ru/lib/14160312/full.htm Accessed August 7, 2014).

93. Sukholesskiy, "Perebal," 315.

94. Kolosov, "Vostok," 301–14.

95. Kenğaev, *Tabadduloti 3*, 93.

96. FBIS-SOV-92–188, 28 September 1992, 41.

97. FBIS-SOV-92–188, 28 September 1992, 41 and FBIS-SOV-92–202, 19 October 1992, 50.

98. FBIS-SOV-92–168, 28 August 1992, 45; FBIS-SOV-92–198, 13 October 1992, 34.

99. FBIS-SOV-92–193, 5 October 1992, 52.

100. FBIS-SOV-92–195, 7 October 1992, 50; FBIS-SOV-92–198, 13 October 1992, 34; FBIS-SOV-92–201, 16 October 1992, 49; FBIS-SOV-92–197, 9 October 1992, 34.

101. FBIS-SOV-92–217, 9 November 1992, 45.

102. FBIS-SOV-92–013, 21 January 1992, 84; FBIS-SOV-02–020, 30 January 1992, 62; FBIS-SOV-92–027, 10 February 1992, 77.

103. FBIS-SOV-92–094, 14 May 1992, 57.

104. FBIS-SOV-92–131, 8 July 1992, 72.

105. Conversation with a former IRPT commander, Dushanbe March 2010.

106. FBIS-SOV-92–137, 16 July 1992, 70; FBIS-SOV-92–141, 22 July 1992, 73.

107. FBIS-SOV-92–143, 24 July 1992, 61–62.

108. FBIS-SOV-93–134, 15 July 1993, 52–54.

109. FBIS-SOV-92–094, 14 May 1992, 58; Karim, *Faryodi*, 445.

110. Yūsuf, *Tāǧīkestān*, 75, 205. Kenǧaev (*Tabadduloti 1*, 87) insinuates that he had arranged his succession earlier (around 5 May 1992). Karim, *Faryodi*, 415; Yūsuf, *Tāǧīkestān*, 75 and 205–206; FBIS-SOV-92–094, 14 May 1992, 58; FBIS-SOV-92–155, 11 August 1992, 57.

111. *Silovik* (plural *siloviki*) means in Russian "person of force," the term s used since the early 1990s for members of the security forces in general and the former KGB (now FSB) in particular. Cf. Rosneft, ed., *Annual Report 2009* (Moscow, 2009), 235.

112. For this version see Kenǧaev, *Tabadduloti 1*, 231–232 and Dudoignon, "Revival," 54.

113. See for instance Sohibnazar, *Subhi 2*, 28–30.

114. In Šar-Šar and Sayyod (two villages on the road between Dushanbe and Kūlob south of the Norak Reservoir) Ġaffur Mirzoev set up a self-defense group he named 'Youth Group of the Saviors of Xatlon' (Karim, *Faryodi*, 453).

115. FBIS-SOV-92–123, 25 June 1992, 71; FBIS-SOV-92–125, 29 June 1992, 58–59; FBIS-SOV-92–127, 1 July 1992, 56; Nasriddinov, *Tarkiš*, 191, 198.

116. Nasriddinov, *Tarkiš*, 201.

117. Qayumzod, "Xudo," 3; Yūsuf, *Tāǧīkestān*, 234.

118. Interview with Odilbek Qurbonbekov: http://millat.tj/component/content/3176.html?task=view Access June 10, 2014.

119. Cf. Kenǧaev, *Tabadduloti 3*, 17–21; FBIS-SOV-92–125, 29 June 1992, 59.

120. Sohibnazar, *Subhi 2*, 249.

121. Sohibnazar, *Subhi 2*, 74.

122. Conversation with a former IRPT commander in Dushanbe (March 2010); GNR representatives, however, denied these reports in 1992 (FBIS-SOV-92–185, 23 September 1992, 46; FBIS-SOV-92–186, 24 September 1992, 48).

123. Sohibnazar, *Subhi 2*, 90, 249.

124. FBIS-SOV-92–125, 29 June 1992, 59; FBIS-SOV-92–143, 24 July 1992, 61;

125. Kosolov, "Vostok," 300–314.

126. Karim, *Faryodi*, 451.

127. Usmonov, *Nabiev*, 82.

128. Kenǧaev, *Tabadduloti 2*, 111–112.

129. FBIS-SOV-82–141, 22 July 1992, 72; FBIS-SOV-92–202, 19 October 1992, 50–51; FBIS-SOV-92–205, 22 October 1992, 53.

130. FBIS-SOV-92–217, 9 November 1992, 46.

131. FBIS-SOV-92–229, 27 November 1992, 54; FBIS-SOV-92–230, 30 November 1992, 67; FBIS-SOV-92–240, 14 December 1992, 21.

132. FBIS-USR-02–050, 1 May 1992, 103.

133. FBIS-URS-92–076, 22 June 1992, 107–109.

134. Yūsuf, *Tāǧīkestān*, 237; FBIS-SOV-92–122, 24 June 1992, 67. Cf. also Nazriev and Sattorov, *Respublika Tadžikistan II*, 215.

135. Karim, *Faryodi*, 469.

136. FBIS-SOV-92–094, 14 May 1992, 54; Sohibnazar, *Subhi 2*, 30.

137. Karim, *Faryodi*, 452.

138. Yūsuf, *Tāǧīkestān*, 214.

139. Yūsuf, *Tāǧīkestān*, 215–216.

140. Safarov hesitated to assume the formal political leadership himself (at some point in September 1992 he presumably had the military power to do so) but organized the appointment of "proxies." The direct assumption of a political office would have constrained Safarov's freedom of action and he sensed that the 'old' political nomenklatura (especially in Uzbekistan and Russia) would not deal with an ex-convict on a par. Tabarov—in some respects—was Rahmonov's predecessor.

141. Xaliliyon, "Se xatoi." See also Yaʿqubov, *Kūlob*, 480. Kalininobod (today Sarband) is east of Qūrġonteppa close to the Airport.

142. Davlat, "Hameša," 11; Mirrahim, *Hamtabaqi*, 243; Yūsuf, *Tāǧīkestān*, 259.

143. Sohibnazar, *Subhi 2*, 76.

144. Medvedev, "Saga," 188; Sohibnazar, *Subhi 2*, 253.

145. FBIS-SOV-92–179, 15 September 1992, 37.

146. A. Šerxond, "Vaqte dar Kūlob sabus [sic: sabūs] nameyoftand … Turaġonzodaro gunahkor medonistand," on *Millat* (7 June 2012) (http://millat.tj/component/content/3166.html?task=view Accessed June 11, 2014).

147. See Nasriddinov, *Tarkiš*, 192–193; Sohibnazar, *Subhi 2*, 250–252.

148. FBIS-SOV-92–185, 23 September 1992, 48.

149. Kenġaev, *Tabadduloti 2* and *Tabadduloti 3*, passim.

150. Nasriddinov, *Tarkiš*, 205–206.

151. Sohibnazar, *Subhi 2*, 56–57.

152. Kenġaev, *Tabadduloti 1*, 329–331.

153. FBIS-SOV-92–125, 29 June 1992, 59–61.

154. FBIS-SOV-92–141, 22 July 1992, 72; FBIS-SOV-92–143, 24 July 1992, 60.

155. Karim, *Faryodi*, 487. Vanġ is a town and river (tributary to the Panġ River) in eastern Tajikistan, the Panġ River is a tributary (with the Vaxš River) to the Amu Darya. From 'Vanġ to Panġ' therefore comprises the mountainous territory of south-eastern Tajikistan.

156. FBIS-SOV-92–169, 31 August 1992, 40; FBIS-SOV-92–170, 1 September 1992, 45.

157. FBIS-SOV-92–173, 4 September 1992, 46; FBIS-SOV-92–174, 8 September 1992, 48–55.

158. Kenġaev, *Tabadduloti 2*, 139, 170–173.

159. FBIS-SOV-92–179, 15 September 1992, 38.

160. FBIS-SOV-92–182, 18 September 1992, 33.

161. FBIS-SOV-92–189, 29 September 1992, 41–44.

162. Kenğaev, *Tabadduloti 2*, 276.

163. FBIS-SOV-82–141, 22 July 1992, 72; FBIS-SOV-92–145, 28 July 1992, 59.Kenğaev, *Tabadduloti 2*, 365. Kenğaev provides data on the combatants (and not the civilians) from Kūlob killed in action (in Kenğaev's diction they were "martyred" [šahid šud]). He lists 530 men killed in the fighting around Qūrğonteppa in September, 56% of them Tajiks, 40.5% Uzbeks and 3.5% other nationalities.

164. *Vahhobī/vahhobov* with the Russian diminutive suffix –[č]*ik vovčik* (= *vahhobovčik*) means "little" Wahhabi, whilst *yorčik'* or *yurčik* refers to the Russian first name Yuri.

165. Sohibnazar, *Subhi 1*, 17.

166. Karim, *Faryodi*, 456.

167. Sohibnazar, *Subhi 2*, 211.

168. Kolosov, "Vostok," 302.

169. Kenğaev, *Tabadduloti 2*, 287.

170. Kenğaev, *Tabadduloti 1*, 340–341.

171. Yūsuf, *Tāğīkestān*, 288, see also 259.

172. Yūsuf, *Tāğīkestān*, 261.

173. Arno J. Mayer, *The furies: Violence and terror in the French and Russian Revolutions* (Princeton: Princeton University Press, 2000), 323.

174. Kalyvas, *Logic*, 59.

175. Kalyvas, *Logic*, 65.

176. Mueller, "Banality," 43.

177. Yūsuf, *Tāğīkestān*, 220.

178. Yūsuf, *Tāğīkestān*, 5.

179. Yūsuf, *Tāğīkestān*, 229.

180. Yūsuf, *Tāğīkestān*, 230, 235.

181. Yūsuf, *Tāğīkestān*, 262.

182. See Amnesty International, *Tadzhikistan: Hidden terror: Political killings, 'disappearances' and torture since December 1992* (London, 1993); Human Rights Watch, *Human Rights in Tajikistan in the wake of the Civil War* (New York, 1993); Panfilov, *Tadžikistan*, passim.

183. Kalyvas, *Logic*, 84.

184. Kalyvas, *Logic*, 85.

185. Many interviews in the Oral History Project refer to forms of sexual violence (cf. for instance TRS/OHT-A1; TRS/OHT-C4; TRS/OHT-L6).

186. Janie Leatherman, *Sexual violence and armed conflict* (Cambridge: Polity, 2011), 9 (italics in the original text).

187. Elisabeth J. Wood, "Sexual Violence during War: Towards an Understanding of Variation," In *Order, conflict, and violence*, Edited by Stathis N. Kalyvas, Ian Shapiro and Tarek E. Masoud (Cambridge: Cambridge University Press, 2008), 340.

188. Oral History Project Tajikistan, OHT-A1: 7

189. OHT-A1: 8–9.

190. Connell, *Masculinity*, 67–86 and Connell and Messerschmidt, "Hegemonic," 845–853.

191. Karim, *Faryodi*, 476.

192. Cf. Karim, *Faryodi*, 519; Sohibnazar, *Subhi 2*, 68–72 & 137–138.

193. For the sequences of events see Nazriev and Sattorov, *Respublika Tadžikistan II*, 213–216. For different versions see Karim, *Faryodi*, 466–467 and Kenğaev, *Tabadduloti 1*, 354.

194. FBIS-SOV-92-131, 8 July 1992, 73; FBIS-SOV-92-139, 20 July 1992, 61.

195. Karim, *Faryodi*, 475–477; FBIS-SOV-92-126, 30 June 1992, 50; FBIS-SOV-92-130, 7 July 1992, 58.

196. FBIS-SOV-92-156, 12 August 1992, 56.

197. Sohibnazar, *Subhi 2*, 114; FBIS-SOV-92-145, 28 July 1992, 57–58.

198. Cf. the reproduction of the protocol in Kenğaev, *Tabadduloti 2*, 21–23 and Karim, *Faryodi*, 490.

199. Nazriev and Sattorov, *Respublika Tadžikistan II*, 271–272. Usmonov, *Nabiev*, 86.

200. FBIS-SOV-92-145, 28 July 1992, 58–59; FBIS-SOV-92-150, 4 August 1992, 73–74.

201. Medvedev, "Saga," 201.

202. FBIS-SOV-92-151, 5 August 1992, 74; FBIS-SOV-92-155, 11 August 1992, 54.

203. FBIS-SOV-92-161, 19 August 1992, 61–62.

204. Sohibnazar, *Subhi 2*, 113.

205. Cf. FBIS-SOV-92-212, 2 November 1992, 71.

206. The Supreme Soviet in February 1990 had 230 deputies, due to death, ill health and migration 5 deputies retired from the Supreme Soviet without by-elections due to the difficult situation (Dostiev, *Toğikiston*, 148–158).

207. Osimī, *Enziklopediyai*, Vol. 8, 581–583.

208. FBIS-SOV-92-155, 11 August 1992, 57.

209. Kenğaev, *Tabadduloti 2*, 27–28; see also: FBIS-SOV-92-154, 10 August 1992, 63–64.

210. Kenğaev, *Tabadduloti 2*, 35.

211. Nazriev and Sattorov, *Respublika Tadžikistan II*, 295–296; see Kenğaev, *Tabadduloti 2*, 30–32; FBIS-SOV-92-092, 12 May 1992, 58.

212. FBIS-SOV-92-155, 11 August 1992, 53; FBIS-SOV-92-158, 14 August 1992, 34.

213. Karim, *Faryodi*, 501; see also FBIS-SOV-92-159, 17 August 1992, 28.

214. FBIS-SOV-92-121, 23 June 1992, 63; FBIS-SOV-92-123, 25 June 1992, 72; Yūsuf, *Tāğīkestān*, 274–275; Sohibnazar, *Subhi 2*, 187–190.

215. Yūsuf, *Tāğīkestān*, 273–274; [Der Spiegel], "Fremder im eignen Land." *Der Spiegel*, September 7, 1992, 37: 184–185.

216. FBIS-SOV-92-170, 1 September 1992, 46.

217. Sohibnazar, *Subhi 2*, 187–201.

218. Nasriddinov, *Tarkiš*, 188.

219. Kenğaev, *Tabadduloti 2*, 47–48, 132. See also FBIS-SOV-92-172, 3 September 1992, 43.

220. FBIS-SOV-92-172, 3 September 1992, 44.

221. Nasriddinov, *Tarkiš*, 180–181; FBIS-SOV-92-172, 3 September 1992, 45.

222. Nasriddinov (*Tarkiš*, 177–179), who was an eye witness, reported about several phone calls between the MVD and the Presidium of the Supreme Soviet and about a TV team ready to film Nabiev's resignation. An armored column of the 201st MRD later arrived at the airport but did not interfere fueling rumors that the Russian administration welcomed Nabiev's exit.

223. Sohibnazar, *Subhi 2*, 225.

224. Sohibnazar insinuated that Abdulloğonov was behind the Nabiev's resignation since he had ambitions to succeed him. See Sohibnazar, *Subhi 2*, 227; Yūsuf, *Tāğīkestān*, 282.

225. Nasriddinov, *Tarkiš*, 180.

226. Sohibnazar, *Subhi 2*, 236.

227. Sohibnazar, *Subhi 2*, 244; FBIS-SOV-92–218, 10 November 1992, 65.

228. FBIS-SOV-92–174, 8 September 1992, 48–55; Sohibnazar, *Subhi 2*, 238; Yūsuf, *Tāğīkestān*, 282–284.

229. Yūsuf, *Tāğīkestān*, 284.

230. Yūsuf, *Tāğīkestān*, 284.

231. Yūsuf, *Tāğīkestān*, 285.

232. Usmonov, *Nabiev*, 102; FBIS-SOV-92–175, 9 September 1992, 47. See also Kenğaev's (*Tabadduloti 2*, 161–167) critique on their legal opinion.

233. http://www.ozodi.org/articleprintview/24319139.html. Accessed June 10, 2014.

234. Sohibnazar, *Subhi 1*, 28.

235. Kenğaev, *Tabadduloti 2*, 55. The *Siyosatnoma* is the 11th century CE treatise on kingship by the Seljuk *vezir* Nizam al-Mulk.

236. Kenğaev, *Tabadduloti 2*, 230.

237. Remarkably, Ibrohim Usmonov (*Nabiev*, 26) came to a similar conclusion with regard to Kenğaev.

238. Kenğaev, *Tabadduloti 2*, 221.

239. Kenğaev, *Tabadduloti 2*, 230.

240. Sohibnazar, *Subhi 2*, 255.

241. FBIS-SOV-92–189, 29 September 1992, 41.

242. FBIS-SOV-92–187, 25 September 1992, 47–48.

243. FBIS-SOV-93–068, 12 April 1993, 62.

244. Nazriev and Sattorov, *Respublika Tadžikistan II*, 381; FBIS-SOV-92–190, 30 September 1992, 41.

245. Sohibnazar, *Subhi 2*, 272.

246. Nabieva and Zikriyoyev, *Tarixi 11*, 93–95.

247. Kenğaev, *Tabadduloti 3*, 12.

248. In Kenğaev's memoirs, the Popular Front is consistently labelled as *fronti xalqī*. In other sources, the terms *sitodi millī* (National Staff) or *ğabhai xalqī* (Popular Front) are also used.

249. Cf. http://millat.tj/component/content/3161.html?task=view Accessed June 11, 2014.

250. Kenğaev, *Tabadduloti 1*, 173, 179.

251. Kenğaev, *Tabadduloti 1*, 305.

252. Kenğaev, *Tabadduloti 1*, 306; as an alternative version: Yūsuf, *Tāğīkestān*, 295.

253. Kenğaev, *Tabadduloti 2*, 190.

254. Sohibnazar, *Subhi 2*, 89.

255. Kenğaev, *Tabadduloti 2*, 236.

256. Kenğaev, *Tabadduloti 2*, 104–105.

257. Kenğaev, *Tabadduloti 2*, 187–189.

258. Kenğaev, *Tabadduloti 2*, 107.

259. Kenğaev, *Tabadduloti 2*, 107–110.

260. Kenğaev, *Tabadduloti 2*, 90–105.

261. Kenğaev, *Tabadduloti 3*, 56.

262. Kenğaev, *Tabadduloti 3*, 68–99.

263. Sohibnazar, *Subhi 2*, 273–275.

264. Kenğaev, *Tabadduloti 3*, 68.

265. Kenğaev, *Tabadduloti 3*, 97.

266. Kenğaev, *Tabadduloti 3*, 112.

267. Kenğaev, *Tabadduloti 3*, 127.

268. Kenğaev (*Tabadduloti 2*, 73) provided only approximate numbers: According to a plan he agreed on with Rizoev, the attack force on Dushanbe should consist of 2,000 men from Kūlob (attacking from the southeast), 1,100 men from Kenğaev's Popular Front (from the west), and 500 men from Leninobod (attacking from Varzob in the north). He later (113) claimed that the Popular Front had some 25,000 men enlisted. Nasriddinov (*Tarkiš*, 196) reported that Kenğaev led only some 500 men in the assault on Dushanbe (which is largely supported by the media coverage). Sohibnazar (*Subhi 2*, 294) reported that Kenğaev's force consisted of 3–4 APCs and 25 army trucks.

269. Kenğaev, Tabadduloti 3, 139.

270. Kenğaev, *Tabadduloti 3*, 142.

271. FBIS-SOV-92–207, 26 October 1992, 71–73. Kenğaev, *Tabadduloti 3*, 144.

272. FBIS-SOV-92–208, 27 October 1992, 59–64; Sohibnazar, *Subhi 2*, 302; Kenğaev, *Tabadduloti 3*, 143–144.

273. Sohibnazar, *Subhi 2*, 285–286. Kenğaev (*Tabadduloti 3*, 124) insinuates that he was aware that the assault on Dushanbe did not come as a surprise for the GNR.

274. Usmonov, *Ta'rixi siyosii*, 85–86; FBIS-SOV-92–206, 23 October 1992, 61. FBIS-SOV-92–210, 29 October 1992, 57.

275. Sohibnazar, *Subhi 2*, 279–280.

276. Kenğaev, *Tabadduloti 3*, 154.

277. Kenğaev, *Tabadduloti 3*, 148–159.

278. Kenğaev, *Tabadduloti 3*, 160–166. Cf. also FBIS-SOV-92–202, 19 October 1992, 51; Nasriddinov, *Tarkiš*, 196. Langariev was evacuated to Xuğand where he died on 9 January 1993 from the wounds sustained in the assault.

279. Kenğaev, *Tabadduloti 3*, 171–173.

280. Kenğaev, *Tabadduloti 3*, 178–188. FBIS-SOV-92–207, 26 October 1992, 68; FBIS-SOV-92–208, 27 October 1992, 59–61.

281. FBIS-SOV-92–207, 26 October 1992, 69; Karim, *Faryodi*, 511.

282. Kenğaev, *Tabadduloti 3*, 247.

283. Yūsuf, *Tāǧīkestān*, 301; see Kenğaev, *Tabadduloti 3*, 172–174.

284. Usmonov, *Nabiev*, 107.

285. Kenğaev, *Tabadduloti 3*, 129

286. Kenğaev, *Tabadduloti 3*, 13.

287. FBIS-SOV-92–202, 19 October 1992, 49; FBIS-SOV-92–203, 20 October 1992, 44–45.

288. Nasriddinov, *Tarkiš*, 286–287.

289. FBIS-SOV-92–202, 19 October 1992, 51. Apparently Kenğaev (*Tabadduloti 2*, 280–284) realized Safarov's change of policy.

290. Sohibnazar, *Subhi 2*, 298.

291. Kenğaev, *Tabadduloti 2*, 308 and *Tabadduloti 3*, 245.

292. Kenğaev, *Tabadduloti 3*, 124.

293. Kenğaev, *Tabadduloti 3*, 312.

294. Yūsuf, *Tāǧīkestān*, 298.

295. Qayumzod, A.:"Az 'a' to 'ya'-I Iǧlosiyai 16 dar guftugū bo Iskandarov". On: Radioi Ozodī (http://www.ozodi.mobi/a/inerviw-with-iskandarov-on-handover/24757203.html Accessed October 14, 2014).

296. Nasriddinov, *Tarkiš*, 198; FBIS-SOV-92–209, 28 October 1992, 56.

297. FBIS-SOV-92–210, 29 October 1992, 56–59; Kenğaev, *Tabadduloti 3*, 192–193.

298. FBIS-SOV-92–209, 28 October 1992, 56. Kenğaev, *Tabadduloti 3*, 193.

299. Kenğaev, *Tabadduloti 3*, 299.

300. Nasriddinov, *Tarkiš*, 197.

301. FBIS-SOV-92–217, 9 November 1992, 46; FBIS-SOV-92–218, 10 November 1992, 65; FBIS-SOV-92–212, 2 November 1992, 71; Kenğaev, *Tabadduloti 3*, 39–50; Sohibnazar, *Subhi 2*, 269; 283–284.

302. FBIS-SOV-92–215, 5 November 1992, 63; FBIS-SOV-92–217, 9 November 1992, 46.

303. Karim, *Faryodi*, 520; Kenğaev, *Tabadduloti 2*, 293. FBIS-SOV-92–212, 2 November 1992, 71; FBIS-SOV-92–227, 24 November 1992, 49.

Chapter 9

The 16th Session of the Supreme Soviet

In September 1992, many Tajik politicians realized that only a session of the Supreme Soviet could resolve the political deadlock and constitutional stand-off. On the cabinet meeting on 7 September (the same day Nabiev was inter-cepted at the airport and forced to resign), Iskandarov suggested to convene the 16th Session in Xuğand for security reasons and in order to reintegrate the northern elites. Tūrağonzoda decidedly opposed the idea since he could not mobilize the same level non-parliamentary support in Xuğand as in Dushanbe, but the majority of Presidium members endorsed Iskandarov's initiative.[1] Not only Tūrağonzoda voiced his concerns, also Davlat Usmon explicitly spoke out against convening the 16th Session in the north: Dushanbe is the capital of Tajikistan and a convention in a different place would increase the civil dis-turbance in the country and further unsettle the population.[2] The resignation of Nabiev delayed the convocation of the 16th Session due to indecisiveness and disagreements among leading politicians. Iskandarov had little interest convening a session after his assumption of office since he was aware that the Supreme Soviet would never confirm his appointment. He intended to consol-idate his position and proliferate as a candidate for the presidential elections later in 1992.[3] Sohibnazar pointed out, that he "did not take a clear position. He thought that if he does not interfere into the affairs of the leaders of the *viloyat,* and if he would stay neutral (*betaraf*), he would see an opportunity to formally stay in office."[4] Finally, the Russian government urged the Tajik government to convene the 16th Session in Xuğand. Throughout September the military situation was confusing and in flux and only in October the situ-ation gradually changed: Safarov had conquered Qūrġonteppa, thousands of refugees crossed into northern Afghanistan or looked for shelter in Dushanbe triggering a severe humanitarian crisis and alarming Tajikistan's neighbors. The Yeltsin administration therefore urged the Tajik government to convene a Supreme Soviet session as soon as possible. The Russian foreign minister, Andrey Kozyrev, even suggested convening a session in Bishkek and sent envoys to Tajikistan to prepare the session.[5] In early November, influential field commanders gave their consent to convene the 16th Session.[6] Iskandarov tried once more to postpone the session suggesting the convocation of a National Assembly with more than 1,000 representatives in a strategy to bypass the majorities in the Supreme Soviet. The nomenklatura from Leninobod and Safarov rejected Iskandarov's plan and there was no constitutional provision for a national assembly. Safarov and the Leninobod nomenklatura were confident to find majorities in the current Supreme Soviet and get through with their agenda.

The final decision on the 16th Session came after a meeting of Iskandarov with the Central Asian neighbors in Almaty, where Uzbekistan's Islam Karimov demanded the convention of the Supreme Soviet. Iskandarov bowed to the pressure and on 9 November 1992, the Presidium formally invited the deputies for the 16th Session in Xuğand. The Government of National Reconciliation was exhausted and had failed politically. The military situation was grim and the Popular Front's marauding soldiery threatened Kofarnihon and Fayzobod, the entry to the Qarotegin Valley and Dushanbe. On 10 November, the government and the Presidium of the Supreme Soviet resigned.[7]

The 16th Session of the Supreme Soviet convened on 16 November 1992 in *qasri* Arbob, a grotesquely large "House of Culture" (*dom kultury*) in a cotton kolkhoz close to Xuğand. Out of 230 deputies of the Supreme Soviet, 193 were present.[8] Except for Sohibnazar, none of the first generation of Glasnost activists and democratic deputies elected in February 1990 was present in Xuğand. Concerned for his security, Tūrağonzoda also did not take part in the session.

Prior to the discussion in the plenum, the deputies agreed to establish a Conciliation Commission (*Komissiyai muroso*) of 40 deputies under the Chairmanship of Qurbon Tūraev (a deputy from Istaravšon). This commission prepared the agenda, decided on the sequence of speakers and the working language (Russian and Tajik). The most important topic of the agenda was the election of a new chairman of the Supreme Soviet who should act until presidential elections as Tajikistan's head of state with the authority to appoint a new government. To accommodate the military clout of Safarov's militia, his protégé Emomalī Rahmonov was the only candidate. In late 1992, the Leninobodī nomenklatura could not ignore Kūlob in the distribution of key positions in the new government. As Davlat Usmon pointed out, Safarov's Popular Front represented the most powerful military formation and 80% of the combatants of the Popular Front were from the Kūlob area. The political leaders in Leninobod and Uzbekistan still expected that the Kūlobī dominance would only last for a brief period of time since internal conflict had already thinned out their ranks. After the defeat of the opposition and the capture of Dushanbe, a younger generation of professional politicians around the Abdulloǧonov brothers expected to return to power.[9]

The deputies decided to suspend the presidential office until elections. Since the chairman of the Supreme Soviet had to be elected by the deputies of the Supreme Soviet, the transition of power was considered as constitutionally acceptable without general elections. Accordingly, Rahmonov announced that the most important objective of the 16th Session would be the re-establishment of constitutional order and not the question of guilt or vengeance—and as such the 16th Session has entered the political historiography of post-conflict Tajikistan.[10] The 16th Session can be interpreted as a transition from situational power based on informal militias to a more institutionalized rule based on an agreement among the field commanders and political elites.[11] The violent non-state actors took their toll: Safarov presented himself as a conciliatory mediator and elder statesman, who publicly celebrated the *oši ošti* with the opposition field commander Ǧumʿaxon Būydoqov. In a solemn ceremony Rahmonov handed over the newly designed national flag and coat of arms of Tajikistan (both devised by Muhammad Osimī) to Safarov who now led his Popular Front with the colors of the new government.[12] Yaqub Salimov, the ex-convict and criminal turned field commander, was rewarded with the position of the Minister of Interior.[13] The 16th Session influenced also the Central Asian and Russian perspective on the conflict and the Session was a prerequisite for the deployment of a CIS peacekeeping force, which provided for the years to come some security for the Rahmonov administration.[14]

Exit Kenǧaev

Imperturbably, Kenǧaev considered the convention of the 16th Session as his personal achievement and result of his military operations.[15] As a deputy of the Supreme Soviet, he was invited to take part in the session and flew to Xuǧand. But upon his arrival in Xuǧand, he was intercepted by KGB officers, escorted to a private residence and held there incommunicado for five days until the Supreme Soviet had adopted the most important decisions.[16] The Leninobodī nomenklatura as well as the Uzbek and Russian governments had a substantial interest in the smooth organization of the session, which should symbolize the return to constitutional order and result in the formation of a legitimate and (from an Uzbek/Russian perspective) acceptable Tajik government without Islamist participation. Kenǧaev should not spoil the course of events by his erratic interventions and divisive behavior. After five days, Kenǧaev reappeared at the Session. He only made vague allusions and announced he would inform the newly elected chairman of the Supreme Soviet, Rahmonov, confidentially about his abduction.[17] Even later Kenǧaev did not explain his absence in his memoirs, but merely insinuated a plot by the political elites in Leninobod and Kūlob, whilst "those who were searching for truth, such as Rustam Abdurahimov, Langarī Langariev or Ğahonxon Rizoev, had been assassinated."[18] In politics, Kenğaev concluded "you sell your mother and brother, your father and sister, for a position."[19] His fall from grace and exit from Tajikistan's political stage became clear after the capture of Dushanbe in December 1992. When Rahmonov formed a new government, he did not consider Kenğaev for a ministerial portfolio and Sohibnazar acidly concluded: "The Kūlobīs did not even give him the position of a gate-keeper to the Yağnob Valley. In fact, they did not even offer him the horseshoe of a dead donkey."[20]

Enter Emomalī Rahmonov

Emomalī Rahmonov entered the republican political stage when he was elected deputy of the Supreme Soviet in the constituency No. 172 in Danğara 1990. Born in 1952 in Danğara, he passed through an inconspicuous career in the local Soviet administration. After his military service in the Soviet Pacific Fleet (1971–1974), he worked as a technician in the Qūrğonteppa Oil Extraction Combine. In 1982 Rahmonov graduated with an economics degree from the Tajik State University and became administrative secretary of the Lenin kolkhoz in Danğara. When the kolkhoz was transformed into a sovkhoz 1987, Rahmonov was appointed director, an office he held until 1992. As a deputy of the Supreme Soviet, Rahmonov was member of a parliamentary committee dealing with regional affairs; therefore, he frequently traveled to the neighboring republics and established contacts with his colleagues in Uzbekistan, Kazakhstan and Kyrgyzstan—perhaps one reason why he was accepted by the regional stakeholders as chairman of the Supreme Soviet in 1992.

Sangak Safarov appointed Rahmonov chairman of the Ispolkom of the Kūlob *viloyat* on 2 November after he had assassinated Rahmonov's predecessor, Rizoev, a few days earlier.[21] Safarov chose Rahmonov in anticipation of the forthcoming 16th Session as his political representative. Safarov realized that he could not seize power himself. His criminal background and the public execution of several high-ranking cadres made him an unacceptable candidate in particular for Uzbekistan and Russia. Furthermore, an official position would have constrained his room for maneuver.

In turn, Rahmonov, as a local collective farm director, did not represent the higher echelons of the Soviet nomenklatura in Kūlob and therefore he did not have an independent political power base in autumn 1992. His inconspicuousness made him also acceptable for Safarov's rivals in Kūlob, Dushanbe, Hisor and Xuğand. Finally, Rahmonov was not a field commander with his own militia and had not been delegitimized by extreme violence. Instead, he had to depend on different field commanders for providing "security"—a situation, which should continue until the early 2000s.

Rahmonov's appointment as Chairman had been prepared carefully in advance and on 18 November 186 deputies (out of the 193 present) elected him chairman of the Supreme Soviet. The remaining agenda of the 16th Session proceeded quietly without controversies or open disputes.[22]

Re-establishing the Constitutional Order:
Evaluating the 16th Session

Rahmonov and his government immediately celebrated the 16th Session as a watershed not only for the armed conflict but also for Tajikistan as a nation. In his first New Year's Address on 31 December 1992, Rahmonov asserted that the session at *qasri* Arbob was the restoration of a constitutional government and a few years later, in his programmatic speech on the history of the Tajiks, he portrayed the event as one of the defining moments in Tajik history in line with the foundation of the Somonid Dynasty (819 CE), the establishment of the Soviet Republic of Tajikistan (1924/1929) and the declaration of independence in 1991.[23] Since then, *qasri* Arbob has been revamped to a national memorial adorned with portraits of Emomalī Rahmonov and Ismoil Somonī evoking the idea of historical continuity (Figure 9.1).

Sohibnazar considered the 16th Session and the rise of Rahmonov not as a fundamental change of the political landscape of Tajikistan, but the take-over of the government by a "third force" alluding to the Uzbek "hidden hand" in Rahmonov's rise to power. He concluded that the political economy of the country largely remained the same: The Supreme Soviet did not transform into a professional parliament but remained an instrument with which the dominant elite could provide their networks with formal positions, which allowed quid pro quo access to state resources.[24] Likewise, Būrī Karim asserted, "the session did not adopt any new laws or took decisions which had to be explained to the people of Tajikistan. Only the politicians were exchanged like chessmen, they continued to work according to the traditional Communist principles."[25] For Yusuf, the 16th Session was a communist coup d'état and not the end of the civil war, instead it marked the destruction of the democratic parties and civil associations:

> The Tajik people should understand that they were deceived by their own parliament. Today, our fatherland is trapped in a fratricidal war, which has killed thousands. The DPT tried to end the war from the first day on [...]. However, the Agreement of Xoruǧ was not honored. And now, the 16th Session of the Supreme Soviet has been convened in the ancient city of Xuǧand and we came with the intention to conclude peace and find reconciliation in this meeting. We also believed that the Communists had understood that it is the wish of all the people in Tajikistan, that peace is concluded. But know we realize that the

Figure 9.1   Entry of the *Qasri* Arbob Close to Xuğand with Portraits of Emomalī Rahmon[ov] (left) and Ismoil Somonī (right).

Source: Tim Epkenhans

> Communists are only interested in power and have betrayed the country and its people. [...] But this government [of Rahmonov] does not have a future and has no place in history, since no one could be truly victorious only with the help of mercenaries and slaves.[26]

A few opposition members even welcomed the suspension of the presidential office since it indicated a gradual change from a presidential to a parliamentary system with a higher degree of participation and inclusiveness.[27] These expectations were finally disappointed with the presidential elections in 1994.

Unsurprisingly, politicians from the south, in particular Kūlob, viewed the 16th Session positively: Nasriddinov celebrated the 16th Session not only as the re-establishment of the rule of law but also as the reconstruction of the "mechanisms of statehood"[28] as well as the "victory of truth, justice and law."[29] For Qurbon Voseʻ, a close associate of Rahmonov, the 16th Session was a reversal of "fortune for the people and the country":

> First, it created our national unity. Second, it saved our people and our country from annihilation and destruction. Third, it gathered the political elite of our country around the Chairman of the Supreme Soviet and later President E[momalī] Š[aripovič] Rahmonov to an extent possible. Fourth, important for the political

culture of our country and the constitutional law, it drafted a program for the future of a secular democratic government, which was accepted by the people. Fifth, it established power structures and extended them. Sixth, it introduced the country to a second round of rebuilding and reconstruction. Seventh, it created a civil society based on mutual understanding and solidarity. Eighth, the peace of the Tajiks and the political school of the President of our country is a shining example for the countries of the region and the entire world.[30]

Shortly after its inauguration, the Rahmonov administration initiated a process of "inventing traditions" and thereby generating legitimation with the 16th Session as the defining date in the imagination of Tajikistan's authentic history.[31] In numerous speeches and writings between 1993 and 1997, the 16th Session equals, if not exceeds, Independence Day (9 September) in importance for the nationalist imagination of the Rahmonov government. With the General Peace Accord 1997, the significance temporarily shifted to the Day of National Unity (*Rūzi vahdati millī* on 27 June). Rahmonov now presented himself as the one who re-established order and peace—a role, albeit, he had to share with Abdullo Nurī until 2006. In recent years—related to the consolidation of Rahmonov's authoritarian government, the marginalization and eventual ban of the IRPT and reconfiguration of the official historical interpretation of 1991—the significance of Independence Day for the invention of the modern Tajik tradition has increased gradually.[32]

In November 1992, the 16th Session resembled perhaps more like a restoration of the "old" Soviet political system and elites centered on the former Soviet institutions including the constitutional order, which was based on the Soviet Tajik constitution from 1978.

THE CAPTURE OF DUSHANBE

At the time, Rahmonov handed over the new national flag and coat of arms to his mentor "Bobo" Sangak, the latter's Popular Front controlled most parts of the south and regrouped for an attack via Yovon on Kofarnihon and Dushanbe. In mid-November, approximately 1,750 men organized in different militias and MVD units maintained security in Dushanbe and were supposed to defend the city against the attack by the Popular Front.[33] After Iskandarov's agreement with the Russian government, the 201st MRD remained neutral and did not intervene in the fighting but guarded several locations in the city.

In late November, Fayzalī Saidov's militia occupied Kofarnihon some 20 km east of Dushanbe and after heavy fighting on 29 November he dislodged Rizvon's men.[34] Until 6 December, militias from Kūlob and Hisor encircled Dushanbe and heavy fighting was reported from the southern and western suburbs.[35] In the early evening of 7 December 1992, the Popular Front under the command of Safarov (from the south), Saidov (from the east/Kofarnihon) and Salimov (from the west/Hisor) started its final assault on Dushanbe.[36] Fighting continued until 10 December, when Rahmonov's government was eventually flown in from Xuğand to Dushanbe in the evening.[37] Shortly after his arrival, Rahmonov addressed the nation in a televised speech stressing the legitimacy of his government:

> The Tajik people have for thousands of years contributed to a worldwide respected civilization with their brilliant sons. Today each of us asks: Why did this catastrophe has befallen our people? The answer is known to all of us. It was a conflict for positions and rule. And the people know how this conflict was provoked. The 16th Session of the Supreme Soviet of the Republic of Tajikistan has vowed to defend the constitution and the laws of the Republic and it has elected the Presidium of the Supreme Soviet of the Republic of Tajikistan according to the laws. A government has been built which takes over its duties today.[38]

The defense of Dushanbe collapsed rapidly and the local networks of organized crime quickly adapted to the new situation. Local groups from Badaxšon in Dushanbe's Avul district, however, refused to surrender their weapons out of concern about reprisals against the population from Badaxšon. Random fighting continued for a few more days, in particular in quarters with strong representation of Pomirī and Ġarmī population.[39] On 18 December, Yaqub Salimov, the racketeer turned minister of interior, declared Dushanbe under full government control.[40] Throughout the next months, however, the various competing militias within the Popular Front exercised a brutal regime in Dushanbe persecuting alleged opposition members in particular from Badaxšon, who were systematically arrested and often executed on the spot.[41] As Sohibnazar reported, public busses were stopped and the male passengers were ordered to repeat the Tajik words for "potato" (= *kartoška*) and "eight" (= *hašt*). Since people from Badaxšon pronounce the words differently (*tuška* and *ašt*), those "identified" in this language test were arrested and summarily executed.[42] An ethnic Russian respondent from Dushanbe remembered how the Pomirī community was attacked after the seizure of Dushanbe:

> There were no Pomirīs in our apartment block. But in the neighboring block, the whole family, which had hidden in the basement, all of them were massacred, slaughtered. Yes, there were many such cases. Our apartment building had one block and on the opposite side there were four blocks of residential buildings with many Pomirīs living there. Some of them left, some were hiding. And some were just killed. It was like ethnic cleansing (*etničeskaya čistka*).[43]

Karim reported that 267 Pomirī disappeared in Dushanbe, but Yusuf maintained that about 1,000 men from Badaxšon were executed and the "dikes of Dushanbe were filled with their blood."[44] The terror against people from

Badaxšon compelled Rahmonov to concede in a duplicitous statement that his government had no control over the situation since "armed groups have infiltrated the interior ministry."[45] At the same time, he asserted that GBAO is an integral part of Tajikistan and condemned the assaults on the population from Badaxšon in Dushanbe. Rahmonov's government indeed had only limited control over the situation and had to negotiate "security" with the Popular Front—in this case with Yaqub Salimov, the newly appointed minister of interior.

For the years to come, Dushanbe remained a contested city and violence flared up frequently until the early 2000s, including numerous assassinations (for instance Otaxon Latifī in 1998 and Safaralī Kenğaev in 1999) and assassination attempts. By the end of 1992, the militias of the IRPT and DPT had been pushed back into the remote mountainous east of Tajikistan. Throughout 1993, the government and its various militias advanced into the Qarotegin Valley. The state media reported diligently about "purging" the valley from *vahhobīs* and Islamic fundamentalists. By early summer 1993, 60% of the local population was expelled and more than 18 villages destroyed only in the Kofarnihon/Fayzobod area.[46] Although Usmonov, Dūstov, Nasriddinov, Sohibnazar and Abdulov consider the capture of Dushanbe as the end of the civil war, the conflict continued with inexorable cruelty for the next four years taking perhaps more than 100,000 lives in total.

Apodosis: Sangak Safarov's Assassination and Rahmon Nabiev's Death

On 29 March 1993 Sangak Safarov and Fayzalī Saidov met in Boxtar to discuss the return of refugees to the Qūrğonteppa area. Reportedly, there had been increasing tensions between the two field commanders[47]: While Safarov tried to broaden his legitimation by adopting a more nationalist tone and by negotiating with UNHCR the return of refugees to Qūrğonteppa and Šahrtuz, Saidov remained the locally entrenched field commander with his personal vendetta and opposed any reconciliation violently. Apparently, Safarov tried to convince Saidov to accept his new policy in a personal meeting. Both field commanders met in an administrative building in Boxtar with their bodyguards and—accidently or not—an exchange of fire killed both.[48] A few days later, on 11 April, Rahmon Nabiev passed away in Xuğand after a cardiac infarction.

NOTES

1. Sohibnazar, *Subhi 2*, 220–222.
2. See the interview with Usmon on http://www.ozodi.org/content/article/24319139.html Accessed July 13, 2014.

3. Karim, *Faryodi*, 542.
4. Sohibnazar, *Subhi 2*, 238.
5. FBIS-SOV-92–217, 9 November 1992, 44.
6. FBIS-SOV-92–217, 9 November 1992, 47; FBIS-SOV-92–218, 10 November 1992, 65.
7. FBIS-SOV-92–219, 12 November 1992, 81–82.
8. Dostiev, *Toğikiston*, 36–37.
9. Conversation with a former CPT official in Xuğand (May 2003 and April 2010). The interview with Usmon on http://www.ozodi.org/articleprintview/24319139.html Accessed June 10, 2014.
10. See Nasriddinov, *Tarkiš*, 232. Dostiev, *Toğikiston*, passim; Nabieva and Zikriyoev, *Ta'rixi 11*, 95; Usmonov, *Toğikon*; 4; Voseʻ, *Az qasri*, 8.
11. Veit and Schlichte, "Legitimierung," 161.
12. Karim, *Faryodi*, 544; FBIS-SOV-92–229, 27 November 1992, 52.
13. FBIS-SOV-92–226, 23 November 1992, 69.
14. FBIS-SOV-92–232, 2 December 1992, 24–25. See Dov Lynch, *Russian peacekeeping strategies in the CIS: The cases of Moldova, Georgia and Tajikistan* (New York: Palgrave, 2000).
15. Kenğaev, *Tabadduloti 3*, 316–321.
16. Karim, *Faryodi*, 538. See [Farağ], "Pisari Kenğaev: 'Padaram farzandi zamoni xud bud…'," *Farağ*, September 26, 2012, 39: 4.
17. Nasriddinov, *Tarkiš*, 216.
18. Kenğaev, *Tabadduloti 3*, 328.
19. Kenğaev, *Tabadduloti 3*, 329.
20. Sohibnazar, *Subhi 2*, 242. Although Kenğaev was never again considered for a government position, he remained in politics. After a brief tenure as persecutor in the town of Qayroqqum (far away from Dushanbe in Leninobod), he was elected to the Parliament in 1994 and founded in 1996 the Socialist Party of Tajikistan. He was assassinated in Dushanbe 1999.
21. Abdullaev and Akbarzadeh, *Dictionary*, 177–178.
22. Voseʻ, *Az qasri*, 18; FBIS-SOV-92–225, 20 November 1992, 54; FBIS-SOV-92–229, 27 November 1992, 53.
23. Rahmonov, *Ehyoi millat*, Vol. 1, 20.
24. Sohibnazar, *Subhi 2*, 214.
25. Karim, *Faryodi*, 541.
26. Yūsuf, *Tāğīkestān*, 312–313.
27. Information based on a conversation with Ašūrboy Imomov, 30 August 2013, Bishkek.
28. Nasriddinov, *Tarkiš*, 234.
29. Nasriddinov, *Tarkiš*, 251.
30. Voseʻ, *Az qasri*, 24.
31. Cf. E. J. Hobsbawm and T. O. Ranger, eds., *The Invention of tradition* (New York: Cambridge University Press, 1983).
32. Cf. Epkenhans, "Mythos," 137–150.

33. Kenğaev, *Tabadduloti 3*, 272. Interviews with eyewitnesses generally support these figures.

34. Karim, *Faryodi*, 544; FBIS-SOV-92–227, 24 November 1992, 50.

35. FBIS-SOV-92–235, 7 December 1992, 20–22.

36. FBIS-SOV-92–234, 4 December 1992, 42.

37. Karim, *Faryod*, 563. FBIS-SOV-92–240, 14 December 1992, 17–18.

38. Emomalī Rahmonov, *Dah soli istiqloliyat, vahdati millī va bunyodkorī* (Dušanbe: Irfon, 2001), 4–5.

39. FBIS-SOV-92–240, 14 December 1992, 20; FBIS-SOV-92–241, 15 December 1992, 41.

40. FBIS-SOV-92–245, 21 December 1992, 69–70.

41. Karim, *Faryodi*, 564; Human Rights Watch, *Human Rights*, 3–10. FBIS-SOV-92–243; 17 December 1992, 58–59; FBIS-SOV-92–247, 23 December 1992, 73.

42. Sohibnazar, *Subhi 2*, 242.

43. OHT-S4: 3–4.

44. Yūsuf, *Tāğīkestān*, 316.

45. FBIS-SOV-92–247, 23 December 1992, 73.

46. Karim, *Faryodi*, 553–554.

47. See the haunting video footage of Saidov's birthday party in February 1993 on: https://www.youtube.com/watch?v=J04qUtpDs_s Accessed October 15, 2014.

48. See Sohibnazar, *Subhi 2*, 209–211; FBIS-SOV-93–060, 31 March 1993, 73–74.

Epilogue

The Nation Imagined and the Civil War Remembered

Omnem memoriam discordiarum oblivione sempiterna delendam[1]

Cicero, *Philippica* 1,1

In August 1996, a year before the General Peace Accord, Rahmonov held a programmatic speech entitled *The Tajiks in the Mirror of History* (*Toğikon dar oinai ta'rix*)[2], which was later extended to a three-volume book. In his speech, Rahmonov reconfirmed and reconfigured the official Tajik national narrative based on the paradigms of Tajik-Soviet historiography but now without ideological constrictions or regional considerateness. Central to Rahmonov's reconstruction of the Tajik nation were the reference to the Aryan ethnogenesis of the Tajiks and the origins of Tajikistan's statehood with the Somonid dynasty. "It is known to all," Rahmonov asserts, "that the Tajiks are genuine Aryans, and from ancient times the original inhabitants of Central Asia."[3] Rahmon describes the Tajiks as peace-loving, altruistic, united, honest and cultured people, who have never used violence against other people—in contrast to their Arab and Turkish neighbors, who repeatedly plundered and occupied the homeland of the Tajiks. The Arabs were the first who destroyed the homeland of the Tajiks in the 8th century CE and either killed or deported the civilized Tajiks to build the cities of the Caliphate. However, the Tajik genius survived the Arabic-Islamic invasion and with the Somonid dynasty the "honorable national civilization reached a new zenith of perfected statehood and consummate personality."[4] The heyday of the Somonids was short-lived and this time the Turks (*turkho*) destroyed the splendid Tajik polity by deception and deceit, establishing their own statehood parasitically on the Tajik model.[5] The Somonid dynasty is presented as the central signifier for Tajik statehood and identity in delimitation to the

351

Uzbek Other.[6] The reference to the Somonids as the first truly Tajik polity has left a visible imprint on the townscape of Dushanbe and other cities. The omnipresent Lenin statues were replaced by statues of Ismoil Somonī, whose idealized pictures also adorn public buildings in pair with pictures of President Rahmonov whose features often conspicuously resemble those of Ismoil (Figure 9.1). Many representatives of the Tajik political and intellectual elite, regardless of their political affiliation, share Rahmonov's appraisal of the Somonid dynasty in Tajik history. Šodī Šabdolov, the chairman of the Communist Party of Tajikistan since 1991, considered the establishment of Soviet Tajikistan in 1924 as a restoration of the Somonid dynasty.[7] The popular poet Šeralī Loiq hailed the Somonids as heroes (*pahlavon*) among the impotent who revived the historical Tajik "Self."[8] And Būrī Karim, celebrating the declaration of independence in September 1991 with an article on the nature of freedom, concluded that the "first time after the fall of the Somonid State we gained our freedom."[9]

While the significance of the Somonid dynasty is widely acknowledged, its relation to other constative elements of the Tajik Self remains conspicuously vague: Rahmonov cherishes the cultural and political achievements of the Somonid dynasty, but he and his academic entourage are silent on an arguably equally important issue: The Somonid advanced the Islamization and promoted the Hanafi-Sunni law school in Central Asia contributing to the Islamic-Iranian symbioses in the 10th and 11th centuries CE.[10] Ibrohim Usmonov—a former advisor to Rahmonov and one of the leading intellectuals in post-conflict Tajikistan—even asserted the alien character of Islam linking the religion with the loss of sovereignty and statehood: "The establishment of alien rule over the territory inhabited by Tajiks begun with the campaign of Qutayba b. Muslim [the commander of the Arab-Islamic forces] in 705 and continued until 1924."[11] Rahmonov's erasure of the Islam in the Somonid's polity explicates the regime's complicated approach to Islam. For years, the government imagination of the Tajik nation excluded Islam as part of its identity by fabricating a pre-Islamic landscape of an official collective cultural memory, only in recent years the government has started to regain its discursive "ownership" of what Islam should mean in the Tajik society.[12]

The mediocre academic establishment in Tajikistan has obediently adopted the Rahmonov's narrative. Only a few raise a dissent voice, such as Hoğī Akbar. Although he acknowledges the importance of the Somonid dynasty as the first Tajik polity, he emphasizes their contribution to the emergence of the Islamicate-Iranian civilization:

> In the 9th century, the Samanids, founders of the first Tajik state, made the belief in God and Islam the building blocks of their country and created an

Islamo-Iranian (some would say Irano-Islamic) spiritual and cultural atmosphere that was preserved for centuries. Though later different Turkic dynasties—Ghaznavid, Timurid, Safavid and Manghyt—rose to power in the region, these foundations laid down by the Samanids were not challenged. It is obvious that the Turkic people of the region had national traits on their own, and that they adapted Islam and, especially Iranian culture in their own ways to serve their own needs. Yet, Islam and Iranian culture were the common bond that united people of Mawarannahr, and in the case of Islam became their way of life.[13]

Likewise, the IRPT had carefully countered official narratives with a more inclusive idea of Tajik history, but these voices have been silenced lately.[14] The impact of the government's identity politics are difficult to measure, but the continuous reproduction of the central tropes of historical imagination— the Aryan ethnogenesis, the antagonism toward the Uzbek Other and the exclusion of Islam—have apparently resulted in an increased receptiveness of the government's discourses on Uzbekistan as a malign neighbor and the ubiquitous Islamic terrorists.

REMEMBERING AND COMMEMORATING THE TAJIK CIVIL WAR

Already at the 16th Session Rahmonov set the parameters for the commemoration (or better oblivion) of the civil war and elliptically remarked, that "in case we want to establish peace and stability, we should not remember the past. The people know very well who was essentially responsible for the outbreak of the fratricide."[15] However, the Rahmonov government was less ready to forget: The Supreme Court banned the DPT, IRPT and La'li Badaxšon and brought up charges against leading opposition representatives.[16] Simultaneously, Rahmonov identified the IRPT and the *qoziyot* as the two groups responsible for the outbreak of the civil war.[17]

However, since 1995 renegade warlords and field commanders, who were initially part of the Popular Front, challenged Rahmonov more seriously than the opposition. Changed parameters for co-option and external developments accelerated the peace negotiations between the government and the UTO, which were finally concluded by Rahmonov and Nurī on 27 June 1997 in Moscow.[18]

The General Peace Accord changed the government's narrative on the origins of Tajikistan's civil war only temporarily. In the Peace Accord, the government and UTO agreed on an integration of opposition representatives into the government. For a few years, Rahmonov conceded to Nurī a share in the peace process by appointing him Chairman of the Joint Committee of National Reconciliation (*Kumissiyai Oštii Millī*). The Committee of national

Reconciliation, however, never pursued reconciliation comparable to the Truth and Reconciliation Commission in South Africa, the National Truth and Reconciliation Commission in Chile or the UN facilitated Justice and Reconciliation Process in Rwanda. The Tajik commission monitored the implementation of the General Peace Accord, in particular, the integration of opposition representatives in government structures as well as the decommissioning of militias. Nurī adopted a similar interpretation of the civil war like Rahmonov as "imposed" by others and between 1997 and 2009 oblivion and suppression of memories dominated the official policy regarding the civil war, albeit with a few exceptions.[19]

In 2004, seven years after the peace accord, Rahmonov had consolidated his power: He secured his re-election in the presidential elections 1999 and a year later his presidential party PDPT won the absolute majority in the parliamentary elections. Nine/Eleven and the subsequent NATO and US operations in Afghanistan fundamentally changed the regional, international and domestic parameters for Tajikistan's government. Despite Western affirmations to support democratization in the region, the authoritarian presidents benefited from the post-9/11 political landscape—including the return of Russia and the rise of China in Central Asia.[20] Rahmonov successively marginalized or eliminated his rivals and consolidated his authoritarian hold on the country. Simultaneously, he re-evaluated his cooperation with the IRPT and the official narrative on the origins of the civil war.

The government and parts of the professional urban civil society display an ambiguous perception of pluralism and the Perestroika/Glasnost years. Rahmonov portrays political parties and the civil society as "economic" projects funded by foreign countries and remarks that "civil associations [...] did not contribute to the unity of our beloved homeland."[21] Since the late 2000s, official narratives started to downplay Nurī's contribution to the General Peace Accord and within the context of the international "war against terror" the Tajik government insinuated that the IRPT—despite its conciliatory rhetoric—is an extremist Islamic party with contacts to insurgents and jihadists.[22] Nurī and other IRPT representatives, such as his political heir Muhiddin Kabirī, positioned the IRPT as a centrist political party and repeatedly reaffirmed their commitment to a secular democratic political system and the General Peace Accord. However, Nurī could not ignore the confrontational politics of the government and expressed his concerns about the future of the reconciliation in Tajikistan.[23]

Official Narratives

Since the death of Nurī in 2006, Rahmonov has begun to portray himself as the one who established peace and—implicitly—the actual winner of the civil war.[24] The modesty with which Rahmonov was attributed in the Parliament's address decorating him with the title "Hero of Tajikistan" in 1999, as the son of a peasant family, whose mother and father brought him up with "work ethics, respect for the homeland, love for humans and modesty,"[25] was gradually replaced by the more assertive role of *ǧanobi olī*—"Your Highness." In December 2015, Tajikistan's parliament bestowed on Rahmonov the title "Leader of the Nation" (*pešvoi millat*) who has established "peace and national unity" (*sulhu vahdati millī*). The new title comes with lifelong immunity for Rahmonov and his family next to a few other privileges. A few months earlier, after the parliamentary elections in March 2015, Rahmonov finally abandoned the (informal) terms of the General Peace Accord: The IRPT was excluded from parliament and on September 29, the Supreme Court banned the party as an extremist and terrorist organization.

Nonetheless, the civil war remains a contentious issue: Despite an increased commemoration of the events by the Tajik media since 2009, the government prefers to suppress any official commemoration of the conflict. In newly built (2013) National Museum of Tajikistan (*Osorxonai millii Toǧikiston*, located on the Ismoil Somonī Street only a few blocks west from the former Šahidon Square) the attentive visitor learns in detail about the pre-Islamic history of Tajikistan, the ethnogenesis of the Tajiks and the origins of their statehood, and perhaps discerns the government's ambiguous perception of Islam. The entire civil war, however, is omitted in the exhibition.[26] Instead of commemorating the Civil War, "national unity (*vahdati millī*)," "peace and stability (*tinǧu subot*)" are central elements in the official discourse on post-conflict Tajikistan with Rahmonov as the one who has established peace, stability and unity in a titanic effort.

There is, however, a notable exception from the official silence on the civil war in form of two interrelated texts on the civil war in contemporary history textbooks for the 9th (published in 2001) and 11th grade (published in 2006). The ministry of education commissioned two veteran Soviet academics, Rohat Nabieva (b. 1936) and Farxod Zikriyoyev (b. 1940), to compile these textbooks.[27] The two versions indicate the shifts in the official narrative on the conflict: While the earlier and shorter version for the 9th grade from 2001 provided a noncommittal summary of the conflict in the spirit of the 1997 General Peace Accord,[28] the second version is far less conciliatory echoing the assertiveness and confidence of a government, which has consolidated its position. Both versions introduce the origins of the civil war in a similar way:

> The tragic events of the early 1990s in the Republic enter as dark pages in the history of the Tajik people. In periodicals, books and articles these events are known as «fratricidal war», «civil war», «regional war» or «suicidal war» etc.

The unfolding war had objective and subjective reasons: First, in the course of Perestroika economic problems intensified on the Union and the republican level. Factories were without work, and products were not sold, salaries not paid, unemployment rose and therefore dissatisfaction in the region increased. Second, in the early 1990s the social discontent intensified and the population of some regions suffered from the lack of food and clothing. Although Tajikistan had the highest population growth [in the Soviet Union], basic services and health care especially for children in rural areas had been neglected. The infant mortality rate rose from year to year. The uneven development (*nohamvorii taraqqiyot*), the malpractice in public office, the undermining of the rule of law on the local level, the increase of corruption and theft increased the discontent of the people as well. Thus, the basis for the tragic events was prepared and it needed only a spark.[29]

In their introduction, Nabieva and Zikriyoyev follow the informal master narrative on the origins of the conflict. However, they soon depart from their noncommittal interpretation and identify those responsible for the outbreak of violence:

Dissatisfaction among the citizens grew and oppositional parties, with the intention to realize their own ambitions, took advantage of the situation. [...] Year-by-year a reactionary orientation increased labelled as «Mothers of the Nation (*modaroni millat*)» and «Fathers of the Nation (*padaroni millat*)»[30], whose poems about the «Culture of Ancestors » revealed tendencies of devotedness to Iran (*Eronparastī*) and nationalism undermining the fabrics and the political structure of the Republic. The IRPT organized protests from 26 March to 17 May 1992 on Šahidon Square with slogans against the government and in favor of Islam. But their struggle was not limited to protests; they also took members of the government and deputies as hostages. In reaction, demonstrations were organized in May 1992 on Ozodī Square in order to support the constitutional government and protect (*himoya*) the president of the republic. As a result of these tensions the first people were killed. [...] In order to counter the activities of the revolutionaries in Dushanbe, advocates of the constitutional system established a people's movement in the provinces of Kūlob, Qūrġonteppa, Hisor and Leninobod. [...] In this Popular Front, all ethnic groups of Tajikistan, Tajiks, Uzbeks, Russian and others, were represented. [...] Nobody could belief that the Tajik people who possess an old culture could embark on such a suicidal path.[31]

In contrast to their textbook for the 9th grade, Nabieva and Zikriyoyev explicitly accuse the opposition in complicity with ominous "foreign forces" for the outbreak of the civil war. The portrait of the Popular Front as a multi-ethnic inclusive organization implicitly marks the opposition as exclusive, narrow-minded regionalists and so forth. The text operates with insinuations and offers a carefully filtered selection of the events withholding central information (for instance the sequence of events, the distribution of arms on

Ozodī Square *before* Bahrom Rahmonov's defection, the divides among the Popular Front commanders and so forth). The text expresses the resentment by the incumbent political elite against the reformist Glasnost era intellectuals (who are vilified as «fathers and mothers of the nation»), the civil society and Islam. As already mentioned, the 16th Session is now presented as the major turning point in Tajik history even dwarfing independence and Emomalī Rahmonov exclusively embodies the restoration of constitutional order and astute political leadership, which saved Tajikistan from annihilation:

> After the 16th Session of the Supreme Soviet [...] life in the republic became more peaceful. Our beloved Republic, Tajikistan, was dragged into the abyss of war by the crimes of political parties and social groups. Some individuals wanted to come to power in an undemocratic and violent way, their abominable deeds resulted in the merciless slaughter of their own people, their fathers and mothers, brothers and sisters and children. As it is remarked in the book *Foundations of a new Statehood* [written by Rahmonov], *«Now it was necessary to have an experienced and able political leadership which took over the responsibility to draft a new constitution and lead the struggle.»* Such a leadership, which accepted the responsibility for the political situation and order, was elected democratically and according to the constitution on the 16th Session of the Supreme Soviet in the city of Xuǧand. [His leadership] played a significant historical role in the elimination of the deep political and structural crisis of Tajikistan which threatened the existence of the national government of the Tajiks.[32]

Counter Narratives

For more than a decade after the Peace Accord, Rahmonov did not face much opposition to his interpretation of the origins of Tajikistan's civil war. The urban civil society in Dushanbe was largely concordant with the official narratives on the civil war. Instead of remembering the civil war, the political elite, civil society and intellectuals preferred to acclaim the peace accord of 1997 as Tajikistan's genuine contribution to post-Soviet Central Asia and the world as such. Official academic institutions reaffirmed the governmental interpretations on Islam and the duplicitous role of the media in the later Soviet Union. The civil society absorbed these official interpretations. Throughout the 2000s, the international community tried to facilitate confidence-building measures between the government and the opposition (in particular the IRPT, which also claimed the exclusive right to represent Islam in these talks); however, the public resonance was limited and the commitment muted.[33] This gradually changed in 2009, on the eve of the 20th anniversary of the February riots, when Tajikistan's independent media started to publish interviews, memories and articles about the events that unsettled the Tajik society 20 years ago.[34] Even the civil society has hesitantly contributed to the debate on the civil war. For instance, Ibrohim Usmonov has established the "Dialogue of Civilizations" format where invited speakers—such as Talbak Nazarov, Akbaršo Iskandarov, Davlat Usmon, Qahhor Mahkamov, Adolat Rahmanova and Būrī Karim—have presented their reading of the events between Perestroika, Independence and the civil war.[35]

Hoğī Akbar Tūrağonzoda was one of the most vocal commentators in recent years. In an interview with *Nigoh* on the occasion of the Day of National Unity on 27 June 2013 he complained that the media did not report objectively about the civil war and challenged the idea that the war was mainly fought for political power or economic resources. Instead he returned to the Perestroika/Glasnost debates:

> We expected that political reforms would save the country from the crisis. Perhaps, some considered this wrong, but it was then the central contentment of the opposition. Actually, we wanted to establish a parliament, which would be accountable and responsive to the people. We wanted to elect deputies who would serve the people, not in a way a chairman (*rais*) or governor acted like a king (*podšoh*).[36]

Even less attentive readers understood the subtext and reference to the contemporary political situation in Tajikistan. Tūrağonzoda—as so many other political commentators—has been targeted by the government and silenced since 2015.

In Tajikistan's cultural field, writers, artists or directors have only carefully addressed the civil war. Unlike the case of the Lebanese Civil War, which has a significant impact on the cultural production in Lebanon and among the Lebanese diaspora[37], only a few movies and other works of art have dealt with the conflict yet: Bakhtyar Khudojnazarov's movie *Kosh ba Kosh* (*Qoš ba Qoš = Odds and Evens*, 1993) uses the actual fighting of the civil war in and around Dushanbe as a surreal setting or background noise for the romance between the two protagonists, Mira and Daler. His *Luna Papa* (1999) includes a short but haunting episode where the main protagonist Mamlakat (played by Chulpan Khamatova) is captured by a marauding militia in an APC. Without many words, the short scene insinuates the abysmal horrors of the civil war and sexual violence against women without addressing the conflict as such. Similarly, Djamshed Usmonov's works, *Farištai kifti rost* (*Angle on the Right*, 2002) and *Bihišt faqat baroi murdagon* (*To get to Heaven First You have to Die*, 2006) do not explicitly refer to the civil war, but portray a deeply traumatized society, in which corruption and fear is part of everyday life and in which gender roles are undermined by the conflict and the post-conflict transformation.

There is, so far, only fragmentary research on how local communities commemorate the civil war. Incidental reports carefully indicate a strong awareness of the conflict and the need for commemoration. The population of a micro-district in Qūrġonteppa, for instance, expressed in an unprecedented move their resentment against the renaming of local kolkhoz, roads and squares after former field commanders such as Safarov, Saidov and Langariev. Those who have lost relatives and friends in the civil war, felt additionally humiliated when their ID cards show as their place of residence the name of the commander responsible for the murder of their loved ones.[38] When the administration of the southern Boxtar *nohiyya* declared Fayzalī Saidov a "national hero" in August 2011, the local population surprisingly criticized the decision triggering a debate on Saidov's role in the civil war's violence.[39] Many other communities in Xatlon, Dushanbe, Hisor, the Qarotegin Valley or in the Pamir remember the civil war in their local context and this local culture of commemoration needs certainly more attention.

From Heroes to Villains

Since the late 2000s, official publications, such as textbooks, statements, local histories or encyclopedic works, intentionally exclude controversial personalities and field commanders. The most prominent example of a *damnatio memoriae* is Sangak Safarov. After his death in 1993 and while the civil war continued, Safarov was portrayed as the embodiment of the Tajik hero (*qahramon*); his grave in Kūlob identifies him in three languages as the "People's Hero of Tajikistan," the Military Academy of Tajikistan was named after him and a memorial complex for Safarov, Langariev, Saidov and Mūrčaev (another field commander of the Popular Front) had been built in Qūrġonteppa in 1994. Throughout the early 2000s, Safarov remained an important symbolic figure for the Rahmonov government indicating the relative success of his legitimation narrative and in 2006 Nabieva and Zikriyoyev portrayed Safarov still in positive terms:

> Sangak Safarov was born 1928 in Šuġnov, Xovaling. His father, Pirnazarov Safar worked in the 1930s in a goldmine in Šuġnov. After his parents' death, he left school and worked as a day laborer. Naturally, he loved the truth (*haqiqatparast*) and was eventually arrested for objectionable activities. As leader of Tajikistan's Popular Front he gained a high reputation among the people. Unfortunately, he was killed by an unknown person on 30 March 1993.[40]

This narrative is symptomatic for the official approach to the Tajik Civil War allowing ambiguities in the interpretation. Ironically, their description of Safarov as somebody who struggled for "truth" echoes Davlat Xudonazar's TV interview after his return from Kūlob in early July 1992.[41] In contrast, Sohibnazar rationalized Safarov by portraying him as the Uzbek Other. He circuitously presented linguistic "evidence" for the Loiq origins of the given name "Sangak" as "hail" or "melting snow" while in Persian it means "little stone," a special "grain" or "bird." Sohibnazar concluded, Sangak Safarov was like his Loiq name,

> he came like hail over the people and thousands of innocent people were killed. He is nothing else. He is not a "national hero" and behind his back his students [Abdumağid] Dostiev, [Narzullo] Dūstov, [Mahmadsaid] Ubaydulloev and Rahmonov do not adorn flower garland.[42]

And indeed, since the mid-2000s Safarov's name silently disappeared from official buildings, such as the Military Academy, and even the monument in Qūrġonteppa was demolished.[43] In the *Encyclopaedia of Kūlob*, published in 2006, the reader finds a short entry for the "Sangak Safarov Road" as the former *ul.* Karl Marx in Kūlob, but there is no explanation who this Sangak Safarov was. Apparently, the Rahmonov administration tries to eradicate the memory of controversial field commanders to conclude the transition of legitimacy to an institutionalized rule and "peace." The former field commanders were marginalized or eliminated and Rahmonov could orchestrate himself as a guarantor of peace and stability in Tajikistan—a man of order.

CONCLUSION

The Tajik Civil War took between 40,000 and 100,000 lives and displaced around one million people. As so often in civil wars the conflict was fought with extreme violence, implacability and mercilessness. The civil war destroyed the physical infrastructure and it deeply affected the social fabrics of the Tajik society—with unpredictable long term consequences compounded by labor migration, authoritarian rule, corruption and a further disintegrating health service and education system. One can only agree with Ibrohim Usmonov who maintained that the civil war was "a disaster for the Tajik nation, a wretched nation, a nation that went astray, which was both, spiritually as well as economically depredated."[44]

My account on the origins of Tajikistan's civil war intended to provide a detailed historical narrative of the events which unfolded since the late 1980s based on autobiographical accounts, a hitherto less consulted source. While the factual validity is often disputed, I consider these autobiographical texts as important sources for the reconstruction of the discursive representation of the conflict's origin and the social imaginaries shared by some of the key actors in the conflict.

The Comparative Perspective

Throughout this manuscript, I operated with a set of explanations on the civil war and scrutinized variables such as regionalism, ideology, the role of predatory or fragmented elites, violent non-state actors, masculinity and the economic crisis compounded by the state breakdown of the USSR with its severe impact on the Central Asian periphery. The disintegration of the USSR's coercive capacity since the late 1980s was exploited by the incumbent elites in complicity with criminal networks in the ubiquitous shadow economy. Violent non-state actors undermined the state's monopoly on violence ultimately leading to privatization of violence in the early months of the conflict. The incumbent elites and their associates rallied support and generated legitimacy by antagonizing opponents and by re-configuring prevalent discourses about social and political grievances in the Tajik society, for instance the societal role of Islam or regionalism in the allocation of political and economic resources. Many Soviet republics and eastern European satellite states of the USSR faced similar challenges. In a few cases, the political and social conflicts descended into violence as in Chechnya, Nagorno-Karabakh, South Ossetia, Georgia, Abkhazia or Transnistria. These conflicts were predominately fought between the remains of the former center and the newly independent nation states (Transnistria), between ethnic groups (Nagorno-Karabakh) or were a struggle for independence (Chechnya).[45] Notably, the Tajik Civil War was the only major post-Soviet conflict, which was fought predominately *within* the majority (titular) ethnic group (the Tajiks) and not against minority nationalities/ethnicities (albeit regionalism functioned as an ordering device similarly to ethnicity on other conflicts) or against the remains of the former center.[46]

A Post-Colonial Moment

In the late 1980s, parts of the Tajik intelligentsia embarked on a post-colonial reading of the Soviet modernization project. The question of an authentic Tajik Self, the status of the Tajik language (in relation to Russian but also to the Farsi in Iran and Dari in Afghanistan), the interpretation of history ("ethnogenesis," origins of statehood and regional ownership) were contentious issues among the representatives of the intellectual field. A younger generation of intellectuals—some of them dealing with the experience of forced resettlement and political marginalization—criticized the complacency as well as mediocrity of the official Soviet-Tajik intelligentsia and challenged the hierarchies and modes of reproduction in the intellectual field. With rising nationalist sentiment—inspired by developments in the Baltic republics—these issues became increasingly relevant in politics and contributed to a generational conflict, which was compounded by perceptions of regionalism, political/economic marginalization, uneven development and rivalry with neighboring Uzbekistan. The discussion about culture and identity eventually supplanted the Glasnost debates about political reform, transparency and democratization. Many Tajik intellectuals who considered themselves as "democrats" exposed their profound incomprehension what an open, pluralistic and democratic society means exhibiting an elitist and exclusive idea about politics and who should be represented in a government. National minorities were excluded, female activists sidelined, civil liberties restricted, political processes and institutions manipulated ad libitum. If nationalism failed in Tajikistan, it was not the lack of nationalist cohesion, which accounted for this "failure," but the inability and unwillingness to transform an ethnic-based, romantic idea of nationalism to its more inclusive civic alternative.

Islam

Islamic concepts of societal and political order proliferated as the most radical alternative to the imagination and realities of the Soviet society in the 1980s. Importantly, the Islamic activists of the *harakat* were not part of the urban Perestroika/Glasnost intellectuals and politicians in the TaSSR; instead, they were entrenched in rural Tajikistan among the *muhoğir* communities representing an authentic Tajik intellectual tradition and identity without alleged dependencies to the (colonial) center. At the same time, Nurī and his followers epitomized a generational change in the religious field, where a younger, post-Stalinist generation of Islamic activists challenged the established *ulamo* on issues such as public religious practice or the societal relevance of religion. While the Soviet system co-opted a small group of loyal *ulamo* and created a docile administration of religious affairs, the activists in the *harakat* resolutely rejected any form of appropriation or co-optation by the SADUM. The societal relevance of religion, its reintegration into the national narrative and public religious practice became the central point of contention between the established *ulamo* and their contenders, while theological and dogmatic issues were less important. The Islamic activists rejected the model of the Soviet society including its morality and emphasized their rootedness in rural Tajikistan, representing themselves as an authentic political/moral/social alternative to both, the incumbent Soviet elites and the secular reformers, who were predominately former CPT cadres.

The conjunction of social relevance and religious practice aggravated the conflict between the established *ulamo* and their contenders. The KGB and the nomenklatura exploited these tensions and adopted an analogue discourse on radical (= *vahhobī*) Islam, which ultimately contributed to the Othering of the *harakat* and its supporters as the *yurčik–vovčik* antagonism demonstrates. Doubtlessly, the *harakat* and the IRPT were not homogenous groups and several criminals and field commanders, such as Mullo Abduğaffur, Rizvon or Ziyoyev, fought as field commanders affiliated with the IRPT. Likewise, many *harakat* activists expressed controversial views on an alleged Islamic social and political order incompatible with concepts of a liberal democracy, gender equality, the freedom of faith or an open society. At the same time, however, the IRPT's leadership, Nurī, Himmatzoda and Usmon, consistently adhered to the Glasnost discourse and advocated for a democratic system, which should be based on vaguely delineated Islamic values and morals. Although the IRPT's official political program reflected the ambivalence of values and morals, it placed the IRPT clearly in a post-Islamist context.[47]

Furthermore, the discussion on the IRPT allows insights in how we view Islamism in the 1970s and 1980s, a time in which "Islam" gained wide dominance as a master signifier in political discourses. That is, Islamic movements, although existing in highly diverse contexts and circumstances (including post-colonial nationalism), did imagine themselves being part of a larger and encompassing transnational movement—and acted to a certain extent following this self-image. Islamism in the 1970s and 1980s has to be clearly situated in its specific regional and national context such as late Soviet/post-Soviet Central Asia, but at the same time asks for transnational comparison, for instance with Iran's revolutionary movement, the transformation of the Muslim Brotherhood or the complicated interaction between conservative Islamists and the military in Turkey. Islamism in the 1970s and 1980s has been a highly variegated venture with variations so obvious and stark that one might make use of Shmuel Eisenstadt's multiple modernities and speak of multiple Islamizations in the distinctive saddle period (Koselleck's *Sattelzeit*). As in the case of modernity, we see a multiplicity of cultural social formations which go far beyond the alleged homogenizing and hegemonizing aspects of the imagined original version of the "one and only true Islam."[48]

By integrating the example of the *harakat* activists and the later IRPT into the broader context of Islamism in this saddle period we might understand the transformation of the religious field (including the shifting value of different forms of social, cultural and symbolic capital[49]), the dynamics of mobilization and recruitment as well as its embeddedness in the larger social sphere in a more differentiated way.

Contingency and Deviance

Many accounts explain the outbreak of the civil war in Tajikistan with the prevalent regionalism (*mahalgaroī*) based on historical animosities between regionally based "clans," which outlived the Soviet system or were created by the Soviet administrative practice in Central Asia. Common regional provenance generates trust as well as solidarity and domestic (republican) politics in the TaSSR—that is, the allocation of positions and resources—reveals regional patterns, but more as an "ordering device" similar to ethnicity in other violent conflicts. The unfolding political confrontation since 1989/1990 clearly shows that regional solidarity and loyalty were neither categorical nor durable: The northern elite from Xuǧand/Leninobod lost within a few months its paramount influence on republican affairs due to *internal* rivalries; "Bobo" Sangak did not unite Kūlob due to the "compelling force" of regionalist solidarity, but by eliminating the political nomenklatura of Kūlob through unrestrained violence and by selecting a new political leadership. These assumptions do not deny the influence of imagined regional communities in the mobilization but invite us to consider the often contingent and confusing local issues which are often disconcerting in their banality and—from an empirical perspective—bewilderingly complex and at times unsatisfyingly contingent.[50]

In the evolving political tensions since February 1990, contingency shaped the dynamics of the conflict. I have emphasized the complexity of the Tajik Civil War, the deviations and cruel contingencies, which are difficult to rationalize and comprehend. My reference to contingency aims at "disaggregating mobilizational acts into their constituent processes and focusing on how casual processes interact and link with one another in the production of macro political outcomes."[51] This approach might help us to consolidate structural models of mobilization with the empirical data and invite us to an intellectual openness including the reflection on the contingency as a potential scope of reality.[52] The rise (and subsequent fall) of Safaralī Kenǧaev, the re-emergence of the Brezhnevite cadre Rahmon Nabiev in 1991, the proliferation of the *qoziyot* under Hoǧī Akbar Tūraǧonzoda or the ascent of "Bobo" Sangak as the most powerful field commander (and eventually kingmaker) cannot be satisfactorily explained by structural determinants. Beyond doubt these actors were embedded into the societal context of the later TaSSR and USSR, but this embeddedness does not cogently explain the rationale behind various decisions and actions by these actors. Arguably, the concurrence of several contingencies diminished the political options and eventually the primacy of politics. Jesse Driscoll impressively demonstrates the importance of local conflict dynamics and decisions by individual field commanders in his model on warlords and coalition politics in Tajikistan and Georgia.[53] The Tajik Civil War can be considered as a good example for a "new" war with its complex mixture of political and criminal elements while external resources were less relevant for the conflict's origins.[54] But first of all, the Tajik Civil War was a post-Soviet conflict and its origins inextricably connected to the disintegration of the Soviet State: Soviet administrative practice and identity politics— reinforced by local perceptions of social hierarchies and loyalties (which rooted reciprocally in a particular Soviet representation of social customs and traditions)—facilitated the delineation of the master narrative (as an elite discourse) legitimating the political confrontation and ultimately the violence in the civil war. Many violent non-state actors came from the margins of the late Soviet society, but acted in complicity with key representatives of the former Soviet nomenklatura. These violent non-state actors were not merely subaltern criminals, but they exploited the ambiguities of the elite discourse for their own protection racket and legitimation project. This phenomenon accentuates the deviance between elite discourses (or the master narrative) and its local adaptions as well as the intricate link between political and criminal motivations in the conflict. The qualitative empirical data analyzed here might contribute to a better understanding of violent conflict in the post-Soviet space and beyond.

NOTES

1. "Every memory of discord should be blotted out in everlasting oblivion."
2. Rahmonov, *Ehyoi millat*, Vol. 2, 3–16.
3. Rahmonov, *Ehyoi millat*, Vol. 2, 4.
4. Rahmonov, *Ehyoi millat*, Vol. 2, 6.
5. Rahmonov, *Ehyoi millat*, Vol. 2, 7. For a similar perception see Kenğaev (*Tabadduloti 1*, 50) who compared his struggle against the Islamist opposition with the Somonids' struggle against the Ġaznavides.
6. See Khudonazar, "Other," 11.
7. FBIS-SOV-92–047, 10 March 1992, 45.
8. Loiq Šeralī, *Varaqi sang* (Dušanbe, 1990), 9.
9. Reprinted in Karim, *Faryodi*, 325.
10. See Fragner, *Persophonie*, passim; Hodgson, *Ventures*, passim; Paul, *Zentralasien*, 201; D. Tor, "The Islamization of Central Asia in the Sāmānid era and the reshaping of the Muslim world," *Bulletin of the School of Oriental and African Studies* 72, no. 2 (2009).
11. Usmonov, *Toğikon*, 168.
12. See Tim Epkenhans, "Islam, Religious Elites and the State in post-Civil-War Tajikistan," In *Islam, society, and politics in Central Asia*. Edited by Pauline Jones Luong (Pittsburgh: University of Pittsburgh Press, 2016).
13. Turajonzoda, "Religion," 266.
14. Epkenhans, "Islamic Revival Party," 341–6.
15. Quoted by Nasriddinov, *Tarkiš*, 217.
16. Among the opposition members, Oynihol Bobonazarova, Gulruxsor Safieva, Bozor Sobir and Mirbobo Mirrahim were imprisoned in the 1990s. Since 2004, several former allies of Rahmonov have been arrested and imprisoned. In September 2015 the IRPT was banned and the entire Presidium of the party imprisoned.
17. FBIS-SOV-93–008, 13 January 1993, 52–53.
18. Driscoll, *Warlords*, 86–122; International Crisis Group (ICG), *Tajikistan's Politics: Confrontation or Consolidation?* (Brussels, 2004).
19. For the General Peace Accord and the Commission on national Reconciliation see United Nations Security Council/General Assembly File A/52/219 S/1997/510 from 2 July 1997; Iji, "Cooperation," 189–204; R. G. Smith, "Tajikistan:

the rocky road to peace," *Central Asian Survey* 18, no. 2 (1999); Usmonov, *Sulh-noma*, passim.

20. Cf. Alexander Cooley, *Great games, local rules: The new great power contest in Central Asia* (New York: Oxford University Press, 2014); David Lewis, *The temptations of tyranny in Central Asia* (London: Hurst, 2008).

21. Emomalī Rahmonov, *Istiqloloyat ne'mati bebahost* (Dušanbe: Šarqi ozod, 2001), 18–19.

22. Epkenhans, "Islamic Revival," 329–340.

23. S. A. Nurī, "Vahdati millī az e'timodi hamdigarī sar-čašmo megirad," *Nigoh*, April 7, 2003, 17: 1–3.

24. Rahmonov's attitude was echoed in the speech he held on the occasion of the official celebration of the Peace Accord in the presidential compound in the Varzob Valley north of Dushanbe in 2007, as a live-recording (in the possession of the author) of the speech illustrates.

25. Nabieva and Zikriyoyev, *Ta'rixi 11*, 155.

26. The exhibition refers to the declaration of independence in September 1991 and immediately jumps to the 16th Session of the Supreme Soviet in November/December 1992, where peace and stability is restored—the visitor, however, does not learn why the restauration of peace was necessary at all.

27. Cf. Helge Blakkisrud and Shahnoza Nozimova, "History writing and nation building in post-independence Tajikistan," *Nationalities Papers* 38, no. 2 (2010).

28. R. Nabieva and F. Zikriyoev, *Ta'rixi xalqi Toğik. Kitobi darsī baroi sinfi 9* (Krasnoyarsk: Ofset, 2001), 117–118.

29. Nabiev and Zikriyoyev, *Ta'rixi 11*, 91.

30. Nabiev and Zikriyoyev refer with 'mothers and fathers of the nation' to the popular poets Gulruxsor Safieva and Bozor Sobir who adopted this title during the demonstrations 1991.

31. Nabiev and Zikriyoyev, *Ta'rixi 11*, 91–94.

32. Nabieva and Zikriyoyev, *Ta'rixi 11*, 95.

33. See Jean-Nicolas Bitter, ed., *From confidence building towards co-operative co-existence: The Tajik experiment of Islamic-secular dialogue* (Baden-Baden: Nomos, 2005).

34. Except for the government mouthpiece Ğumhuriyat and the PDPT's *Minbari xalq*, most of the Tajik periodicals published feature articles, memoirs and interviews with eye-witnesses of the events between 1989 and 1992.

35. The papers *Farağ* and *Ozodagan* as well as *Radioi Ozodī* have covered the dialogue forum.

36. Tūrağonzoda, "Ivazšavii," 16.

37. See for instance Sune Haugbolle, *War and memory in Lebanon* (New York: Cambridge University Press, 2010).

38. See http://www.ozodi.org/content/article/24625965.html. Accessed January 17, 2016.

39. The discussion has continued online, see http://www.ozodi.org/content/article/24295680.html. Accessed January 17, 2016. More than a 110 readers commented on the online article by *Ozodī* indicating the relevance of the topic.

40. Nabieva and Zikriyoyev, *Ta'rixi 11*, 93.

41. Karim, *Faryodi*, 477.

42. Sohibnazar, *Subhi 2*, 102.

43. See http://www.ozodi.org/content/article/1767734.html [last access 25.01.2014].

44. Usmonov, *Nabiev*, 105.

45. Zürcher, *Post-Soviet wars*, 213–224.

46. Rogers Brubaker and David Laitin, "Ethnic and Nationalist Violence," *Annual Review of Sociology* 24 (1998).

47. For the post-Islamist context see Asef Bayat, *Making Islam democratic: Social movements and the post-Islamist turn* (Stanford: Stanford University Press, 2007).

48. Cf. Eisenstadt, S.N. "Multiple Modernities in an Age of Globalization." Canadian Journal of Sociology / Cahiers canadiens de sociologie 24, no. 2 (1999): 283–95; Reinhart Koselleck, "Über die Theoriebedürftigkeit der Geschichtswissenschaft," In *Theorie der Geschichtswissenschaft und Praxis des Geschichtsunterrichts*. Edited by Reinhart Koselleck and Werner Conze (Stuttgart: Klett, 1972), 10–28; Mandaville, *Transnational*, 152–191.

49. Pierre Bourdieu, "The Forms of Capital," In *Handbook of theory and research for the sociology of education*. Edited by John G. Richardson (New York: Greenwood Press, 1986), 241–258; id., "Genèse et structure du champ religieux," *Revue française de sociologie* 12, no. 3 (1971): 295–334.

50. Cf. Stathis N. Kalyvas, "Promises and pitfalls of an emerging research program: the microdynamics of civil war," In *Order, conflict, and violence*. Edited by Stathis N. Kalyvas, Ian Shapiro and Tarek E. Masoud (Cambridge: Cambridge University Press, 2008), 397–421.

51. Beissinger, "Mechanisms of Maidan," 40.

52. See Arnd Hoffmann, *Zufall und Kontingenz in der Geschichtstheorie: Mit zwei Studien zu Theorie und Praxis der Sozialgeschichte* (Frankfurt am Main: V. Klostermann, 2005).

53. Driscoll, *Warlords*, 173–196, 213–220.

54. Kaldor, *Wars*, 202–221; Kalyvas, "New and Old," 117–18.

Bibliography

Abduğabbor, Tohir. "Muhiti zist va zabon [Environment and Language]." In *Darsi xeštanšinosī. Daftari duyum [A Lesson in Self-Awareness. The Second Notebook]*. Edited by A. Mahmadnazar, 200–47. Dušanbe: Irfon, 1991.

Abdullaev, K. N. *Ot Sin'czyanya do Xorasana. Iz istorii sredneaziatskoy emigracii XX veka*. Dushanbe: Irfon, 2009.

Abdullaev, Kamoludin and Shahram Akbarzadeh. *Historical dictionary of Tajikistan*. Lanham, MD: Scarecrow Press, 2002.

———. *Historical dictionary of Tajikistan*. 2nd edn. Lanham Md.: Scarecrow Press, 2010.

Abdulloh, Masrur. "Či tavr ba xati millii Toğikī bargardem [How should we return to the national Tajik Script]?" *Adabiyot va San'at*, August 15, 1991. 33.

Abdulov, Karim. *Rohi behbud [The Path of Improvement]*. Dušanbe, 1995.

Abrahamian, Ervand. *Khomeinism: Essays on the Islamic republic*. Berkeley: University of California Press, 1993.

Adams, Laura L. "Can We Apply Postcolonial Theory to Central Eurasia?" *Central Eurasian Studies Review* 7, no. 1 (2008): 2–7.

Adirim, I. "A Note on the Current Level, Pattern and Trends of Unemployment in the USSR." *Soviet Studies* 41, no. 3 (1989): 449–461.

Aitmatov, Chingiz. *The day lasts more than a hundred years*. Bloomington: Indiana University Press, 1983.

Akbarzadeh, Shahram. "Why Did Nationalism Fail in Tajikistan?" *Europe-Asia Studies* 48, no. 7 (1996): 1105–1129.

Akiner, Shirin. *Tajikistan: Disintegration or reconciliation?* Central Asian and Caucasian prospects. London: Royal Inst. of Internat. Affairs, 2001.

Algar, Hamid. "The Naqshbandi Order: A Preliminary Survey of Its History and Significance." *Studia Islamica* 44 (1976): 123–152.

Allen, Frank J. *Dictionary of Central Asian islamic terms*. Springfield: Dunwoody Press, 2002.

Amiršohī, Nurmuhammad. *Fehristi nomi mahalhoi Toğikiston [List of Toponyms in Tajikistan]*. Dušanbe: Ensiklopediyai Millii Toğik, 2013.

Amnesty International. *Tadzhikistan: Hidden terror: Political killings, 'disappearances' and torture since December 1992.* London, 1993.

Anderson, Benedict. *Imagined communities: Reflections on the origin and spread of nationalism.* London: Verso, 2006.

Anderson, John. *Religion, state and politics in the Soviet Union and successor states.* Cambridge, New York: Cambridge University Press, 1994.

Anonymus. "Čegūne ʿalaye enqelāb-e Irān touṭeʿe mīkonand [How they conspire." *Eṭṭelāʿāt*, 23 Dey 1358hš = January 13, 1980. 16049.

Arbatov, Georgij A. *Das System: Ein Leben im Zentrum der Sowjetpolitik.* Frankfurt am Main: Fischer, 1993.

Asimov [see also: Osimī], Mukhammad, ed. *Tadžikskaya sovetskaya socialističeskaya respublika [The Tajik Socialist Republic].* Dušanbe: SIEST, 1984.

Atabaki, Touraj and Erik J. Zürcher, eds. *Men of order: Authoritarian modernization under Atatürk and Reza Shah.* London: I.B. Tauris, 2004.

Atkin, Muriel. *The subtlest battle: Islam in Soviet Tajikistan.* The Philadelphia papers. Philadelphia: Foreign Policy Research Institute, 1989.

———. "The Survival of Islam in Soviet Tajikistan." *Middle East Journal* 43, no. 4 (1989): 605–18.

———. "Tajikistan: Ancient Heritage, New Politics." In *Nation and politics in the Soviet successor states.* Edited by Ian Bremmer and Ray Taras, 361–83. Cambridge, New York: Cambridge University Press, 1993.

———. "The Politics of Polarization in Tajikistan." In *Central Asia: Its strategic importance and future prospects.* Edited by Hafeez Malik, 211–31. New York: St. Martin's Press, 1994.

———. "Tajikistan: Reform, Reaction, and Civil War." In *New states, new politics: Building the post-soviet nations.* Edited by Raymond C. Taras and Ian A. Bremmer, 600–27. Cambridge: Cambridge University Press, 1997.

———. "Thwarted Democratization in Tajikistan." In *Conflict, cleavage, and change in Central Asia and the Caucasus.* Edited by Karen Dawisha and Bruce Parrott, 277–311. Cambridge, New York: Cambridge University Press, 1997.

Aynī, Sadriddin. *Yoddoštho [Memoirs].* 2 vols. Dušanbe [Stalinobod]: Našri davlatī, 1954/55.

———. "Maʿnoi kalimai «Toğik» [The Meaning of the Word «Tajik»]." *Adabiyot va Sanʿat*, September 13, 1992. 37.

Ayubzod, S. *Sad rangi sad sol. Toğikiston dar qarni bistum [A hundred colors of a hundred years. Tajiki-stan in the 20th Century].* Prague: Post Skriptum Imprimatur, 2002.

Babadjanov, Bakhtiyar and Kamilov Muzaffar. "Muhammadjan Hindustani (1892–1989) and the Beginning of the 'Great Schism' among the Muslims of Uzbekistan." In *Islam in politics in Russia and Central Asia.* Edited by Stéphane A. Dudoignon and Hisao Komatsu, 195–220. London: Kegan Paul, 2001.

Babajanov, B. M., A. Muminov, and von Kügelgen. *Disputes on Muslim Authority in Central Asia in 20th century.* Almaty: Daik-Press, 2007.

Babak, Vladimir, Demian Vaisman, and Aryeh Wasserman, eds. *Political organization in Central Asia and Azerbaijan: Sources and documents.* London, Portland, OR: Frank Cass, 2004.

Barfield, Thomas J. *The Central Asian Arabs of Afghanistan: Pastoral nomadism in transition.* Austin: Univ. of Texas Press, 1981.

Barthold, V. V. *Four Studies on the history of Central Asia.* 3 vols. Leiden: Brill, 1962.

Bashiri, Iraj. *Prominent Tajik figures of the twentieth century.* Dushanbe, 2002.

Bauer, Henning, Andreas Kappeler, and Brigitte Roth, eds. *Die Nationalitäten des russischen Reiches in der Volkszählung von 1897.* Stuttgart: F. Steiner, 1991.

Bayat, Asef. *Making Islam democratic: Social movements and the post-Islamist turn.* Stanford, Calif: Stanford University Press, 2007.

Beissinger, Mark. "Mechanisms of Maidan: The Structure of Contingency in the Making of the Orange Revolution." *Mobilization: An International Quarterly* 16, no. 1 (2011): 25–43.

———. "Elites and Ethnic Identities in Soviet and Post-Soviet Politics." In *The Post Soviet nations: Perspectives on the demise of the USSR.* Edited by Alexander J. Motyl, 141–69. New York: Columbia University Press, 1992.

———. *Nationalist mobilization and the collapse of the Soviet State.* Cambridge: Cambridge Univ. Press, 2002.

———. "Soviet Empire as 'Family Resemblance'." *Slavic Review* 65, no. 3 (2006): 294–303.

Bennigsen, Alexandre. "Unrest in the World of Soviet Islam." *Third World Quarterly* 10, no. 2 (1988): 770–86.

Bennigsen, Alexandre and Chantal Lemercier-Quelquejay. "'Official' Islam in the Soviet Union." *Religion in Communist Lands,* no. 7 (1979): 148–59.

Bennigsen, Alexandre and S. E. Wimbush. *Mystics and commissars: Sufism in the Soviet Union.* London: Hurst, 1985.

Bennigsen, Alexandre A., ed. *Soviet strategy and Islam.* Basingstoke, Hampshire: Macmillan, 1989.

Bergne, Paul. *The birth of Tajikistan: national identity and the origins of the Republic.* London: Tauris, 2007.

Bhabha, Homi K. *The location of culture.* London, New York: Routledge, 1994.

Bitter, Jean-Nicolas, ed. *From confidence building towards co-operative co-existence: The Tajik experiment of Islamic-secular dialogue.* Baden-Baden: Nomos, 2005.

Blakkisrud, Helge and Shahnoza Nozimova. "History writing and nation building in post-independence Tajikistan." *Nationalities Papers* 38, no. 2 (2010): 173–89.

Bosworth, Clifford E. *The Ghaznavids: Their empire in Afghanistan and Eastern Iran 994-1040.* Edinburgh: Edinburgh University Press, 1963.

Bourdieu, Pierre. "Genèse et structure du champ religieux." *Revue française de sociologie* 12, no. 3 (1971): 295–334.

———. "The Social Space and the Genesis of Groups." *Theory and Society* 14, no. 6 (1985): 723–44.

———. "The Forms of Capital." In *Handbook of theory and research for the sociology of education.* Edited by John G. Richardson, 241–58. New York: Greenwood Press, 1986.

———. *The logic of practice.* Cambridge: Polity Press, 1990.

———. *Distinction: A social critique of the judgement of taste.* New York: Routledge, 2008.

———. *Religion.* Berlin: Suhrkamp Verlag, 2011.

Brown, Bess A. "The Civil War in Tajikistan, 1992–1993." In *Tajikistan: The trails of independence.* Edited by Mohammad-Reza Djalili, Frédéric Grare and Shirin Akiner, 86–96. Richmond: Curzon, 1998.

Brubaker, Rogers and Frederick Cooper. "Beyond 'Identity'." *Theory and Society* 29, no. 1 (2000): 1–47.

Brubaker, Rogers and David Laitin. "Ethnic and Nationalist Violence." *Annual Review of Sociology* 24 (1998): 423–52.

Buškov, Valentin and D. Mikul'skiy. *Anatimiya graždanskoy voyny v Tadžikistane: etno-social'niye processy i političeskaya bor'ba: 1992–1996.* Moskva, 1996.

Buškov, Valentin I. *'Tadžikskaya revolyuciya' i graždanskaya voyna: (1989–1994 gg.).* Moskva: CIMO, 1995.

Chatterjee, Partha. *The nation and its fragments: Colonial and postcolonial histories.* Princeton, N.J: Princeton University Press, 1993.

Clapham, Christopher S. "Introduction: Analysing African Insurgencies." In *African guerrillas.* Edited by Christopher S. Clapham, 1–18. Bloomington: Indiana University Press, 1998.

Clarke, Killian. "Unexpected Brokers of Mobilization: Contingency and Networks in the 2011 Egyptian Uprising." *Comparative Politics* 46, no. 4 (2014): 379–97.

Collins, Kathleen. *Clan politics and regime transition in Central Asia.* Cambridge: Cambridge Univ. Press, 2006.

Connell, R. W. and James W. Messerschmidt. "Hegemonic Masculinity: Rethinking the Concept." *Gender & Society* 19, no. 6 (2005): 829–59.

Connell, Raewyn. *Masculinities.* Cambridge: Polity Press, 2005.

Cook, Michael. *Commanding right and forbidding wrong in Islamic thought.* Cambridge: Cambridge Univ. Press, 2000.

Cooley, Alexander. *Great games, local rules: The new great power contest in Central Asia.* New York: Oxford University Press, 2014.

Critchlow, James. "'Corruption', Nationalism, and the Native Elites in Soviet Central Asia." *The Journal of Communist Studies* 4, no. 2 (1988): 142–61.

Croissant, Michael P. *The Armenia-Azerbaijan conflict: Causes and implications.* Westport, Conn.: Praeger, 1998.

Crone, Patricia. *God's rule: Government and Islam.* New York: Columbia University Press, 2004.

Dave, Bhavna. *Kazakhstan: Ethnicity, language and power.* London, New York: Routledge, 2007.

Davlat, Nuralī. "Istiqloliyate ki onro xudi deputatho dark nakardand [An independence even the deputies did not imagine]." *Farağ*, September 18, 2013. 38.

———. "'Hameša zinda'-e, ki faramūš šud [Those who lived forever and were forgotten]." *Nigoh*, January 8, 2014. 41.

———. "Qozī [The Qadi]." *Nigoh*, February 25, 2014. 48.

———. "Qozikalon dar girdobi siyosat [The qozikalon in the political maelstrom]." *Nigoh*, March 5, 2014. 49.

———. "Qozikalon. Kommuniston boyad ğanoza našavand? [Qozikalon. Communists should not receive a funeral?]." *Nigoh*, March 11, 2014. 50.

———. "Qozikalon. Siyosati mustaqili Hoğī Akbar [Qozikalon. The independent politics of Hoğī Ak-bar]." *Nigoh*, March 26, 2014. 1.

Davlat, Rahmatkarim. "Bahmanmoh: Hadaf – ğangi šimolu ğanub [Bahmanmoh: The intention – a war between the North and the South]." *Millat*, February 17, 2011.

[Der Spiegel]. "Fremder im eignen Land." *Der Spiegel*, September 7, 1992. 37.

———. "Tadschikistan: Stalins Blut." *Der Spiegel*, no. 4 (1993): 143–50.

DeWeese, Devin. "Islam and the Legacy of Sovietology: A Review Essay on Yaacov Ro'i's Islam in the Soviet Union." *Journal of Islamic Studies* 13, no. 3 (2002): 298–330.

Dobson, Richard B. "Youth Problems in the Soviet Union." In *Soviet social problems*. Edited by Anthony Jones, Walter D. Connor, and David E. Powell, 227–51. Boulder: Westview Press, 1991.

Dostiev, Abdulmağid. *Toğikiston – šikastanho va bastanho [Tajikistan – Fractures and Bonds]*. Dušanbe: Irfon, 2005.

Driscoll, Jesse. *Warlords and coalition politics in post-Soviet states.* Cambridge studies in comparative politics. New York, NY: Cambridge University Press, 2015.

Dudoignon, Stéphane A. "Une Segmentation peut en Cacher une Autre: Regionalismes et Clivages politico-economiques au Tadjikistan." *Cahiers d'étues sur la Méditerranée orientale et le monde turco-iranien*, no. 18 (1994): 73–129.

———. *Communal solidarity and social conflicts in late 20th century Central Asia: The Case of the Tajik Civil War*. Islamic Area Studies Project. Tokyo: University of Tokyo Press, 1998.

———. "Political Parties and Forces in Tajikistan, 1989–1993." In *Tajikistan: The trails of independence*. Edited by Mohammad-Reza Djalili, Frédéric Grare, and Shirin Akiner, 52–85. Richmond: Curzon, 1998.

———. "From Revival to Mutation: The Religious Personnel of Islam in Tajikistan, from De-Stalinization to Independence (1955-91)." *Central Asian Survey* 30, no. 1 (2011): 53–80.

Dudoignon, Stéphane A. and Sayyid A. Qalandar. "They Were All from the Country: The Revival and Politicisation of Islam in the Lower Wakhsh River Valley of the Tajik SSR (1947-1997)." In *Allah's Kolkhozes: Migration, De-Stalinisation, Privatisation, and the New Muslim Congregations in the Soviet Realm (1950s–2000s)*. Edited by Stephane A. Dudoignon and Christian Noack, 47–122, 314. Berlin: Klaus-Schwarz-Verlag, 2013.

Dūstov, Narzullo. *Zaxm bar ğismi vatan [The Wound in the Body of the Homeland]*. Dušanbe: Irfon, 1994.

EBRD. *Tajikistan: 2000 Country Investment Profile*. London: EBRD.

Eisener, Reinhard. *Auf den Spuren des tadschikischen Nationalismus: Aus Texten und Dokumenten zur Tadschikischen SSR*. Berlin: Verl. Das Arab. Buch, 1991.

Eisenstadt, S.N. "The Breakdown of Communist Regimes and the Vicissitudes of Modernity." *Deadalus* 121, no. 2 (1992): 21–41.

———. "Multiple Modernities in an Age of Globalization." *Canadian Journal of Sociology / Cahiers canadiens de sociologie* 24, no. 2 (1999): 283–95.

Epkenhans, Tim. "Defining normative Islam: some remarks on contemporary Islamic thought in Tajikistan - Hoji Akbar Turajonzoda's Sharia and society." *Central Asian Survey* 30, no. 1 (2011): 81–96.

———. "Zwischen Mythos und Minenfeld: Historiographie in Tadschikistan." *Osteuropa* 62, no. 3 (2012): 137–50.

————. "The Islamic Revival Party of Tajikistan: Episodes of Islamic Activism, Postconflict Accommodation, and Political Marginalization." *Central Asian Affairs* 2 (2015): 321–46.

————. "Islam, Religious Elites and the State in post-Civil-War Tajikistan." In *Islam, society, and politics in Central Asia*. Edited by Pauline Jones Luong. Pittsburgh: University of Pittsburgh Press, 2016.

Erlikhman, Vadim. *Poteri narodonaseleniia v XX veke: Spravochnik*. Moskva: Russkaia panorama, 2004.

[Farağ]. "Pisari Kenğaev: 'Padaram farzandi zamoni xud bud...' [The Son of Kenğaev: 'My father was a man of his time...']." *Farağ*, September 26, 2012. 39.

Feldbrugge, F. J. M., ed. *The Constitutions of the USSR and the union republics: Analysis, texts, reports*. Alphen aan den Rijn, Netherlands, Germantown, Md: Sijthoff & Noordhoff, 1979.

Fenster, Mark. *Conspiracy theories: Secrecy and power in American culture*. Minneapolis: University of Minnesota Press, 2008.

Fierman, William and Martha B. Olcott. "Youth Culture in Crisis." *Soviet Union/ Union Soviétique* 15, 2/3 (1988): 245–62.

Figes, Orlando. *The whisperers: Private life in Stalin's Russia*. New York: Metropolitan Books, 2007.

Filatochev, Igor and Roy Bradshaw. "The Soviet Hyperinflation: Its Origins and Impact throughout the Former Republics." *Soviet Studies* 44, no. 5 (1992): 739–59.

Fitzpatrick, Sheila. *Everyday stalinism: Ordinary life in extraordinary times; Soviet Russia in the 1930s*. Oxford: Oxford Univ. Press, 2000.

Fragner, Bert G. "'Glasnost' in einem fernen Land: die tadschikische Literaturzeitschrift Adabijot va San'at als Meinungsforum." In *Presse und Öffentlichkeit im Nahen Osten*. Edited by Christoph Herzog, Raoul Motika, and Anja Pistor-Hatam, 45–57. Heidelberg: Heidelberger Orientverlag, 1995.

————. *Die "Persophonie": Regionalität, Identität und Sprachkontakt in der Geschichte Asiens*. Berlin: Das Arab. Buch, 1999.

Frazer, Glenda. "Basmachi (Part I & II)." *Central Asian Survey* 6, 1 & 2 (1987): 1.

Friedman, T. "Tajikistan Agrees to Curbs on Arms." *The New York Times*, February 14, 1992.

Fulbrook, M. and U. Rublack. "In Relation: The 'Social Self' and Ego-Documents." *German History* 28, no. 3 (2010): 263–72.

Fürst, Juliane. *Stalin's last generation: Soviet post-war youth and the emergence of mature socialism*. Oxford, New York: Oxford University Press, 2010.

Gafurov, Bobodžan G. *Istoriya tadžikskogo naroda [The History of the Tajik People]*. Moskva: Gosudarstv. Izdat. Polit. Literatury, 1949.

Ġafurov, Boboğon. *Toğikon [The Tajiks]*. Dušanbe: Irfon, 1998.

Gambetta, Diego and Steffen Hertog. "Why are There so Many Engineers Among Islamic Radicals?" *A.E.S.* 50, no. 2 (2009): 201–30.

Ganev, Venelin I. "Post-Communism as an Episode of State Building: A Reversed Tillyan Perspective." *Communist and Post-Communist Studies* 38 (2005): 425–45.

Gilmour, Julie and Barbara E. Clements. "'If You Want to Be like Me: Train!': Contradictions of Soviet Masculinity." In *Russian masculinities in history and culture*.

Edited by Barbara E. Clements, Rebecca Friedman and Dan Healey, 210–22. New York: Palgrave, 2002.

Gray, Matthew. *Conspiracy theories in the Arab world: Sources and politics*. London, New York: Routledge, 2010.

Gretsky, S. "Qadi Akbar Turajonzoda." *Central Asia Monitor* 1 (1994): 16–24.

Greyerz, K. von. "Ego-Documents: The Last Word?" *German History* 28, no. 3 (2010): 273–82.

Ǧumhurii Toǧikiston. *Sarqonuni Ǧumhurii Toǧikiston [The Constitution of the Republic of Tajikistan]*. Dušanbe: Šarqi ozod, 2000.

Gurov, A. I. *Professional'naja prestupnost': Prošloe i sovremennost' [Organized Crime. History and Present]*. Moskva: Juridičeskaja literatura, 1990.

Habibov, Abdullo. *Vaqte amr qonunro ivaz mekunad...[When an order changes the law...]*. Dušanbe: Vatanparvar, 2009.

Hallaq, Wael B. *Shari'a: Theory, practice, transformations*. Cambridge: Cambridge Univ. Press, 2009.

Hamad, Sulton. *Dar payrahai nur [On the path of light]*. Dušanbe: Muattar, 2013.

Harris, Colette. *Muslim youth: Tensions and transitions in Tajikistan*. Boulder: Westview Press, 2006.

Haugbolle, Sune. *War and memory in Lebanon*. New York: Cambridge Univ. Press, 2010.

Havemann, Axel. "Männerbünde im islamischen Orient: Soziale Bewegungen in Iran, Irak und Syrien." In *Geregeltes Ungestüm: Bruderschaften und Jugendbünde bei indogermanischen Völkern*. Edited by Rahul P. Das and Gerhard Meiser, 68–90 Bd. 1. Bremen: Hempen, 2002.

Heathershaw, John. *Post-conflict Tajikistan: The politics of peacebuilding and the emergence of legitimate order*. London: Routledge, 2009.

———. "Central Asian Statehood in Post-Colonial Perspective." In *Stable outside, fragile inside? Post-Soviet statehood in central Asia*. Edited by Emilian Kavalski, 87–106. Farnham, Surrey, Burlington, VT: Ashgate Pub., 2010.

———. "Of National Fathers and Russian Elder Brothers: Conspiracy Theories and Political Ideas in Post-Soviet Central Asia." *Russian Review* 71, no. 4 (2012): 610–29.

———. "The Global Performance State." In *Ethnographies of the state in Central Asia: Performing politics*. Edited by Madeleine Reeves, Johan Rasanayagam, and Judith Beyer, 29–54. Bloomington: Indiana University Press, 2013.

Heathershaw, John and David W. Montgomery. *The myth of post-soviet Muslim radicalization in the Central Asian republics*. London: Chatham House, 2014.

Helsinki Watch. *Conflict in the Soviet Union: Tadzhikistan*. New York, NY: Human Rights Watch, 1991.

Henry Dunant Centre for Humanitarian Dialogue. *Humanitarian engagement with armed groups: The Central Asian Islamic opposition movements*. Geneva, 2003.

Herzig, Edmund. "Regionalism, Iran and Central Asia." *International Affairs* 80, no. 3 (2004): 503–17.

Hirsch, Francine. "Toward an Empire of Nations: Border-Making and the Formation of Soviet National Identities." *Russian Review* 59, no. 2 (2000): 201–26.

————. *Empire of nations: Ethnographic knowledge & the making of the Soviet Union.* Ithaca: Cornell Univ. Press, 2005.

Hobsbawm, E. J. and T. O. Ranger, eds. *The Invention of tradition.* New York: Cambridge Univ. Press, 1983.

Hodgson, Marshall G. S. *The venture of Islam: Conscience and history in a world civilization.* 3 vols. Chicago: University of Chicago Press, 1974.

Hoffmann, Arnd. *Zufall und Kontingenz in der Geschichtstheorie: Mit zwei Studien zu Theorie und Praxis der Sozialgeschichte.* Frankfurt am Main: V. Klostermann, 2005.

Hofstadter, Richard. *The paranoid style in American politics and other essays.* New York: Vintage Books, 1967.

Horkheimer, Max. *Gesammelte Schriften.* Vol. 12, Frankfurt am Main: Fischer, 1985.

Human Rights Watch. *Human rights in Tajikistan in the wake of the Civil War.* New York, 1993.

Humphrey, Caroline. "Russian Protection Rackets and the Appropriation of Law and Order." In *States and illegal practices.* Edited by Josiah M. Heyman, 199–232. New York: Berg, 1999.

Husaynī, Saidumar. *Xotiraho az naxust ošnoiyam ba Harakati Islomii Toğikiston to rasmiyati on [Memoirs from the first Acquaintance with the IRPT until its registration].* Dušanbe: Muattar, 2013.

Iji, Tetsuro. "Cooperation, Coordination and Complementarity in International Peace-making: The Tajikistan Experience." *International Peacekeeping* 12, no. 2 (2005): 189–204.

Ikromī, Ğalol. *Onči az sar guzašt [Those things which have happened].* Dušanbe: Šarqi ozod, 2009.

Imomov, Ašūrboy. *Administrativno-territorial'noe ustroystvo Tadžikistana [The administrative-territorial Organization of Tajikistan].* Dušanbe: Ofset Imperiya, 2013.

International Crisis Group (ICG). *Tajikistan's Politics: Confrontation or Consolidation?* Asia Briefing. Brussels, 2004.

————. *The curse of cotton: Central Asia's destructive monoculture.* Osh/Brussels, 2005.

International Monetary Fund (IMF), World Bank, OECD, and EBRD. *A study of the Soviet economy.* 3 vols. Paris: OECD, 1991.

Irkaev, Mullo I. *Istoriya Graždanskoy Voyny v Tadžikistane.* Dušanbe: Irfon, 1971.

Istad, Adaš. "Sohibi in zamin kist [Who owns this land]." *Adabiyot va San'at*, August 15, 1991. 33.

————. "Musohibai Adaš Istad bo Muhammadğon Šukurov. Ziyoī ravšangari aqlhost [Adaš Istad's interview with Muhammadğon Šukurov. The Intellectual inspires the Intellect]." *Adabiyot va San'at*, September 19, 1991. 38.

————. "Davlati millī [The National Government]." *Adabiyot va San'at*, May 21, 1992. 21.

————. "Davlati millī čī guna boyad? [What kind of national government is needed?]." *Adabiyot va San'at*, July 4, 1992. 23.

Jawad, Nassim and Shahrbanou Tadjbakhsh. *Tajikistan: A forgotten civil war.* London: Minority Rights Group, 1995.

Jolly, Margaretta, ed. *Encyclopedia of life writing: autobiographical and biographical forms*. 2 vols. Encyclopedia of life writing. London: Fitzroy Dearborn, 2001.

Jones Luong, Pauline. *Institutional change and political continuity in Post-Soviet Central Asia: Power, perceptions, and pacts*. Cambridge, New York: Cambridge Univ. Press, 2002.

Kabirī, Muhiddin, ed. *Muğaddidi asr [The Renovator of the Age]*. Dušanbe: ŠKOS HNIT, 2007.

Kaldor, Mary. *New & old wars: Organized violence in a global era*. 3rd edn. Stanford, Calif: Stanford University Press, 2012.

Kalyvas, Stathis N. "'New' and 'Old' Civil Wars. A Valid Distinction?" *World Politics* 54 (2001): 99–118.

———. "The Ontology of 'Political Violence': Action and Identity in Civil Wars." *Perspectives on Politics* 1, no. 3 (2003): 475–94.

———. "Promises and pitfalls of an emerging research program: the microdynamics of civil war." In *Order, conflict, and violence*. Edited by Stathis N. Kalyvas, Ian Shapiro, and Tarek E. Masoud, 397–421. Cambridge: Cambridge Univ. Press, 2008.

———. *The logic of violence in civil war*. Cambridge: Cambridge Univ. Press, 2009.

Kandiyoti, Deniz. "The Politics of Gender and the Soviet Paradox: Neither Colonized, nor Modern?" *Central Asian Survey* 26, no. 4 (2007): 601–23.

Karim, Būrī. *Dar girdobi zindagī. Yoddošt, maqolaho, musohibaho [In the Maelstrom of Life. Memories, articles and interviews]*. Možaysk: Terra, 1995.

———. *Faryodi solho. Huğğat, dalel, tabsira, xulosa [The Cry of Years. Evidence, Reasons, Comment, Summary]*. Moskva: Transdornauka, 1997.

Karimov, I. A. *Uzbekistan on the threshold of the twenty-first century: Challenges to stability and progress*. New York: St. Martin's Press, 1998.

Kassymbekova, Botakoz. "Humans as Territory: Forced Resettlement and the Making of Soviet Tajikistan, 1920–38." *Central Asian Survey* 30, 3–4 (2011): 349–70.

Kassymbekova, Botakoz, and Christian Teichmann. "The Red Man's Burden: Soviet European Officials in Central Asia in the 1920s and 30s." In *Helpless imperialists: Imperial failure, fear and radicalization*. Edited by Maurus Reinkowski and Gregor Thum, 163–86 6. Göttingen: Vandenhoeck & Ruprecht, 2013.

Keddie, Nikki R. "The Origins of the Religious-Radical Alliance in Iran." *Past and Present* 34, no. 34 (1966): 70–80.

Keller, Shoshana. *To Moscow, not Mecca: The Soviet campaign against Islam in Central Asia, 1917–1941*. Westport: Praeger, 2001.

Kellner-Heinkele, Barbara and Jacob M. Landau. *Language politics in contemporary Central Asia: National and ethnic identity and the Soviet legacy*. London: Tauris, 2012.

Kemper, Michael. "Ljucian Klimovič: Der ideologische Bluthund der sowjetischen Islamkunde und Zentralasienliteratur." *Asiatische Studien/Études Asiatiques* 63, no. 1 (2009): 93–133.

Kendžaev [Kenğaev], Safarali, and Kutfiniso Mirzoeva. *Očerk istorii prokuratury Tadžikistana [Historical Digest on the Procurator's Office in Tajikistan]*. Dušanbe: Fondi Kendžaeva, 1995.

Kenğaev, Safaralī. *Huquq va ozodihoi graždaninho [Laws and Freedoms of Citizens]*. Dušanbe: Irfon, 1988.

———. *Sūzi dil [Burning Heart]*. Dušanbe: Irfon, 1991.

———. Ğinoyatnoma [The Book of Crime]. Dušanbe: Maorif, 1993.

———. *Tabadduloti Toğikiston 1 [Coup d'état in Tajikistan 1]*. Dušanbe: Fondi Kenğaev, 1993.

———. *Tabadduloti Toğikiston 2 [Coup d'état in Tajikistan 2]*. Toškand: Fondi Kenğaev, 1994.

———. *Tabadduloti Toğikiston 3 [Coup d'état in Tajikistan 3]*. Toškand: Fondi Kenğaev, 1995.

Khalid, Adeeb. *The politics of Muslim cultural reform: Jadidism in Central Asia*. Berkeley: Univ. of California Press, 1998.

———. "Introduction: Locating the (Post-) Colonial in Soviet History." *Central Asian Survey* 26, no. 4 (2007): 465–73.

———. *Islam after communism: Religion and politics in Central Asia*. Berkeley: Univ. of California Press, 2007.

———. *Making Uzbekistan: Nation, empire, and revolution in the early USSR*. Ithaca, London: Cornell University Press, 2015.

Khudonazar, Anaita. "The Other." Berkeley Program in Soviet and Post-Soviet Studies, 2004.

Khudonazar, Davlat. "The Conflict in Tajikistan: Questions of Regionalism." In *Central Asia: Conflict, resolution, and change*. Edited by Roald Sagdeev and Susan Eisenhower, 249–63. Washington, DC: The Eisenhower Institute, 1995.

King, Diane E. "The Personal is Patrilineal: Namus as Sovereignty." *Identities* 15, no. 3 (2008): 317–42.

Kirkwood, Michael. 'Glasnost', 'the National Question' and Soviet Language Policy." *Soviet Studies* 43, no. 1 (1991): 61–81.

Kisch, Egon E. *Asien gründlich verändert*. Berlin: Erich Reiss Verlag, 1932.

Kislyakov, Nikolay. *Tadžiki karategina i darvaza [The Tajiks of Qarotegin and Darvoz]*. 3 vols. Dušanbe: Doniš, 1966–1976.

Klimovič, Lyucian I. *Islam*. Moskva: Nauka, 1965.

Kolosov, S. "Vostok - delo tonkoe [The East - a delicate Affair]." In *Spetcnaz GRU: Pyat'desyat let istorii, dvadcat' let voyny [50 Years of History and 20 Years of War]*. Edited by Sergey N. Kozlov, 300–14. Moskva: Russkaya panorama, 2001.

Korf, Benedikt, and Timothy Raeymaekers. "Geographie der Gewalt." *Geographische Rundschau* 64, no. 2 (2012): 4–11.

Koselleck, Reinhart. "Über die Theoriebedürftigkeit der Geschichtswissenschaft." In *Theorie der Geschichtswissenschaft und Praxis des Geschichtsunterrichts*. Edited by Reinhart Koselleck and Werner Conze, 10–28. Stuttgart: Klett, 1972.

———. *Futures past: On the semantics of historical time*. New York: Columbia University Press, 2004.

Košlakov, G. "Roğun: Čī boyad kard [Roğun: What has to be done]?" *Adabiyot va San'at*, January 5, 1989. 1.

Kügelgen, and Anke von. "Buchara im Urteil europäischer Reisender des 18. und 19. Jahrhunderts." In *Muslim Culture in Russia and Central Asia to the Early 20th*

Centuries. Edited by Michael Kemper, 415–30. Islamkundliche Untersuchungen 200. Berlin: Schwarz, 1996.

Kul'čik, Y., S. Rumyantsev, and N. Čičerina. *Graždanskie dviženiya v Tadžikistane*. Moskva, 1990.

Kunitz, Joshua. *Dawn over Samarkand: The Rebirth of Central Asia*. London: Lawrence and Wishart, 1936.

Kupatadze, Alexander. *Organized crime, political transitions and state formation in post-Soviet Eurasia*. New York: Palgrave Macmillan, 2012.

Kurbanova, Š. I. *Pereselenie. Kak eto bylo [The Resettlement. How it was]*. Dušanbe: Irfon, 1993.

Latifī, Otaxon. "Sarband [Scarf]." In *Darsi xeštanšinosī [A Lesson in Self-Awareness]*. Edited by A. Mahmadnazar, 197–210. Dušanbe: Irfon, 1989.

Leatherman, Janie. *Sexual violence and armed conflict*. Cambridge, Malden, MA: Polity, 2011.

Lebow, Richard N. "Contingency, Catalysts, and International System Change." *Political Science Quarterly* 115, no. 4 (2000): 591–616.

Ledeneva, Alena V. *Russia's economy of favours: Blat, networking, and informal exchange*. New York: Cambridge University Press, 1998.

Lewis, David. *The temptations of tyranny in Central Asia*. London: Hurst, 2008.

Ligachev, Yegor. *Inside Gorbachev's Kremlin: The memoirs of Yegor Ligachev*. Boulder, Colo: Westview Press, 1996.

Louw, Maria E. *Everyday Islam in post-Soviet Central Asia*. London: Routledge, 2007.

Löwenhardt, John, James R. Ozinga, and Erik van Ree. *The rise and fall of the Soviet Politburo*. London: UCL Press, 1992.

Lozo, Ignaz. *Der Putsch gegen Gorbatschow und das Ende der Sowjetunion*. Köln: Böhlau Köln, 2014.

Lynch, Dov. *Russian peacekeeping strategies in the CIS: The cases of Moldova, Georgia and Tajikistan*. New York: Palgrave, 2000.

———. "The Tajik Civil War and Peace Process." *Civil Wars* 4, no. 4 (2001): 49–72.

Mahmadnazar, A., ed. *Darsi xeštanšinosī [A Lesson in Self-Awareness]*. Dušanbe: Irfon, 1989.

———, ed. *Darsi xeštanšinosī. Daftari duyum [A Lesson in Self-Awareness. The Second Notebook]*. Dušanbe: Irfon, 1991.

Mamadazimov, Abdugani. *Političeskaya istoriya Tadžikskogo naroda [Political History of the Tajik People]*. Dušanbe: Doniš, 2000.

Mamadšoev, Farrux. "Tūrağonzoda – agenti KGB [Tūrağonzoda – an agent of the KGB]?" Ğumhuriyat, March 15, 2009.

Mandaville, Peter G. *Transnational Muslim politics: Reimagining the umma*. London, New York: Routledge, 2001.

———. *Islam and politics*. Second edition. New York: Routledge, 2014.

Mandel, David R. "Simulating History: The Problem of Contingency." *Analyses of Social Issues & Public Policy* 3, no. 1 (2003): 177–80.

Markowitz, Lawrence P. *State erosion: Unlootable resources and unruly elites in Central Asia*. Ithaca, N.Y: Cornell University Press, 2013.

Martin, Terry. *The affirmative action empire: Nations and nationalism in the Soviet Union, 1923-1939.* Ithaca, London: Cornell University Press, 2001.

Masov, R. M. *Istoriya topornogo razdelenija [The History of territorial Demarcation].* Dušanbe: Irfon, 1991.

———. *Tadžiki: istoriya c grifom 'sovershenno sekretno' [Tajik History with the Seal 'Top Secret'].* Dušanbe: Payvand, 1995.

———. «Nasledie» Mangytskoy dinastii [The «Heritage» of the Manghit Dynasty]. Dušanbe, 2002.

Masov, Rahim. "Emomali Rahmon: ‹The Architect of Peace›." *Diplomatic World,* no. 36 (2012): 64–8.

Mayer, Arno J. *The furies: Violence and terror in the French and Russian Revolutions.* Princeton: Princeton University Press, 2000.

Medvedev, Vladimir. "Saga o bobo Sangake, voine [The Saga of Bobo Sangak, warrior]." *Družba Narodov,* no. 6 (1993): 187–204.

Meier, Christian. *Das Gebot zu vergessen und die Unabweisbarkeit des Erinnerns: Vom öffentlichen Umgang mit schlimmer Vergangenheit.* München: Siedler, 2010.

Menashri, David. "Iran's Regional Policy: Between Radicalism and Pragmatism." *Journal of International Affairs* 60, no. 2 (2007): 153–67.

Metcalf, Barbara. "The Madrasa at Deoband: A Model for Religious Education in Modern India." *Modern Asian Studies* 12, no. 1 (1978): 111–34.

Mirrahim, Mirbobo. *Hamtabaqi Šodmon Yusupov va Xul'kar Yusupov pūkid [The Companionship with Šodmon Yusupov and Xul'kar Yusupov emptied].* Dušanbe: Buxoro, 2012.

Mirzorahmatov, S. "Šumo kisted [Who are you]?" Ğumhuriyat, July 17, 2012. 94.

Mosalmāniyān-Qobādiyānī, Raḥīm. *Tāǧīkestān: āzādī yā marg [Tajikistan: Freedom or Death].* Tehrān: Daftar-e našr-e farhang-e Eslāmī, 1373hš=1994/95.

Mueller, John. "The Banality of 'Ethnic War'." *International Security* 25, no. 1 (2000): 42–70.

Munkī, Rağab and Amiršoh Xatlonī. *Nomus [Honor].* Dušanbe: Paik, 1994.

Nabieva, R., and F. Zikriyoev. *Ta'rixi xalqi Toǧik. Kitobi darsī baroi sinfi 9 [History of the Tajik People. Textbook for the 9th grade].* Krasnoyarsk: Ofset, 2001.

———. *Ta'rixi xalqi Toǧik. Kitobi darsī baroi sinfi 11 [History of the Tajik People. Textbook for the 11th grade].* Dušanbe: Sobiriğon, 2006.

Najmabadi, Afsaneh. "The Erotic Vaṭan [Homeland] as Beloved and Mother: To Love, To Possess, and To Protect." *Comparative Studies in Society and History* 39, no. 3 (1997): 442–67.

Narzikulov, I. and K. Stanyokovič. *Atlas Tadžikskoy sovetskoy socialističeskoy respubliki [Atlas of the TaSSR].* Dušanbe: GUGiK, 1968.

Nasriddinov, Hikmatulloh. *Tarkiš [Explosion].* Dušanbe: Afsona, 1995.

Naumkin, Vitaliy V. *Radical Islam in Central Asia: Between pen and rifle.* Lanham: Rowman & Littlefield, 2005.

Nazarzoda, Nosir. "Fayzullo Saidov (1959–1992)." *Qonun,* January 14, 2016. 2.

Nazarzoda, S. *Farhangi tafsirii zaboni Tojikī.* Dushanbe: Pažūhišgohi zabon va adabiyot ba nomi Rūdakī, 2008.

Nazriev, Davlat and Igor Sattarov. *Respublika Tadžikistan: Istoriya nezavisimosti god 1992-y (Tom II) [Republic of Tajikistan: History of Independence, the year 1992 (Volume II)].* Dušanbe: Nur, 2005.

————. *Respublika Tadžikistan: Istoriya nezavisimosti god 1993-y (Tom III) [Republic of Tajikistan: History of Independence, the year 1993 (Volume III)]*. Dušanbe: Irfon, 2006.

————. *Respublika Tadžikistan: Istoriya nezavisimosti god 1991-y (Tom I) [Republic of Tajikistan: History of Independence, the year 1991]*. Dušanbe: AK-94, 2002.

Negmatov, N. [. *Gosudarstvo samanidov (Maverannahr i Khorasan v IX-X vv.) [The Samanid State (Central Asia and Khorasan in the 9-10th Century)]*. Dušanbe: Doniš, 1977.

Ne'matov, Nū'mon. *Ta'rixi xalqi Toǧik. Kitobi yakum. Az insoni oqil to Toǧiki barkamol [History of the Tajik Peo-ple. First Volume. From the first people to the completion of the Tajiks]*. Dušanbe: Sarparast, 2003.

Niyazi, Aziz. "The Year of Tumult: Tajikistan after February 1990." In *State, religion and society in Central Asia: A post-Soviet critique*. Edited by Vitalij V. Naumkin, 262–89. Reading (GB): Ithaca Press, 1993.

————. "Migration, Demography and Socio-Ecological Processes in Tajikistan." In *Migration in Central Asia: Its History and Current Problems*. Edited by H. Komatsu et al., 169–78. Tokyo, 2000.

Northrop, Douglas. *Veiled empire: Gender & power in Stalinist Central Asia*. Ithaca, NY: Cornell Univ. Press, 2004.

Nourzhanov, Kirill, and Christian Bleuer. *Tajikistan: A political and social history*. Canberra: ANU Press, 2013.

Nozimova, Shahnoza, and Tim Epkenhans. "Negotiating Islam in emerging public Spheres in contemporary Tajikistan." *Asiatische Studien/Études Asiatiques* 67, no. 3 (2013): 965–90.

Nurī, S. A. *Oštinoma [Book of Peace]*. Dušanbe: Nodir, 2001.

————. "Vahdati millī az e'timodi hamdigarī sar-čašmo megirad [National Unity originates in mutual trust]." *Nigoh*, April 7, 2003. 17.

Obiya, Chika. "When Faizulla Khojaev Decided to Be an Uzbek." In *Islam in politics in Russia and Central Asia*. Edited by Stéphane A. Dudoignon and Hisao Komatsu, 99–118. London: Kegan Paul, 2001.

Olcott, Martha B. *A Face of Islam: Muhammad-Sodiq Muhammad-Yusuf*. Carnegie Papers 82. Washington, 2007.

Olney, James, ed. *Studies in autobiography*. New York: Oxford University Press, 1988.

————. *Memory & narrative: The weave of life-writing*. Chicago, London: University of Chicago Press, 2007.

Ortmann, S., and J. Heathershaw. "Conspiracy Theories in the Post-Soviet Space." *Russian Review* 71, no. 4 (2012): 551–64.

Orzu, Muhammad, ed. *40 soli Nahzat. Xotira, andeša, didgoh [40 Years of IRPT. Memories, Thoughts, Observations]*. Dušanbe: Muattar, 2013.

Osimī, Muhammad, ed. *Enziklopediyai sovetii Toǧik*. 8 vols. Dušanbe: SIEST, 1978-1988.

Panfilov, Oleg. *Tadžikistan: Žurnalisty na graždanskoy voyne (1992-1997)*. Moskva: Izd-vo "Prava cheloveka", 2003.

Parkes, Peter. "Milk kinship in Islam. Substance, structure, history." *Social Anthropology* 13, no. 3 (2005): 307–29.

Patnaik, Ajay. "Agriculture and Rural Out-Migration in Central Asia, 1960–91." *Europe-Asia Studies* 47, no. 1 (1995): 147–69.

Paul, Jürgen. *Die politische und soziale Bedeutung der Naqsbandiyya in Mittelasien im 15. Jahrhundert.* Berlin: de Gruyter, 1991.
————. *Zentralasien.* Frankfurt: S. Fischer, 2012.
Penati, Beatrice. "The reconquest of East Bukhara: the struggle against the Basmachi as a prelude to Sovietization." *Central Asian Survey* 26, no. 4 (2007): 521–38.
Perry, John R. "Script and Scripture: The Three Alphabets of Tajik Persian, 1927–1997." *Journal of Central Asian Studies* 2 (1997): 2–18.
Petkelʿ, Vladimir V. *Žiznennye ukhaby čekista [A bumpy life as a Čekist].* Donetsk: Astro, 2010.
Pianciola, Niccolò, and Paolo Sartori. "Waqf in Turkestan: The Colonial Legacy and the Fate of an Islamic Institution in Early Soviet Central Asia, 1917-1924." *Central Asian Survey* 26, no. 4 (2007): 475–98.
Poljakov, Sergej P. *Everyday Islam: Religion and tradition in rural Central Asia.* Armonk, NY: Sharpe, 1992.
Qayumzod, A. "Xudo bo most, pirūzī niz [God is with us, victory too]." *Čaroǧi rūz,* 1992. 24.
Qayumzod, Abduqayum. *40 soli muboriza, muqovimat va talošho [40 Years of Struggle, Opposition and Efforts].* Dušanbe: Baxt, 2013.
Qiyompur, S., and P. Ǧahongir. "Raisi ǧumhur čī kase bošad? [The President will be what kind of person?]." *Adabiyot va Sanʿat,* September 12, 1991. 37.
Qosim, Nizom. "Farǧomi prezidenti bexalq [The end of a president without people]." *Adabiyot va Sanʿat,* September 5, 1991. 36.
Radnitz, Scott. *Weapons of the wealthy: Predatory regimes and elite-led protests in Central Asia.* Ithaca, N.Y.: Cornell University Press, 2010.
Rahmonov, Emomalī. *Toǧikon dar oinai taʾrix: Az Oriyon to Somoniyon [The Tajiks in the Mirror of History: From the Aryans to the Somonids].* 3 vols. London/Dušanbe: Irfon, 1999–2008.
————. *Dah soli istiqloliyat, vahdati millī va bunyodkorī [10 Years of Independence, national Unity and Creation].* Dušanbe: Irfon, 2001.
————. *Istiqloloyat neʿmati bebahost [Independence a priceless Grace].* Dušanbe: Šarqi ozod, 2001.
————. *Istiqloliyati Toǧikiston va Ehyoi millat [The Independence of Tajikistan and the Revival of the Nation].* 7 vols. Dušanbe: Irfon, 2002-2008.
Rahnamo, Abdullo. *Ulamoi Islomī dar Toǧikiston [The ulamo in Tajikistan].* Dušanbe: Irfon, 2009.
Rakowska-Harmstone, Teresa. *Russia and nationalism in Central Asia: The case of Tadzhikistan.* Baltimore: Hopkins Press, 1970.
————. "The dialectics of nationalism in the USSR." *Problems of Communism* 23, no. 1 (1974): 1–22.
Raleigh, Donald J. *Soviet baby boomers: An oral history of Russia's Cold War generation.* The Oxford oral history series. Oxford, New York: Oxford University Press, 2012.
Rasanayagam, Johan. *Islam in post-Soviet Uzbekistan: The morality of experience.* Cambridge: Cambridge University Press, 2010.
Rasulī, Abdurahmon. "… va gaphoi digar. Rahmon Nabiev […with other words. Rahmon Nabiev]." *Adabiyot va Sanʿat,* August 22, 1991. 34.

————. "Marde, ki dar ġami millat ast [A Man, who is among the people]." *Adabiyot va San'at*, September 19, 1991. 38.

Rasuliyon, Qahhor. "Vahhobiho kistand? [Who are the Vahhobī?]." *Adabiyot va San'at*, July 2, 1992. 27.

Raximov, R. R. *'Mužskie doma' v tradicionnoy kul'ture tadžikov ['The male House' and the traditional Culture of the Tajiks]*. Leningrad: Nauka, 1990.

Reeves, Madeleine. "Staying put? Towards a relational politics of mobility at a time of migration." *Central Asian Survey* 30, 3–4 (2011): 555–76.

Riordan, James, ed. *Soviet youth culture*. Bloomington: Indiana University Press, 1989.

————. *Sport, politics, and communism*. Manchester, New York: Manchester University Press, 1991.

Roche, Sophie. *Domesticating youth: Youth bulges and its socio-political implications in Tajikistan*. New York: Berghahn Books, 2014.

Ro'i, Yaacov. *Islam in the Soviet Union: From the Second World War to Gorbachev*. London: Hurst, 2000.

Rosneft. *Annual report 2009*. Moscow, 2009.

Rowe, William C. "Kitchen Gardens in Tajikistan: The Economic and Cultural Importance of Small-Scale Private Property in a Post-Soviet Society." *Human Ecology* 37, no. 6 (2009): 691–703.

Roy, Olivier. *The new Central Asia: Geopolitics and the birth of nations*. London: Tauris, 2007.

Roziq, Zubaydulloh. *HNIT dar masiri ta'rix [The IRPT on the Path of History]*. Dušanbe: Muattar, 2013.

Rubin, Barnett R. "The Fragmentation of Tajikistan." *Survival* 35, no. 4 (1993): 71–91.

————. "Russian Hegemony and State Breakdown in the Periphery: Causes and consequences of the Civil War in Tajikistan." In *Post-Soviet political order: Conflict and state building*. Edited by Barnett R. Rubin and Jack L. Snyder, 128–61. London, New York: Routledge, 1998.

Rzehak, Lutz. *Tadschikische Studiengrammatik*. Wiesbaden: Reichert, 1999.

————. *Vom Persischen zum Tadschikischen: Sprachliches Handeln und Sprachplanung in Transoxanien zwischen Tradition, Moderne und Sowjetmacht (1900–1956)*. Wiesbaden: Reichert, 2001.

Rzehak, Lutz and Chairullo Saifulloejew. *Wörterbuch Deutsch-Tadschikisch*. Dushanbe: Šarqi ozod, 2010.

Sa'dī, Samd. "Bedorii siyosī lozim! Davlati Toǧik či xel bud va či xel xohad šud? [A political Awakening is necessary! How was the Tajik state and how will it be?]." *Adabiyot va San'at*, August 22, 1991. 32.

Sadriddinzoda, Hoǧī Q. *HNIT: Sabziš, laǧžiš va pešraft [IRPT: Flourishing, sliding and progressing]*. Dušanbe: Muattar, 2013.

Safieva, Gulruxsor. "Yak Rūzi Xudšinosī [One Day of Self-reflection]." In *Darsi xeštanšinosī [A Lesson in Self-Awareness]*. Edited by A. Mahmadnazar, 129–38. Dušanbe: Irfon, 1989.

————. "Xudšinos [Self-Awareness]." *Adabiyot va San'at*, January 5, 1989. 1.

————. "Panǧ soli xudšinosī [5 Years of Self-Awareness]." *Adabiyot va San'at*, April 9, 1992. 15.

Said, Edward W. *Orientalism.* New York: Vintage Books, 2003.

Saidbaev. *Islam i obščestvo. Opyt istoriko-sotsiologičeskogo issledovaniya [Islam and Society. A historical-sociological Essay].* Moskva: Nauka, 1978.

Šakurī, Muhammadǧon. "Naǧoti mo az davlati millist! [Our Salvation is the national Government!]." *Adabiyot va San'at,* June 25, 1992. 26.

Šakurī (Buxoroī), Muhammadǧon. *Xuroson ast in ǧo: Ma'naviyat, zabon va ehyoi millii Toǧikon [Khorasan is here: Culture, Language and the Resurrection of the Tajik's Nation].* Dušanbe: Olii Somon, 1997.

———. *Har suxan ǧoevu har nuqta maqome dorad. Čande az mas'alahoi farhangi suxan [Every word and every dot has its place. Some examples from the Issue of Speech Culture].* Dušanbe: Irfon, 2005.

———. *Panturkizm va sarnivišti ta'rixii Taǧikon [Panturkism and the historical Destiny of the Tajiks].* Dušanbe: Adib, 2010.

Salimov, Yakub. *Aziyatskiy sindrom [The Asian Syndrome].* Moskva: CNETR, 2001.

Salom, Talabšoh. "Amirbek Atobek – Vahdati mellī nadorem [We do not have national Unity]." *Naǧot,* June 6, 2012. 23.

Saroyan, Mark. "Rethinking Islam in the Soviet Union." In *Beyond Sovietology: Essays in politics and history.* Edited by Susan G. Solomon, 23–52. Armonk, N.Y: M.E. Sharpe, 1993.

———. "Authority and Community in Soviet Islam." In *Accounting for fundamentalisms: The dynamic character of movements.* Edited by Martin E. Marty and R. S. Appleby, 513–30. Chicago: Univ. of Chicago Press, 1994.

Saroyan, Mark, and Edward W. Walker. *Minorities, mullahs, and modernity: Reshaping community in the former Soviet Union.* Berkeley, Calif.: Univ. of California, 1997.

Sattorī, Qiyomiddin, ed. *HNIT – Zodai ormoni mardum [IRPT – Born by the Will of the People].* Dušanbe: ŠKOS HNIT, 2003.

Savčenkov, N. G. *Nurekskaya GĖS: Tadzhikistan ėnergogigant na Vakhshe.* Moskva: Speckniga, 2009.

Schiffauer, Werner. *Die Bauern von Subay: Das Leben in einem türkischen Dorf.* Stuttgart: Klett-Cotta, 1987.

Schmemann, Serge. "War Bleeds Ex-Soviet Land at Central Asia's Heart." *The New York Times,* February 21, 1993.

Schmitt, Rüdiger. *Die iranischen Sprachen in Geschichte und Gegenwart.* Wiesbaden: Reichert, 2000.

Schneckener, Ulrich. "Fragile Statehood, Armed Non-State Actors and Security Governance." In *Private actors and security governance.* Edited by Alan Bryden and Marina Caparini, 23–40. Wien: Lit, 2006.

Schoeberlein-Engel, John. "Conflict in Tajikistan and Central Asia: The Myth of Ethnic Animosity." *Harvard Middle Eastern and Islamic Review* 1, no. 2 (1994): 1–55.

———. "Identity in Central Asia: Construction and contention in the conception of 'Özbek,' 'Tajik,' 'Muslim,' 'Samarquandi' and other groups." PhD diss., Harvard University, 1994.

Schulze, Winfried, ed. *Ego-Dokumente: Annäherung an den Menschen in der Geschichte.* Berlin: Akad.-Verl, 1996.

Šeralī, Loiq. "Dar duroha [At the Crossroad]." In *Darsi xeštanšinosī [A Lesson in Self-Awareness]*. Edited by A. Mahmadnazar, 148–53. Dušanbe: Irfon, 1989.

———. "Šinosnomai millat [The ID Card of the Nation]." In *Darsi xeštanšinosī [A Lesson in Self-Awareness]*. Edited by A. Mahmadnazar, 20–28. Dušanbe: Irfon, 1989.

———. *Varaqi sang [Leaf of Stone]*. Dušanbe, 1990.

Šerxond, A. "Vaqte dar Kūlob sabus [sic: sabūs] nameyoftand ... Turaǧonzodaro [sic] gunahkor medonistand [When no grain reached Kūlob ... they consider Tūraǧonzoda as the culprit]." *Millat*, July 7, 2012. 27.

Shelley, Lousie I. "Crime in the Soviet Union." In *Soviet social problems*. Edited by Anthony Jones, Walter D. Connor and David E. Powell, 252–69. Boulder: Westview Press, 1991.

Slezkine, Yuri. "The USSR as a Communal Apartment, or How a Socialist State Promoted Ethnic Particularism." *Slavic Review* 53, no. 2 (1994): 414–52.

———. "N. Ia. Marr and the National Origins of Soviet Ethnogenetics." *Slavic Review* 55, no. 4 (1996): 826–62.

Smith, R. G. "Tajikistan: The Rocky Road to Peace." *Central Asian Survey* 18, no. 2 (1999): 243–51.

Sohibnazar, Asliddin. *Subhi sitorakuš. Kitobi avval. Nazare ba rūydodhoi oxiri Toǧikiston [The Morning the Star is killed. First Volume. An Opinion of the latest Events in Tajikistan]*. Dušanbe: Doniš, 1997.

———. *Subhi sitorakuš. Kitobi diyom. Nazare ba rūydodhoi oxiri Toǧikiston [The Morning the Star is killed. Second Volume. An Opinion of the latest Events in Tajikistan]*. Dušanbe: Mahmadǧon, 2000.

Sokolov, Vladimir. "Zona molčaniya [The Zone of Silence]." *Literaturnaya Gazeta*, January 20, 1988. 3.

Soucek, Svatopluk. *A history of inner Asia*. Cambridge, New York: Cambridge University Press, 2000.

Stalin, Joseph. *Marxism and the national and colonial question*. Moscow: Co-Operative Publishing Society of Foreign Workers in the USSR, 1935.

Stone, Richard. "Combating Radioactive Risks and Isolation in Tajikistan." *Science* 309, no. 5731 (2005): 44–5.

Stover, Eric and Elena O. Nightingale, eds. *The Breaking of bodies and minds: Torture, psychiatric abuse, and the health professions*. New York: Freeman, 1985.

Subtelny, Maria E. "Husayn Va'iz-i Kashifi: Polymath, Popularizer, and Preserver." *Iranian Studies* 36, no. 4 (2003): 463–67.

Sukholesskiy, A. "Perebal Šar-Šar [The Šar-Šar Pass]." In *Spetcnaz GRU: Pyat'desyat let istorii, dvadcat' let voyny [50 Years of History and 20 Years of War]*. Edited by Sergey N. Kozlov, 315–19. Moskva: Russkaya panorama, 2001.

Šukurov, Muhammadǧon. "Nazare ba taʿrix [An Opinion on History]." In *Darsi xeštanšinosī [A Lesson in Self-Awareness]*. Edited by A. Mahmadnazar, 139–46. Dušanbe: Irfon, 1989.

———. "Zaboni millī ǧamxorii maxsus xohon ast [Special Care is needed for the National Language]." In *Darsi xeštanšinosī [A Lesson in Self-Awareness]*. Edited by A. Mahmadnazar, 3–19. Dušanbe: Irfon, 1989.

————. "Du silsilağunboni madaniyati Toğik [The two civilizational Dynamics of the Tajiks]." In *Darsi xeštanšinosī. Daftari duyum [A Lesson in Self-Awareness. The Second Notebook]*. Edited by A. Mahmadnazar, 118–29. Dušanbe: Irfon, 1991.

Sunstein, Cass R. and Adrian Vermeule. "Conspiracy Theories: Causes and Cures*." *Journal of Political Philosophy* 17, no. 2 (2009): 202–27.

Suyarkulova, Mohira. "Between National Idea and International Conflict: The Roghun HHP as an Anti-Colonial endeavor, Body of the Nation, and National Wealth." *Water History* 7, no. 1 (2015): 1–17.

Tabarov, Nur. "Nilufare rūi gūri orzu [A Water Lily on the Grave of Hope]." *Adabiyot va San 'at*, February 13, 1992. 7.

Tabarov, Sohib. *Spor 'derevenskogo intelligenta' s 'gorodskim intelligentom' [The Disputation between a 'rural intellectual' and an 'urban intellectual']*. Dušanbe, 2004.

Taeschner, Franz. *Zünfte und Bruderschaften im Islam: Texte zur Geschichte der futuwwa*. Zürich: Artemis-Verlag, 1979.

TAJSTAT [Agentii omor/Agency for Statistics under the President], ed. *Hayati millī, donistani zabonho va šahrvandii aholii ğumhurii Toğikiston [National Figures on Language Proficiency and the Status of the Citizens of the Republic of Tajikistan]*. Dušanbe: RMT MKH, 2010.

————, ed. *Demografiyai solonai ğumhurii Toğikiston [Annual Demographics of the Republic of Tajikistan]*. Dušanbe: RMT MKH, 2013.

Tasar, Eren M. "Muslim Life in Central Asia, 1943–1985." Social Research Center / AUCA, 2007.

————. "Soviet and Muslim: The Institutionalization of Islam in Central Asia, 1943-1991." Dissertation, Harvard University, 2010.

Taylor, Charles. *Modern social imaginaries*. Durham: Duke University Press, 2004.

Tilly, Charles. "War Making and State Making as Organized Crime." In *Bringing the state back in*. Edited by Peter B. Evans, Dietrich Rueschemeyer and Theda Skocpol, 169–91. New York: Cambridge University Press, 1985.

Tor, D. G. "The Islamization of Central Asia in the Sāmānid Era and the Reshaping of the Muslim World." *Bulletin of the School of Oriental and African Studies* 72, no. 2 (2009): 279–99.

Tunçer-Kılavuz, İdil. "The Role of Networks in Tajikistan's Civil War: Network Activation and Violence Specialists*." *Nationalities Papers* 37, no. 5 (2009): 693–717.

————. "Understanding Civil War: A Comparison of Tajikistan and Uzbekistan." *Europe-Asia Studies* 63, no. 2 (2011): 263–90.

————. *Power, networks and violent conflict in Central Asia: A comparison of Tajikistan and Uzbekistan*. London: Routledge, 2014.

Tūrağonzoda, Hoğī A. *Miyoni obu otaš. Tarhi sulh andoxtam, ammo...[Between Water and Fire. I had a plan for peace, but...]*. Dušanbe, 1998.

————. *Šariat va omea [Sharia and Society]*. Dušanbe: Nodir, 2006.

————. "Ivazšavii hokim naboyad nišonai noamnī bošad [A Change of Government does not have to be an indication for Instability]." *Nigoh*, July 10, 2013. 16.

Turajonzoda, Akbar. "Religion: The Pillar of Society," In *Central Asia: Conflict, Resolution, and Change*. Edited by Roald Sagdeev and Susan Eisenhower, 265–71. Washington, DC: The Eisenhower Institute, 1995.

Tursunov, Akbar. "Oye metavon ba ob nadaromada šinovarī omūxt? [Can you learn swimming without water?]." In *Darsi xeštanšinosī [A Lesson in Self-Awareness]*. Edited by A. Mahmadnazar, 88–99. Dušanbe: Irfon, 1989.

———. "Padidahoi millatgaroī [Manifestations of Nationalism]." In *Darsi xeštanšinosī [A Lesson in Self-Awareness]*. Edited by A. Mahmadnazar, 49–57. Dušanbe: Irfon, 1989.

Uehling, Greta. "Dinner with Akhmet." In *Everyday life in Central Asia: Past and present*. Edited by Jeff Sahadeo and Russell G. Zanca, 127–40. Bloomington: Indiana Univ. Press, 2007.

Usmonov, Ibrohim. *Soli Nabiev [The Year of Nabiev]*. Dušanbe, 1995.

———. *Sulhnoma [The Book of Peace]*. Dušanbe: Matbuot, 2001.

———. *Toǧikon. Surudi ta'rixi xalq va zamin [The Tajiks. A Hymn on the History of the People and the Territory]*. Dušanbe: Payvand, 2001.

———. *Ta'rixi siyosii Toǧikistoni sohibistiqlol [Political History of independent Tajikistan]*. Xuǧand: Nuri ma'rifat, 2003.

V. Ponomarev. "Kolokola nadeždy [Chimes of Hope]." *Pravda*, May 11, 1990. 131.

van Atta, Don. "'White Gold' or Fool's Gold? The Political Economy of Cotton in Tajikistan." *Problems of Post-Communism* 56, no. 2 (2009): 17–35.

Veit, Alex and Klaus Schlichte. "Zur Legitimierung bewaffneter Gruppen." In *Bürgerkriege erzählen: Zum Verlauf unziviler Konflikte*. Edited by Sabina Ferhadbegović and Brigitte Weiffen, 153–76. Paderborn: Konstanz University Press, 2011.

Vose', Qurbon. *Az qasri Arbob to koxi Vahdat [From the Arbob Palace to Koxi Vahdat]*. Dušanbe: Devatič, 2004.

———. *Adabiyoti ǧavonmardii Toǧiku Fors [The Tajik and Persian Literature on ǧavonmardī]*. 2 vols. Dušanbe: Doniš, 2007.

Voslensky, M. S. *Nomenklatura: The Soviet ruling class*. New York: Doubleday, 1984.

Weber, Max. *Wirtschaft und Gesellschaft: Grundriß der verstehenden Soziologie*. Tübingen: Mohr, 1990.

Wedel, Janine R. "Corruption and Organized Crime in post-communist States: New Ways of Manifesting old Patterns." *Trends in Organized Crime* 7, no. 1 (2001): 3–61.

Wennberg, Franz. *On the edge: The concept of progress in Bukhara during the rule of the later Manghits*. Uppsala: Uppsala University Library, 2013.

Whitlock, Monica. *Land beyond the river: The untold story of Central Asia*. New York: Thomas Dunne Books, 2003.

Williams, Christopher, V. I. Chuprov, and I. Zubok. *Youth, risk, and Russian modernity*. Burlington, VT: Ashgate, 2003.

Wilson, Andrew. *Virtual politics: Faking democracy in the post-Soviet world*. New Haven: Yale Univ. Press, 2005.

Wood, Elisabeth J. "Sexual Violence during War: Towards an Understanding of Variation." In *Order, conflict, and violence*. Edited by Stathis N. Kalyvas, Ian Shapiro, and Tarek E. Masoud, 321–51. Cambridge, UK, New York: Cambridge University Press, 2008.

World Bank Group, ed. *Statističeskiy sbornik, 1993 god*. Washington, DC, 1992.

Xaliliyon, S. "Se xatoi Sangak Safarov. Musohiba bo sobiq komandiri gordi millii Kūlob Ismoil Ibrohimov [The three mistakes of Sangak Safarov. Interview with the former Commander of the National Guard of Kūlob Ismoil Ibrohimov]." *Farağ*, August 22, 2011. 34.

Xoliqnazar, Ūktam. "Donistani ta'rix vağib ast [To know history is an obligation]!" In *Darsi xeštanšinosī. Daftari duyum [A Lesson in Self-Awareness. The Second Notebook]*. Edited by A. Mahmadnazar, 137–44. Dušanbe: Irfon, 1991.

Xolnazar, Mullonazar. *Dar čašmoni xotiraho [In the Eyes of Memories]*. Dušanbe: Kayhon, 2011.

Ya'qubov, Y., ed. *Kūlob Ensiklopediia*. Dušanbe: Ensiklopediyai millii Tojik, 2006.

Yemelianova, Galina, ed. *Radical Islam in the former Soviet Union*. London: Routledge, 2010.

Yofučī, Mirzo Y., ed. *HNIT sarvaron – dar hadisi digaron [The Leaders of the IRPT – in the words of others]*. Dušanbe: Muattar, 2013.

Yountchi, Lisa. "The Politics of Scholarship and the Scholarship of Politics: Imperial, Soviet, and Post-Soviet Scholars studying Tajikistan." In *The heritage of Soviet Oriental studies*. Edited by Michael Kemper and Stephan Conermann, 217–40. Abingdon, Oxon, New York, NY: Routledge, 2011.

Yurchak, Alexei. *Everything was forever, until it was no more: The last Soviet generation*. Princeton: Princeton Univ. Press, 2006.

Yūsuf, Šādmān. *Tāğīkestān. Bahā-ye āzādī [Tajikistan: The Price of Freedom]*. Tehrān: Daftar-e našr-e farhang-e Eslāmī, 1373hš = 1994/1995.

Zaman, Muhammad Q. *The ulama in contemporary Islam: Custodians of change*. Princeton: Princeton University Press, 2002.

Zürcher, Christoph. *The post-Soviet wars: Rebellion, ethnic conflict, and nationhood in the Caucasus*. New York: New York Univ. Press, 2007.

Index

About the Author

Tim Epkenhans is professor for Islamic studies at the University of Freiburg (Germany). After completing his PhD on Iranian Modernist Thought in Bamberg (Germany) in 2002, he worked for the German Ministry of Foreign Affairs in Tajikistan and as the director of the OSCE Academy in Bishkek.

Lightning Source UK Ltd.
Milton Keynes UK
UKHW020156121218
333811UK00016B/640/P